Support for
Caregiving Families

Support for Caregiving Families
Enabling Positive Adaptation to Disability

edited by

George H.S. Singer, Ph.D.
Larry K. Irvin, Ph.D.
Oregon Research Institute
Eugene

·P A U L·H·
BROKES
PUBLISHING C°

BALTIMORE · LONDON · TORONTO · SYDNEY

Paul H. Brookes Publishing Co.
Post Office Box 10624
Baltimore, Maryland 21285-0624

Typeset by Brushwood Graphics, Inc., Baltimore, Maryland.
Manufactured in the United States of America by
Thomson-Shore, Inc., Dexter, Michigan.

Library of Congress Cataloging-in-Publication Data

Support for caregiving families: Enabling positive adaptation to
disability.

  Bibliography: p.
  Includes index.
  1. Mentally handicapped children—Home care—United States.
2. Parents of handicapped children—Services for—United States.
3. Parents of handicapped children—United States—Psychology.
4. Family social work—United States. I. Singer, George H. S.
II. Irvin, Larry K.
HV894.S86   1989   362.4′088054   88-30386
ISBN 1-55766-014-X

Table of Contents

Contributors

John Agosta, Ph.D.
Human Services Research Institute
Todd Hall (Room 231)
Western Oregon State College
Monmouth, OR 97361

Jacki Anderson, Ph.D.
Department of Educational Psychology
A&E Building
California State University-Hayward
Hayward, CA 94542

Tony Apolloni, Ph.D.
California Institute on Human Services
Sonoma State University
Rohnert Park, CA 94928

Shirley K. Behr, Ph.D.
Project Coordinator, Family Perceptions Research
   Project
Beach Center on Families and Disability
University of Kansas
348 Haworth
Lawrence, KS 66045

Anthony Biglan, Ph.D.
Oregon Research Institute
1899 Willamette Street
Eugene, OR 97401

Valerie Bradley, M.A.
Human Services Research Institute
2336 Massachusetts Avenue
Cambridge, MA 02140

Diane Bricker, Ph.D.
Center on Human Development
University of Oregon
901 E. 18th Avenue
Eugene, OR 97403

Randy V. Campbell
Project Ecosystems
Box 2396
Costa Mesa, CA 92628-2396

Elizabeth Cooley, doctoral student
Oregon Research Institute
1899 Willamette Street
Eugene, OR 97401

Janet Deppe, M.S.
Special Infant Services, Department of Special
   Education
San Francisco State University
1600 Holloway Avenue
San Francisco, CA 94132

Katherine Doering, M.A.
San Francisco State University
4 Tapia Way
San Francisco, CA 94132

Carl Dunst, Ph.D.
Director
Family, Infant and Preschool Program
Western Carolina Center
300 Enola Road
Morganton, NC 28655

Lynne Ellis, M.Ed.
Department of Special Education
San Francisco State University
1600 Holloway Avenue
San Francisco, CA 94132

Felicia Farron-Davis, M.S.
San Francisco State University
4 Tapia Way
San Francisco, CA 94132

Lori Goetz, Ph.D.
San Francisco State University
612 Font Boulevard
San Francisco, CA 94132

Nancy J. Gordon, M.A.
Community Liaison Specialist
Family, Infant and Preschool Program
Western Carolina Center
300 Enola Road
Morganton, NC 28655

Rolf Habersang, M.D.
Department of Pediatrics
Texas Tech University
Health Sciences Center
1400 Wallace Boulevard
Amarillo, Texas 79106

Ann Tiedemann Halvorsen, Ed.D.
Statewide Integration Project
Department of Educational Psychology, Special
  Education Option
California State University-Hayward
Hayward, CA 94542

Marci Hanson, Ph.D.
Department of Special Education
San Francisco State University
1600 Holloway Avenue
San Francisco, CA 94132

Mark Harrold
Project Ecosystems
Box 2396
Costa Mesa, CA 92628-2396

Nancy E. Hawkins, Ph.D.
Oregon Research Institute
1899 Willamette Street
Eugene, OR 97401

Larry K. Irvin, Ph.D.
Oregon Research Institute
1899 Willamette Street
Eugene, OR 97401

A. Blair Irvine, Ph.D.
Oregon Research Institute
1899 Willamette Street
Eugene, OR 97401

James A. Knoll, Ph.D.
Human Services Research Institute
2336 Massachusetts Avenue
Cambridge, MA 02140

Sherry Laten, Ph.D.
Consultant and Family Advocate
630 North Kenilworth
Oak Park, IL 60302

Sue Lehr, M.S.
Center on Human Policy
Syracuse University
Syracuse, NY 13210

John Lutzker, Ph.D.
University of Judaism
15600 Mulholland Drive
Los Angeles, CA 90077

Maury Martinez, R.N., M.S.N.
Department of Pediatrics
Texas Tech University
Health Sciences Center
1400 Wallace Boulevard
Amarillo, TX 79106

Nancy A. Neef, Ph.D.
The Devereux Foundation
Institute of Clinical Training and Research
19 South Waterloo Road, Box 400
Devon, PA 19333-0400

Maxine Newman
California School of Professional Psychology
2235 Beverly Boulevard
Los Angeles, CA 90057

J. Macon Parrish, Ph.D.
Associate Professor of Psychiatry and Pediatrics
The Johns Hopkins School of Medicine
The Children's Hospital of Philadelphia
34th & Civic Center Boulevard
Philadelphia, PA 19104

Lynda L. Pletcher, M.Ed.
Case Coordinator
Family, Infant and Preschool Program
Western Carolina Center
300 Enola Road
Morganton, NC 28655

Wayne Sailor, Ph.D.
Department of Special Education
San Francisco State University
612 Font Boulevard
San Francisco, CA 94132

George H.S. Singer, Ph.D.
Oregon Research Institute
1899 Willamette Street
Eugene, OR 97401

Mary A. Slater, Ph.D.
Department of Pediatrics
Texas Tech University
Health Sciences Center
1400 Wallace Boulevard
Amarillo, TX 79106

Kristine L. Slentz, Ph.D.
Center on Human Development
University of Oregon
901 East 18th Avenue
Eugene, OR 97403

Jo-Ann Sowers, Ph.D.
Oregon Research Institute
1899 Willamette Street
Eugene, OR 97401

Jean Ann Summers, Ph.D.
Director, Kansas University Affiliated Program
University of Kansas
Lawrence, KS 66045

Steven J. Taylor, Ph.D.
Center on Human Policy
Huntington Hall
Syracuse University
Syracuse, NY 13210

Carol M. Trivette, M.A.
Coordinator, Family Ecology Laboratory
Family, Infant and Preschool Program
Western Carolina Center
300 Enola Road
Morganton, NC 28655

Ann P. Turnbull, Ed.D.
Co-Director, Beach Center on Families and
    Disability
Acting Associate Director, Bureau of Child
    Research
Professor, Department of Education
University of Kansas
Lawrence, KS 66045

Ruth Usilton, M.Ed.
San Francisco State University
4 Tapia Way
San Francisco, CA 94132

Barbara Walker, M.S.
Oregon Research Institute
1899 Willamette Street
Eugene, OR 97401

Pamela Walker, doctoral student
Center On Human Policy
Syracuse University
Syracuse, NY 13210

Frank Warren
Director, Full Citizenship of Maryland, Inc.
3205 Cheverly Avenue
Cheverly, MD 20785

Sandra Hopfengardner Warren
Community Programs Monitor
DC Association for Retarded Citizens
7826 Eastern Avenue NW, Suite 6630
Washington, DC 20012

Foreword

When I was approached to write the Foreword for this book, I was of course flattered. After reading the book I felt not only flattered, but deeply honored. Let me explain why.

It has long been recognized that families who have a child with a disability, especially a severe disability, have a different set of circumstances than other families. However, only recently have professionals begun to look at how to help those families meet their unique and individualized needs. As that examination has occurred, family support has emerged as a concept that is frequently more amorphous than specific. This book provides a definitive structure for family support.

A number of years ago, there were many efforts to provide training to parents of children with disabilities. As I look back on my own part in those efforts, I must today be somewhat embarrassed, for so often we failed to recognize the emotional and psychological support, which many of those families required and we were unprepared to give. Our major focus was on providing the skills that would help them to teach their child. Fortunately, we professionals have begun to listen to the families, and have learned that training is not their primary need. We have begun to recognize that support comes in many forms and degrees of intensity. This book provides that recognition.

Therein lies the strength of this book. It recognizes the broad implications of family support and succeeds in providing a comprehensive discussion of the subject, through an array of chapters written by some of the more renowned authors in special education and psychology. The editors compile a series of chapters in the opening portion of the book that carefully make the case for the need for family support. Yet, I was pleased to see the chapter by Summers, Behr, and Turnbull, who review some of the ways in which families positively appraise the effect of handicapped relatives on the family. Without this chapter, readers might get the impression that a child with a disability brings only stress to a family, and yet those of us who have such a child know that he or she can bring us the happiest times of our lives.

The book then discusses coping skills and informal social support, and distinguishes these types of support from more formal support systems. John Agosta discusses with great clarity the issues of using cash assistance, a controversial subject according to many professionals and legislators. Family support is then discussed at each of the major life cycles of the family, and even after the family is no longer able to care for the child. Finally, evaluation and policy issues are examined. Thus, one has to be impressed by the comprehensive treatment that these editors have provided for this subject.

And would anyone expect anything different from these two editors, who have demonstrated over the years the highest degree of scholarship? They have succeeded once again in providing a complete examination of a very complex subject. They have done so by compiling the best practices and ideas that exist about family support. This book is truly a state-of-the-art volume.

H. D. Bud Fredericks, Ed.D.
Oregon State System of Higher Education
Teaching Research Division

Preface

We intend for this book to present an overview of a social movement that is in its infancy: family support services for families of individuals with developmental disabilities. During the past quarter of a century, community services have begun to reflect social ideals of normalization, empowerment, and enfranchisement for persons with disabilities. But families have not been included actively in efforts to open the mainstream of society to citizens with disabilities, despite the fact that they are the primary and lifelong source of support for most persons with developmental disabilities. Parents, siblings, and other extended family members perform a host of caregiving tasks that cannot (and, in most cases, should not) be replaced by formal services. The family support services that are described in this book aim to create productive *partnerships* between social services and families, in order to assist families to succeed in their caregiving roles without supplanting them.

We have organized the book around two major ideas that have emerged from the study of families: the roles of family stress and the concept of the family life cycle. Current stress and life cycle theories acknowledge the importance of family coping skills and community resources for facilitating positive adaptation to disability. Throughout this book, we and other contributors have emphasized the idea that many families can and do adapt successfully and, as a consequence, view their disabled relative as an important and valued member of the family. At the same time, however, stress theory has directed our attention to circumstances that weaken families and exacerbate distress. Preventive as well as ameliorative services are needed to assist families. When both family stress and the life cycle are considered, the need for changing services over time is apparent.

This book is intended to be useful for family service providers, students who are preparing for work with families, and parents and their allies who are advocating for support services. Each contribution is meant to be scholarly enough to provide intelligent rationales for the services described, and practical enough to provide a clear sense of what is required for implementation of services. The contributions are not "cookbook" manuals, however, for want of space. Most of the chapter authors have prepared more detailed manuals that can be obtained upon request.

In developing this book, we have been guided also by our conviction that empiricism belongs in the gallery of values that ought to shape family support services. Along with ideals of normalization, pluralism, empowerment, and consumerism, we believe that there is an important place for applied research, both to test new service elements and to evaluate programs in their entirety. Toward that end, we have asked authors to provide whatever data are available on the efficacy of their work.

Acknowledgments

Many people have contributed to this book. We feel fortunate indeed that the contributors we sought agreed to share their work, and that their efforts are of such high quality. We would like to offer special thanks to our colleagues at the Oregon Research Institute both for their contributions to the book and for accommodating us as we devoted time and energy to editing this volume. Elizabeth Cooley, Nancy Hawkins, Barbara Walker, Blair Irvine, and Tony Biglan contributed chapters as well as helpful suggestions. Mona Bronson, as the technical editor, kept us from slipping into chaos.

And finally, we would like to thank the families who have opened their lives, homes, and hearts to us over the past several years. We hope that some of their dignity and commitment may grace the pages of this book.

AN ORIENTATION toward FAMILIES AND SUPPORT SERVICES

Context, Structure, and Goals

CHAPTER 1

Family Caregiving, Stress, and Support

George H.S. Singer and Larry K. Irvin

Parents and their professional allies have prompted the creation of family support services throughout the country. Since early 1988, some 27 states have created at least rudimentary family support services (Agosta & Bradley, in press). At the same time, a number of model demonstration projects have been federally funded for fieldtesting innovative support services. In this book, the authors present descriptions of a number of these model demonstration projects, and discussions of some innovative state programs. These efforts vary tremendously in terms of the kinds of family needs that they address. To provide a template for organizing presentation of these diverse projects, this initial discussion focuses on family stress, which serves as a conceptual framework for the themes that weave through many of the contributions in this volume. Consequently, this chapter consists of two major sections: 1) an overview of contemporary stress theory as a way to draw together recent research on caregiving families, and 2) and overview of the common themes that unify the various descriptions of support services in this volume.

The first portion of this chapter describes a view of stress and coping as it applies to individuals as well as families. A brief discussion of recent evidence on the effects of caregiving on individuals and families follows.

THE PROBLEM

All families experience stress from time to time. Many caregiving families are subject to added stressors or reduced coping resources because of the demands of caring for a family member with disabilities. Stress theory provides a normative framework for understanding family problems, and it offers a basis for organizing preventive and ameliorative support and education efforts.

Families are the primary providers of caregiving services for vulnerable individuals in our society (Moroney, 1986). Although billions of dollars are spent on public and private programs for people who are not able to care for themselves without frequent assistance, the bulk of this daily human work takes place in family homes and is performed as a matter of course by concerned relatives. Families provide assistance with basic activities of daily living to approximately 4 million handicapped, elderly, and chronically ill individuals in the United States (Perlman, 1983). If all of this daily help had to be turned over to paid caregivers, the fiscal costs alone—not to mention the psychosocial ones—would be immense. Moroney (1983) has called caregiving families "a precious national resource."

This chapter focuses on one important group of caregivers—families of individuals with severe handicaps. Although many of the issues and services that are described in this volume apply to a much larger population, many of the authors have concentrated upon families of individuals with severe disabilities or mental retardation (i.e., those that include individuals who have difficulty learning to accomplish the routines of daily living, and whose IQs measure at less than 50). Estimates of the prevalence of severe mental retardation vary from 3 per 1,000 to 7 per 1,000, depending upon the method of screening (McLaren & Bryson, 1987). Moroney (1983) estimates that there are at least 165,000 households in the United States in which relatives care for children under age 14 with severe disabilities. Most young people with severe disabilities continue to live at home well into their adult years. Thus, the total number of caregiving households is actually considerably higher.

The focus on this poulation reflects the fact that most of the model demonstration projects described in this volume were designed to serve this group of families. Family support services are equally important for a much broader range of caregiving families, including families of children with mild mental retardation, neuromuscular disorders, and chronic illnesses. The issue of eligibility for services is discussed later in this chapter.

Many individuals with severe mental retardation also experience additional disabling conditions, particularly epilepsy, cerebral palsy, and sensory impairment (McLaren & Bryson, 1987). Most need some degree of assistance with activities of daily living. Although many individuals with severe mental retardation require increased levels of caregiving, some need little assistance to carry on a normal life. The need for assistance in daily activities does not preclude participation in normal community living. With the benefit of effective special education services and ongoing community supports, many individuals with severe handicaps can and do live with substantial autonomy and independence as adults. Increasingly, individuals with severe handicaps contribute productively to society and live as neighbors in their communities.

Because all people with severe mental retardation need at least some extra assistance, family members are an important source of assistance, advocacy, and affection during the adult years. To foster those long-term bonds, society must nurture family cohesion and adaptation in caregiving families from the inception of the caregiving.

Individuals with severe handicaps experience an unusually prolonged period of dependence in childhood because they learn basic skills much more slowly than other age mates. The effect of this prolonged period of dependency on families is highly variable. Overall, these families experience more stress and resultant distress than do similar families of nonhandicapped children and

young adults (Breslau & Davis, 1986; Quine & Pahl, 1985).

Averages, however, obscure differences. Summarized data from studies of families of persons with severe handicaps provide only a broad comparison of the group as a whole with groups of similar families of nonhandicapped persons. Such data tell us little about the people who do well or those who are extremely distressed or, for that matter, those whose morale varies substantially over time. With these reservations in mind, a review of recent research on stress in caregiving families is presented.

Effects of Stress on
Individuals in Caregiving Families

In the United States, some of the best research on families with children who have handicaps has been conducted by Naomi Breslau and her colleagues (Breslau & Davis, 1985, Breslau, Staruch & Mortimer, 1982). They have used adequate sample sizes, well established measures, and carefully selected control groups to investigate psychological problems among mothers and siblings of handicapped children. Breslau et al. (1982) found that, as a group, mothers of handicapped children reported being more depressed than mothers of nonhandicapped children. The best predictor of maternal distress was the amount of help that the child needed with activities of daily living such as eating, dressing, and grooming. The researchers followed this study with another large scale effort to determine whether or not there was a higher rate of clinical depression in caregiving families than in control group families.

A brief digression will be useful here. Psychologists make a distinction between clinical depression (Major Depressive Disorder) and depressive symptoms. They refer to Major Depressive Disorder (MDD) as a mental illness that is usually incapacitating, whereas depressive symptoms indicate that a person is quite unhappy but does not exhibit all of the necessary behavioral problems to acquire the status of a case. That is, a person can have depressive symptoms without having MDD. Such a person would report being very unhappy but would most likely continue to function in social roles, albeit with reduced energy. This kind of unhappiness has been labeled "demoralization" and is characteristic of people under unusual stresses (Dohrenwend, Oksenberg, Shrout, Dohrenwend, & Cook, 1979).

Breslau and Davis (1986) found that 15% of the mothers of nonhandicapped children and 30% of the mothers of handicapped children were demoralized. However, there were no differences between each group's rates of actual mental illness or MDD. While the number of women with MDD was comparable in the two groups, the mothers of the handicapped children often attributed the onset of their first severe depressive episode to the birth of the handicapped child. These findings suggest that mothers of handicapped children are more at risk for feeling discouraged and unhappy than are mothers of nonhandicapped children. However, two-thirds of the mothers of handicapped children were not demoralized. And as a group, they are not more vulnerable to major depression.

In a five-year, longitudinal study of siblings in families of handicapped children, Breslau and Prabucki (1987) had similar findings. The siblings of handicapped children, as a group, were more demoralized and more aggressive than children in control group families. Again, rates of disabling mental illness were not different between the groups.

Data on emotional distress in fathers of handicapped children are more limited than that available for mothers and siblings. Cummings (1976), using a control group design and standardized measures of distress, found higher rates of demoralization among fathers of handicapped children. Thus, the same pattern of elevated levels of distress seems also to apply to fathers, as well as to mothers and siblings.

The picture that emerges from these data confirms the findings of a number of other studies indicating that many families of handicapped children experience intermittent or chronic stress, and that a significant number of family members describe themselves as unhappy as a result. The samples in these studies included children with a wide range of handicapping conditions. Given that the best predictor of depressive symptoms was the handicapped child's need for assistance with activities of daily living (Breslau, Staruch & Mortimer, 1982), it is likely

that a group composed solely of family members of individuals with severe mental retardation would report higher rates of demoralization. Indeed, a large-scale study from England by Pahl and Quine (1987) found that the highest levels of psychological distress occurred in parents of the most severely handicapped children. These are important reasons for being concerned about the well-being of individuals in caregiving families.

These same studies also document that many family members are doing at least as well as matched controls. And research on siblings of severely handicapped children suggests that some children benefit from growing up with a handicapped sibling (Simeonsson & Bailey, 1986). These studies also show that the problem for family members of handicapped persons is not one of mental illness, but rather of difficulties in daily living that, for some members, are demoralizing.

At the same time, the full range of reaction and adaptation that these families experience must not be ignored. As a social issue, it is important to determine what kinds of interventions might prevent caregiving families from falling into difficult straits, and what kinds might help those who are already experiencing difficulty.

Psychologists and sociologists have created models of stress that demonstrate how it affects individuals and family units (Hill, 1958, Lazarus & Folkman, 1984). They have developed a general theory for understanding stress that provides a basis, at least implicitly, for designing interventions. Such models help to organize a large and diverse body of knowledge about parental and family reactions to living with an individual with severe handicaps (Cole, 1987). A review of these models of stress follows, and is intended to serve as a framework within which the remainder of this volume is organized.

Figure 1 presents a model of individual stress (Billings & Moos, 1984) that shows how events affect a person's morale and functioning and how individuals can react very differently to similar events. The model illustrates that the effects of environmental stressors are determined in part by resources available for dealing with challenging events and, in part, by the ways that individuals appraise and cope with stressors. Therefore, the resources, appraisal and coping responses,

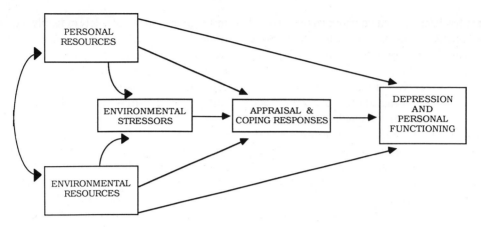

Figure 1.   Model of individual stress and functioning. (From A.G. Billings & R.H. Moos [1982]. Psychosocial theory and research on depression: An integrative framework and review, *Clinical Psychology Review, 2*, pp. 213–237; reprinted by permission.)

and the nature of the stressors all combine to determine an individual's morale and functioning under difficult circumstances. Figure 2, adapted from the work of Olson et al. (1983), presents a similar model applied to families. In this model, a family's interpretation of the stressfulness of events interacts with the family's coping skills and their resources, in order to produce positive or negative family adaptation. The following discussion defines and illustrates each of the components of these models, with recent evidence concerning caregiving individuals and families.

STRESS: A CONTEXTUAL MODEL

Stress and coping theory is a way of structuring information about individual and group reactions to difficult circumstances. Stress theory has

been most carefully defined in terms of individuals rather than groups (Lazarus & Folkman, 1984). Because the nature and effects of individual stress have been studied more thoroughly than those at the family level, the following discussion focuses on individuals.

Individual Stress

Stress has become an enormously popular concept in both native psychology (what the "person on the street" thinks) and in the life sciences (Lazarus & Folkman, 1984). In a recent Harris Poll, 80% of the respondents reported that they experience high stress at least once a week, and 30% said they were greatly stressed daily (Harris, 1987). Stress is often tied to physical and emotional reactions. The people who responded to the Harris poll listed several ways

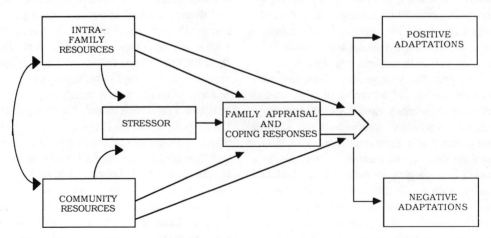

Figure 2.   Model of family stress.

that stress affected them, including headaches, anger, fatigue, and depression.

Other research has linked stressful events to emotional problems, such as anxiety and depression (Billings & Moos, 1984). Stressful contexts, such as a troubled marriage or a conflicted work environment, predict low morale, which is often described as depression.

In order to avoid confusion with the clinical definition of depression, the term *demoralization* is used to refer to a negative affect that has not been identified as mental illness according to current psychological standards (DSM-III). Demoralization often characterizes people who live with chronic strains (e.g., it is prevalent among disadvantaged minority groups, adults with chronic illness, and people who have lost their employment [Link & Dohrenwend, 1980]). In these circumstances, stressful life events often take the form of a series of relatively minor but painful problems. Researchers have dubbed these irksome events, such as having a flat tire or getting an unexpected bill, as *daily hassles.* Stressors do not have to be large-scale catastrophic events in order to have a negative impact on an individual's morale. Kanner, Coyne, Schaefer, and Lazarus (1980), showed that daily hassles are better predictors of demoralization than are major life events such as a death in the family or a divorce. Thus, for some family caregivers, the daily routine of feeding, dressing, lifting, and transporting a child with severe handicaps can be a source of fatigue and demoralization (Breslau & Davis, 1986).

In the scientific study of stress, researchers often look at the effect of aversive stimuli on physiology (Seyle, 1976). In the early work on stress, researchers devised a very simple model of stress and stress reactions. The model consisted of unpleasant events, called *aversive stimuli,* and of unhealthy physiological consequences. From this tradition, the relationship of stressful life events and physical health has been studied. For example, early researchers explored the effect of unavoidable shock on the physical health of rats, and found that unpredictable and inescapable aversive stimuli led to severe adverse health changes in these lab animals. This model was then applied to humans in investigations of the relationship of negative life events to

physical health (Sarason, Johnson, & Siegel, 1978). Consistent but relatively weak correlations have been documented between major life events and poor health.

Stressors

To understand stress in individual family members, researchers need to identify which events are stressors and whether or not exposure to these unpleasant events leads to physical or emotional problems. Identification of these events has important implications for the design of services. Many studies of families are based on the assumption that simply having a member of the family who is handicapped is itself a stressor (Embry, 1984). The effects of living with a severely handicapped person cannot be defined so narrowly; there are many different events that change in content or intensity with time.

A large-scale study from England contributes important information about the sources of stress in caregiving families with a severely handicapped child. Pahl and Quine (1987), using a psychometrically established measure of demoralization, determined that parents of severely handicapped children had unusually high rates of distress. They then conducted interviews with parents in order to determine the specific events that parents found to be most stressful. They found that a combination of variables was predictive of distress. Table 1 presents a list of these stressors. Clearly, most of these stressors are directly related to the child's condition, although other family problems also contribute to an accumulation of stressors. These findings are consistent with contemporary theories of family stress that hold that family distress is most extreme when chronic problems amass and an

Table 1. List of family stressors

Behavior problems in child

Night time disturbance

Social isolation

Adversity in family

Multiplicity of child's impairments

Child's ill health

Problems with child's appearance

Parents' money worries

Source: Pahl and Quine (1987).

acute stressor is encountered (McCubbin & Patterson, 1982). Similar findings about stressful child characteristics have been reported in studies of stressors conducted in the United States (e.g., Beckman, 1987).

Many individuals with severe mental retardation are likely to experience other medical and behavioral problems. Associated significant costs accrue for the family due to medical expenses, special equipment, special clothing, or diets. Breslau, Salkever, & Staruch (1982) found that low socioeconomic status (SES) and middle income families were hardest hit by the financial costs of caregiving. They also found that costs increased with the severity of the child's handicapping condition.

The amount of daily supervision that an individual with severe handicaps requires varies with many factors, including age, severity of disability, architecture and safety of the home, medical conditions, behavioral problems, and the availability of effective educational and support services. Again, there is a wide range of variability in the population. Some individuals with handicaps are able to stay by themselves and help with daily chores; others require constant supervision in order to ensure their safety. Stress theory would predict that as supervision needs increase, so do stress reactions in caregivers. As noted earlier, Breslau, Mortimer, and Staruch (1984) found just that result in a survey of 300 parents of handicapped children—the best predictor of maternal depression or demoralization was the amount of daily care that the child required.

So far, stressors have been discussed at a microlevel of analysis—life events and daily "hassles." Large-scale (more "macro") demographic and economic trends also make caregiving at home increasingly problematic for many families. These trends are best understood by adopting the rather narrow perspective of economists. From this point of view, caregiving is a commitment of labor resources. That is, it takes *person hours* to provide assistance to a severely handicapped relative. Traditionally, these caregiving tasks were performed by mothers and older daughters. Despite the influence of the women's movement, mothers are still the primary caregivers for handicapped children (Ka-

zak & Marvin, 1984). This traditional reliance on women as unpaid caregivers is becoming problematic; a majority of mothers of young children now work outside of the home. The combination of inflation and rising expectations has brought women into the labor force in enormous numbers, thereby depleting the pool of person resources available for home caregiving.

At the same time, families have been declining in size since the 1950s (U. S. Dept. of Commerce, Census Bureau, 1987). Today, the average family has fewer children and is likely to live at a distance from extended family members. As a consequence, fewer family members are available to perform the work involved in assisting severely handicapped relatives. Furthermore, with the aging of the general population, increasing numbers of young families are taking on the responsibility of caring for elderly relatives. When a family is also providing caregiving to a child with severe handicaps, the demands of caregiving are amplified. A severely handicapped family member, in many cases, represents a dramatic increase in the work required to make a home.

Caregiving demands are often so great, and adequate day-care or after-school care so rarely available, that mothers elect not to work. When one parent foregoes work, families accrue what economists call *opportunity costs,* or losses of wealth that could have accrued if resources were used in a diferent way (Breslau, Salkever, & Staruch, 1982). When mothers stay home to care for a relative, they lose the opportunity to raise the family's standard of living. As a result, many caregiving families are less upwardly mobile and less wealthy than families with nonhandicapped chidren (Moroney, 1986). At a time when expectations and the cost of living are rising steadily, the economic penalty involved in caregiving can serve as a significant stressor and disincentive. Low SES parents are particularly vulnerable to this problem. Lower income mothers are often caught in a bind in which they want to work, but cannot afford the costs of day-care for a handicapped child or the costs of replacing public medical insurance with private insurance (Breslau, Salkever, & Staruch, 1982). Many private insurance companies will not cover families with a child with severe handicaps. The ensuing economic loss itself becomes a source of distress, and may weaken commitments to caregiving.

Some of the major stressors that caregiving families may encounter in living with a relative with severe handicaps have been discussed thus far. However, people do not have a uniform reaction to these problems; some parents do not find these concerns to be stressful, whereas others find them intolerable. In order to account for individual and family differences, the verbal and affective behavior involved in assigning meaning to events through appraisals and values must be understood.

Appraisal People vary tremendously in how they respond to the same events. Aversive stimuli to one person may be perceived as neutral or even benign to another. In order to account for the different ways that individuals respond to potential stressors, psychologists have described the importance of cognitive appraisal or perceptions (Lazarus & Folkman, 1984). Whether or not an event acts as a stressor, and to what extent it does so, is partly determined by the kinds of attributions that it brings to mind. For example, one parent of a severely handicapped child may view the child's attempts to communicate through gestures as a source of frustration and annoyance, while another may be elated by similar behaviors. These variations grow out of individuals' very different learning histories, in which ways of interpreting events and giving them meaning come from personal experiences and from the cultural communities that have shaped them. Different parents appraise their life with their handicapped child differently. In Chapter 2, Summers, Behr, and Turnbull review some of the ways in which family members positively appraise the effect of handicapped relatives on the family. These positive attributions are important to our understanding of family caregiving and support services because they point out the positive adaptations that many families work out over time and that may serve as goals for supported family living. In Chapter 5 on stress management, Hawkins and Singer present a technique that some parents have found useful for deliberately altering negative attributions. For example, parents in their stress classes reported that they learned to redefine their children's problem behaviors as a sign that they

needed to change a given situation, rather than as evidence that they were incompetent parents.

To this point, appraisals have been discussed at an event-by-event level. The role(s) of larger, more abstract, appraisals and viewpoints—or values—are also important.

Some of the sociocultural emphasis on individual fulfillment may function as a set of guidelines for living that are incompatible with caregiving. For some parents, the birth of a severely handicapped child may be experienced as a social and emotional trauma that plunges them into a tumultuous new world of professional helpers, uncertain expectations, odd and often painful reactions from friends and relatives, and laborious caregiving. The ongoing demands of caring for the child may conflict with parents' desires for personal fulfillment through a career or self-expression. Popular values centering on personal growth, achievement, and self-realization do not necessarily account for drudgery, enduring commitment, and confrontation of socially inflicted pain (Bellah, Madsen, Sullivan, Swidler, & Tipton 1986). For some parents, a sense of loss and grief recurs for many years. For others, the limitations imposed by a life devoted primarily to caregiving are intolerable, and are eventually escaped through family break-up or placing the child out of the home.

However, perhaps hearkening back to more traditional values, many parents do weather the difficulties involved in family caregiving. Indeed, many families simply take life with a severely handicapped relative in stride. They would be uncomfortable with the use of the word *caregiving* as a descriptor of what they do. That is, they simply live with their child, sibling, or grandchild as another member of the family; they manage what needs to be accomplished as a matter of course. Similarly, many parental accounts describe personal growth as a result of raising a handicapped child (Ferguson & Asch, in press; Simons, 1987). These parents report that they have gradually gained a sense of perspective and mastery (see Chapter 2 by Summer, Behr, & Turnbull). Even in the individualist modern language of personal growth and self-fulfillment, some parents and siblings describe acquiring more depth precisely as a result of life with a handicapped relative. Others whose values are shaped more by their church describe a growing understanding of faith and love. Still others experience what Goode (1980) called *profound ambiguity*—a mixture of changing positive and negative perceptions of the child and family. In summary, many events and conditions are not inherently stressful. Instead, stress is partly determined by individual learning histories as manifested in attributions and values.

The context in which a stressor occurs is also important. Major aspects of the context for caregiving families are the resources available to them, and the coping skills they possess. These are discussed next.

Resources   Individual reactions to stressors are not only a matter of appraisals but also of the kinds of resources available to a person. For example, the loss of a job may have a different effect on a person who already owns a home than on one who has high monthly house payments. Many kinds of resources are possible, including personal skills, social support, informal social ties, formal services, and money. This book emphasizes ways to ensure that families have these kinds of resources.

Some of the most important resources are social. It is clear from more than a decade of research that social support can buffer people from stressful events and that people who believe they are supported are less adversely affected by stressors than are people who are more isolated (Gottlieb, 1981). Intimate social support is particularly important. For example, Friedrich, Wilturner and Cohen (1985) have demonstrated that one of the best predictors of adjustment in mothers of handicapped children is marital satisfaction. By contrast, mothers who are single and socially isolated are likely to be at risk for a number of psychosocial problems (Wahler & Dumas, 1984). Similarly, informal social support from extended family members and friends can make an important difference in how a person reacts to stressors. Various chapters in this volume document the roles of informal social support. In Chapter 8, Dunst, Trivette, Gordon, and Pletcher discuss the way informal social supports are emphasized in one family intervention program. In Chapter 9, Cooley describes the value of volunteers as sources of help to families. And in Chapter 2, Summers, Behr, and

Turnbull describe the role that religion can play in helping parents to make positive appraisals. Usually, religiosity is accompanied by social support from clergy and fellow congregants. Several of the programs described in this volume make use of parent-to-parent groups or networks in order, in part, to establish mutual supports.

Coping Skills   Coping skills, or ways of responding to stressors once they have already caused some distress, are another important element in the psychosocial model of stress. Coping skills have been classified in several ways. One useful way has three categories: emotion-focused coping, problem-focused coping, and passive coping. In Chapters 5 and 19, Hawkins and Singer, and Biglan, respectively, describe the ways that they teach coping skills to parents. In a broader sense, many of the parenting skills that are described in Chapters 6 (Singer, Irvine, & Irvin), 13 (Hanson, Ellis, & Deppe), and 14 (Slentz, Walker, & Bricker) are problem-focused coping skills applied to specific parenting problems.

An important reason for emphasizing coping skills is that they can be taught and readily learned by many people. Such skills as progressive muscle relaxation, self-monitoring, cognitive reframing, covert rehearsal, problem solving, assertiveness, increasing pleasurable events, and communication have been taught effectively to various populations. These skills have proven effective in alleviating a wide range of stress-related problems, including depression, generalized anxiety, headaches, gastrointestinal problems, hypertension, and insomnia (Woolfolk & Lehrer, 1984). The skills can be learned in a relatively short period of time and are highly portable (i.e., they can be used in a variety of situations as active ways of responding in real life to potentially difficult situations). Once someone has acquired these skills, little need exists for an instructor or therapist; the skills can help to foster independence and a sense of self-efficacy.

FAMILY STRESS THEORY

Following a model of stress as it affects individuals, social scientists try to explain the ways that families react to difficult circumstances. In this model, family stress reactions are defined as crises marked by change in the family's structure, such as divorce or family break-up, or by distress between family members, rather than as individual physical or psychological distress. The work of Hill (1958) and McCubbin and Patterson (1982) illustrates the application of stress and coping theory to family issues. They have followed the lives of families in which fathers were missing as prisoners of war, families in which a child had a chronic illness, and families in which children had a developmental disability. In these studies, the researchers looked at changes in structure, roles, conflict, and supportiveness within the family as an entity. Hill's (1949) now classic ABCX theory posits an interaction of three factors: A, a stressor; B, a family's resources for dealing with stress; and C, the family's appraisal of the stressor. These three factors produce X, either the family crisis or the successful family adaptation.

In many ways, Hill's theory involves the same constructs for stress theory as it applies to individuals. The primary difference is that, in Hill's ABCX theory, each component of the model refers to a group, the family, as the object of study. Although there are a number of conceptual problems when families serve as the unit of analysis, one part of the model that is relatively well defined is the X factor—family crisis or adaptation. A number of researchers have identified and measured family structural changes tied to caregiving.

A study by Bristol (1987) illustrates the application of family stress theory to families with developmentally disabled children. The study also demonstrates some of the conceptual problems that arise when moving from the study of individuals to the study of families as a unit. The dependent variables in Bristol's study were: the quality of parenting, marital satisfaction, and maternal depression. The first two variables involved more than one person—parents and children, and spouses—and may rightly be called indicators of family stress. The third variable, maternal depression, relates to an individual rather than to a family. For the A, or stressor factor, Bristol measured stressful life events, characteristics of handicapped children, and restrictions on family opportunities because of caregiving demands. For family resources, the B

factor, Bristol measured formal and informal sources of social support and the family's coping strategies. For the C factor, Bristol measured the way that the family appraised the stressors. By combining the ABC variables in a regression analysis, Bristol was able to account for 38% of the variance in quality of parenting scores and 61% of the variance in marital adjustment scores.

In this example, Hill's model produced a powerful set of predictors of family stress. As with most family research, only mothers filled out the questionnaires so that what was measured was one individual's view of her family. Nevertheless, Bristol's study illustrates how family stress theory can predict some kinds of distress and adjustment for the family as a unit. Other affects on the family unit have also been documented. McCubbin and Patterson (1982) have built upon this theory by recognizing that stressors can accumulate, that family resources can include coping skills, and that encounters with stress can have positive as well as negative outcomes. In this book, the authors use a modified version of ABCX theory to make it parallel to the Billings and Moos (1984) model of individual stress, and to incorporate positive as well as negative adaptation to stressors. Figure 2 (mentioned previously) presents the chapter authors' model of family stress, adapted from McCubbin and Patterson (1984) and Billings and Moos (1984).

Family Stress Reactions

Four major indicators of distress have emerged from relevant research on families: early out-of-home placement, divorce, social isolation, and child neglect or abuse. Over time, stress in families of handicapped children appears to lead to higher than normal rates of family break-up. Children with severe mental retardation are frequently placed out of their natural home into institutional and foster care settings (Seltzer & Krauss, 1984). While out-of-home placement is an important option for many families, policymakers have begun to recognize some of the social and fiscal costs of allocating resources exclusively to out-of-home settings. In Chapter 3, Taylor, Knoll, Lehr, and Walker discuss the importance of permanancy planning for all children. Of central concern is the way in which early separation from natural families may sever the social ties that, under other conditions, might help to sustain and enrich an individual with severe handicaps.

There is also some evidence that rates of divorce may be higher among families with children with severe handicaps (Gath, 1977). The data are equivocal though, because other studies have found no difference in divorce rates (e.g., Williams & McKenry, 1981). Some indirect evidence may be relevant here. A recent census bureau survey found that 14% of children with intensive care needs lived in single-parent households, compared with 7% of children who do not have special care needs. (This finding does not directly confirm the idea that divorce rates are higher, since there are other reasons why children live in single-parent families.) Some studies report high rates of marital distress in caregiving families (Murphy, 1982; Tew, Payne, & Lawrence, 1974). Again, however, other research has produced contradictory findings (Kazak & Marvin, 1984). These mixed results suggest that there is considerable variability in family reactions, that some marriages in caregiving families are adversely affected, and that, at the very least, marital distress is an important concern for support services.

Social isolation has also been documented as a problem for some families of handicapped children (Moroney, 1986). In a longitudinal study of siblings, Breslau and Prabucki (1987) found that brothers and sisters of handicapped children were more socially isolated than those of non-handicapped children. Isolation can be attributed to various causes, including the scarcity of respite care, perception of negative community attitudes, lack of time and money for recreation, and depression. Social isolation is of concern because it has been implicated repeatedly as a contributor to health and emotional problems in adults and children (e.g., Breslau & Prabucki, 1987).

Finally, there is the troubling suggestion that handicapped children are at greater risk for child abuse and neglect than is the general population (Frodi, 1981; Garbarino, Broehhauser, & Authier, 1987). Reliable data on child abuse are extremely difficult to collect; prevalence figures are, at best, broad estimates. Problems of accuracy are compounded when individual differences, such as IQ or physical abilities, must also be measured. Nevertheless, higher rates of abuse have been documented in the population of handicapped children (Meier & Sloan, 1984). In extensive work with school-age children with severe handicaps, the authors have encountered problems of abuse and neglect in some families. Abuse often appears to be related to a child's problem behaviors, whereas neglect seems to be related more to the lack of available extensive caregiving that many children with severe handicaps require. Incidents of abuse and neglect indicate a breakdown in one of the major functions of a family—to provide basic care and reasonable socialization experiences to children. In Chapter 20, Lutzker, Campbell, Neuman, and Harrold describe in greater detail some of the causes of abuse and neglect, as well as a treatment model.

Individual and Family Adaptation to Stress

The interaction of stressors, appraisals, resources, and coping skills can also have positive outcomes for individuals and families. Until the late 1980's, research has focused primarily on the various negative outcomes associated with caregiving stress in families of severely handicapped children. This chapter has already discussed some common negative stress reactions, ranging from tension headaches to demoralization at the individual level, and from divorce to abuse or neglect at the family level. Many adaptive and life-enhancing responses to stress are also common. Some individuals and families seem to thrive in challenging circumstances (McCubbin, Sussman, & Patterson, 1983). Many parents and siblings come to perceive their life with a handicapped relative as mutually beneficial (Simons, 1987). Some marriages are strengthened, in part, through cooperation and a joint sense of purpose in parenting a handicapped child (Kazak & Marvin, 1984). And some families become more cohesive and adaptive in response to stressors linked to a handicapped member of the family (McCubbin, McCubbin, et al., 1983).

Stress reactions are not necessarily stable and unvarying. People can experience demoralization or illness, and then gradually gain resolve or strength. Many descriptions of parental adaptation to the birth or diagnosis of a handicapped child present the view that parents pass through various stages of adjustment, from those marked by negative affect to those that include a sense of acceptance (Blacher, 1984). This progression resonates with some of the traditional tenets of Greek and Judeo-Christian thought (i.e., through challenge and/or suffering, self-knowledge, acceptance, or faith can be achieved). In current psychological terminology, successful coping can lead to an enhanced sense of well-being and self-efficacy. For example, in many parental accounts of living with a handicapped child, mothers and fathers describe the ways in which they were gradually strengthened by facing many challenges (Simons, 1987).

Knowledge of the contexts that permit parents to move from demoralization to acceptance and mastery is limited. Often, the process is described as if it has a life of its own and is, apparently, unaffected by social or environmental circumstances. For example, Simons (1987) describes parents moving out of depression in their own time, as if signaled by an inner clock. The problem with this view is that it leaves out the *context* of personal change and, as a result, provides little information about the kinds of social and environmental resources that nurture the process.

Some findings from previous research can be pieced together to create a better understanding of the contexts of positive adaptation. A strong marital relationship and a supportive social network are associated with positive adaptation (Friedrich, Wilturner, & Cohen, 1985). A shared view of the child's handicapping condition (congruence) has been linked to positive adaptation (Bristol, 1987), as has a strong religious affiliation (Fewell, 1986). Provision of community services, such as respite care and public school services, has been linked to declines in rates of institutionalization (Hill, Lakin, & Bruininks, 1984). Knowledgeable professionals have sometimes been described as instrumental in assisting parents to accept their child realistically, and as important sources of social support (Moehler, 1987). And effective behavioral interventions in homes have alleviated stress at least temporarily, thus indirectly facilitating long-term familial adaptation (Baker, 1984).

Turnbull and Turnbull (1986) have highlighted two dimensions of family interaction that appear to be important for the well-being of all family members: family cohesion, and family adaptability. Adaptability refers to family members' ability to change roles or routines in order to respond effectively to environmental demands. Family cohesion refers to the way in which relatives cooperate in order to achieve shared goals. Members of cohesive families have reported that: 1) "family members really help and support one another," 2) "we really get along well with each other," and 3) "there was a feeling of togetherness in our family" (Bloom, 1985, p. 232). Family cohesiveness is associated with both positive parental outcomes and positive outcomes for the handicapped family member (McCubbin et al., 1983). In cohesive families, the teamwork and shared sense of responsibility that the family accomplishes appear both to strengthen the marriage and to encourage the handicapped child's health status and adaptation to school and community. In McCubbin et al.'s (1983) studies of families of children with cystic fibrosis, family characteristics were correlated with improvements in children's weight and other important indicators of thriving in that population. The children who made the most progress came from families in which a sense of teamwork and cohesion was emphasized. Similarly, Nihira, Meyers, and Mink (1980) found that family cohesion was an important indicator of school adjustment for a sample of moderately retarded children.

Unfortunately, little is known about how families develop cohesion and sustain it. Some initial efforts to assist family members to work together cooperatively have emphasized group problem solving (Goldfarb, Brotherston, Summers, & Turnbull, 1986). As yet, however, no conclusive evidence has demonstrated that group problem solving assists family members in families of handicapped children to cooperate more effectively as caregivers.

In a more theoretical vein, researchers have suggested that a family's fit with the community is an important contributor to adjustment (Cole, 1986; Reiss & Oliveri, 1983). Presumably, a community that is accepting, accessible, and generous in providing services will promote family adaptation. The model demonstration projects that are described in this volume represent pioneering efforts to create supportive communities for families of individuals with severe handicaps.

After illustrating stress theory with findings from research on caregiving and disability have been presented. In the next section, major themes are presented that unify emerging efforts to support caregiving families. The model demonstration projects that are described in this volume represent a variety of services. Despite their diversity, the services are based on many common values and methods. The next section begins with a brief discussion of changing societal values and with a working definition of supported family living.

ADDRESSING THE PROBLEM

Family stress and coping theory provides the conceptual foundation for the presentation of innovative family support projects in this volume. The interventions described in the following chapters were designed to enhance family adaptation. Their focus is on preventing or alleviating stress by providing resources, including fiscal assistance, social support, positive perceptions of individuals with severe handicaps, coping skills, contact with families that have made positive adaptations, and treatment for families who experience maladaptive reactions to stress.

VALUES

The discussion of family support services begins with a simple values statement. The authors believe that families, when given proper societal assistance, can provide the best residential environments for severely handicapped children and the best context for creating lifelong social support for these individuals.

The authors recognize that there will always be some families that are unable or unwilling to provide for their severely handicapped relative and that, in these cases, other permanent family-like arrangements need to be created. In Chapter 3, Taylor, Knoll, Lehr, and Walker discuss a set

of family-like residential options for children who must be placed outside of their natural home.

Transferring public resources to caregiving families in the form of direct payments or services is a phenomenon of the 1980s. It represents an abrupt change of focus in societal commitments for individuals with severe handicaps and their families.

Historically, the lion's share of public resources for this population was allocated for large congregate-care institutions. Public resources were tapped only after parents decided to place their child out of home. The institutional population reached its zenith in the mid-1960s and has been declining since then (Lakin, 1979). For the first time in history, expenditures for community programs for individuals with developmental disabilities have reached parity with institutional expenditures, although per capita federal expenditures still favor the minority in large institutions (Braddock, 1987). The historic commitment to institutions is odd, to say the least, given the fact that 8 of every 10 persons with severe retardation live outside of an institution (Moroney, 1986). The majority live in natural and foster homes well into adulthood.

Importance of Home

An assumption of public discourse, as well as popular belief, has been that the quality of family life affects the success of young people in public school and the ultimate adjustment of adult citizens. The importance of families for the life careers of severely handicapped individuals comes as no surprise to their parents and siblings. However, interest in supporting families is relatively new in both research and practice. Although there is, perhaps, a much larger effect of a severely handicapped child's physical and mental constitution on his or her development, these children are also substantially molded by their home environments. In a large-scale study of families of moderately retarded children, Nihira et al. (1980) found that the best predictors of a child's adjustment in public school were the extent of harmony within the family and the family's educational values.

The family often continues to influence the life course of individuals with severe handicaps for many years after completion of school. For example, Jo-Ann Sowers (Chapter 17) summarizes research showing that parental beliefs are an important predictor of success in competitive employment settings for handicapped adults. Later in life, siblings often take over the role of guardianship, advocacy, and daily living assistance that parents once provided (Zetlin, 1986). The extent and quality of this benefactor role can have a critical impact on a person's success as a member of the community (e.g., Edgerton, 1976).

In the absence of these family supports, the responsibility for caregiving devolves to the state. Public funds are required to take over the tasks that are performed gratis by families for the majority of vulnerable persons. Consequently, when home caregiving fails, public costs rapidly begin to accrue.

Other enduring human losses occur when the family unit can no longer provide care. Unfortunately, no ready calculus exists for the social and emotional losses acquired when a family dissolves, or when family members become so discouraged as a result of ongoing strains that they relinquish their supportive role. Both in terms of public costs and private loss, there are important reasons for society to be concerned about the role that families play as primary caregivers and supporters of individuals with severe handicaps.

DEFINING SUPPORTED FAMILY LIVING

Supported family living is an example of creating *extended supportive environments*. These are the relatively permanent arrangement of socioenvironmental conditions that provide ongoing support for behavior (Lindsley, 1966). For the purposes of this volume, the socioenvironmental conditions are created around the family unit. They are ongoing in that they respond to changing family needs with the passage of time. They must be relatively permanent because the extra demands placed upon families by their caregiving roles are enduring. The behavior that they support is a complex mix of changing actions that together create family caregiving.

Family caregiving consists of a large class of behaviors and events that enable an individual with severe handicaps to live as normal a lifestyle as possible, within the context of positive familial relationships. Effective family supports will assist families to perform their caregiving functions with less psychosocial distress and more satisfaction than would be possible without the supports. These extended supportive environments for families can be designed to help families to care for their severely handicapped relatives at home until a normal age for leaving home is reached, and to continue in a supportive relationship with their relative for a lifetime.

In general, family caregiving fulfills traditional family functions. Turnbull and Turnbull (1986) have provided a useful taxonomy of these family functions: economic, domestic/health care, recreation, socialization, self-identity, affection, and educational/vocational care. Each of these functions can become problematic for families because of the challenges sometimes posed by individuals with severe handicaps. For example, economic activities such as earning an income for the family can be disrupted by a child's frequent illnesses or by extremely costly bills for medical treatments or adaptive equipment. Family recreational activities may be reduced because of perceived negative attitudes of others, inaccessible buildings, or a child's inappropriate behavior or lack of skills. The normal giving and receiving of affection between family members can be reduced by a caregiver's fatigue or demoralization.

This book's definition of family supports as "relatively permanent socioenvironmental conditions designed to maintain family caregiving" focuses on the family as a caregiving agent. In a sense, the authors are viewing the family as a social service that prevents or limits the need for more costly formal social services, such as residential institutions (Moroney, 1986). This view of the family is certainly debatable on both aesthetic and practical grounds.

An aesthetic objection to this perspective might be that the home is usually thought of as a place where subjective meanings and informal interactions prevail. Thinking of a family as a social service raises the specter, at least conceptually, of converting the family dinner table into a hospital cafeteria, and converting family leisure time into a scheduled and officially designated family recreational activity. The authors acknowledge that by adopting this emphasis on caregiving, the observations of families are from the point of view of outsiders. Many family members would not use the term *caregiver* to describe themselves. This book's intent is in no way to distort the informal, subjective, and affective nature of family living, but is instead to emphasize the importance that researchers illuminate families in ways that preserve this subjective world; qualitative analyses as well as first hand accounts are well suited to this task (Ferguson & Asch, in press; Goode, 1980; Simons, 1987). And perhaps these approaches ought to be used, in part, as a way to evaluate the impact of service programs on family life.

There is reason to be concerned, however, about the practical implications of the kinds of claims on public resources that family support services can make in order to continue to receive societal support. The authors believe that the closer that family support services stay to helping families as caregivers, the stronger and safer the claim will be on public dollars. Those entitlements that remain relatively close to the caregiving acts of the family are most likely to be created in the first place and supported by society over the long term. A danger of this view is that too narrow a focus on caregiving may ignore other family variables that ultimately contribute to a stable and positive social network for individuals with severe handicaps. For example, as described in Chapters 6 and 20, adjunctive treatments may enhance parents' implementation of behavioral parent training. One way to give families maximum leeway in selecting resources that they see as most contributory to effective caregiving is to provide cash support; Agosta describes cash assistance programs in Chapter 12.

FAMILY FUNCTIONS AND CAREGIVING

Families perform multiple functions for their members, including providing guidance, assisting with educational and vocational goals, creating a sense of belonging and identity, providing basic physical needs, and providing recreational activities (Turnbull & Turnbull, 1986). An undue emphasis on one family function may deplete the time and energy needed for another. For example, special educators have ex-

pressed concern that too much emphasis on training parents to teach skills to their handicapped children may divert parents from providing the family with time for recreational activities or from attending to other family members. Or, such an emphasis may inadvertently orient parents toward focusing on child change at the cost of affection for and enjoyment of the child (Kaiser & Hayden, 1984). When caregiving is the center of concern, is it too narrow a focus?

For many purposes, a multifaceted view of the family is necessary in order to recognize the complexity and uniqueness of each family. Indeed, the authors believe that in order to enhance the caregiving capacity of families, the families need support and assistance in a variety of functions. In Chapter 6 on parent training, the authors describe how they try to link families to needed services, and to teach general stress reduction skills prior to introducing more traditional parent training to family members. Similarly, Lutzker, Campbell, Newman, and Harrold (Chapter 20) describe a comprehensive, ecobehavioral treatment for troubled families.

Parents and professionals who work with families are well aware that often the most pressing concerns of a parent or a sibling may be far removed from caregiving. At the same time, these concerns may be the greatest impediment to sustained or successful caregiving. The key to enhancing one family's caregiving capacity may be to help a parent obtain treatment for alcoholism, while for another it might be to provide assistance with obtaining decent housing, while for yet another family it may be to assist parents to manage a child's problem behavior. From this point of view, the purpose of societal intervention—from whatever source—is to assist the family to maintain and nurture a vulnerable family member who would otherwise become fully dependent upon the community.

This view recognizes the value of the family's efforts and allies the community with them. It recognizes the need for a partnership between private, familial human resources and society. It also provides some standard for determining what kinds of family needs are legitimate concerns for the public and which ones are not. As discussed by Bradley in Chapter 22, an emerging policy issue concerns which services ought to be provided to families and which ones should not. It is important to understand what conditions enhance the caregiving capacities of families and what conditions appear to weaken or disrupt these capacities.

NEEDS OF FAMILIES ACROSS THE LIFE CYCLE

Supports for families can be organized into two broad categories: those that meet relatively continuous and stable needs, and those that meet needs that emerge at different stages of the family lifecycle. Sociologists have charted the ways that families change with time (Olson et al., 1983). Just as individuals develop and change through discernable phases of life, so do families. At each stage of the life cycle, family members have different developmental tasks to accomplish. For example, in the first stage of forming a couple, two individuals need to build a relationship and learn to live together cooperatively. Later in life, when children are leaving home, family members must adapt to people exiting the family.

Turnbull and Turnbull (1986) have related life cycle phases to common concerns that relatives have about a handicapped family member. When a child first enters the family through birth or adoption, parents are often concerned about obtaining an accurate diagnosis and information about the effects of a handicapping condition. When an individual with handicaps is finishing school years, parents and siblings are more likely to be concerned about employment and residential options.

Some kinds of family support services are targeted to specific phases in the life cycle. Obvious examples are the infant and toddler program that Hanson, Ellis, and Deppe describe in Chapter 13, the early intervention model presented by Slentz, Walker, and Bricker in Chapter 14, and the educational and transition from school to adulthood models defined by Goetz, Anderson, and Laten, and Halvorsen, Doering, Farron-Davis, Usilton, and Sailor in Chapters 15 and 16 respectively.

Other support services meet functional needs that do not vary much with time. For example,

fiscal assistance is not tied logically to the life cycle; the extra expenses involved in raising a severely handicapped child are likely to be relatively stable or to fluctuate unpredictably in ways unrelated to the child's age. In Chapter 12, Agosta discusses alternative fiscal assistance approaches. Similarly, the need for linkage to generic community services is unlikely to change; the case management model described in Chapter 10 by Slater, Martinez, and Habersang, as well as the Direction Service model described in Chapter 6 by Singer, Irvin, and Irvine, discusses services that meet more continuous family concerns.

PARENT-PROFESSIONAL PARTNERSHIPS

Another theme that runs through the contributions to this volume concerns the way in which professionals and parents relate to one another, both in terms of communication and in terms of basic assumptions about their roles. More than a decade of research provides clear evidence regarding the pitfalls of some modes of parent-professional interaction (Ferguson & Asch, in press; Turnbull & Turnbull, 1986). In the worst cases, parents have reported feeling intimidated, unheard, or dismissed by the professionals who are trying to help them (e.g., Doernberg, 1982).

A second and related concern grows out of the recognition that some modes of helping can inadvertently reduce family members' ability to solve their own problems. In a recent line of research, Fisher (1983) and other social psychologists have explored the impact of helping relationships on recipients' perceptions of themselves and others. Some of this research documents that help-seeking, in some cases, can reduce an individual's sense of self-efficacy. Dunst and Trivette (in press) have expressed concern that traditional modes of assisting parents of handicapped infants may potentially induce helplessness. They have proposed several guidelines for providing family supports that empower family members, instead of reducing their self-confidence.

Contributions to this volume report on a variety of strategies and assumptions to address these problems. Several programs offer parents choices of roles (Slentz, Walker, & Bricker, Chapter 14; Singer, Irvine, & Irvin, Chapter 6; Slater, Martinez, & Habersang, Chapter 10). Other programs emphasize the importance of cooperative professional values, as well as accepting and empathetic communication styles (Hawkins & Singer, Chapter 5; Walker, Chapter 7; Slater, Martinez, & Habersang, Chapter 10; Biglan, Chapter 19; Lutzker, Campbell, Newman, & Harrold, Chapter 20). Several other programs attempt to assist parents in ways that enable them to feel more competent and effective in managing their concerns, and to avoid some of the traditional assumptions that tend to place parents and professionals at odds (Hawkins & Singer, Chapter 5; Biglan, Chapter 19; Dunst, Trivette, Gordon, & Pletcher, Chapter 8; Singer, Irvine, & Irvin, Chapter 6; Goetz, Anderson, & Laten, Chapter 15; Agosta, Chapter 12; Walker, Chapter 7). For example, Hawkins and Singer (Chapter 5) and Biglan (Chapter 19) present approaches to treating stress reactions and depression that assume that parents are essentially healthy and knowledgeable people who may benefit from listening to one another, and who may benefit from learning skills that others have found effective. Both approaches encourage parents to set their own goals within a group setting, with the group leader assuming the role of an ally in helping parents to reach these goals. Warren (Chapter 4) describes the critical role that parents play in advocating for services and high standards in innovative programs.

RECOGNITION OF THE VALUE OF INFORMAL SUPPORT

Boggs (1984) has described how some of the most vital kinds of family support come from "the person to person, one-to-one, free association, caring support and assistance that family members and neighbors give to each other through transactions that leave no market trace" (p. 70). Friends, relatives, neighbors, and acquaintances offer some of the most essential and potent kinds of support (Fewell & Vadasy, 1986). A substantial body of evidence suggests that perceived, informal social support buffers people from the effects of negative life events (Gottlieb, 1981). Social support networks can provide fam-

ily members with several kinds of assistance including information, linkage to other individuals and groups, emotional support, financial and material assistance, and respite (Stagg & Catron, 1986).

Several of the models described in this book explicitly recognize the importance of informal social supports to families, and represent recent efforts to form partnerships between helping professionals and more organic social networks including extended families, church congregations, parent/teacher organizations, and other voluntary associations. Dunst, Trivette, Gordon, and Pletcher devote Chapter 8 to informal social support, and Cooley presents a description of community volunteers as informal family assistants in Chapter 9. Several of the models utilize parent-to-parent support groups as vehicles for communicating skills and for fostering supportive social linkages.

Other models recognize the importance of making generic community institutions open to families of individuals with severe handicaps. For example, Goetz et al. (Chapter 15) discuss the potential benefits of integrated public schools as sources of family support. Halvorsen, Doering, Farron-Davis, Usilton, and Sailor (Chapter 16) and Sowers (Chapter 17) discuss how opening up the competitive job market to severely handicapped individuals has potential benefits for other family members. Similarly, several contributors in this volume discuss the importance of full social integration of individuals with severe handicaps as an essential way of creating the proper adaptive fit between families and their communities.

MODEL DEMONSTRATION

Most of the programs described in this book are social experiments. Researchers or pioneering program developers and administrators have created them in order to demonstrate that a given constellation of techniques in a given service delivery system can alleviate a specific set of problems. This process has been dubbed *model demonstration,* and is an important way in which social innovations are introduced into our society (Paine, Bellamy, & Wilcox, 1980).

Paine et al. (1980) have identified several features of successful model demonstration projects. These efforts have clarified their purposes and established measurable goals concerning an important social problem. They incorporate techniques that have already proven effective in research studies. The model designers develop highly specified procedures for creating the service and then "package" the model so that it can be delivered by a specified service agency. The model is tested in real world circumstances and evaluated empirically to determine whether or not it accomplishes its purposes. Finally, the model is replicated and again evaluated when it is operated by people who are not connected with the original development and demonstration.

Most of the chapters in this volume present discussions of the purposes and components of their model demonstrations. Techniques as well as service settings are described, as are results from evaluative studies. The critical role(s) that evaluation plays in social innovation are described by Irvin in Chapter 21. As new services are created for families, the developers must determine whether or not these services are achieving their stated goals and whether or not unanticipated positive or negative effects have occurred. Because of their newness, some of the services described in this book have not been evaluated thoroughly as of Spring 1988. In other cases, well designed studies lend considerable credibility to the claims of model efficacy. The absence of broad evaluative data for all of the service models in this book represents a limitation that hopefully will be overcome as the contributors continue their development, demonstration, and evaluation efforts.

Implications of Model Demonstrations for Public Policy

The projects described in this volume are products of an inductive process of creating public policy. There is no overriding political or social movement that has provided a comprehensive rationale and program for supporting caregiving families, although theorists such as Moroney (1986) and Rodgers (1982) have stated positions that are compatible with traditional American liberal social policy. The social democratic movements in Western Europe have fueled pro-

gressive social innovations on behalf of most vulnerable members of society, as part of a general orientation toward cooperation between families and then nations (Rodgers, 1982). By contrast, this nation's innovative programs are created one at a time, usually in response to the grassroots efforts of interested groups of citizens. Societal support for home caregiving has advanced incrementally in the United States— often in response to highly specialized citizens' lobbies. Consequently, implications for public policy emerge more inductively from efforts at the state level and from program implementation, rather than deductively from preordinate political philosophy. Three of the chapters in this volume have policy issues as a major focus. Agosta (Chapter 12) discusses the issues involved in creating fiscal assistance services. Taylor, Knoll, Lehr, and Walker (Chapter 3) describe the values base of the emerging policy trends surrounding the issue of out-of-home placement and permanency planning for children with handicaps. Bradley (Chapter 22) describes some of the overall policy implications of the movement for family support, including illustrations from the other contributions to this book.

Castellani (1987) has identified several public policy issues that must be resolved if effective and efficient family support services are to be created. They include questions such as: Which families should be eligible? Which services should be provided? To what extent should public resources be directed to private families? Under which level of our government—local, state, or federal? Furthermore, there are questions about what sort of administrative arrangements ought to be established. For example, are there ways to prevent the establishment of complex bureaucracies as individuals go about setting up new programs? How might public resources best be used to strengthen local voluntary associations, if at all? These and other issues are posed by the movement to assist families.

These service design issues are being addressed on the state and national levels. As of 1988, twenty-seven states reported having established some form of a family support program. Generally, three forms of programs have been created; cash supports, payment for specific services, and combinations of the two. In Chapter

12 on cash supports, Agosta describes the characteristics of some of the state programs as well as unresolved policy issues. Programs that assist families with specific services differ widely in the kinds of services that they will buy, the eligibility criteria, and the amounts of money available. Figure 3 presents the range of services that are provided to some families in seventeen states. It shows a great deal of variability in state level programs; the diversity of these programs demonstrates that, as of the late 1980s, no widely held consensus has emerged as to how the government should assist families. The states also vary in terms of their experience with family

Services	States																
	ND	FL	ID	CT	MI	IL	PA	MN	NB	CA	MD	WA	MT	CH	NV	SC	RI
Transportation	•	•	•	•	•	•	•	•	•	•		•	•		•	•	
Respite Care	•	•	•	•	•	•	•	•	•			•	•	•	•		
Adaptive Equipment	•	•	•	•	•	•		•		•		•	•	•	•	•	
Education and Training	•	•		•	•	•	•	•	•	•							•
Sitter/Companion	•	•	•		•		•	•		•	•		•	•	•	•	
Family Counseling	•	•	•	•	•	•		•	•				•	•			
Medical/Dental	•	•	•		•	•		•	•		•			•	•	•	
Home Barrier Removal	•	•	•		•	•		•	•	•			•	•		•	
Special Clothing	•	•	•	•	•	•		•							•	•	
Special Diet	•	•	•		•	•					•			•			
Individual Counseling	•	•	•	•		•			•								
Medication		•		•	•	•		•	•		•						
Diagnosis and Assessment	•	•	•		•	•		•	•								
Physical Therapy*	•	•	•	•	•		•					•					
Occupational Therapy*	•	•	•	•	•		•					•					
Speech/Hearing Therapy*	•	•	•	•	•		•					•					
Homemaker						•	•	•	•	•	•						
Home Health Care	•		•		•	•		•	•		•						
Behavior Management*	•	•	•	•			•					•					
Personal Care				•	•			•	•	•	•						
Chore						•		•	•	•	•						
Day Care		•	•	•		•											
Visual/Mobility Training*	•	•		•			•										
Vocational Therapy*	•	•		•			•										
Recreational Therapy*	•	•		•			•										
Recreation/Leisure	•		•				•										
Housekeeping										•	•						
Basic Care Subsidy	•																•
Information and Referral													•				
Other/Innovative	•	•	•	•	•		•	•		•	•	•	•		•	•	
Number of Services Offered	23	22	19	18	18	16	14	14	13	10	10	8	8	7	7	7	2

Figure 3.   Services offered in 17 Family Support Programs. (*, delivered as an in-home service). (From Bird, W.A. [1984]. *A survey of family support programs in 17 states.* Albany, NY: New York State Office of Mental Retardation and Developmental Disability; reprinted by permission.)

support programs. For example, Pennsylvania started its program in 1972, Montana in 1975, and Florida in 1978, whereas other states are only beginning to create programs at the end of the 1980's. Some states are in the process of revising their family service system, while others are testing pilot projects, and still others are limiting family support services. The issues are also presently before the United States Congress as advocates push for revisions in Medicare legislation to permit federal funds to be used for home based care. In this atmosphere of innovation, the experience of a number of model demonstration projects around the country might provide an important resource for those who are trying to serve caregiving families.

LIMITATIONS OF THIS VOLUME

It is impossible to fit descriptions of all of the component services of a comprehensive family support program into one voume. As a result, decisions had to be made about some important omissions. Descriptions of programs aimed specifically at siblings, grandparents, or other extended family members were not included. Fewell and Vadasy (1986) provide information on model demonstration projects with these emphases. In addition, discussion(s) of effective and necessary services for mildly handicapped children and youth have not been included. Prevention and treatment efforts have been demonstrated for these families (e.g., Gallagher & Ramey, 1987). Other kinds of services that are vital to specific populations are also not addressed; for example, services for families of technology-dependent children, who require access to up-to-date equipment along with maintenance and repair services, or those for families of physically handicapped children who may require assistance in making architectural modifications are not specifically discussed.

Finally, the authors must acknowledge that the descriptions in this volume do not present much detail about programs for ethnic and racial minorities and for people in poverty. Several of the projects described in this volume do provide services to poor and minority families. However, a full discussion of the impact of poverty and ethnicity on family needs awaits another book.

This concern leads to a brief discussion of the limitations of family support services as presently conceived. Families of handicapped children encounter all of the larger-scale social problems of our society: poverty, unemployment, family break-up, homelessness, substance abuse, and so on. Just like all members of society, these families have to cope with high crime rates, environmental pollution, inflation, and economic uncertainty. Some of these problems are so devastating that they may easily override the impact of even the most comprehensive and generous family support service. Tausig (1988) has cautioned that new family support services may not mitigate the effects of the absence of an employed wage earner in a family, or of single parenthood. In addition, families must contend with the legacy of exclusion and prejudice that has characterized society's attitudes toward persons with handicapping conditions. These societal barriers take many forms, including negative attitudes, segregated schools and services, and extremely limited employment.

Services that have been created in the late 1980s in a majority of states represent a minuscule proportion of the total expenditures for individuals with developmental disabilities. While promising as social innovations, their scope is still quite limited. Resources remain insufficient to serve all caregiving families and to address some of the more stubborn and destructive social problems that enmesh many families.

The authors believe that support services for caregiving families will need, ultimately, to join with a broader movement for distributive justice within the society. Some of the industrial democracies in Western Europe devote proportionately far higher percentages of national resources to support the well-being of all families. For example, when Sweden offers fiscal support to caregiving families, it is with the assurance that none of them suffer from homelessness or life in rat-infested tenements, because Sweden has a history of assisting all citizens with adequate housing (Rodgers, 1982). In the United States, 30 million children currently live in poverty (Rodgers, 1982). Somewhere between 30,000 and 210,000 of these children experience severe mental retardation. None of the programs described in this book are likely to be effective in overriding the burdens placed on families by the convergence of poverty and caregiving. Such programs await larger-scale social innovation in the United States.

The programs described in this volume do offer hope for creating imaginative and effective partnerships between caregiving families and

society. They represent a significant break from the past and reflect a growing national commitment to vulnerable citizens and their families. The authors hope that they will be the forerunners of future, enduring partnerships between the community and families in sharing the responsibility of nurturing all citizens.

REFERENCES

Agosta, J.M., & Bradley, V.J. (Eds.). (1985). *Family care for persons with developmental disabilities: A growing commitment*. Boston: Human Services Research Institute.

Agosta, J.M., & Bradley, V.J. (Eds.). (In press). *Survey of state family support programs*. Boston: Human Services Research Institute.

Allen, D.A., & Hudd, S.S. (1987). Are we professionalizing parents? Weighing the benefits and pitfalls. *Mental Retardation, 25* (3), 133–139.

Baker, B. (1984). Intervention with families with young, severely handicapped children. In J. Blacher (Ed.), *Severely handicapped young children and their families*. Orlando, FL: Academic Press.

Beckman, P.J. (1983). Influence of selected child characteristics on stress in families of handicapped infants. *American Journal of Mental Deficiency, 88* (2), 150–156.

Bellah, R.N., Madsen, R., Sullivan, W.M., Swidler, A., & Tipton, S.M. (1985). *Habits of the heart: Individualism and commitment in American life*. New York: Harper & Row.

Billings, A.G., & Moos, R.H. (1982). Psychosocial theory and research on depression: An integrative framework and review, *Clinical Psychology Review, 2*, 213–237.

Billings, A.G., & Moos, R.H. (1984). Coping, stress, and social resources among adults with unipolar depression. *Journal of Personality and Social Psychology, 46* (4), 877–891.

Billings, A.G., & Moos, R.H. (1985). Psychosocial stressors, coping, and depression. In E.W. Beckham & W.R. Leber (Eds.), *Handbook of depression: Treatment, assessment, and research*. Chicago, IL: Dorsey Press.

Bird, W.A. (1984). *A survey of family support programs in 17 states*. Albany, NY: New York State Office of Mental Retardation and Developmental Disability.

Blacher, J. (1984). Sequential stages of parental adjustment to the birth of a child with handicaps: Fact or artifact? *Mental Retardation, 22* (2), 55–68.

Blacher, J. (Ed.). (1984). *Severely handicapped young children and their families*. Orlando, FL: Academic Press.

Blacher, J., Nihira, K., & Meyers, C.E. (1987). Characteristics of home environment of families with mentally retarded children: Comparison across levels of retardation. *American Journal of Mental Deficiency, 91* (4), 313–320.

Blaney, P.H. (1985). Stress and depression in adults: A critical review. In T.M. Field, P.M. McCabe, & N. Schneiderman (Eds.), *Stress and coping* (pp. 263–278). Hillsdale, NJ: Lawrence Erlbaum Associates.

Bloom, B.L. (1985). A factor analysis of self-report measures of family functioning. *Family Process, 24*, 225–239.

Boggs, E. (1984). Feds and families: Some observations on the impact of federal economic policies of families with children who have disabilities. In M.A. Slater &

P. Mitchell (Eds.), *Family support services: A parent professional partnership*. Stillwater, OK: National Clearinghouse of Rehabilitation Training Materials.

Braddock, D. (1987). *Federal policy toward mental retardation and developmental disabilities*. Baltimore: Paul H. Brookes Publishing Co.

Breslau, N., & Davis, G.C. (1986). Chronic stress and major depression. *Archives of General Psychiatry, 43*, 309–314.

Breslau, N., & Prabucki, K. (1987). Siblings of disabled children: Effects of chronic stress in the family. *Archives of General Psychiatry, 44*, 1040–1046.

Breslau, N., Salkever, D., & Staruch, K.S. (1982). Women's labor force activity and responsibilities for disabled dependents: A study of families with disabled children. *Journal of Health and Social Behavior, 23*, 169–183.

Breslau, N., Staruch, K.S., & Mortimer, E.A. (1982). Psychological distress in mothers of disabled children. *American Journal of the Disabled Child, 136*, 682–686.

Bristol, M.M. (1987). The home care of children with developmental disabilities: Empirical support for a model of successful family coping with stress. In S. Landesman & P. Vietz (Eds.), *Living environments and mental retardation*. Washington, DC: American Association on Mental Retardation.

Castellani, P.J. (1987). *The political economy of developmental disabilities*. Baltimore: Paul H. Brookes Publishing Co.

Cole, D.A. (1986). Out-of-home child placement and family adaptation: A theoretical framework. *American Journal of Mental Deficiency, 91* (3), 226–236.

Cummings, S. (1976). The impact of the child's deficiency on the father: A study of fathers of mentally retarded and of chronically ill children. *American Journal of Orthopsychiatry, 46*, 246–255.

Dangel, R.F., & Polster, R.A. (Eds.). (1984). *Parent training*. New York: Guilford Press.

Darling, R.B. (1983). Parent-professional interaction: The roots of misunderstanding. In M. Seligman (Ed.), *The family with a handicapped child: Understanding and treatment*. New York: Grune & Stratton.

Depue, R.A., & Monroe, S.M. (1986). Conceptualization and measurement of human disorder in life stress research: The problem of chronic disturbance. *Psychological Bulletin, 99*(1), 36–51.

Doernberg, N.L. (1982). Issues in communication between pediatricians and parents of young mentally retarded children. *Pediatric Annals, 11*(5), 438–444.

Dohrenwend, B.P., Oksenberg, L., Shrout, P.E., Dohrenwend, B.S., & Cook, D. (1979). *What brief psychiatric screening scales measure: Health survey research methods: Third biennial research conference* (Publication [PHS] 81–3268, pp 188–198). Washington, DC: Department of Health and Human Services.

Dunst, C.J., Cooper, C.S., & Bolick, F.A. (1987). Supporting families of handicapped children. In J. Garbarino, P.E. Brookhouser, K.J. Authier (Eds.), *Special children—special risk: The maltreatment of children with disabilities* (pp. 17–46). New York: Aldine Publishing.

Dunst, C.J., & Trivette, C.M. (in press). Helping, helplessness and harm. In J. Witt, S. Elliott, & F. Gresham (Eds.), *Handbook of behavior therapy in education.* New York: Plenum.

Edgerton, R.B. (1976). *The cloak of competence.* Berkeley: University of California.

Embry, L. (1984). What to do? Matching client characteristics and intervention techniques through a prescriptive taxonomic key. In R.F. Dangel & R.A. Polster (Eds.), *Parent training.* New York: Guilford Press.

Ferguson, P.M., & Asch, A. (in press). Lessons from life: Personal and parental perspectives on school, childhood, and disability. In D. Biklen, D. Ferguson, & A. Ford (Eds.), *Schooling and disability: NSSE yearbook.* Chicago: National Society for the Study of Education.

Fewell, R.R. (1986). Supports from religious organizations and personal beliefs. In R.R. Fewell & P.F. Vadasy (Eds.), *Families of handicapped children: Needs and supports across the life span.* Austin, TX: PRO-ED.

Fewell, R.R., & Vadasy, P.F. (1986). *Families of handicapped children: Needs and supports across the life span.* Austin, TX: PRO-ED.

Fisher, J.D. (1983). Recipient reactions to aid: The parameters of the field. In J.D. Fisher, A. Nadler, & B.M. DePaulo (Eds.), *New directions in helping: Vol. 1. Recipient reactions to aid.* New York: Academic Press.

Friedrich, W.N., Wilturner, L.T., & Cohen, D.S. (1985). Coping resources and parenting mentally retarded children. *American Journal of Mental Deficiency, 90*(2), 130–139.

Frodi, A.M. (1981). Contribution of infant characteristics to child abuse. *American Journal of Mental Deficiency, 85*(4), 341–349.

Gallagher, J.J., Beckman, P., & Cross, A.H. (1983). Families of handicapped children: Sources of stress and its amelioration. *Exceptional Children, 50*(1), 10–19.

Gallagher, J.J., Cross, A., & Scharfman, W. (1981). Parental adaptation to a young handicapped child: The father's role. *Journal of the Division for Early Childhood, 3,* 3–14.

Gallagher, J.J., & Ramey, C.T. (Eds.). (1987). *The malleability of children.* Baltimore: Paul H. Brookes Publishing Co.

Gallagher, J.J., & Vietze, P.M. (Eds.). (1986). *Families of handicapped persons: Research, programs, and policy issues.* Baltimore: Paul H. Brookes Publishing Co.

Gath, A. (1977). The impact of an abnormal child upon the parents. *British Journal of Psychiatry, 130,* 405–410.

Goldfarb, L.A., Brotherson, M.J., Summers, J.A., & Turnbull, A.P. (1986). *Meeting the challenge of disability or chronic illness—A family guide.* Baltimore: Paul H. Brookes Publishing Co.

Goode, D.A. (1980). *Deaf-blind: An examination of extraordinary communication and its significance to the sociology of knowledge.* Unpublished doctoral dissertation, University of California.

Gottlieb, B.H. (Ed.). (1981). *Social networks and social support.* Beverly Hills: Sage Publications.

Harris, L. (1987). *Inside America.* New York: Vintage Books.

Hill, R. (1958). Generic features of families under stress. *Social Casework, 39,* 139–150.

Hill, B.K., Lakin, K.C., & Bruininks, R.H. (1984). Trends in residential services for people who are mentally retarded: 1977–1982. *Journal of The Association for Persons with Severe Handicaps, 9*(4), 243–250.

Intagliata, J., & Doyle, N. (1984). Enhancing social support for parents of developmentally disabled children: Training in interpersonal problem solving skills. *Mental Retardation, 22*(1), 4–11.

Kaiser, A.P., & Fox, J.J. (1986). Behavioral parent training research: Contributions to an Ecological Analysis of Families of Handicapped Children. In J.J. Gallagher & P.M. Vietze (Eds.), *Families of handicapped persons: Research, programs, and policy issues.* (pp. 219–235). Baltimore: Paul H. Brookes Publishing Co.

Kaiser, C.E., & Hayden, A.H. (1984). Clinical research and policy issues in parenting severely handicapped infants. In J. Blacher (Ed.), *Severely handicapped young children and their families.* Orlando, FL: Academic Press.

Kamerman, S., & Kahn, A. (1976). *Social services in the United States.* Philadelphia: Temple University Press.

Kanner, A., Coyne, J., Schaefer, C., & Lazarus, R. (1980). Comparison of two modes of stress measurement: Daily hassles and uplifts versus major life events. *Journal of Behavioral Medicine, 4,* 1–39.

Kazak, A.E., & Marvin, R.S. (1984). Differences, difficulties and adaptation: Stress and social networks in families with a handicapped child. *Family Relations, 33,* 66–77.

Lakin, K.C. (1979). *Demographic studies of residential facilities for the mentally retarded: An historical review of methodologies and findings.* Minneapolis: Department of Psychoeducational Studies, University of Minnesota.

Landesman, S., Vietze, P.M., & Begab, M.J. (Eds.). (1987). *Living environments and mental retardation.* Washington, DC: American Association on Mental Retardation.

Lazarus, R.S., & Folkman, S. (1984). *Stress, appraisal, and coping.* New York: Springer-Verlag.

Lewinsohn, P.M., Youngren, M.A., & Grosscup, S.J. (1979). Reinforcement and depression. In R.A. Depue (Ed.), *The psychology of the depressive disorders: Implications for the effects of stress.* Orlando, FL: Academic Press.

Lindsley, O.R. (1966). Geriatric behavioral prosthetics. In R. Ulrich, T. Stachnik, & J. Mabry (Eds.), *Control of human behavior: Vol. 1.* Glenview, IL: Scott Foresman.

Link, B., & Dohrenwend, B.P. (1980). Formulation of hypotheses about the true prevalence of demoralization in the United States. In B.P. Dohrenwend, B.S. Dohrenwend, M.S. Gould, B. Link, R. Neugebauer, & R. Wunsch-Hitzig (Eds.), *Mental illness in the United States: Epidemiologic estimates.* New York: Praeger.

Longo, D.C., & Bond, L. (1984). Families of the handicapped child: Research and practice. *Family Relations, 33,* 57–65.

Matheny, K.B., Aycock, D.W., Pugh, J.L., Curlette, W.L., & Cannella, K.A.S. (1986). Stress coping: A qualitative and quantitive synthesis with implications for treatment. *The Counseling Psychologist, 14*(4), 499–549.

McCubbin, H.I. (1979). Integrating coping behavior in family stress theory. *Journal of Marriage and the Family, 41*(1,2), 237–244.

McCubbin, H.I., McCubbin, M.A., Patterson, J.M., Cauble, A.E., Wilson, L.R., & Warwick, W. (1983). CHIP—Coping Health Inventory for Parents: An assessment of parental coping patterns in the care of the chronically ill child. *Journal of Marriage and the Family, 45*(2), 359–370.

McCubbin, H.I., & Patterson, J.M. (1982). Family adaptation to crises. In H.I. McCubbin, A.E. Cauble, & J.M. Patterson (Eds.), *Family stress, coping, and social support*. Springfield, IL: Charles C Thomas.

McCubbin, H.I., Sussman, M.B., & Patterson, J.M. (1983). Introduction. In H.I. McCubbin, M.B. Sussman, & J.M. Patterson (Eds.), *Social stress and the family: Advances and development in family stress theory and research*. New York: Haworth Press.

McLaren, J., & Bryson, S.E. (1987). Review of recent epidemiological studies of mental retardation: Prevalence, associated disorders, and etiology. *American Journal of Mental Retardation, 92*(3), 243–254.

Mederer, H., & Hill, R. (1983). Critical transitions over the family life span: Theory and research. *Marriage and Family Review, 6*(1/2), 39–60.

Meier, J.H., & Sloan, M.P. (1984). The severely handicapped and child abuse. In J. Blacher (Ed.), *Severely handicapped young children and their families*. Orlando, FL: Academic Press.

Moehler, C.M. (1986). The effects of professionals on the family of a handicapped child. In R.R. Fewell & P.F. Vadasy (Eds.). *Families of handicapped children: Needs and supports across the life span*. Austin, TX: PRO-ED.

Monroe, S.M. (1983). Major and minor life events as predictors of psychological distress: Further issues and findings. *Journal of Behavioral Medicine, 6*(2), 189–205.

Moroney, R.M. (1983). Families, care of the handicapped, and public policy. In R. Perlman (Ed.), *Family home care*. New York: Haworth Press.

Moroney, R.M. (1986). *Shared responsibility: Families and social policy*. Chicago: Aldine.

Moroney, R.M. (1987). Social support systems: Families and social policy. In Kagan, Powell, Weissbourd, & Ziglar (Eds.), *America's family support programs: Perspectives and prospecies*. New Haven, CT: Yale University Press.

Murphy, A.T. (1982). The family with a handicapped child: A review of the literature. *Developmental and Behavioral Pediatrics, 3*(2), 73–82.

Nihira, K., Meyers, C.E., & Mink, I.T. (1980). Home environment, family adjustment, and the development of mentally retarded children. *Applied Research in Mental Retardation, 1*, 5–24.

Olson, D.H., McCubbin, H.I., Barnes, H.L., Larsen, A.S., Muxen, M.J., & Wilson, M.A. (1983). *Families: What makes them work*. Beverly Hills, CA: Sage Publications.

Pahl, J., & Quine, L. (1987). Families with mentally handicapped children. In J. Orford (Ed.), *Treating the disorder, treating the family*. Baltimore: Johns Hopkins University Press.

Paine, S., Bellamy, T., & Wilcox, B. (Eds.). (1980). *Human services that work: From innovation to standard practice*. Baltimore: Paul H. Brookes Publishing Co.

Pearlin, L.T., & Schooler, C. (1978). The structure of coping. *Journal of Health and Social Behavior, 19*, 2–21.

Perlman, R. (Ed.). (1983). *Family home care: Critical issues for services and policies*. New York: Haworth Press.

Quine, L. (1986). Behavior problems in severely mentally handicapped children. *Psychological Medicine, 16*, 895–907.

Reiss, D., & Oliveri, M.E. (1983). Family stress as community frame. *Marriage and Family Review, 6*(1/2), 61–83.

Rodgers, H.R. (1985). *The cost of human neglect*. Armonk, NY: M.E. Sharpe, Inc.

Roesel, R., & Lawlis, G.F. (1983). Divorce in families of genetically handicapped/mentally retarded individuals. *American Journal of Family Therapy, 11*(1), 45–50.

Sarason, I.G., Johnson, J.H., & Siegel, J.M. (1978). Assessing the impact of life changes: Development of the Life Experiences Survey. *Journal of Consulting and Clinical Psychology, 46*, 932–946.

Schaefer, C., Coyne, J.C., & Lazarus, R.S. (1981). Health-related functions of social support. *Journal of Behavioral Medicine, 4*(4), 381–406.

Seltzer, M.M., & Krauss, M.W. (1984). Placement alternatives for mentally retarded children and their families. In J. Blacher (Ed.), *Severely handicapped young children and their families*. Orlando, FL: Academic Press.

Selye, H. (1976). *The stress of life* (rev. ed.). New York: McGraw-Hill.

Sherman, B.R., & Cocozza, J.J. (1984). Stress in families of the developmentally disabled: A literature review of factors affecting the decision to seek out-of-home placements. *Family Relations, 33*, 95–103.

Simeonsson, R.J., & Bailey, D.B., Jr. (1986). Siblings of handicapped children. In J.J. Gallagher & P.M. Vietze (Eds.), *Families of handicapped persons: Research, programs, and policy issues.* (pp. 67–77). Baltimore: Paul H. Brookes Publishing Co.

Simons, R. (1987). *After the tears: Parents talk about raising a child with a disability*. San Diego: Harcourt Brace Jovanovich.

Singer, G.H.S., Irvin, L.K., & Hawkins, N. (in press). Stress management training for parents of severely handicapped children. *Mental Retardation*.

Slater, M.A. (1986). Modification of mother-child interaction processes in families with children at-risk for mental retardation. *American Journal of Mental Deficiency, 91*(3), 257–267.

Slater, M.A., Bates, M., Eicher, L., & Wikler, L. (1986). Survey: Statewide family support programs. *Applied Research in Mental Retardation, 7*, 241–257.

Stagg, V., & Catron, T. (1986). Networks of social supports for parents of handicapped children. In R.R. Fewell & P.F. Vadasy (Eds.), *Families of handicapped children: Needs and supports across the life span*. Austin, TX: PRO-ED.

Suelzle, M., & Keenan, V. (1981). Changes in family support networks over the life cycle of mentally retarded persons. *American Journal of Mental Deficiency, 86*(3), 267–274.

Tausig, M. (1988). Personal support networks: Benefits and liabilities (Letter in forum section). *Mental Retardation*, 47–49.

Tew, B.J., Payne, E.H., & Lawrence, K.M. (1974). Must a family with a handicapped child be a handicapped family? *Developmental Medicine and Child Neurology, 16*(Suppl. 32), 95–98.

Turnbull, A.P., & Turnbull, H.R. (1986). *Families, professionals, and exceptionality: A special partnership*. Columbus, OH: Charles E. Merrill.

U.S. Department of Commerce. (1987). *Statistical abstract of the United States, 1987*. Washington, DC: Bureau of the Census.

Wahler, R.G., & Dumas, J.E. (1984). Changing the observational coding styles of insular and noninsular mothers: A step toward maintenance of parent training effects. In R.F. Dangel & R.A. Polster (Eds.), *Parent training: Foundations of research and practice* (pp. 379–417). New York: Guilford Press.

Wikler, L.M. (1986). Family stress theory and research on

families of children with mental retardation. In J.J. Gallagher & P.M. Vietze (Eds.), *Families of handicapped persons: Research, programs, and policy issues.* (pp. 167–195). Baltimore: Paul H. Brookes Publishing Co.

Williams, R.G., & McKenry, P.C. (1981). Marital adjustment among parents of mentally retarded children. *Family Perspective, 15*(4), 175–178.

Woolfolk, R.L., & Lehrer, P.M. (Eds.). (1984). *Principles and practice of stress management.* New York: Guilford Press.

Wyngaarden, M.K. (1986). Patterns and trends in public services to families with a mentally retarded member. In J.J. Gallagher & P.M. Vietze (Eds.), *Families of handicapped persons: Research, programs, and policy issues.* Baltimore: Paul H. Brookes Publishing Co.

Zetlin, A.G. (1986). Mentally retarded adults and their siblings. *American Journal of Mental Deficiency, 91*(3), 217–225.

CHAPTER 2

Positive Adaptation and Coping Strengths of Families Who Have Children with Disabilities

Jean Ann Summers,
Shirley K. Behr, and Ann P. Turnbull

Families who have a member with a disability have long been objects of pity. Society as a whole tends to view the presence of a child with a disability as an unutterable tragedy from which the family may never recover. Researchers and service providers in the field of developmental disabilities have mirrored this societal perception, and tend to view the family as a whole as embroiled in a series of acute crises interspersed with chronic sorrow (Olshansky, 1962). Thus the task of family support is seen as ameliorating the deadly pall of tragedy that hangs over the family.

The day-to-day experiences of many thoughtful service providers, however, cast doubt on the universal validity of that perception about families who have members with disabilities. To be sure, one encounters families who seem to fit the stereotype—who are unable to cope with the emotional implications of the disability and/or the daily demands that are placed on them as a consequence of the disability. But there are other families who do quite well, with or without interventions from service providers. These are the families who roll up their sleeves and get on with the task of finding the best available services for their child: who both accept the reality of the disability and are able to love the child for who she or he is; who manage to have successful marriages and emotionally well-adjusted children, both with and without disabilities. Many of them have enough energy left over from coping with the demands of their own lives to provide support to other families, and even to give encouragement now and again to weary educators and service providers. These families are said to have made a *positive adaptation* to their child with a disability. We meet these families every day in the course of our educational or health practices.

Yet seldom, if ever, are they presented in the research literature or the textbooks designed to prepare practitioners to work with families who have members with disabilities. The typical portrait is one of families who are in distress, and the goal of the practitioner is to alleviate that stress, to "fix" the problems associated with a child with a disability (Turnbull, Blue-Banning, Behr, & Kerns, 1986; Turnbull & Turnbull, 1986). This perception is, in the authors' opinion, a great loss. Families who successfully meet the challenge of a child with a disability have much to teach us, not only about what works, so that we may provide support to those who are struggling, but also about our own attitudes toward people with disabilities. Furthermore, a focus on distress makes the practitioner's task more difficult since there is less opportunity to build on family strengths as a part of the overall intervention strategy.

The purpose of this chapter is to explore some of these success stories. It begins by considering ways in which the experience of having a child with a disability may strengthen families as well as create distress. Second, the chapter describes some of the cognitive coping strategies that families may use to meet the challenges of a child with a disability. Finally, it considers some of the implications of these positive contributions and cognitive coping strategies for practitioners who will be supporting those families.

EVIDENCE OF POSITIVE CONTRIBUTIONS BY PEOPLE WITH DISABILITIES TO THEIR FAMILIES

Family Narratives and Anecdotal Reports

Perhaps because of the focus on distress that has been pervasive in research on families of persons with disabilities (Summers, 1988; Turnbull & Turnbull, 1986), the vast majority of evidence for positive contributions lies not in the empirical literature but in parent narratives and anecdotal literature. One of the earliest voices to be raised in this vein was from Murray (1959), a mother of a child with mental retardation:

> It has been my privilege to have talked with hundreds of parents of retarded children. One of the favorite themes which permeates our conversation is how much our children have meant to us. This thought runs like a bright golden thread through the dark tapestry of our sorrow. We learn so much from our children . . . in patience, in humility, in gratitude for other blessings we had accepted before as a matter of course; so much in tolerance; so much in faith—believing and trusting where we cannot see; so much in compassion for our fellow man; and yes, even so much in wisdom about the eternal values of life. (pp. 1087–1088)

Similar observations have been shared through conversations with family members, newsletters of consumer organizations, and the popular media. For example, the *Down Syndrome News* (Watson, 1986) printed a portion of an essay written for a college entrance application by the sister of a girl with Down syndrome. A portion of that essay reads:

> My sister . . . is truly one of the most wonderful human beings in the world. Melissa has taught me to accept all people and respect their feelings. She enables me to realize, in a moment of panic, that a homecoming date will not determine my future happiness. She reminds me to slow down, when my schedule gets so frantic I lose time for my family. (Watson, 1986, p. 54)

Another sibling described the contribution of her sister with mental retardation as giving her family a sense of strength and identity:

> I always felt there was something very special about our family. . . . Because of [Cathy's] difference there was a degree of specialness or closeness that made us all very, very close. We all pitched in and helped each other out and Cathy was the one thing in difficult times that we could focus on. (Klein, 1972, p. 25)

The themes of narratives written by family members include those mentioned above—tolerance, faith, strength, professional and personal growth and development, and understanding the meaning of life (see, e.g., Featherstone, 1980; Turnbull & Turnbull, 1985).

In a content analysis of 60 books written by parents of children with a wide variety of disabilities, Mullins (1987) identified four major themes: 1) a realistic appraisal of the disability, 2) extraordinary demands on families, 3) extraordinary emotional stress, and 4) resolution and growth. With regard to this last theme, Mullins (1987) found that the majority of authors felt their lives were enriched and made more meaningful, regardless of the type or severity of their child's disability. Mullins cites a comment from one parent that she notes as typical of the prevailing attitude of most of the authors:

> I write now what fifteen years past I would still not have thought possible to write: that if today I were given the choice to accept the experience, with everything that it entails, or to refuse the bitter largess, I would have to stretch out my hands—because out of it has come, for all of us, an unimagined life. And I will not change the last word of the story. It is still love. (Park, 1982, p. 320, cited in Mullins, 1987, p. 33)

Empirical Studies

A few empirical studies have found evidence of positive contributions, in some cases as an incidental finding to the major interest of the investigation. Wikler, Wasow, and Hatfield (1983), in the conduct of a study concerning chronic sorrow experienced by parents, included a question asking whether the respondents felt that raising a child with a developmental disability made them stronger or weaker. A total of 75% of this small sample ($n = 27$) indicated that their experiences had made them stronger, with 46% indicating that they had been made *much* stronger. In contrast, only 9% of the professionals surveyed in this study $n = 43$), believed that parents would feel that their experience had made them much stronger.

In a study of coping resources of families who have children with mental retardation, Abbott and Meredith (1986) found that 88% of a sample of 36 parents reported positive contributions of their child with a disability. These included a closer and stronger family (55%); personal growth, such as more patience, compassion, and unselfishness (41%); and a greater appreciation for the small and simple things of life (17%).

Turnbull, Guess, and Turnbull (1988) content-analyzed letters sent to the Select Subcommittee on Education in the United States House of Representatives in support of regulations concerning treatment of newborns with disabilities. The 174 letters sent by parents, relatives, and individuals with disabilities were coded as to type of respondent, reasons for supporting the regulations, and the inclusion of recommendations pertaining to providing parent support or adoption options. Thirty-five percent of the respondents identified, as a reason for supporting the regulations, at least one positive contribution (usually to the family) by the person with a disability. Furthermore, approximately two-thirds of persons with disabilities and one-third of family members mentioned positive attributes of people with disabilities. In the 61 letters mentioning positive contributions to the family, six subcategories of contribution emerged: 1) source of joy (39% of 61), 2) source of learning life's lessons (28%), 3) source of love (28%), 4) source of blessing or fulfillment (28%), 5) source of pride (8%), and 6) source of family strength (5%). (Percentages exceed 100% because many respondents identified more than one contribution.)

Turnbull, Behr, and Tollefson (1986) conducted unstructured interviews with 18 parents who have a child with a disability, and 10 parents who have children with no disabilities. These parents were asked to describe the areas of their life (e.g., marriage, other children, extended family) that had been affected by their child, how their life would be different without their child, what pleases and displeases them about their child, an example of a positive and a negative experience with their child, and some of the positive contributions the child may have made to the family, friends, and society. Responses of parents of children with disabilities were coded, initially using the six categories of contribution generated in the Turnbull et al. (1988) study described above. Eight new categories were identified; parents of children with disabilities now identified their children as either sources of or reasons for:

1. Increased happiness
2. Greater love
3. Strengthened family ties
4. Strengthened religious faith
5. Expanded social network
6. Greater pride and accomplishment
7. Greater knowledge about disabilities
8. Learning not to take things for granted
9. Learning tolerance and sensitivity
10. Learning to be patient
11. Expanding career development
12. Increased personal growth
13. Assuming personal control
14. Living life more slowly

The sample of parents whose children had no disabilities contributed similar responses, except that they had no responses related to "living life more slowly" or "strengthening religious faith," but these parents added new categories of "source of energy and enthusiasm," and "source of practical help." (The category "source of knowledge about disability" was reconstituted to a more general category, "source of knowledge about child-rearing and family life.") These findings suggest that parents not only perceive their children with disabilities as making positive contributions to their lives, but also that those perceived contributions are relatively similar to perceptions about positive contributions of children without disabilities.

Theoretical Rationale
for Positive Contributions

The idea that families might derive some positive effects from an event that is considered stressful and undesirable is plausible from the perspective of stress theory. To understand a rationale for positive growth deriving from stressful events, it is necessary to consider some of the current thinking in social stress theory.

Stress theory has its roots in the work of Hill (1949), who formulated the ABCX model of stress. That theory postulates that a family's reaction (X) to an event (A) is mitigated by the family's resources (B) and its perceptions of the significance of the event (C). Hill's theory has undergone numerous modifications and elaborations since 1949 (McCubbin et al., 1980), but the basic structure remains. McCubbin, Sussman, and Patterson (1983), however, have called attention to the need for stress theory to accommodate the possibility of positive outcomes as a reaction to stress. They note:

> Our review of the field has left us with some discomfort regarding the lack of recognition, on the conceptual and empirical levels, that stress can be productive in some instances. Researchers have tended to use a unidirectional, pathological model which implies that the recipient experiencing stress as a consequence of one or more stressors must adapt, reach a steady state, recover, or if not destroyed will function less than adequately afterwards . . . few workers can visualize stress in a more positive framework. It can be postulated that creativity, effective communication in interpersonal relationships, motivation, and increased competence in brain, verbal and physical skills are outcomes of stress experience. (pp. 1–2)

McCubbin and Patterson (1983) attempt to rectify this problem through their proposed Double ABCX model, in which the family's reactions (X) create multiple events (Aa), and additional resources as well as altered perceptions, in a continuous cycle. Thus, the process of reacting to a stressful event is not seen as a single event but as an ongoing process in the life of a family. Depending on the family's reactions, this could lead to adaptation or accommodation resulting in a progressively upward spiral of growth ("bonadaptation," in McCubbin and Patterson's [1983] terms), or a downward spiral of dysfunction and crisis ("maladaptation"). McCubbin and Patterson (1983) define bonadaptation as follows:

> The positive end of the continuum of family adaptation, called bonadaptation, is characterized by a balance at both levels of functioning which results in (a) the maintenance or strengthening of family integrity; (b) the continued promotion of both member development and family unit development; and (c) the maintenance of family independence and its sense of control over environmental influences. (p. 20)

In short, current thinking in stress theory suggests that a given family's reaction to a challenging event could cause it to marshall its resources and focus its perceptions on positive aspects of its life, and, in the process of solving the initial problem, employ that event as a catalyst to improve other aspects of family life.

Beyond stress theory, it should be acknowledged that a child with a disability encompasses a multitude of characteristics, some related to the disability and some not. Some characteristics or personality traits may lead to stress in the family, while others may yield nonstressful effects that may be either positive or negative. In this regard, a child with a disability may be similar to children without disabilities. For example, an adolescent may have no disabilities but may experience special problems such as drug or alcohol use, sexual exploitation, eating disorders, or a multitude of other possibilities creating stress in the family; and *at the same time* the adolescent may provide assistance with household chores, serve as a source of pride in accomplishments, and become a participant in shared hobbies with parents. Children with disabilities may offer their own mixtures of positive and negative contributions (Turnbull, 1985). The tendency to define *impact* in terms of a unitary construct such as stress, may obscure the multiplicity of effects of the total human personality (Summers, 1988).

Summary and Conclusion
about Positive Adaptation

The consistency of parent narratives reporting positive growth, love, and other benefits invites a more systematic program of investigation. The studies reported above should be considered first steps in that direction. They should be considered hypotheses of types of positive contributions to be validated by more extensive research. Nevertheless, parent narratives and empirical studies consistently suggest that children with disabilities do contribute positively to their families, and that some families may not only survive their experience with disability, but also grow stronger. Theoretically, such positive contributions are possible within the context of stress and coping theory because the family utilizes stress as a catalyst to improve its functioning, and because stress and coping theory recognizes multiple outcomes that allow for a variety of positive and negative effects.

On a substantive level, the contributions of children with disabilities are usually seen as some type of intangible value or resource, such as greater strength, closer family ties, personal or career growth, and love. In short, in the experience of many families who have children with disabilities, those children are not devalued objects, but active and contributing members of their families, whose presence makes a real contribution to an improved quality of life.

All of this is not to deny, however, that all children, including those with disabilities, do present a special challenge to their families. And, those who successfully meet the challenges of a child with a disability may be equipped with particular coping skills and resources that allow them to do so. The next section of this chapter considers coping skills and resources that may contribute to success.

COPING SKILLS AND RESOURCES THAT ARE PREDICTIVE OF FAMILY SUCCESS

In the mid 1980s, a new strand of research on families who have children with disabilities has diverged from the documentation of distress in these families, to an identification of factors that may contribute to successful coping in families (see, e.g., Abbott & Meredith, 1986). This shift has in essence required a reversal of the dependent and independent variables under study. For example, rather than considering the impact of a

child with a disability on the quality of the parents' marriage, the question becomes: What is the impact of the quality of the marriage on the ability of the family to cope successfully with the demands of the child with a disability (Friedrich & Friedrich, 1981)? This line of inquiry is fairly recent, but has produced results that point the way toward an understanding of how families may successfully cope.

Investigators concerned with families of people with disabilities have increasingly adopted the ABCX stress and coping model described previously, in order to explain variances in family responses to a child with a disability. The ABCX model has been utilized by several reviews of literature and analyses of impacts of events in families who have children with disabilities (Bristol & Schopler, 1983; Cole, 1986; McDonald-Wikler, 1986; Turnbull, Summers, et al., 1986).

Concerning family resources (B in the ABCX model), a number of potentially effective resources and interpersonal skills that may lead to successful coping have come to the attention of investigators. These include: problem solving and behavior management skills (see Chapters 4 and 5, this volume); negotiation and communication skills in working with professionals (see Chapter 6, this volume); informal social support, including other family members (see Chapter 7); and generic community support (see Chapter 8). Similarly, all of the formal service programs designed to provide family support, such as respite care and family subsidies, might be conceptualized as programs intended to enhance family resources for coping.

Family perceptions (the C factor in the ABCX model) have been much less extensively explored as they relate to families of children with disabilities. McDonald-Wikler (1986) notes that "we are very far . . . from developing instruments or even concepts that can confidently be employed in the study of family perceptions" (p. 190). Yet perceptions may be powerful predictors of successful family coping. In fact, some theorists have suggested that resources such as social support may enable people to gain access to perceptions that reduce feelings of threat or stress associated with an event; for example, comparisons with others may lead a person to perceive his or her problem as less difficult than those faced by others (Shumaker & Brownell, 1984).

The key to a study of perceptions may lie in the work of cognitive coping theorists. Cognitive coping strategies refer to the ways in which individual family members may change their subjective perceptions of stressful situations (McCubbin et al., 1980). Taylor (1983) proposes a theory of cognitive adaptation in which she hypothesizes that adjustment to threatening events is mediated by three dimensions of cognitive adaptation: 1) attributing a cause for the event, 2) establishing a sense of mastery or control over the event in particular and over one's life more broadly, and 3) enhancing one's self-esteem. This chapter utilizes Taylor's framework to consider how these cognitive coping strategies may improve successful adjustment in families who have children with disabilities.

Causal Attributions

The first construct might be seen as an initial or related step toward either or both of the other dimensions of establishing mastery or enhancing self-esteem. Theory suggests that people who encounter a threat or an aversive experience may initiate a search for the cause of that experience in order to establish or re-establish a sense of control (Taylor, Lichtman, & Wood, 1984) and/or a sense of the orderliness and predictability of the environment (Rothbaum, Weisz, & Snyder, 1982). Similarly, people may tend to interpret the meaning of an event (the "why me" question) in such a way as to preserve or enhance their self-esteem (Taylor, 1983).

Investigators have found that people who have experienced a variety of threatening events tend to assign a cause or find some meaning in those events (Affleck et al., 1985; Bulman & Wortman, 1977; Patterson, 1985; Silver, Boon, & Stone, 1983). There is support for the notion that finding meaning, purpose, or cause in a child's disability is correlated with better psychological and physical health (Affleck, Tennen, & Gershman, 1985). Commentators have remarked that parents may be overly preoccupied (from the perspective of the service provider) with a search for the cause of their child's problems (Blacher,

1984), and may engage in "shopping behavior"; that is, parents may contract with a series of professionals to conduct diagnostic assessments of their child. Rather than a dysfunctional response based on denial, however, attribution theory suggests that identifying a cause may be a part of the adaptive process. For example, Bernheimer, Young, and Winton (1983) found that mothers of children with Down syndrome tended to experience less stress than mothers whose children were diagnosed with a developmental delay of unknown origin.

Whether the specific content of a causal attribution has a relationship to positive adjustment is not as clear. One may blame a variety of sources for an event, including oneself, other people, the environment, a spiritual entity (God), or, more nebulously, fate or luck. Some research suggests that self-blame is associated with positive adjustment (e.g., Affleck, Allen, McGrade, & McQueeney, 1982), presumably because it serves as a basis for establishing control of the situation in the future. Consistent with this notion, other research has found that blaming others is associated with poorer adjustment (Bulman & Wortman, 1977; Taylor et al., 1984). Still other research suggests that the content of the cause is not as important as the fact of perceiving a cause in and of itself (Lowery, Jacobsen, & Murphy, 1983; Taylor, 1983), and that finding a cause may not be as important immediately after the onset of the crisis as it is at a later point in time (Bulman & Wortman, 1977; Taylor et al., 1984).

Mastery

The second construct, mastery, involves "gaining a feeling of control over the threatening event so as to manage it or keep it from occurring again" (Taylor, 1983, p. 1163). In the perspective of some commentators, one of the ultimate aims of humanity is to predict and control events (Kelly, 1967); thus, the ability to maintain control of a situation, or to perceive that one has control, may be a powerful factor in reducing feelings of stress. Affleck et al. (1985) found that mothers of newborns in intensive care who believed they had greater personal control over their child's recovery tended to experience significantly less depression and significantly fewer major stress reactions (e.g., troubled dreams, blunted sensations). Other studies have found that parents with an internal locus of control tended to be better adjusted, to seek services for their children more actively, and to participate more actively in their child's treatment program (Affleck et al., 1982). Individuals may also perceive that others, such as doctors, service providers, or God, have the power to influence positively the outcome of a traumatic event. Taylor et al. (1984) found that belief in one's own control and in the control of others were both significantly associated with positive adjustment in women who have cancer. This line of research leads to the hypothesis that families of children with disabilities who perceive the future course of a situation as controllable may tend to experience better adjustment.

A further issue to be explored is the form of control a person may take. Two types of control suggested by Thompson (1981) are *information control* (learning about the situation) and *behavioral control* (taking direct action to change or improve the situation). An analysis of the relationship to adjustment by cancer patients to information control and various specific types of behavior control (e.g., changing diet, exercising more) yielded ambiguous results (Taylor et al., 1984). Future research might focus on the degree to which particular control strategies, such as participating in a child's educational program or becoming active in advocacy groups, may enhance positive adjustment in families of children with disabilities.

Enhancing Self-Esteem

The third major construct of cognitive adaptation theory, enhancing self-esteem, is generally achieved through selectively attending to the positive aspects or benefits of a situation, and/or comparing oneself positively to others. Selective attention, that is, focusing on positive attributes, has been identified as a coping strategy (Pearlin & Schooler, 1978), and a component of cognitive reframing (McCubbin, Larsen, & Olson, 1982). Taylor (1983) labels construing positive benefit as establishing cognitive or retrospective control of a situation. For example, deriving a sense of pride in a child's accomplishments can center around the nature of the accomplish-

ments, the perceived innate ability of the child, or the child's level of effort. Since level of effort may be more highly valued in this culture (Lavelle & Keogh, 1980), a perception that a child with a disability is working hard to achieve what might be considered by an outside observer to be a minimal gain might serve as a source of pride for families (see, e.g., Turnbull & Turnbull, 1985, for anecdotal reports that families do feel a sense of pride in the accomplishments of their child with a disability). Focusing on the benefits of a situation involves a "search for a silver lining" (Venters, 1980). Researchers have found that people may construe positive benefits from a number of traumatic experiences, including cancer (Taylor, 1983), incest (Silver et al., 1983), paralysis (Bulman & Wortman, 1977) and cystic fibrosis (Venters, 1980). Families who have a child with a disability may be no exception, given the number and variety of positive contributions that were described earlier in this chapter. A hypothesis emerging from these findings and self-reports is that families who are able to identify benefits from their experiences may have greater levels of family well-being. Whether the specific content of or the number of benefits identified has a relationship to well-being or positive adjustment is a further question to be pursued.

Self-esteem may also be enhanced by comparing oneself favorably to others. The idea is that people may feel better about their own situation if they perceive others as less fortunate in some way. An example of this phenomenon is the commonly held belief that wealthy people lead neurotic, shallow, and unhappy lives; the concomitant of this belief is that the observer is, by comparison, more fortunate to be poor but happy. Making positive comparisons is a coping strategy identified by Pearlin and Schooler (1978). Taylor (1983) found in her studies of women with breast cancer that women differentially chose their referent for comparison so that they could see themselves advantageously; for example, women with lumpectomies felt better off than women with radical mastectomies, and married women with mastectomies felt they were better off than single women with mastectomies. Taylor's (1983) findings are paralleled by findings in a qualitative study conducted by

Turnbull, Summers, and Brotherson (1984). Parents of children with disabilities in this sample either compared their children favorably to children without disabilities (e.g., believing that their child was easier to raise than the typical teenager), or compared their child's disability favorably to other disabilities (e.g., grateful that their child's disability was less severe or, alternatively, grateful that their child's disability was so severe that he or she could not be aware of and hurt by community stigma and rejection). These findings lead to the hypothesis that families who compare themselves favorably to others may tend to experience greater levels of family well-being.

In summary, people may employ a variety of cognitive coping strategies designed to reduce feelings of stress. First, individuals may search for the meaning or cause of a stressful event, either to render it more controllable in their minds, or to enhance their self-esteems. Second, copers may seek to gain a sense of mastery or control over a situation, to convince themselves that they may be able to either prevent the recurrence of a situation or relieve or solve the problem. Third, copers may seek to enhance feelings of self-esteem in the face of stressful events by looking for the positive aspects of a situation (i.e., the positive contributions of a child with a disability), and by comparing themselves favorably to others in similar situations. All of these coping strategies have implications for family support services, which are considered in the final section of this chapter.

IMPLICATIONS OF COGNITIVE COPING STRATEGIES FOR FAMILY SUPPORT SERVICES

Implications for Support Services

All types of family support services have the potential to enhance the use of cognitive coping strategies, to the extent that they may reduce stress enough to allow families to engage in calm reflection. Respite care programs, for example, may give families a chance to relax and view the situation from a more detached perspective. Two types of family support services, however, may have a more direct ability to encourage the use of

cognitive coping strategies. These are social support groups and family education or informational services.

Social Support Groups Social support or self-help groups have become increasingly popular forms of family support among families who have children with disabilities (Pearson & Sternberg, 1986; Walsh, 1987). Support groups may be organized by a professional or may arise informally through associations among family members, but their chief characteristic is the provision of support among the peer members of the group (Scott & Doyle, 1984).

Support groups may serve a number of functions that enhance cognitive coping strategies. For example, the validation of one's feelings by other group members (Oster, 1984) might be seen as an enhancement of self-esteem. Also, family members who meet others in similar situations have opportunities to make comparisons with others, to share positive experiences, and to look at situations with a humorous eye, all of which relate to self-esteem. Finally, support groups, especially those whose members participate in advocacy, may help the participants achieve a sense of mastery or control through group accomplishment. The sharing of information that often occurs in support groups may also lead to a greater sense of empowerment (Oster, 1984). In addition, group leaders may directly explain the use of these coping strategies and encourage the members of the group to share their own effective strategies with one another (see Chapters 5 and 6, this volume, for a description of how this intervention may be helpful to some families). It may be useful for professionals or consumer volunteers who facilitate support groups to consider how the group can best enhance feelings of mastery and self-esteem.

Family Education and Informational Services A number of curricula for parent education have been developed that may serve to enhance cognitive coping strategies. Behavior modification training, for example, may enhance parents' sense of control and mastery over their child's behavior. Similarly, training and/or counseling programs designed to teach problem-solving and communication may increase control as well as self-esteem through increased feelings of competence. Finally, educational programs providing family members with information about participating in decisionmaking for their child's educational or habilitation program may directly enhance a sense of mastery and control through empowering family members.

A further question to be considered is whether these cognitive coping strategies can be taught directly. Stress-management training materials often contain sections on cognitive coping or reframing as a part of the curriculum (see, e.g. Hawkins, Chapter 5; Summers, Turnbull, Shaffer, & Brotherson, 1987); however, to the authors' knowledge there has been no attempt to systematically teach families who have members with disabilities to use coping strategies directly related to causal attribution, mastery, and enhancement of self-esteem, or to evaluate whether this or any other type of training results in increased use of cognitive coping strategies.

The question of whether these strategies can be taught or are an integral part of an individual's personality traits is an empirical one requiring further investigation. Such a research agenda would require, first, a study of families who are good copers to identify the types of strategies they use, how they use them, and how they learned those strategies. Second, these results might be used to develop a curriculum to teach coping strategies. A careful evaluation of such a curriculum would also require a well-designed and psychometrically valid measure of the extent to which participants utilize these cognitive coping strategies. The curriculum could then be evaluated in the context of a controlled research design, comparing gains in the use of cognitive coping strategies by participants in the training with those who participate in peer support groups, and with those who receive no interventions.

Implications for Family-Professional Relationships

One of the most important aspects of family support is the relationship between the professionals serving a child with a disability and the family. Unfortunately, family members have often cited interactions with professionals as a source of stress as well as help (see, e.g., Warren, 1985). Kupfer (1984) notes that a certain amount of animosity between parents and professionals may

be endemic, since professionals are unable to fulfill parents' ultimate wish, that their child be cured. Kupfer (1984) also notes that professionals may choose to work with people with disabilities and find that they gain self-esteem from their work; however, since families do not choose to have a child with a disability, they may not have that foundation of strong confidence and self-esteem.

Also, family members and professionals may have stressful interactions due to negative attitudes about disability that may be held by the professional, by the family, or by both. Those attitudes include beliefs that the family is in part the cause of the child's problem, that the child is a devalued object of no worth to the family, and/or that the family is responsible for everything that happens to the child. All of these assumptions at best lead to poor family-professional relationships (Turnbull & Summers, 1987), and at worst lead to self-fulfilling prophecies in which families experience crisis based on the expectation that they should feel that way (Blackard & Barsh, 1982).

While there are still many unanswered questions about the function and use of cognitive coping strategies in families who have children with disabilities, there are several implications about the information that is known for family-professional relationships. Professionals who understand the function and value of these coping strategies may not only be able to help families enhance their use, but may also gain insights into the family's behavior that may enhance the professional's ability to respect and collaborate with the family. There are implications for family-professional interactions in all three of the major types of cognitive coping strategies.

Causal Attributions The search for the meaning or a cause of an event appears to be an important coping strategy. Families who are able to attribute some cause to the problems that their child is experiencing may have a stronger foundation for their later ability to cope, since the attribution of cause may be part of the resassertion of a sense of control or mastery of the problem. Professionals who perceive families as locked into the process of searching for a cause should not immediately infer that the family is unable to accept the child's disability; rather, the family may simply be attempting to reassert control of the situation.

The family's need to identify a cause of the problem and to attach a comprehensible label or name to the child's condition may come into conflict with the values of some professionals who believe it is important to avoid labeling, especially in the case of young children. In this case it is important for professionals to realize that labels may be unimportant in relation to the type of service to be provided and to the child's potential in society, and in fact a label may become unimportant to the family at a later point in life. However, at an early stage, when the family is newly aware of the child's disability and is struggling to make sense of the problem, it is vital to provide as much information in as clear a fashion as possible. This requires careful and complete explanations of all diagnostic information. When the cause of the disability is unknown, as it often is in the case of cognitive disorders like mental retardation and learning disabilities, it is important to provide families with as much information as possible.

One might ask, however, about the appropriate stance of a professional working with a family member who ascribes a "magical" cause to the disability. A "magical" cause is an illusory or unsubstantial belief about the cause of an event that may range from a spurious association (e.g., taking cold medicine in the first trimester of pregnancy) to a belief in divine intervention. It should be noted that magical causal attributions are distinct from denial or passive appraisal, which is yet another type of coping strategy (McCubbin et al., 1982). Denial is an avoidance of the stressful event or a refusal to believe that a problem exists; denial has not been discussed in this chapter because its prolonged use may too often result in problems (see, e.g., Pollner & McDonald-Wikler, 1985), and thus may not be part of the coping arsenal of successful families. Nevertheless, magical causal attributions may also be dysfunctional if they lead to a lowering of self-esteem or a reduction of a sense of mastery (e.g., believing that the child's disability is a punishment from God). The dilemma for professionals is how to distinguish between constructive and destructive causal at-

tribution. And, in the case of the latter, how might professionals guide families in more constructive directions?

It is at this point that the lack of research information begins to impede practice. There are a number of empirical questions yet to be examined: whether the specific content (i.e., whether the attributed cause is illusory or not) is significant in enhancing coping; and whether the specific identified causal agent (i.e., self or others) is significant. The relationship between causal attributions and self-esteem or mastery is also unknown. Furthermore, there are no empirical studies, to the authors' knowledge, relative to the efficacy of interventions designed to change causal attributions. All of these issues require a long-term research effort before professionals can have definitive guidance in working with families who make dysfunctional causal attributions.

Gaining Mastery A sense of mastery or control may be a vital coping strategy for families who have children with disabilities. People who believe that they can control what happens to them in life are more likely to persist in spite of the difficulties, and may be less likely to be debilitated by stress (Brickman et al., 1982). Without a sense that interventions or actions on the part of family and professionals will actually be useful, the family may not only fall prey to feelings of anxiety and helplessness, but could fail to participate fully in programs that could be of great value to the child. Thus it is important for professionals to take every possible opportunity to point to progress that the child is making. Even more importantly, professionals should try to link that progress to some action taken by the family. For professionals who regularly employ behavior modification in their service settings, the principle is simple: pair the reward (e.g., improvements by the child, greater happiness or satisfaction on the part of the child) with the behavior of the family.

In the long run, the establishment of a sense of mastery and control may be one of the most important outcomes of parent participation in educational/program decisionmaking. For this reason, all of those principles related to encouraging meaningful participation in decisionmaking, as well as attending to parent and consumer preferences for educational or habilitative objectives, take on an importance beyond mere legal compliance. The concept that the professional is essentially in charge has the effect of reducing families to clients, or helpless recipients of intervention (Barnard, 1984). A shift in attitude, placing the family at the center of the universe with professionals seen as consultants, can lead to empowered families who truly make a difference in the developmental and medical outcomes of their children (Barnard, 1984; Oster, 1984; Turnbull & Summers, 1987).

Enhancing Self-Esteem As noted in the previous section, the identification of positive aspects of a situation—the "silver lining" effect—may be one of the most powerful cognitive coping strategies of all. As noted in the description of positive contributions made by people with disabilities to their families, it is clear that families do recognize positive contributions, and in fact often do choose to focus on those positive aspects as a part of their coping effort. Service programs that adopt positive and optimistic attitudes can go a long way toward enhancing the family's capacity to focus on the positive (Dyson & Fewell, 1986).

A question that may arise is whether the positive contributions described earlier in this chapter are indeed *real* contributions to families, or whether the families' perceptions of those intangible contributions are, like magical causal attributions, mere rationales designed to relieve feelings of stress. While attributions of positive benefits may indeed be coping strategies, those attributions need not in any way be considered mythical or illusory. To the authors of this chapter, the question is irrelevant, as long as the attribution of positive benefits is not accompanied by prolonged denial (once again, a distinction is drawn between denial and cognitive coping). To the extent that the attribution of positive benefits leads to enhanced self-esteem and reduced distress, then their objective reality is irrelevant. In fact, due to the intangible nature of most of the positive contributions that families identify (e.g., unconditional love, pride, tolerance), the objective reality or unreality of these contributions may be impossible to prove. If they are real to the family, then professionals must accept that they are, in essence, real.

Helping families identify positive contributions of their experiences with a child with a disability, and enhancing self-esteem through appreciation of positive aspects of the situation requires that professionals themselves hold these positive attitudes. Professionals should examine their own feelings about the value of people with disabilities (Dudley, 1983) and should be able to identify ways in which particular children and adults with whom they have worked have enhanced their own life. There is no way to pretend a positive attitude; families and people with disabilities can spot insincere statements as easily as anyone else. Therefore, to the extent that professionals actually enjoy their work and actually believe in the intrinsic worth of the people they serve, they will be able to enhance the family's ability to see positive worth in both themselves and in their child with a disability.

CONCLUSION

An understanding of the coping strengths of families and an appreciation of the positive contributions of people with disabilities and their families also has implications for societal change and generally held attitudes about disability. In many ways, the message of this chapter is that it is the attitude of society, rather than the families and/or the people with disabilities, that needs to be addressed. It is not the nature of the handicap itself, but the way it is interpreted, that determines the impact on individuals (Grossman, 1972), and stress may largely be a product of a community's expectations about how people "should" react to particular events (Reiss & Oliveri, 1983).

An appreciation of successful families who have adapted positively should be achieved without sanctifying these families. Many parents have commented that they resent implications that they are somehow superhuman or saintly as much as they do the implications that their lives must be endless tragedies (Willette, 1987). Such sanctification of families who succeed suggests that adaptation requires heroic efforts beyond the reach of an "ordinary" family, and again leads back to the assumption that the impact of children with disabilities is pervasively negative. It is important to emphasize that these coping strengths are available to most families, and that families who cope successfully are simply ordinary people who are doing the job of raising a child with a handicap much the same as they would approach raising any other child. As one parent put it, "You just do it and you are not more special than anyone else because of it" (Yudenfriend-Glaser, 1987, p. 7).

Much has been written about disability as a social value judgment, and about handicaps as socially imposed limitations (Meyerson, 1963). Stigma is a result of social attitudes about the

negative impact of disabilities and about the worthlessness of persons with disabilities (Goffman, 1963). For this reason, it is vital to continue investigations of positive contributions of people with disabilities to their families and to society as a whole. Empirical evidence of positive value will go a long way toward strengthening the value that all persons in this society are worthy and useful human beings. Indeed, "when we look for the good in people, we will find ways to make the world better" (Blatt, 1987, p. 46).

REFERENCES

Abbott, D.A., & Meredith, W.H. (1986). Strengths of parents with retarded children. *Family Relations, 35,* 371–375.

Affleck, G., Allen, D., McGrade, B.J., & McQueeney, M. (1982). Maternal causal attributions at hospital discharge of high-risk infants. *American Journal of Mental Deficiency, 86,* 575–580.

Affleck, G., Tennen, H., & Gershman, K. (1985). Cognitive adaptations to high-risk infants: The search for mastery, meaning, and protection from future harm. *American Journal of Mental Deficiency, 89*(6), 653–656.

Barnard, K. (1984). Toward an era of family partnership. In National Center for Clinical Infant Programs (Ed.). *Equals in this partnership: Parents of disabled and at-risk infants and toddlers speak to professionals* (pp. 4–5). Washington, DC: National Center for Clinical Infant Programs.

Bernheimer, L.P., Young, M.S., & Winton, P.J. (1983). Stress over time: Parents with young handicapped children. *Developmental and Behavioral Pediatrics, 4,* 177–181.

Blacher, J. (1984). Sequential stages of adjustment to the birth of a child with handicaps: Fact or artifact? *Mental Retardation, 22,* 55–68.

Blackard, M.K., & Barsh, E.T. (1982). Parents and professionals' perceptions of the handicapped child's impact on the family. *Journal of The Association for the Severely Handicapped, 7,* 62–70.

Blatt, B. (1987). *The conquest of mental retardation.* Austin, TX: PRO-ED.

Brickman, P., Rabinowitz, V.C., Karuza, J. Coates, D., Cohen, E., & Kidder, L. (1982). Models of coping and helping. *American Psychologist, 37*(4), 368–384.

Bristol, M.M., & Schopler, E. (1983). Stress and coping in families with autistic adolescents. In E. Schopler & G.B. Mesibov (Eds.), *Autism in adolescents and adults* (pp. 251–278). New York: Plenum Press.

Bulman, R.J., & Wortman, C.B. (1977). Attributions of blame and coping in the 'real world': Severe accident victims react to their lot. *Journal of Personality and Social Psychology, 35*(5), 351–363.

Cole, D.A. (1986). Out-of-home placement and family adaptation: A theoretical framework. *American Journal of Mental Deficiency, 91,* 226–236.

Dudley, J.R. (1983). *Living with stigma: The plight of people who we label mentally retarded.* Springfield, IL: Charles C Thomas.

Dyson, L., & Fewell, R.R. (1986). Stress and adaptation in parents of young handicapped and nonhandicapped children: A comparative study. *Journal of the Division for Early Childhood, 10*(1), 25–35.

Featherstone, H. (1980). *A difference in the family.* New York: Basic Books.

Friedrich, W.N., & Friedrich, W.L. (1981). Psychological assets of parents of handicapped and nonhandicapped children. *American Journal of Mental Deficiency, 85,* 551–553.

Goffman, E. (1963). *Stigma: Notes on the management of spoiled identity.* Englewood Cliffs, NJ: Prentice-Hall.

Grossman, F.K. (1972). *Brothers and sisters of retarded children: An exploratory study.* Syracuse: Syracuse University Press.

Hill, R. (1949). *Families under stress.* New York: Harper & Row.

Kelley, H. (1967). Attribution theory in social psychology. In D. Levine (Ed.), *Nebraska Symposium on Motivation* (Vol. 15, pp. 192–238). Lincoln: University of Nebraska Press.

Klein, S.D. (1972). Brother to sister/Sister to brother. *Exceptional Parent, 3*(2), 24–27.

Kupfer, F. (1984). Severely and/or multiply disabled children. In National Center for Clinical Infant Program (Eds.), *Equals in this partnership: Parents of disabled and at-risk infants and toddlers speak to professionals* (pp. 18–25). Washington, DC: National Center for Clinical Infant Programs.

Lavelle, N., & Keogh, B.K. (1980). Expectations and attributions of parents of handicapped children. In J.J. Gallagher (Ed.), *New directions for exceptional children: Parents and families of handicapped children* (Vol. 4, pp. 1–57). San Francisco: Jossey-Bass.

Lowery, B.J., Jacobsen, B.S., & Murphy, B.B. (1983). An exploratory investigation of causal thinking of arthritics. *Nursing Research, 32*(3), 157–162.

McCubbin, H.I., Joy, C.B. Cauble, A.E., Comeau, J.K., Patterson, J.M., & Needle, R.H. (1980). Family stress and coping: A decade review. *Journal of Marriage and the Family, 42,* 855–871.

McCubbin, H.I., Larsen, A.S., & Olson, D.H. (1982). *F-COPES*. St. Paul, MN: Family Social Science, University of Minnesota.

McCubbin, H.I., & Patterson, J.M. (1983). The family stress process: The double ABCX model of adjustment and adaptation. In H.I. McCubbin, M.B. Sussman, & J.M. Patterson (Eds.), *Social stress and the family: Advances and developments in family stress theory and research* (pp. 7–38). New York: The Haworth Press.

McCubbin, H.I., Sussman, M.B., & Patterson, J.M. (1983). Introduction. In H.I. McCubbin, M.B. Sussman, & J.M. Patterson (Eds.), *Social stress and the family: Advances and development in family stress theory and research* (pp. 1–6). New York: The Haworth Press.

McDonald-Wikler, L. (1986). Family stress theory and research on families of children with mental retardation. In J.J. Gallagher & P.M. Vietze (Eds.), *Families of handicapped persons: Research, programs, and policy issues* (pp. 167–196). Baltimore: Paul H. Brookes Publishing Co.

Meyerson, L. (1963). Somatopsychology of physical disability. In W.W. Cruickshank (Ed.), *Psychology of exceptional children and youth* (2nd Ed., pp. 1–52). Englewood Cliffs, NJ: Prentice-Hall.

Mullins, J.B. (1987). Authentic voices from parents of exceptional children. *Family Relations, 36,* 30–33.

Murray, M.A. (1959). Needs of parents of mentally retarded children. *American Journal on Mental Deficiency, 63,* 1078–1093.

Olshansky, S. (1962). Chronic sorrow: A response to having a mentally defective child. *Social Work, 43,* 190–193.

Oster, A. (1984). Keynote address. In National Center for Clinical Infant Programs (Ed.), *Equals in this partnership: Parents of disabled and at-risk infants and toddlers speak to professionals* (pp. 26–32). Washington, DC: National Center for Clinical Infant Programs.

Patterson, G. (1985). Ministering to the family of the handicapped child. *Journal of Religion and Health, 14*(3), 165–176.

Pearlin, L.I., & Schooler, C. (1978). The structure of coping. *Journal of Health and Social Behavior, 19,* 2–21.

Pearson, J.E., & Sternberg, A. (1986). A mutual-help project for families of handicapped children. *Journal of Counseling and Development, 65,* 213–215.

Pollner, M., & McDonald-Wikler, L. (1985). The social construction of unreality: A case study of a family's attribution of competence to a severely retarded child. *Family Process, 24,* 241–254.

Reiss, D., & Oliveri, M.E. (1983). Family stress as community frame. In H.I. McCubbin, M.B. Sussman, & J.M. Patterson (Eds.), *Social stress and the family: Advances and developments in family stress theory and research* (pp. 61–84). New York: The Haworth Press.

Rothbaum, F., Weisz, J.R., & Snyder, S.S. (1982). Changing the world and changing the self: A two-process model of perceived control. *Jounal of Personality and Social Psychology, 43*(1), 5–37.

Scott, S., & Doyle, P. (1984). Parent-to-parent support. *Exceptional Parent, 14*(1), 15–22.

Shumaker, S.A., & Brownell, A. (1984). Toward a theory of social support: Closing conceptual gaps. *Journal of Social Issues, 40*(4), 11–36.

Silver, R.L., Boon, C., & Stone, M.H. (1983). Searching for meaning in misfortune: Sense of incest. *Journal of Social Issues, 39*(2), 81–102.

Summers, J.A. (1987). *Defining successful families with and without children with disabilities.* Unpublished doctoral dissertation, University of Kansas, Lawrence.

Summers, J.A. (1988). Family adjustment: Issues in research on families with developmentally disabled children. In V.B. Van Hasselt, P.S. Strain, & M. Hersen (Eds.), *Handbook of developmental and physical disabilities* (pp. 79–90). Elmsford, NY: Pergamom.

Summers, J.A., Turnbull, A.P., Shaffer, H., & Brotherson, M.J. (1987). *Stress and coping for families of persons with disabilities.* Lawrence: Kansas University Affiliated Facility.

Taylor, S.E. (1983). Adjustment to threatening events: A theory of cognitive adaptation. *American Psychologist, 38,* 1161–1173.

Taylor, S.E., Lichtman, R.R., & Wood, J.V. (1984). Attributions, beliefs about control, and adjustment to breast cancer. *Journal of Personality and Social Psychology, 46*(3), 489–502.

Thompson, S.C. (1981). Will it hurt less if I can control it? A complex answer to a simple question. *Psychological Bulletin, 90,* 96–101.

Turnbull, A.P. (1985, October). *What is the impact of a child with a disability on the family?* Paper presented at the Hastings Center Colloquium on Disability, Hastings-on-the-Hudson, NY.

Turnbull, A.P., Behr, S.K., & Tollefson, N. (1986, May). *Positive contributions that persons with mental retardation make to their families.* Paper presented at American Association on Mental Deficiency, Denver, CO.

Turnbull, A.P., Blue-Banning, M., Behr, S., & Kerns, G. (1986). Family research and intervention: A value and ethical examination. In P.R. Dokecki & R.M. Zaner (Eds.), *Ethics of dealing with persons with severe handicaps* (pp. 119–140). Baltimore: Paul H. Brookes Publishing Co.

Turnbull, H.R., Guess, D., & Turnbull, A.P. (1988). Vox populi and Baby Doe. *Mental Retardation 26,* 127–132.

Turnbull, A.P., & Summers, J.A. (1987). From parent involvement to family support: Evolution to revolution. In S.M. Pueschel, C. Tingey, J.E. Rynders, A.C. Crocker, & D.M. Crutcher (Eds.), *New perspectives on Down syndrome* (pp. 289–306). Baltimore: Paul H. Brookes Publishing Co.

Turnbull, A.P., Summers, J.A., Bronicki, G.J., Backus, L.H., Goodfriend, S.J., & Roeder-Gordon, C. (1986). *Stress and coping in families having a member with a disability.* Washington, DC: D:ATA Institute (NARIC Rehabilitation Research Review).

Turnbull, A.P., Summers, J.A., & Brotherson, M.J. (1984). *Working with families with disabled members: A family systems approach.* Lawrence: Kansas University Affiliated Facility, University of Kansas.

Turnbull, A.P., & Turnbull, H.R. (1986). Stepping back from early intervention: An ethical perspective. *Journal of the Division for Early Childhod, 10*(2), 106–117.

Turnbull, H.R., & Turnbull, A.P. (1985). *Parents speak out: Then and now.* Columbus, OH: Charles E. Merrill.

Venters, M.H. (1980). *Chronic childhood illness/disability and familial coping: The case of cystic fibrosis.* Unpublished thesis, University of Minnesota, Minneapolis.

Walsh, J. (1987). The family education and support group. A psychoeducational aftercare program. *Psychosocial Rehabilitation Journal, 10,* 51–61.

Warren, F. (1985). A society that is going to kill your children. In H.R. Turnbull & A.P. Turnbull (Eds.), *Parents speak out: Then and now* (pp. 201–220). Columbus, OH: Charles E. Merill.

Watson J. (1986). A sibling essay. *Down Syndrome News, 10* (4), 54.

Wikler, L., Wasow, M., & Hatfield, E. (1983, July-August). Seeking strengths in families of developmentally disabled children. *Social Work,* 313–315.

Willette, J. (1987). Just an ordinary parent. *The Exceptional Parent, 17*(3), 12–13.

Yudenfriend-Glaser, R. (1987). Response to "Just an ordinary parent." *The Exceptional Parent, 17*(5), 7.

CHAPTER 3

Families
for All Children

Value-Based Services
for Children with Disabilities
and Their Families

Steven J. Taylor,
James A. Knoll, Susan Lehr, and Pamela M. Walker

Historically, society has largely treated people with disabilities as if they fell into a special class of human beings not entitled to the same rights and opportunities accorded to other individuals. This devaluation was, and often still is, reflected in the services available to them and their families (Biklen & Knoll, 1987; Wolfensberger, 1975). Fortunately, the late 1980s have seen a growing awareness of the abuse that can be fostered by this differential treatment and a concomitant growth in the movement of parents and self-advocates demanding recognition and respect. These forces have contributed to a reorientation of services to people with special needs and their families away from the specialized and segregated and toward the typical and integrated. The values underlying this redirection are some of the basic principles that political leaders often harken to as the cornerstones of society. Specifically, in the area of services for families one might see a reaffirmation of the fundamental rights of children and families.

In this chapter the authors assert that there are certain fundamental values that should form the foundation for a comprehensive system of family supports. Furthermore, this chapter attempts to demonstrate, by reference to an ongoing search for the best practices in community services for people with severe disabilities (Taylor, Biklen, & Knoll, 1987; Taylor, Racino, Knoll, & Lutfiyya, 1987), that the degree to which service providers are committed to this core of values largely determines the quality of services available to families.

A STATEMENT IN SUPPORT OF FAMILIES AND THEIR CHILDREN

In 1979, the Center on Human Policy released "The Community Imperative" declaration that affirmed the right to community living for people with mental retardation. This declaration was subsequently endorsed by professionals, parents, and concerned people throughout the country.

At that time, this right to community living for adults and children with severe disabilities was, and in most regions still is, translated as a mandate for small "homelike" group homes. Yet

This research was supported in part through Cooperative Agreement No. G0085C03503 between the Center on Human Policy, Syracuse University, and the National Institute on Disability and Rehabilitation Research, U.S. Department of Education. The opinions expressed herein do not necessarily represent those of the U.S. Department of Education and no endorsement should be inferred. The authors would like to thank Larry Irvin, George Singer, Julie Racino, Bonnie Shoultz, Hank Bersani, and Naomi Karp for their assistance in the preparation of this chapter.

the efforts of people who have attempted to make the principles of the community imperative a reality have moved the field to realize that people with mental retardation should not be accorded simply the right to "homelike environments." Rather, they should have the same right as everyone else—to a *home*. Thus, the Macomb-Oakland Regional Center in Michigan, which has developed more community living arrangements for people with severe disabilities than any other service system in the country, has stopped placing children in group homes, let alone institutions. As one administrator has explained, "There isn't a kid in the world who can't do better in a family than a group home (personal communication)."[1] In the Seven Counties Services Region in Kentucky, children with complex medical needs and "challenging behaviors" are also being matched with foster families. Many of the families have become legal guardians or adoptive parents. The sentiment that children belong in a family rather than a group home is gradually taking root around the country.

Unfortunately, while some of the most forward-looking service systems have discarded a model of group services for children with disabilities, most areas of the country have seen little change in the service system. As of 1988, thousands of children with developmental disabilities remain in public institutions, while thousands of others have been placed in nursing homes, group homes, and other facilities. In most states, families receive some token level of support, often restricted to limited access to respite services, rather than all of the supports they need to keep their children at home.

In May of 1986, in an effort to identify some of the principles underlying individualized family-centered services for children with disabilities, the Center on Human Policy convened a meeting of representatives from states, universities, parent and consumer associations, and service agencies from around the country. The position statement, *A Statement in Support of Families and Their Children,* grew out of that meeting, as an expression of the basic values that should guide services for children with disabilities (see Table 1).

The sections that follow elaborate on the principal points of this statement and point out how these values have found expression in a number of states, regions, and agencies around the country.

Permanency Planning

Permanency planning provides a policy context for the various programs that support families with a child who has a severe disability. It reflects a conscious decision to abandon the policies of the past that essentially required that a child be placed outside of a home to receive specialized services. As applied in the field of developmental disabilities, a permanency planning perspective also represents a realization that the presence of a disability should not affect a child's basic right to a home and family.

At root, permanency planning is no more than a policy affirmation of the basic fact that children develop best in a secure, nurturing environment—what is usually called a family home. The fact that the birth home, for any number of reasons, may not be able to provide a child with this nurturing climate does not alter this fact nor obviate a child's right to a home, positive enduring relationships with adults, and an individual advocate who is committed to his or her best interests.

In child welfare, permanency planning has been the dominant perspective for many years. It is required in any program receiving assistance under Public Law 96-272, *The Adoption Assistance and Child Welfare Act of 1980,* which redirected:

> . . . current federal fiscal incentives away from out-of-home care and towards alternatives to placement, and . . . provide(d) protection for children to insure they enter care only when necessary, are placed appropriately, provided quality care, reviewed periodically, and provided permanent families in a timely fashion.

Since most children with developmental disabilities have received services from a different funding source, this concept has not had an impact on their lives until recently.

The mid- to late 1980s have seen numerous states reorder their priorities for services to chil-

[1]Quotes from agency personnel (i.e., personal communication) are based on visits to Michigan and Kentucky in 1985, and Wisconsin in 1987. For further information, see reports on these site visits (Racino, 1985; Taylor, 1985a, 1985b, 1987).

Table 1.   The Center on Human Policy's *Statement in Support of Families and Their Children* (1987)

THESE PRINCIPLES SHOULD GUIDE PUBLIC POLICY TOWARD FAMILIES OF CHILDREN WITH DEVELOP-
MENTAL DISABILITIES . . . AND THE ACTIONS OF STATES AND AGENCIES WHEN THEY BECOME INVOLVED
WITH FAMILIES:

All children, regardless of disability, belong with families and need enduring relationships with adults.

When states or agencies become involved with families, permanency planning should be a guideline philosophy.
As a philosophy, permanency planning endorses children's rights to a nurturing home and consistent relationships with adults. As a guide to state and agency practice, permanency planning requires family support, encouragement of a family's relationship with the child, family reunification for children placed out of home, and the
pursuit of adoption for children when family reunification is not possible. Families should receive the supports
necessary to maintain their children at home.

Family support services must be based on the principle "whatever it takes."

In short, family support services should be flexible, individualized, and designed to meet the diverse needs of
families.

Family supports should build on existing social networks and natural sources of support.

As a guiding principle, natural sources of support, including neighbors, extended families, friends, and community associations, should be preferred over agency programs and professional services. When states or agencies become involved with families, they should support existing social networks, strengthen natural sources,
and help build connections to existing community resources. When natural sources of support cannot meet the
needs of families, professional or agency-operated support services should be available.

Family supports should maximize the family's control over the services and supports they receive.

Family support services must be based on the assumption that families, rather than states and agencies, are in
the best position to determine their needs.

Family supports should support the entire family.

Family support services should be defined broadly in terms of the needs of the entire family, including children
with disabilities, parents, and siblings.

Family support services should encourage the integration of children with disabilities into the community.

Family support services should be designed to maximize integration and participation in community life for children with disabilities.

When children cannot remain with their families for whatever reason, out-of-home placement should be viewed initially as a temporary arrangement and efforts should be directed toward reuniting the family.

Consistent with the philosophy of permanency planning, children should live with their families whenever possible. When, due to family crisis or other circumstances, children must leave their families, efforts should be directed at encouraging and enabling families to be reunited.

When families cannot be reunited and when active parental involvement is absent, adoption should be aggressively
pursued.

In fulfillment of each child's right to a stable family and an enduring relationship with one or more adults, adoption
should be pursued for children whose ties with their families have been broken. Whenever possible, families
should be involved in adoption planning and, in all cases, should be treated with sensitivity and respect. When
adoption is pursued, the possibility of "open adoption," whereby families maintain involvement with a child,
should be seriously considered.

While a preferred alternative to any group setting or out-of-home placement, foster care should only be pursued when
children cannot live with their families or with adoptive families.

After families and adoptive families, children should have the opportunity to live with foster families. Foster family
care can provide children with a home atmosphere and warm relationships and is preferable to group settings
and other placements. As a state or agency sponsored program, however, foster care seldom provides children
the continuity and stability they need in their lives. While foster families may be called upon to assist, support, and
occasionally fill in for families, foster care is not likely to be an acceptable alternative to fulfilling each child's right
to a stable home and enduring relationships.

From Center on Human Policy. (1987b). Statement in support of families and their children. Syracuse, NY: Author; reprinted by
permission.

dren with developmental disabilities. Increasingly, the emphasis has shifted from services
that focus exclusively on the disability to a more
holistic perspective that sees the child first. The
state of Michigan has been in the forefront of the
states that have used permanency planning as a

vehicle for giving expression to this change in
priorities.

In Michigan, permanency planning for children with developmental disabilities expands on
the basic concept and recognizes the special demands that a child with a disability can place on

a family. The state regulations describe the process as supporting both children and families. The first priority is to provide what is needed to maintain the child within the birth family. If this fails, the service system begins working toward reunifying the family. If reunification is not possible, and there is no active parental involvement, services focus on facilitating the adoption of the child. When these other goals cannot be achieved, a plan is developed for a permanent foster family, with arrangements for ongoing involvement with the birth family (if appropriate) and a guardian or advocate to see that the best interests of the child are being met. Institutionalization is not considered for any child and, in general, children are no longer placed in any group setting in Michigan.

Implementation of the permanency planning program requires not only changes in policy and procedure, but also changes in attitudes toward birth families. It requires a change in the purposes of out-of-home placement. Placement is used as a temporary support to families, not a long-term answer for children whose families are experiencing stress and difficulty in parenting their developmentally disabled child. That is to say, out-of-home placement initially is defined as an opportunity for families and agencies to work together to alleviate the circumstances that led to the removal of the child from the home. Michigan's Department of Mental Health defines permanency planning as follows:

> A planning process undertaken by public and private agencies on behalf of developmentally disabled children and their families with the explicit goal of securing a permanent living arrangement that enhances a child's growth and development. Permanency planning for children is directed to securing:
> 1) a consistent, nurturing environment;
> 2) an enduring, positive adult relationship; and
> 3) a specific person who will be an advocate for the child into adulthood.
> Underlying assumptions:
> 1) It is generally in the best interest of children to remain at home with their family. Therefore, public agencies should first attempt to plan, provide and coordinate services in such a manner that the integrity of the family unit may be *maintained.*
> 2) If a child cannot be maintained in the

> home, it is assumed that a public agency should then give priority attention to the provision and coordination of those services that will facilitate *reunification* of the child with his/her family at the earliest possible time after placement out of the natural home.
> 3) If reunification of the child with his/her family is not possible, and there is no active parental involvement with the child, the feasibility of adoption planning should be rigorously pursued.
> 4) For some children, already in care, strengthening the ties with the birth family by increasing the quality of involvement while the child remains in foster care may be the most appropriate permanency planning option. For certain other children, the permanency planning path may include such alternatives as long-term foster care, supplemented by securing an advocate or a guardian.
> 5) Institutionalization is not considered to be an appropriate permanency planning option. (Michigan Department of Mental Health, 1986, p. 5–6)

The Michigan Permanency Planning Project has provided extensive training to mental health staff of those agencies involved in the project about such topics as the permanency planning philosophy and concept, the importance of the parent/child relationship, how to maintain and reunite children with their families, the processes of attachment and separation, and adoption processes and procedures. Permanency planning casework activity has also been initiated for those children in care with the project agencies; 250 children in foster care with three agencies in metropolitan Detroit were screened and permanency objectives identified. As a result of efforts initiated through the project, 45 individuals have returned to their families from out-of-home placements and 18 children have been adopted.

Whatever It Takes

Permanency planning cannot work without having concrete services and resources to support children living with their families. As Jerry Provencal (personal communication), Director of the Macomb-Oakland Regional Center, put it:

> We don't believe in giving lip-service to the concept of family support; the important thing is to

make good the concept. Our purpose is to help families re-establish contact with a member of the family with whom they may have lost contact, and to give them whatever support they may need to enable the member with disabilities to return home permanently as a full member of the family. So we ask families what they need to keep their son or daughter with disabilities at home or to help them to return home. The shopping list may include anything like help with getting on and off the bus, constructive use of leisure time, or assistance at mealtimes.

In looking for the best approaches to serving people with severe disabilities in the community, the authors have identified a number of family support programs that have adopted a *whatever it takes* policy. They are all marked by placing much of the control of services into the hands of families and by flexibility to respond to each family's situation. Essentially the people involved in providing these services believe that cost effectiveness and human benefit are both best served by providing families with at least the range of services that traditionally have been available in out-of-home placements. These systems use a variety of approaches for getting resources to families and ensuring that the families' needs are being met. These models of providing support are not mutually exclusive and, in fact, can be used together to meet families' needs more effectively. Here the authors would like to highlight the cash subsidy provided in the state of Michigan, and Wisconsin's use of service vouchers as two examples of programs that realize that the needs of families are not always addressed by a professionally determined list of available services.

Cash Subsidy In Michigan, the state pays direct cash subsidies to families of children with severe disabilities. The subsidy is designed to help parents pay for the extra expenses incurred in having a child with severe disabilities (e.g., equipment, respite, home renovation, diapers, sitters). The subsidy amounts to $255 per month, an annual subsidy of $2,700 for eligible families (Taylor, 1985b).

Passed by the Michigan legislature with strong support from parent and advocacy groups, the Family Subsidy Act appealed to people with diverse political persuasions (liberal, conservative, right-to-life). As an economic measure, supporters argued that passage of the legislation would result in cost savings to the state by preventing out-of-home placements and encouraging families to take their children home from institutions and nursing homes. As a philosophical rationale, they pointed out that the legislation supported traditional family values.

Some agencies were not supportive of the legislation. They took the position that families would be better off if funds were provided to agencies to operate family support programs. They also questioned whether families might use the funds for things not related to their children with disabilities. Supporters countered that families themselves were in the best position to determine their needs. As one of the key legislators supporting the Family Subsidy Act put it (Taylor, 1985b), "We made the assumption that families are capable of making good decisions." It might also be argued that even if families used the subsidy for general household expenses, this can make it easier to maintain their children at home.

The eligibility criteria for Michigan's family subsidy program are as follows (Taylor, 1985b):

1. The family's annual income must be less than $60,000.
2. The child must be 0 to 18 years of age (after that age, he or she is eligible for Supplemental Security Income).
3. The child must have a severe disability. This includes children with severe mental impairments, autism, and severe multiple disabilities, as identified by public schools in accord with state education law.

As with any categorical program targeted to a specific population, the family subsidy program creates potential inequities in terms of beneficiaries. Families of children with severe physical disabilities and moderate mental disabilities are not eligible for subsidies. Surely, many of these families incur extraordinary expenses in caring for their children at home. Yet the Michigan Family Subsidy Act is an important step in the right direction. The program encourages, rather than discourages, families to maintain their children at home, reversing the traditional pattern of developmental disabilities services. Over 2,000 families participate in the Family Subsidy Program throughout the State of Michigan (Taylor, 1985b).

Service Vouchers   Wisconsin has one of the most innovative family support programs in the country. While many states have begun to establish respite and other programs for families, the Wisconsin Family Support Program with its use of a voucher system stands out for its responsiveness to the needs of individual families. Unlike many other schemes, the program is flexible, individualized, and family-centered.

The Family Support Program provides up to $3,000 in services for families of children with severe disabilities (Taylor, 1987). The state is authorized to approve additional funds to families upon the request of the local administering agency. Under state legislation, 10% of the funds allocated to a county may be used to pay for staff and other administrative costs; the remainder must be spent directly for family support services.

The Family Support Program can be used to pay for a broad range of services that families may need. As Linda Brown (personal communication), one of the parents participating in the program, has stated, families of children with severe disabilities can have a variety of extraordinary expenses:

> Along with the stress that arises from living much of the time on the edge of life, we families deal with things most families never have to consider: occupational, physical, and speech therapy; special feeding techniques, utensils, and foods; special equipment like wheelchairs, bolsters, wedges, seats, splints, braces, and hearing aids; and life support equipment like oxygen, apnea monitors, ventilators, nebulizers and compressors, various tubing, trachs, trach masks, and suctioning equipment. There are even special dressings for all of the tubes inserted and sterile water for all the special techniques. On top of these are countless medications, diapers (usually far past the normal toilet training stage), and often special clothing.

The Family Support Program lists 15 specific categories of services that a family can receive (Taylor, 1987):

1.   Architectural modifications to the home
2.   Child care
3.   Counseling and therapeutic resources

4.   Dental and medical care not otherwise covered
5.   Specialized diagnosis and evaluation
6.   Specialized nutrition and clothing
7.   Specialized equipment and supplies
8.   Homemaker services
9.   In-home nursing and attendant care
10.   Home training and parent courses
11.   Recreation and alternative activities
12.   Respite care
13.   Transportation
14.   Specialized utility costs
15.   Vehicle modification

In addition, the program can pay for the costs of their goods or services as approved by the state.

As the authors spoke with people involved in these and other service systems, the depth of their commitment to supporting the children with disabilities within their families became clear. Regardless of the variety of services listed on the official list, their attitude toward families is, "You tell us what you need and we'll try to get it for you." They view all of these programs as just the first steps in redirecting funds away from out-of-home placement and toward real support of families. In Michigan, Wisconsin, Calvert County in Maryland, and other places, a growing array of special assistance is also available. These include services and resources like "as needed" respite care, in-home aides, in-home nursing, counseling, adaptive equipment, assistance with physical plant modifications to the home, and training to deal with their child. Certainly, helping families to keep their developmentally disabled child at home is, even with the most extensive supply of services, a less costly alternative to out-of-home placement, but more important is the fact that home is the best place for that child to be.

Existing Social Networks and Natural Supports

A recurring theme in much of the writing by parents of children with disabilities is the parents' sense of isolation from the extended family, the neighborhood, and the larger community (see, e.g., Featherstone, 1982). There is a growing sense in the field of human services that, while this isolation may partially be a result of social prejudice against people with disabilities and the demands of caring for a child with special needs, it may be exacerbated by the traditional approach to services.

Recent years have witnessed the publication of compelling arguments on the importance of unpaid relationships and informal social supports in the lives of people with disabilities and their families (McKnight, 1987; O'Brien, 1987). As McKnight (1987) argues, human services agencies may actually undermine natural support systems and sever ties with community associations and relationships with typical community members. The most extreme example of this is found when a person is physically removed from the community and placed in an institution. However, agencies can also undermine informal supports in more subtle ways, for example, by providing professional services rather than encouraging families to turn to neighbors, extended family members, and community associations for support.

An awareness of the need for people with disabilities and their families to stay connected with their communities has been the impetus behind some of the more innovative approaches to family supports. The emerging perspective is that the professional supports are a safeguard or a buttress for natural resources that, at least hypothetically, are available in the community. In Michigan, one program administrator (personal communication) said that, "We succeed to the extent that we see people become less and less dependent on our services." It is instructive that this statement was made within the context of perhaps the most extensive array of family support services in the country, a system that will do "whatever it takes" to support families.

Some family support services try to take the informal support systems into account as part of determining a family's need for formal services. In Wisconsin, for example, all families being served by the Family Support Program initially receive a needs assessment and family plan. The needs assessment looks at the family's existing formal and informal support networks, and the family plan attempts to build upon these. For example, a neighbor may be called upon to provide transportation for a child. The plan then specifies what services a family will receive through the

program and what will be obtained from other sources. In addition to providing support services, the Family Support Program is intended to help coordinate other resources that a family may need. According to documents describing the Family Support Program (Taylor, 1987):

> An important role for the family support coordinator or case manager is to act as a kind of service broker assisting the family through the bureaucratic maze of available programs and services. The worker can also act as an advocate in helping the family to make maximum use of community services, such as community recreation programs, medical and dental services, public transportation, and other generic service providers (p. 18).

Family Control

Just as many human services programs have tended to emphasize professionalized services to the exclusion of informal supports, they have also tended to control the services offered to families. In the area of family supports, the available services have tended to be determined by the agency or professionals, rather than the family itself.

Gunnar Dybwad (1984) describes how this state of affairs developed. He points out that in the years after World War II parents became tired and resentful of society's discrimination against their children, and finally they rebelled. They wanted services for their children where none were available, and so they created them. They started their own schools and recreation programs, and, in some communities, they began sheltered workshops. It did not take them long to realize that this was no easy task—they needed help, and they sought it from educators and other professionals. The educators and professionals were the experts, and parents turned to them for expert guidance and information. However, in the process, authority passed from parent to expert, a pronounced shift that left the family lost and forgotten. "For many years, we (the professionals) essentially ignored and devalued the family as a focal point of helping children with severe handicaps" (Dybwad, p. 3).

An inherent danger of family support programs is for families to come to believe that experts have all of the answers, and that they cannot trust their own instincts based on their knowledge of themselves and their child. Although agencies may not intend to undermine the role of the family in the life of their child, they can fall into the habit of telling families what they need rather than working with them to help them identify their needs. A failure to listen carefully to the needs of families, as the families define them, can lead to a situation in which families must fit the program, rather than the program or service being designed to fit the family. The following case study illustrates this point.

> Jane and Carl Baker (pseudonyms) are parents of Alicia, a 13 year old girl who has been labeled autistic and emotionally disturbed. Those who know the Bakers know that they love Alicia and try to do what they think is right. Despite her aggression toward others and her constant attempts to hurt herself, Alicia is lovable. But the Bakers are tired, they are getting older, Carl's health is poor, and Alicia is getting tougher to handle.
> Alicia was refusing to bathe, dress, or get on the bus to go to school. The Bakers had tried everything, but each morning became a greater confrontation than the one before. Exhausted and frustrated, the Bakers requested family support services from a local agency.
> They asked for someone to come in the morning for about an hour to help get Alicia up, dressed, and off to school. In addition, they saw the need for a psychologist or social worker to do some problem-solving with the family and provide some ongoing support for Jane and Carl.
> The agency denied their requests, claiming that they were unable to find someone who could go into the home during the morning hours, and that their psychological services were not equipped to deal with people at home who had disruptive behaviors. Instead, the agency recommended placement for Alicia in an institution or a group home.

Families throughout the country tell variants of the same story. The agency worker listens as the family outlines its needs, or the family responds to a survey, questionnaire, or checklist. Then the agency describes what services it has available, who is eligible to receive the services, and at what cost. From this array, ideally, the family should be able to choose what it needs. In reality, it often has to accept whatever the agency can offer. In some cases, families are put on waiting lists, referred to other agencies, or simply denied services.

The main problem seems to be that the professionals have assumed the role of telling the parents not only what they need, but what they can

have, in spite of what the families say they need. To many parents this is not family support or case management, but attempts by professionals to manage a family. Families know best what will make their lives easier, more productive, and secure for their children. Unfortunately, professionals usually feel that they know better what the family should have, and often make decisions accordingly.

If "family support" is to be just that, it must be determined and directed by the family with the assistance of the professionals, and not the other way around. Agencies should be the case managers, not the family managers. Professionals need to stop telling the families that they, the professionals, know better what is needed. Their role should be to help the family identify what long- and short-term support services it needs and to assist the family in obtaining these services. If the services do not exist, then the professionals should be compelled to find or provide the technical assistance to generic community-based agencies, in order to create the service or augment already existing services.

Support the Whole Family

Of all the values underlying the new approaches to family supports, the most significant is perhaps the least apparent, and certainly the least conscious to the people involved in these services. What is distinctive here is the perspective from which "the problem" is addressed.

Many family support programs have identified the problems of families as occurring in one of three areas: 1) the disability that needed to be cured, contained, or accepted; 2) the person with the disability who needed to be rehabilitated or removed; and 3) the family that had to overcome its unrealistic expectation, its disorder, or its denial (Taylor, Racino, Knoll, & Lutfiyya, 1987). In each of these three instances, the problem was traditionally seen as a pathology residing in the individual or the family. To simplify this perspective, the person with a disability and/or the family was seen as the problem. This approach to defining the problem led to the development of services that focused very narrowly on the pathology. Some examples of this can be seen in behavioral interventions that attempt to eliminate a troublesome behavior without considering the total context within which it occurs, or family supports that only offer respite one weekend a month so the family can be temporarily relieved of the 'burden' of caring for the child.

The more recently developed services of the 1980s are marked by a broader, more holistic approach to the problems confronting people with disabilities and their families. For these services, the problems are encountered as the person with the disability and the family (with its unique constellation of strengths, weaknesses, needs, and desires) confront the demands of everyday life in their community. From this perspective, problems are properly identified as issues to be dealt with, and not as people. Furthermore, the person with a disability and the members of the family are no longer passive recipients of services, but rather active participants in solving problems.

The holistic perspective has a number of major implications that can be seen running through the principles outlined in the Family Statement (see Table 1). A holistic vision leads parents to an increasingly activist role in the formal service system. Some agencies, for example, are responsible for the administration of family support programs and require that more than 50% of their governing board be actual consumers of the services that they offer. In addition, service agencies are recruiting "experienced" parents to play a formal role in the delivery of services. For example, in Calvert County, Maryland, family support services for an individual family are coordinated by a parent counselor, who is the parent of a child with a disability and works as a counselor for the project. Most of the parents say that they find it easier to communicate with another parent.

Another result of the broader vision is a more expansive definition of the services that are seen as family supports. A concern for the functioning of the family unit, the environment within which a child with a disability grows and develops, has led to parent-to-parent self-help groups, financial advisors, grandparent groups, and sibling groups being brought under the family support canopy. Also, the realization that parents may occasionally need respite from their children is the motivator for a flexible approach

to respite services. Services that have adopted this approach may allow a neighborhood babysitter to be paid with respite care funds, help recruit and train a respite worker from the neighborhood, or permit an agency respite worker to babysit all of the children in a household rather than restricting him or her to only watching the child with a disability.

On the surface, the changes in services outlined in this section can be written off as rather insignificant. In fact, similar elements can be found in some traditional services. Nevertheless, when they are viewed in context with everything else that innovative agencies and programs are doing, they seem to herald a fundamentally different attitude toward the needs of families.

Encourage Community Integration

A major implication of the critique that McKnight (1987) and others level against traditional services is that as services become less invasive in the life of the community and the family, they should actively foster the integration of the individual with a disability into the life of the community. Helping to forge the connection with the community has the potential for being the greatest contribution any service can provide for an individual or a family. Services and case workers come and go, but the resources of the community—especially family ties and friendships—remain.

One example of this approach is found in an *integrated recreation* program. It is funded as a type of respite care, but at the same time, gives a child with disabilities the chance to spend time and make friends with people outside the family. The Dunbar Community Center, a private, nonprofit neighborhood center located in an inner-city section of Syracuse, New York, provides such an opportunity. Here, 40–50 neighborhood children and teenagers participate in a variety of recreational, educational, and cultural activities. Among them are three girls with disabilities, all of whom are labeled mentally retarded and attend special education classes, who come to Dunbar on a regular basis. For Tracy, this participation includes arts and crafts, games, browsing in the library, going on field trips to community sites such as museums and swimming pools, movies, and being in a poetry group. For Michelle and Pam, too, this is a time to make friends as they join their nondisabled peers in making ceramics, on the playground, or in the game room.

Participation by Tracy, Pam, and Michelle at Dunbar is made possible by the presence of a support person, Bertha Jones. Bertha is paid through respite funds provided by the New York State Office of Mental Retardation and Developmental Disabilities to work part-time assisting the girls. Bertha continually makes efforts to involve them in activities with other nondisabled children. For instance, she will help them engage in activities that are of interest to others also, and invite others to participate. She assists other staff at the center to get to know them and learn to assist them. At Dunbar, these girls are forming friendships and acquaintances with other children from their neighborhood. Pam's mother commented, "It's really great that she can come here. She comes here every day."

Family Reunification

As one Michigan state official (personal communication) described it, "Permanency planning is a fundamental change in the way we do business." As it should be, permanency planning starts with the family, to provide the services that families need to keep their children at home.

Even with the best support services, some families cannot care for their children at home. This is where the permanency planning approach makes all the difference in the world. In most communities, out-of-home placement signals an end to the family's responsibility for the child. Indeed, many service systems actually discourage family involvement with the child after placement, while permanency planning supports the family's ongoing relationship with the child and aims toward family reunification.

Macomb-Oakland has closed what one person there referred to as the "smorgasbord" of placements commonly presented to families (institution, group home, foster care). For children, there is only one option: foster care. As one administrator (personal communication) stated:

We tell families when they can't care for their children, "If you're looking for out-of-home place-

ment, we can help you. What we have available is a foster family." Parents are approached with empathy and understanding: We try to break down parents feeling threatened by foster care. We tell them, "A foster parent is different. You didn't choose to have a child with a disability, you didn't choose the type of child, you didn't have training prior to having the child, you didn't choose the time of life to have a child with a disability, and you didn't have an out clause."

When a child is placed in foster care, this is viewed as a temporary placement, and plans are made to reunite the family. Macomb-Oakland, together with other agencies, develops a written memorandum of understanding with the family and the foster family. This specifies the reason for the placement, the conditions necessary for the child to return home, the parents' responsibilities to change things to enable the child to return home, the parents' agreement to visit the child regularly, Macomb-Oakland's and other agencies' responsibilities to provide services to families to enable them to take their children home, and the foster parents' agreement to encourage and cooperate with parental visits. In short, permanency planning aims at encouraging continued parental involvement during placement, with the goal of returning the child to the natural family. When this is not possible other options are pursued.

Adoption

Adoption is being increasingly viewed as the option of choice for children who cannot live with their families (Nelson, 1985). Macomb-Oakland, Seven Counties Services in Kentucky, and other service systems around the country are finding parents to adopt children with disabilities. Contrary to conventional wisdom, they are finding that even children with severe disabilities are adoptable. According to an administrator at Seven Counties Services, age is a more important factor than severity of disability in finding families to adopt children. In other words, the younger the child, the easier it is to find adoptive families, regardless of severity of the child's disability.

As part of the permanency planning approach, Macomb-Oakland and Michigan are looking for adoptive families for children whose natural parents are no longer involved in their lives. As Macomb-Oakland administrators explain, they push hard for adoption for children who do not have involved families. Macomb-Oakland also explores *open adoption* for some children. This is a nonlegal arrangement whereby a family gives a child up for adoption, but the adoptive family agrees to cooperate with the birth parents' visits and continuing involvement.

In Michigan, as in several other states, adoptive families can qualify for a range of subsidies, including a special adoption subsidy equivalent to the rate paid to specialized foster care providers and either a medical care subsidy or the state's family support subsidy. These subsidies are designed to help adoptive parents pay for the extra expenses entailed in taking care of the child.

Foster Care

Although foster care is the placement of last resort in the outline in *A Statement in Support of Families and Their Children,* it remains a crucial element in a family-centered system of support services and should remain a priority for service providers. Children who for whatever reason cannot live with their birth families or adoptive parents should be in foster homes. For most children, foster placement will be a temporary arrangement. But, for some children, foster placement is likely to be a long-term arrangement. Even those children who cannot live with their families or be freed for adoption should have the opportunity to live with a family that not only cares for them, but cares about them as well.

As part of its permanency planning approach, Macomb-Oakland pursues options known as *shared care* and *permanent foster care* when family reunification or adoption are not possible. *Shared care* is an arrangement in which the natural and foster parents agree to share responsibility for raising the child; for example, the child might spend weekdays with the foster family and weekends with the natural family. Permanent foster care refers to a nonlegal agreement by foster families to serve as primary parents for children until adulthood.

The problem of finding enough good foster families is a common lament among agencies. A Macomb-Oakland resource manual (Dewey,

1980) is entitled: *Recruitment of Foster Homes . . . Can Good Homes Really Be Found?* In characteristic fashion, the last sentence of the manual reads, "Yes! They can be found!" Places like Macomb-Oakland have found ways to accomplish what many others say cannot be done.

According to the Macomb-Oakland staff, there is a foster parent somewhere for every child. As one administrator (personal communication) explained:

> There's somebody for everybody. Foster parents aren't interchangeable, though. Some aren't good with kids with behavior problems, but they're good with medically fragile kids. You have to match the kid with the family. The toughest kid will be taken in by someone who likes him.

Macomb-Oakland has placed 35 children with severe multiple disabilities and medical involvements in foster homes. Several of these children have subsequently been adopted by their foster parents.

So where are these wonderful foster parents, these "saints," found? First, it is not necessary to be a saint to be a foster parent. To be sure, foster parents should be caring and committed people, and willing to treat the child "as their own." According to people at Macomb-Oakland, however, the image of the foster parent as a saint has driven many otherwise good people away from being foster parents. In looking for foster parents, they try to downplay the romanticized version of foster parenting. As long as foster parents are decent people, they do not mind if they are attracted to foster parenting by the opportunity to supplement family income or to practice professional skills.

Second, case managers need to be prepared to stand behind foster parents. Good service systems offer a variety of support services to foster parents: respite, home aide services, consultation, in-home nursing and professional services, and financial assistance for purchasing equipment and supplies and making necessary modifications to a house. Perhaps the biggest support to foster parents is being available when help is needed. This is what good case managers do. At Macomb-Oakland, case managers stay in close touch with foster parents. Part of the reason for this is to monitor foster homes, to ensure that people placed in foster care are doing well. It is also a matter of supporting foster parents. As one Macomb-Oakland case manager (personal communication) commented, "I'll stop by during the evening or on weekends. They also know they can call me anytime, day or night. You can't just drop in unannounced without reciprocating." In Louisville, Kentucky, another director (personal communication) described how important it was to families to be able to reach someone at the time they need help. As he said, "It is often not important to do anything; just being there and caring seems most important."

Third, it helps to pay foster parents a decent stipend. For some people, especially those who view themselves as professionals, this will mean the difference between becoming a foster parent or not. Many states and service systems today offer foster parents both a payment for room and board and a stipend to provide training and services within the home. Region V in Nebraska recruits both foster parents who receive from $322.00 to $359.50 per month for room and board and *extended families* who are paid an additional $125–$500 per month for training and services. Macomb-Oakland refers to foster homes as *community training homes,* and this creates an expectation of what foster families are supposed to do. Community training homes receive between $25 and $35 per day ($9,125–$12,775 per year) and higher in some instances. While it is true that many good people can be attracted to being foster parents for children with severe disabilities by the opportunity to supplement family income, it is equally true that some people neither need nor want to be paid a salary for being a loving parent to a child. These people, too, have to be sought out.

Finally, it is important to know where and how to look for foster parents. Agencies that have been successful in finding foster homes for children with severe disabilities seem to start with the assumption that there are decent people in the world and proceed to look for them. Those that have not been successful seem to assume that only people who are merely interested in the money will become foster parents. Macomb-Oakland makes foster parent recruitment an agency priority, and employs three full-time specialists who recruit and screen foster families. Macomb-Oakland's strategy is to achieve high

visibility for foster care. It attempts to generate a large number of phone calls and inquiries in order to come up with a small number of good families. As Nancy Rosenau (personal communication) explained:

> What we need to do is generate thousands of inquiries about foster care. You have to get large numbers. Then you need a staff of people to call and stay in touch with them, to nurture and shape them into being able to give what a kid needs.

CONCLUSION

Values play an elusive role in the formation of social policy. Literally everyone engaged in the conversation about policy as it relates to people with disabilities acknowledges that values influence decisions. However, there are major differences in the role assigned to values.

There is a position that sees values as having secondary importance in the decisionmaking process. The research literature in human services often seems to convey the impression that policy should be primarily guided by the findings of value-neutral research that can empirically determine the most effective mode of service. Similarly, management literature points to cost-effectiveness, obtaining a desirable outcome for the lowest cost, as the major factor in the policy equation. From this point of view, broad societal values (e.g., services should not hurt people) provide a context for the decisionmaking process, but the actual determination of policy is purely a management decision informed by the hard data of the researcher and the accountant.

The authors contend that this approach to policy formation, research, and management, with values writ small and in the background, is fundamentally flawed. In this process, the voice of the recipient of services is silent and the human benefit of a policy can be lost in a spreadsheet.

The alternative is modeled by the various services cited in this chapter. In these situations the values were clearly stated at the outset and held up as a standard for all that followed. From this perspective, research serves as a tool for exploring how the goals expressed in the initial value statement can be realized. It does not enter into an interminable academic debate over whether it can be achieved. The administrators of these services use their value base as a major factor in their budgeting. For them the question is cost-benefit, not mere cost-effectiveness: How can limited funds be used to achieve the greatest degree of human benefit for the individuals involved with this program?

REFERENCES

Adoption Assistance and Child Welfare Act of 1980, §623, 42 U.S.C. §671 (1981).

Biklen, D., & Knoll, J. (1987). The disabled minority. In S. J. Taylor, D. Biklen, & J. Knoll (Eds.) *Community integration for people with severe disabilities* (pp. 3–24). New York: Teacher's College Press.

Center on Human Policy. (1987a). *Families for all children*. Syracuse, NY: Author.

Center on Human Policy. (1987b). Statement in support of families and their children. Syracuse, NY: Author.

Dewey, J. (1980). *Recruitment of foster homes: An instructional manual on foster home recruitment techniques: Can good homes really be found?* Mt. Clemens, MI: Macomb-Oakland Regional Center.

Dybwad, G. (1984). *Coalition Quarterly, 4*(1), 3–7.

Featherstone, H. (1982). *A difference in the family*. New York: Penguin Books.

McKnight, J.L. (1987). Regenerating community. *Social Policy*, Winter, 54–58.

Michigan Department of Mental Health. (1986). Permanency planning for children with developmental disabilities in the mental health system. Lansing, MI: Author.

Nelson, K.A. (1985). *On the frontier of adoption: A study of special-needs adoptive families*. New York: Child Welfare League of America.

O'Brien, J. (1987). Embracing ignorance, error, and infallibility: Competencies for leadership of effective services. In S.J. Taylor, D. Biklen, & J. Knoll (Eds.) *Community integration for people with severe disabilities* (pp. 85–108). New York: Teacher's College Press.

Racino, J. (1985). *Report on Seven Counties' Services*. Syracuse, NY: Center on Human Policy.

Taylor, S.J. (1985a). *Report on Macomb-Oakland Regional Center*. Syracuse, NY: Center on Human Policy.

Taylor, S.J. (1985b). *Report on the State of Michigan*. Syracuse, NY: Center on Human Policy.

Taylor, S.J. (1987). *Community living in three Wisconsin counties*. Syracuse, NY: Center on Human Policy.

Taylor, S.J., Biklen, D., & Knoll, J. (Eds.). (1987). *Community integration for people with severe disabilities*. New York: Teacher's College Press.

Taylor, S.J., Racino, J., Knoll, J., & Lutfiyya, Z. (1987). *The nonrestrictive environment: On community integration for people with the most severe disabilities*. Syracuse, NY: Human Policy Press.

Wolfensberger, W. (1975). *The origin and nature of our institutional models*. Syracuse, NY: Human Policy Press.

CHAPTER 4

The Role
of Parents in Creating
and Maintaining Quality
Family Support Services

Frank Warren and Sandra Hopfengardner Warren

The role of parents in creating and maintaining quality services should be obvious. Their participation should be pervasive, limited only by the express will of their adult son or daughter in areas involving personal choice. Every aspect of the creation, quality assurance, and maintenance of services ought to be open to parental and family participation. Parents have the keenest motivation for bringing about both individual and systemic change for people with developmental disabilities, and, banding together, they have the power to change the actions of governments and the attitudes and daily functions of society.

It should be a basic assumption of agencies and professionals that parents love their children, wish to provide for them, and are their best advocates. They want good lives for them, good homes, good occupations, and a fulfilling human existence. Unfortunately, this is not a basic assumption, and, in many instances, sets the stage for ongoing distrust and difficulty between parents and professionals. Parents are still seen by many service providers as part of the problem rather than part of the solution.

Almost reflexively, parents begin to plan support systems so that they and the children with disabilities when they become adults, may progress toward conventional life goals in spite of any challenges they may face. Parents plan as a conventional function of parenting; as naturally as they feed, comfort, teach, provide warmth, nurture, and shelter so that children may grow

and develop. They try to provide for their offspring individually or within the context of support systems, in supportive environments or surrounded by hostile public opinion. They succeed or fail to every imaginable degree. All individuals experience either or both aspects of the parent-child relationship, therefore, the perspective of professional persons encompasses that of parents.

The examination of any family support service will reveal the work of parents who care and plan for a child who is approaching or has reached adulthood. This chapter examines some of the ways that parents plan and care for children with disabilities, and discusses how they create support services and develop systems and policies to maintain them, as well as to assure quality within them. It also examines some of their successes and failures and outlines areas for future parent and family activity.

DEVELOPMENTS AND CHANGES

A Change in Focus

Support services for people with developmental disabilities and their families have moved dramatically, in the late 1970s and during the 1980s, from supporting families by removing children with disabilities from family care to providing community-based services such as schools, homes, jobs, and support systems that help to integrate children with disabilities. These services

have developed not only as a result of an expanded understanding that people with disabilities are entitled to the same rights as other citizens, but also as a result of parental advocacy to
influence public policy that, in turn, has made
available certain funding sources for the development of services in home communities.
Service providers have responded to the availability of funding, and have acted in concert
with the wave of opinion sweeping the developmental disabilities field that provides positive reinforcement for such development and negative
responses for the continuation of institutional
services.

However, in some cases the development of
community support services has reflected the desire of providers to expand services because the
funding and climate for growth was present,
rather than as a manifestation of concern for the
rights and well-being of persons with disabilities. Unfortunately, in the early years of this
change, many individuals exchanged wards and
walls for other kinds of equally segregated and
isolated conditions as some service providers, at
significant public expense, created new forms of
segregation while abandoning other, more obvious ones. Institutionalized devaluation, poor
quality programming, neglect, abuse, and systemic failure have been found in both the traditional forms of support and the newer ones in
communities (Bercovici, 1983; Bicklen, 1977;
Braddock, 1987; Gettings, 1986; Warren, 1987).

Quality Assurance System Changes

Coinciding with the growing awareness of problems within traditional and new support systems, much attention has turned to quality
assurance systems. Standards and survey approaches have been altered so that they can more
accurately address service environments, conditions, and value structures in a dynamic state of
flux (Accreditation Council on Services for People with Developmental Disabilities [ACDD],
1987; The Commission on Accreditation of Rehabilitation Facilities [CARF], 1986; Hemp &
Braddock, 1985; Hemp, Fujiura, & Braddock,
1986; Wolfensberger & Glenn, 1975). These
changes are taking place in spite of the fact that,
as Braddock (1987) observed at the conclusion

of his extensive analysis of federal policy toward
services to the developmentally disabled, "A
clearly articulated and well-financed federal policy commitment to community integration is
. . . lacking" (p. 184).

The involvement of parents in creating and
maintaining quality services for members of
their families who are developmentally disabled
is essential while change is taking place; such
efforts are likely to be more effective than when
public policy has been solidified. For many who
have not been active—the parents of young children, the families of those whose living arrangements are changing, the relatives of those who
remain unserved in the community or who are
coming out of institutions with no reasonable
support services in place—the field may seem
distant and full of unfamiliar forces. But many
avenues of access exist. It is not an exaggeration
to say that the lives of those who have disabilities
may depend upon the use of those avenues for
their benefit, whether it is to correct an untenable
situation for an individual, create the necessary
atmosphere for change within an agency, influence the development of a public policy, or add
one voice or one letter to a lobbying effort.

INVOLVEMENT OF FAMILY MEMBERS

Family Perspectives

Aside from the legally mandated involvement of
parents in the process of planning and delivering
services to their child with developmental disabilities (The Developmental Disabilities Assistance and Bill of Rights Act of 1975 [PL
94-103]; The Education for All Handicapped
Children Act, [PL 94-142], 1975), parents and
family members are valuable participants because they bring a common-sense perspective to
the evaluation and enhancement of services that
is often seen as unique to these processes
(Boggs, 1985a, 1986; Cutler, 1984; *Monitoring
Community Residences,* 1984; Schopler, 1984;
Schopler & Reichler, 1971; Taylor, 1980; Turnbull, 1985; Warren, 1979, 1985a).

It is understandable that families approach
services with different expectations and concerns. For example, one parent who had suffered
many disappointments in a long search for ser-

vices answered the question, "What are your expectations from this program?" with a single word: "Nothing." Some parents have organized programs based entirely upon need and then sought funding for them after they were established, rather than following the more accepted process of creating a program that will mesh with the ideas of certain sources of money or established provider agencies.

Professional Merry-Go-Round

Parents have often been angered, frightened, and discouraged by service providers. Many have undergone what Ritvo (1976) calls "the professional merry-go-round (p. 274)" at the hands of individuals and agencies charged with assisting them and their disabled offspring. *The National Society for Children and Adults with Autism* (1981) cites a common experience of many parents:

> The pediatric clinic says the child is "slow in developing," the parents must wait. Try a mental retardation specialist.
> The mental retardation specialist finds the child is not testable. It must be a brain dysfunction. Try pediatric neurology.
> Pediatric neurology comes up with "funny wiggles" on the EEG. Nothing specific. See a psychiatrist.
> The psychiatrist decides the child is too ill for testing and must be retarded. Try special education.
> Special education refers the child back to the pediatric clinic for diagnosis and treatment (pp. 18–19).

Ritvo charges that professionals, out of ignorance, often mismanage parents who come to them for help: "I, for one, feel . . . that if brought to trial we (professionals) would be found guilty on many grounds (1981, p. 18)."

The implication of this statement is interesting. Perhaps many professionals, after having spent years in training, feel they must have answers to the multiplicity of problems that parents bring them, and when they find that no answers exist, they feel guilt. Parents and professionals together, acknowledging the paucity of systemic answers to a multitude of daily life problems, can turn frustration and anger into tools for change rather than experience these feelings as personal guilt. By examining needs, planning,

and working together, families and professionals can find answers, change policy, and create support systems—particularly support systems that can exist between individual parents and professionals who trust and respect one another.

Extreme Cases As a result of service problems, or because needed services were not available, or as a result of their own fear and mistrust of available persons and agencies, some parents have faced extreme situations. Support services in the situations that follow were nonexistent, fragile, inadequate, and offered these parents harsh choices or compelled them to side with extremists who promoted questionable goals. For example:

> The mother of a young adult with autism in Prince George's County, Maryland, tried for years to find a residential placement for her son who was severely handicapped and often ran away from home. She applied to every agency, including the state institution nearby, without success. She was unable to find respite care when her son's day placement closed for a holiday. In January, 1987, he left her house, dashed across a busy highway on his way to a local fast-food store, and was struck by an automobile. On February 18, 1987, he died in a local hospital. Her efforts to sue for damages were unsuccessful. "We have buried him now. It is over. I'm just going to try to put it behind me," she said.

> The physician father of a young man with a behavior disorder (the young man was committed to a psychiatric hospital after being criminally charged for injuring a child in a grocery store) reported that his son was being drugged to death in the institution. "He is tied to his bed. He is bleeding from his esophagus. The dosage and variety of drugs he is being given is so powerful it is killing him. There is no behavioral program for him. Every time I go to a state agency for help, they do nothing. No one can help me. They are killing my son." (Warren, 1985b, p. 221).

> In 1986 the state of Massachusetts closed an institution on the grounds that its "treatment" amounted to nothing more than severe abuse. The parents of a young man with severe and challenging behavior who was being treated by aversive procedures at the institution organized a class action suit to challenge the state's efforts. The parents and their attorney were successful in their efforts to maintain the aversive procedures, and on May 27, 1987, were presented the *humanitarian award* of the Association for Behavior Analysis (ABA) for their efforts (Etzel et al., 1987). Yet there were also

many who expressed outrage at the inappropriateness of this action, which reinforces the importance of parent's advocating on their own behalf, particularly where issues of controversy are involved.

Among those who responded to the events cited in the last example was Dick Sobsey of the University of Alberta. He noted that state action was initiated when the youth died, "after experiencing a seizure while restrained by arm and leg cuffs, with staff sitting on him, while wearing a specially designed helmet that covered his face to block his vision, while forced to listen to static through earphones, and while exposed to ammonia vapors (Sobsey, 1987, p. 2; TASH Newsletter, August, 1986)." Sobsey wrote: "Criminals and prisoners of war are protected against such procedures, but . . . individuals labeled as handicapped do not enjoy the same protection. Being handicapped is not a crime. If it were, society would be forced to treat people with handicaps as well as it treats criminals—undoubtedly a major improvement (p. 2)."

As these examples illustrate, problems facing parents and families with disabled members can be quickly transformed from daily concerns to matters of life and death. Fortunately, these examples do not represent the actual experiences of most families, although most families can relate to the sense of rapidly escalating frustration that can drive one to desperation. The tragic situations noted previously are reminders of how fragile current support systems can be, and how close families can come to disaster.

Service providing agencies are not inherently emphathetic to the needs of their constituencies. A variety of forces contribute to the performance of agencies, including the naturally occurring inclination for agencies to perpetuate themselves, sometimes in spite of and at variance with their founding purposes (Wolfensberger, 1972). Thus, they cannot be expected to institute procedures or to establish services that are sensitive to and supportive of consumer and parental needs without consumer and parental input and involvement.

Families of persons with disabilities have historically served to identify unmet needs and to advocate for the resolution of problems (Principles of community integration, 1986; Provencal & Taylor, 1983). In short, parents have the most

information about their children with disabilities, and have a lifelong commitment to them. They interact with professionals and service providers, and depending upon how they view the value of professional advice and service provision, often create powerful alliances that can have far reaching effects—or sometimes engage in destructive behavior out of desperation. It is incumbent upon professionals and parents, therefore, to collaborate, actively seeking to plan not only for the future of children with disabilities, but also to draw upon their considerable resources to influence broader systemic change that would benefit all persons with disabilities.

Avenues for Involvement

Many avenues exist for families and parents to become involved in the establishment and maintenance of quality services. For example, they could hold positions on agency boards of directors and committees; in governmental oversight agencies and their various volunteer appendages; in volunteer advocacy organizations and networks; in monitoring groups of all sorts; in local, state, and national organizations formed for the purpose of suggesting, influencing, or directing policy; or in agencies or interest groups created from the imagination and motivation of interested parents, family members, or others.

Numerous service agencies have been founded, developed, or taken over by parents who, after examining the human services landscape for a support system to meet specific needs and finding none (or finding existing ones inadequate), are determined to make changes on their own. Few parents become involved in service provision because that is what they have originally planned to do. Initially they expected to find these services already in place. One example involves Jane Salzano, a Rockville, Maryland, schoolteacher, who established Community Services for Autistic Adults and Children (CSAAC), a nationally recognized agency serving over 60 adults with autism and mental retardation in integrated apartments, townhouses, and homes in the Washington, DC suburbs. CSAAC also pioneered supported employment for persons severely handicapped with autism and behavior problems, finding jobs for them in businesses and industry where they work alongside their nonhandicapped peers, making wages, receiving company benefits, and becoming taxpayers (Warren, 1987).

"I heard the statement so many times: '*Somebody* ought to do something,' " Salzano (personal communication) said. "Finally I decided *I am that somebody.* I am going to have to do something (Warren, 1987, p. 9)." She adopted the phrase as a personal motto.

Salzano, like many others, visited the existing options for placement before deciding to organize and create a separate program.

In 1968 I visited . . . (a Maryland institution). That, more than anything else, got me going. I took a group of parents, and we visited King's Cottage—"cottage" is the euphemism used—where they kept the 'low-functioning' people. We observed the day room. It was bare, with a concrete floor. There were about 60 people milling around. They wore no shoes for 'safety reasons.' They did not have their own clothes, but institutional clothes, some tattered and torn. There were two staff persons in that room, and they had no interaction with the clients, except to move in and take out those who were injured or who injured themselves.

When I went in, many of the people came up to me, tugging at me, begging 'Mommy! Mommy! Take me home. Take me home, Mommy!' I didn't sleep for three nights after that visit. Then I made a vow that my son, Brian, would never become one of those people (Warren, 1987, p. 9).

After this experience, Salzano used skills that she acquired as a teacher to organize parents and professionals in creating and directing a new agency. Her story is not unique. Many parents have had similar experiences, and have reacted to them in a variety of ways by creating new programs, establishing service agencies, organizing coalitions for the purpose of changing laws, influencing legislation, changing or establishing policy at all levels of government, founding national advocacy groups and networks, providing motivation for lawsuits to broaden the rights of individuals with disabilities and their families, and writing about their own and others' experiences so that teachers, educators, and policymakers will be influenced to work toward better lives for disabled persons.

Parent-Professional Alliances

Numerous examples of parent-professional alliances exist, both individual and organizational, through which skills and resources are joined to produce benefits that would have been difficult, if not impossible, alone. For example:

Barbara C. Cutler, parent of a severely handicapped son, has worked with Martin A. Kozloff of the Department of Sociology at Boston University since 1977. Influencing one another, they have produced numerous books and articles, have trained hundreds of parents and students, and have become a force to reckon with, not only in their home state of Massachusetts, but nationwide. In Cutler's (1981) basic manual for individual parent advocacy, Kozloff writes: "This book [will] help parents institute and maintain a productive relationship with special education systems . . . [it] will be equally useful for educators and other professionals, helping them to . . . enlist parents as partners . . ." (p. xi).

Working in close alliance with families associated with the North Carolina Society for Autistic Children (now the State Chapter of the Autism Society of America) Eric Schopler, Ph.D., of the University of North Carolina at Chapel Hill and his associate, Robert J. Reichler, M.D., in 1971 created Division TEACCH (Treatment and Education of Autistic and Related Communication Handicapped Children), the first statewide program designed to support families with autistic children and to provide community integrated education for them in public schools. Schopler and Reichler broke with traditional approaches to the treatment of autism when they developed the concept of "parents as cotherapists" in working with their children. This idea grew from their observation of parents who were coping not only with the direct problems caused by the disability of autism, but also with blame-inflicting and stigmatizing problems created for parents by traditional professional ideas, including the once commonly accepted view that *poor parenting* caused the disability. Schopler sees parents as "advocates, developmental agents, and the primary cure for the problems of autism" (Schopler & Mesibov, 1984, p. 3). He writes (Schopler & Marcus, 1987, p. 509): "The importance of working collaboratively cannot be emphasized enough, nor can the necessity of maintaining a flexible attitude and willingness to avoid building barriers."

The role of parents and families and their productive collaboration with professionals in the creation of educational opportunities for handicapped children is traced by Levine and Wexler (1981), who cite the involvements of the National Association for Retarded Citizens (now the Association for Retarded Citizens of the United States [ARC-US]) and the Council for Exceptional Children (CEC) in the advocacy effort that resulted in passage of PL 94-142. ARC-US, primarily a parent organization, and CEC, made up of teachers and educators, collaborated in this effort, bringing in other groups of both parents and professionals to meet the needs of legislative strategy. In this case, education became the vehicle for collaboration between parents and professionals toward the goal of a better life for persons with disabilities. Largely as a result of this successful effort, a coalition of parent and professional organizations working at the federal level was formed and continues to influence legislation and government policy. The Consortium for Citizens with Developmental Disabilities (CCDD) is composed of various groupings of organizations that come together to address specific issues. CCDD task forces involve every significant agency representing the interests of persons with disabilities with a presence in Washington.

The previous examples, and many others like them, represent the way that parents and professionals, working together toward common goals, make up the fabric of the developmental disabilities movement.

Creating Order Out of Chaos

The role of parents in creating and maintaining quality services is essentially one of creating order out of chaos, or creating an arrangement—environmentally, sequentially, and/or longitudinally—that serves particular family needs. What may appear to be chaos is, in reality, a multitude of orders created by others to serve a multiplicity of purposes, almost none of which neatly mesh with the needs of a particular family. Parents of children who are not handicapped may expect to find the order of things somewhat amenable to their family needs. But parents of children who have any one of a great variety of labels attached to them such as mental retardation, autism, cerebral palsy, and epilepsy, have already begun to understand that the order of things is much more chaotic, ill-fitting, and not arranged in the best interest of their family or of their child in particular.

Perhaps these parents have discovered by prenatal tests that the next member of their family is likely to be mentally retarded, have spina bifida, or have Down syndrome. The mother may have heard the suggestion, either directly or by implication: "You really must have an abortion. It is up to you. You have a choice, you know." Or, she may have heard the opposite: "If you do so, you

and all those who may assist you will have committed murder. You will have to bear that guilt as long as you live, and you will never be spared from the terrible result of your decision. Take care." Already the "order" of things, arranged by others for other purposes, has come brutally to bear upon such parents, and has presented them with difficult, stressful, and frightening choices that cannot be seen in any way as supportive. To change chaos to order to benefit family members with disabilities, parents must have the power to do so. Parents should understand that they *have* that power.

Individual action can sometimes solve the problem. It may take no more than a clearly articulated explanation of the problem and a proposed solution presented to the right official or agency. Often, however, it takes concerted, cooperative action. Individuals involved in a common effort, planning and acting together, can create an appropriate order of things that will bring about solutions. For example, one parent working to resolve an issue with a school board may meet little success when acting alone. The board may have other agendas, and one person seeking change can be ignored more easily than a group of people. Imagine the attention that will be focused upon the problem if 10 people arrive, or 20 or 75, accompanied by representatives of the press.

As Levine and Wexler (1981) observe, the developmental disabilities movement has its roots and much of its impetus in the civil rights upheaval of the 1960s. The power of parents—not upper or middle class people, but ordinary working class parents who band together because they recognize injustice—has been felt in both the developmental disabilities and the civil rights movements. A classic example of how an effective confrontation carried out by well organized and motivated parents can change an entire system follows.

In 1969, Kinston, a city in North Carolina of 15,000 people, was under pressure to integrate its public school system. The board of education was controlled by individuals who believed that races should be segregated. Over the years the system had responded as little as possible to federal urging to comply with the law, and had brought individuals who were not white into tra-ditional white schools, but no traditionally black schools had been integrated. In early 1969 the school board submitted a plan to the federal gov-ernment that integrated 49 white students—all from the poor, blue collar section of town—into all black schools.

The monthly school board meeting was scheduled to be held at the administration build-ing on September 8, 1969. The local paper, the *Kinston Daily Free Press,* reported the meeting. The headline read: *Angry East Kinston Parents Demand Fair Play.* "Some 250 to 300 parents from East Kinston flocked into Lewis School Auditorium Monday night for an eye-to-eye con-frontation with the Kinston City School board (Warren, 1969, p. 1, 12)." The parents, objecting to the way that the school board chose to selec-tively integrate students from a lower income section, argued for complete integration of all the schools in the system. They announced that they would not leave the meeting until the school board agreed.

The same issue of the local paper announced the resignation of a long-time conservative member of the board. The chairperson resigned shortly thereafter, and a new configuration of power within the board emerged. A liberal chair-person was elected, and a new plan submitted and approved. Under the new plan integration was accomplished, and students were assigned to schools by grade rather than by race. That in-cident and many others demonstrate that policy changes can be made when parents are willing to work together to achieve their goals. Parents of children with disabilities can have the same kind of impact if they see their roles as clearly as these parents did.

Individual Planning Process

One of the primary tools for parents to use in "creating order out of chaos" is the individual planning process. In its legal form this process is the result of parental insistence that families be intimately involved in program planning for their members who have disabilities, rather than leav-ing the planning entirely in the hands of paid professionals.

Federal regulations as well as nationally ac-cepted standards (ACDD, CARF, Program Anal-ysis of Service Systems [PASS]) emphasize the necessity for active participation by the individ-ual that is served and his or her family in the de-velopment of individual program plans. This participation is even more crucial as planning begins to address functional living in the com-munity and long-term planning for the future (ACDD, 1987).

Haring and Billingsley (1984) observe that the individual planning process has evolved from the notion of a *multidisciplinary* to an *inter-disciplinary* to a *transdisciplinary* team ap-proach. The shades of meaning between these terms, while seeming slight, have significant im-plications. When the *multidisciplinary* model was popular, several specialists saw the individ-ual, did not consult with each other, and sent separate recommendations for implementation. This approach was replaced by the *inter-disciplinary* model, in which many specialists were members of a team that met, discussed findings, and devised a single set of recommen-dations. Nevertheless, many professionals still carried out their own programs. Under the *trans-disciplinary* model, the following principles are followed:

1. The team members are chosen based on the needs of the particular individual.
2. Individuals on the team trade skills and learn from one another.
3. Accountability is provided through frequent meetings and cross-skill training.

In the transdisciplinary approach, those with the most frequent contact with the individual who is receiving services, including family members and direct-care staff, must take an ac-tive part in implementing the team's recommen-dations. These are the people who are exposed to many more opportunities and settings, such as leisure activities and meals, in which they can not only carry out the program, but also observe and collect data for program decisions made by the team. Parents and family members involved in team functions can influence the team toward a broader understanding of individualized pro-gram planning, and can facilitate in-service training and skill sharing.

Historically, individualized program planning has been accomplished primarily by professional teams, rather than by parents, family members, or the individual served. More recently, however, parental and individual access to these teams has been mandated by law, and strengthened by accrediting mechanisms. But the notion that planning for an individual with disabilities is primarily a function of the individuals themselves, along with family, friends, and persons or agencies whose purpose is to provide a variety of paid *services,* has been slow to emerge in practice.

PARENTS AND "LIFE AFTER SCHOOL"

Transitional Planning

Parents and family members that are engaged in the individual planning process with a student with disabilities must address planning for "life after school." It is generally assumed that education has as its goal the provision of skills and resources that are necessary for adult employment and community living. Until recently, most students with disabilities were not included in this functional preparation for adult life (Sowers, Jenkins & Powers, 1988). However, with the passage of PL 98-199 *The Education of the Handicapped Act Amendments of 1984* and PL 99-457 *The Education of the Handicapped Act Amendments of 1986,* specific categorical incentives have been developed to encourage educational agencies to provide transitional services leading to employment and life in the community for young adults with disabilities.

What Are Transitional Services? *Transition* refers to activities that prepare an individual for subsequent environments, expectations, norms, and rules (Falvey, 1986) and is an outcome-oriented process (Will, 1984). One of the most crucial periods of a person's life begins at the point of exiting from school, either by means of "aging out" or graduation (Haring & Billingsley, 1984). Transitional services assist individuals in making the adjustments that are necessary to function successfully in the community environment.

Will (1984) has outlined various levels of transition services. These include: 1) minimal support (e.g., similar to that offered students without

disabilities), 2) time-limited supports designed to lead to independence, and 3) ongoing services enabling an individual to receive all necessary services (indefinitely) for continued, successful employment. Bellamy, Rhodes, and Albin (1986) further clarify the role of transitional services in their findings that such supports should begin during training and continue throughout the employment duration, rather than ending at the point of employment, as is the traditional vocational rehabilitation approach.

Elements of Transitional Services Numerous transitional service programs for young adults have developed in the mid 1980s, offering an opportunity to study the effectiveness of these programs (Bellamy et al., 1986). Central to any effective service delivery system is a coordinated (Haring & Billingsley, 1984), holistic (Elder, Conley, & Noble, 1986) approach. This requires communication and cooperation among parents or families and educational, vocational rehabilitation, transportation, housing, and social service agencies.

Educational curricula leading toward future employment for youth with disabilities should focus on personal decision- or choice-making (Brown, Halpern, Hasazi, & Wehman, 1987; Will, 1984) and community integration for educational (Falvey, 1986) and related services (Rainforth & York, 1987). Parental and family involvement in these areas is essential. Instruction for teenagers and young adults should continue to emphasize personal decisionmaking and community integration, while increasing the focus upon pregraduation employment (Sowers et al., 1988). Opportunities for employment while an individual is still in school have been shown to be among the strongest determinants for successful, continued employment after school (Hasazi, Gordon, & Roe, 1985).

Any actual transitional employment program should be designed to provide: 1) early, continued employment preparation throughout a student's entire academic career (Sowers et al., 1988); 2) work skills training based on actual jobs available in the work force (Brown et al., 1987); 3) systematic, direct, and behaviorally based vocational instruction ensuring that students learn to perform to their maximum potential (Sowers et al., in press); and 4) adaptations in the natural environment designed and used to assist a student in performing employment tasks (Hofmeister & Friedman, 1986).

Principles of Integrated Employment Historically, professionals and even family members have made decisions for individuals with disabilities that were not always in their best interest, often despite their good intentions. Fortunately, service agencies are beginning to view people with disabilities as individuals who have much to offer, and who retain their rights and responsibilities like all citizens. And like all citizens, they need *opportunities* more than protection, *support* more than shelter, and *training and assistance* rather than charity and pity.

The following principles of integrated employment are based on such changing attitudes:

Everyone has an inherent right to full participation in society, *including the right to work;* the fact that an individual has a disability should in no way preclude him or her from taking full advantage of the benefits of employment.

Tests and assessments are made *only* for the purpose of achieving a proper match between job and individual skill or preference, not for exclusionary purposes.

Separate prevocational or vocational training for adults is of little use, and presents an unnecessary delay to actual work; training *on the job* works best.

The presence of a worker with disabilities is the most effective way to dispel fear and prejudice that may occasionally be found among co-workers.

The belief that the integration of people with disabilities into all walks of life is a *moral issue,* not just an interesting exercise, generates energy, enthusiasm, and commitment on the part of individuals and organizations trying to bring it about.

Parents' Roles during Transition Parents and families may become involved in transition programs at all levels, including the review of individualized education programs (IEPs) for their son or daughter to ensure that vocational goals include functional activities in the natural environment. Parents and family members can also advocate for and assist in the development of

curricula designed to prepare students for community life (social interaction and employment strategies are of particular importance), and insist upon teaching environments and practices that maximize student contact with nondisabled peers (Falvey, 1986). Essential to any smooth transition from school to work is continued contact and coordination among parents or families, and social service, employment, housing, and transportation agencies.

EVALUATING EXISTING FAMILY SUPPORT PROGRAMS

Parents as Monitoring Team Members

The participation of parents and family members in monitoring service programs is a valuable way for assessing quality in existing services, and for gathering information for the development of additional services.

Parents and family members can offer a viewpoint that is often lacking in standard evaluation efforts; that is, they can offer one that reflects local community values (Turnbull, Blue-Banning, Behr, & Kerns, 1986). Teams comprising family members, recipients of services, and interested citizens can provide an alternative (or adjunct) to conventional monitoring systems. Their focus is on *service quality from the perspective of values* (Association for Retarded Citizens-U.S., 1987; Provencal & Taylor, 1983). Team members can ask such questions as: "How does this home compare with my own and other homes in the area?"; "Do the people that are being served live, work, play, shop, and go to school in the same places I would go to do these things?", "Do these people perform real work for pay?"; "Does this agency demonstrate a commitment to normalization and community integration?"; "Do the planning activities of the agency and the daily interactions of staff valorize the roles that service recipients play?"; "Does the agency recognize the need of all people for real (unpaid) friends and a feeling of belonging?"; "Are recipients of services and their families treated as equal citizens?"; "Do they participate as partners in service planning?" (Principles of Community Integration, 1986; Wolfensberger, 1983; Wolfensberger & Glenn, 1975); "Do the people served have sufficient opportunity for reciprocal

interaction with people who love them?" (Bronfenbrenner, 1973). By asking such questions,
teams can evaluate the "feel" of a program, the
atmosphere of an environment, the warmth of a
home, the individuals' freedom to express varied
tastes, the agency's commitment to rights and
role valorizing functions, and the overall sensitivity of the agency.

Parents and Quality Assurance

Quality assurance simply means a guarantee of
quality or excellence (Morris, 1970). It refers to
a variety of evaluative and corrective processes
that are designed to encourage service providers
to assist individuals in ways that coincide with
philosophical, ethical, or government policy
goals and objectives (Boggs, 1986; Gold, 1979;
Hoover-Dempsey, 1986; Schopler, 1984; Warren, 1979; Wolfensberger, 1983). Elements of
quality assurance include standard setting, performance measurement, feedback, and control
(Human Services Research Institute [HSRI],
1983). The ultimate indicator of quality is
whether individuals in a particular program
achieve personal and social milestones that reduce dependence and enable them to exercise
citizenship rights and responsibilities (ACDD,
1987).

Representatives of both the public and private
sectors commonly participate in quality assurance systems (ACDD, 1987; Dokecki &
Zaner, 1986; Martin, 1980; *Principles of Community Integration,* 1986, Turnbull & Turnbull,
1985; Wiegerink & Pelosi, 1979). Public sector
participants often include those responsible for
licensing, providers of funding, case managers,
and protective service workers. Private sector
participants should include those who receive
services; parents and families of recipients; and
friends, lawyers, advocates, neighbors, and interested citizens.

Every parent of an individual with a disability
who depends upon a service provider should remember certain basic goals about quality assurance. Any such system should have at least
six goals of assurance: 1) providers are capable
of delivering quality services, 2) services are
consistent with good practices, 3) the commitment of resources necessary to produce quality
services is adequate, 4) services are designed to

meet individual needs, 5) agency planning and
staff interaction enhances the value of the roles
that clients play in the community, and 6) individual rights and well-being are protected
(HSRI, 1983; Wolfensberger, 1983).

PARENTS AND SYSTEMIC CHANGE

Systemic Advocacy

The importance of parent and family involvement in systemic advocacy and lobbying is
widely recognized (Bowe & Williams, 1979;
Martin, 1980; Turnbull & Turnbull, 1985; Warren, 1984, 1987). Parents and family members
have always played important roles in systemic
issues, including the development of (and the
creation of driving energy behind) legislative initiatives, policy formulation, governmental budget alterations, and service evaluation.

Parental membership on advisory boards and
planning councils is mandated by the PL 94-103
and PL 94-142, providing additional avenues for
participation. These laws, as well as every major
act of Congress affecting people with disabilities, bear the imprint of family members acting
individually, as members of organizations, as
elected officials, or as public servants holding
appointed government positions. Here are some
well known examples:

John F. Kennedy provided impetus for current
federal government involvement in the developmental disabilities movement; he was the brother of
a person with mental retardation.

Lowell Weicker, a United States Senator from Connecticut, both during his term as Chairman of the
Senate Subcommittee on the Handicapped and as a
subcommittee member, played a leading role in
Senate action to benefit persons with developmental disabilities, and is continuing efforts to enact
major Medicaid program reform. He is the father of
a son with mental retardation.

Madeleine Will, Assistant Secretary for Special
Education and Rehabilitative Services (OSERS) of
the U.S. Department of Education during the Rea-
gan Administration, authorized major funding initiatives in the area of transitional services and supported employment. She is the mother of a son with
Down syndrome.

Elizabeth Boggs, author and founder and former
president of the Association for Retarded Citizens

of the United States has, since 1949, played a major and uninterrupted role in the formulation of public policy toward persons with developmental disabilities by way of her involvement with ARC-US. Also a veteran member of the board of directors of the Accreditation Council on Services for People with Developmental Disabilities (ACDD), she describes herself (Boggs, 1985b) as "a social synergist with a predisposition toward communication and collaboration rather than confrontation (p. 40)." She is the mother of a son with profound retardation and multiple handicapping conditions.

Impact on Judicial Decisions

Families have played a major role in formulating public policy to benefit their relative with a disability by influencing legislative and administrative actions. Their efforts have also been felt in the judicial arena. They have initiatied or been active participants in legal actions to guarantee education, to close institutions, to mandate habilitation, to protect rights, to ensure pay for work, to guarantee due process, to prevent abuse, and to increase services to individuals in the community. The pattern has been a familiar one. Family members have observed an injustice or have experienced one themselves. They have sought redress in a variety of ways, and when they have failed, they have brought lawsuits, either as individuals, on behalf of family members, or in collaboration with advocacy organizations. Their success in this arena has been dramatic and has changed the configuration of our system of rights and the way the public understands persons with handicapping conditions and their role in society.

Some of the major cases that have been instigated by, or received significant impetus from, parents and family members follow. In *Armstrong v. Kline* (1979), the Federal Court of Appeals affirmed a district court holding that restricting the education of handicapped children to the regular 180-day school year violates their right to an appropriate education. In *Covington v. Harris* (1969), the Federal Court of Appeals for the District of Columbia held that whenever an alternative placement is considered, within or outside an institution, the *least restrictive alternative* must be explored first. In *Donaldson v. O'Conner* (1974), the Federal Court of Appeals for the Fifth Circuit held that there is a constituional right to individual treatment. If treat-

ment is the reason for commitment, it violates due process for no treatment to be provided; and if an individual's dangerous behavior is the reason for commitment, then treatment is the price that society must pay for the safety it derives from the denial of liberty.

In *Halderman v. Pennhurst State School and Hospital* (1977), the U.S. Court of Appeals affirmed a lower court holding that individual programs must be devised for individuals in a large Pennsylvania institution, and that each resident must be provided habilitation in the least restrictive, most integrated environment possible. The court ruled that the instituion was "incapable" of providing constitutionally appropriate care and habilitation, thus setting off a wave of similar actions in 20 other states. In *Knecht v. Gilman* (1973), a federal appeals court noted that labeling the administration of a vomit-inducing drug as a "treatment" (contingent upon swearing and not standing when told) did not insulate it from Eighth Amendment scrutiny, and held that it was "cruel and unusual punishment" unless administered with residents' approval. In *Lake v. Cameron* (1966), the principle of "least restrictive alternative" emerged. The Federal Court of Appeals for the District of Columbia held that government cannot involuntarily confine a person simply because he or she needs care, and is not entitled to compel an individual to accept help at the price of freedom.

In *Mills v. Board of Education* (1972), the court held that all school-age children are entitled to public education, and should be assigned to regular public classrooms. In *New York Association for Retarded Children v. Rockefeller* (1973), the residents of a New York institution were found to be in worse condition after entering the institution than before, and the court held that there is a constitutional right to protection from deterioration. In *Pennsylvania Association for Retarded Children v. Commonwealth of Pennsylvania* (1971), the court struck down a law excluding children from school if they could not "benefit" from education. The court held that all children, no matter how handicapped, could benefit from a program of education and training. *Rouse v. Cameron* (1966), viewed as the genesis of the right to treatment cases, established that an individual who is committed must have treatment or be released. *Souder v. Brennan* (1973) established that an individual in an institution must be paid the minimum wage for work performed.

The Fifth Circuit Court of Appeals held in *Wyatt v. Stickney* (1972) that there is a constitutional right to adequate care for individuals who are institutionalized. This case was instigated when a cut in the Alabama cigarette tax led to the firing of 99 employees in state institutions. Overcoming Alabama's argument that the notion of treatment presents questions not susceptible to the judiciary, the court held that institution-wide standards could be formulated. Many rights were enumerated, including the right to the least restrictive conditions necessary for treatment, the right to be free from isolation, the right not to be subjected to experimental research without consent, the right not to be subjected to hazardous or unusual treatment procedures without express and informed consent after consultation with counsel, the right to keep and use personal possessions, the right not to be required to perform institutional maintenance work and to receive minimum wage for such work if done voluntarily, the right to a comfortable bed and privacy, the right to recreational facilities, the right to adequate staff and meals, and the right to individualized treatment plans with projected timetables, specific goals, and criteria for discharge.

These court cases, and many others, bear the mark of parents and families joining with or acting on behalf of individuals with disabilities to reclaim the rights that handicapped citizens should have as a matter of course.

Program Enhancement and Sensitization

Parent and family involvement brings commonsense perspectives and an infusion of commu-

nity values into the operation of services, and provides networks for information sharing and policy change activities, all of which serve to enhance program quality (Provencal & Taylor, 1983; Surratt, 1984; Wallitt, 1978; Warren, 1984).

Parents and family members, working individually or in association with other parents and professionals, can sensitize communities to the value of individuals with disabilities (Wolfensberger, 1983) both informally and by collaborative action. They can bring about increased value perception, acceptance, and appreciation of persons with disabilities by providing education to neighbors and friends, businesses, and community organizations, and by using their imaginations to enable individuals with disabilities to become more involved in the regular daily social activities of the neighborhood, and thus to become more fully integrated into their communities.

SUMMARY

Families with members who have disabilities have been the primary instigators in all areas of policy, quality assurance, program development, and service delivery to persons with developmental disabilities. Their continued involvement is essential if services are to enable children and adults to play valuable roles in their communities, become franchised citizens, and hopefully to escape dependency. Professionals and other service providers can increase the quality of their efforts by understanding the common links that they share with parents and family members of persons with disabilities. They can cultivate trust and seek collaboration so that combined family and professional resources can be used most efficiently to improve life conditions for persons with disabilities.

REFERENCES

Accreditation Council on Services for People with Developmental Disabilities. (1987). *Standards for services for people with developmental disabilities.* Boston: Author.

ARC facts: Citizens monitoring. (1987, August). Arlington, TX: Association for Retarded Citizens of the United States.

Armstrong v. Kline, 476 F. Supp. 583 (E.D.Pa.1979).

Association for Retarded Citizens/Ohio. (1984). *Monitoring community residences.* Columbus, OH: Author.

Bellamy, G.T., Rhodes, L.E., & Albin, J.M. (1986). Supported employment. In W.E. Kiernan & J.A. Stark (Eds.), *Pathways to employment for adults with developmental disabilities* (pp. 129–138). Baltimore: Paul H. Brookes Publishing Co.

Bercovici, S. (1983). *Barriers to normalization: The restrictive management of retarded persons*. Baltimore: University Park Press.

Bicklen, D. (1977). The politics of institutions. In B. Blatt, D. Bicklen, & R. Bogan (Eds.), *An alternative textbook in special education* (pp. 29–84). Denver: Love Publishing Company.

Boggs, E. (1985a). Update: Whose head is in the clouds? In H.R. Turnbull & A. Turnbull (Eds.), *Parents speak out: Then and now* (2nd ed.) (pp.55–63). Columbus, OH: Charles E. Merrill.

Boggs, E. (1985b). Who's putting whose head in the sand? In H.R. Turnbull & A. Turnbull (Eds.), *Parents speak out: Then and now* (2nd ed.) (pp. 39–54). Columbus, OH: Charles E. Merrill.

Boggs, E.M. (1986). Ethics in the middle of life: An introductory overview. In P.R. Dokecki & R.M. Zaner (Eds.), *Ethics of dealing with persons with severe handicaps: Toward a research agenda* (pp. 1–15). Baltimore: Paul H. Brookes Publishing Co.

Bowe, F., & Williams, J. (1979). *Planning effective advocacy programs*. Washington, DC: American Coalition of Citizens with Disabilities.

Braddock, D. (1987). *Federal policy toward mental retardation and developmental disabilities*. Baltimore: Paul H. Brookes Publishing Co.

Bronfenbrenner, U. (1973). The split-level American family. In H. Kirschenbaum & S. Simon (Eds.), *Readings in values clarification* (pp. 249–264). Minneapolis: Winston Press.

Brown, L., Halpern, S., Hasazi, S., & Wehman P. (1987). From school to adult living: A forum on issues and trends. *Exceptional Children, 53*(6), 546–559.

Commission on Accreditation of Rehabilitation Facilities. (1986). *Standards manual for organizations serving people with disabilities*. Tucson, AZ: Author.

Covington V. Harris, 419 F. 2d.617 (D.C. Cir. 1969).

Cutler, B.C. (1981). *Unraveling the special education maze*. Champaign, IL: Research Press.

Cutler, B.C. (1984). The parent as trainer of professionals: Attitudes and acceptance. In E. Schopler & Mesibov (Eds.), *The effects of autism on the family* (pp. 247–262). New York: Plenum.

Dokecki, P.R., & Zaner, R.M. (Eds.). (1986). *Ethics of dealing with persons with severe handicaps: Toward a research agenda*. Baltimore: Paul H. Brookes Publishing Co.

Donaldson v. O'Conner, 493 F.2d.507 (CA5 1974).

Elder, J.K., Conley, R.W., & Noble, J.H.J. (1986). The service system. In W.E. Kiernan & J.A. Stark (Eds.), *Pathways to employment for adults with development disabilities* (pp. 53–66). Baltimore: Paul H. Brookes Publishing Co.

Etzel, B.C., Hineline, P.N., Iwata, B.A., Johnson, J.M., Lindsley, O.R., McGrale, J.E., Morris, E.K., & Pennypacker, H.S. (1987). The ABA humanitarian awards for outstanding achievement in pursuit of the right to effective treatment. *The Behavior Analyst, 10*(2), 235–237.

Falvey, M.M. (1986). *Community-based curriculum: Instructional strategies for students with severe handicaps*. Baltimore: Paul H. Brookes Publishing Co.

Gettings, R. (1986). *Assuring the quality of institutional and community-based services for developmentally disabled persons: An identification of relevant federal policy issues*. Alexandria, VA: National Association of State Mental Retardation Program Directors.

Gold, M. (1979). Preparing for a meaningful adult life. In *Proceedings of the 1979 Annual Meeting and Conference of the National Society for Autistic Children* (pp. 35–42). Washington, DC: National Society for Autistic Children.

Halderman v. Pennhurst State School and Hospital, 446 F. Supp. 1295 (E.D.Pa. 1977).

Haring, N., & Billingsley, F. (1984). Systems-change strategies to ensure the future of integration. In N. Certo, N. Haring, & R. York (Eds.), *Public school integration of severely handicapped students: Rational issues and progressive alternatives* (pp. 83–105). Baltimore: Paul H. Brookes Publishing Co.

Hasazi, S., Gordon, L., & Roe, C. (1985). Factors associated with the employment status of handicapped youth exiting from high school from 1979 to 1983. *Exceptional Children, 51*, 455–469.

Hemp, R., & Braddock, D. (1985). *ACMRDD accreditation: Analysis of nationwide survey results, 1980–1984* (Monograph No. 20). Chicago: University of Illinois at Chicago, Institute for the Study of Developmental Disabilities.

Hemp, R., Fujiura, G., & Baddock, D. (1986). *CARF accreditation: Summary of 50 surveys, 1982–1984* (Monograph No. 21). Chicago: University of Illinois at Chicago, Institute for the Study of Developmental Disabilities.

Hill, M., Wehman, P., Kregel, J., Banks, D., & Metzler, H. (1987) Employment outcomes for people with moderate and severe disabilities: An eight-year longitudinal analysis of supported competitive employment. *Journal of The Association for Persons with Severe Handicaps, 12*. 182–189.

Hofmeister, A.M. & Friedman, S.G. (1986). The application of technology to the education of persons with severe handicaps. In R.H. Horner, L.H. Meyer, & H.D. Fredericks (Eds.), *Education of learners with severe handicaps: Exemplary service strategies* (pp. 351–367). Baltimore: Paul H. Brookes Publishing Co.

Hoover-Dempsey, K.V. (1986). Family-responsive policy and mental retardation. In P.R. Dokecki & R.M. Zaner (Eds.), *Ethics of dealing with persons with severe handicaps: Toward a research agenda* (pp. 233–238). Baltimore: Paul H. Brookes Publishing Co.

Human Services Research Institute. (1983). *Assuring the quality of services to persons with developmental disabilities in Colorado: System design recommendations*. Boston: Author.

Knecht v. Gillman, 488 F.2d 1136 (8Cir. 1973).

Lake v. Cameron, 364 F.2d 657 (D.C. Cir. 1966).

Levine, L.L., & Wexler, E.M. (1981). *P.L. 94-142, an act of Congress*. New York: Macmillan.

Martin, R. (1980). *Educating handicapped children: The legal mandate*. Champaign, IL: Research Press.

Mills v. Board of Education of the District of Columbia, 348 F.Supp. 866 (DC 1972).

Morris, W. (Ed.). (1970). *The American heritage dictionary of the English language*. Boston: American Heritage Publishing and Houghton Mifflin.

National Society for Children and Adults with Autism (NSAC) (1981). *How they grow: A handbook for parents of young children with autism* (2nd ed.). Washington, DC: Author.

New York Association for Retarded Children v. Rockfeller, 357 F.Supp.752 (E.D.N.Y. 1973).

Noble, J., & Conley, R. (1987). Accumulating evidence on the benefits and costs of supported and transitional employment for persons with severe disabilities. *Journal of The Association for Persons with Severe Handicaps, 12,* 163–174.

Pennsylvania Association for Retarded Children v. Commonwealth of Pennsylvania, 334 F.Supp 1257 (1971).

Principles of community integration. (1986, July). *Community News,* 5.

Provencal, G., & Taylor, R. (1983). Security for parents: Monitoring of group homes by consumers. *Exceptional Children, 13*(6), 39–44.

Rainforth, B., & York, J. (1987). Integrating related services in community instruction. *Journal of The Association for Persons with Severe Handicaps, 12,* 190–198.

Rhodes, L., Ramsing, K., & Hill, M. (1987). Economic evaluation of employment services: A review of applications. *Journal of The Association for Persons with Severe Handicaps, 12,* 175–181.

Ritvo, E. (1976). *Autism: Diagnosis, current research and management,* New York: Spectrum Publications.

Rouse v. Cameron, 125 U.S. App. D.C. 366, 373 F.2d 451 (1966).

Schopler, E. (1984). My great teachers. In E. Schopler & G. Mesibov (Eds.), *The effects of autism on the family* (pp. 227–232). New York: Plenum.

Schopler, E., & Marcus, L. (1987). Working with families: A developmental perspective. In D. Cohen & A. Donnellan (Eds.), *Handbook of autism and pervasive developmental disorders* (pp. 499–512). New York: John Wiley & Sons.

Schopler, E., & Mesibov, G.B. (1984). *The effects of autism on the family.* New York: Plenum.

Schopler, E., & Reichler, R. (1971). Parents as cotherapists in the treatment of psychotic children. *Journal of Autism and Childhood Schizophrenia, 1,* 87–102.

Snell, M. (1987). *Systematic instruction of persons with severe handicaps.* Columbus, OH: Charles E. Merrill.

Sobsey, D. (1987). Non-aversive behavior management: The verdict is in. *News and Notes, a quarterly newsletter of the American Association on Mental Retardation, 1*(2), pp. 2, 8.

Souder v. Brennan, 367 F. Supp. 808 (D.D.C. 1973).

Sowers, J., Jenkins, C, & Powers, L. (1988). Vocational education of persons with physical handicaps. In R. Gaylord-Ross (Ed.), *Vocational education for persons with handicaps* (pp. 387–416). Palo Alto, CA: Mayfield Publishing Co.

Staff. (1986, August). An update on the BRI Case. *TASH Newsletter,* p. 3.

Surratt, J. (1984). Advocacy: Effectively changing the system. In E. Schopler & G. Mesibov (Eds.), *The effects of autism on the family* (pp. 129–141). New York: Plenum.

Taylor, S. (1980). *A guide to monitoring residential settings.* Syracuse, NY: Syracuse University, Center on Human Policy.

TransCen, Inc. (1987). *Building bridges from school to work for persons with disabilities.* Rockville, MD: Author.

Turnbull, A. (1985). Update: The dual role of parent and professional. In H.R. Turnbull & A. Turnbull (Eds.), *Parents speak out: Then and now* (2nd ed.) (pp. 137–141). Columbus, OH: Charles E. Merrill.

Turnbull, A.P., Blue-Banning, M., Behr, S., & Kerns, G. (1986). Family research and intervention: A value and ethical examination. In P.R. Dokecki & R.M. Zaner (Eds.), *Ethics of dealing with persons with severe handicaps: Toward a research agenda* (pp. 119–140). Baltimore Paul H. Brookes Publishing Co.

Turnbull, H.R., & Turnbull, A. (Eds.). (1985). *Parents speak out: Then and now* (2nd ed.), Columbus, OH: Charles E. Merrill.

Wallitt, W. (1978). *Handbook for developing local child advocacy systems.* Ithaca, NY: Cornell University Press.

Warren, F. (1969, September 9). Angry East Kinston parents demand fair play. *Kinston Daily Free Press,* pp. 1, 12.

Warren, F. (1979). Role of the consumer in planning and delivering services. In R. Wiegerink & J.W. Pelosi (Eds.), *Developmental disabilities: The DD movement* (pp. 141–149). Baltimore, Paul H. Brookes Publishing Co.

Warren, F. (1984). The role of the National Society in working with families. In E. Schopler & G. Mesibov (Eds.), *The effects of autism on the family* (pp. 99–115). New York: Plenum.

Warren, F. (1985a). A society that is going to kill your children. In H.R. Turnbull & A. Turnbull (Eds.), *Parents speak out: Then and now* (2nd ed.) (pp. 201–219). Columbus, OH: Charles E. Merrill.

Warren, F. (1985b). Update: Call them liars who would say all is well. In H.R. Turnbull & A. Turnbull (Eds.), *Parents speak out: Then and now* (2nd ed.) (pp. 221–229). Columbus, OH: Charles E. Merrill.

Warren, F. (1987). Advocacy and lobbying: Strategies and techniques for obtaining services and influencing policy for people with autism. In D. Cohen & A. Donnellan (Eds.), *Handbook of autism and pervasive developmental disorders* (pp. 643–652). New York: John Wiley & Sons.

Warren, F. (Winter, 1987). Jane Salzano: 'A Canny, Tenacious Pioneer' *Community News, 3*(1), p. 9.

Warren, F. (November, 1987). Social role valorization: An enabling principle. *News and Notes, a quarterly newsletter of the American Association on Mental Retardation, 1,*(2), pp. 2, 5.

Wiegerink, R., & Pelosi, J. (Eds.). (1979). *Developmental disabilities: The DD movement.* Baltimore: Paul H. Brookes Publishing Co.

Will, M. (1984). *OSERS programming for the transition of youth with disabilities: Bridges from school to working life.* Washington, DC: U.S. Department of Education.

Wolfensberger, W. (1972). *The principle of normalization in human services.* Toronto: National Institute on Mental Retardation.

Wolfensberger, W. (1983). Social role valorization: A proposed new term for the principle of normalization. *Mental Retardation, 21*(6), 234–239.

Wolfensberger, W., & Glenn, L. (1975). *Program analysis of service systems* (3rd ed.). Toronto: National Institute on Mental Retardation.

Wyatt v. Stickney, 344 F.Supp. 373, 344 F. Supp. 387 (M.D.Ala. 1972)

COPING SKILLS AND INFORMAL SOCIAL SUPPORT

CHAPTER 5

A Skills Training Approach for Assisting Parents to Cope with Stress

Nancy E. Hawkins and George H.S. Singer

According to a substantial body of evidence already cited in Chapter 1, parents of severely handicapped children experience higher than average levels of stress due to child rearing. The particular stresses experienced by these parents vary a great deal (Schilling & Schinke, 1984).

THE NEED FOR STRESS MANAGEMENT

Autobiographical accounts emphasize the difficulties in coping with the child's diagnosis and daily care, with contacts with the social service system, with intense and chronic sorrow, with isolation, with the child's added physical care, with sleep disturbance, and with the child's behavior problems (Quine & Pahl, 1985).

The autobiographical accounts are substantiated by surveys of parents as well (Breslau & Davis, 1986). The surveys indicate that parents of handicapped children experience more stress than parents of nonhandicapped children, and that the distress (i.e., negative attitudes, worries, and daily difficulties) increases with the severity of the child's handicapping condition.

Parent Counseling and Training

Until relatively recently, reviews of the literature indicated that parents of handicapped children were provided with two types of assistance to aid them in coping with this stress: behaviorally oriented approaches to help them change their child's behavior, and nondirectively oriented groups designed to give them emotional support.

Implicit in the behavioral parent training is the assumption that if a child's behavior improves, parental distress will decrease (Baker, 1984).

Reviews by Baker (1984) and Snell and Beckman-Brindley (1984) report studies in which parents, given behavioral training, have successfully reduced their child's aberrant behavior and increased their skills. Although the effects on the children have been documented, the effects on the parents have rarely been reported in a systematic fashion.

Reflective Group Therapy

The other treatment approach for parents of handicapped children has consisted of nondirective counseling support groups. These groups have centered around goals of reducing feelings of isolation and grief, establishing friendships, providing information, and permitting emotional expression (Shapiro, 1983; Wright, Granger, & Sameroff, 1984). The approach emphasizes the value of empathy, sympathy, and self-expression of feelings (Buscaglia, 1975; Shapiro, 1983). Although this approach has been very popular, virtually no empirical validation exists for its effectiveness in reducing distress (Shapiro, 1983; Wright et al., 1984).

Stress Management: A Behavioral/Educational Approach

Behavior therapists have used such methods as self-monitoring, relaxation training, coping self-statements, and modeling to treat anxiety (Suinn, 1977), depression (Biglan & Campbell,

1981; Lewinsohn & Hoberman, 1982), and psychosomatic disorders (Leigh, 1982) in adults. These behavioral approaches emphasize skill training rather than emotion and empathy. The effectiveness of behavioral approaches has been tested in controlled outcome studies. Reviewers of studies employing cognitive-behavioral approaches to the treatment of depression, for example, have unanimously concluded that these treatments are efficacious (e.g., Blaney, 1981; DeRubeis & Hollon, 1981; Hersen & Bellack, 1982; Lewinsohn & Hoberman, 1982; Rehm & Kornblith, 1979).

People who experience depression often live or work in aversive environments (Biglan, Hops, & Sherman, 1988). The environmental conditions associated with depression and those experienced by parents of severely handicapped children bear similarities.

Stress-management training, consisting of self-monitoring, identification of environmental stressors, relaxation training, and coping self-statements, is shown to be effective in a variety of studies (Woolfolk & Lehrer, 1984). It has been used to treat people who suffer from insomnia, migraine headaches, peptic ulcers, generalized anxiety, and essential hypertension (Leigh, 1982; Stoyva & Anderson, 1982). These ailments are associated with environmental stresses that may be similar to the daily challenges faced by parents of severely handicapped children. That is, these parents often have to cope with difficult circumstances that tax their physical and mental resources (Schilling & Schinke, 1984).

Since parents of handicapped children have demonstrated more symptoms of depression and stress disorders than matched groups of parents of nonhandicapped children (Breslau & Davis, 1986), and behavioral treatments for depression and stress have been demonstrated in controlled studies to be helpful for other groups of adults, the next logical step is to use the skill-oriented treatments with parents of handicapped children. In 1984 Schilling and Schinke called for parent-focused interventions that provide parents with both personal coping skills and enhanced social supports.

The study described in the remaining portion of this chapter evaluates the use of stress-management skill training in reducing the distress of parents with severely handicapped children.

SERVICE DESIGN

Philosophy and Goals of Skills-Based Treatment

The stress-management and social skills treatment discussed in this chapter is one component of a model demonstration project designed to develop and evaluate support services for families with severely handicapped children. The goal of the service studied was not only to provide assistance for the families while working with them, but also to teach them to continue to function with less distress long after the treatments ended. Consequently, the focus was on teaching skills and on assisting participants to build the skills into their daily lives while they were still involved in the treatment groups. Participants were not only given practice with the skills during the weekly sessions, but they were also encouraged to do systematic behavioral assignments or activities that were designed to promote home-practice of the skills in between sessions as well. As Shelton and Levy (1981) emphasize, these assignments are a crucial part of intervention, and the therapist's efforts should focus on ways to maximize this home practice. By practicing coping skills between sessions, individuals have the chance to apply the skills in their own natural settings while they still have the possibility of feedback from other group members as to different methods of adapting the skills.

In the study, rather than focusing on providing treatment only to parents with identified mental health problems, the services were offered to any parents of severely handicapped children who were interested in learning skills for coping with stress. Consequently, the emphasis was on teaching skills in a supportive, class-like environment, rather than on providing group therapy for people with problems. The major goal of the class was to assist parents of severely handicapped children in learning to better manage their own stress through skill training. The assumption was made that these skills would directly benefit parents, and indirectly benefit their children by providing an environment that maximizes the child's learning of appropriate behaviors. A comment from a mother during one of the follow-up interviews illustrates the point (personal communication):

> I didn't change anything about Mark, I just changed my behavior. Before, he would start crying as soon as the bus showed up and he'd go to school crying . . . and now, he might do it three or four times a year, compared to maybe every other day before. I didn't change anything as far as him . . . I was less anxious about it and my voice was different, and when I took care of him in the morning and got him ready, my attitude was better.[1]

Although the agenda for the class was to address a specific set of goals through a known repertoire of skills, participants were given support for coping behaviors that they had previously found to be useful as well. The group leaders encouraged members to interact and to share their own variations and adaptations of coping behaviors. The leaders tried to convey the message throughout the class that they did not have solutions, but rather had skills for members to try and ways to guide people in observing and discovering what could be most useful for them as individuals.

To set a supportive atmosphere that would encourage members to participate in the discussions and guided skill practice, the group leaders engaged in active listening with an empathic nonjudgmental style. They were friendly and informal, frequently interspersing humorous examples from their own lives to illustrate relevant points. In discussing stressful life events, they provided examples of a variety of stressors, only some of which revolved around coping with a handicapped child.

The coping strategies that were presented included both altering the events preceding a stressful reaction, and managing reactions to the events. For example, rather than simply teaching a parent to relax and think differently about feeling lonely when uninvolved with other people, skills for increasing social support were also ad-

dressed. When skills for changing the child's behavior were needed, parents were encouraged to wait until the next set of classes to proceed, because 8 weeks would be devoted to presenting a detailed child behavior–management program.

Population Served

The participants of the program were either natural or adoptive parents of moderately and severely handicapped children. The participants of the initial groups (totaling 70 participants) volunteered as a result of recruitment by a case management staff from whom they were already receiving services in a local direction services agency. Participants in the replication site groups volunteered as a result of recruitment within their child's school district. They were all provided with written and oral information about the nature of the classes and the assignments between sessions, and the study used fully informed consent procedures.

Although 70 parents received stress-management services at the model demonstration project site, the effects of the stress-management component alone were evaluated for only the first 36 parents. The characteristics of these 36 parents are further described in the evaluation section of this chapter.

Organizational Structure

The participants attended 2-hour classes once a week for 8 weeks. The classes were held in the conference room of a research institute in the evening, as a convenience for working parents. In-home respite care was provided for the handicapped child through a local respite care agency. When both parents in a two-parent family attended, they were assigned to the same group. The groups consisted of 8–10 participants and 2 leaders.

For the purposes of being able to replicate the content of the classes and to evaluate their effectiveness, a training manual for group leaders was developed. This manual not only covers the content of the class, but also provides informa-

---

[1]This quote and all others from parents that are interspersed throughout this chapter have been reproduced verbatim from the transcripts of third-party evaluator interviews. The interviews with the parents took place from six months to a year after parents' involvement in the project. See page 80 for a fuller description of the third party evaluation.

tion on organization, group process, and rationale for various procedures.

Staff Skills

The classes in the model demonstration project were co-led by a licensed clinical psychologist and a certificated special educator. Classes in the replication sites were led by professionals with training and experience in working with adults and with severely handicapped children. Their professional training varied, from clinical psychology to social work, to special education; at least one co-leader in each group had extensive experience working with severely handicapped children, a criterion that was deemed important to the parents in order to add professional credibility.

The authors recommend that prospective trainers are well versed in the use of behavior analysis. Graduate work in social learning theory or a considerable amount of supervised field experience is a necessary prerequisite for leading this type of group. In addition, the trainer should demonstrate good clinical skills such as active listening, paraphrasing and empathizing, and the ability to give instructions in a personable and understandable manner. The trainer must also be able to adjust the sophistication of his or her language to that of the group members.

Methods and Techniques of Service Provision

Session Format   As mentioned earlier, the major emphasis in the stress-management class was skill training. The goal of the class was to teach participants to use coping skills for handling stressful situations that occurred in their daily lives. Assisting them to practice the skills in between sessions was crucial to the learning process. Consequently, the format of the sessions was designed to enhance compliance with between-session homework assignments. The sessions all followed a set format, regardless of the content taught. The rationale for each of the session components is described below in terms of its intended effects on learning and practicing the skills.

Overview   Each session began with a brief overview of the session plan for the evening. The importance of practicing skills at home each week is emphasized at the beginning of each session. The choice that each participant has over which assignments to select is also emphasized. Since choice of program has been shown to play a role in the effectiveness with which people acquire skills (Kanfer & Grimm, 1978), choices were offered in order to increase the practice of relevant skills between sessions.

Presenting an overview of the session also re-emphasizes the educational nature of the class. This emphasis can assist participants to anticipate that by learning and practicing new skills, they will be able to manage their stress better. By believing that their efforts will pay off, participants are more likely to practice skills between sessions.

Homework Review   After a brief overview of the session, at least 15–20 minutes were spent on reviewing details of the participants' between-session practice. During this time, the leaders listened to each participant, paraphrased their comments, and reinforced their efforts. They also encouraged group members to support each other by pointing out common experiences whenever possible. The leaders avoided spending much time on excuses that participants gave for not completing assignments. They politely acknowledged these, and then focused on the positive efforts. Certainly, the effect of positive reinforcement on behavior needs no elaboration. Meichenbaum and Turk (1987) review the literature relating to the effect of reinforcement on treatment compliance.

Presentation and Discussion of New Skills   Each new skill was presented to the group by describing it, giving a rationale for learning it, and presenting examples of situations in which it could be useful. Examples were also elicited from the participants who were already familiar with the skill whenever possible. After presenting the skill the leaders encouraged questions and discussion. Since participants enter the classes with different levels of experience with stress-management skills, the leaders made themselves aware of these differences in order to assist people to integrate the new techniques with those that already worked for them in their daily lives.

Guided Practice   After presenting the new skill in a session, the leaders provided some guided practice. The practice involved activities such as asking each participant to think through his or her day to identify stressful situations as an exercise in pinpointing, taking the group through a progressive muscle relaxation experience, and asking group members to identify negative self-talk that might occur for a person in various stressful situations, and coaching statements that would be appropriate for those situations. The guided practice provided assistance with the skills that participants would be trying on their own in between sessions. During practice, the leaders would reinforce correct examples of skills and give corrective feedback in a supportive way for nonexamples. Such a practice allowed leaders to make sure that the material was clearly understood to ensure that participants would be successful in applying the skills by themselves at home.

Between-Session Assignments Supported by research findings, Shelton and Levy (1981) identify a number of factors that appear to enhance treatment compliance. In setting up the between-session assignments for the class, these factors were incorporated: ". . . Assignments should contain specific detail . . . should begin with small homework requests and gradually increase . . . clients should make a public commitment and a private commitment to comply . . . therapist should monitor and reinforce compliance. . ." (Shelton & Levy, 1981, p. 77).

After modeling and rehearsing the new skill with the participants, the leaders distributed homework assignment sheets. Each item on the page was read aloud and the reason for practicing the skill was explained. Some of the items asked participants to decide how many times they would rehearse a given skill, and what time of day they would practice. The leaders then asked each person to decide on the assignments that he or she agreed to do between sessions. (Assignments for earlier sessions were briefer than those for later sessions.) While participants were encouraged to be diligent with their practice, they were also encouraged to be realistic in their self-expectations—that is, to agree only to assignments that they felt they could complete (developing a private commitment). The leaders emphasized that although the practice was important, individuals should not commit for so much that they might have difficulty finding time

in their busy schedules to accomplish their goals and then feel discouraged with themselves for failing to keep their commitments.

After group members had chosen the assignments they agreed to do, and turned in a copy of the assignment commitments, each was asked to tell the rest of the group about his or her plans. The leaders listened actively to each member and reinforced his or her decisions about the assignments.

Reactions to the homework varied. Comments by participants who were asked their opinions six months to two years later follow.

> . . . the homework was never a problem for me . . . I looked forward to doing it because then I could see how I was doing and how I reacted to that day . . . I learned from it as I was doing it, 'cause I really had to sit down and think, 'Did that really drive me crazy or not?' 'How did I like this?', or 'Did I really behave well when this happened?'. . . .

> . . . it was a problem to remember to do it, so what we did, cuz my husband and I both took the class, was do it before we went to bed. We went out to the kitchen table and both got the charts out and sat down and did them . . . sometimes we talked about them and shared, sometimes we just did them and went to bed. . . .

> . . . at first, I didn't keep up with it too good . . . and then I would try to catch up and that was hard, so then I started doing it in the morning when my son was at school and that seemed to work well. . . .

The Lottery The behavioral parent training literature suggests that attrition rates in group training are high (Dangel & Polster, 1984). As many as 40%–80% of parents who enroll in parent training groups may drop out. Some researchers have attempted to improve attendance by offering financial rewards (Baker, 1984). To attempt to decrease the dropout rate and increase compliance with between-session assignments in the stress-management groups in the program, a weekly lottery prize was offered. Participants received one lottery ticket for attendance and a second for completing all the assignments that they had agreed to complete during the previous week. Lottery prizes were donated from local businesses and restaurants.

Follow-Up Phone Calls Follow-up phone calls were made to each parent's home within 6 days (ideally within 3–4 days) of each group session. The purpose of the calls was to review the content of the previous meeting, to answer any questions that had arisen, and to prompt and reinforce efforts taken toward completing assignments.

The caller, who was the same person each week, was familiar with the course content and assigned homework, and was also comfortable communicating on the phone. He or she focused on making the contact brief and pleasant, using a few directive questions to see how the assignment was going, listening carefully, and responding to any concerns. If the participant had not started the homework, the caller encouraged a revision of the commitment in order to increase the person's chance of success in completing some portion of the assignment before the next class session.

Content of Stress-Management Lessons
Stress-management intervention includes a number of individual components and their interrelationships. The components focus on identifying individual stressors, learning relaxation skills and how to apply them to the natural setting, identifying and modifying cognitive responses to difficult situations, and evaluating and increasing support from other people. Each of the components is described briefly below, along with some reactions from participants interviewed 6 months to 2 years after the stress-management training sessions were over.

Self-Monitoring The primary goal of introducing pinpointing or self-monitoring was to encourage participants to view stress as a series of separate events or stressors. By understanding that there are specific antecedents to the feelings of stress that they experience, participants begin to see that there are also specific coping skills that may be useful. They then begin to understand the importance of keeping track of stressful events in their lives as a first step in learning to cope with stress.

Self-monitoring is a widely utilized component of behavioral therapy (Karoly & Kanfer, 1982). In the present model, parents were asked to identify stressors three times each day, rate their stress level on a seven-point scale, and note the successes that they had in coping with stressful situations. They were also asked to mark any stress symptoms they noted throughout the day

on a list provided. Further details on the tracking and other aspects of the treatment are available in the Stress-Management Treatment Manual written for group leaders of the present project.

Participants were generally diligent about following through with self-monitoring for at least the first few weeks. Their reactions to the usefulness of the task were usually positive, although some found the tracking hard to do with regularity. Examples of their comments are provided for illustration.

> . . . When we started keeping track, we did notice that there were some definite stress patterns. The one that was real surprising to me was in the morning. I found that I was doing about 90% of our getting together in the morning, and after our classes, we decided that we would split that. So instead of me doing everything, we had particular jobs to do and that really has saved tremendous stress on myself, my son, and my husband.

> The tracking actually helps you see where your areas of stress are by actually citing, three times a day, areas that were really stressful, be it home, the work area, or the evening schedule. We found out right away that our biggest stress time was between 7 and 8 o'clock in the morning. In identifying that, we were both real surprised because we did our homework separately . . . we found that we both had the same concerns and the same anxieties, but yet by the time we left for work, we were both furious with each other.

Relaxation Relaxation was taught as a coping skill by emphasizing the ways that it could be used throughout the day to keep tension from building. It was taught in stages. At first participants were coached through a modified form of progressive muscle relaxation. They were directed to alternately tense and release large muscle groups while simultaneously breathing deeply. While tensing and releasing, they were asked to direct their attention to the sensation of tension and the feeling of relaxation in each of the muscle groups. They were also given some brief practice in visualizing a relaxing place.

After being coached on relaxation in the group setting, participants were given an audio tape of the same version with which to practice at home. After learning the 20- to 25-minute version of relaxation, participants were aided in developing their own briefer forms of relaxation to use throughout the day. They were also aided in developing personal cues that could serve as frequent reminders to check for tension and relax to relieve it.

Most participants found some form of relaxation to be useful. As can be seen in the following examples, many of the participants found ways to make relaxation a permanent part of their lives, even after the classes were over.

> I work a rotating shift . . . when I come home from swing shift at 11:00, its hard to go to sleep after being so wound up . . . I got to using that tape and I'd get to sleep before 12:00 instead of being up til 2:00.

> In the beginning I tried to use the tape and I found it took much more time than I had wanted to use . . . so I started doing it on my own. I would use it in the beginning just at home, and then I started using it at work. I would take a few minutes and just stop and mentally relax starting at the head and just working down . . . that was a really helpful time . . . it really changed a lot of tight situations. . . .

> I did those comfort checks on a regular basis . . . I put a dot [a cue to relax] at work . . . and when I noticed it I would just relax . . . release a lot of weight off my shoulders or whatever. . . .

> I find myself taking myself out of a particular tense situation, taking some deep breaths or daydreaming for a few minutes . . . and then I go back to the situation and I can deal with it a lot better. It keeps tempers down. In the evening when the kids are down . . . I will make a point of sitting down . . . putting my feet up and just relaxing the muscles in the neck and everything . . . and just drift away into the day . . . reviewing the day very quietly with no interruptions . . . just kinda float away . . . and I have a lot better nights' sleep than going to bed all tensed up.

Cognitive Modification The focus in teaching people cognitive skills was on identifying and then modifying cognitive responses to stressful situations. This technique has proven to be effective in assisting people to reduce anxiety (Deffenbacher & Suinn, 1982). Participants were first given examples to illustrate the effect of self-talk on feelings in particular situations. They were taught to monitor their self-talk by recording in a log what they said to themselves about stressful events. Then they were taught ways to criticize negative or irrational self-talk and to replace it with more positive responses. Just as with the relaxation skills, emphasis was

placed on learning to generalize cognitive skills as well—that is, developing brief thought change strategies that could be used in stressful situations throughout the day.

A few examples of the ways that participants adapted the cognitive skills to their lives are illustrated below.

> In an IEP (Individualized Education Plan) meeting . . . because that's a real stressful time, I'd go through and write down and practice it (what to say) in my head . . . because with a lot of people you know what they're going to say and then what you'd say back to that. . . .

> [When a son is having a tantrum] . . . Just by giving myself positive messages and taking a few deep breaths to calm myself down and not trying to bring myself to the 2-year-old level . . . I stop and think "Okay, I'm just going to be acting like he is and that's not going to get us anywhere, I need to calm down and distract him and then we'll be O.K. . . ."

> . . . changing my thought patterns was the most important part . . . I had trained myself for years to project disaster. I mean it didn't matter what the situation was—I walked into the doctor's office and it wouldn't matter what he said, I thought, "he's going to die" . . . I spent a lot of my time reacting to things that I decided were going to happen. Night time was always my fearful time . . . He'd wake up in the middle of the night, he'd turn and go "a-a-h-h," my first response was that he's sick . . . Now, when he does wake up and make noise, I'm not afraid. I'll go in the room and maybe he's uncovered and can't cover himself up and he's cold, but I deal with it then. And I don't get that feeling in my stomach any more . . . I deal with whatever's going on . . . and don't panic over it . . . You know there're appropriate times to worry and with me it's learning the appropriate times.

Social Support As discussed earlier, information from the literature suggests that many families with severely handicapped children experience social isolation (Roos, 1978). The goal of introducing a component on social support in the model was to increase participants' awareness of the role of support from others in managing their own stress.

A portion of this awareness was provided by the very nature of the social support in the class itself. By the time this component was introduced in the sixth session, participants had already had a chance to share personal information about their families and themselves in a supportive atmosphere. One father summed up his feelings as follows:

> We found it very very helpful also listening to other parents who had similar problems, where we could nod our heads and say, "Oh yeah, our son is doing this," or "No, this is not the same way," but we could question the parents and say, "Is your daughter or son doing this way?" or whatever . . . I believe the combination between the stress-management classes in an organized fashion, doing the homework, and also the opportunity to listen to other parents and talk to them . . . we found that we were able to come to grips with our problems and find better solutions which worked.

Setting the supportive atmosphere in the classes was accomplished in a purposeful manner. Five group agreements were adopted in the first session. With these, members agreed to keep confidential any personal information divulged in the group, to be supportive of other members, to not pressure others to talk, to share time equally, and to address each other by first names. The leaders referred to these agreements when necessary to keep the tone of the group supportive. The leaders also pointed out common experiences of different members, and asked for ideas from members of the group rather than just providing solutions from a professional viewpoint. A break in the middle of each session also provided time for members to socialize.

The social support component of the class first asked participants to keep track of both the frequency and the satisfaction of their contacts with other people. After examining their contacts, those who desired more support set some goals and identified steps they could take between sessions toward those goals. An example of one mother's discovery and plan illustrates the point:

> Before I started tracking, I thought I was socially very active. When I started tracking, I realized that because of our son . . . we were becoming hermits. We would use him as the reason for not going out . . . because he can't speak, we were afraid of leaving him with someone . . . I started out with calling a friend that I hadn't seen in a while . . . like one person a week . . . I thought I'd like to reach a family member out of town once a month. I'm one of six kids . . . now they return the calls and we've kind of reunited. In fact we had our

first family portrait in 22 years, since this class, just because we're communicating again.

Common Problems and Processes for Addressing Them

Although providing skill training in groups has the benefit of providing social support from other parents of severely handicapped children, group training also presents some potential problems. Some of the difficulties that group treatment presented in the current study, as well as ways in which those problems were addressed, are described.

Previous Experience with Coping Skills Participants entered the class with varying levels of skill for managing stress. In working with individuals or families, these differences could be taken into account in both presentations and homework assignments. However, the class presentations assumed little or no previous exposure to the specific skills taught, in order to provide basic information to people on an entry level. Some of the participants had previous experience with skills such as relaxation. The leaders tried to encourage those with previous experience to assume the role of mentor, and at the same time to assist them to learn more subtle nuances within the specific skill. Although the homework assignment sheets were the same for each participant, the leaders encouraged individuals to select or modify assignments to meet their own needs.

Couples' Issues Sometimes marital discord was an issue that led to increased stress for participants. The leaders encouraged couples in two-parent families to come to the classes together. When one parent refused to come, the potential risks to the relationship were pointed out, and the participating member was also encouraged to share information with the absent member whenever possible.

In the initial class session, one of the group agreements accepted by all participants was to be supportive to others in the group. Specific examples relating to members of a couple putting aside their differences during the class to give each other support were cited. When partners had conflict between them during a class, they were gently reminded of the group agreement, and privately offered the opportunity to meet as a couple outside the group for additional assistance.

Nonreaders Since much of the homework between sessions required reading and completing self-monitoring forms, participants who were unable to read or were poor readers required extra help. When the leaders were informed of the problem, they provided additional help before and during each session with the materials, while trying to be as inconspicuous as possible. Of course, some people who were poor readers may have been overlooked if they didn't mention the problem. In the future, videotapes accompanying the written materials will be made available to all, and these materials will lessen the emphasis on reading. In addition, the written materials are being revised to simplify them and include illustrations wherever possible.

Issues with Chaotic Families The group format appeared to be less effective with families whom the authors describe as *chaotic families.* These families were usually from a lower income level, and had less educational experience; they often lived in a somewhat chaotic household, with extra people outside the family coming and going. These parents had trouble just attending weekly sessions, let alone following through with assignments between sessions. For families such as these, stress-management skills may need to include assistance with more basic needs prior to, or in lieu of, learning skills of the sort taught in these classes. Lutzker, Frame, and Rice (1982) provides a model for the types of services that may be helpful for these families.

EVALUATION

The discussion that follows briefly describes one study designed to evaluate the short-term effects of the stress-management course. A more detailed description of the study (Singer, Irvin, & Hawkins, in press) and a treatment manual (Hawkins, 1986) are available. The stress-management course was evaluated by comparing two groups of parents of children with severe handicaps who were randomly assigned to treatment or a waiting list control group.

Thirty-six parents were recruited by social workers from a local direction service agency. All parents had children who were served by the local public school program for severely handicapped students. The median age of the handicapped children was 11 years, with a range from 4 to 16 years. Two-thirds of the parents were from two-parent families and one-third were from single-parent families. In the two-parent families both of the spouses participated. The median income for the sample was $12,500; 11 of the families had poverty-level income ($10,600 for a family of four). The parents were assessed on several variables in order to ensure that the groups were equivalent. There were no significant differences between the groups on any demographic variables, measures of social isolation, depression, anxiety, or family stress. The groups did differ in one way; the treatment group had children whose adaptive behavior was significantly lower than that of the control group. In order to statistically control for this difference, adaptive behavior scores were used as a covariate in an analysis of covariance.

The treatment group received the stress-management class described previously. The groups were led by a clinical psychologist and a special educator. Meetings were held at night in order to accommodate working parents, and respite care was provided during those meetings. The treatment group was divided into two classes of nine parents each. The classes met for 2 hours, one night a week, for 8 weeks.

The dependent variables in this study were measures of psychological distress associated with stress. The State Trait Anxiety Inventory (STAI) (Speilberger, Gorsuch, & Lushene, 1970) and the Beck Depression Inventory (Beck, Ward, Mendelson, Mock, & Erbaugh, 1961) are mood-symptom inventories that have been widely used in stress research (Dcrogatis, 1982). All of the parents completed them immediately before the first class and at the end of the last class.

The results were analyzed using analysis of covariance. With pretest scores and child adaptive behavior scores as covariates. A significant difference was found between the two groups at the posttest on the state and trait scales of the STAI and on the Beck Depression Inventory. All differences were significant at the .03 level or below.

Follow-up measures on the stress-management class alone are not available because parents went on to participate in the other components of a package of interventions that are described in Chapter 6. One-year follow-up measures for the whole treatment model are presented there.

In order to learn whether or not parents continued to use any of the stress-management techniques, a third party evaluator conducted open-ended structured interviews with 25 parents who participated in the stress-management class. Parents were interviewed between six months and one year following the last class. All parents reported that they continued to use some of the stress-management techniques. When asked if their lives were less stressful as a result of the classes, most parents answered no, but added that they felt better able to cope with the stress as a result of the classes. When asked how the classes could be improved, several parents said that they would find instruction on time management to be helpful. Some parents reported that they would have preferred to have help with behavior management skills before learning stress management techniques, since their primary source of stress was their child's problem behaviors. All parents who were interviewed continued to recommend the classes to other parents.

FUTURE DIRECTIONS

Public Policy

Increasingly, parents of severely handicapped children are raising their children at home. At the same time, there are growing numbers of severely disabled children who are surviving as a result of improvements in medical technology. As parents assume the burden of care for these children, they encounter serious stress. Preliminary evidence such as that provided in the present study suggests that assisting parents with skill training, such as training in stress-management, can reduce parental distress just as behavioral parent training can reduce the child's aberrant behaviors and increase the child's skills. If parental distress is reduced, parents are more likely to be able to maintain the child at

home and provide the type of environment that can maximize the child's future functioning as well. Providing necessary assistance to parents so that children can be maintained in the home is a part of fulfilling society's obligation to provide the least restrictive environment to children with handicapping conditions. Although effective assistance for parents initially may be costly, it would likely be cost effective in the long-term by keeping more children out of institutions.

The current findings present only preliminary data with a small sample of parents with severely handicapped children; however, the evidence for the effectiveness of stress-management techniques with other adult populations is corroborated. Such efforts as model demonstration projects that can further develop services and can continue to collect ongoing data as the projects are gradually taken over by existing community agencies hold promise. These projects could then follow participants over time as well, in order to evaluate and further refine procedures that enhance maintenance of the skills.

Direct Service Practices

The goal of treatment in the present study was to teach participants some specific skills that they would be able to apply in their daily lives to help them cope better with stressful life events. The model for teaching the skills was to provide information and rationale, to prompt by use of examples, to assist with guided rehearsal, to provide structured practice at home, and to suggest ideas for integrating the skills into daily activities. Certainly the model is one that is involved in many teaching situations. Just as a classroom teacher must examine the different steps in the model that can discourage an individual child and result in that child dropping out or failing, the leaders must examine where the model may break down for parents who do not succeed in learning or maintaining the skills for coping with stress, or who do not manage to come to the class sessions regularly.

As mentioned previously, parents from families that were somewhat chaotic and unorganized had difficulty following through with regular class attendance. Perhaps for the classes to be helpful, a parent needs certain preconditions to exist (e.g., having enough money to take care of food, clothes, and shelter; not being dependent on drugs or alcohol; and being able to take care of family health problems). When a parent has missed more than one class session, the leader should meet with him or her individually to discover how to best meet the needs of the family. With more research in the area, a screening tool might be developed to identify those families that would be best served in other ways.

In the stress-management class discussed in this chapter, some of the information was presented in writing and many of the assignments involved written responses. To accommodate those who have difficulty reading, audio and video materials will need to be developed to assist in teaching the skills.

Because participants enter the classes with different levels of previous experience with coping skills, participants could be screened and grouped by skill level in order to focus on the most needed skills. More advanced level classes could be designed for those participants who were already familiar with the stress-management skills taught in the current classes. Such topics as time-management, problem-solving skills, or leisure planning could be beneficial for these parents as well.

Once the skills are taught and practiced in the reinforcing atmosphere of the group setting, the next hurdle is ensuring that participants will put forth the effort to work on them at home between sessions as well. As reviewed earlier, much of the focus of the intervention format was designed to facilitate adherence to homework assignments. Further efforts are still needed in this area, so that skills are well established by the time the classes have finished. Perhaps one way to increase practice of skills would be to provide structured contact between participants (i.e., a buddy system) between sessions. Another possibility would be to stretch out the time between the last few sessions and ask participants to do homework on only a few prescribed days. The additional time would allow more opportunities for new stressful situations to arise so that participants could see how well they were able to apply their skills.

With any newly learned skill, the biggest question involves what will happen to its use when the reinforcers provided for learning it are withdrawn. Hopefully some of the reinforcers continue—that is, participants in the classes will continue to notice that they experience less distress and are more successful in dealing with their handicapped child when they remember to relax and talk to themselves more positively. Certainly some of the couples who have been in our classes together have shared ways in which they reinforce each other for maintaining the skills. Other members have maintained the friendships that they formed in the classes, and socializing with these friends serves as a reminder to use the coping skills. Some created specific cues in their environments that will serve as reminders to relax or change thoughts and so forth. Others have remarked that they have difficulty remembering to use the skills without the class structure.

While parents of nondisabled children have many child-centered activities that bring them together periodically for support (e.g., school plays, sports, orchestras, clubs), parents of severely handicapped children have few child-related gatherings. Consequently, they have few occasions on which to compare notes on their children and to assist each other in adapting to new issues that arise. Some of the parents that have been in the program have expressed an interest in an ongoing bimonthly group that could assist them in maintaining coping skills and also deal with new issues as needed. A model for training parents as leaders of such an ongoing follow-up group is currently being developed. The training will likely entail 3–4 hours of class time and will focus on basic communication skills, coping with values conflicts, structuring a group agenda, and identifying "red flags" or times to call for some help from a professional.

Research

Although the results of the present study suggest that stress-management training may be a useful addition to the clinical procedures available to help parents of severely handicapped children, further research is needed to determine the long-term effects of the program. A component analysis is also needed to determine which parts of the treatment package are most effective with which parents. Some parents appear to need additional one-on-one counseling for depression or marital problems, and some may need intense parent training in the home for dealing with severe behavior problems of their child. Others may need extended respite care for their child, or other types of back-up services. Being able to determine in advance the most effective services for each parent would be of considerable help, both in providing the best treatment and in delegating resources efficiently.

Another question for research involves the effect of training only one member of a couple. Sometimes a father was unable to come to the groups because of alternating shifts of work, or in other instances was unwilling to participate. Does involving only one member lead to increased marital conflict? If so, are there some ways of systematically involving the other parent that will lessen that conflict?

REFERENCES

Baker, B.L. (1984). Intervention with families with young, severely handicapped children. In J. Blancher (Ed.), *Severely handicapped young children and their families* (pp. 319–375). Orlando: Academic Press.

Beck, A.T., Ward, C.H., Mendelson, M., Mock, J.E., & Erbaugh, J.K. (1961). An inventory for measuring depression. *Archives of General Psychiatry, 4,* 561–571.

Biglan, A., & Campbell, D.R. (1981). Depression. In J. Shelton & R. Levy (Eds.), *Behavioral assignments and treatment compliance* (pp. 111–146). Champaign, IL: Research Press.

Biglan, A., Hops, H., & Sherman, L. (1988). Coercive processes and maternal depression. In R.J. McMahon & R. DeV. Peter (Eds.), *Social learning and systems approaches to marriage and the family* (pp. 72–103). New York: Brunner/Mazel.

Blaney, P.H. (1981). Cognitive and behavioral therapies for depression: A review of their effectiveness. In L.P. Rehm, (Ed.), *Behavior therapy for depression: Present status and future directions* (pp. 1–32). New York: Academic Press.

Breslau, N., & Davis, G.C. (1986). Chronic stress and major depression. *Archives of General Psychiatry, 43,* 309–314.

Buscaglia, L. (1975). *The disabled and their parents: A counseling challenge.* Thorofare, NJ: Slack, Inc.

Dangel, R.F., & Polster, R.A. (Eds.). (1984). *Parent training: Foundations of research and practice.* New York: Guilford Press.

Deffenbacher, J.L., & Suinn, R.M. (1982). The self-control of anxiety. In P. Karoly & F.H. Kanfer (Eds.), *Self-management and behavior change.* Elmsford, NY: Pergamon.

Derogatis, L.R. (1982). Self-report measures of stress. In L. Goldberger & S. Breznitz (Eds.), *Handbook of stress: Theoretical and clinical aspects* (pp. 270–294). New York: Free Press.

DeRubeis, R.J., & Hollon, S.D. (1981). Behavioral treatment of affective disorders. In L. Michelson, M. Hersen, & S. Turner (Eds.), *Future perspectives in behavior therapy* (pp. 103–129). New York: Plenum.

Hawkins, N.E. (1986). Stress-management training manual. Unpublished manuscript, Oregon Research Institute, Eugene.

Hersen, M., & Bellack, A.S. (1982). Perspectives in the behavioral treatment of depression. *Behavior Modification, 6,* 95–106.

Kanfer, F.H., & Grimm, L.G. (1978). Freedom of choice and behavioral change. *Journal of Consulting and Clinical Psychology, 46,* 873–878.

Karoly, P., & Kanfer, H. (Eds.). (1982). *Self-control and behavior change.* Elmsford, NY: Pergamon.

Leigh, H. (1982). Evaluation and management of stress in general medicine: The psychosomatic approach. In L. Goldberger & S. Breznitz (Eds.), *Handbook of stress: Theoretical and clinical aspects* (pp. 733–744). New York: Free Press.

Lewinsohn, P.M., & Hoberman, H. (1982). Depression. In A.S. Bellack, M. Hersen, & A.E. Kazdin (Eds.), *International handbook of behavior modification and therapy* (pp. 173–207). New York: Plenum.

Lutzker, J.R., Frame, R.E., & Rice, J.M. (1982). Project 12-Ways: An ecobehavioral approach to the treatment and prevention of child abuse and neglect. *Education and Treatment of Children, 5,* 141–155.

Meichenbaum, D., & Turk, D.C. (1987). *Facilitating treatment adherence.* New York: Plenum.

Quine, L., & Pahl, J. (1985). Examining the causes of stress in families with severely mentally handicapped children. *British Journal of Social Work, 15,* 501–517.

Rehm, L.P., & Kornblith, S.J. (1979). Behavior therapy for depression: A review of recent developments. In M. Hersen, R.M. Eisler, & P.M. Miller (Eds.), *Progress in behavior modification* (Vol. 7, pp. 277–318). New York: Academic Press.

Roos, P. (1978). Parents of mentally retarded children—misunderstood and mistreated. In A.P. Turnbull & H.R. Turnbull (Eds.), *Parents speak out* (pp. 12–27). Columbus, OH: Charles E. Merrill.

Schilling, R.F., & Schinke, S.P. (1984). Personal coping and social support for parents of handicapped children. *Children and Youth Services Review, 6,* 195–206.

Shapiro, T. (1983). Family reactions and coping strategies in response to the physically ill or handicapped child: A review. *Social Science and Medicine, 17*(14), 913–931.

Shelton, J.L., & Levy, R.L. (Eds.). (1981). *Behavioral assignments and treatment compliance, a handbook of clinical strategies.* Champaign, IL: Research Press.

Singer, G.H.S., Irvin, L.K., & Hawkins, N.E. (1988). Stress-management training for parents of severely handicapped children. *Mental Retardation, 26*(5), 269–277.

Snell, M.E., & Beckman-Brindley, S. (1984). Family involvement in intervention with children having severe handicaps. *Journal of The Association for Persons with Severe Handicaps, 9*(3), 213–230.

Spielberger, C.D., Gorsuch, R.C., & Lushene, R.E. (1970). *Manual for the State Trait Anxiety Inventory.* Palo Alto: Consulting Psychologists Press.

Stoyva, T., & Anderson, C. (1982). A coping-rest model of relaxation and stress-management. In L. Goldberger & S. Breznitz (Eds.), *Handbook of stress: Theoretical and clinical aspects* (pp. 745–763). New York: Free Press.

Suinn, R.M. (1977). *Manual: Anxiety management train-*

ing. Fort Collins, CO: Rocky Mountain Behavior Sciences Institute.

Woolfolk, R.L., & Lehrer, P.M. (Eds.). (1984). *Principles and practices of stress management*. New York: Guilford Press.

Wright, J.S., Granger, R.D., & Sameroff, A.J. (1984). Parental acceptance and developmental handicap. In J. Blacher (Ed.), *Severely handicapped young children and their families: Research in review* (pp. 51–90). Orlando: Academic Press.

CHAPTER 6

Expanding the Focus of Behavioral Parent Training
A Contextual Approach

George H.S. Singer, A. Blair Irvine,
and Larry K. Irvin

This chapter presents a rationale for expanding traditional behavioral parent training (BPT) to address important determinants of parenting practices. It reviews recent BPT studies that have included a focus on the context of parent-child interactions. Finally, it presents an example of a BPT program embedded in a multi-element intervention for families of individuals with severe handicaps.

BEHAVIORAL PARENT TRAINING

Since the early 1970s researchers and practitioners have been using principles of applied behavior analysis and social learning theory to help parents teach and manage their children with handicaps. The contributions are impressive, including procedures for training self-help, communication, play, self-feeding, mobility, toilet training, and a wide array of other developmental skills (Baker, 1984). Furthermore, behavioral parent training has assisted parents to ameliorate a variety of behavior problems (Snell & Beckman-Brindly, 1984). These efforts are particularly important for families of children with severe handicaps.

Children with severe handicaps often have difficulty in acquiring basic communication and social skills as well as normal self-help and daily living skills. Partially as a consequence of such skill deficits, some of these children are at risk for developing severe problem behaviors including aggressive and self-injurious behavior. Both skill deficits and problem behaviors pose serious challenges for family members; Breslau, Staruch, and Mortimer (1982) found that the best predictor of demoralization in a large sample of mothers was the amount of assistance that their handicapped children required to perform activities of daily living. Similarly, parents have rated aberrant behavior as highly stressful (Quine, 1986). Levels of parental demoralization correlate strongly with perceived difficulties of aberrant behavior (Erickson, 1986).

Demoralization is defined as a complex of negative affect (e.g., sorrow and hopelessness) and somatic complaints (insomnia and indigestion) that is characteristic of many people who are exposed to persistent stressors such as chronic illness, sustained unemployment, or poverty (Depue & Monroe, 1986). When psychological distress becomes unbearable, parents often seek-out-of-home placement for their disabled child.

Behavioral parent training offers a relatively inexpensive and effective set of interventions for many of these problems. In reviewing the various treatment and support services for parents of handicapped children, Turnbull and Turnbull (1986) concluded that behavioral parent training was the most developed and best researched of any set of interventions to date. They

The chapter was funded in part by Grants #G008430093 and #G008730149 from the U.S. Department of Education. The views expressed herein do not necessarily reflect those of the funding agency.

also noted many limitations of the technology. Before these limitations are discussed, some of the premises underlying early BPT are examined.

Microanalysis

Behavioral parent training emerged, in large part, from laboratory work in the field of operant psychology (Baer, Wolf, & Risley, 1987). Operant theory diverged from earlier forms of behaviorism in that its basic unit of analysis, the operant, is defined functionally. Any unit of behavior that can be shown to reliably covary with contextual variables can be studied as an operant. The size and complexity of the unit under study can range from small-scale discrete movements such as pushing a button to large-scale phenomenon such as the collective actions of a community in using electricity. Until the 1980s the focus within behavioral parent training has been on moment-to-moment social interactions between parents and children. The operants have been behaviors of relatively short duration by one or two individuals at a time. This focus on discrete, time-limited interactions is referred to as microanalysis.

For example, Forehand and McMahon (1981), working with mothers of nonhandicapped children, have studied parental commands and consequences for child compliance in order to help parents with their noncompliant children. To help parents change noncompliant child behavior, Forehand and colleagues teach parents to give fewer commands, to state commands clearly, and to reinforce compliance with praise and to discourage noncompliance with time out. Forehand and McMahon (1981) have demonstrated the efficacy of this treatment package with parents and their nonhandicapped young children. They have demonstrated that maintenance of treatment effects over time, generalization across settings, and generalization to new problem behaviors can be accomplished. Efforts to use these same procedures with groups of parents of handicapped children have had more equivocal results (Brenner & Beck, 1984). However, microanalysis of noncompliance has allowed other researchers to demonstrate the effectiveness of other compliance procedures with severely handicapped individuals (e.g., Cataldo, 1984; Singer, Singer, & Horner, 1987).

Patterson (1982) has made a major contribution to our understanding of family dynamics by describing coercive interactions between parents and aggressive children. These interactions are escalating two-way engagements in which each party tries to control the other through rapidly intensifying levels of aggression. Similar coercive processes have been identified as operating in demand situations for some severely handicapped children who are aggressive or who have tantrums (Carr & Durand, 1985; Singer et al., 1987).

Patterson's (1982) treatment package consists of a set of alternative parental responses that terminate the child's aggressive actions effectively. Parents of aggressive boys are taught to reduce their child's hostile outbursts by using praise and rewards for prosocial behavior and time out for aggression. Patterson (1982) has demonstrated the efficacy of the intervention when it is taught by highly trained therapists.

Microanalysis has been highly effective in these two lines of research. In their work with noncompliant children and aggressive children, Forehand and McMahon (1981) and Patterson and colleagues were able to isolate critical parent-child interactions that characterized many problematic interactions across many times and settings. By identifying these key interactions they were able to develop strategic interventions that have a great deal of treatment economy; that is, a relatively simple intervention facilitates significant change.

Limitations of
Behavioral Parent Training (BPT)

As the behavioral parent training (BPT) technology has matured, many of the researchers who originally developed microanalyses and micro-level interventions have turned their attention to larger units of analysis, or a more macroanalytic perspective. They have begun to study and intervene on a wider range of variables that make up the ecology or context for troubled parent-child relationships. These contextual variables include social isolation, depression, and the adverse effects of poverty. They have turned in this direction because of mounting evidence that BPT, like many other treatment procedures, has severe limitations. Some enduring problems continue to be troublesome to behavioral parent trainers, including recruitment, attrition, generalization, and maintenance.

Recruitment and Attrition The few studies of recruitment of parents of children with handicaps for BPT programs suggest that only a small percentage of parents volunteer to learn BPT. Baker (1983) reviewed three studies on BPT with parents of children with handicaps. Recruitment rates in these three studies were low; of the parents who were contacted about the training, 18%, 11%, and 24% actually attended the first meeting.

Once parents agree to attend BPT classes, many drop out. Reported dropout rates vary widely, from under 10% to over 50%, depending in part on how the criterion for completion is defined, on the design of the program, and on the population of parents served (Baker, 1983).

The difficulties in achieving successful outcomes from BPT do not end with low recruitment and completion rates. Of those parents who do complete training, a substantial number do not successfully implement the techniques in their homes, or they do not continue using them with the passage of time (O'Dell, 1984).

Generalization Stokes and Baer (1977) defined generalization as "the occurrence of relevant behavior under different, nontraining conditions (i.e., across subjects, settings, people, behaviors, and/or time without the scheduling of the same events in those conditions as had been scheduled in the training conditions)" (p. 350). Parent training must generalize across all five conditions if it is to be broadly effective in these dimensions. The literature on BPT for parents of handicapped children has few exemplars of successful generalization across these dimensions. This chapter focuses on three dimensions of generalization: subjects, settings, and behaviors.

Subject Generalization One form of subject generalization occurs when parents or family members who do not attend BPT sessions change their behavior as a result of another family member using BPT techniques. Subject generalization is important in BPT because published BPT studies focus almost entirely on mothers of children with handicaps. Fathers, grandparents, and older siblings rarely appear as change agents in the literature, despite the fact that they are often influential in shaping the context for maternal/child interactions. This problem can be addressed as a recruitment issue by enrolling fathers and other family members in the training, or as a generalization issue by encouraging mothers to share information and skills with their family members. Without the support of other family members, mothers are at risk of generating family conflict by unilaterally attempting to alter parenting practices.

Setting Generalization Setting generalization is also an important issue. In research with parents of children without handicaps, there is considerable evidence to suggest that training conducted in clinics can generalize to the home (Sanders & James 1983). However, there is little methodologically sound evidence regarding setting generalization in BPT for parents of children with handicaps (Kaiser & Fox, 1986). Apparently, no research has yet demonstrated successful BPT with parents of children with handicaps in a variety of home settings and community locations.

A home environment is not a static entity. Conditions change with the time of day as well as with more infrequent events. For example, the time between awakening and leaving the house on a work day is likely to have very different characteristics than the same amount of time during the afternoon on a weekend.

Busy and stressful times are likely to bring out competing and interfering behavior from parents as well as children. Sanders and Dadds (1982) identified stressful times of day for parents of children without handicaps who have conduct disorders. They found that when parents learned to use behavioral techniques in a relatively low-key training setting (the home dining room and kitchen at a low stress time of day), they did not use the techniques during more stressful times in the home until they were provided with specific training on how to cope with their child during more demanding time periods.

This chapter is unable to identify comparable research concerning parents of children with handicaps. Furthermore, no one has reported on successful BPT in the community settings that are the locations for many daily activities.

Behavior Generalization Behavior generalization concerns transferring behavioral parenting techniques from one problem child behavior or skill deficit to another. Enabling parents to generalize behavioral parenting techniques is particularly important because the target for change is usually a moving one. For example, a parent of a preschooler may learn how to use milieu teaching techniques to encourage a child to label objects. A mother might learn to delay giving a toy to a child until the child says "car." Eventually, the child learns to routinely use single word statements to ask for desirable items and activities. At that point the target for instruction needs to shift in order to assist the child to respond with more complex language. Unless the parent is able to apply the same principles to a new target, such as teaching the child to say "I want the car," the initial teaching procedure may inadvertently serve as an impediment to the child's development (because the parent may persist in reinforcing one-word utterances when the child, with continued teaching, might well learn to utter short sentences.)

Problems of generalization across behaviors are compounded when working with parents of children with severe handicaps. The children often encounter difficulty in transferring new learning from one setting to another, even when there are no competing problem behaviors. Successful interventions for generalization can require fairly complex instructional design (e.g., Horner, Meyer, & Fredericks, 1986). Many tasks may need to be modified or simplified with adaptive devices in order to make them possible for some children with severe handicaps to learn. Thus, general training principles may not be sufficient to enable parents to apply their teaching skills across different tasks.

Other examples of the need for behavioral generalization arise in regard to problem behaviors (Kaiser & Fox, 1986). For example, a parent of a 10-year-old child learned to manage her daughter's tantrums by rewarding her for following directions, and by having the child sit in the corner for 3 minutes when she had a tantrum. A year later, the child began pinching her younger brother when he went near her toys. Although the parents had been successful at dealing with the first target behavior, they did not use their BPT skills to address the new problem. Unles parents have access to someone who can

help them develop a new intervention or they have learned to apply general principles to a range of problems, they are likely to resort to other learned ways of parenting, such as scolding and spanking.

Maintenance Individuals with severe handicaps often live at home well into their adult years. Their need for skill training or for behavior management may endure for much of this time. Consequently, the issue of generalization of treatment over time is an important one. This kind of generalization is often referred to as maintenance. As with other issues in BPT for children with handicaps, the long-term or maintenance effects of behavioral parent training are not well documented. Some studies have shown that short-term changes fail to endure over time for a sizeable percentage of parents (Dumas & Wahler, 1983; O'Dell, 1984). Others are more encouraging (Kaiser & Fox, 1986). Maintenance of BPT is important because parents are likely to live with their child with severe handicaps well into the child's adulthood.

Baker (1984) has conducted one of the longest-term follow-up studies on parent training with children with handicaps. In Baker's study, parents reported that they continued to use behavioral techniques at 17 months after the termination of group parent training classes. Parents reported continuing to utilize teaching skills for incidental (naturally occurring) instruction, rather than for formal teaching. Because the study relied upon parent interviews, these results are tentative and await further documentation via direct observation. Maintenance procedures such as booster sessions, intermittent telephone calls, and perhaps novel uses of video and computer media need to be studied, using longitudinal designs that focus on following families over long periods of time.

Improving the Microlevel Approach

In order to address problems of generalization and maintenance, researchers and developers of parent training approaches have attempted to improve teaching procedures and methods of implementation. One approach to improving outcomes related to response generalization is to teach parents general behavioral principles in order to give them a basis for developing new interventions as needed. Researchers have used this approach with both parents of nonhandicapped and parents of handicapped children (Forehand et al., 1979; Koegel, Glahn, & Nieminer 1978). Along with specific treatment programs to use with their children, parents learn general rules about influencing child behavior. The premise on which this approach is based is ideally, that parents can learn to apply general rules to create new treatments when new problem child behaviors arise.

Another means of encouraging response generalization has been to teach parents techniques that have broad applicability. For example, there is growing evidence that teaching children with severe handicaps to follow simple directions can have positive spillover effects, in which problem behaviors decline without being specifically targeted for reduction (Cataldo, 1984). Furthermore, since many parent-child interactions involve parental directives, simple compliance training procedures can have broad applicability. Some compliance training techniques also can be used as a proactive intervention to prevent problem behaviors (Singer, Singer, & Horner, 1987). By learning a relatively simple procedure for encouraging children to follow directions, parents can, in some cases, generalize their instructional and behavior management skills over time, settings, and behaviors (Forehand & McMahon, 1981).

Some cautions must be observed in choosing compliance training as a focal point for BPT. An excessive emphasis on parental directives and child compliance may reduce the opportunities for children with handicaps to initiate their own behavior, to request preferences, and to make choices. These outcomes may be averted by combining compliance training with another intervention that holds promise for having broad treatment effects, that of teaching functional communication skills to children with severe handicaps as an alternative to problem behaviors (Carr & Durand, 1985). However, as yet no research has applied this combined treatment approach in behavioral parent training.

A final approach for improving the technology involves strengthening corollary skills that assist parents to use BPT. Behavioral parent training requires a certain level of self-control. Parents

need to be able to observe and identify their child's behaviors and their own ways of interacting with their child. Similarly, many parents may lack the prerequisite skills to set goals, to move in progressive steps toward accomplishing them, or to find rewards in the process (Blechman, 1984). In order to deal with these problems, Blechman (1984) has added self-control training as a component of BPT. Parents learn to monitor their own actions, record their own behavior, and arrange contingencies to support behavior change. These correlative skills seem to enhance BPT for some parents. For other parents, however, the obstacles that impede successful use of BPT appear to be larger, and involve characteristics of the social and physical environments that serve as the daily context for parenting.

The Larger Context of Parent Behavior

Applied behavior analysis can be explained as part of a philosophical paradigm called "contextualism (Pepper, 1942). Contextualism involves determining the conditions or context surrounding a particular phenomenon, and then trying to predict or control the phenomenon by manipulating some of the variables in the context. The success of a contextualist venture is measured by whether or not prediction or control is attained. A foundation of BPT is the assumption that parents can create an important context for child behavior. For example, if a parent gives clear commands and rewards for following directions, he or she may establish the proper context for child compliance. A parent who learns to use time out, and not to be drawn into coercive interactions with a child, may alter the context that normally elicits child aggression. A therapist achieves these changes in child problem behavior by assisting parents to change their behavior. Unfortunately, adult behavior change is often difficult to achieve. BPT classes or clinical sessions often do not provide a potent context for obtaining and maintaining adult behavior change. There are many competing contingencies that operate upon parents as well as entrenched habits of responding to children (O'Dell, 1984).

The contextualist approach suggests that individuals examine the context that governs the parents' behavior. In order to determine which contextual variables may be impeding parental acquisition and implementation of behavioral techniques, researchers have tried to identify factors that predict attrition or treatment failure. Once identified, these contextual variables are manipulated in order to establish and document the conditions that enable parents to learn and use BPT. Four sets of contextual impediments have been identified, including low socioeconomic status or poverty, social isolation, maternal depression, and marital discord; some parts of these contexts have been successfully manipulated.

Poverty Poverty can be an impediment to parent training (Baker, 1984; Dumas & Wahler, 1983; Szykula, Fleischman, & Shilton, 1982). Dumas and Wahler (1983) studied ($n = 67$) parent-child pairs. They divided them into two groups: parents who successfully completed parent training and those who did not. They found that an index of socioeconomic status (SES) was highly predictive of completion of training as an outcome. They found that the poorer and less educated the parent, the more likely that parent training would not work. Poor parents are less likely to seek assistance from parent trainers, more likely to drop out of treatment, and less likely to implement procedures at home than are higher SES parents.

Baker (1984) has reported successful efforts in working with poor, urban parents of handicapped children. In order to overcome some of the obstacles associated with poverty, Baker and his colleagues recruited parents with the help of counselors who had already developed a trusting relationship with the families. These counselors ran the training groups; they also provided the parent training in neighborhood centers, provided transportation and respite care when it was needed, and supplemented group activities with individual modeling and individual coaching (Baker, 1984). Similarly, Szykula et al., (1982) described a program to reduce attrition and treatment failure in a program serving low socioeconomic status (SES) urban parents of nonhandicapped children. They were able to reduce dropout rates from 46% to 26% by adding several adjuncts to behavioral parent training including establishing personal rapport with referrals, employing contracting and "salaries" for participation, teaching self-control training, uti-

lizing frequent telephone contacts, and helping with housing, legal, and medical problems.

Social Isolation Behavioral parent trainers also have identified social isolation as an obstacle to successful acquisition and implementation of parenting skills (Baker, 1983; Wahler, 1980). One specific social circumstance stands out as an impediment to effective parent training: single parenthood. Single parents who have few positive social contacts and frequent conflicts with relatives and social service agents are prone to drop the use of new parenting skills. In response to these problems Depue and Monroe (1986) have created an adjunctive treatment called *mand review,* an interview process in which the therapist guides a single mother through a process of reviewing and identifying unpleasant interactions that set the stage for her to act coercively with her children. This process of recognizing the external social stressors appears to assist mothers to continue to implement BPT. Another strategy has been to recruit friends or relatives to take the BPT classes along with single mothers. They are encouraged to act as allies with mothers by showing interest and giving encouragement for using new skills (Baker, 1983).

Demoralization A third contextual variable associated with treatment failure in BPT is maternal demoralization. Mothers who describe themselves as very unhappy on self-report measures such as the Beck Depression Inventory (Beck, Ward, Mendelson, Moch, & Erbaugh, 1961) and the State-Trait Inventory (Spielberger, Gorsuch, & Lushene, 1970) are more likely to drop out of treatment than are mothers who rate themselves as less demoralized (Forehand, Furey, & McMahon, 1984). Demoralized mothers are also more likely to perceive their children as difficult and as sources of stress (Erickson, 1986). Quine and Pahl (1985) found that the more caregiving demands and behavior management problems that mothers of children with severe handicaps encounter, the more distressed they are likely to feel.

As with all correlational research, the nature of causality here is unknown. However, whether child-related problems cause depression, or depression influences negative perceptions of children, as many as one-third of mothers of children with handicaps report that they are discouraged and unhappy (Breslau & Davis, 1986). There is evidence that parents who report this kind of distress do poorly with BPT (Forehand et al., 1984).

In order to improve BPT outcomes with demoralized parents, some behavioral parent trainers have added adult therapies to BPT. These adjunctive treatments aim to improve the contexts that shape parental behavior. Griest et al. (1982) added a package of adjunctive treatments to their BPT treatment for child noncompliance. They provided behavioral counseling to mothers of nonhandicapped children to increase their positive interactions in the community, to decrease their conflicts with others outside the family, to improve their communication with their spouses, to help them develop more realistic perceptions of their children, and to change their cognitions in order to improve their outlooks. Demoralized mothers who participated in the adjunctive treatments plus BPT achieved significantly better results in their efforts to improve child behavior than did demoralized mothers who participated solely in BPT. By assisting mothers to alter both the elements of their environment *and* their habitual ways of thinking about it, the therapists were able to help mothers improve their child's behavior with parent training.

Marital Discord Researchers have begun to explore the benefits of addressing marital problems as an adjunct to BPT. Once again this concern is relevant to parents of children with severe handicaps because of the stresses that caregiving places on some marriages (Gath, 1977). Marital discord is correlated with maternal depression, and may be one of its primary causes (Billings & Moos, 1985). Marital discord has been linked to problematic parenting behavior, negative perceptions of the child's behavior, and independently assessed child problem behavior (Dadds, Schwartz, & Sanders, 1987). In a recent study, Dadds, Schwartz, et al., (1987) found that marital discord predicted poor treatment outcomes at a 6-month follow-up in parents of nonhandicapped children with conduct disorders. They concluded that a troubled marriage interferes with the long-term implementation of BPT.

As an adjunct to parent training, Dadds, Schwartz, et al. (1987) combined BPT with a brief form of behavioral marital therapy. They gave parents four sessions, $1\frac{1}{2}$ hours each, of marital communication and problem-solving training. They focused primarily on couples' discussions and problem solving pertaining to their child (behavioral marital therapy generally covers many more issues and takes longer). In order to test whether or not the marital treatment enhanced treatment effects of BPT they compared three groups of maritally distressed parents of children with conduct disorders: a BPT only group, a BPT plus brief marital therapy group, and a no treatment control. At a 6-month follow-up, the BPT plus marital treatment group maintained significantly lower rates of child problem behavior. Although researchers have not conducted similar studies with parents of handicapped children, this line of research is promising because of the likelihood that many caregiving families will experience strain in their marriages.

Adjunctive Treatments

Evidence has gradually accumulated to show that adjunctive treatments enhance the effectiveness of behavioral parent training. Several contextual variables (poverty, isolation, etc.) have been identified as impediments to successful parent training, and a few studies have indicated that these can be at least partially overcome. Dealing with these impediments may be particularly important in programs for parents who are likely to experience a variety of chronic and intermittent stressors that may undermine morale and strain relationships (Gallagher, Beckman, & Cross, 1983). Furthermore, a disproportionate number of handicapped children come from poor families. Adjunctive treatments appear to be important for this population. They are expensive, however, and resources for parent training are often difficult to obtain—individualized treatment for depression or marital discord is costly and time consuming.

To further complicate the problem, some poor, depressed, or unhappily married parents do benefit from BPT alone. For example, in a study by Dadds, Sanders, and Behrens (1987), three couples were successful in reducing problem child behavior without any specific marital counseling. But one couple did not improve their parenting skills until they were able to control their fighting in front of the child. Currently, no method of differential diagnosis permits us to match family needs with interventions. In the case of the Dadds, Sanders, et al. (1987) study, the treatments were over-inclusive, in that marital communication training was unnecessary for some parents even though all four couples were diagnosed as maritally distressed based upon a clinical assessment.

Well-tested diagnostic instruments are helpful for accurate identification of people who need adjunctive treatments and those who do not. Some researchers have attempted to develop such screening procedures (Embry, 1984); however, these approaches are still highly experimental and have not yet achieved sufficient power to be useful for the prognosis of individual treatment outcome. For example, it may be accurate to say that a group of depressed parents is likely to have more treatment failures than a group of nondepressed parents. However, identifying a specific parent and concluding that he or she needs therapy for depression *prior to* behavioral parent training is not yet possible.

In the absence of accurate screening tools, how should treatment be organized? Until a more substantial body of knowledge is developed about who will benefit from which treatment, one interim tool that can be used is what Miller (1975) called criterion assessment. In this approach, each parent is assessed broadly in order to devise a treatment. The parent and the interventionist jointly agree on criteria for determining when parent training has been successful. At first the treatment that is available at the lowest cost is provided. If that training is not successful, then more costly methods are applied. When a parent fails to meet a criterion, the assessment is broadened in order to determine the obstacles to successful intervention. The treatment is then altered to address these barriers (O'Dell, 1984).

This approach to assessment and treatment gives rise to a way of structuring service delivery. Initial levels of service are designed to accommodate a range of problems in group settings. Groups of parents may meet together with a paraprofessional or, if need be, with a professional as group leader. If the group classes are not sufficient to help parents meet their goals,

they may attend another group that addresses their obstacles to goal attainment. For example, a socially isolated parent who does not benefit from BPT might attend a group with other isolated individuals; this second group might focus on social skills training, using respite care, and increasing opportunities for social interactions. If the group approach is not successful, then individual counseling, therapy, or in-home coaching for BPT can be offered. This approach to services may provide a relatively cost-effective means of enhancing the outcomes of BPT—at least, until more is known about matching treatments to individuals.

In the discussion that follows, a description of a model demonstration program that is organized around this approach to addressing the contextual problems of parents of children with severe disabilities is presented.

DESIGN OF SERVICES

The Support and Education for Families Model (Project SAEF) was designed to address four problems, including parental demoralization, parental failure to obtain needed community services, child maladaptive behavior, and low rates of participation by children with severe handicaps in home and community activities.

The model was designed to serve the needs of families with children with severe handicaps and to be implemented cooperatively by public school personnel and social workers or therapists from community mental health agencies. A sample of parents was deliberately recruited in which single parents and low SES families make up a large percentage of those served. The staff tried to balance needed adjunctive treatments with cost containment.

Figure 1 presents a diagram of the flow of the SAEF model services for parents. The services were designed so that all parents were initially linked to generic assistance through a caseworker from a local Direction Service (information and referral agency). The case managers helped families with some of their needs for income, medical care, respite care, and other community services. They also helped parents to resolve conflicts that arose with community

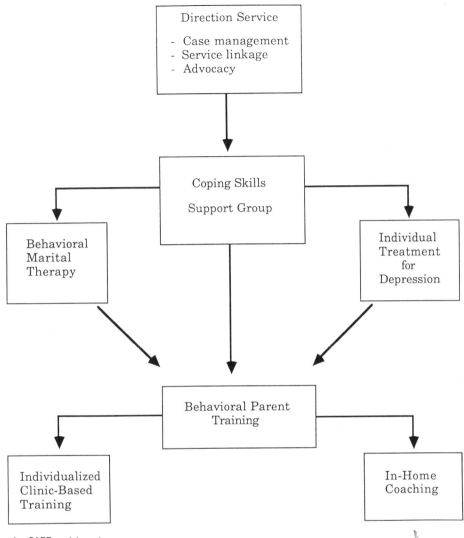

Figure 1. SAEF model services.

agencies such as public schools or local health care clinics.

Parents participated in coping skills training via two group-training programs including eight classes on stress and mood management, and another eight classes on behavioral parent training. Individual treatments were provided to those who expressed any of three specific problems: depression, marital discord, or severe aberrant child behavior.

In addition, the services were designed to mitigate attrition and keep failure rates low, especially for the substantial number of parents who were poor. Families were recruited by case managers from a Direction Service agency and by special education teachers. The personal familiarity that the case managers and teachers had with the parents allowed the recruitment of approximately 25% of the families with school-aged children with severe handicaps living in Lane County, Oregon (total metro population 200,000). Respite care and carpooling were arranged for all families who requested this assistance. Most classes were held at night in order to permit fathers to attend; other classes were presented during the noon hour to serve the needs of working families or those who found it easiest to meet while children were in school. The case manager assisted some parents in obtaining leave from work in order to attend the meetings that were held in neighborhood centers and neighborhood schools.

Most parents attended classes on stress-management first and then BPT classes. The content of the stress-management class is described in detail in Chapter 5 by Hawkins and Singer. In the stress-management class several treatment components were combined that have been used as adjuncts to BPT, including self-management training as well as social skills and relaxation training.

In each class, the ways in which procedures needed to be altered in order to accommodate the varying skill levels and physical conditions represented by the heterogenous mix of children were discussed. For example, the staff discussed the use of tangible and sensory reinforcers as well as verbal and symbolic reinforcement. When homework was assigned, the staff carefully explored with each parent how they would use a technique with their particular child. Lessons were also designed to teach strategies that have been developed specifically for use with children with severe handicaps, for example, partial participation in home and community activities, use of inexpensive adaptive devices, and task modifications (Brown et al., 1979).

Class Organization

The parent training classes were organized into an eight-session curriculum, with each meeting scheduled weekly for 1½–2 hours. Parents were recruited via flyers or phone contacts with special education teachers and community service agencies. Class size was limited to 12 people, to facilitate discussions. When couples were recruited, both members of a couple were urged to attend the classes together with the rationale that parenting techniques can be applied most effectively if both partners use the same approach.

When the class met, parents shared experiences and learned new skills to adapt for use with their children. Discussions on homework assignments were encouraged and class interactions were informal, within the constraints of the following rules:

1.   Confidentiality was respected; members agreed to use first names only in class, and not to discuss experiences of other parents outside of class.
2.   All class members agreed to be supportive of others.
3.   Individual privacy was respected; parents could elect to "pass" during class discussions.
4.   Each participant was entitled to equal time to express views and relate experiences.

During each class session, parents individually shared their home practice experiences with the class and new content was presented to increase the skills of the parents incrementally. Problems that had occurred were discussed, and, as necessary, new strategies were proposed. As part of this process, plans for upcoming home practice assignments were developed, and any required forms were partially completed during class; this approach gave parents a "head start" on the assignment. It also alerted parents to some planning needs associated with a home practice activity, such as arranging to have other children watched or otherwise engaged, and finding appropriate toys and a suitable location before a practice activity began.

New material was presented in class as a combination of lecture/discussion with the aid of videotapes produced by the staff to complement the lessons. Most of the videos showed parents who have "graduated" from the classes and their child with a handicap modeling target parenting behaviors in naturalistic activities and settings. For some lessons, such as those involving how to give clear directions and how to give time outs, role-play practice was built into the class sessions. To conclude each session, a small lottery prize was awarded. It was intended as a motivational tool to encourage attendance and compliance on the home practice assignment.

Personnel   The classes were designed to be led by a professional counselor or a lay person with considerable experience in training parents and leading groups. Knowledge of applied behavior analysis and its uses with children with severe handicaps is essential for the parent trainer.

Other important staff assignments included clerical tasks to prepare meeting logistics, and phone calling to prompt home practice compliance several days after each class. The purpose of calling is twofold, to both remind the parents of their commitments to complete the home practice assignment, and probe for comprehension problems related to class content or completing the assignment. The responsibilities of the phone caller, depending on the level of skill, ranged from that of an advisor giving tips on how to complete the home practice assignment forms, to simply prompting parents to complete home practice assignments and referring other questions to the class leader. In different classes, callers with a range of skill levels have been used, including the class leader, a graduate student, a lay person with no counseling skills, and a parent of a handicapped child. All four types of callers in the study elicited satisfactory responses from the parents, although the least-trained callers required more supervision.

Course Content

The content of the BPT program was designed to reflect a set of explicitly stated values as well as to present techniques that have been demonstrated to be effective in influencing the behavior of children with severe handicaps. The values behind the classes were: 1) a commitment to integrating children with severe handicaps into the community and into the daily activities of the family; 2) a belief that parents are teachers, but that homes are different from schools and other service settings and that the uniqueness of each home and family must be acknowledged and respected; 3) a commitment to effective behavior change procedures that offer alternatives to physical punishment; and 4) a commitment to recognizing and remediating contextual problems that interfere with BPT. The parent training class is based conceptually on behavior modification principles that apply to nonhandicapped as well as to developmentally disabled children. In addition, the ways in which common techniques need to be modified for children of different ages and ability levels are described. Behavior changes motivated by positive reinforcement in the form of praise and attention are encouraged, while forms of physical punishment are discouraged.

In the first session, parents are taught to observe their child's behavior carefully. Parents learn the a-b-c's of the behavioral model: antecedent, behavior, and consequence. The group leader introduces the idea of behavioral chains and coercive interactions using the a-b-c model as a template. Parents are asked to observe their child and to record one antecedent-behavior-consequence relationship each day. The importance of positive antecedents such as parent/child play and activity times, inclusion in enjoyable family activities, and frequent praise and attention are emphasized.

In the second session, parents are taught to integrate behavioral analysis skills that they learned during session one with reinforcement concepts. Positive reinforcement is introduced as a key to generating positive changes. A videotape demonstrating positive reinforcement techniques for children with handicaps is shown, and then parents develop a list of potential reinforcers for their own child and discuss ways to give praise and attention paired with more tangible activities and rewards.

In the third session, reinforcement principles continue to be emphasized, and the concept of teaching their child to follow directions is taught. After a review of home practice experiences by each parent, class members see a videotape entitled, *How to Give Clear Directions*. The video presents the following principles: initially getting the child's attention; giving one direction at a time; using short, simple statements; prompting if necessary; and praising compliance. These procedures are a modification of Forehand and McMahon's (1981) techniques for nonhandicapped children. This model has added a component on prompting procedures, as well as a discussion of children's receptive language skills, in order to accommodate some of the needs of children with severe handicaps.

By session four, the class members have had practice in observing their child's behavior closely, giving praise and attention, and giving clear directions. After reviewing these principles, the concept of using back-up rewards as a supplemental reinforcement is presented, and parents are introduced to the concept of using a token system for children who have a symbolic expressive communication repertoire. If appropriate, the class sees a videotape called *A Star Chart*, which demonstrates use of a chart to represent accumulation of rewards for child behavior. Using class discussion and a handout for ideas, the parents identify behaviors that can be performed easily by their child to earn stars. Likewise they choose suitable back-up rewards as part of the home practice assignment. The direction-following procedures from the previous lesson are reviewed because the token system incorporates their use.

In classes that are provided for parents of children who are not able to respond to tokens because of severe mental retardation, a video lesson on receptive communication for children with sensory impairments and/or extremely limited receptive language is substituted. The video lesson describes ways of indicating to children when an interaction or activity is going to start, what is going to happen, and when it is completed. As a homework assignment, parents are asked to structure at least one interaction per day in the fashion described in the video lesson.

In the fifth session, parents are taught to deal with minor problem behaviors. Parents learn to interrupt problem behaviors and redirect the child by asking that simple directions be followed. The lesson also describes how to plan activities to establish positive interactions between parents and children. Then parents are given ideas on how to spend brief periods of quality time with their child. The activity, dubbed the "Child's Game," allows the child to make choices about what activities are chosen; the adult pays attention, gives clear directions as necessary, and praises good behavior. Parents see a videotape called *A Child's Game* that demonstrates the principles and additionally shows how parents might deal with minor problem behaviors that occur.

In the sixth session, parents learn to use time out techniques that are offered as an appropriate strategy for dealing with major problem behaviors. The principles of time out are explained and include interrupting the behavior, giving a short, clear explanation about why the time out is being given, placing the child in an uninteresting location such as a corner, using a clock to limit the duration to 3 minutes, and redirecting the child to a praiseworthy task immediately afterward. Parents view a videotape demonstrating proper techniques and then role-play the activity. During discussions, in the role-plays, and

in home-practice assignments, using time out as a last resort is emphasized, and contrasted against a positive home atmosphere where praise and attention for appropriate behavior are the norm. The group leader also explains that time out is ineffective or inappropriate for some children with severe handicaps (e.g., children who are both deaf and blind). Alternative decelerative procedures are discussed with parents of these children privately before or after class. The use of response interruption and other nonaversive procedures are emphasized. BPT as well as in-home coaching usually has been necessary, in addition to the group classes for parents of children who exhibited dangerous forms of aberrant behavior. The classes are presented to these parents as a necessary foundation for using other interventions to meet their children's needs.

In the seventh session, integrating the handicapped child into home activities by using the principles of partial participation (Brown et al, 1979) is stressed. Our *Partial Participation* video shows children with handicaps helping with meal preparation by stirring, assisting with laundry by unloading the clothes dryer, and using some adaptive devices to join in family leisure activities. Parents choose everyday activities in which their child may participate at appropriate skill levels. Class discussion provides parents with ideas about how to organize partial participation activities in the home. The purpose is to help the child feel included in family activities and to increase the number of cooperative parent-child interactions.

The final class session is called, "Children in the Community." In this last class, a general review of the course content is offered, with a group discussion of how skills learned in classes may be generalized to a variety of situations and behaviors. Parents are provided with written suggestions about including their child with severe handicaps on trips to supermarkets and restaurants. These procedures represent slight modifications of methods developed for nonhandicapped young children (Clark et al., 1977). Class discussion focuses on how to plan ahead for visits, with parents sharing useful ideas from their own experiences. Parents are encouraged to talk about ways of coping with strangers or difficult situations that arise when they go to community settings with their child with severe handicaps.

Maintenance   Ideally, behavioral parent training would equip parents with a flexible and enduring set of skills that would serve them through the many years of living with their child. Little research is available that describes a technology for ensuring durability of BPT (Sanders & James, 1983). Using interview data, Baker (1983) has established that parents report continuing to use incidental teaching techniques with their handicapped children at 17 months following the termination of group training. Baker found that parents reported that they continued informal, incidental teaching methods, but did not report that they continued to give more formal (planned and structured) instruction to their children. Thus, Baker (1983) recommends emphasizing incidental training during initial BPT as a way to encourage maintenance.

The program staff are currently experimenting with a maintenance strategy that involves a combination of periodic mailed and telephoned reminders to parents, group booster sessions, and contacts from trained parents who serve as leaders of the initial BPT group. Evaluation of this maintenance package will require longitudinal data that are not yet available.

Generalization   Several strategies were used in order to enhance the chances of generalization across settings and behaviors. For most of the BPT classes, videotapes demonstrated the application of the techniques with both non-handicapped and children with severe handicaps. The tapes about nonhandicapped children were purchased commercially (Dangel & Polster, 1982). Video lessons were developed to show applications of the techniques with children who have severe handicaps. These tapes showed children of different ages and with a variety of handicapping conditions. Exemplars were chosen that illustrated the children in age-appropriate activities in home and integrated community settings.

EVALUATION OF THE SAEF MODEL

A series of evaluation studies have been designed to determine if the model has had measurable effects on families, and if families perceive it as useful. All of the components of the model presented in Figure 1 have been evaluated for the purpose of describing the processes of implementation and determining the efficacy of each component. In addition, the impact of the model as a "package treatment" on parents and children over time has been studied. The overall evaluation model was designed to capture the perspectives of various model consumers, including families, service providers, funders, and so forth. Irvin (Chapter 21) describes this approach to evaluation in detail. Hawkins and Singer describe the stress-management component of their model and evaluation data in Chapter 5. Cooley (Chapter 9) describes the community volunteer component and its results from the perspectives of parents and volunteers. Individual behavioral therapy for depression is described by Biglan in Chapter 19, along with some case histories. The Oregon Research Institute is currently conducting research on behavioral marital therapy for parents of children with severe handicaps. The following discussion evaluates group training for parents of children with severe handicaps as well as evaluating the effects of the model on parental distress.

Evaluation of Group Parent Training

In order to assess the impact of our BPT classes on parent and child behavior, parents were randomly assigned to a treatment or waiting-list comparison group. Thirteen parents completed BPT classes and nine were in the comparison group.

The median annual income for all participants was $10,000–$15,000, reflecting the fact that the majority of parents were from poverty-level or lower middle class SES families. Detailed demographic information, as well as descriptions of the handicapped children, have been reported elsewhere (Singer, Irvin, Irvine, & Hawkins, 1987). In order for the parents to be eligible for the classes, the children had to be classified as severely handicapped by the state department of education. This classification includes children with moderate, severe, and profound mental retardation, individuals with autism, children with dual sensory impairments, and children with severe neuromotor disabilities.

To assess the impact of treatment, parents and

their children were observed at home in play and instructional interactions. Videotapes of the parent-child interactions were coded by trained observers using a short version of the LIFE (Living in Familiar Environments) code (Arthur, Hops, & Biglan, 1982). The LIFE code is a real-time, direct observation data collection system that can be used to record the nature and effect of social interactions. Reliability data on 30% of the sessions was collected. Inter-observer agreement reached acceptable levels for this kind of real-time code. Inter-observer agreements averaged 73% for content of interactions and 85% for affect of interactions. Kappa (Cohen, 1960) was also calculated and averaged .65 for content and .69 for affect.

Parent affect, child affect, child compliance, noncompliance and aberrant behavior, and parental use of clear commands and praise were measured. Following the procedures recommended by Hops and Lewin (personal communication, March, 1985), program staff analyzed the data with ANCOVA analyses in which two covariates were used: pretest direct observation measures, and pretest ratings of demoralization on the Beck Depression Inventory. The analysis of the direct observation data revealed significant changes in parent behavior in the home settings. As compared with the control group, the BPT treatment group parents exhibited significantly fewer instances of negative affect and behavior toward their children at posttest. Similarly, at posttest the BPT parents used significantly more praise statements. The frequency of unclear commands was very low at baseline and remained low after treatment; no significant change occurred in this variable or in parental use of clear commands.

The direct observations did not reveal significant changes in child behavior as a result of treatment. However, once again, the initial base rate of child noncompliance and aberrant behavior was very low and the baseline rate of child compliance was high. Thus, direct observations indicated some changes in parenting behavior but no observable changes in child behavior.

Parents, however, reported significant improvements in child problem behavior. Parents were asked to record the frequency of 13 prob-

lem behaviors during the week prior to treatment and during the last week of intervention. Pre- and postchanges were evaluated using a Mann-Whitney U test (Siegel, 1956). A nonparametric statistic was used because program staff combined and averaged the reports of spouses in two-parent families; thus reducing substantially the number of observations. According to parental reports, child problem behavior decreased significantly in the treatment group and increased in the control group.

Parents also completed social validation measures of each behavioral technique. They rated all techniques as useful, with the exception of ignoring mild problem behaviors. And they unanimously recommended the class to other parents.

The fact that very low rates of child problem behaviors were found in baseline observations meant that there was little room for improvement as a result of treatment. The lack of direct observation evidence for child change is problematic, but observed parent behavior change in the home setting is an important outcome, as are improved parent ratings of problem behaviors.

All parents reported that they began to include their child with a severe handicap in more domestic activities as a result of the classes. Reported partial participation activities included helping with laundry, setting the table, feeding the family pet, and putting away groceries. All parents in the intervention group also reported spending increased amounts of play time with their child with a severe handicap as a result of the training classes. In ongoing research program staff are collecting direct observation data as well as parent daily reports on these variables because they are important outcome measures; future research will investigate parent and child behavior in the community settings that were the focus of the last class in this series.

Evaluation of Parental Distress Intervention

In Chapter 5, Hawkins and Singer describe the results of a coping skills intervention for parental demoralization. The discussion that follows presents expanded evaluation data from intervention with parents that included all the major elements of the model program, including BPT as well as case management, community volunteers, respite care, coping skills, and a parent support group. Although evaluations from individual program components are presented elsewhere in the volume (Chapters 5, 9, 17), this discussion presents data from an overall evaluation of the program.

As discussed earlier, successful BPT may depend upon identifying and treating other contextual problems that impede effective implementation of behavioral parenting techniques. In this parent training model, group stress-management training was provided as a set of adjunctive treatments for adult problems that have been identified as common for many parents of handicapped children.

In order to assess the impact of the SAEF model on stress-related psychological distress, the State-Trait Anxiety Inventory (Spielberger et al., 1970) and the Beck Depression Inventory (Beck et al., 1961) were administered. These measures are widely used in stress research, and are generally accepted indicators of demoralization (Derogatis, 1982).

Forty-nine parents of severely handicapped school-age children participated during the first 2 years of the SAEF project. Twenty-eight parents were randomly assigned to an intensive treatment group and twenty-one to a less intensive level of support, consisting of case management and weekly respite care services. The less intensive services were already available to all families with children with severe handicaps in the community. Parents in the intensive treatment group participated in stress-management and behavior-management classes as well as receiving weekly respite care, assistance from community volunteers, and case management services from a direction service agency.

In order to ensure that the treatment and comparison groups were equivalent at pretest, parents were tested on a variety of dimensions that have been shown to predict distress. The groups were equivalent on all measures except for children's adaptive behavior. This variable was controlled statistically in an ANCOVA analysis.

The ANCOVA analysis demonstrated significant posttest effects for the Beck Depression Inventory and for the State-Trait Anxiety Inven-

tory-Trait Scale. That is, parents who participated in the full support model showed significantly reduced levels of demoralization. Data collected 1 year following the treatment showed that these treatment gains maintained over the year. In addition, when the comparison group parents received the full treatment consisting of all major model components, they experienced similar reductions in distress.

To determine if parents were actively using any of the skills that were taught in the stress-management and behavior-management classes after 1 year, 25 parents who were randomly selected from a sample that was stratified according to initial levels of demoralization were interviewed. In order to credit parents for actively using a skill, they had to answer questions about the skills with very specific examples of their use. The interviews were conducted by a third party evaluator who was unknown to the parents. All parents interviewed said that they still used some of the skills from stress-management and BPT training. There was a wide range of variability in which skills they found helpful and which ones they continued to use; most continued to use some form of stress management, usually progressive muscle relaxation and cognitive management procedures. Similarly, most parents reported that they continued to use praise and rewards with their children as well as some form of partial participation.

IMPLICATIONS FOR FUTURE RESEARCH

As described earlier, future research needs to utilize more direct observation measures of parent and child behavior change across settings and over time. Repeated observations of parent-child interactions in various home situations and community settings are necessary to demonstrate generalized parent and child behavior change. Furthermore, direct observations of interactions over time are needed to demonstrate maintenance of treatment effects.

A component analysis of the SAEF model would be valuable as one way to determine which treatment elements are effective for which parents. As described earlier, large-scale comparison studies are needed in order to develop reliable diagnostic screening procedures for assigning parents to necessary adjunctive treatments.

Policy Implications

The authors' research suggests that a cascade model for delivering services may be a useful approach. Parental support groups that focus on coping skills and parenting techniques appear to be a useful way to reduce parents' emotional distress and to assist parents to interact more positively with their children with severe handicaps. More intensive, and consequently more expensive, individual and in-home services can be provided to those parents for whom the group sessions are not sufficient. This work and that of others (Szykula et al., 1982) demonstrate the importance of providing a range of services to parents, with particular emphasis on the additional needs of low-income and socially isolated parents.

Research on ways to assist parents with maintenance of coping and BPT skills over time is likely to yield some important implications for the design of services. Parents will desire ways in which they can obtain access to assistance as their needs change through the family life cycle. For example, in current work the chapter authors are modifying their classes to accommodate the needs of parents of teenagers and young adults with severe handicaps. Perhaps this research needs to evolve toward a model of a stable resource center for families that offers educational and psychological services on an on-call basis, with training and counseling programs that change with the changing needs of families.

REFERENCES

Allen, D.A., & Hudd, S.S. (1987). Are we professionalizing parents? Weighing the benefits and pitfalls. *Mental Retardation, 25*(3), 133–139.

Arthur, J.A., Hops, H., & Biglan, A. (1982). *LIFE (Living in Familial Environments) coding system.* Unpublished manuscript, Oregon Research Institute, Eugene, Oregon.

Baer, D.M., Wolf, M.M., & Risley, T.R. (1987). Some still-current dimensions of applied behavior analysis. *Journal of Applied Behavior Analysis, 20,* 313–327.

Baker, B.L. (1984). Intervention with families with young, severely handicapped children. In J. Blacher (Ed.), *Severely handicapped young children and their families* (pp. 319–375). Orlando, FL: Academic Press.

Baker, B.L. (1983). Parents as teachers: Issues in training. In J.A. Mulnick & S.M. Pueschel (Eds.), *Parent-professional partnerships in development disability services* (pp. 55–74). Cambridge, MA: Ware Press.

Baker, B.L., & Brightman, R.P. (1984). Training parents of retarded children: Program-specific outcomes. *Behavior Therapy & Experimental Psychiatry, 15,* 255–260.

Beck, A.T., Ward, C.H., Mendelson, M., Moch, T.E., & Erbaugh, J.H. (1961). An inventory for measuring depression. *Archives of General Psychiatry, 4,* 561–571.

Billings, A.G., & Moos, R.H. (1985). Psychosocial stressors, coping, and depression. In E.W. Beckham & W.R. Leber (Eds.), *Handbook of depression: Treatment, assessment, and research* (pp. 940–976). Homewood, IL: Dorsey Press.

Blechman, E.A. (1984). Competent parents, competent children. Behavioral objectives of parent training. In R.F. Dangel & R.A. Polster (Eds.), Parent training (pp. 34–63). New York: Guilford Press.

Breiner, J., & Beck, S. (1984). Parents as change agents in the management of their developmentally delayed children's noncompliant behaviors: A critical review. *Applied Research on Mental Retardation, 4,* 259–278.

Breslau, N., & Davis, G.C. (1986). Chronic stress and major

depression. *Archives of General Psychiatry, 43,* 309–314.

Breslau, N., Staruch, K.S., & Mortimer, E.A. (1982). Psychological distress in mothers of disabled children. *American Journal of the Disabled Child, 136,* 682–686.

Brighton, R.P., Baker, B.L., Clark, D.B., & Ambrose, S.A. (1982). Effectiveness of alternative parent training formats. *Journal of Behavior Therapy and Experimental Psychiatry, 13,* 113–117.

Brown L., Branston, M.G., Hamre-Nietupski, S., Pumpian, I., Certo, N., & Gruenewald, L. (1979). A strategy for developing chronological age appropriate and functional curricular content for severely handicapped adolescents and young adults. *Journal of Special Education, 13*(1), 81–90.

Carr, E.G., & Durand, V.M. (1985). The social-communicative basis of severe behavior problems in children. In S. Reiss & R. Bootzin (Eds.), *Theoretical issues in behavior therapy* (pp. 219–254). New York: Academic Press.

Cataldo, M.F. (1984). Clinical considerations in training parents of children with special problems. In R.F. Dangel & R.A. Polster (Eds.), *Parent training* (pp. 329–356). New York: Guilford Press.

Christophersen, E.R., Arnold, C.M., Hill, D.W., & Quilitch, H. (1972). The home point system: Token reinforcement procedures for application by parents of children with behavior problems. *Journal of Applied Behavior Analysis, 5,* 485–497.

Clark, H., Greene, B., Macrae, J., McNees, M., Davis, J., & Risley, T. (1977). A parent advice package for family shopping trips: Development and evaluation. *Journal of Applied Behavior Analysis, 10,* 605–624.

Cohen, J. (1960). A coefficient of agreement for nominal scales. *Educational and Psychological Measurement, 20*(1), 37–46.

Csapo, M. (1979). The effect of self-recording and social reinforcement components of parent training programs. *Journal of Experimental Child Psychology*, *27*, 479–488.

Dadds, M.R., Sanders, M.R., & Behrens, B.C. (1987). Marital discord and child behavior problems: A description of family interactions during treatment. *Journal of Clinical Child Psychology*, *16*, 192–203.

Dadds, M.R., Schwartz, S., & Sanders, M.R. (1987). Marital discord and treatment outcome in behavioral treatment of child conduct disorders. *Journal of Consulting and Clinical Psychology*, *55*, 396–403.

Dangel, R.F., & Polster, R.A. (Producers). (1982). *Winning!: Child management skills* [Videotapes]. Arlington: University of Texas.

Depue, R.A., & Monroe, S.M. (1986). Conceptualization and measurement of human disorder in life stress research: The problem of chronic disturbance. *Psychological Bulletin*, *99*(1), 36–51.

Derogatis, L.R. (1982). Self-report measures of stress. In L. Goldberger & S. Breznitz (Eds.) *Handbook of stress: Theoretical and clinical aspects* (pp. 270–294). New York: The Free Press.

Dumas, J.E., & Wahler, R.G. (1983). Predictors of treatment outcome in parent training: Mother insularity and socioeconomic disadvantage. *Behavioral Assessment*, *5*, 301–313.

Embry, L. (1984). What to do? Matching client characteristics and intervention techniques through a prescriptive taxonomic key. In R.F. Dangel & R.A. Polster (Eds.), *Parent training* (pp. 443–473). New York: Guilford Press.

Embry, L.H. (1984). What to do? Matching client characteristics and intervention techniques through a perspective taxonomic key. In R.F. Dangel & R.A. Polster (Eds.), *Parent training: Foundations of research and practice* (pp. 443–475). New York: Guilford Press.

Erickson, A.M. (1986). Construct validity of the Parent Stress Questionnaire for parents of handicapped preschool-age children. *Dissertation Abstracts International*, *47*/07B, 3158.

Erickson, A.M., & Irvin, L.K. (1985). *Parent Stress Questionnaire*. Unpublished manuscript, Oregon Research Institute, Eugene.

Forehand, R., Furey, W.M., & McMahon, R.J. (1984). The role of maternal distress in a parent training program to modify child non-compliance. *Behavioural Psychotherapy*, *12*, 93–108.

Forehand, R., & McMahon, R.J. (1981). *Helping the non-compliant child: A clinician's guide to parent training*. New York: Guilford Press.

Forehand, R., Sturgis, E.T., McMahon, R.J., Aguar, D., Green, K., Wells, K.C., & Breiner, J. (1979). Parent behavioral training to modify child noncompliance: Treatment generalization across time and from home to school. *Behavior Modification*, *3*, 3–25.

Forehand, R. (1977). Child noncompliance to parental requests: Behavioral analysis and treatment. In M. Hersen, R.M. Eisler, & P.M. Miller (Eds.), *Progress in behavior modification* (Vol. 5, pp. 111–147). New York: Academic Press.

Forehand, R., & Atkeson, B.M. (1977). Generality of treatment effects with parents as therapists: A review of assessment and implementation procedures. *Behavior Therapy*, *8*, 575–593.

Gath, A. (1977). The impact of the abnormal child on the parents. *British Journal of Psychiatry*, *130*, 405–410.

Gallagher, J.J., Beckman, P., & Cross, A.H. (1983). Families of handicapped children: Sources of stress and its amelioration. *Exceptional Children*, *50*(1), 10–19.

Griest, D.L., Forehand, R., Rogers, T., Breiner, J., Furey, W., & Williams, C.A. (1982). Effects of parent enhancement therapy on the treatment outcome and generalization of a parent training program. *Behavior Research Therapy*, *20*, 429–436.

Griest, D.L., Forehand, R., & Wells, K.C. (1979). Follow-up assessment of parent behavioral training: An analysis of who will participate. *Child Study Journal*, *11*, 221–228.

Hops, H., Biglan, A., Sherman, L., Arthur, J., Friedman, L., & Osteen, V. (1987). Home observations of family interactions of depressed women. *Journal of Clinical and Consulting Psychology*, *55*(3), 341–346.

Hornby, G., & Singh N.N. (1984). Behavioural group training with parents of mentally retarded children. *Journal of Mental Deficiency Research*, *28*, 43–52.

Horner, R.H., Meyer, L.H., & Fredericks, H.D.B. (1986). *Education of learners with severe handicaps: Exemplary service strategies*. Baltimore: Paul H. Brookes Publishing Co.

Kaiser, A.P., & Fox, J.J. (1986). Behavioral parent training research. Contributions to an ecological analysis of families of handicapped children. In J.J. Gallagher & P.M. Vietze (Eds.), *Families of handicapped persons* (pp. 219–235). Baltimore: Paul H. Brookes Publishing Co.

Koegel, R.L., Glahn, T.J., & Nieminen, G.S. (1978). Generalization of parent-training results. *Journal of Applied Behavior Analysis*, *11*, 95–109.

Koegel, R.L., Schreibman, L., Johnson, J., O'Neill, R.E., & Dunlap, G. (1986). Collateral effects of parent training on families with autistic children. In R.F. Dangel & R.A. Polster (Eds.), *Parent training* (pp. 358–378). New York: Guilford Press.

McDonald, M.R., & Budd, K.S. (1983). "Booster Shots" following didactic parent training: Effects of follow-up using graphic feedback and instructions. *Behavior Modification*, *7*, 211–223.

McMahon, R.J., Forehand, R., Griest, D.L., & Wells, K.C. (1981). Who drops out of treatment during parent behavioral training? *Behavioral Counseling Quarterly*, *1*, 79–85.

Miller, W.H. (1975). *Systematic parent training: Procedures, cases and issues*. Champaign, IL: Research Press.

Miller, S.J., & Sloane, H.N. (1976). The generalization effects of parent-training across stimulus settings. *Journal of Applied Behavior Analysis*, *9*, 355–370.

Mulnick, J.A., & Pueschel, S.M. (1983). *Parent-professional partnerships in developmental disability services*. Cambridge, MA: Ware Press.

Neef, N.A., Shafer, M.S., Egel, A.L., Cataldo, M.F., & Parrish, J.M. (1983). The class specific effects of compliance training with "do" and "don't" requests: Analog analysis and classroom application. *Journal of Applied Behavior Analysis*, *16*, 81–99.

O'Dell, S.L. (1985). Progress in parent training. In M. Hersen, R.M. Eisler, & P.M. Miller (Eds.), *Progress in behavior modification* (Vol. 19, pp. 57–108). New York: Academic Press.

Patterson, G.R. (1982). *Coercive family processes*. Eugene, OR: Castalia Press.

Patterson, G.R. (1982). *A social learning approach, Vol. 3: Coercive family process*. Eugene, OR: Castalia.

Patterson, G.R. (1975). *Families: Applications of social learning to family life.* Champaign, IL: Research Press.

Pepper, S.C. (1942). *World hypotheses, a study in evidence.* Berkeley: University of California Press.

Quine, L. (1986). Behaviour problems in severely mentally handicapped children. *Psychological Medicine, 16,* 895–907.

Quine, L., & Pahl, J. (1985). Examining the causes of stress in families with severely mentally handicapped children. *British Journal of Social Work, 15,* 501–517.

Russo, D.C., Cataldo, M.F., & Cushing, P.T. (1981). Compliance training and behavioral covariation in the treatment of multiple behavior problems. *Journal of Applied Behavior Analysis, 14,* 209–223.

Sanders, M.R., & Dadds, M.R. (1982). The effects of planned activities and child management procedures in parent training: An analysis of setting generality. *Behavior Therapy, 13,* 452–461.

Sanders, M.R., & Glynn, T. (1981). Training parents in behavioral self-management: An analysis of generalization and maintenance. *Journal of Applied Behavior Analysis, 14,* 223–237.

Sanders, M.R., & James J.E. (1983). The modification of parent behavior. *Behavior Modification, 7,* 3–27.

Seltzer, M.M., & Krauss, M.W. (1984). Placement alternatives for mentally retarded children and their families. In J. Blacher (Ed.), *Severely handicapped young children and their families* (pp. 143–175). Orlando, FL: Academic Press.

Siegel, S. (1956). *Nonparametric statistics for the behavioral sciences.* New York: McGraw-Hill.

Singer, G.H.S., Irvin, L.K., Irvine, B., & Hawkins, N. (1987). *Group behavior management training for parents of severely handicapped children.* Manuscript submitted for publication.

Singer, G.H.S., Irvin, L.K., & Hawkins, N. (1988). Stress management training for parents of severely handicapped children. *Mental Retardation, 26*(5), 269–277.

Singer, G.H.S., Singer, J., & Horner, R.H. (1987). Using pretask requests to increase the probability of compliance for students with severe disabilities. *Journal of The Association for Persons with Severe Handicaps, 12,* 287–291.

Snell, M.E., & Beckman-Brindley, S. (1984). Family involvement in intervention with children having severe handicaps, *9*(3), 213–230.

Spielberger, C.D., Gorsuch, R.C. & Lushene, R.E. (1970) *Manual for the State-Trait Anxiety Inventory.* Palo Alto: Consulting Psychologists.

Stokes, T.F., & Bear, D.M. (1977). An implicit technology of generalization. *Journal of Applied Behavior Analysis, 10,* 349–367.

Szykula, S.A., Fleischman, M.J., & Shilton, P.E. (1982). Implementing a family therapy program in a community: Relevant issues on one promising program for families in conflict. *Behavioral Counseling Quarterly, 2,* 67–78.

Tavorima, J.B. (1975). Relative effectiveness of behavioral and reflective group counseling with parents of mentally retarded children. *Journal of Clinical and Consulting Psychology, 43,* 22–31.

Tawney, J.W., & Sniezek, K. (1985). Educational programs for severely mentally retarded elementary-age children: Progress, problems, and suggestions. In D. Bricker & J. Filler (Eds.), *Severe mental retardation: From theory to practice* (pp. 76–96). Lancaster: Lancaster Press.

Turnbull, A.P. & Turnbull, H.R. III. (1986). *Families, professionals, and exceptionality: A special partnership.* Columbus, OH: Charles E. Merrill.

Wahler, R.G. (1980). The insular mother: Her problems in parent-child treatment. *Journal of Applied Behavior Analysis, 13,* 207–219.

Wahler, R.G., & Dumas, J.E. (1984). Two conceptualizations of parental deficit in child management. In R.F. Dangel & R.A. Polister (Eds.), *Parent training* (pp. 379–416). New York: Guilford Press.

Webster-Stratton, C. (1985). Predictors of treatment outcome in parent training for conduct disordered children. *Behavior Therapy, 16,* 223–243.

Webster-Stratton, C. (1981). Videotape modeling: A method of parent education. *Journal of Clinical Child Psychology, 10,* 93–98.

Williams, W., Vogelsberg, R.T., & Schutz, R. (1985). Programs for secondary-age severely handicapped youth. In D. Bricker & J. Filler (Eds.), *Severe mental retardation: From theory to practice* (pp. 97–118). Lancaster: Lancaster Press.

Zeller, R.W. (1980). Direction service: Collaboration one case at a time. In J.O. Elder & P.R. Magrab (Eds.), *Coordinating services to handicapped children: A handbook for interagency collaboration* (pp. 65–98). Baltimore: Paul H. Brookes Publishing Co.

CHAPTER 7

Strategies for Improving Parent-Professional Cooperation

Barbara Walker

A serious failure occurs in service delivery when the two most influential agents for change in the child's learning experience—parents and teachers—do not collaborate successfully in the planning and monitoring of the child's educational program. When this happens, the essential connection between home and school is lost. Unresolved conflict often leads to severed communication or adversarial encounters, and produces a great deal of stress for many parents and teachers. Ultimately, both parties may feel ineffective in their efforts on the child's behalf, and the student is cheated of the benefit of a coordinated learning experience.

NEED FOR SERVICE

The trends in educational theory and federal legislation have begun to support and expand parental involvement in educational planning for children with a disability (e.g., PL 94-142, *The Education for All Handicapped Children Act of 1975* and PL 99-457, *The Education of the Handicapped Act Amendments of 1986*). Nevertheless, continuing difficulty in achieving cooperative partnerships between parents and educators is apparent (Baker & Brightman, 1984; Goldstein, Strickland, Turnbull, & Curry, 1980; Maxman, 1983; Turnbull & Turnbull, 1986). The need to comply with federal mandates to translate educational theory into practice compels researchers to seek effective strategies for improving cooperation between home and school.

Obstacles to Home-School Cooperation

Although there is evidence that parents are generally satisfied with the laws that provide for parent involvement, there are several reasons why federal mandates for parent-professional collaboration have not succeeded in bringing about the hoped for partnerships between home and service settings. Darling (1983) and Roos (1979) describe problems in parent-professional relationships that result from competition for control of the child's activities. Others (Schulz, 1985; Shulman, 1980; Turnbull & Turnbull, 1986) attribute difficulties to such factors as: 1) poor communication skills and unfavorable attitudes; 2) lack of professional training for dealing effectively with parent concerns and emotions; 3) parental disinterest and lack of experience in dealing with educational and medical systems, as well as a lack of awareness of the expectation for active parent involvement; 4) lack of coordination among various professionals and agencies working with families; and 5) logistical problems in arranging contacts, including lack of time on both sides.

A number of educators have expressed reservations about eliciting active parental participation in the IEP (Individualized Education Program) (Fuqua, Hegland, & Karas, 1985; Gerber, Banbury, Miller, & Griffen, 1987; Yoshida, Fenton, Kaufman, & Maxwell, 1978). Their arguments emphasize parents' lack of expertise and knowledge regarding educational assessment and programing for students with disability. In-

This research was supported in part by a grant from the U.S. Department of Education, Grant # G008730149.

deed, some parents report that they prefer passive or uninvolved roles in the formal IEP process. These parents prefer that professionals take the responsibility for making decisions and carrying out plans for treatment or education (Lusthaus, Lusthaus, & Gibbs, 1981; Winton & Turnbull, 1981).

Strategies for Increasing Home-School Collaboration

Training efforts have been directed at educators' communication and conference skills (Flake-Hobson & Swick, 1984; Henniger, 1984; Kroth, 1985; Losen & Diament, 1978; Salett & Henderson, 1980; Simpson, 1982; Turnbull & Turnbull, 1986; Wolf & Troup, 1980), but their effects are not well documented. Efforts designed to stimulate greater parental participation at IEP meetings have had disappointing results when intervention has unilaterally targeted parents (Goldstein & Turnbull, 1982; Maxman, 1983). Furthermore, increased parental activity in the IEP process often has translated into an increase in adversarial rather than cooperative interactions between parents and school personnel (Pfeiffer, 1980; Roos, 1979; Seligman, 1983; Strickland, 1982; Turnbull & Turnbull, 1978).

However, Brinckerhoff and Vincent (1986) reported success in increasing both parent participation and home-school collaboration with a strategy emphasizing interactive activities between parents and teachers. Training for both parents and school staff stressed the importance of an IEP that links educational program goals to the child's daily routine. This strategy resulted in a significant increase in parents' participation in discussions, decision-making and goal-setting, an increase in joint parent-teacher decisions, and a decrease in unilateral staff decisions. These findings suggest that interventions are more likely to encourage parental participation in planning meetings and to increase instances of parent-professional cooperation in general when they: 1) target both parents and professionals, 2) emphasize consistent communication, 3) encourage an active exchange of information, and 4) incorporate both parent-generated observations on child functioning and related goals into programming for the child.

Broadening the Focus for Evaluating Home-School Relationships

Evaluations of parent participation in activities directly related to the IEP process provide useful information on parent and educator behavior in one important arena of home-school interactions. However, since IEP meetings have been described frequently as inadequate by both parents and teachers (Turnbull & Turnbull, 1986), these encounters may provide a misrepresentative view of parent-teacher interactions in general. Furthermore, many parents who have not actively contributed to IEP meetings may be involved actively with school personnel in less formal ways. Winton and Turnbull (1981) found that parents often preferred informal contacts with teachers to formal IEP meetings. And yet, the formal IEP process remains the primary focus of evaluations of home-school relationships.

The more informal, day-to-day contacts that occur between parents and teachers as they exchange information about the child and negotiate their own relationship may be more representative of the development of productive and satisfying parent-teacher relationships than are behaviors observed at IEP meetings. Part of the focus of the project described in the Service Design section of this chapter was to document parent-teacher interactions as they occur on a daily basis. More than half of those contacts were of a personal, individualized nature. Teachers and their aides initiated nearly three times as many contacts as did the parents. Nearly all of the contacts were neutral or positive in tone. The proportion of talk-time that was attributed to teachers was slightly higher than that attributed to parents, but the proportions were clearly more equal than those reported from observations of IEP meetings (e.g., Gilliam & Coleman, 1981; Goldstein, et al., 1980).

Improving Cooperation in Relationships

Educators and organizational psychologists have achieved considerable success in promoting cooperation among participants in problem-solving groups in both classroom and adult work settings (Johnson & Johnson, 1975; Tjosvold, 1984, 1986). Managers of group activities can elicit more cooperative interpersonal behaviors among group members by arranging working conditions so that participants in problem-solving activities are rewarded for finishing their work tasks only when others in their group are also successful in completion of assigned tasks. Under such work conditions, participants learn to perceive a connection between attaining personal rewards or goals and the successful attainment of goals for others with whom they are linked. Over time, participants in this cooperative work context develop more open communication with one another; demonstrate increased use of problem-solving behaviors; display greater empathy, concern, and liking for one another; and develop more positive attitudes toward themselves and others.

Viewed from this perspective, the style of parent-teacher relationships most likely depends on the degree to which parents and teachers see themselves as competitors (i.e., in conflict), individuals (i.e., independent), or cooperative collaborators (i.e., interdependent) in the task of setting and attaining goals pertaining to the child's educational experience.

Competitive Parent-Teacher Relationships When a parent-professional relationship is characterized by competition, unresolved conflict and adversarial relationships are more likely to occur, and neither parent nor teacher is likely to demonstrate support for the concerns, priorities, or efforts of the other. Individual efforts by either party to promote personally valued goals for the child are more likely to be contested or undermined by the other.

A parent and teacher, for example, who are engaged in a competitive disagreement about the child's mental status, might invest considerable energy in arguments about appropriate placement for the child. The teacher might argue for a specialized, segregated setting while the mother could insist on mainstreaming. In this competitive relationship, parent and teacher soon would be polarized on many issues relating to the child's education. Any opportunity for the development of a working relationship between them would thus be thwarted.

Individualistic Parent-Teacher Relationships In instances where the parent-teacher relationship is characterized by individualization,

little interaction between teacher and parent occurs. There is little purposeful collaboration or support for each other's concerns, priorities, and efforts on behalf of the child. Any reinforcement at home for efforts at school, and vice versa, is coincidental, not intentional. In this situation, a relationship between home and school is unlikely, and the benefit to the child is random.

In an individualistic relationship, the parents might be unaware of an effort occurring in the classroom to encourage their daughter to vocalize when she wants something. At home, the parents might continue to respond to her nonverbal gestures, and be pleased that their increasing ability to anticipate their daughter's needs seems to decrease her frustration when she is trying to communicate. In the absence of any collaboration between home and school, these parents and the teacher would be working unwittingly at cross purposes with one another.

Cooperative Parent-Teacher Relationships When parent-teacher relationships are cooperative, there is a commitment to constructive resolution of conflict and collaboration in efforts on behalf of the child. Parents and teachers are likely to demonstrate genuine interest in each other's concerns and priorities for the child, and to engage in purposeful reinforcement of each other's efforts. For example, in the first situation described previously, the teacher and parent might agree on a mainstream placement where a language program could be incorporated into the child's school routine in the mainstream setting. In the second example cited previously, more frequent communication would allow the parents to be aware of and possibly supportive of the teacher's work on vocalization. In addition, the teacher would have the opportunity to help the parents plan interactions to encourage their daughter to vocalize. Working cooperatively, the teacher and the parents would have a greater opportunity to arrive at a plan that reflected both the teacher's and the parents' goals for the child.

Unfortunately, the due process mechanisms currently used to settle disagreements can promote adversarial rather than cooperative home-school relationships. Furthermore, the ability to control the awarding of tangible rewards for team efforts does not exist in the home-school context, as it did in the intervention settings described in the cooperation studies (Johnson & Johnson, 1975). It may be possible, however, to motivate parents and teachers to build more cooperative relationships by developing for them a picture of the success that they could feel by collaborating on the child's behalf. The following section describes an intervention aimed at convincing parents and teachers to use cooperative strategies in their interactions.

SERVICE DESIGN

Philosophy and Goals

The cooperation intervention described in this section was an experimental component of a model demonstration project designed to develop and evaluate support services for families whose children have severely handicapping conditions. The belief that parent-teacher collaboration is fundamental to successfully planning educational programs for students with special needs provides the guiding philosophy of the intervention design. Failures in parent-teacher collaboration are seen as environmental and skill deficits. Since many factors that seem to influence interactions are specific to individual parent-teacher relationships, an intervention that allowed staff to work individually with parent-teacher pairs was chosen. By adopting more proactive, cooperative attitudes and skills, it was assumed that parents and teachers would be more likely to negotiate collaborative relationships.

Thus the goals of the cooperation intervention were to induce cooperative intentions and to teach cooperative interaction skills to both parents and teachers. Another goal was to increase the rate of positive interactive behaviors in parent-teacher conversations. And finally, the intervention was designed to improve parents' and teachers' attitudes toward home-school communication and the importance of parent-teacher conversations about the child.

Population Served

Parents and teachers who participated in the cooperation intervention responded voluntarily to an invitation to take part in a project designed to improve cooperation between home and school. Invitations were issued to teachers and parents in classrooms for moderately and severely handicapped children through both a county education service district office and a preschool program director.

Organizational Structure

Individual intervention sessions were scheduled for teachers and parents separately. An interventionist met first with the teacher, and within a week met with each of the participating parents from the teacher's classroom. The interventionist coordinated all aspects of the intervention, including development and distribution of packets containing information about cooperation strategies, as well as schedules, instructions, and forms needed for completing intervention activities. In addition, the interventionist conducted follow-up contacts, monitored participants' completion of activities, and designed and implemented an evaluation of the training program.

Staff Skills

The interventionist for this study was an advanced graduate student in counseling psychology, with training and experience in family counseling, and in communication and problem-solving interventions. In addition, she had experience with parents and teachers in special education settings.

Experience in adult education and counseling, as well as training in mediation and/or negotiation strategies, are important skills for instructors of cooperation strategies. Effective communication and problem-solving skills are critical to encourage participant involvement in the intervention activities. The instructor's credibility can be established with participants by familiarity with: 1) laws and practices that affect service delivery in the local community, and 2) issues and problems faced by both parents and teachers in their efforts to collaborate. A working knowledge of behavioral principles (especially of reinforcement strategies) and of cooperation theory is critical to effective delivery of the intervention. The ability to individualize the intervention experience for many different parent-teacher pairs is also important for eliciting participants' commitment and for increasing the likelihood of adherence to intervention activities.

METHODS AND TECHNIQUES OF SERVICE PROVISION

Format

The intervention activities were developed as mechanisms to engage parents and teachers in cooperative exchanges regarding the child's educational needs and progress. Sessions for parents and teachers were planned around similar general content agendas that called for presentation of the rationale for cooperation and the goals of the intervention components, and instruction in completing activities associated with the intervention. For each parent and teacher, an intervention session was designed to address the specific concerns presented by individual participants. This session lasted approximately 2 hours, and was scheduled at a time and site convenient to individual participants. After the intervention session, informal phone or mail contact was maintained between the interventionist and participants until all intervention activities were completed. This format for follow-up was designed to clarify any confusion about how to carry out intervention activities, to resolve problems in completing intervention activities, and to reinforce progress toward activity completion.

Training Content and Materials

A similar agenda for the intervention session was followed for both parents and teachers. Each participant's packet contained a schedule for completing intervention activities, all forms to be used in assigned activities, and informational handouts with tips for successful completion of activities.

Introduction and Overview   Introductions were handled in an informal manner. The interventionist framed her role as that of an agent for positive change within the broader context of concern for improved collaboration between home and school. As soon as participants demonstrated comfort in talking about their own experiences in home-school interactions, the inter-

ventionist shifted the focus toward a discussion of the purpose of the training session.

A brief overview of the objectives of the intervention session and activities associated with it was presented first. Emphasis was placed on the primary service objective—the acquisition of specific skills for increasing cooperation in relationships. Those skills were defined as follows:

1. *Perspective-taking:* understanding the position taken by another and appreciating the good intentions that motivate behavior
2. *Positive reinforcement:* expressing appreciation or offering other rewards for behaviors in others that are pleasing
3. *Maintaining frequent contact:* sustaining communication between home and school through notes, phone calls, and personal visits

The forms that served as the mechanisms for initiating and maintaining such cooperative communication activities between specific pairs of teachers and parents were briefly presented, in order to familiarize participants with some of the work that would occur during the intervention period.

It was important to present a rationale that would stimulate participants' interest in learning cooperation strategies; therefore, the pitfalls of adversarial relations were contrasted with the merits of cooperation. Illustrations of particular rewards associated with cooperative parent-teacher interactions in special education settings were generally effective in gaining both parent and teacher commitment to participation in the service program. The interventionist often provided the first example, usually one drawn from a hypothetical case where parents and teacher held conflicting ideas. It was pointed out that when due process measures are initiated in these situations, competition usually develops between home and school advocates and parent-teacher partnerships are threatened. Often, one party emerges as the winner and the other as the loser. By contrast, when a cooperative environment is established for resolving disagreements, the parties involved will be more likely to work to prevent disagreements that undermine important partnerships. In addition, there is a far greater likelihood that individuals will be willing to assist one another in reaching a resolution in which everyone feels satisfied. The legal mandate for parent involvement was also presented, in the light of its intent to encourage home-school collaboration, not competition. When participants could provide examples from their own experiences illustrating how competitive or adversarial strategies had failed and cooperation had proven productive for their own goal attainment, the interventionist moved into the next phase of the intervention session.

Participants' specific concerns regarding home-school collaboration were then assessed. Teachers were asked to specify three areas of concern where they desired information from each parent. These concerns were registered on a *Request for Information* form and forwarded to parents. Parents registered their concerns on an *Educational Concerns Questionnaire (ECQ)*. Their concerns were recorded in five separate categories: 1) the child's educational goals, 2) the child's progress, 3) current method for getting information from school, 4) current method for providing information to be used by the teacher, and 5) information desired from the teacher. The *ECQ* was then forwarded to teachers. This exchange of information provided a communication strategy for a systematic exchange of information in areas considered important by each participant in the transaction.

Skills Training A systematic skills training approach was then followed in teaching participants the three skills targeted in this intervention. The definition of each skill was repeated (from the definition used in the overview of the session).

Perspective Taking Several kinds of illustrations were used to provide examples of how the skills apply to parent-teacher relationships. Examples of *perspective taking* were drawn from hypothetical situations in which parent and teacher might disagree about the child's school placement. It was pointed out that learning more about why another person is invested in a different course of action does not mean giving up one's own position.

Participants were then asked to identify a problem they had had or were having in communicating effectively with their counterpart in the home-school relationship. The interventionist first validated participants' feelings and perceptions as understandable, then modeled perspective taking by speculating out loud about the various positive motives for behaviors to which participants were reacting negatively. Participants were then invited to imagine positive motives for a variety of behaviors that occur frequently during times of discord in the home-school relationship.

Positive Reinforcement When participants could acknowledge positive motives and identify situations from their own experience in which thinking about positive motives would be useful, the intervention focus shifted to learning how to apply *positive reinforcement* in parent-teacher relationships. It was not difficult to generate examples of opportunities for reinforcing one another. Participants were then asked to note when they had last been complimented by their counterpart. Few could report frequent instances of positive reinforcement. Together the interventionist and individual participants generated examples of reinforcers they could use in their interactions. Examples often included: commenting on the other's efforts on the child's behalf, writing thank-you notes for acts of kindness or compliance with the other's requests, being considerate in complying with requests, and acknowledging the other's enjoyment or positive interest in the child or in oneself.

Maintaining Frequent Contact The importance of *maintaining frequent contact* as a strategy for ensuring the exchange of accurate information was then emphasized. It was pointed out that many breakdowns in parent-teacher relationships occur in circumstances where involved parties lack accurate information, especially when emotions are a factor. Both the interventionist and parents could usually present vivid examples of problems caused by infrequent contact. Many of the examples focused on home-school misunderstandings that occur during the IEP process. Teachers and parents both described confusion and frustration with efforts involving lack of communication as well as ambiguous roles and purpose within IEP meetings.

Role-Play Activities After examples typical to many home-school situations were presented, the interventionist engaged participants in a problem-solving process in order to select a situation in which they would be willing to apply the cooperation skills presented in the intervention session. Usually, a situation previously identified during the session was selected.

After illustrating the targeted cooperation skills, the interventionist then engaged participants in *role-play activities*. Initial roles were assigned depending on how confident the participant was in the use of the targeted skill. If the participant seemed reluctant to take a role, he or she was invited to play the role of the counterpart and the interventionist assumed the role of the participant. The interventionist would then set the scene, soliciting information from participants for the purpose of engaging them in the activity. Initial role-plays involved hypothetical situations; however, eventually the role-plays focused more directly on a problem area identified by participants, and the participants played their own roles. The primary objectives of the role-play exercises were to model willingness to experiment with new behaviors, demonstrate appropriate use of cooperation strategies, and coach participants until they demonstrated accurate use of targeted strategies. Care was taken to empathize with difficulties that participants were having and to positively reinforce any progress made in using the new strategies. Participants were encouraged to experiment, expect some failure and some success, evaluate the effect of new behaviors, and be prepared to make changes in order to get a more desirable result. The interventionist offered her future assistance to participants, both to reinforce adherence to scheduled activities and to provide support.

Written Communication After role-playing, participants were instructed in the use of written forms associated with intervention activities. Drawing on concerns presented during assessment, both parents and teachers completed the "Specific Information Requested" section of the *Child's Activity Record* form. Care was taken to help both parents and teachers make entries that were stated in behavioral terms and that focused on observations of successful functioning rather than on failures. For instance, if either wanted information on the child's progress with tantrums, they were asked to word that request so that the information provided would focus on the desired substitute for tantrum behavior, rather

than solely on the undesirable act of having a tantrum. This more positive focus was expected to lead to more opportunities for a positive focus in parent-teacher exchanges of information.

Participants were then coached on how to make observations over a three-day period and record information in the appropriate space on the *Child Activities Record*. They were instructed to exchange the forms with one another within one week. In the meantime, the interventionist encouraged participants to comply with intervention activities.

Summary and Review Brief explanations were given for the informational handouts included in the packets provided to participants. Teachers received a handout developed by the interventionist describing typical communication dilemmas confronted by teachers, with tips for effective communication with parents. Parents received a description of parent involvement, rights, and responsibilities, published by a state task force.

The training session ended with a brief summary and review of the rationale for increasing cooperation among parents and teachers, the skills that had been practiced, and the activities that were to be completed by participants. Time was allowed for questions.

Identifying and Dealing with Problems During Training

Problems Common to Both Parents and Teachers There were a number of factors that contributed to difficulties in planning and implementing this intervention program. Many parents and teachers were excessively busy, making the scheduling of sessions difficult. Some resistance to participation could be attributed to negative expectations; for example, several participants reported that they did not have much hope for improvement, because they believed they had already tried every alternative. And pessimistic perceptions about their counterpart's interest in collaboration and ability or desire to cooperate were voiced by a number of participants.

Value conflicts often existed between parents and teachers, and created barriers to the cooperation intervention. Several instances of value conflict occurred over the issue of appropriate punishment for children. For example, some parents felt criticized by teachers who argued for alternatives to spanking, while teachers resented parents who criticized classroom punishment strategies such as isolation and removal of food.

Similar difficulties occurred during sessions when participants were resistant to the intervention agenda and attempted repeatedly to redirect the session toward their own agenda. In these instances staying "on task" with the cooperation intervention was difficult. Participants who were engaged in a current conflict with a counterpart commonly had difficulty shifting their focus away from their polarized orientation and to consider ways to improve cooperation in home-school interactions.

Addressing Problems Common to Parents and Teachers   To overcome the problems associated with participants' busy schedules, the session was planned to accommodate their schedules and take place at a location that was convenient for them. Sessions took place at sites near participants' place of work, including participants' homes, the center sponsoring the training, and conveniently located restaurants or coffee shops. An effort was made to create a relaxed social atmosphere during sessions, to enhance their appeal. Additional enticements included payments for completion of intervention and evaluation activities.

In situations where parents' and teachers' expectations or values were in conflict, the interventionist engaged more actively in listening strategies at the beginning of the session, with the intent of demonstrating empathy and validating participants' concerns. Care was taken to avoid supporting polarized positions in the conflict and, eventually, to point out the added difficulties that often arise when parents and teachers engage in extended conflict. The presentation of the cooperation rationale included many individualized examples of benefits that might be derived from determining a strategic way to gain a counterpart's cooperation in attaining important personal goals. In addition, extra time was devoted to the perspective taking activity for the purpose of diminishing negative perceptions. Frequently, the interventionist helped participants state one or two positive outcomes they would like to work toward in their relationships with their counterpart.

Problems Related to Parent Factors   The problems attributable to parent characteristics seem to have been related primarily to lifestyle and parenting behaviors. Parents without phones and those who did not respond to written messages presented special problems in setting up meetings and in making follow-up contacts. Transportation and child care needs presented occasional barriers to scheduling sessions. Some families had very unstable living situations and moved frequently, making contact difficult. For parents who were experiencing unemployment, change of marital status, illness, and/or difficulties with law enforcement authorities, participation in this project was a low priority in their lives. The concerns they presented related to problems that seriously threatened financial and family survival. In a number of situations, these concerns seemed much more pressing than the home-school relationship.

Some parents reported negative past experiences with schools and service agencies. Others with parenting problems were generally distrustful of service providers because of histories of being monitored for abusive or neglectful parenting practices, and their involvement with the intervention activities was guarded. Other parents simply had difficulty understanding the concepts involved or, because of literacy difficulties, found the printed materials and activity forms problematic.

Addressing Parent-Related Problems   Extra attention was devoted to soliciting the participation of parents who were difficult to reach and those who were distrustful cf the intervention service. The interventionist enlisted the help of teachers in contacting these parents and finding telephone numbers of relatives or neighbors who could take messages. Frequent reminders were sent through the mail with requests to call or send a message through the teacher. Occasionally, with the consent of a parent, the interventionist would drop by the parent's residence to leave a message. The informal setting of the sessions helped to establish the intent to provide the service under conditions that were most comfortable to participants. In some cases, child care and transportation were provided to permit a parent to attend the intervention session.

When parents were distrustful of the service offer, special care was taken to win their trust before attempting intervention. Additional information was provided about the project and the expectations of parents, and considerable time was devoted to answering questions. During the intervention period, frequent contact was maintained with these parents.

For parents with more demanding social problems, the interventionist abbreviated the presentation and session activities. A decision was made in those cases to attend to the presenting issues, to support the parent in moving in directions that would alleviate the more pressing problems in life, and to offer the current service as an option that they might want to consider in more depth in the future. For parents in this situation who were still interested in carrying out the home-school cooperation activities, additional assistance was provided to make their participation a success.

When the issue of parenting practices created problems in the parent-teacher relationship (e.g., when teachers had recently reported suspicion of child abuse or neglect), the interventionist took a more active role as a facilitator for a constructive relationship between the two. The primary goal of the intervention became to encourage the two parties to maintain contact and remain open to cooperating on the resolution of the problem. The interventionist spent considerable time listening to both parent and teacher, validating feelings and positive social concerns, ascertaining how the participants had managed to work cooperatively in the past, and eventually presenting plausible reasons and strategies for maintaining a relationship.

For parents who had difficulty understanding the concepts presented in the cooperation intervention, descriptions of the rationale were simplified and more examples that were tailored to the parent's individual experiences were presented. Additional assistance in using the forms and completing training activities was provided. While assisting these parents, care was taken to label evidence of competence in the use of new skills and to reinforce all behaviors which demonstrated adherence to intervention activities.

Problems Related to School Factors Frequently teachers were unable to complete activities on schedule. Contacting teachers for follow-up was difficult because few teachers had easy access to phones during their workday; nor did they generally have times in their workday set aside for this type of activity.

One of the most difficult problems was the hesitation of school administrations to support this kind of service project. Considerable wariness was evident regarding negative repercussions that might arise from involving parents and teachers in activities that might address areas of discord between home and school. While these objections were understandable, they also presented very real barriers to providing a service aimed at decreasing the tendency to use adversarial strategies to resolve conflicts between home and school.

Addressing School-Related Problems In order to gain support for the training program from school administrators, program directors modified the activities of the intervention to de-emphasize assertive communication skills and to stress instruction in cooperative strategies. By adapting the intervention to accommodate school administrators' concerns, greater support was also gained from teachers who were understandably reluctant to participate in service activities that were not supported by their employers.

SUMMARY OF KEY FINDINGS

Subjects

This experimental service project attracted a diverse sample of parents and teachers from special education settings for severely handicapped students in a metropolitan area of 200,000 in the Northwest. A total of 8 teachers and 37 parents of children in classes serving students with severe disability participated in the cooperation intervention project. Four teachers and 19 parents represented preschool settings; 3 represented teachers and 14 parents represented elementary school settings; and one teacher and four parents represented a middle school setting. Of the parents, all were mothers or female guardians except one, who was the natural father of his child. The teachers ranged in age from 27 to 40, with an average age of 33; 62% reported a master's degree in special education. Forty-six percent of the parents were between 30 and 39 years old; twenty-seven percent reported ages lower than 30; and twenty-seven percent, 40 years or older.

Parents reported a range of educational levels, with 51% having some high school or less, 21% with high school degrees and/or some college, and 27% with college degrees. Incomes for parents varied, with 39% earning under $10,000 a year; 22% earning between $10,000 and $20,000; and 37% earning over $20,000. Household structure was divided. with 57% of parent participants reporting households with married parents and 38% with single parents. (Note: Missing data account for percentages that equal less than 100%.)

Evaluation Design

Within the classrooms, pairs of parents were formed by matching them on demographic and home-school interaction variables measured prior to intervention. One member of each pair was then randomly assigned to the intervention group, the other to the nonintervention group. In addition, a blocking procedure was used to ensure that teachers were not informed about the intervention during the period when their interactions with nonintervention parents were evaluated.

Both pre- and post- and post- only designs were used to evaluate the impact of the intervention. Daily logs maintained by teachers over ten school days at both pre- and posttreatment provided measures of frequencies of parent-teacher contact at pre- and post-treatment times, as well as information on several additional dimensions of parent-teacher contacts, including topics discussed, initiators of contacts, and tone and duration of interactions. In addition, transcripts of parent-teacher phone conversations completed at pre- and post-treatment were separated into *message units*. *Message units* were defined as utterances that contained both a distinct subject and predicate, or that implied a completed thought. For example, "I agree with you," and "Okay," were both considered complete message units. Message units were coded on two dimensions: 1) speaker (parent or teacher), and 2) message type, as defined by Bales' (1950) Interaction Process Analysis coding system. Interrater reliability tests for point by point agreement exceeded levels of .70.

Using a questionnaire containing four 5-point Likert-type scales, participants provided independent ratings at post-treatment of their feelings subsequent to a parent-teacher phone conversation. The ratings provided information on the participants' evaluation of four dimensions of a recent parent-teacher interaction: 1) respondents' own effectiveness in communicating, 2) the effectiveness of counterpart during the conversation, 3) the comfort level, and 4) the importance (i.e., the social validity) they attach to effective parent-teacher communication.

Analysis and Results

The cooperation strategies intervention was very successful in obtaining participant adherence to intervention activities. Ninety-five percent of parents and 100 percent of teachers assigned to the experimental intervention completed at least the minimum of suggested activities.

With performance during pre-treatment measurement as a covariant, analyses of covariance were conducted to evaluate the impact of the cooperation intervention on selected dimensions of parent-teacher *daily contacts* at post intervention. For a period of 10 school days, eight teachers of students with severe handicaps kept logs on their contacts with parents. Table 1 provides a summary of these records (parents who had no contact are not represented in this summary).

Some expected effects on parents and teachers participating in the intervention were documented in teachers, including: 1) increases in personal, individualized contacts; 2) more frequent discussions about the student's progress and testing activities; and 3) more interactions that were rated as positive in tone.

Several unexpected effects were documented as well. Parents and teachers engaged in more lengthy contacts following intervention, rather than in more frequent contact, as expected. A plausible explanation of the occurrence of lengthier contacts is that the intervention component stressing maintenance of regular communication did not sufficiently differentiate the concepts of frequency and length. It is equally possible that specific extraneous circumstances elicited lengthier contacts among intervention group participants. In another area, for example, a review of cases suggests that the circumstances of individual students' health problems, rather than effects of the intervention condition, con-

Table 1. Contacts between parents and teachers for 10 school days

	Total group (N = 36 pairs)						Intervention (n = 18 pairs)		Nonintervention (n = 18 pairs)	
	Pre			Post			Post		Post	
	Number	Mean	SD	Number	Mean	SD	Mean	SD	Mean	SD
Total contact	288	8.00	3.96	235	6.53	3.47	7.06	3.69	6.00	3.31
Personal contacts	165	4.58	2.94	175	4.86	3.05	5.72c	2.95	4.00	3.00
Other	123	3.42	—	60	1.67	—	—	—	—	—
Topics^a	350			454	12.61	—	—	—	—	—
School events	110	3.06	1.72	61	1.70	1.35	1.44	1.20	1.94	1.47
Health, medicine	74	2.06	1.90	60	1.67	2.27	.94	1.39	2.39*	2.75
Student progress	61	1.69	2.18	81	2.25	2.34	3.06*	2.01	1.44	2.41
Parent involvement	26	.72	.91	14	.39	.84	.33	.84	.44	.86
Behavior, emotions	16	.44	1.10	11	.36	1.07	.33	.97	.39	1.20
Other	63	1.75	—	227	6.31	—	—	—	—	—
Initiations	288			235						
Teacher	132	3.67	2.50	120	3.33	2.58	3.78	2.21	2.89	2.89
Aide	81	2.25	2.60	43	1.20	1.41	.78	.88	1.61d	1.72
Parent	69	1.92	2.57	67	1.86	2.17	2.28	2.61	1.44	1.58
Other	6	.17	—	5	.14	—	—	—	—	—
Tone	288			235						
Neutral	189	5.25	2.58	161	4.47	3.33	4.72	3.72	4.22	2.99
Positive	91	2.53	2.99	62	1.72	1.32	2.17e	1.30	1.28	1.23
Negative	2	.06	.23	8	.22	.87	.06	.27	.39	1.20
Other	6	.17	.45	4	.11	—	—	—	—	—
Duration (Personal contacts)	165			175						
Under 5 minutes	65	1.81	2.51	72	2.00	2.22	2.72	2.76	1.28	1.18
5–15 minutes	52	1.44	2.09	53	1.47	1.89	1.39	1.14	1.56	2.45
16–30 minutes	24	.67	1.04	20	.56	.84	.44	.62	.67	1.03
Over 30 minutes	15	.42	.73	23	.64	2.26	1.00*	1.14	.28	.58
Other^b	9	.25	.84	7	.19	.71	—	—	—	—

^aTeachers reported multiple topics for many contacts; hence n topics $> n$ contacts.

^bContact occurred with another member of household.

$^c p = .108.$

$^d p = .055.$

$^e p = .06.$

$^* p < .05.$

tributed substantially to the greater frequency of discussions related to health and medical topics among *non*intervention parent-teacher pairs. The lower proportion of contacts initiated by teachers' aides among intervention pairs suggests that the intervention stimulated teachers to initiate more contacts themselves, rather than delegate this activity to aides. This finding could be seen as further evidence of the intervention's positive effects; that is, teachers' initiations of individualized, personal contacts with parents was increased.

Phone conversations between parent-teacher pairs were coded using Bales' (1950) system for analyzing interaction process. Mean base rates calculated at pretest for three broad commu-nication categories of *Information Exchange*, *Positive Social* messages, and *Negative Social* messages are summarized in Table 2. Not surprisingly, the highest proportion of message types for both teachers and parents fell into the *Information Exchange* category. In the categories of communication that affect the social/emotional needs of a relationship, however, there was considerably less activity. While the mean rates of social/emotional communication were nearly equal for teachers and parents, the overall occurrence of *Positive Social* messages (those that function to promote, build, and support the relationship) was relatively infrequent when compared to the usage of *Information Exchange* messages, especially when the data show that

Table 2. Mean base rates[a] of teacher and parent message usage at pre-test[b]

	Teachers (Proportion of talktime = 54%)		Parents (Proportion of talktime = 46%)	
	Mean	SD	Mean	SD
Informational exchange message	68.8	6.0	66.6	8.3
Positive social messages	19.4	6.1	23.0	8.4
Negative social messages	11.8	3.6	10.0	2.2
Uncodable	0.0	—	.4	—

[a]Base rate = n of individual's utterances (message units) of message type/sum of individual's utterances.
[b]N = 23 parent-teacher pairs.

the vast majority of *positive social* messages were categorized as minimal encouragers such as "um hum," "yeah," and "okay." The low base rates for message types that serve the social/emotional needs of developing relationships documents an infrequent occurrence of the kinds of interactive behaviors that typically work to demonstrate positive feelings and support between communicants. The even lower proportion of *Negative Social* behaviors indicates that there was relatively little obvious disagreement, animosity, or assertive behavior between the parents and the teachers in these conversations.

Analysis of covariance tests, with the base rates at pretest as covariate, indicated no significant differences at posttest in base rates of *message type usage* (in the three broad categories of *Positive Social, Negative Social,* and *Informational* communication messages) between participants under intervention and *non*intervention conditions. These findings indicate that the intervention was not successful in changing actual communication behaviors, and attest to the

strength of personal habits in communication behavior. Indeed, message usage at premeasurement time contributed significantly in most instances to variances at postmeasurement time ($p<.05$). The consistency from premeasurement to postmeasurement in observed message usage makes the findings of more positively rated interactions documented in teachers' reports all the more intriguing. Could it be that the intervention strategy of perspective taking worked to induce teachers to view their interactions with parents more empathetically, and perhaps more positively, despite a lack of change in actual message usage?

Analysis of variance tests also indicated that while intervention pairs reported higher ratings in terms of their perceptions of *communication effectiveness and comfort,* the between-group differences were not significant at the .05 level. When parents' mean scores on these two dimensions were contrasted with those of teachers, parents' ratings were significantly higher (t test $p=.03$).

Table 3. Social validity ratings on the importance of parent-teacher communication[a]

	Moderately important[b]		Quite important		Very important	
	Teachers	Parents	Teachers	Parents	Teachers	Parents
Intervention (n = 17 pairs)	18% (n = 3)	6% (n = 1)	29% (n = 5)	23% (n = 4)	53% (n = 9)	71% (n = 12)
Nonintervention (n = 10 pairs)	10% (n = 1)	0% (n = 0)	50% (n = 5)	50% (n = 5)	40% (n = 4)	50% (n = 5)

[a]N = 27 parent-teacher pairs.
[b]Moderately important = score <9; quite important = score 9–12; very important = score >12. Scores ranged from 3–15, with 15 being the highest score possible.

Table 3 shows ratings on the *social validity* scale indicating that a high percentage of all participants rated parent-teacher interactions as "quite" or "very" important in influencing the quality of the child's educational experience. Intervention participants had significantly more ratings in the "very important" category, while *non*intervention participants had proportionally more ratings in the "quite important" category ($\chi^2 p < .05$). A higher percentage of parents rated parent-teacher communication as "very important", compared to teachers (t-test $p = .12$). The findings suggest that the intervention had more effect on perceptions of social validity than on perceptions of communication effectiveness and comfort, which were only slightly higher after intervention. The discrepancies in overall ratings for parents and teachers as groups are consistent with other reports on teachers' relatively pessimistic evaluations of the importance of home-school collaboration and parents' history of reporting relatively high satisfaction with services.

Individual Case Findings

Three individual case findings are presented to illustrate the types of changes that occurred in parent-teacher interaction. These findings are not necessarily reflected in measurement of group effects, but provide an additional basis for evaluating program effects. Case records provided information from which these summaries are drawn.

A Case of No Contact In one instance, there had been no personal contact between a teacher and a parent in the seven months prior to the training project. The parent had no phone, and her response to routine written messages from school was infrequent. The teacher was pessimistic about the parent's ability to complete evaluation activities that required participation in phone conversations. Surprisingly, this parent was one of the most cooperative in completing the phone conversation exercises. A message phone was identified and instructions were given to place calls at specific times of the day that were convenient to the teacher. Moreover, in the course of their four telephone conversations, the parent commented to the teacher that some of the information on parental rights and responsibilities mailed to her as part of the project was new

to her. She was particularly impressed with changes that had occurred in provisions for special instruction in the fifteen years that had passed since her own experience as a student with significant developmental delays. The teacher was impressed with the mother's desire to improve her own skill level and actively helped the mother locate some services for adults with developmental delays. The teacher subsequently acknowledged that she had had no idea that the mother was as observant of her child's behaviors as she indicated in the phone conversations. This case illustrates how providing a structure for regular contact between parent and teacher can modify pessimistic impressions and lead to more active cooperation between parent and teacher, not only in terms of the child's needs, but in terms of mutual assistance.

Conflict over Parenting Competence In one situation, the parent-teacher relationship faltered after the teacher reported her suspicion of severe child neglect. In this same case, the role assumed by the interventionist in facilitating cooperative interactions between the two seemed to be influential in reestablishing positive feelings and communication between parent and teacher. Less than a week after the disruption, the teacher followed the interventionist's suggestion to initiate a conversation with the parent, present her good intentions, and express her concern for the negative impact her action was having on their parent-teacher relationship. In addition, she acknowledged the conflict of interest she felt in her dual role as a professional required to act as the child's advocate at the same time that she wanted to be a support person for the parent. She reiterated her desire to work cooperatively with the parent to create a solution that was positive for both child and parent, and suggested some activities that the two of them could undertake to get their working relationship back on track. At last report, the parent perceived the teacher in a positive light and was receptive to continued interaction with her.

Conflict about Placement In the course of the intervention program, a parent reported feeling troubled by the teacher's recommendation for placement following preschool. The parent expressed frustration at her inability to present her preference effectively to the teacher. She held a very high opinion of the teacher's skills and interest in her child's progress and was afraid of alienating her if she disagreed with her. The interventionist encouraged this parent to address this concern through the cooperation intervention activities. She did so, and sought frequent coaching from the interventionist in ways to state her case firmly without offending the teacher. The parent managed to ask for and get another planning meeting in which she presented her preference, with her husband's support.

Prior to this activity, the teacher had interpreted the parent's silence as acceptance of her placement recommendation. After the meeting, she reported having a better understanding and appreciation of the parents' goals for their child. She modified her appraisal of the child's needs to include more information about parental priorities and became more active in assisting the parents to obtain adequate services in a placement of their choice. In this instance, cooperation training activities contributed to effective confrontation of a difference of opinion and to a resolution that preserved a cooperative relationship between parents and teacher.

Summary

Many questions remain about the ability of the experimental cooperation intervention to effect significant changes in attitudes and behaviors that are critical to productive parent-teacher relationships. Data reported here must be interpreted with caution, because they are gathered from measures for which psychometric qualities have not been established with this population. Nonetheless, the positive changes documented in evaluation of the project are encouraging. The diverse sample of parents and teachers who participated voluntarily in the intervention suggest that it has appeal to a wide population of parents and teachers. In general, the intervention appears to have been effective in increasing positive perceptions toward parent-teacher cooperative interactions and the importance of parent-teacher communication to planning services for children with disability. While there was no apparent impact on specific communication behaviors, approaches to cooperative settlement of misunderstandings and disputes were documented in several individual cases.

FUTURE DIRECTIONS

Research

Parent involvement continues to be an important research focus. It remains important to find strategies that are effective in increasing parent participation in service planning and implementation processes. It would seem appropriate as well that the survey research documenting negative attitudes among professionals toward parent involvement be follwed by research on methods, if they exist, for alleviating this barrier to home-school collaboration. Additionally, it seems appropriate to develop a corresponding research tradition focused on professional involvement in family settings. What are the family characteristics, behaviors, or attitudes that encourage or discourage professional involvement in educational planning programs and include balanced consideration of the needs and resources of families as well as the child with disability? What encourages professionals to consider parental appraisal of the child's needs on an equal footing with appraisals derived from formal evaluations conducted in educational settings? What are the mechanisms that work to promote professional participation in family-based efforts, in order to create a healthy environment and integrated life experience for a disabled child within his or her particular family setting?

Although there is considerable research in educational settings on the participation behaviors exhibited by parents and school personnel at IEP meetings, this project appears to be the first effort to describe the nature of less formal interactions between parents and teachers. These daily contacts may be the arena in which many effective relationships evolve or dissolve. Further empirical study is needed to describe the content of these contacts, as well as the interactive processes by which parents and teachers typically develop or fail to develop collaborative relationships. A better understanding of how the content of parent-teacher conversations relates to the relationship behaviors demonstrated by either party, and how communication behaviors affect subsequent interactions, is needed. Are there, for example, ways to assess the impact of a teacher's communication style while making suggestions to different parents? If so, teachers may be able to learn ways to adjust the delivery of their suggestions to be more effective with individual parents. Similarly, a careful study of the impact of parents' communication patterns—both in terms of content and process—might shed light on how parent communication styles affect parent-teacher relationships. And finally, long-term studies are needed to document the maintenance of intervention effects.

Public Policy

If educators are to assist parents in assuming roles of increased responsibility in service planning for students with disability, as current policy stipulates, additional policies are needed to encourage the role changes implied. Policy is needed that presents meaningful incentives for parents to assume more responsibility for care, or for roles as teachers, child advocates, decision makers, case managers, or policy planners. It seems equally important that emerging policy provide clear direction to educators and other professionals as to how they might assume roles within the existing service structure that allow greater involvement in practices that are responsive to family needs and goals.

And finally, more explicit policy is needed to encourage cooperation and partnership development between home and school. Current policies that promote the use of due process of the resolution of service provision disputes often create a climate of competition between parents and educators, and prevent the development of collaboration that is essential to the desired home-school partnership outlined in federal legislation. This trend in adversarial processes could be countered by a new policy that stipulates mediation and problem-solving strategies as procedures of choice for disputes between service providers and parents. Public policy should reinforce structures and processes that ensure that the evolution of changing roles occurs within an atmosphere of collaboration, rather than competition.

Direct Service Practices

It is becoming apparent that educators will need to become more family-oriented in conceptualizing goals for their students. In addition, they will need to become skilled in roles that call for more frequent interaction with parents, where they function less as decisionmakers and more as consultants and advocates for family needs and priorities. These role changes imply changes in administrative practice for many existing educational systems. Teachers and other professionals in school systems will need greater administrative support than is currently reported to accept the challenge of broadening their responsibilities to include more parent-teacher interactions.

Perhaps greater use could be made of existing resources within school systems. School counselors with training that includes addressing parent-related concerns could facilitate greater home-school collaboration between teachers and parents in special education settings.

It seems likely, as well, that school systems will need to seek mechanisms to allow more flexibility in intervention practices, as efforts are made to accommodate the evolution of more broadly defined and more complex roles for educators and parents. Staff positions may need to be expressly created within education systems to facilitate more frequent interaction between teachers and parents; staff with training in mediation and problem-solving skills would be a boon to many school systems beleaguered with home-school disputes. Expertise in adult and family counseling procedures could facilitate the evolution of satisfying and productive parent-professional relationships.

Any changes in roles for teachers imply corresponding alterations in current personnel preparation for special educators. Increased training in communication and adult relationship management skills should become available in special education training programs. In addition to the currently available courses on understanding the needs of the parent and family, more opportunities for skills training in such areas as problem solving, values clarification, support-giving, and role clarification would assist teachers in becoming more confident and skilled in dealing with concerns presented by parents.

Likewise, parents should have more opportunities to learn problem-solving techniques and cooperation methods, as a preferable alternative to due process, for resolving issues with service systems. Both parents and teachers could benefit from more opportunities to learn strategies and skills to assist them to be negotiators and peace-makers with those who work closely with the child on a daily basis.

And finally, increased opportunities are needed for parents and professionals to learn *to-gether* in interactive forums about new legislation, changes in service options, and about one another's ability to contribute to the child's progress. Currently, conferences and educational forums are typically designed for segregated audiences and do little to promote the use of cooperative processes or to teach the skills that would equip parents and professionals to be more collaborative in their relationships. Part of their mutual education could include strategies for countering the adversarial effects of due process mechanisms. The effectiveness of skills training courses would be compounded if parents and teachers could participate together in learning these skills in an interactive format.

CONCLUSION

Surveys show that many teachers are not as positive as they might be about the feasibility of constructive collaboration between parents and teachers under current conditions. Parents also give accounts of continuing frustrations and failure in achieving their objectives in interactions with school personnel. Current due process approaches of settling disagreements present barriers to the use of cooperative strategies in home-school disputes. At the same time, there is evidence that methodologies exist which hold promise for improving cooperative partnerships between parents and teachers. Recent legislation (e.g., PL 99-457) reiterates federal commitment to a system of service provision in which parents assume increasing responsibility for service decisions and parent-professional collaboration is central to planning interventions for children with disabilities.

Improving cooperation in parent-teacher relationships is vital to the success of current policy trends that support greater integration between family and education systems in planning and providing appropriate services for students with disability. If parents and teachers are to become proficient collaborators in this endeavor, they will need opportunities to become more skilled in cooperation strategies designed for home-school partnerships. The climate is ripe for some innovation in service delivery and for thoughtful evaluation of the impact intervention strategies have on parents, educators, and the home-school system. The experimental project reported here documents some positive effects of an intervention aimed at increasing parent-teacher cooperation in informal day-to-day contacts and suggests the need for the incorporation of service components that are designed to facilitate cooperation among parents and educators into existing education systems.

REFERENCES

Baker, B.L., & Brightman, R.P. (1984). Access of handicapped children to educational services. In M.D. Repucci, L.A. Withorn, E.P. Mulvey, & J. Honahan (Eds.), *Children, mental health, and the law* (pp. 289–307). Beverly Hills: Sage Publications.

Bales, R.F. (1950). *Interaction process analysis: A method for the study of small groups.* Reading, MA: Addison-Wesley Publishing Company.

Brinckerhoff, J.L., & Vincent, L.J. (1986). Increasing parental decision-making at their child's individualized educational program meeting. *Journal of the Division for Early Childhood, 11*(1), 46–58.

Darling, R.B. (1983). Parent-professional interaction: The roots of misunderstanding. In M. Seligman (Ed.), *The family with a handicapped child* (pp. 95–121). New York: Grune & Stratton.

Gilliam, J.E., & Coleman, M.C. (1981). Who influences IEP committee decisions? *Exceptional Children, 47*(8), 642–644.

Flake-Hobson, C., & Swick, K.J. (1984). Communication

strategies for parents and teachers, or how to say what you mean. In M.L. Henniger & E.M. Nesselroad (Eds.), *Working with parents of handicapped children: A book of readings for school personnel* (pp. 141–149). Lanham, MD: University Press of America, Inc.

Fuqua, R.W., Hegland, S.M., & Karas, S.C. (1985). Processes influencing linkages between preschool handicap classrooms and homes. *Exceptional Children, 51*(4), 307–314.

Gerber, P.J., Banbury, M. Miller, J.H., & Griffen, H.C. (1986). Special educators' perceptions of parental participation in the Individual Education Plan process. *Psychology in the Schools, 32*, 158–163.

Gilliam, J.E., & Coleman, M.C. (1981). Who influences IEP committee decisions? *Exceptional Children, 47*(8), 642–644.

Goldstein, S.E., Strickland, B., Turnbull, A.P., & Curry, L. (1980). An observational analysis of the IEP conference. *Exceptional Children, 46*(4), 278–386.

Goldstein, S., & Turnbull, A.P. (1982). The use of two strategies to increase parent participation in IEP conferences. *Exceptional Children 46*(4), 278–286.

Henniger, M.L. (1984). Building parent/teacher relations through written communication. In M.L. Henninger & E.M. Nesselroad (Eds.), *Working with parents of handicapped children* (pp. 151–157). Lanham, MD: University Press of America.

Johnson, E.W., & Johnson, R.T. (1975). *Learning together and alone: Cooperation, competition, and individualization.* Englewoods Cliffs, NJ: Prentice-Hall.

Kroth, R.L. (1985). *Communicating with parents of exceptional children* (2nd ed.). Denver: Love Publishing Company.

Losen, S.M., & Diamant, B. (1978). *Parent conference in the schools: Procedures for developing effective partnership.* Boston: Allyn & Bacon.

Lusthaus, C.S., Lusthaus, E.W., & Gibbs, H. (1981). Parents' role in the decision process. *Exceptional Children, 48*(3), 256–257.

Maxman, B. (1983). *Parent participation in special education decisionmaking: The parent member's role on the committee on the handicapped.* Unpublished doctoral dissertation, Columbia University Teachers College, New York.

Pfeiffer, S.I. (1980). The school-based interprofessional team: Recurring problems and some possible solutions. *Journal of School Psychology, 18*(4), 388–394.

Roos, P. (1979). Parents of mentally retarded children: Misunderstood and mistreated. In A.P. Turnbull & H.R. Turnbull (Eds.), *Parents speak out: Growing with a handicapped child* (pp. 12–27). Columbus, OH: Charles E. Merrill.

Salett, W., & Henderson, A. (1980). *A report on the Education for All Handicapped Children Act: Are Parents involved?* Columbia, MD: National Committee for Citizens in Education.

Schulz, J.B. (1985). The parent-professional conflict. In H.R. Turnbull & A.P. Turnbull (Eds.), *Parents speak out: Then and now* (pp. 3–11). Columbus, OH: Charles E. Merrill.

Seligman, M. (1983). *The family with a handicapped child.* New York: Grune & Stratton.

Shulman, B.H. (1980). An administrator's view. *The Exceptional Parent, 10*(4), 24–27.

Simpson, R.L. (1982). *Conferencing parents of exceptional children.* Rockville, MD: Aspen Systems.

Strickland, B. (1982). Parental participation, school accountability, and due process. *Exceptional Education Quarterly, 3*(2), 41–49.

Tjosvold, D. (1984). Cooperation theory and organizations. *Human Relations, 37*(9), 743–767.

Tjosvold, D. (1986). *Working together to get things done: Managing for organization productivity.* Lexington, MA: Lexington Books.

Turnbull, A.P., & Turnbull, H.R., III. (1986). *Families, professionals, and exceptionality: A special partnership.* Columbus, OH: Charles E. Merrill.

Turnbull, H.R., & Turnbull, A.P. (1978). *Free appropriate public education: Law and implementation.* Denver: Love Publishing Co.

Winton, P., & Turnbull, A.P. (1981). Parent involvement as viewed by parents of preschool handicapped children. *Topics in Early Childhood Special Education, 1*(3), 11–19.

Wolf, J.S., & Troup, J. (1980). Strategy for parent involvement: Improving the IEP process. *Exceptional Parent, 10*(1), 31–32.

Yoshida, R.K., Fenton, K.S., Kaufman, J.J., & Maxwell, J.P. (1978). Parental involvement in the special education pupil planning process: The school's perspective. *Exceptional Children, 44*(7), 531–534.

CHAPTER 8

Building and Mobilizing Informal Family Support Networks

Carl J. Dunst, Carol M. Trivette, Nancy J. Gordon, and Lynda L. Pletcher

According to Hobbs et al. (1984), interdependent, supportive communities are the primary and principal contexts for enhancing and promoting human development in general, and strengthening family functioning in particular. The operationalization of the characteristics of supportive communities that Hobbs et al. (1984) described forms the basis for the family support project described in this chapter.

In their descriptions of the meaning of community, Hobbs et al. (1984) noted that a:

community is an immediate social group that promotes human development. . . . In communities, individuals experience a sense of membership, influence members of the group and are themselves in turn influenced by others, have *personal needs fulfilled,* and share a psychologically and personally satisfying connection with other people. . . . Community basically involves the coming together of people around shared values and the pursuit of common cause . . . that involves *reciprocal obligations.* (p. 41, emphases added)

A sense of community, in turn, promotes the exchange of resources and supports that constitute the range of aid and assistance that are necessary for enhancing and maintaining individual, family, and community well-being. Bronfenbrenner (1979), for example, noted that:

whether parents can perform effectively in their child-rearing roles within the family depends upon the role demands, stresses, and supports emanating from (community) settings. . . . The availability of supportive settings is, in turn, a function of their existence and frequency in a given culture or subculture. (p. 7)

In their discussion of the criteria that ought to guide social policy and practice for strengthening families, Hobbs et al. (1984) specify a number of conditions that they believe must be met in order to optimize the development of individual family members and the family itself. According to these investigators, the policy and practice that strengthen family functioning should:

1. Promote supportive exchanges among people that highlight human commonalties rather than individual differences.
2. Emphasize the common needs of all people and avoid the conspicuous setting apart of people or groups.
3. Avoid unwarranted advantage in distribution of resources based upon social class or individual differences.
4. Promote diversity in the bringing together of people.
5. Create opportunities for enhancing the ac-

The work reported in this chapter was supported, in part, by grants from the U.S. Department of Health and Human Services, Administration on Developmental Disabilities (90DD0113) and the National Institute on Mental Health, Prevention Research Branch (MH38862). Appreciation is extended to Clara Hunt for assistance in preparation of the chapter and to Tom Fite, Debbie Williams, Wilson Hamer, Tammy Moss, Dolores Pittman, Michelle Davis, Ron Davis, and Pat Condrey for data collection, coding, and analysis.

quisition of competencies that are necessary to promote individual and family development.

6. Create linkages among people that can be of mutual benefit to one another.

7. Permit and encourage families to make informed decisions about themselves and their children.

8. Ensure that families have the necessary resources (time, energy, information, etc.) to perform child-rearing functions well.

9. Employ partnerships and parent-professional collaboration that explicitly enable and empower families to become more capable and competent.

10. Promote both interdependence among community members and family self-reliance with respect to identifying and meeting needs.

11. Protect individual family members and the family itself from neglect, abuse, isolation, and other developmental deterrents.

Collectively, Hobbs et al. (1984) persuasively argue that these 11 characteristics of *family support programs* are the essential ingredients for strengthening family functioning.

The project described in this chapter uses the majority of the above 11 characteristics, together with formulations from the social support and help-giving literatures as a foundation for conceptualizing, operationalizing, implementing, and evaluating efforts designed to build and mobilize informal family support networks. Project SHaRE (*S*ource of *H*elp *R*eceived and *E*xchanged) was conceived in response to work with poor families and families with disabled members who had needs that went continually unmet due to a host of social, economic, and personal factors that impinged upon their daily lives. Needs were met through Project SHaRE by building informal social support networks that enhanced the exchange of resources, aid, and assistance among network members. The SHaRE Network operated much like a barter program (e.g., Lloyd & Segal, 1978; Tobin & Ware, 1983, 1984) in which persons or groups provided different products and services to one another based upon the principle of reciprocal obligations (see Fisher, Nadler, & Wichter-Alagna,

1983). The goal of the project was to enable and empower families to identify their needs and strengths, to employ strengths as a basis for mobilizing resources to meet needs, and to help families acquire the capabilities necessary to become more interdependent and self-sustaining (Dunst, Trivette, & Deal, 1988; Hobbs et al., 1984).

NEED FOR PROJECT SHaRE

Project SHaRE is located in Morganton, North Carolina in the foothills of the Blue Ridge Mountains. The project is operated as a model demonstration project of the Family, Infant and Preschool Program (FIPP) (Dunst & Trivette, 1988a). FIPP is a family support program that serves disabled, handicapped, and developmentally at-risk children and their parents in rural western North Carolina. The program began in 1972, and since that time more than 1,200 children and families have received home-, center-, and community-based services.

Project SHaRE evolved from efforts to identify effective ways to support and strengthen family functioning. The project was developed in response to four major concerns and considerations. First, families who have substantial numbers of unmet needs are repeatedly encountered, despite the efforts of FIPP, other social agencies, and community help givers (clergy, volunteer organizations, etc.). Families from the poorest social economic background often lack basic resources (adequate housing, food, clothing, etc.), and families with disabled children often have additional burdens and demands (e.g., lack of appropriate child care, excessive medical expenses) that place enormous stresses and strains on the parents.

Second, attempts by help givers to assist and aid these families often result in noncontingent giving (Skinner, 1978) and increased dependence (Merton, Merton, & Barber, 1983) upon the help givers. Well-intentioned professionals and other social groups (volunteer organizations, churches, etc.) have a tendency to rush in and try to "fix" these families by filling in missing resources. And although needs may be met, the methods for doing so only reinforce the families' already negative images of themselves as being incapable and unable to take care of themselves. Helpers who act in this way often view the families as "broken," and see their job in terms of "putting the broken pieces back together."

Third, efforts to be helpful with these families often have negative consequences (e.g., attenuation of self-esteem and self-efficacy). The families sometimes withdraw from not only the helpers, but friends and relatives as well. Interactions with others increasingly become negative and confrontative, or families simply refuse or avoid the efforts of others to reach out and be helpful. Help givers often interpret the families' reactions as a sign of being ungrateful for what was given or offered.

Fourth, the increased isolation on the part of the families, together with inadequate resources for meeting needs, result in even greater stress and more frequent dysfunctional family interactions, as well as other negative consequences (lack of attention to childcare and child development, abuse and neglect, etc.). Many of these families become increasingly characterized as rearing children that are at-risk for out-of-home placements (foster care, institutionalization, etc.).

An analysis of the ways in which help givers interact with the families demonstrates that most attempts to be helpful run counter to the 11 principles described previously (Hobbs et al., 1984). In Project SHaRE, considerable effort was and is placed on reversing the ways in which help givers viewed these families, and how they went about intervening and assisting these families to meet their needs.

CONCEPTUAL BASES OF PROJECT SHaRE

A social and family systems framework was used to guide project conceptualization and implementation (Dunst & Trivette, in press). The problems that these families faced were viewed not as inherent personal deficits, but rather as the result of broad-based social influences that prevent the families from acquiring and using the competencies necessary to mobilize resources to meet needs.

The major features of Project SHaRE are based upon conceptual and theoretical formulation-derived from human ecology (Bronfenbrenner, 1979; Cochran & Brassard, 1979; Garbarino, 1982; Hobbs et al., 1984), social support and social network theory (Cohn & Syme, 1985; Gottlieb, 1981; Hall & Wellman, 1985; Mitchell & Trickett, 1980; Sarason & Sarason, 1985), and help-seeking and help-giving theory (Brickman et al., 1983; Brickman et al., 1982; Coates, Renzaglia, & Embree, 1983; Gourash, 1978; Gross & McMullen, 1983; Rabinowitz, Karuza, & Zevon, 1984). Collectively, these three theoretical orientations provide a framework for understanding how resources and support either directly or indirectly affect family functioning, as well as suggest the conditions under which the influences of support are likely to have their greatest positive impact.

Human Ecology and Human Development

Human ecology provides the type of social systems framework that both explicates the relationships between and within social units and explains how human development is influenced by broad-based community experiences. According to Bronfenbrenner (1979), ecological and social units may be conceived topologically as a nested arrangement of concentric circles, each embedded within one another. The innermost level comprises individual families and their members (mother, father, children, etc.). The family unit is embedded in broader ecological systems consisting of relatives, friends, neighbors, and other acquaintances. These formal and informal kinship units are further embedded in larger social units, including neighborhoods, churches, social and human service organizations, the parents' place of work, school, and so forth.

One tenet of social system theory is that events in different ecological units do not occur in isolation, but interact both within and between levels so that changes in one unit or subunit reverberate and affect other units. Another tenet of social system theory is the contention that the behavior of individuals and social groups (e.g., the family) is affected by a host of forces emanating from different ecological systems and units, indicating that a person's development is influenced both directly and indirectly by different people and events. "Network influences come

directly to (a person) through the range and variety of (individuals and groups) with whom (he or
she) has contact on a recurring basis, either together with other family members or independently" (Cochran & Brassard, 1979, p. 602).
Less obvious but no less powerful are the indirect influences that bear upon a person's development. These influences emanate from the different social settings or networks within which
the family is embedded. Personal social networks can and often do impinge upon a person's
or family's behavior and development, depending upon the types of social experiences that network members provide to one another. These social experiences are most often referred to as
social support.

Personal Social
Networks and Social Support

Social network and social support theorists emphasize the study of the relationships among social units and how these different relationships
promote or impede the flow and exchange of resources and social support. Social support refers
to the resources—potentially useful information
and materials—provided to individuals or social
units (e.g., a family) in response to the need for
aid and assistance (Cohen & Syme, 1985; Dunst,
Trivette, & Deal, 1988). Social support is considered a multidimensional construct that includes physical and instrumental assistance, attitude transmission, resource and information
sharing, and emotional and psychological assistance. The persons and institutions with
which a family and its members come in contact—either directly or indirectly—are referred
to as the family's *personal social network,* and it
is this network that is the primary source of support to families and individual family members.

The importance of social support derives
from its empirical relationship with individual
and family functioning, and the potential that it
holds as a major form of intervention. The stress-
buffering and health-promoting influences of social support have been so well documented (see
e.g., Cohn & Syme, 1985; Sarason & Sarason,
1985) that it is now almost axiomatic to state that
social support both enhances well-being and
lessens the likelihood of emotional and physical

distress. There is a growing body of evidence
that social support directly and indirectly influences other aspects of individual and family
functioning, including family well-being (Patterson & McCubbin, 1983), adaptations to life
crises (Moos, 1986), satisfaction with parenting
(Crnic, Greenberg, Ragozin, Robinson, & Basham, 1983), attitudes toward one's child (Colletta, 1981), parental styles of interaction (Trivette & Dunst, 1987a), aspirations for self and
child (Lazar, Darlington, Murray, Royce, &
Snipper, 1982), and child behavior and development (Affleck, Tennen, Allen, & Gershman,
1986; Crnic, Greenberg, & Slough, 1986).

The extent to which different aspects of social
support and resources influence parent, family,
and child functioning has been a major focus of
the authors' research efforts with families of
handicapped, disabled, and developmentally at-
risk children (Dunst, 1985; Dunst, Cooper, &
Bolick, 1987; Dunst & Leet, 1987; Dunst, Leet,
& Trivette, 1988; Dunst & Trivette, 1986, 1987,
1988a, 1988b, in press; Dunst, Trivette, &
Cross, 1986a, 1986b, in press; Dunst, Vance, &
Cooper, 1986; Trivette & Dunst, 1987a, 1987b,
in press). These data have shown that the adequacy of different types and forms of support,
*especially aid and assistance that match family
identified needs,* enhances parent and family
well-being, decreases time demands placed
upon a family by a disabled or at-risk child, promotes positive caregiver interactive styles,
decreases the display of interfering caregiver interactive styles, enhances positive parental perception of child functioning, and indirectly influences a number of child behavior characteristics,
including affect, temperament, and motivation.

Help Seeking and Help Giving

The extent to which help seeking and help giving
is likely to have either positive or negative consequences on individual and family functioning
depends upon the intertwining of a host of intrapersonal, interpersonal, and situational factors.
These include the perception of the need for
help, the manner in which help is offered, the
source of the help, the response costs involved in
accepting help, and the sense of indebtedness
that recipients feel toward help providers (De-

Paulo, Nadler, & Fisher, 1983; Fisher, Nadler, & DePaulo, 1983; Nadler, Fisher, & DePaulo, 1983).

In many respects, help seeking and help giving (i.e., social support) may be considered as interactive. The help-seeking process considers the help seeker's behavior and the conditions that set the occasion for perceiving a problem and the need for assistance (see especially Gross & McMullan, 1983), whereas help giving (social support) considers the manner in which members of a personal social network are mobilized and provide help and assistance to the help seeker.

Several investigators have recently attempted to integrate help-seeking and social support concepts (Antonucci & Depner, 1982; Dunst & Trivette, 1988b; Gourash, 1978; Hobfoll, 1985; Wilcox & Birkel, 1983). Gourash (1978), who made one of the first attempts to integrate the help-seeking and social support literature, placed particular emphasis on how the provision of help from members of a person's social network influenced help seeking from formal support sources. According to Gourash (1978):

(personal) social networks can affect help seeking in a number of ways: (a) by buffering the experience of stress which alleviates the need for help, (b) by precluding the necessity for professional assistance through the provision of instrumental and affective support, (c) by acting as screening and referral agents to professional services and (d) by transmitting attitudes, values, and norms about help seeking. (p. 416)

This set of conditions suggests an inverse relationship between the need for help from members of formal support sources and the extent to which members of personal social networks can provide or mediate the provision of resources necessary to affect personal and family functioning. It is known, for example, that in most cases people turn to professionals for help only when necessary assistance is not available from members of their personal social networks (Gurin, Veroff, & Feld, 1960). Additionally, help giving is most likely to have positive influences when it comes from people with whom the help seeker has positive emotional ties, most notably, personal social network members (Clark, 1983).

A review and integration of the help-seeking literature points clearly to the fact that there are certain characteristics of help seeker–help giver exchanges that are necessary for help giving to have positive consequences (see Dunst & Trivette, 1987, 1988b; Dunst, Trivette, Davis, & Cornwell, 1988). Fisher, Nadler, and Whitcher-Alagna (1983), for example, have accumulated evidence that indicates that help seekers are more likely to respond favorably to help giving if: 1) positive attributions are ascribed to help givers by help seekers, 2) help seekers are afforded the opportunity to reciprocate and repay help giver favors, 3) help-giving exchanges minimize the social differences between help seekers and help givers, and 4) help seeking neither implies lost freedoms nor threatens self-esteem or autonomy.

Helping Relationships and Empowerment
Specification of the characteristics of effective helping has constituted a major focus of the authors' own work with poor families and families with disabled members (Dunst, 1987, 1988; Dunst & Trivette, 1987, 1988b; Dunst, Trivette, Davis, & Cornwell, 1988). This work has culminated in the development of an enabling and empowering model of helping relationships that defines the parameters of empowerment and the conditions that set the occasion for help seeker–help giver exchanges to have positive consequences. The model is based upon Rappaport's (1981) contention that:

empowerment implies that many competencies are already present or at least possible. . . . Empowerment implies that what you see as poor functioning is a result of social structure and lack of resources which make it impossible for the existing competencies to operate. It implies that in those cases where new competencies need to be learned, they are best learned in a context of living life rather than in artificial programs where everyone, including the person learning, knows that it is really the expert who is in charge. (p. 16)

Rappaport's contention includes three conditions that reflect the ways in which helping relationships and empowerment were operationalized as part of Project SHaRE. First, it states that people are already competent or that they have the capacity to become competent. This is re-

ferred to as a positive, *proactive stance* toward
help seekers. Second, it states that the failure to
display competence is not due to intrinsic deficits within the help seeker, but rather the failure
of social systems to create opportunities for
competencies to be displayed. Opportunities for
competence to be displayed are referred to as *enabling experiences*. Third, it implicitly states
that the person who is the learner or client must
be able to deploy competencies to obtain resources to meet needs, and attribute behavior
change to his or her own actions, in order to acquire a sense of control over life events. This is
what is meant by *empowerment*. This stance toward help seekers suggests a new and expanded
definition of effective helping as the:

> act of enabling individuals or groups (e.g., family)
> to become better able to solve problems, meet
> needs, or achieve aspirations by promoting acquisi-
> tion of competencies that support and strengthen
> functioning in a way that permits a greater sense of
> individual or group control over its developmental
> course. (Dunst, 1987 p. 1)

Empowerment and Effective Helping
The above perspectives of empowerment and effective helping have guided the authors' attempts
to better understand how helping acts and helping relationships influence help-seeking behavior. Table 1 shows the particular help-giver attitudes, beliefs, behaviors, and responses that
are most consistent with positive, competency-
producing influences. The three clusters of behaviors shown in Table 1 are organized according
to: 1) prehelping attitudes and beliefs, 2) help-
giving behaviors, and 3) posthelping responses
and consequences. According to this model,
prehelping attitudes and beliefs influence help-
giver behavior, and help-giver attitudes, beliefs,
and behaviors influence posthelping responses
and consequences. Together, these three clusters
of variables are seen as determinants of a help-
seeker's sense of control and efficacy resulting
from help seeker–help giver exchanges that, in
turn, are seen as exerting an influence on the
well-being of the person receiving help.

Both direct and corroborative theoretical and
empirical evidence shows that individual help-
giving characteristics within and across clusters
tend to occur simultaneously and exclude the use
of characteristics incongruent with competency

producing attitudes, beliefs, and behaviors
(e.g., Brickman et al., 1982, 1983; DePaulo et
al., 1983; Fisher, Nadler, & DePaulo, 1983;
Fisher, Nadler, & Wichter-Alagna, 1983; Hobbs
et al., 1984; Nadler et al., 1983; Rappaport,
1981, 1987). This model of effective helping provided the background for the ways in which
Project SHaRE staff went about enabling and
empowering families with the knowledge and
skills necessary to identify their needs and mobilize resources to meet their needs.

MAJOR CHARACTERISTICS
OF THE PROJECT DESIGN

Project Philosophy
The material described in the preceding section
was used as the foundation for specifying the
philosophy of Project SHaRE and its underlying
principles. The philosophy and principles were
derived from a family and social systems model
of functioning (Dunst & Trivette, 1988a; Dunst,
Trivette, & Deal, 1988) that guided the development and implementation of the project. Project
SHaRE was based upon the belief that all families have the capacity to meet their needs if adequately supported and strengthened in ways that
make them intrapersonally self-reliant and self-
sufficient, and interpersonally interdependent.
The underpinnings of the philosophy include the
following nine principles.

 1. Empowerment of Families   The major
emphasis of all project activities and efforts was
the empowerment of families. Empowerment is
operationally defined as the ability to identify
needs, deploy competencies to mobilize resources to meet needs, and gain a greater sense
of intrapersonal and interpersonal control over
life events involving interactions with personal
social network members (Bandura, 1978, 1982;
Dunst, 1987, 1988; Rappaport, 1981, 1987).

 2. Family Strengths and Capabilities
The project was based upon the premise that *all*
families have strengths and capabilities that constitute resources that could be used to meet the
needs of others, and that building upon strengths,
rather than correcting deficits, is the best way to
strengthen and empower families. Additionally,
it was a basic assumption of the project that *all*

Table 1. Help-giver attitudes, beliefs, and behaviors associated with empowerment and competence

Prehelping attitudes and beliefs	Help-giving behaviors	Posthelping responses and consequences
1. Positive attributions toward help seekers and helping relationships.	1. Employs active and reflective listening skills.	1. Accepts and supports help-seeker decisions.
2. Emphasis on help-seeker responsibility for meeting needs and solving problems.	2. Helps client clarify concerns and needs.	2. Minimizes the help seeker's sense of indebtedness.
3. High expectations regarding the capacity of help seekers to become competent.	3. Proffers help in response to help-seeker needs.	3. Permits reciprocity as part of help giver–help seeker exchanges.
4. Emphasis upon building on help-seeker strengths.	4. Offers help that is normative.	4. Minimizes the psychological response costs of accepting help.
5. Proactive stance toward helping relationships.	5. Offers help that is congruent and matches the help-seeker's appraisal of needs.	5. Enhances a sense of self-efficacy regarding active involvement in meeting needs.
6. Promotion emphasis as the focus of help giving.	6. Promotes acquisition of competencies to meet needs, solve problems, and achieve aspirations.	6. Maintains confidentiality at all times; shares information only with help-seeker permission.
	7. Employs partnerships and parent-professional collaboration as the mechanism for meeting needs.	
	8. Allows locus of decisionmaking to rest with the help seeker.	

families have existing capacities and competencies as well as the ability to become more capable of managing life events if adequately supported and strengthened (Hobbs et al., 1984; Rappaport, 1981, 1987; Stoneman, 1985).

3. Enhancement and Promotion of Family Functioning Primary emphasis was placed upon the enhancement and promotion of all aspects of positive family functioning as opposed to the prevention of negative outcomes or the treatment of a problem or disorder (Cowen, 1985; Hoke, 1968; Zautra & Sandler, 1983). A promotion or competency-enhancement approach to empowering families was chosen because it is more likely to lead to "greater individualization and self-reliance, and less, not more, dependence" (Zautra & Sandler, 1983, p. 39) upon professionals for meeting needs.

4. Informal Support Networks Informal support networks were viewed as primary sources of resources for meeting needs (Gottlieb, 1985), and building and mobilizing informal support systems were seen as the ways of bringing people together for the purpose of ex-

changing resources (Hobbs et al., 1984). Formal sources of support were used only to the extent that informal sources did not have the necessary resources to meet family identified needs (e.g., medical treatment).

5. Diversity Among Project Members From the very beginning, the project emphasized heterogeneity among the SHaRE members with respect to socioeconomic status, income, family structure, and so forth, despite the fact that the project was conceived primarily in response to two distinct social groups (families with disabled members and poor families rearing preschool and school-age children). This heterogeneity was emphasized for several reasons. First, broad-based representation highlighted the commonalities among project participants (i.e., all people have needs and strengths). Second, heterogeneous representation increased the likelihood that the network members would have the assets and resources that other members required to meet their needs. If, for example, only families from poor backgrounds were included as members, the needs of these families would be similar, and the resources required to meet those needs might not be available as part of SHaRE exchanges.

6. *Variety of Resources* In contrast to many bartering and exchange programs that basically focus on the give-and-take of one service or product (e.g., respite care or companionship), few restrictions were placed on the types of resources that could be requested or exchanged; evidence suggests that the variety of resources available for exchange among personal social network members increases the likelihood of the flow of resources among people and groups (Hall & Wellman, 1985).

7. *Simplicity of the SHaRE Exchange Program* Many bartering and exchange programs assign points and values to the types of aid and assistance that program participants exchange among one another. This was avoided as part of Project SHaRE in order to keep the exchange system as simple and normative as possible. Members involved in particular exchanges were allowed to decide among themselves what constituted a fair and equitable exchange. However, normative exchanges that promoted a sense of community were emphasized, rather than a business atmosphere surrounding the exchange of resources.

8. *Enabling Experiences* The exchange of resources among the Project SHaRE participants was promoted using a number of different types of enabling experiences. Enabling experiences were opportunities afforded participants as part of their participation in the project that emphasized the meeting of people with mutually identified needs, and the acquisition of knowledge and skills that promote social exchanges, the flow of resources, and the likelihood of future interactions.

9. *Contingent Helping and Reciprocity* The exchange of resources among SHaRE participants was guided by two helping principles: contingent helping and reciprocity (see Dunst, 1987, 1988; Dunst & Trivette, 1987, 1988b). The provision of resources and support to one SHaRE member by another person or group was always made contingent upon the active involvement on the part of the project participant in terms of identifying needs and procuring re-

sources, and the provision of a resource in exchange for what was received (i.e., reciprocity). Noncontingent helping was neither sanctioned nor approved. Skinner (1978) called noncontingent helping unethical because it "postpones the acquisition of effective behavior and perpetuates the need for help" (p. 251). Meeting needs is likely to have long-term positive effects only when individuals "take pride in their accomplishments [and] ascribe successes to their own abilities and efforts" (Bandura, 1978, p. 349). Therefore, major emphasis was placed upon *reciprocal obligations* as part of SHaRE exchanges. Reciprocity involves giving in order to receive, and occurs because in this culture debts are expected to be paid by persons who enter into exchange arrangements. By not allowing reciprocity, indebtedness accrues, and help becomes potentially harmful (Greenberg & Westcott, 1983).

Project Goal and Objectives

As previously noted, the major goal of the project was to enhance family well-being and other aspects of family functioning by enabling and empowering the family unit and individual members to meet needs in ways that were competency producing, which in turn made the families more self-reliant and less dependent upon formal sources of support. Project SHaRE activities were designed to accomplish the following major objectives:

1. Identify family needs as a basis for determining the resources necessary for supporting and strengthening family functioning.
2. Identify family strengths that constitute resources that could be exchanged for aid and assistance to meet family needs.
3. Develop a SHaRE Exchange Program as a basis for creating reciprocal interactions and obligations among project participants.
4. Promote linkages among SHaRE Exchange Program members by enhancing acquisition of competencies (e.g., resource procurement skills) that permit project participants to become better able to obtain aid and assistance necessary to meet needs.
5. Employ help-giving behaviors that enhance

self-sufficiency and decrease the need to depend upon professional help givers for aid and assistance for meeting family needs.

6. Develop and refine an assessment and intervention model for promoting the families' ability to identify their needs and strengths, use existing and newly acquired competencies to mobilize resources, and engage in reciprocal exchanges that further strengthen family functioning.

7. Disseminate information about Project SHaRE and promote utilization of the project materials as a way of replicating the SHaRE Exchange Program with other populations of families in other parts of the country.

Attainment of these objectives was expected to strengthen family functioning and result in enhanced self-esteem and self-efficacy with respect to procurement of resources to meet needs.

Description of the Project Participants

The project participants were divided into three separate groups. The first included families with a child who had a disability, or an individual adult with a disability. This group is hereafter referred to as the DD (developmentally disabled) target group. The second group included families from poor socioeconomic backgrounds rearing a preschool or school-age child, families caring for a dependent adult, or an individual adult with extremely limited physical, financial, and other basic resources. This group is hereafter referred to as the AT-RISK target group. The third group included families or individuals from middle to upper socioeconomic backgrounds. This group is hereafter referred to as the CONTRAST group.

Selected characteristics of the three groups are shown in Table 2. Examination of the data shows that the two target groups were remarkably similar on nearly all of the demographic measures. The subjects in the two target groups, on the average, completed less than a twelfth grade education, were from the lowest socioeconomic background, and had gross monthly incomes that placed them below the poverty level. An analysis of maternal work status showed that only about 25% of the mothers in the two target groups worked outside the home compared to 83% for the CONTRAST group. Particularly noteworthy is the fact that less than half of the mothers in the target groups were married, and

Table 2. Selected characteristics of project participants

| | | | | | Group | | | | | |
| | | DD | | | At-risk | | | Contrast | | |
Characteristics	N	Mean	SD	N	Mean	SD	N	Mean	SD	P-level
Mother's age	43	39.02	15.07	34	30.79	12.43	30	36.23	11.17	.03
Mother's education	43	11.33	1.20	34	10.94	2.76	30	15.33	2.92	.0001
Mother's occupation level	43	0.95	1.62	34	0.78	1.19	30	5.60	2.42	.0001
Father's age	19	35.96	9.13	19	34.13	10.60	9	41.73	13.72	.09
Father's education	19	10.36	2.41	19	10.13	2.16	9	14.68	2.51	.0001
Father's occupation level	19	2.77	2.32	19	2.56	1.63	9	5.46	2.57	.0001
Social economic status	43	21.27	9.57	34	19.97	8.71	30	48.67	9.65	.0001
Gross monthly income	43	773.84	471.85	34	607.82	317.39	30	1964.14	685.91	.0001
		%			%			%		
Mother's work status (working)	43	73.00	—	19	81.00	—	9	91.00	—	.228
Mother's marital status (married)	43	28.00	—	34	24.00	—	30	83.00	—	.0001
Father's work status (working)	19	48.00	—	34	40.00	—	30	65.00	—	.128

that about two-thirds of the mothers in the CON-TRAST group were married. Overall, the DD and AT-RISK groups were best characterized as having limited personal resources and limited informal supports with respect to the existence of social ties and relationships.

In addition to the primary project participants, other individuals and groups participated in the project whenever needed resources could not be provided by SHaRE members. These included physicians, dentists, pharmacists, store merchants, churches, and community groups who were willing to provide services (e.g., surgery, dental care) or products (e.g., prescription drugs, furniture) in exchange for a SHaRE member providing a service (e.g., house painting) or product (e.g., baked goods) to these help givers. In all but a few cases, a person or group could be located who had a resource that a SHaRE member needed and who was willing to enter into a reciprocal arrangement.

Organizational Structure

Program Management Activities within the program management component of Project SHaRE included the specification of the project goal and objectives, development and refinement of the conceptual framework and service-delivery system, staff training and performance measurement, physical and human resource allocation, and the monitoring of activities within each of the other project components. The major function of activities in this component was to ensure that plans, methods, and strategies used to achieve project goals were carried out in ways that were consistent with the conceptual and philosophic assumptions upon which the project was based.

Public Awareness The major function of the activities in the public awareness component was to foster enrollment in the project by the target and contrast groups. Local newspaper articles, distribution of the project brochure, a project poster, presentations to church and civic groups, recruitment letters, and individual contacts with potential project participants were the primary strategies used to promote project involvement.

Demonstration The major emphasis of the demonstration component of the project was to

demonstrate how a SHaRE Exchange Program could be used to identify and meet needs in ways that supported and strengthened individual and family functioning. The demonstration activities of the project included methods and procedures for enrollment of project participants; for assessment of needs, strengths, and social support; for enabling opportunities that had competency enhancing influences; for network building and promotion of reciprocal exchanges; and for evaluation of the project by SHaRE participants.

Utilization The major emphasis of the project utilization activities was promoting and enhancing the adoption of strategies and techniques for building and mobilizing informal support networks. The activities within this component included: the distribution and dissemination of information about the project to professional audiences; presentations at local, state, regional, and national conferences; workshops describing the philosophy, methods, and expected outcomes for the project; publications on various aspects of the project; development of an instruction manual for persons and groups desiring to establish a SHaRE Exchange Program; and on-site training in methods for replication of the project.

Program Evaluation The major emphasis of the program evaluation activities for the project was to determine the extent to which goals and objectives were met, how well planned activities were carried out, and whether project activities had the anticipated effects on the project participants. The evaluation model defined four types of evaluation: context, input, process, and products (Stufflebeam, 1971). Context evaluation is concerned with the identification of unmet project participant needs, and the delineation of the goals and objectives to meet these needs. Input evaluation involves the identification of strategies and approaches for meeting needs, and the implementation of appropriate plans to meet family identified needs. Process evaluation involves monitoring the implementation of the plan, and the collection of data to determine when, how often, and the degree to which proposed activities were implemented as planned. Product evaluation is designed to assess the effectiveness of planned activities, determine whether or not anticipated goals and objectives were achieved, and, last and most difficult, determine what factors or variables were responsible for observing changes (Campbell & Stanley, 1966; Cook & Campbell, 1979).

Operational Structure of the Project

The operational structure of the project was kept as simple as possible to increase the likelihood that the advantages and benefits of participation would be immediately realized. Enrollment of project participants was followed by an assessment of a number of aspects of individual and family functioning. Once needs and strengths were determined, strategies were used to both enhance the acquisition of competencies and promote resource mobilization as a way of meeting needs. SHaRE exchanges were evaluated in terms of participant satisfaction and the accumulated influences that participation in the project had on individual and family functioning.

Enrollment   The ways in which participants were enrolled in the project proved to be extremely important with respect to promoting active involvement. Enrollment always began with a full description and explanation of the project, with particular emphasis on the personal benefits that could be realized by a reciprocal exchange of resources as opposed to payment for services or resources. Additionally, the roles and expectations of both the SHaRE members and project staff were also described and discussed to ensure that participants fully understood the concepts of reciprocal obligations and contingent giving.

Assessment Procedures   The procedures used to assess needs, strengths, social support, and family functioning were divided into two phases. In Phase I the project participants completed a number of self-report scales that measured the need for certain resources (services, products, information, etc.), adequacy of existing family resources (housing, job, medical care, etc.), and intrafamily resources (strengths) that could be exchanged for needed aid and assistance. Phase II involved the completion of a number of additional self-report measures that assessed social support, well-being, and other aspects of family functionings.

Needs and adequacy of resources were assessed by the Resource Exchange Scale (RES) (Dunst, Pletcher, & Gordon, 1986), Family Re-

source Scale (FRS) (Dunst & Leet, 1987), and Support Function Scale (SFS) (Dunst & Trivette, 1988c). The RES measures the need for certain services (childcare, home maintenance, transportation, etc.) and products (food, clothing, tools, etc.). The FRS measures the degree to which existing resources (food, shelter, financial resources, childcare, etc.) are adequate in the household of the respondent. The SFS assesses the extent to which a respondent has a need for 12 different types of aid and assistance. All three scales were used as a basis for enabling project participants to identify concerns, translate concerns into need statements, and specify the resources necessary to meet needs. This was implemented as part of the interactions between project staff and project participants, during which staff employed interview techniques that created opportunities for families to engage in the process of needs identification (see Dunst, Trivette, & Deal, 1988).

The particular resources that project participants were able to provide in exchange for resources (services, products, etc.) furnished by other SHaRE members were identified using the Provision of Resources Scale (PRS) (Pletcher, Dunst, & Gordon, 1986). The PRS includes 35 categories and subcategories of services and products that project participants used to identify the contributions that they were willing to make as part of reciprocal obligations. The scale was also used for the development of a SHaRE Directory (see below) that was employed as part of competency enhancement activities.

The Inventory of Social Support (ISS) (Trivette & Dunst, 1988) was used to identify both the members of the project participants' social networks and the types of aid and assistance that were generally provided by network members. The ISS also provided a basis for determining the amount of support that was available to the respondent, and from whom different types of support are requested or offered. The scale was used not only for assessment purposes but also for network mapping and resources network mobilization (see below) as part of exploring support source options for meeting needs.

The SHaRE members also completed a number of other scales primarily for program evaluation purposes. These included the Personal Well-

Being Index (Trivette & Dunst, 1985), Personal Time Commitment Scale (Dunst & Trivette, 1985), Parent Rating Scale (Dunst & Bolick, 1985), and Family Inventory of Resources and Management (McCubbin, Comeau, & Harkins, 1981). All the scales and measurement tools were completed at entry into the project and at 6-month intervals thereafter.

Competency Enhancement The enhancement of competencies that were necessary for participants to engage in the reciprocal exchange of resources was accomplished using a number of different types of enabling experiences. The first involved nothing more than providing opportunities to discuss with project staff what project participants needed and what they could provide in exchange for the receipt of a product or service (see the previous ***Assessment*** subsection).

The second strategy that was used to promote exchange of resources is best described as strengthening resource procurement skills. Enhancement of these skills always began with a discussion of the meaning of reciprocal obligations, what constitutes a fair and equitable exchange, what a SHaRE exchange involves, and what expectations are placed upon SHaRE Exchange Program members. This provided the necessary backdrop for all members to follow as part of participation in the project.

Modeling ways to arrange and engage in SHaRE exchanges was the primary strategy used for competency enhancement. Several types of modeling techniques were used. The first involved a project staff member and SHaRE participant approaching another person or group to arrange and engage in a reciprocal exchange. The second technique concerned the steps that were followed in using the SHaRE Directory to identify a person who had a resource that could be procured in exchange for another service or product. The third technique involved modeling how to call or approach another SHaRE member to arrange a SHaRE exchange.

A number of concrete materials were also used to increase the likelihood of arranging and engaging SHaRE exchanges. A simply written document, "Steps to SHaRE Exchanges," was provided to all members as a way of reminding them of their responsibilities in arranging and

engaging in exchanges. A SHaRE Directory was the primary tool used to promote the exchange of resources. The directory was organized much like the yellow pages of a phone book, with 35 categories of services and products, and the persons willing to provide those resources in exchange for other types of aid and assistance listed under each heading and subcategory; this directory was revised and updated every 2–3 months. In addition, on a monthly basis all SHaRE members received a newsletter that listed all new members and the resources that they could provide and offered useful information about arranging SHaRE exchanges. A bulletin board in the SHaRE office and an "Exchange File" also listed the directory information. Staff members were always available to show project participants how to use those resource guides for arranging an exchange.

Network Mobilization The building and mobilization of informal support networks in Project SHaRE was characterized by several features. The first involved network mapping and network building. This called for project participants to identify existing personal social network members as well as potential but untapped resources. The latter included SHaRE members, but also other persons and groups who might be willing to provide a needed resource in exchange for a service or product by the project participant. Network mapping was accomplished through the completion of both the Inventory of Social Support (see previous discussion) and project staff and project participant discussions designed to identify personal social network members whom they thought would be willing to engage in a reciprocal exchange.

The mediation of exchanges was accomplished by using the competency enhancement strategies described above. Promoting the project participant's understanding of the types of exchanges that were possible proved helpful in terms of the range of resources that were requested and offered. Most exchanges involved two parties, although occasionally three-party exchanges were used to meet the SHaRE member needs. Two-party exchanges involved a person seeking resources to meet his or her needs directly interacting with another person or group as part of arranging a SHaRE exchange (Tobin &

Ware, 1983). A three-party exchange involved the person seeking resources providing a resource to a second party who in turn provided a resource to a third party, who then in turn provided a resource to the person initiating the exchange. Three-party exchanges were necessary whenever a mutual agreement could not be reached between a SHaRE member and another party; although project staff were generally involved in arranging three-party exchanges, many SHaRE members learned to arrange these more complicated exchanges themselves.

Three types of exchanges were mediated by SHaRE members once they acquired the necessary competencies to arrange exchanges and had broadened their perceptions of their informal support network. The first involved two SHaRE members arranging an exchange between each other. This type of exchange was promoted through use of the SHaRE Directory and other project resource guides. The second involved a SHaRE member arranging and engaging in an exchange with a nonSHaRE member whom the project participant already knew, and with whom that person generally had a close personal relationship (e.g., friend or relative). Once the benefits of SHaRE exchanges were realized by project participants, they often used the methods and strategies for arranging reciprocal exchanges to obtain and provide resources with their informal network members. The third type of exchange involved a SHaRE member exchanging resources with a nonSHaRE member whom the person did not know, but who was willing to be involved in a reciprocal exchange. This usually involved a physician or service merchant who was the only individual able to provide a resource (e.g., prescription medicine) needed by a project participant. A project staff member was usually involved in assisting the SHaRE member to arrange this type of exchange. The extent to which SHaRE members' needs were met on a continuous basis was, in part, determined by their abilities to mediate and engage in these various types of exchanges.

Network building and mobilization were found to occur most often in situations where the SHaRE members and project staff were able to work together in a partnership capacity. Partnership not only provided the mechanism for competency enhancement, but also provided the necessary environment for support and strengthening family functioning. Staff-to-SHaRE member collaboration was often the basis for project participants eventually becoming able to engage in independent exchanges.

Exchange Evaluation Ongoing evaluation of SHaRE exchanges was conducted in a number of ways. First, each exchange was evaluated in terms of whether it was completed as planned and whether it was done in a timely manner. Second, each exchange was evaluated with respect to whether it was independent (without any staff involvement), assisted (staff helped only to identify a support source), or arranged (staff initiated and arranged the exchange). Third, each exchange was evaluated in terms of whether the persons giving and receiving resources were satisfied with the outcome of the exchange. Fourth, the personal benefits accrued from each exchange were determined by maintaining case records of the descriptions provided by SHaRE members in terms of self-esteem, well-being, self-efficacy, and any other interpersonal benefits resulting from participation in the project.

Staff Roles and Responsibilities

As one might suspect, the roles and responsibilities that staff assumed as part of assessment, competency enhancement, and network mobilization activities were quite different compared to those typically employed in human service programs. Six major roles evolved from efforts designed to attain Project SHaRE goals and objectives. Each and every contact with a family usually involved a staff member employing several of the different roles simultaneously.

Empathetic Listener The role of the empathetic listener involved the use of active and reflective listening skills in order for the staff member to both learn about the families' needs and strengths, and develop trust and rapport. Staff members used empathetic listening skills with SHaRE members during home visits, office visits, phone contacts, and any other time the staff member interacted with project participants. The staff *listened* to the persons' concerns and needs, past histories with respect to their successes and failures in getting needed help, problems encountered in arranging exchanges, and so forth. In some instances, this was the only role that was used when a family wanted only to share their concerns rather than to take action at a particular time. In most instances, the empathetic listener role was used as a basis for determining what other roles needed to be used with the family.

Resource One of the most important roles that SHaRE staff members assumed was that of a resource to the family. In this capacity, the staff member functioned as a source of information about available supports and resources that the family could use as possible ways of meeting needs. This is especially true with regard to the types of services and products that were available as part of SHaRE exchanges. Families often were not aware of the types of aid and assistance that could be obtained in exchange for needed resources. In a resource capacity, the staff member functioned as a natural clearinghouse of information about Project SHaRE, different types of products and services available from SHaRE members, and so forth.

Consultant In the consultant role, the SHaRE staff member provided information and opinions in response to requests made by the family or individual family members. Information was provided to families in order to help them make informed decisions about how best to go about meeting their needs. As a consultant, the SHaRE staff member answered questions about the project, explained the benefits of using informal support networks and reciprocal obligations, participated in discussions with the family that promoted a sharing of information to learn about needs and strength identification and the meaning of social support networks, and mobilized resources to meet needs.

Mobilizer In the mobilizer role, the SHaRE staff member not only made the family aware of potential but untapped resources and helped them acquire the ability to mobilize support and access resources, but additionally linked the family to others (individuals or groups) that could provide new or alternative perspectives about ways to meet needs. As part of the process of helping families identify persons in their personal social networks and the SHaRE Exchange Network, staff members and the family explored

ways in which individuals and groups could be used as a source of aid and assistance. As a mobilizer of personal social support networks, the staff member worked to bring together the individuals needed in order for the family to gain access to resources and support.

Enabler Beyond a familiarity with various services and programs, SHaRE members needed to be able to acquire those resources. As an enabler, the staff member created opportunities for families to gain experience in obtaining resources and support. In this capacity, the staff moved beyond simply making SHaRE members aware of services and products to helping them become effective and successful in acquiring resources and support. The critical element in performing this role was that the project participants become able to take action rather than needing the staff member to act for the family.

Mediator In instances where families had experienced many negative encounters with their personal social network members, it was necessary for the SHaRE members and project staff to work directly with individuals or groups in a manner that promoted cooperation between the respective parties. One of the purposes of these encounters was to encourage more positive, task-oriented, and mutually reinforcing exchanges between the family and other network members. Mediating interactions and exchanges between the family and others was a function that was performed only long enough for the family to develop its own capacity for mobilizing support and acquiring resources more effectively.

Promoting the ability of staff to engage in these different roles as well as to shift from one role to another occurred primarily through on-the-job training and experience combined with numerous and repeated case reviews that explored why certain efforts to enhance exchanges succeeded or failed. The opportunity to explore staff roles and discuss their applications and implications proved extremely helpful as part of improving the day-to-day implementation of project activities. Staff with differing years of education from differing disciplines and backgrounds have all been able to learn these roles, but only if they fundamentally believed that the goal of intervention with families should be competency enhancement, and not simply non-contingent provision of missing resources (Maple, 1977; Skinner, 1978).

Problems and Challenges

Five major problems continually surfaced with respect to implementation of the project. The first problem related to certain beliefs held by members of the two target groups, particularly those who had a long history of involvement with social agencies and human services programs that engaged in noncontingent helping. More specifically, a number of people who enrolled in the project expected to be provided with whatever resources they needed, and failed to recognize the importance of reciprocal obligations. These individuals would arrange exchanges and obtain resources without fulfilling their reciprocal obligations. It became clear from interactions with these persons that the passive acceptance of services had become a learned expectancy, and appeared to be the direct consequence of the types of professional service-delivery systems that they had become dependent upon for provisions of needed resources. Continual dialogue with these SHaRE members proved necessary to instill the value and importance of reciprocal obligations as a part of each and every SHaRE exchange.

The second problem also involved a sizable number of project participants in the two target groups. During the assessment process that was used to identify individual and family strengths, there were many persons who literally stated that they did not have any resources from which they believed others might benefit. Comments like, "There isn't anything I can do for someone else," and, "Nobody would want anything from me," were quite common from the family members when assessing personal and family assets and strengths. Apparently, based upon conversations with these people, these negative images about themselves had been learned as well. These individuals generally described their interactions with others (particularly professionals) in terms of being told what they could not do, rather than what they were capable of doing. It was not uncommon for these individ-

uals to tell project staff that they were the first professionals who had ever said anything good about their families or conveyed the belief that they had competencies and strengths that would benefit others. The solution to this problem required continual dialogue and interaction between project staff and SHaRE members as a way of making them aware of their capabilities and competencies and supporting them to use strengths and mobilize resources.

The third problem that was encountered was somewhat unexpected and proved to be particularly difficult to resolve. It involved a number of members of the contrast group and members of community and civic groups that participated in the project. These individuals were primarily from upper-middle and upper class backgrounds who had adequate personal resources, and who indicated that they participated in the project to fulfill a civic duty. Whenever these individuals became involved in an exchange with a target group member, particularly a very poor family with extremely limited resources, the more affluent family not only refused to accept a resource in exchange for their assistance (reciprocal obligations) but also wanted to assist by providing other missing resources (noncontingent giving). This opposed every principle upon which the project was based, and upset the target group members because they were not permitted to reciprocate. Although most individuals were able to understand how they would be defeating the purposes of the project if they provided resources noncontingently, a few eventually needed to be removed from the SHaRE membership rolls because they were so insistent upon noncontingent giving.

The fourth problem related to maintaining interest and involvement in the project. Project staff quickly became aware of the fact that active participation waned if certain activities were not implemented to promote exchanges once initially identified needs were met. A number of strategies were used to overcome this problem, including monthly phone calls to the project participants, the distribution of a monthly newsletter, occasional letters providing information about new exchange opportunities, and the frequent updating and distribution of the SHaRE

Directory. The secret to maintaining ongoing involvement of project participants seemed to be at least twice monthly contact using different means.

The fifth problem related to a program evaluation issue. One outcome measure used to judge the effectiveness of the project was the number of independent exchanges completed among SHaRE members. This information was obtained through direct, phone, and written (post cards) contacts with the project participants. As part of the efforts to obtain this information, an interesting problem surfaced that posed a dilemma between ensuring project success and the ability to document project efficacy. A large number of project participants who learned the benefits of using informal exchanges for meeting needs began using the principles of reciprocal obligations and contingent helping in other aspects of their lives with neighbors, friends, and relatives. These exchanges became such a natural part of their day-to-day activities that they often failed to report when an exchange transpired. While this did attest to the success of the project, it also posed a problem in terms of documenting project efficacy.

SUMMARY OF PRELIMINARY FINDINGS

A multimethod, multitrait approach is being used to evaluate the efficacy of the project. This approach allows for independent demonstrations of the extent to which the project activities have anticipated impacts (Campbell & Stanley, 1966). The methods that are being used to evaluate the

project include comparative group analyses, multivariate regression procedures, single-subject research designs, and case study methodologies. Data are being analyzed in terms of the extent to which the DD and AT-RISK groups are similar or different from the CONTRAST group on the needs and resources measures; whether there are changes in the needs of project participants over time; whether the project participants become more capable of mobilizing resources to meet needs; whether there are discernible changes in the structure of the project participants' social networks, adequacy of resources, and social support; and whether enhancement of the participants' competencies influences personal well-being, family well-being, and other aspects of individual and family functioning.

Comparative Analysis

The extent to which the three groups of project participants (DD, AT-RISK, CONTRAST) were similar or different on a number of different demographic variables was shown previously in Table 2. Table 3 shows the results of the comparative analyses for the DD, AT-RISK, and CONTRAST groups on the Resource Exchange Scale (Dunst, Pletcher, et al., 1986), the Family Resource Scale (Dunst & Leet, 1987), the Support Function Scale (Dunst & Trivette, 1988c), and the Provision of Resources Scale (Pletcher et al., 1986). As Table 3 shows, the DD and AT-RISK groups had very similar scores, and when compared to the contrast group had more needs and less adequate resources. These results simply reflect the fact that the two target groups

Table 3. Needs, adequacy of resources, and strengths scores for the three groups of project participants

| | | Group | | | | | | | | |
| | DD | | | At-risk | | | Contrast | | | |
Measure	N	Mean	SD	N	Mean	SD	N	Mean	SD	P-level
Resource Exchange Scale[a]	44	8.29	4.34	35	8.77	4.59	30	6.03	4.06	.03
Family Resource Scale[a]	44	92.45	20.18	34	89.67	24.19	30	108.40	17.67	.001
Support Functions Scale[a]	35	21.43	9.06	29	21.07	10.56	24	14.37	8.51	.01
Provision of Resources Scale[b]	45	15.13	10.56	34	18.88	10.02	32	13.28	8.16	.06

[a]Higher scores reflect a greater number of needs.
[b]Higher scores reflect a willingness to exchange a greater number of products and services for needed resources.

faced more challenges at the time of entry into the project, which was not surprising given the characteristics of the families in these groups.

Number of Needs Met

An anticipated finding was that the needs of the project participants would decrease as a result of the time they spent in the project. This anticipated decrease was expected to reflect the fact that participation in the project promoted an exchange of resources that resulted in the provision of aid and assistance necessary to meet needs.

Available data were analyzed using a 3 Between Group X 3 Time Period repeated measures analysis of variance design. The between factor included the subjects in the DD ($n = 21$), AT-RISK ($n = 14$), and CONTRAST ($n = 13$) groups. The time period factor included the data collected at entry into the project and at 6 and 12 months following entry. The dependent measure was the Resource Exchange Scale (RES) (Dunst, Pletcher, & Gordon, 1986). The RES specifically measures the need for 18 types of services (e.g., child care, house cleaning, transportation) and 14 types of products (e.g., food, clothing, furniture). The sum of the service and product needs yields a total needs score.

The analysis for the total needs score yielded a significant main effect for the time period, $F(2,90) = 8.07$, $p<.001$. As expected, there was a decrease in the mean number of needs from entry ($M = 7.53$) to the 6-month ($M = 6.36$) to the 12-month ($M = 4.09$) data collection points. The analysis of the service needs data also produced a significant main effect for time period, $F(2,90) = 5.55$, $p<.01$, again showing a decrease in needs over time. The analysis of the product needs data yielded a main effect for groups, $F(2,39) = 4.31$, $p<.02$, and a main effect for time period, $F(2,90) = 5.08$, $p<.01$. The CONTRAST group had half as many product needs ($M = 1.82$) compared to either the DD ($M = 3.76$) or AT-RISK ($M = 3.79$) groups. There also was a progressive decrease in the number of product needs over time.

Taken together, these results indicated that despite the fact that the target groups had more needs and less adequate resources at the time of entry into the project, the DD and AT-RISK groups nonetheless benefited in the same way as

the CONTRAST group did as a result of engaging in reciprocal exchanges of resources.

Percentage of Needs Met

As the project participants became more capable of engaging in reciprocal exchanges, project staff expected that the percentage of needs that were met would increase over time. This increase was hypothesized to reflect a greater capacity to locate needed resources and arrange an exchange that would result in the exchange of resources necessary to meet needs.

The data were analyzed using a 3 Between Group X 3 Time Period repeated measures analysis of variance design with the percentage of needs met as the dependent variable. The percentage of needs that were met were computed for the total scale scores, and services and products subscale scores, on the Resource Exchange Scale (RES) (Dunst, Pletcher, et al., 1986). The analysis of the percentage data for the total RES scores yielded a main effect for time period, $F(2,90) = 6.10$, $p<.01$, as did the analysis for the percentage of product needs met, $F(2,90) = 2.82$, $p<.06$. In every case, the percentage of needs met increased during each time interval, confirming expectations that the project participants would become more able to meet their needs as a result of engaging in reciprocal exchanges. The results for the percentage of total needs met, for example, increased from 53%, to 57%, to 63%, over the course of the first 12 months of participation in the project.

Percentage of Independent Exchanges

One of the major measures of the success of the project was predicted to be the increase in the ability to independently arrange and engage in reciprocal exchanges. This was determined as part of program evaluation efforts by assessing the percentage of all exchanges that were independently arranged by project participants. A 3 Between Group X 6 Time Period repeated measures analysis of variance was used to test for changes in the types of exchanges that transpired over time. Data were available for six 2-month time intervals, beginning from program entry to 12 months. Two different dependent measures were computed: 1) the percentage of independent exchanges for each 2-month time interval, based upon the total exchanges for that interval (Total Number of Independent Exchanges for the 2-Month Time Period / Total Number of Exchanges for the 2-Month Interval), and 2) the percentage of independent exchanges for each 2-month time interval based upon the total number of exchange for the entire 12-month period (Total Number of Independent Exchanges For the 2-Month Interval/Divided by the Total Number of Exchanges for the 12-Month Period).

The analyses of the data yielded significant main effects for both the 2-month, $F(5,315) = 8.07$, $p<.001$, and the 12-month, $F(5,315) = 4.67$, $p<.001$, percentage of independent exchanges measures. Overall, there was a 20% increase in independent exchanges from the first 2-month to the last 2-month interval for the percentage data based upon each 2-month interval. Similarly, there was a 12% increase during the same time period for the percentage data based upon the number of exchanges for the entire 12-month interval. Both analyses demonstrated that, regardless of group membership, *all* project participants become better able to independently arrange exchanges to meet their needs.

SUMMARY AND IMPLICATIONS

The description of a model demonstration project for building and mobilizing informal family support networks constitutes the focus of this chapter. Project SHaRE was developed and operated as a resource exchange program based upon the principles of reciprocal obligations and contingent giving. Reciprocal obligations involved giving services and products in exchange for receiving needed resources, and was the basis for developing a sense of "community" among the project participants. The exchange of resources was done in a contingent manner so that project participants were actively involved in identifying and mobilizing support and resources. The goal of the project was to enable and empower families to identify their needs and strengths, employ strengths as a basis for mobilizing resources to meet needs, and help families acquire the capabilities necessary to become more interdependent and self-sustaining. Project SHaRE differed from other family support programs in several important respects, the methods

and outcomes of which suggest alternative ways to go about enhancing community support and promoting family development among populations typically provided resources noncontingently. The project proved effective in terms of influencing a number of aspects of family structure and functioning.

The material described in this chapter has implications in at least three areas: policy, practice, and research. The lessons learned from Project SHaRE point to the necessity for using a backward mapping approach for developing programs designed to build supportive communities (Dokecki & Heflinger, 1987; Elmore, 1979–80). In this approach, policy development begins at the consumer level with knowledge of what consumers need and what organizational structures are required to be in place in order for consumer specified outcomes to be realized. This is what Project SHaRE did in order to be responsive to the desires, needs, and hopes of the project participants. This approach was based upon "an empowerment model of human services as a substitute for the paternalistic model that has dominated human service delivery during this century" (Swift, 1984, p. xi). Building family and community support programs from this alternative perspective reverses the trend and pervasive belief that experts should decide not only what people need but what they can have by enabling and empowering families to take control over important events in their lives (Dunst et al., 1988c; Rappaport, 1981). A shift in policy toward an empowerment model should prove to be successful in developing and building family support programs.

The lessons learned from Project SHaRE have a number of implications for practice. First, to be successful, resource mobilization should be needs-based, family identified, and consumer driven. Second, major emphasis should be placed upon building on family capabilities as a way of strengthening family functioning and promoting supportive resource exchanges. Third, to the extent possible, exchange of resources that enhances a sense of community should occur among individuals and social groups that involve the coming together of people around shared interests and common causes. Fourth, professionals who interact with families concerning each of the above should not mobilize resources on behalf of the families but rather should create opportunities for them to become better able to do so for themselves. Collectively, these principles of practice constitute a unique way of supporting and strengthening family functioning (Dunst et al., 1988c).

The experiences from Project SHaRE have at least one major implication for researchers involved in documenting the effects of building and mobilizing family support systems. Applied research like that conducted as part of Project SHaRE must be multimethod and multitrait in order to fully describe and depict the influences of project activities. On the one hand this means the use of a variety of research methodologies for studying project impact, and on the other hand means the use of a range of behavior indicators that reflect predicted outcomes. Efforts to document the efficacy of Project SHaRE, as well as

other family support demonstration projects, demonstrates that only a broad based and wide scoped research approach can provide the necessary lens from which to see all that occurs in this type of support building initiative.

The message that the authors wish to convey was perhaps best stated by Wilkinson (1980) in a presentation made at a meeting of the Family Services Association of America. He noted that:

> In a (supportive) community, people are interdependent; everyone has a function and everyone has a role to play, and that's what keeps the people together and forms a community. When outsiders run things, suddenly no one in the . . . community has any function or role because everyone is controlled by outsiders. As a result people tend to be worth little or nothing to each other.

Supportive community building is what Project SHaRE has been all about.

REFERENCES

Affleck, G., Tennen, H., Allen, D.A., & Gershman, K. (1986). Perceived social support and maternal adaptation during the transition from hospital to home care of high-risk infants. *Infant Mental Health Journal, 7,* 6–18.

Antonucci, T.C., & Depner, C.E. (1982). Social support and informal helping relationship. In T.A. Wills (Ed.), *Basic processes in helping relationships* (pp. 233–254). New York: Academic Press.

Bandura, A. (1978). The self system in reciprocal determinism. *American Psychologist, 33,* 344–358.

Bandura, A. (1982). Self-efficacy mechanism in human agency. *American Psychologist, 37,* 122–147.

Brickman, P., Kidder, L.H., Coates, D., Rabinowitz, V., Cohn, E., & Karuza, J. (1983). The dilemmas of helping: Making aid fair and effective. In J.D. Fisher, A. Nadler, & B.M. DePaulo (Eds.), *New direction in helping: Vol. 1. Recipient reactions to aid* (pp. 18–51). New York: Academic Press.

Brickman, P., Rabinowitz, V., Karuza, J., Coates, D., Cohn, E., & Kidder, L. (1982). Models of helping and coping. *American Psychologist, 37,* 368–384.

Bronfenbrenner, U. (1979). *The ecology of human development: Experiments by nature and design.* Cambridge, MA: Harvard University Press.

Campbell, D.T., & Stanley, J. (1966). *Experimental and quasi-experimental designs for research.* Chicago: Rand McNally & Co.

Clark, M. (1983). Reactions to aid in communal and exchange relationships. In J.D. Fisher, A. Nadler, & B.M. DePaulo (Eds.), *New directions in helping: Vol. 1. Recipient reactions to aid* (pp. 281–304). New York: Academic Press.

Coates, D., Renzaglia, G.J., & Embree, M.C. (1983). In J.D. Fisher, A. Nadler, & B.M. DePaulo (Eds.), *New di-*rections in helping: Vol. 1. Recipient reactions to aid (pp. 251–279). New York: Academic Press.

Cochran, M., & Brassard, J. (1979). Child development and personal social networks. *Child Development, 50,* 601–616.

Cohen, S., & Syme, S.L. (1985). *Social support and health.* New York: Academic Press.

Colletta, N. (1981). Social support and the risk of maternal rejection by adolescent mothers. *The Journal of Psychology, 109,* 191–197.

Cook, T., & Campbell, D.T. (1979). *Quasi-experimentation: Design and analysis issues for field settings.* Chicago: Rand McNally & Co.

Cowen, E.L. (1985). Person-center approaches to primary prevention in mental health situation-focused and competence-enhancement. *American Journal of Community Psychology, 13,* 31–48.

Crnic, K.A., Greenberg, M., Ragozin, A., Robinson, N., & Basham, R. (1983). Effects of stress and social support on mothers of premature and full-term infants. *Child Development, 54,* 209–217.

Crnic, K.A., Greenberg, M.T., & Slough, N.M. (1986). Early stress and social support influences on mothers' and high-risk infants' functioning in late infancy. *Infant Mental Health Journal, 7,* 19–48.

DePaulo, B., Nadler, A., & Fisher, J. (Eds.) (1983). *New directions in helping: Vol. 2. Help-seeking.* New York: Academic Press.

Dokecki, P.R., & Heflinger, C.A. (1987, June). *Strengthening families of young handicapped children with handicapping conditions: Mapping backward from the "street level" pursuant to effective implementation of PL 99-457.* Paper presented at the 1987 Bush Colloquium on the Implementation of Public Law 99-457, Chapel Hill, N.C.

Dunst, C.J. (1985). Rethinking early intervention. *Analysis and Intervention in Developmental Disabilities, 5,* 165–201.

Dunst, C.J. (1987, December). *What is effective helping?* Paper presented at the Plenary Session "What is Helping?" held at the Fifth Biennial National Training Institute of the National Center for Clinical Infant Programs, Washington, DC.

Dunst, C.J. (1988, March). *Enabling and empowering families: Caveats, considerations and consequences.* Paper presented at the Early Intervention: Innovations in Service Delivery Conference, Danbury, CT.

Dunst, C.J., & Bolick, F.A. (1985). *Child Behavior Rating Scale.* Unpublished scale, Family, Infant and Preschool Program, Western Carolina Center, Morganton, NC.

Dunst, C.J., Cooper, C.S., & Bolick, F.A. (1987). Supporting families of handicapped children. In J. Garbarino, P.E. Brookhouser, & K.J. Authier (Eds.), *Special children, special risk: The maltreatment of children with disabilities* (pp. 17–46). New York: Aldine Publishing.

Dunst, C.J., & Leet, H. (1987). Measuring the adequacy of resources in households with young children. *Child: Care, Health and Development, 13,* 111–125.

Dunst, C.J., Leet, H., & Trivette, C.M. (1988). Family resources, personal well-being and early intervention. *The Journal of Special Education, 22,* 108–115.

Dunst, C.J., Pletcher, L., & Gordon, N. (1986). *Resource Exchange Scale,* Unpublished scale, Family, Infant and Preschool Program, Western Carolina Center, Morganton, NC.

Dunst, C.J., & Trivette, C.M. (1985). *Personal Time Commitment Scale.* Unpublished scale, Family, infant, and Preschool Program, Western Carolina Center, Morganton, NC.

Dunst, C.J., & Trivette, C.M. (1986). Looking beyond the parent-child dyad for the determinants of maternal styles of interaction. *Infant Mental Health Journal, 7,* 69–80.

Dunst, C.J., & Trivette, C.M. (1987). Enabling and empowering families: Conceptual and intervention issues. *School Psychology Review, 16,* 443–456.

Dunst, C.J., & Trivette, C.M. (1988a). A family systems model of early intervention with handicapped and developmentally at-risk children. In D.P. Powell (Ed.), *Parent education and support programs: Consequences for children and families* (pp. 131–179). Norwood, NJ: Ablex Publishing Corp.

Dunst, C.J., & Trivette, C.M. (1988b). Helping, helplessness and harm. In J. Witt, S. Elliott, & F. Gresham (Eds.), *Handbook of behavior therapy in education* (pp. 221–268). New York: Plenum.

Dunst, C.J., & Trivette, C.M. (1988c). Support Functions Scale. In C.J. Dunst, C.M. Trivette, & A.G. Deal, *Enabling and empowering families: Principles and guidelines for practice* (pp. 143–145). Cambridge, MA: Brookline Books.

Dunst, C.J., & Trivette, C.M. (1988d). Toward experimental evaluation of the Family, Infant and Preschool Program. In H. Weiss & F. Jacobs (Eds.), *Evaluating family programs* (pp. 315–346). Hawthorne, NY: Aldine de Gruyter.

Dunst, C.J., & Trivette, C.M. (in press). Assessment of social support in early intervention programs. In S. Meisels & J. Shonkoff (Eds.), *Handbook of early intervention.* New York: Cambridge University Press.

Dunst, C.J., Trivette, C.M., & Cross, A.H. (1986a). Mediating influences of social support: Personal, family, and child outcomes. *American Journal of Mental Deficiency, 90,* 403–417.

Dunst, C.J., Trivette, C.M., & Cross, A.H. (1986b). Roles and support networks of mothers of handicapped children. In R. Fewell & P. Vadasy (Eds.), *Families of handicapped children: Needs and support across the lifespan* (pp. 167–192). Austin, TX: PRO-ED.

Dunst, C.J., Trivette, C.M., & Cross, A.H. (in press). Social support networks of Appalachian and nonAppalachian families with handicapped children. In S. Keefe (Ed.), *Appalachian mental health.* Lexinton, KY: University Press of Kentucky.

Dunst, C.J., & Trivette, C.M., Davis, M., & Cornwell, J. (1988). Enabling and empowering families of children with health impairments. *Children's Health Care, 17*(2), 71–81.

Dunst, C.J., Trivette, C.M., & Deal, A.G. (1988). *Enabling and empowering families: Principles and guidelines for practice.* Cambridge, MA: Brookline Brooks.

Dunst, C.J., Vance, S.D., & Cooper, C.S. (1986). A social systems perspective of adolescent pregnancy: Determinants of parent and parent-child behavior. *Infant Mental Health Journal, 7,* 34–48.

Elmore, R.F. (1979–80). Backward mapping: Implementation research and policy decisions. *Political Science Quarterly, 94,* 601–616.

Fisher, J.D., Nadler, A., & DePaulo, B.M. (Eds.). (1983). *New directions in helping: Vol. 1. Recipient reactions to aid.* New York: Academic Press.

Fisher, J.D., Nadler, A., & Wichter-Alagna, S. (1983). Four conceptualizations of reactions to aid. In J.D. Fisher, A. Nadler, & D.M. DePaulo (Eds.), *New directions in helping: Vol. 1. Recipient reactions to aid* (pp. 51–84). New York: Academic Press.

Garbarino, J. (1982). *Children and families in the social environment.* New York: Aldine Publishing.

Gottlieb, B.H. (1981). Social networks and social support in community mental health. In B.H. Gottlieb (Ed.), *Social networks and social support* (pp. 11–42). Beverly Hills: Sage Publications.

Gottlieb, B.H. (1985). Assessing and strengthening the impact of social support on mental health. *Social Work, 3,* 293–300.

Gourash, N. (1978). Help seeking: A review of the literature. *American Journal of Community Psychology, 6,* 499–517.

Greenberg, M.S., & Westcott, D.R. (1983). Indebtedness as a mediator of reactions to aid. In J.D. Fisher, A. Nadler, & B.M. DePaulo (Eds.), *New directions in helping: Vol. 1. Recipient reactions to aid* (pp. 85–112). New York: Academic Press.

Gross, A.E., & McMullen, P.A. (1983). Models of the help-seeking process. In B. DePaulo, A. Nadler, & J. Fisher (Eds.), *New directions in helping: Vol. 2. Helping-seeking* (pp. 45–70). New York: Academic Press.

Gurin, G., Veroff, J., & Feld, S. (1960). *Americans view their mental health.* New York: Basic Books.

Hall, A., & Wellman, B. (1985). Social networks and social support. In S. Cohen & S. L. Syme (Eds.), *Social support and health* (pp. 23–42). New York: Academic Press.

Hobbs, N., Dokecki, P.R., Hoover-Dempsey, K.V., Moroney, R.M., Shayne, M.W., & Weeks, K.H. (1984). *Strengthening families.* San Francisco: Jossey-Bass.

Hobfoll, S.E. (1985). Limitations of social support in the stress process. In I.G. Sarason & B.R. Sarason (Eds.),

Social support: Theory, research, and applications (pp. 391–416). Dordrecht, The Netherlands: Marticus Nijhoff.

Hoke, B. (1968). Promotive medicine and the phenomenon of health. *Archives of Environmental Health, 16,* 269–278.

House, J.S., & Kahn, R.L. (1985). Measures and concepts of social support. In S. Cohen & S.L. Syme (Eds.), *Social support and health* (pp. 83–108). New York: Academic Press.

Lazar, I., Darlington, R., Murray, H., Royce, J., & Snipper, A. (1982). Lasting effects of early education: A report from the consortium for longitudinal studies. *Monographs of the Society for Research in Child Development, 47* (2–3, Serial No. 195).

Lloyd, A., & Segal, P. (1978). *The barter research project.* Madison: University of Wisconsin Extension.

Maple, F.F. (1977). *Shared decision making.* Beverly Hills: Sage Publications.

McCubbin, H.I., Comeau, J.K., & Harkins, J.A. (1981). Family Inventory of Resources for Management. In H.I. McCubbin & J.M. Patterson (Eds.), *Systematic assessment of family stress, resources and coping* (pp. 67–69). St. Paul, MN: Family Stress and Coping Project.

Merton, V., Merton, R.K., & Barber, E. (1983). Client ambivalence in professional relationships: The problem of seeking help from strangers. In B. DePaulo, A. Nadler, & J. Fisher (Eds.), *New directions in helping: Vol. 2. Help seeking* (pp. 13–44). New York: Academic Press.

Mitchell, R.E., & Trickett, E.J. (1980). Task force report: Social networks as mediators of social support: An analysis of the effects and determinants of social networks. *Community Mental Health Journal, 16,* 27–44.

Moos, R.H. (Ed.). (1986). *Coping with life crisis: An integrated approach.* New York: Plenum.

Nadler, A., Fisher, J.D., & DePaulo, D.M. (Eds.). (1983). *New directions in helping: Vol. 3. Applied perspectives on help-seeking and -receiving.* New York: Academic Press.

Patterson, J.M., & McCubbin, H.I. (1983). Chronic illness: Family stress and coping. In C.R. Figley & H.I. McCubbin (Eds.), *Stress and the family: Vol. II. Coping with catastrophe* (pp. 21–36). New York: Brunner/Mazel.

Pletcher, L., Dunst, C.J., & Gordon, N. (1986). *Provision of Resources Scale.* Unpublished scale, Family, Infant and Preschool Program, Western Carolina Center, Morganton, NC.

Rabinowitz, V.C., Karuza, J., Jr., & Zevon, M.A. (1984). Fairness and effectiveness in premediated helping. In R. Folger (Ed.), *The sense of injustice* (pp. 63–92). New York: Plenum.

Rappaport, J. (1981). In praise of paradox: A social policy of empowerment over prevention. *American Journal of Community Psychology, 9*(1), 1–25.

Rappaport, J. (1987). Terms of empowerment/exemplars of prevention: Toward a theory for community psychology. *American Journal of Community Psychology, 15*(2), 121–128.

Sarason, I.G., & Sarason, B.R. (Eds.). (1985). *Social support: Theory, research, and applications.* Dordrecht, The Netherlands: Martinus Nijhoff.

Skinner, B.F. (1978). The ethics of helping people. In L. Wispe (Ed.), *Sympathy, altruism and helping behavior* (pp. 249–262). New York: Academic Press.

Stoneman, Z. (1985). Family involvement in early childhood special education programs. In N.H. Fallen & W. Umanskyn (Eds.), *Young children with special needs* (2nd ed.) (pp. 442–469). Columbus, OH: Charles E. Merrill.

Stufflebeam, D.L. (1971). The use of experimental design in educational evaluation. *Journal of Education Measurements, 8,* 268–274.

Swift, C. (1984). Empowerment: An antidote for folly. In J. Rappaport, C. Swift, & R. Hess (Eds.), *Studies in empowerment: Steps toward understanding action* (pp. xi–xv). New York: Haworth Press.

Tobin, D., & Ware, H. (1983). *The barter network handbook: Building community through organized trade.* Arlington, VA: National Center for Citizen Involvement.

Tobin, D., & Ware, H. (1984). *Supporting your barter network: A preview of a new volunteer handbook.* Arlington, VA: National Center for Citizen Involvement.

Trivette, C.M., & Dunst, C.J. (1985). *Personal Well-Being Index.* Unpublished scale, Family, Infant and Preschool Program, Western Carolina Center, Morganton, NC.

Trivette, C.M., & Dunst, C.J. (1987a). *Caregivers styles of interaction: Child, parent, family and extra-family influences.* Unpublished manuscript, Family, Infant and Preschool Program, Western Carolina Center, Morganton, NC.

Trivette, C.M., & Dunst, C.J. (1987b). Proactive influences of social support in families of handicapped children. In H.G. Lingren, L. Kimmons, P. Lee, G. Rowe, L. Rottmann, L. Schwab, & R. Williams, (Eds.), *Family strengths, Vol. 8–9: Pathways to well-being* (pp. 391–405). Lincoln: University of Nebraska Press.

Trivette, C.M., & Dunst, C.J. (1988). Inventory of Social Support. In C.J. Dunst, C.M. Trivette, & A.G. Deal, *Enabling and empowering families: Principles and guidelines for practice* (pp. 158–163). Cambridge, MA: Brookline Books.

Trivette, C.M., & Dunst, C.J. (in press). Characteristics and influences of role division and social support among mothers of handicapped preschoolers. *Parenting Studies.*

Wilcox, B.L., & Birkel, R.C. (1983). Social networks and the help-seeking process: A structural perspective. In A. Nadler, J.D. Fisher, & B.M. DePaulo (Eds.), *New directions in helping: Vol. 3. Applied perspectives on help-seeking and -receiving* (pp. 235–253). New York: Academic Press.

Wilkinson, J. (1980). On assisting Indian people. *Social Casework: Journal of Contemporary Social Work, 61,* 451–454.

Zautra, A., & Sandler, I. (1983). Life events needs assessments: Two models for measuring preventable mental health problems. *Prevention in Human Services, 2*(4), 35–58.

CHAPTER 9

Community Support

The Role of Volunteers and Voluntary Associations

Elizabeth Cooley

S upport for families of children with disabilities comes from a variety of sources—formal and informal, generic and specialized, financial and emotional. People who provide that support can be experts or amateurs, paid or unpaid, strangers or friends.

This chapter will provide a discussion of some of the roles that volunteers have played in supporting families. Before describing those roles, however, a broader picture of volunteerism in America will be presented. This more global view is helpful not only for gaining a better understanding of the benefits that volunteers can impart to families, but also for appreciating certain drawbacks and cautions regarding the use of volunteers (as defined in the traditional sense) in serving families.

Volunteering has been defined as "any relatively uncoerced work, intended to help, and done without primary or immediate thought of financial gain" (Scheier, 1982, p. 33). Webster's Dictionary defines a volunteer as "one who enters into or offers himself for a service of his own free will" (*Webster's Ninth New Collegiate Dictionary*, 1987, p. 1322). Quite simply, a volunteer can be thought of as almost anyone doing almost anything for another's benefit without pay. The range of activities is infinite, and can include anything from babysitting a child to soliciting donations for a cause, or from organizing a church picnic to fighting a fire.

NEED FOR SERVICE

Volunteers and voluntary associations such as churches, civic clubs, and voluntary action centers, have been and continue to be a significant source of support to individuals, families and communities across the country; many billions of dollars in services are provided by volunteers every year. A 1983 Gallup Survey (Gallup Survey, 1984) on volunteering found that 55% of adults in America had volunteered during the previous year, and nearly half of these volunteered through structured programs. (Volunteering was defined for the survey as "working in some way to help others for no monetary pay"; thus, the figure would include someone who regularly helped an elderly neighbor as well as someone who volunteered in a nursing home.) The largest areas of volunteer involvement included church, health-related, and educational services (Gallup Survey, 1984).

In a 1982 report, the National Forum on Volunteerism identified five types of volunteer activity: 1) service to others, 2) advocacy/action-oriented (such as circulating petitions), 3) citizen participation in government, 4) administrative governance (such as serving on a Board of Directors), and 5) self-help (such as neighborhood improvement programs) (Manser, 1982). These types of volunteer activities can be broadly divided into two categories: 1) providing needed services and 2) promoting social change.

In both of these areas, volunteers have been used increasingly to serve the needs of individuals with disabilities and their families. In the area of social change, many efforts have taken the form of lobbying activities that promote legislation aimed at improving the quality of life (e.g., through parent networks and organizations such as The Association for Severely Handicapped Persons and the Association for Retarded Citizens).

This chapter focuses on the various roles that volunteers have played in direct service (i.e., person-to-person assistance) to families of children with disabilities, with particular emphasis on one program developed at the Oregon Research Institute. Before presenting specific examples of the use of volunteers in helping to meet family needs, however, an examination of those needs is useful.

Family Needs

There is as much variability among families who have children with disabilities as there is among other families. For some, raising a child with disabilities poses no particular difficulty, while for others the challenges are extreme. Undoubtedly, there is a high degree of overlap in the kinds of stresses experienced by families of handicapped children and families of nonhandicapped children; even within the same family, stressors are apt to change over time (Turnbull & Turnbull, 1986).

On the average, however, families of children with severe disabilities face common challenges, including chronic stress, grief, financial costs and losses in financial opportunities, extraordinary time demands, difficulties with normal family routines, marital discord, absence of services, and difficulty with physical management of the child (Bradley & Agosta, 1985). These stressors are bound to affect the quality of life in these families. The effects on quality of family life are not only a cause for concern in and of themselves, but are also pressing because of the fact that the quality of home life has an enormous impact on the developmental outcomes of children with disabilities (Nihira, Meyers, & Mink, 1980).

In addition to facing these stressors, parents of a child with disabilities may also experience considerable isolation from their community (Barsh, Moore, & Hamerlynck, 1983) and anxiety over the limited opportunities available to their child to participate in integrated community activities (Turnbull & Turnbull, 1986). Moreover, they may worry about the child's deficit (or even total lack) of relationships with others who are neither relatives nor paid service

workers (Seaver-Reid, 1986; Turnbull & Turnbull, 1986). Strully and Strully (1985) discuss the need for individuals with handicaps to have people in their lives who are not paid to be there. Friendships are important for everyone, not only individuals with handicaps and their families. As Perske (1988, p. 2) puts it, "If a person is breathing, [he or she] needs a friend."

Clearly, families of children with disabilities may experience a multitude of needs. Equally clear, though disturbing, is the reality of ever-present shortages in fiscal resources available to agencies dedicated to serving those needs. An effective volunteer program, then, can be a cost-effective, adjunctive option for service delivery systems (Calkins, Dunne, & Kultgen, 1986; Marrs, 1984; Powers & Goode, 1986).

In addition to their cost-effectiveness, volunteers can also be of great value in serving families for another reason. Their status as ordinary individuals may be a comfortable alternative for parents who are uneasy with professionals. For a variety of reasons, parents and professionals may not always agree (Darling, 1983); volunteers, because of their nonprofessional status, may be able to provide support in ways that professionals cannot.

Formal versus Informal Support Roles

In looking at the direct-service roles that volunteers have played in supporting families, a distinction needs to be made between formal and informal support services. Kozlowski, Phipps, and Hitzing (1983) defines formal support services as organized services provided by a variety of agencies or providers that assist people with disabilities (and their families) to live in the community. He defines informal supports as networks such as families, friends, neighbors, churches, and clubs that may offer friendship and assistance in problem-solving and obtaining needed services. These informal supports are not *professionalized,* in that they are performed by individuals who do not necessarily possess any particular expertise in a particular type of 'problem.' Such supports are, for the most part, unpaid.

Volunteers have been engaged to support individuals with disabilities and their families within a variety of formal support settings including agencies, schools, and institutions (Creekmore & Creekmore, 1983; Essex, Walter, Bonham, Gallo, & Golledge, 1974; Frith & Wood, 1983; Moore & Willems, 1987).

In this chapter, the primary focus is on roles that volunteers have played as *informal* supports to families. There are certain inherent advantages to this kind of support. For example, as Kozlowski et al. (1983) have pointed out, an important distinction between the two types of services is that informal supports often reflect a more reciprocal relationship than that encountered in formal support systems. That is, both parties are at once givers and receivers; the relationship is not one-sided. Dunst (1987) asserts that this kind of relationship between a provider and a receiver of assistance is actually more effective in the delivery of services, because of the empowering effect it has upon the recipient.

Informal supports have an additional benefit over formal systems in that they are often perceived as less threatening to a family's sense of self-sufficiency (Kendrick, 1981). They may create a sense of community that in turn promotes a family's sense of competence and well-being (Dunst, 1987).

Kozlowski et al. (1983) have further underscored the importance of these informal networks by pointing out that even when all formal supports are in place there may be deficiencies in the quality of life, and a lack of support can increase the likelihood of a child's placement in a more restricted environment.

In part due to the potential for reciprocity in informal supports, these kinds of supports are perhaps more "normal" than formalized services, in that they more closely emulate the customary give-and-take that exists in most naturally occurring relationships. They might, therefore, be more apt to last longer over time.

Despite the benefits that volunteers can impart to families, some potential drawbacks must be addressed concerning their role, as traditionally defined. As mentioned earlier, a volunteer is often thought of as one who provides service to another person without thought of personal gain. The danger in this definition as it applies to volunteers serving individuals with disabilities and their families is that it implies a unidirectional relationship, in which the role of the volunteer is

to assist and the role of the individual or family is to be assisted. Such roles, even if only subtly apparent, may serve to perpetuate the societal myth that individuals with disabilities have very little to offer. Romney (1980) explains:

> The danger is that one person's empowering will be another's disempowering. Citizens who occupy relatively stable, relatively empowered positions in society must be careful that what they intend as positive acts of volunteering do not inadvertently impede the efforts of other citizens to gain their full standing in the society. (p. 4)

Therefore, when engaging volunteers as informal supports, care must be taken, when describing the volunteer's role, to point out the possible mutual benefits and stress the reciprocal nature of the relationship.

Current Approaches

Following are brief descriptions of a few examples of the types of programs which connect volunteers to families in more or less informal support roles. Later in the chapter, the Support and Education for Families (SAEF) volunteer program is described and discussed in more depth, as an example of another such program.

In a Vermont project called Volunteers for Families (Seaver-Reid, 1986), volunteers were paired with families in an effort to assist parents of children with developmental disabilities. This assistance took the form of working directly with the children in order to achieve home and community Individualized Education Program (IEP) objectives, to provide social integration opportunities within the neighborhood, and to create opportunities to practice leisure and social skills.

In a program called Volunteers in Partnership with Parents, volunteer partners were paired with families and, with the help of the volunteer coordinator in a process similar to developing an IEP, identified the families' needs and goals for meeting them. The goals that were most often worked on by volunteers in this project related to respite services, transportation to children's appointments, child stimulation activities, and behavior management (Nelson, 1986).

In an interesting proposal combining the use of volunteers as formal and semi-informal supports, Powers and Goode (1986) describe a three-tiered model in which volunteers could be "incentivized" with such benefits as an invested annuity, theatre tickets, free meals, and insurance coverage. Level One would include lay volunteers who would be paired with families in order to determine which direct-support services would most directly address those families' particular needs (in most cases, respite and transportation). Level Two would consist of professional volunteers (psychologists and social workers) who would provide case management services to families. Medical, law, and accounting professionals would constitute Level Three volunteers, and their function would be to provide technical assistance and consultation to the case managers and families. While this model of volunteer services has not yet been implemented, it poses interesting possibilities.

In a project called the Foster Extended Family (FEF) (Barsh et al., 1983), foster families' resources were expanded by recruiting friends, relatives, neighbors, and community volunteers to provide support and assistance to foster parents of children with severe handicaps. The project provided all volunteers and extended family members with training and stipends for their participation; the services that were provided included respite care, in-home training for the child, transportation, and construction of special equipment and home adaptations to facilitate caring for the child. Service contracts were drawn up between FEF members and families, and their contents were determined by the particular needs of the children and families.

The results of the FEF project are promising; not only were families and FEF members satisfied with the experience, but many of the children's school skills subsequently generalized to the home setting, and the amount of teaching time per child was increased due to the FEF members' in-home interventions (Hamerlynck & Moore, 1982).

In a spin-off from the FEF project, the Extending Family Resources (EFR) project helped 16 biological families to incorporate "underutilized" family members, neighbors, and friends into their existing support network. If supplemental assistance was needed, community volunteers were recruited and assigned to families as well.

In roughly one year, 115 extended family members participated in EFR, with the number of support persons per family ranging from 4 to 14. Family stress was reduced across all participating families, and several of the families that had previously been considering foster placement for their child were able to keep their child at home (Barsh et al., 1983).

Following is a model of family support developed at Oregon Research Institute that connects university volunteers as community companions to children and youth aged 2–21 with severe disabilities.

SERVICE DESIGN: THE SUPPORT AND EDUCATION FOR FAMILIES (SAEF) VOLUNTEER PROGRAM

Philosophy and Goals

The SAEF Volunteer Program was created in order to respond to several of the family needs described earlier, including a brief reprieve from caretaking demands, more opportunities for the child to engage in community activities, and a chance for the child to establish a friendship. In addition to its goal of supporting families, the program was intended to provide meaningful experiences and valuable training to the volunteers who participated in the program.

Specifically, volunteers in the SAEF program were responsible for working one-on-one with a child with disabilities for approximately three hours per week for a minimum of six months. In their time together, the volunteers and the children participated in a wide range of community activities.

Although SAEF volunteers received training, the fact that they were not professionals, and that the child and family were not to be treated as clients was carefully emphasized. The fundamental focus of the volunteer program was to establish meaningful friendships between volunteers and children, while at the same time providing opportunities for the children to participate to a greater extent in the community at large. As a result of the time away from home that the child spent with the volunteer, parents were provided with limited respite from caretaking responsibilities.

Participants

Families Since the volunteer program was only one element of a larger family support program, most of the families who participated were already receiving one or more service options (such as coping skills classes and case management) at the time that they were offered a volunteer. Thirty-seven moderately and severely handicapped children of families who participated in the SAEF program (in three different groups over 2 years) were paired with volunteers; eleven of these children had at least two volunteers over time because their families requested continued involvement with the program. The children had diagnoses ranging from moderate to profound mental retardation, and many had additional developmental disabilities including cerebral palsy, autism, Down syndrome, and sensory impairments. The children's ages averaged 9.5 years, with a range of 2 to 16 years.

Volunteers Volunteers were recruited from a local university via posted fliers and in-class presentations in relevant departments such as special education, therapeutic recreation, clinical services, psychology and human services.

Of the 54 university volunteers engaged over a 2½ year period, 43 were undergraduates and 11 were graduate students. Volunteers ranged in age from 19 to 47, with a mean of 24 years. There were 45 female and 9 male volunteers.

Organizational Structure and Program Procedures

Following is a brief outline of the selection, training and supervision procedures employed in the SAEF volunteer program. For a more in-depth description of the volunteer program procedures, the Community Volunteer Program Manual is available (Cooley, 1986).

Selecting Volunteers To facilitate drawing on university students as volunteers, instructors and department heads were contacted and arrangements were made for volunteers to have the option of receiving academic practicum credit for their participation in the project. In several classes, the SAEF program was listed as one of the field-placement options open to students.

During the in-class recruitment presentations,

recruiters emphasized the reciprocal nature of the relationships and pointed out the various benefits to the volunteers and children. They also clearly stated the minimum level of commitment that was expected of volunteers who were accepted into the program.

The volunteer screening process was virtually the same as that used for many paid positions; each volunteer completed an application, was interviewed individually for 30–45 minutes, and listed two relevant references that were then checked. At first glance, it may appear somewhat incongruous that in a program that promoted such informal relationships, these somewhat formal screening procedures were followed. It is important to keep in mind, however, that the volunteers were being selected to engage in one-on-one activities with a child in the absence of the parents. Therefore, in light of the flagrantly widespread risk of child abuse, this level of precaution becomes necessary.

Prior relevant experience was not required of new volunteers because of the training provided by the SAEF project and because of the program's focus on friendship as opposed to formal instruction. However, volunteers were carefully selected on the basis of perceived conscientiousness, commitment, capability for working with children, and motivation for participation. Thus, while academic credit was always available to volunteers, applicants whose primary motivation for participation was to receive credit were deliberately not selected. In fact, many volunteers did not receive credit for their involvement at all.

Training Volunteers Numerous sources have noted that volunteers who are new to relationships with people with disabilities often need help to overcome whatever fears, discomforts, and insecurities they may initially have regarding handicapping conditions (Calkins et al., 1986; Essex et al., 1974; Marrs, 1984; Sharow & Levine, 1984). This was true for this program as well. One volunteer explained:

> I had never worked with handicapped kids. I worked with kids all my life, but I never worked with handicapped kids. I was sure, since you hear of 'special ed classes', that there was a way to deal with them, and I wanted to be told how to deal with

handicapped kids. I wanted a course. I wanted you to tell me. . . . I thought I had to be a professional of some sort. And then I went out, and right away I found out that the only thing you have to do is be their friend and experience them as another person, not as a handicapped person.

Thus, the focus of the training and supervision procedures was to equip volunteers with enough knowledge and support to feel comfortable and competent in their friendship with the child—not to make them teachers or experts.

SAEF volunteer training consisted of a combination of group and individual instruction. Upon acceptance into the program, new volunteers attended a 3½-hour orientation session in which the following topics were discussed by project staff and volunteers:

1. Philosophy and goals of the program and the organization as a whole
2. Basic behavior-management concepts and techniques, with an emphasis on providing clear directions and positively reinforcing appropriate behavior
3. Readings pertaining to various disabilities, as well as readings concerning the "people first" concept
4. Confidentiality and child-abuse reporting obligations
5. Tips for fostering enjoyable interactions with children
6. Suggestions for possible activities
7. Administrative business (e.g., reimbursement procedures)

At this orientation session, several videotaped lessons developed within the project were shown to illustrate key ideas, such as: *The Volunteer Experience: Working with a Handicapped Child,* (Cooley & Singer, 1986), *Partial Participation,* (Marquez, Singer, & Irvin, 1987a) *Prompting,* (Marquez, Singer, & Irvin, 1987b) and *Reinforcement* (Marquez, Irvin, & Singer, 1987). In addition, for volunteers working with children who were deaf/blind, another video was also shown, *Getting in Touch: Communicating with a Child who is Deaf/Blind* (Cooley & Singer, 1987).

In order to match volunteers to children, practical and family/volunteer preferences were considered, and both the volunteer and the family

had input toward the decisions. Practical considerations consisted of transportation issues, volunteer and family schedules, and prior experience of the volunteer in relation to the expected difficulty of accommodating the child's special needs. Preferential considerations for families and volunteers consisted of age, gender, type of disability, and interests.

Once a volunteer was matched to a child, an introductory visit with the child and family occurred. Project staff accompanied the volunteer on this visit to make introductions and observe the interactions. Each volunteer brought along a standard list of questions to ask parents regarding such considerations as safety concerns on outings with the child, preferred activities, medical issues, adaptive equipment, emergency instructions, and so forth. This visit also served as an informal opportunity for the family and the volunteer to become acquainted. Of particular benefit in some instances was the input from parents of nonverbal children regarding how to read their child's unique communicative style. One volunteer explained:

Part of the problem that I had when I started was that he (the child) is nonverbal, and I didn't know how I would contend with that, how I would deal with his needs, and things he wanted, and his expression without being able to talk to him very well. One of the things that was real helpful was when I went and visited his mother. He was included, and I got to see them interact. I got some sense of how he expressed himself when he liked something, and how he behaved when he didn't like something. Plus, she had a lot of helpful suggestions (which) made it much easier to take him out the first time.

After the introductory visit, volunteers had the option of contacting the child's teacher at school in order to ask many of the same questions asked at the parent visit, and also to have the opportunity to observe the child in another setting and see how any problem behaviors were handled and appropriate behaviors rewarded by the teacher.

Volunteer-Child Activities The role of a volunteer in the SAEF program was to spend time one-on-one with a severely handicapped child for approximately three hours per week for a minimum of six months. In their time together, the volunteer and the child participated in a wide range of community activities, such as bowling, swimming, shopping, dining in restaurants, roller-skating, and going to movies. Reimbursement was provided by the project to the volunteers for mileage ($.10/mile) and limited activity costs ($2.00/outing).

Supervision of Volunteers Each volunteer was accompanied by project staff on the first outing with the child, so that help would be available to the volunteer in case any difficulty arose. In addition, this supervised visit served as a mechanism for providing feedback and support to the volunteer after the visit was completed.

After the supervised first outing, volunteers conducted their weekly outings independently with the child, but were asked to maintain weekly phone contact with project staff for the first two or three months to discuss experiences and problems when necessary.

Monthly group meetings were held for all volunteers. At these meetings volunteers shared their experiences with each other, problem-solved as a group, and shared ideas for activities to engage in with the children. These sessions also served as ongoing training opportunities for volunteers; new topic areas, such as interacting with parents and normalization were discussed, and guest speakers were occasionally invited.

Staffing

The program was run by a volunteer coordinator employed by the project at .75 full-time employment who also had additional job duties unrelated to the volunteer program. The time commitment required for coordinating the program was roughly 15 to 20 hours per week. In a subsequent replication, the coordinator recruited both undergraduate and graduate student interns (whose qualifications and experience varied widely) to assist in the running of the program. These assistant coordinators each contributed from 3 to 12 hours per week. In addition, the program was replicated by two respite care agencies, as well as a local division of the Big Brother/Big Sister program. The previous experience of the coordinators at these sites included a range from experienced case workers having no background in disabilities to veteran special education teachers. Duties undertaken by the volunteer coordinator(s) included:

1. Establishing volunteer recruitment sources
2. Recruiting and screening volunteers
3. Training and supervising volunteers
4. Maintaining ongoing contact with families and volunteers
5. Seeking out activity ideas for volunteers
6. Keeping necessary records and participating in data collection

Program Evaluation

Measures To evaluate the efficacy of the volunteer program in providing community participation opportunities for the children, support to the families, and valuable experiences for the volunteers, social validation and process measures were used. In addition, costs associated with the program were summarized.

Social validation measures were constructed to measure parent and volunteer perceptions of the goals and outcomes of the volunteer program. The parents' evaluation form enumerated a list of the goals of the volunteer program. For each goal, parents were asked to make *two ratings* on a Likert scale: 1) the importance of each goal, and 2) how successful the program was in reaching each goal. Parents completed this form after the closure of involvement with a particular volunteer.

A 12-item social validation instrument was also developed for volunteers to assess their satisfaction with their training, involvement with families, and level of program staff support. Again, Likert scales were provided on which the volunteers made their ratings.

To document the activities of volunteers and children, volunteers were asked to complete a brief form at the time of each outing describing the type and length of the activity. (This form also served as a request for parent permission). The frequency of activities by type across volunteers and children was summarized.

Finally, costs involved in reimbursing volunteers for mileage and activity fees were documented by summarizing reimbursement request forms turned in by volunteers.

Results The results of the social validation evaluation of parents' perceptions of the importance of the volunteer program goals and of the success of the program regarding those goals are presented in Table 1. All goals were regarded by

Table 1.   Mean ratings on parent evaluations of volunteer program (*n* = 45).

	X̄
1. The volunteer will provide reliable assistance.	
a. How important is this as a goal?	3.77
b. How successful was your volunteer in meeting this goal?	3.70
2. Volunteers will be adequately trained to deal with handicapped children.	
a. How important is this as a goal?	3.95
b. How successful was your volunteer in meeting this goal?	3.84
3. The children will enjoy the time spent with the SAEF volunteer.	
a. How important is this as a goal?	3.91
b. How successful was your volunteer in meeting this goal?	3.82
4. The child's participation in community activities will increase as a result of the efforts of the SAEF volunteer.	
a. How important is this as a goal?	3.66
b. How successful was your volunteer in meeting this goal?	3.37
5. The activities of the SAEF volunteer will enable parents to have some time away from the child.	
a. How important is this as a goal?	3.50
b. How successful was your volunteer in meeting this goal?	3.39
6. The ideas and suggestions of the parents will be respected and followed by the volunteer.	
a. How important is this as a goal?	3.73
b. How successful was your volunteer in meeting this goal?	3.81
7. Parents will recommend the SAEF volunteer program to other parents.	
a. How important is this as a goal?	3.84
b. How successful was your volunteer in meeting this goal?	3.82

Rating scale: 4 = highly, 3 = moderately, 2 = mildly, 1 = not at all.

parents as "highly important" (means of 3.5 to 3.9 on 1 to 4 scales).

The means of parent ratings of the success of volunteers in meeting the various goals ranged from 3.4 to 3.8 ("successful" to "highly successful") on 1 to 4 scales.

The results of volunteers' evaluations are presented in Table 2. Volunteers evaluated the training, supervision, and other resources provided to them as generally "very satisfactory." On scales of 1 to 4, where 4 was "very satisfactory" and 1 was "very unsatisfactory," the means of

Table 2.   Mean ratings on volunteer satisfaction questionnaire (*n* = 50).

	X̄
1. How would you rate the amount of training you received?	3.3
2. How would you rate the quality of training you received?	3.6
3. How would you rate the *amount* of supervision/follow-up provided by the project coordinator?	3.7
4. How would you rate the *quality* of supervision/follow-up provided by the project coordinator?	3.8
5. How would you rate the amount of support and suggestions available to you?	3.8
6. How would you rate the usefulness to you of the supervised first and second visits to the family?	3.7
7. How would you rate the *amount* of group meetings?	3.4
8. How would you rate the *quality* of group meetings?	3.5
9. How would you rate your understanding of "Partial Participation", (that is, the concept of allowing the child to participate in an activity as much as possible)?	3.7
10. How would you rate your ability to implement "Partial Participation" (as defined above) with your child?	3.3
11. How would you rate your overall volunteer experience?	3.6
12. How would you rate the quality of your learning about handicapped people from this experience?	3.6

Rating scale: 4 = very satisfactory, 3 = satisfactory, 2 = unsatisfactory, 1 = very unsatisfactory.

Table 3. Volunteer activity summary.

Activity category	(Number of times engaged in by all volunteers and children)
Movies	29
Sports (participative)	73
Sports (spectator)	16
Shopping	98
Restaurants	57
In-home activities	75
Outdoor recreation	69
Social visits	32
Library/museum/exhibits	44
Activities with pets and other animals	32
Miscellaneous activities	14
Total number of volunteers	54
Total number of *reported* activities with handicapped children	534
Average number of activities per volunteer	10

Table 4. Incidental costs associated with volunteer program.

Mileage costs	$731.19
Activity costs	$208.63
Insurance costs	$14.00
Total costs	$953.82

satisfaction responses by 50 volunteers were all between 3 and 4, with 9 of the 12 items having means between 3.5 and 4.

Table 3 presents a summary of the frequency and variety of activities that volunteers engaged in with children. Volunteers, in several cases, have noted informally that they did not report all of their activities. At least two reasons exist for this underreporting. One is that some volunteers simply forgot to complete the forms. Another reason may stem from the program's emphasis on the development of informal friendships, as opposed to formal service. Referring to the procedure of obtaining written permission prior to each outing, one volunteer explained, "He's my friend, so it feels kind of funny to have to 'check him out' every week like a library book." (This remark points to a very interesting paradox regarding some inherent difficulties posed by the process of fostering *informal* relationships via a *formal* program. This issue is discussed in more depth in the section on Limitations).

Community-based activities such as shopping, outdoor recreation and participative sports were the most frequent types of activities engaged in, followed by in-home activities (such as playing together with games or toys).

Table 4 summarizes the total mileage, activity, and supplementary auto insurance costs for 54 volunteers, and provides the average total cost per volunteer. Total costs amounted to $953.82; thus the per-volunteer average total cost was $17.66. It is important to note, however, that of the 54 participating volunteers, 24 never requested any reimbursement at all and chose to pay for any expenses themselves. Perhaps, then, a more accurate average total cost per volunteer would include only those volunteers requesting reimbursement: 30 of the 54 volunteers requested reimbursement, so the *adjusted* average total cost per volunteer came to $31.79. Figuring at an average of 10 outings per volunteer over a six-month minimum period, the adjusted average cost per outing was $3.18.

In figuring the cost of reimbursing volunteers for mileage and activities, the author was somewhat surprised to find that almost half of the volunteers did not request any reimbursement at all, even though it was made available to them. This may also have been partially due to the program's emphasis on friendship as opposed to service. Several volunteers explained that since they did not get reimbursed when they socialized with their other friends, they saw no reason to accept money from the program. Making reimbursement available, however, may enable some potential volunteers to participate rather than exclude themselves from the opportunity on the basis of monetary cost considerations.

The author was also surprised by the somewhat limited extent of the volunteers' acceptance of academic credit for their participation with the children. While the majority of volunteers did make use of this incentive for the first term of their involvement, they frequently did not wish to continue receiving credit beyond the first term, even though it was available to them. Perhaps providing incentives for volunteers in the form of academic credit or reimbursements may be most useful for helping to draw people into the program, but these incentives may not have a lasting effect on the volunteers' motivation to continue their involvement.

In evaluating the success of the program, it is also important to look at some other indications of participants' satisfaction in addition to the social validation measures, namely the length of volunteer commitment as well as parents' repeated requests for additional volunteer assistance. This information was not formally documented, but it was clear that many of the volunteers continued their involvement with the child beyond the six-month minimum, with most of them stopping after nine months (the end of the academic year). One volunteer continues to see her friend regularly after two years. Almost all of the parents who have had volunteers told us that they would like another after the first one left, because the child had enjoyed the relationship so much. And indeed, 11 families have had at least two volunteers.

Limitations Encountered

One limitation that was faced involves the paradox that was alluded to earlier concerning the programming of informal relationships via a formal program. Although volunteers were asked to complete activity-record forms at every outing, they did not always do so. Therefore, in the assessment of the number of activities engaged in by volunteers and children, the reported figures are low. (Nevertheless, they do convey an accurate representation of the general nature of the activities).

The required documentation, however minimal, may have appeared to some volunteers to be incongruous with the emphasis on the development of informal, mutually fulfilling friendships. Nevertheless, this program has a need for certain information to be able to report on the program's scope and effectiveness. It may be that data collection methods need to match more closely the nature of the program; thus, it may be more appropriate to gather data on activities via personal interviews instead of through regularly completed paperwork.

Another limitation that was encountered in data collection had to do with capturing the success of the program in establishing meaningful friendships between volunteers and children in the data. Repeatedly, parents told us of their child's delighted anticipation of outings and of the value to their child of having, perhaps for the first time, a *friend*—someone outside of the family—take an interest in developing a relationship with him or her. One parent explained:

> I don't think that parents that do not have handicapped children give their children's friends a second thought. They are just a part of the unit, part of life. You always have friends. Well, that's not true with handicapped people. It's very hard for them to get friends. Cindy's peers have no patience for her because she is younger-acting. Her little brain just does not compute like theirs. They can be nice to her but there's no true friendship, and there's no one special just for Cindy. And this (the volunteer program) has taken care of that. There is complete friendship between Amy and Cindy. It's just wonderful.

Although volunteers were encouraged to and did take children on a wide variety of community activities, some of the experiences most valued by the children themselves had to do with simply spending time together, regardless of the nature of the activity. One volunteer said:

> When I first started, I thought I'd need to keep her entertained all the time. But what I found out was that my friend didn't need that much entertainment. What she needed was just the time spent with her, like playing cards or talking. Some of the best times we had were the talks we had on the bus rides taking us to our activities.

Possibly because of the program's emphasis on mutual friendship rather than service delivery, some nice examples of reciprocity developed in the relationships formed. As one volunteer put it: "It didn't feel like something I had to do. It was something I looked forward to doing. Spending time with her was good for her, I imagine, but great for me. She was my buddy!" This same volunteer was a student who lived in a dormitory, and she described the child's family as her "extra family. I am far away from home and in college, and I could go over there, eat a real dinner, and be part of the family. It was neat." Another volunteer expressed the following:

> It makes me feel good to be doing good for someone else, but it's important to remember that when you're volunteering you get a lot out of it too. It's a

two-way street—I've probably gotten as much or more out of it as Chris has. It's a lot of fun . . . he's just one of my friends.

Still another volunteer, speaking of the child and his mother, said, "I don't feel I've so much volunteered as that I've made some dear friends." One particularly poignant example of reciprocity came when one of the volunteers tragically lost her mother in a car accident. She later said that the child's family became a great source of support to her in her grief.

One aspect of the program that deserves greater attention and improvement is that of closure of the volunteer-family relationships. While guidelines for handling closure were discussed with volunteers after about five months (such as discussing upcoming closure in advance with children and families, and fading involvement gradually), and parents were told at the time that volunteers were assigned of the approximate length of a volunteer's involvement, several families told us that they felt as if they were "left hanging" when the volunteer left. Perhaps if closure were discussed with the volunteers much closer to the beginning of their involvement, and if families were contacted by project staff toward the end of volunteers' involvement specifically to discuss closure, this type of discomfort could be alleviated.

However, even if closure is handled appropriately, a sense of loss may be an inherent drawback in a program that seeks to encourage friendships between individuals. There may always be a certain sadness as friends come and go. But hopefully, the benefits of these friendships ultimately outweigh the costs.

FUTURE DIRECTIONS

Research

Due to some of the limitations encountered in this data collection, it seems that model demonstration programs such as this one should include as part of their evaluation component more qualitative procedures in addition to quantitative measures. The essence of something as intangible and personal as friendships between individuals is difficult, if not impossible, to quantify;

the perceptions of all involved parties are crucial in rendering an accurate account of the phenomenon. A friendship consists in large part of the individual's perspectives of it—perspectives that are often incongruous, as Rubin (1986) has demonstrated. In Rubin's (1986) interview study, she asked 44 people to give her the names of their closest friends. Rubin then contacted those people and asked them to list *their* closest friends. Surprisingly, 64 percent of the latter group made no mention of the people originally interviewed! Allen (1987), in speaking of client-focused volunteer programs, cited a similar incongruity, within a correctional program, between the volunteers' and clients' perceptions of each other, and warned that mutual positive perceptions cannot be *assumed* simply because interactions are taking place.

Thus, it seems that in a program such as the SAEF Project described here, it would be necessary to measure the program's success largely by the views voiced by parents, children and volunteers, in addition to a tally of the number of activities and other such quantitative measures. In examining relationships between volunteers and nonverbal children, field observations could provide valuable information concerning the nature and quality of the interactions.

Further research is needed in developing more satisfactory procedures for handling the process of closure when volunteers need to exit children's lives. Ways need to be developed to somehow communicate to the children the reasons that the volunteers are leaving, or at least to alleviate the children's disappointment. One child who was interviewed clearly did not understand that his volunteers left because they graduated or moved away; he expressed anxiety that his current volunteer would leave too if he "disappointed her." On the subject of closure, one mother told us:

> I think it's hard for Lucy because she doesn't understand or know why they quit. . . . I think if it ended and I were to mention her (the volunteer's) name, she would still get excited and want to go see her.

A related area of consideration involves the source of volunteer recruitment. Perhaps if volunteers were drawn from more stable populations (e.g., retirees, church, and service groups) as opposed to the student population, the commitments might be of a more permanent nature.

Program Implications

To avoid the aforementioned pitfalls associated with engaging volunteers as helpers of families of children with disabilities, caution should be exercised during the recruiting phase to ensure that the mutual benefits and opportunities for reciprocity are stressed. Such an emphasis serves to empower families to the fullest extent by describing and treating them as givers as well as receivers.

The term *volunteer* may in itself be of diminishing and questionable value in programs striving to provide informal support, due to its historic association with charitable, unidirectional, helping acts. Programs may prefer instead to employ terms that are less laden with such associations and more suggestive of naturally occurring relationships, such as "special friends" (Voeltz et al., 1983) or "parent partners" (Nelson, 1986).

Part of the paradox of programming informal support via formal volunteer programs is that at first glance it appears somehow peculiar, even distasteful, to attempt to formalize relationships that for many people occur naturally. However, until families of children with disabilities no longer experience a deficit in naturally occurring support systems, formal programming for such support may be a necessary step toward more complete community integration. One implication for programs designed to pair volunteers with families concerns the sources of recruitment. It may prove worthwhile, as was done in the FEF project (Barsh et al., 1983) to recruit volunteers from a family's existing informal support network (e.g., neighbors or civic, church, and scouting groups with which the family may already have ties). The aim of this practice would be to intentionally "blur the lines" between supports available to families with handicapped children and those utilized by families of non-handicapped children, perhaps paving the way for such formalized programs to become obsolete.

Another avenue toward this end concerns the location of such formalized programs. To whatever extent possible, programs serving individuals with handicaps and their families should be incorporated into *generic* programs, meaning comparable programs serving the rest of the community. For example, in determining replication sites for the SAEF volunteer program, staff did not limit themselves to agencies serving only special populations. A generic program having similar aims (Big Brothers/Big Sisters) was also contacted and offered training materials and technical assistance. In so doing, it is possible for a program that was previously unavailable to children with disabilities to become accessible to them.

Another implication stemming from this program and others concerns the focus of volunteer training. Certainly enough information about disabilities, behavior management, and safety issues should be presented to enable volunteers to feel comfortable being with someone who has special needs. Equally important, however, is an emphasis on the fact that individuals with disabilities are really much more similar to non-handicapped individuals than they are different from them, and that medical kinds of issues need not be overplayed. One volunteer described her initial worries and subsequent realizations in this way:

> I was concerned about medical things. Cindy has seizures and medical problems I didn't know how to deal with. I later found out that the only way to learn was to spend time with her, becoming familiar with her problems, and all that worry is just wasted. If I was training the volunteers, I would tell them to just go do it!

In keeping with this focus, a training segment covering the "people first" language concept is helpful in sensitizing volunteers to the ways that they think and talk about those members of the community who have disabilities. That is, volunteers need to be reminded that their language should emphasize the person first rather than the disability (e.g., the "boy with Down syndrome" rather than the "Down's child"; "people with retardation" rather than "the retarded").

Policy

Implications for public policy stemming from this work and that of others involved in the administration of volunteer programs tend to point to two rather broad aims: the promotion of volunteerism in general and the provision of practical guidelines and information to potential and existing volunteer program administrators.

In a series of recommendations published by a Governor's Task Force on Voluntarism[1] (Atiyeh, 1980), several objectives were presented that serve as a basis for future policy decisions regarding the promotion of volunteerism in the state of Oregon. These goals, though developed with regional needs in mind, certainly would apply in any area of the country and are thus helpful as general guidelines, particularly in encouraging the continued use of volunteers in *formal* support services. (A note of caution: As McKnight (1987) has warned, extensive government involvement in *informal* volunteer efforts may in fact be counterproductive, in that it may only serve to detract from the naturalness of such support systems).

By striving to keep volunteerism alive through action at both state and federal governmental levels, the society at large will continue to reap the benefits of volunteerism, and consequently, so too will the families of children with disabilities.

Three of the goals outlined in the task force's report include:

1. To Encourage Greater Utilization of Volunteers to Enrich the Services of State Agencies Despite the cost-effectiveness of employing volunteers in formal support programs, barriers such as a lack of knowledge about implementing a volunteer program may preclude many agencies from making use of volunteers. Key recommendations of the task force included ways of providing specific information and support to programs wishing to supplement their resources with volunteer assistance.

2. To Raise the General Awareness of the Public about Voluntarism and to Specifically Encourage People to Volunteer Encouraging people to volunteer can be accomplished in any number of ways—by providing social recognition, mileage and expenses tax deductions, tax-deferred annuities, and so on. (Currently, the mileage deduction allowed for program volunteers is only about half—$.12/mile vs. $.21/mile—the deduction afforded to people who use their cars for business purposes).

Another option not mentioned in the report consists of providing volunteers with some protection against civil liability suits (except in cases of clear negligence or wrong-doing). While the SAEF program covered all volunteers with the same liability insurance that was issued to other employees, not all volunteer programs do this. With the increasing frequency of lawsuits, some volunteers may decline to participate in a program if such coverage is not offered. Even in informal volunteer involvements, this issue poses a threat. One state has lobbied for a "Volunteer Protection Act" that would grant immunity from civil liability to volunteers who were acting in good faith (Counterman, 1987). The passage of such an act would be an encouraging step toward removing the barriers between families of children with disabilities and others in the community.

3. To Improve the Management of Volunteer Resources throughout the State in Both Public and Private Sectors According to the report:

> Many volunteer program managers . . . have inadequate training and experience in the management skills necessary to administer programs. In addition, other volunteer organizations such as service clubs, neighborhood groups and churches lack the resource information and organizational skill training necessary for adequate impact (Atiyeh, 1980, p. 17).

Specific recommendations made by the report included at-cost dissemination of training materials and sponsorship of cooperative training events.

Not mentioned in the report, but potentially very useful, would be the issuance of a position paper concerning the minimal level of support that ought to be provided to volunteers in the form of materials and supervision. Too often, volunteer programs are inadequately budgeted for, due to the common but erroneous notion that they are "free."

Also not mentioned, but of critical impor-

---

[1]For the purposes of this chapter, *volunteerism* and *voluntarism* are used interchangeably. Voluntarism has been retained only in specific references where that spelling was originally used; the preferred spelling for this text is volunteerism.

tance, is the issuance of minimal screening procedures to be used in selecting volunteers. Often, volunteer program managers have trouble turning down potential volunteers because of the ever-present shortage of services. However, particularly in programs in which volunteers are working in unsupervised settings with children or other individuals, thorough screening is essential.

Summary

Volunteers and voluntary associations have been and continue to be a significant source of support to families of children with disabilities and to society at large. By understanding the various roles they have played in formal and informal support systems, their future involvement in supporting families can be better promoted in ways that are fulfilling not only to the families, but to the volunteers themselves. Such reciprocity will not only make the experiences more valuable to volunteers and more empowering to families, it will ultimately "blur the lines" between recipient and helper, handicapped and nonhandicapped, and volunteer and friend.

REFERENCES

Allen, N.J. (1987). The role of social and organizational factors in the evaluation of volunteer programs. *Evaluation and Program Planning, 10,* 257–262.

Atiyeh, V. (1980). *The Governor's Task Force on Voluntarism.* Portland, OR: Pacific Northwest Bell.

Barsh, E.T., Moore, J.A., & Hamerlynck, L.A. (1983). The foster extended family: A support network for handicapped foster children. *Child Welfare, 62*(4), 349–359.

Bradley, V.J., & Agosta, J. (Eds). (1985). *Family care for persons with developmental disabilities: A growing commitment.* (Technical Report). Cambridge, MA: Human Services Research Institute.

Calkins, C., Dunne, W., & Kultgen, P. (1986). A comparison of preschool and elderly community integration/demonstration projects at the University of Missouri Institute for Human Development. *Journal of The Association for Persons with Severe Handicaps, 11*(4), 276–285.

Cooley, E. (1986). *Community volunteer program manual.* Unpublished manuscript, Oregon Research Institute, Eugene.

Cooley, E. (Writer/Producer), & Singer, G.H.S. (Project Director). (1986). *The volunteer experience: Working with a handicapped child* [Videotape]. Eugene, OR: Oregon Research Institute.

Cooley, E. (Writer/Producer), & Singer, G.H.S. (Project Director). (1987). *Getting in touch: Communicating with a child who is deaf/blind* [Videotape]. Eugene, OR: Oregon Research Institute.

Counterman, B. (1987, June). Voluntarism protection act. *TASH DC Update,* p. 3.

Creekmore, W.N., & Creekmore, N.N. (1983, November). *Community volunteers as paratherapists for significantly handicapped children.* Paper presented at the Annual Conference of The Association for Persons with Severe Handicaps, San Francisco, CA.

Darling, R.B. (1983). Parent-Professional interaction: The roots of misunderstanding. In M. Seligman (Ed.), *The family with a handicapped child—understanding and treatment.* New York: Grunhe and Stratton.

Dunst, C.J. (1987). Enabling and empowering families: Conceptual and intervention issues. *School Psychology Review, 16*(4), 443–456.

Essex, M.W., Walter, F.B., Bonham, S.J., Jr., Gallo, N.P.,

& Golledge, M.R. (1974). *Utilizing volunteers for children with behavioral disabilities.* Columbus, OH: Ohio Department of Special Education, Columbus Division of Special Education.

Frith, G.H., & Wood, J.W. (1983). The emerging role of foster grandparents in serving handicapped individuals. *The Pointer, 27*(4), 33–35.

Gallup Survey. (1984). The 1983 Gallup Survey on volunteering. *Voluntary Action Leadership,* Winter, 1984, 20–26.

Hamerlynck, L.A., & Moore, J.A. (1982). *Contingent Involvement of Parents, Siblings, and Kin Volunteers in Special Education Programming.* Charles R. Strother Lecture, Child Development and Mental Retardation Center, University of Washington, Seattle.

Kendrick, M. (1981). *Promising practices: Reaching out to families.* Washington, DC: Administration for Children, Youth, and Families. (ERIC Document Reproduction Service No. ED 209 843)

Kozlowski, R.E., Phipps, C., & Hitzing, W. (1983). *Promoting quality community living through formal support services and informal supports.* Columbus, OH: Ohio State University, Herschel W. Nisonger Center. (ERIC Document Reproduction Service No. ED 250 900)

Manser, G. (1982). Report of the second session of the national forum on volunteerism. In G. Romney (Chair), *Shaping the future: A report of the National Forum on Volunteerism.* Appleton, WI: Aid Association for Lutherans.

Marquez, K.R. (Producer), Irvin, L.K. (Writer), & Singer, G.H.S. (Cowriter). (1987). *Reinforcement* [Videotape]. Eugene, OR: Oregon Research Institute.

Marquez, K.R. (Producer), Singer, G.H.S. (Writer), & Irvin, L.K. (Cowriter). (1987a). *Partial Participation* [Videotape]. Eugene, OR: Oregon Research Institute.

Marquez, K.R. (Producer), Singer, G.H.S. (Writer), & Irvin, L.K. (Cowriter). (1987b). *Prompting* [Videotape]. Eugene, OR: Oregon Research Institute.

Marrs, L. (1984). Should a special educator entertain volunteers? Interdependence in rural america. *Exceptional Children, 50*(4), 361–366.

McKnight, J.L. (1987). Regenerating community. *Social Policy, 17*(3), 54–58.

Moore, B., & Willems, J. (1987, Spring). *A history of success: The use of volunteers—Ten years of experience.*

Newsletter article for the Teaching Research Infant and Child Center, Monmouth, OR.

Nelson, L. (1986). *Volunteerism: A manual for implementation.* Greenville, NC: East Carolina University.

Nihira, K., Meyers, C.E., & Mink, I.T. (1980). Home environment, family adjustment, and the development of mentally retarded children. *Applied Research in Mental Retardation, 1,* 5–24.

Perske, R. (1988, January). Friends circle to save a life. *TASH Newsletter,* p. 1–3.

Powers, J., & Goode, D. (1986). *Partnerships for people.* Unpublished manuscript. Albert Einstein College of Medicine, Bronx, NY.

Romney, G. (1980). Empowerment. In K.K. Allen, J.L. Dutton, G. Manser, L.J. Peterson, & W.D. Rydberg (Eds.), *The shape of things to come: 1980–1990/A report from the National Forum of Voluntarism.* Appleton, WI: Aid Association for Lutherans.

Rubin, L.B. (1986). *Just friends: The role of friendship in our lives.* New York: Harper & Row.

Scheier, I.H. (1982). Other-than-national organizations and volunteering. In G. Romney (Chair), *Shaping the future: A report of the National Forum on Volunteerism.* Appleton, WI: Aid Association for Lutherans.

Seaver-Reid, M.E. (1986). *Preparation of trainers of volunteer parent service providers (including parents) for Vermont's school-age learners with severe developmental disabilities.* Final report of Vermont University at Burlington, Center for Developmental Disabilities.

Sharow, N., & Levine, S. (1984). *Training babysitters and volunteers for children with disabilities.* Springfield, IL: Charles C Thomas.

Strully, J., & Strully, C. (1985). Friendship and our children. *Journal of the Association for Persons with Severe Handicaps, 10*(4), 224–227.

Turnbull, A.P., & Turnbull, H.R. (1986). *Families, professionals, and exceptionality: A special partnership.* Columbus, OH: Charles E. Merrill.

Voeltz, L.M., Hemphill, N.J., Brown, S., Kishi, G., Klein, R., Fruehling, R., Levy, G., Collie, J., & Kube, C. (1983). *The special friends program: A trainer's manual for integrated school settings.* Hawaii Integration Project, College of Education, University of Hawaii. (ERIC Document Reproduction Service No. ED 256 128).

Webster's Ninth New Collegiate Dictionary. (1987). Springfield, MA: Merriam-Webster, Inc.

RECURRENT NEEDS FOR FORMAL SUPPORT

CHAPTER 10

Normalized Family Resources
A Model for Professionals

*Mary A. Slater,[1] Maury Martinez,
and Rolf Habersang*

Caring for a family member with a disability or chronic illness is stressful. However, family reactions vary. For some this situation appears to pull the family together, with each member marshalling internal and external resources to assist the disabled member. For others, dysfunctional family patterns emerge. The formation of ineffective cross-generational alliances is also a possibility, but as of the late 1980s no studies have been identified that delineate the characteristics of well-adjusted families who are caring for a chronically ill or disabled child. The majority of the research literature focuses on programs and concerns that the families raising these children face daily. This chapter focuses on an approach that helping professionals may employ to assist families in living as normal a family life as possible while caring for the child with a disability. Through this model, professionals are encouraged to view the disabled child within the family's social context. Programing focuses not simply on the child but on the family as a whole.

NORMALIZED FAMILY RESOURCES

Professionals from many fields are being called upon by families to assist them in raising their children who have special health care and be-

havioral needs. Pediatricians, nurses, educators, social workers, and psychologists are being asked by families with special care children for assistance. Although professionals tend to be well trained in discipline-specific roles, few service models exist to guide them in providing and/or coordinating comprehensive services that meet the whole child's needs as well as the needs of the family. The normalized family resource model was developed as one such model. It was originally described and designed for mental health workers who were concerned with families caring for a developmentally disabled child (Slater, 1986; Slater & Wikler, 1984). Within this chapter these principles and applications are discussed as they apply to children with special behavioral as well as health-care needs who may be served by a wide range of professionals from the health care to the educational and social service fields.

Families raising children with special needs require services that are provided within a family framework. These families desire and strive to maintain as normal a life as possible while assisting their special needs children in attaining their potential. The normalization principle was proposed in the late 1960s as a service ideology for directing the physical and social integration

This research was supported in part by grants from the National March of Dimes Clinical Services Program and the US Department of Education Early Childhood Demonstration Division Grant #G009630367.

[1]At the time of her death, Dr. Slater was a professor of Pediatrics at Texas Tech University Health Sciences Center in Amarillo. Her contributions to this article and the area of children and families will continue to influence service providers for years.

of individuals with disabilities into the main-stream of society (McCubbin, 1980). The normalized family resources model is being proposed in the same way: to assist families that are caring for a child with special needs to live as normal a family life as possible. Resource programs designed within the normalized family resource model strive to attain the following goals:

1. Individual family members should maintain normally autonomous lives.
2. Individual family members should relate to each other in a flexible, nonjudgmental fashion.
3. The family should maintain a normal daily routine and schedule vacations normally.
4. Adult family members should pursue normal employment opportunities.
5. All family members should maintain normal social relationships with relatives, friends, and neighbors.
6. Family members, including the special needs member, should have their needs met through normal generic service programs.

Basic to this position is the belief that all families require a triad of support that includes flexible internal family relationships supported by both informal and formal social supports, to function optimally. Just as normal families require reliable childcare arrangements and help from neighbors and relatives, so too do families with a chronically ill or disabled member. Recent demonstration projects suggest that assistance by extended family members, combined with limited financial support, promotes family harmony and allows all family members to attain their own personal goals as well as family goals (Berger & Fowlkes, 1984; Moore, 1982).

Professionals working within the normalized family resource model view themselves as resources to the family, rather than solely as case managers; parents choose an array of services from which their children should benefit, including medical, educational, and social services. Within the normalized family resource model, parents act as the co-case managers (with the professionals) for their special needs child, weighing the pros and cons of various types of services. Professionals working within this model assist parents by employing problem-solv-ing communication patterns, taking on family support roles in addition to discipline-specific roles, planning for the future through anticipatory guidance, and measuring progress through the development of individualized family support plans.

Areas of Concern

There are three major areas of concern that professionals must address when involved with families who have a chronically ill member.

Chronic or Acute Stress Raising a chronically ill or developmentally disabled child often leads to additional chronic and acute stresses for the family. Sources of these stressors may include the need for special-care skills such as suctioning, or financial strain resulting from continuing medical needs. Additionally, few families have ever seen other families raise children with these types of disorders and have little knowledge of avenues of assistance. The greatest initial stress is dealing with the loss of the hoped for "normal child".

Social Isolation Decreased social contact has been found to be a significant and distinguishing variable between families of normal children and those with a mentally retarded child (Davis & McKay, 1973). There is often an absence of rituals such as birth announcements or birthday parties. There may also be less extended family support due to discomfort with the situation.

Reduced Autonomy Raising a delayed or chronically ill child reduces a parent's feelings of control over one of life's major endeavors, that of raising a child. Parents of chronically ill children report feeling uncertain and threatened by a family member whom they are unprepared to nurture.

COMMUNICATION PATTERNS

Persons under stress have difficulty communicating both verbally and nonverbally. Parents under stress frequently eliminate everyday civilities such as greetings and handshakes when talking with professionals; similarly, well-trained professionals tend to use stilted, professional jargon that provides limited meaning to the parent regarding what caused the child's disorder, what types of service alternatives are available, and what short-term and long-term problems are to be expected.

Few parents question the competence and expertise of professionals such as pediatricians, nurses, social workers, and teachers who are serving their children. Many, however, are dissatisfied with the human element. Medical professionals have been frequently criticized by parents with handicapped children for their lack of understanding and empathy, and their communication patterns. Recently, members of the pediatric community have begun to investigate these concerns. Korsh and her colleagues at the University of Southern California videocassette-recorded 800 pediatric outpatient visits followed by detailed interviews with the parents (Korsh & Negrete, 1972). Analyses of the outpatient video recordings revealed that common greetings and expressions of friendliness were rare. Mothers appeared tense with the physicians who primarily reported medical findings. During the postoutpatient interviews mothers noted that their emotional concerns had not been addressed. One-fourth noted that their primary concern had not been discussed. One-fourth had no understanding of their child's disorder, and over half had left the physician's office not understanding what caused their child's disorder.

Within the normalized family resource model, professionals and parents are encouraged to use a problem-solving communication format. In assisting parents to become effective consumers, the following eight basic primary steps to effective consumer communication are suggested. These steps attempt to guide parents in a timely, easy-to-understand fashion (Carmen, 1987). Parents do need help, initially, in using this format but gradually gain confidence in their skills. Professionals must also understand and utilize this communication format.

STEPS TO EFFECTIVE COMMUNICATION BETWEEN PARENTS AND PROFESSIONALS

Step 1: Identify Concerns in Advance

Prior to talking with a physician, parents should try to itemize the concerns and worries they may be having about their young child. During these stressful times it usually helps parents to talk these concerns over with other family members. Family members who can openly discuss their concerns are a great source of emotional support for each other and will help them understand their concerns better and state them more clearly to the physician.

It can be helpful to write a list of concerns, enabling both the parents and the physician to maximize the quality of the appointment.

Step 2: Greeting the Physician

Physicians and consumers alike are human beings first and parents or professionals second. As with opening any conversation, it is always polite to say, "Hi, good afternoon; how has your day been going?". Adding simple everyday greetings to conversations with medical professionals tends to add a touch of relaxation and courtesy to our dialogues.

Step 3: Body Language

Many times when individuals experience high levels of stress they tend to convey their discomfort through body language (e.g., facial expressions, posture, eye contact). Although it may be very difficult for a parent to relax during stressful times, he or she should try to be aware that feelings of worry, concern, and anger may get in the way of effectively communicating with the physician.

Step 4: Arrange the Environment

Talking with the physician may occur with or without planning. When parents unexpectedly encounter their physician, asking him or her to walk down the hall to a quiet conference room or empty patient room can make everyone feel more relaxed while discussing important information.

If time and circumstances permit, parents might plan a physician conference. Enough chairs should be obtained for all participants to be seated. The family spokesperson should sit next to the physician. At these times it is good to have at least two family members present; because a friend or relative is usually less emotionally affected by the infant's illness he or she tends to absorb more of the details from the physician's conversation. After the family conference, they can restate the physician's viewpoints and clarify his or her thoughts.

Step 5: Active Participation

The overall care of an infant or young child lies in parents' hands. While the physician is talking with parents regarding their child's condition, the should listen intently and ask probing questions. Many times parents feel like they know very little about what is happening to their child because basic medical terminology gets in the way. Physicians may not even realize when they are using terms that parents may not understand completely. As the infant's physician uses these words, parents can ask for an explanation. If they wait until the end of the discussion they may have missed understanding many vital concerns.

Step 7: Living with Ambiguity

Many times in caring for the critically ill infant no definitive answers exist. Frequently parents want to know when their child may be able to come home, whether their child will be brain damaged, or how many more days he or she may need outside oxygen. These concerns, although very well founded, may not have specific answers. What will happen specifically to your infant is sometimes most difficult to tell. Frequently time and faith are your best hope.

Step 8: Decisions

Parents are frequently asked to make many decisions regarding the care of their critically ill infant. If time permits, they should try to obtain all the basic facts, then go home and weigh the pros and cons. In times of noncrisis, a second opinion may be valuable. Again, a family friend who is not intimately involved in the situation can often assist with clarifying possible solutions and patterns of action.

If the decision must be made immediately, parents may want to rely heavily upon the physician's advice. He or she has probably faced these situations and circumstances many times in the past, and can probably offer the best prognosis.

Closing

As the discussion conference comes to an end, it is helpful to summarize the main points covered.

This allows parents to cement the main points of the discussion into memory and gives the physician a chance of clarify major points that may not have been fully understood. In addition, it is always courteous to close the meeting with general farewells and thank the physician for taking the time to meet.

A basic description of the roles some key hospital-based medical professionals may play in the care of an infant follows.

Primary Nurse Most modern hospitals today assign one primary nurse to the care of critically ill infants and young children. The child's nurse is able to answer any parent's basic questions. The primary nurse who comes to care for the infant usually becomes a very important human being in his or her life. The baby's nurse is usually most grateful to hear about his or her progress once parents take him or her home.

Social Worker A hospital-based social worker can assist you with basic necessities such as help with hotels, restaurants, and funding options to help pay hospital bills if insurance does not cover all these expenses. Additionally, they tend to be well-informed about local resources that may be needed when parents begin to care for him or her at home. By making information like this available to families, professionals can assist them in becoming active consumers.

Summary and Examples

Consumers who become active partners in the communication process tend to receive more personal attention and obtain a fuller range of services for their child than those who employ a more passive style. Because cure is not an issue for chronically handicapped children, the quality of services these children and families receive becomes critical. Informal and personalized communication, not technological advances, form the basis of humanistic and normalized care.

CROSS-PURPOSE VERSUS PROBLEM-SOLVING COMMUNICATION

Studies have reported the frequent use of cross-purpose rather than problem-solving communication patterns between allied health professionals and their clients (MacKinnon, 1984).

Cross-purpose communications are characterized by a monologue approach in which facts and figures are relayed in a matter-of-fact manner with few personal concerns or comments made, and limited interpersonal discussion ensues. In contrast, the *problem-solving* approach is based upon a dialogue in which a mutual exchange of information takes place among members, with each sharing their own personal experiences, building upon one another's ideas, and jointly developing a plan of action. The problem-solving style includes nonverbal communication patterns as well, such as smiling and maintaining a relaxed body posture (MacKinnon, 1984).

The following synopsis is provided to highlight the differences between parents and professionals who employ a problem-solving versus cross-purpose communication style.

The Problem-Solving Case between Nurse (N) and Parent (P)

N—How are you today?

P— Fine.

N—And your child, Todd?

P— He does not seem to feel very good.

N—I'm sorry to hear that. Could you tell me about some of the things you've noticed?

P— He's restless during sleep, has a temperature, and is only drinking and eating a little bit.

N—It doesn't sound like he feels very good. I'm going to ask you some more specific questions and as we're talking if you remember noting anything else please feel free to let me know. How high has his temperature been and how long has he been running one?

P— He had one of 102.4 this morning and about 2 days ago he ran a temperature, but that went down. I guess I should have paid more attention at that time.

N—It sounds like you pay a lot of attention. You must have noticed something two days ago that prompted you to take his temperature.

P— Well I guess I did. He was a little fussy and thirstier than usual for the wintertime.

N—I think you probably did what most of us would do if our child ran a 99.6 temperature—just watch him for other symptoms—which you did and today those other signs showed up. Now when is the last time he ate or drank?

P— This morning he had a quarter of a slice of toast and some 7–up.

N—Do you recall any other symptoms besides tiredness, temperature, and poor appetite?

P— No, but a child at his day care has AIDS; we just found out.

N—AIDS? Obviously you're well informed. A lot of parents would have pulled their child out of a school if another child there had AIDS. You must already realize that it is highly unlikely that anyone else could contract AIDS by going to school with a child who does. Have there been any chicken pox, or other childhood diseases that you know of at his school or in your neighborhood?

P— No, not that I know of.

N—Good, thanks for your help. The doctor may order some tests to see if your child has a bug of some kind that needs to be treated with an antibiotic, or if it is a virus that we have to ride out. As soon as I know I'll come and explain to you what the tests are and how they are done, as well as when the results will be back. Do you have any questions or any other information that you think we should know about?

The Cross-Purpose Case of Nurse (N) and Parent (P)

N—Hi! What's the problem?

P— I think my son is sick.

N—You think, don't you know? (Laughs)

P— Well, hum . . .

N—Let's take a look at him. Has he got a runny nose, diarrhea, vomiting, etc.?

P— No Ma'am.

N—Well there is a flu virus going around, you know. Do you think he has been exposed to someone who has that?

P— Probably, I guess.

N—During these winter months you have got to be careful about taking this little boy out in crowds. Is he in day care?

P— Yes, I work . . .

N—Well, I guess that can't be helped. Does he have a temp?

P— Yes.

N—Any nausea?

P— No.

N—How long has he been sick?

P— Mostly today.

N—What have you done about the fever?

P— Just watched him. I gave him aspirin in the middle of the night.

N—That's okay, but you should really never give aspirin. It is just not a good idea with children. Get some Tylenol for your medicine cabinet. Aspirin can cause a big problem in some kids. I highly recommend you be careful about aspirin.

P— Okay, how much Tylenol should I give?

N—There are directions on the bottle. Just follow those recommendations and you will be fine.

N—So, he's got a temp. Does he seem lethargic?

P— No.

N—I'll let the doctor know you're here. He'll probably want to run some tests. Okay, be back in minute.

ROLES OF NORMALIZED FAMILY RESOURCE PROFESSIONALS

To work effectively within the family resource model, professionals take on new roles. In addition to providing discipline-specific services, the normalized family resource professionals assist the family as a systems assessor, a systems convener, an activator of informal social support, a provider of information and training to nuclear and extended family members, and, when appropriate, a family therapist. Through this program professionals serve as support to the families' own internal and external social supports.

Role 1: Systems Assessor

The initial task of a family resource professional is to determine the needs of the child within the family system. Within the normalized family resource model, the needs of the whole child can only be fully met as the family's needs are being addressed. Assessment proceeds on a multi-tiered basis, beginning with parental perceptions and concerns regarding the chronically ill or developmentally delayed child, and continuing through identification of more global family issues such as financial and personal stability, depth of informal and formal support mechanisms, and future concerns of individual family members.

Child assessment encompasses a determination of the child's medical and behavioral strengths as well as weaknesses. If a professional is working within an interdisciplinary structure, a team of professionals usually completes this task. If a professional resource person is working alone, complete assessment is usually accomplished through referrals. It is important to determine, for instance, the child's behavioral profile across major areas of development, including cognitive, language, motor, neurosensory, emotional, and independent functioning. Medical needs must be covered in detail in the areas of medications, equipment dependencies, nutritional needs, and home safety regimens. Finally, and probably most important, it is essen-

tial to determine the family's perceptions of the child's needs. Family perceptions are rarely measured, yet it is thought that how the family views the child will be a major determining factor in the degree to which the family participates in needed programs.

Age-appropriate medical and behavioral assessment guides are available commercially. However, standardized guides to measuring family perceptions of their child's development are not available. A Parental Perception Guide has been developed by the chapter authors. This guide is completed by parents and assists resource professionals in prioritizing services.

Part two of the assessment process involves assisting families in identifying informal and formal means of support. This assessment process begins through identification of individual family members' strengths and concerns, and proceeds in highlighting means of informal and formal support. A Family Perception Checklist that may be useful in obtaining this information is also available. This checklist is designed to identify the family's financial and information needs, the current mental health needs of individual family members, and the availability of informal and formal means of support.

Although more detailed and formal means of assessing family concerns are available, these are not recommended as an initial assessment device for a number of reasons. First, traditional family assessment instruments are very time-consuming for the family and the professional to complete and score. Second, few non-mental-health professionals who serve the majority of families with chronically ill children, such as pediatricians and infant educators, are trained in administration of these more extensive types of assessment methodology. Third, highly distressed families tend to become more distressed simply through participation in detailed and lengthy family assessment sessions.

Role 2: Systems Convener

In this role, the professional assists the family in identifying external, informal sources of support. Eco-maps (Dunst, 1985) are utilized to depict the family within its supportive relationships. Relationships that could be reactivated and new relationships that could be developed are pinpointed. As the eco-map is developed, family members' perceptions of those relationships are discussed. The professional discusses the possibility of improving troubled relationships and developing relationships where gaps exist, and acknowledges the strengths of ongoing relationships. The function of the systems convener is to support and extend a family's support network.

Role 3: Systems Activator

As the child and family needs are identified, the professional resource person takes on a new role. This role encompasses activating the appropriate informal and formal support systems needed for this child and family. In this role, the professional assists the family in developing a coherent family plan that denotes individual roles. All too frequently the mother takes on the major responsibility of the time-consuming daily tasks, depleting herself of the energy to meet her own personal goals. Extended family members such as neighbors, friends, and relatives may be enlisted to assist with some of the day-to-day child care, transportation, and special training exercises that the child may require. These same friends and relatives may be enlisted as confidants who listen, provide emotional support, and help the family problem-solve. As informal sources of support are obtained, dysfunctional family patterns begin to be corrected. Social isolation and lack of emotional support is diminished through the involvement of informal support members. Feelings of empowerment and autonomy grow, as individual family members begin to attain personal as well as family goals.

Complementing informal support is the wide range of formal supportive services that many chronically ill and handicapped children require. Most require educational programming, special therapies, in-home nursing care, and specialized medical services from a number of subspecialists. Working within this capacity, the normalized family resource professional assists the family in identifying generic, quality service providers who believe in assisting the child and family to live as normal a life as possible. The normalized resource professional plans for these children to participate in regular educational programs, with special services provided as an adjunct. Medical services are provided through typical pediatric service systems, not state-institutionalized programs for the developmentally delayed. Generic home health-care services are employed where needed, instead of placing the child in a restricted medical setting such as a nursing home or other chronic care facility.

Role 4: Systems Trainer

Parents, siblings, and extended family members require information about their family member's medical and behavioral needs. Families frequently note that information is more vitally needed than therapy. Persons who could provide formal as well as informal means of support to families are reluctant to do so, feeling that they do not possess the special knowledge that caring for these children sometimes requires. A professional resource person working within the normalized family resources model views himself as a clearinghouse for information and pertinent training programs. Just as they recommend service providers to the families, the professional resource person ensures that these providers have the latest information available to serve these children with disabilities. Normalized family resource professionals develop an information and referral system with local educational, medical, and social service personnel who may be specially trained to assist the disabled child. Some may also arrange special training sessions in newly developed techniques such as home monitoring or effective mother-child interaction patterns, to enhance the skills of the family and extended family members.

Preparing the family for upcoming changes in the child's development is another essential part of the systems training role. Anticipatory guidance is a basic tenant of mainstream pediatric practice. Pediatricians have found that by informing parents of soon-to-emerge behavior changes in their child, the parent will have time to prepare emotionally to develop appropriate behavioral responses. Normal children, for example, become fearful of strangers near 8 months of age and tend to become highly distressed in their mother's absence. Informing parents of this normal occurrence and explaining the duration of this behavior assists them in coping.

Role 5: Family Therapist

Raising a chronically ill or handicapped child may disturb internal and external family relationships. Although many parents who have a disabled child do not develop marital conflicts, some do (Rueveni, 1979). Intergenerational alliances may develop in which the mother, for example, becomes over-involved with the handicapped child to the exclusion of the husband or other siblings. Cross-generational alliances may also evolve in which a grandparent may become overprotective of the chronically ill child and label the parent as incompetent.

Because families tend to function as essentially private units, they do not have access to the ways that other families problem-solve during crises. To assist the family in overcoming internal conflicts, the normalized family resource professional may need to assume some traditional family therapy roles. Family discussions may be initiated in which the concept of shared-role responsibility is introduced. The understanding that each family member needs assistance in developing some of his or her own personal goals must be fostered, and the importance of individual members maintaining a degree of personal autonomy must be emphasized.

Family restructuring may be needed in which all members are allowed to participate in major decisions, with all family members helping to perform some undesirable tasks to allow time for each member to pursue personal interests.

The following discussion will illustrate Baby E's case through the normalized family resource model.

CASE STUDY

Baby E was born in a car enroute to the hospital some 85 miles from home at 28 weeks gestation, weighing 800 grams. The first 3 days involved intense observations by an in-house NICU (neonatal intensive care unit) staff, a project nurse specialist, and an infant educator. The initial plan was formulated to avoid overstimulating the baby. This plan included terminating bedside discussions, covering the isolette to minimize sound and light, therapeutic positioning, enhancing the neonate's approach behaviors, and

preventing avoidance behaviors that caused disruption in blood pressure, pulse, and oxygen consumption. As the infant improved and matured, weekly assessments with plan updates were discussed among the interdisciplinary team members. The plans grew to include normalizing sleep/wake patterns by clustering care and scheduling sleep time. Educational concepts were incorporated into daily care routines, such as visual tracking activities during diaper changes and maximum support measures during and after periods of distress. The social-emotional support for this infant was provided throughout the NICU stay by rocking sessions and baby massages.

The family members spoke only Spanish, but were incorporated into the plan through an interpreter. They performed procedures when possible, and learned the individual cues of their baby. The family was unable to visit frequently due to constraints with finances and childcare; however, project staff arranged for home visits during the NICU stay to assess the home environment and to keep the family aware of the child's progress. (The groundwork was laid for the in-home portion of the Extended Clinical Services Program.) Project staff arranged for a home visit during the baby's first week at home, taking care to time the visit so that the family would have a chance to incorporate the baby into the home and establish routines.

Since this child was medically stable, the educational therapist became the contact person for the family. Other professionals were involved through home and office visits at the discretion of parents and the educator. The nurse examined the baby, obtained measurements, and coordinated medical referrals. The infant medical/education plan (IMEP) was expanded to include preventive teaching, nutrition assessments, feeding schedules, well-child care routines, and home safety measures. The infant educator performed periodic assessments to evaluate the child's development in order to formulate appropriate home activities for the parents. Activities were designed around daily tasks to prevent the parents from becoming teachers. Instead the idea was reinforced that learning takes place from moment to moment—not in a 10-minute play session twice daily. The simply written activities were placed on a board and displayed as reminders of developmental objectives. Some examples included fine motor activities (picking up Cheerios during snack time), and language activities (singing nursery rhymes during rocking periods before or after naps). The parents were also encouraged to design their own activities.

Effectively supporting this family was an important component of the IMEP. Such support included securing appropriate medical documentation to prevent deportation to Mexico due to family members' expiring visas. Positive reinforcement was important for the mother and father to improve their self-concepts. Information was regularly ascertained to ensure that the family's basic needs were met in the form of food, housing, and so on. Follow-up after the family's contact with referral agencies that did not have access to a translator helped the family to stay aware of each service provider's plan and observations. The superceding goals in this plan were to assist the family in becoming effective consumers while they provided an optimum environment that would enhance their child's development.

Baby E remains at high risk for developmental delays. However, the baby's scoring was normal to above normal on developmental assessments at 8 months of age. The family is following all plans and suggestions, and the child has been accepted into the family structure without overpowering any one family member. Family members have had their visas extended through the combined efforts of the co-case manager, and will be allowed to stay in this country legally until the baby is no longer at high risk. Tentatively, that will be at about 4 years of age, when lung damage should be repaired and developmentally the child will have a strong foundation on which to build.

Systems Assessor

The child was the subject of intense observation during her stay in the hospital. In this case, the systems assessor was a clinical nurse specialist (CNS). The neonate was assessed and various tools, such as the Newborn Behavior Assessment Scale (NBAS), the 24 hour movement in-

ventory, and daily neurological/physical exams, were used. The systems assessor performed portions of the assessment process and coordinated with the primary nurse and neonatologist to derive the plan.

The CNS referred parental assessment procedures to the infant educator. Again, the results of nursing observations, parental requests, and formal assessments were all utilized in deriving a plan. Home visits were made in an effort to put the family at ease during these intake procedures. The appropriate needs were then identified for the child (Table 1) and the family (Table 2).

Systems Convener

The interpreter and educator were able to locate a friend's family that lived 10 miles away and could provide some emotional support to family. A family friend agreed to relay messages to and provide transportation for the family since she had a phone, a car, and was bilingual. She also was available during home visits. Arrangements were made for the maternal grandparents to come for one month to help with the other children. In addition, an NICU nurse who was bilingual was assigned to this baby, and was available to talk with the parents during hospital visits or talk on the phone when they were able to call.

Table 1. Child's assessment

Strengths		Needs and Concerns	
Medical	Educational	Medical	Educational
Improving lung status	Has clear approach/ avoidance cues	Premature infant	Premature infant
Responding to medical treatment	Visual system intact	No state regulation	No state regulation
Clear cues	Auditory system intact	Respiratory Distress Syndrome	Decreased range of motion of extreme
Intraventricular hemorrhage		Poor muscle tone	Unable to hold/cuddle

Table 2. Family's assessment

Strengths	Concerns
1. Third child	1. No transportation
2. Two-parent family	2. No phone
3. Mother/father interactive when visiting	3. Nearest neighbor 2 miles
4. Other children in school doing well	4. Rural address
5. On Maternal and Infant Health Improvement Act-Maternal Assistance Program	5. Extended family in Mexico
6. Public health nurse available to family	6. Visas expiring soon
7. Nuclear family supportive of one another	7. Spanish speaking only
8. Warm parent/child interaction patterns	8. Not United States citizens
	9. Need for interpreter during parent/physician conference
	10. Limited visitation due to financial and transportation difficulties
	11. Quality of parenting skills low

Systems Activator

The infant educator activated the previously mentioned sources of informal support. The clinical nurse specialist made arrangements for the in-hospital informal support measures.

Formal systems were also identified. The Maternal and Infant Health Care Assistance program was notified of the child's birth by the clinical nurse specialist. Procedures were clarified regarding the medical coverage that this service provides. Through the interpreter, the family was given the necessary information and followed through with all the requests received.

The Public Health Department was a referral agency through which personal contact made by the clinical nurse specialist with a public health nurse relayed the child's medical status and family needs. The contact information was given to the parents so that they had access to the public health nurse.

The neonatologist contacted the general practitioner, who was the family's doctor in their community, and he also relayed the status of the child and/or family, as well as his recommendations for follow-up. All of these formal contacts were coordinated through the infant educator since the parents were most familiar with her. She was responsible for following up with team members to make sure that all identified contacts were made.

Systems Trainer

As each person came in contact with the family, the professional co-case manager served as a liaison. She assisted the family in developing questions for the physician, learning about the equipment involved in their daughter's care, and understanding the educational plan. She helped the parents learn to take an active role during their visits, encouraging them to do diaper changes and feedings when possible.

She also reinforced the teaching initiated by the hospital staff. By being a part of the NICU staff and serving as the professional co-case manager, the infant educator was able to serve as a clearinghouse for both the staff and the family. She could relay to staff the concerns that the family had or critical information derived during home visits; and by being a nonmedical background person she could address issues from a lay-term perspective for the parents.

As the child progressed, she was able to begin discharge planning—making the referrals indicated through the interdisciplinary assessment. The service agencies were contacted prior to discharge, and the referral and intake process was completed so that there was no lapse in service after discharge; intervening agencies were able to begin service immediately.

Family Therapist

Within this family, it was necessary to consider cultural modes when attempting to assist them in the acceptance of this child. In the Hispanic culture, it is the mother's responsibility to perform most of the day-to-day childcare and housekeeping. The goal for this family was to monitor and make sure that the father was included at least passively in all teaching sessions during the NICU stay. It was also necessary to include him in the CPR training. Financial counseling was done with the father privately, because he believed that he is solely responsible for finance matters, which is also culturally induced.

PROGRAM FORMAT: THE INDIVIDUAL SERVICE PLAN (ISP)

Coordinating services for any one child and family requires in-depth planning and periodic reassessment and monitoring. Development of an individual service plan (ISP) is one method that may assist professional resource personnel in providing optimum services. An ISP contains three basic elements. First, the ISP includes a cover sheet with a summary of the child's and family's identification information, accompanied by a concise listing of the child's medical and behavioral strengths and weaknesses, as well as the family's strengths and weaknesses. Second, the ISP provides a delineation of goals matched to service agency objectives for each child and family weakness. Goals and objectives are written in concrete, measurable terms. A service agency that will primarily be responsible for the completion of the program objectives is noted, and a summary statement of the program activities and a projected service duration are listed. Finally, the ISP includes a signature sheet that all major participating persons sign, acknowledging their involvement and agreement with the ISP.

The ISP is similar to a child's individualized education program, but also different in some essential respects. An IEP is designed to plan the child's educational programming in-depth. For instance, detailed language and cognitive activities are written. In contrast, the ISP is a coordinating plan in which all services that the individual child and family may require are listed. No detailed program plans are included for individual services; rather the ISP is an overall road map for the major services that the child and family require. Individual behavioral and medical plans are developed by professionals in each of these areas.

Program Efficacy

Data on the effectiveness of this approach has come from two research-based clinical pro-

grams. One program, the Texas Tech Neonatal Follow-up Clinic, provides specialized pediatric monitiring services to critically ill, low birth-weight infants and their families from the time of hospital discharge through the child's preschool years. These children tend to have a wide range of continuing medical problems upon hospital discharge and are at heightened risk for delayed development. The clinic is staffed by a multidisciplinary team of medical and behavioral professionals. The goals of the program are three-fold: 1) to assess the child's and family's needs, 2) to provide in-home programing when needed, and 3) to refer infants and other family members to community-based programs as required.

Slater, Andrew, Naqvi, and Haynes (1987) recently reported on child and family differences existing between two groups of these children at 36 months of age: monitored and nonmonitored. Monitored participants were defined as those who participated at least annually in the follow-up services. Nonmonitored participants were those who did not attend the follow-up service once each year. At birth the two groups had similar medical and socioeconomic status characteristics. However, by the third year of life the monitored children had a 14 point General Cognitive Index advantage over the nonmonitored group. Examination of process variables revealed significant differences between the two groups, suggesting that the monitored children were raised in more normal, supportive home environments. The monitored home environments were led by parents who reported fewer signs of mental health problems, maintained flexible internal family relationships, and had developed and maintained a more extensive network of informal social supports.

Caution must be exercised, however, in interpreting these results. Since the infants in the above study had not been randomly assigned to monitored versus nonmonitored groups (the groups were formed retrospectively at age 3), it is not possible to determine if the follow-up program was the only significant determining factor. It may well be that the monitored families were somehow more inherently motivated to obtain services.

To determine whether the long-term follow-up care that is based upon the principles of the Normalized family resource model is a primary factor in promoting more normalized infant and family development, Texas Tech Medical School has recently embarked upon a long-term early intervention project in which two sets of high-risk infants and young children are being randomly assigned to experimental and control group status. This program, entitled *Extended Clinical Services*, is designed to provide long-term medical and behavioral programing to two groups of children and their families, including those at risk for delayed development due to very low birthweight and related medical complications, and infants and young children (birth through 6 years of age) who have suffered a documented head injury. The program maintains a family focus, beginning services from the moment of birth (or within 48 hours of head injury or diagnosis of meningitis or encephalitis), and continuing for 36 months after hospital discharge. Throughout all project phases, child and family goals are maintained.

In the short time that this model has been utilized in a federally funded follow-up project for NICU graduates and head-injured children in Amarillo, Texas, it has been proven to be highly successful. Parents have expressed a high level of satisfaction in written evaluations. They also explain that they feel confident in independently addressing the resources that are available to them. Professionals have experienced a high rate of compliance with regard to parents keeping appointments, following through with suggestions, initiating contact in order to troubleshoot problems, and so on. The normalized family resource model has led to an extremely comfortable, highly functional, parent-professional relationship.

Implications for Service Providers

The normalized family resources model provides a workable framework for both in-patient and out-patient services. It can apply to center-based or home-based projects, urban or rural. The model provides one professional who is identified *by the family,* which strengthens that professional's role tremendously. Families are protected from duplicating service agencies and from outdated or unrealistic plans set by agen-

cies who may be unfamiliar with the entire patient/family assessment and history, and most important, they are not overwhelmed by a large number of people intervening in their family. The Normalized family resource model can provide a well-founded, sound plan of service for each individual family through its case management system.

Implications for Future Research

Within the normalized family resource model, the selection of the co-case manager is left up to the family. This would require the family to be aware of the various resources and choose one person to work with them. It may not always be the case that families are aware of the service alternatives. A question that probably needs to be further investigated involves how families find their co-case managers.

The second question is how to ensure that the person selected to be the professional co-case manager has the broad-base knowledge necessary to function in that role. There would have to be some sort of system to ensure that such co-case managers are satisfactory representatives and could provide the necessary expertise.

These are questions that can be answered through the implementation of the proposed model. There are certainly enough positive benefits to convince agencies and families to adopt this method of case management and to begin to research these two questions.

Conclusion

In many respects, the time is right for the implementation of normalized family resource principles by professionals from many disciplines. Many states have presently instituted family support programs; these states provide state dollars or state-supported services to families caring for a developmentally delayed child within their home. Many of these programs assist the family in maintaining stable family relations while the family cares for the disabled child in a home setting. Similarly, federal and state medical professionals are promoting the concept of coordinated, case-managed care for chronically ill children. These professionals also work to assist the family in identifying and coordinating services for the young child. There is even some discussion that private insurance companies and federal Medicaid laws may allow professional re-

imbursement for time and effort spent on coordinated care.

REFERENCES

Berger, M., & Fowlkes, M.A. (1984). A family network model for serving young children with handicaps. In M.A. Slater & P. Mitchell (Eds.), *Family support services: A parent-professional partnership.* Stillwater, OK: National Clearinghouse of Rehabilitation Training Materials.

Carmen, S. (1987). *Personal communication.* Unpublished manuscript, Extended Clinical Services, Texas Tech University Health Services Center, Amarillo, Texas.

Davis, M., & McKay, D. (1973). Mentally subnormal children and their families, *Lancet, 2,* 974.

Dunlap, W.R., & Hollingsworth, J.J. (1977). How does a handicapped child affect the family? Implications for practitioners. *The Family Coordinator, 26*(3), 286–293.

Dunst, C.J. (1985). Rethinking early intervention. *Analysis and Intervention in Developmental Disabilities, 5,* 165–201.

Farber, B., & Ryckman, P.S. (1965). Effects of severely mentally retarded children on family relationships. *Mental Retardation Abstracts, 2,* 1–17.

Heifetz, L.J. (1977). Behavioral training for parents of retarded children: Alternative formats based upon instructional manuals. *American Journal of Mental Deficiency, 82,* 194–203.

Hill, R. (1949). *Families under stress.* New York: Harper & Row.

Hill, R. (1958). *Generic features of families under stress.* Social Casework, Y9, 139–150.

Holroyd, J. (1974). The questionnaire on resources and stress: An instrument to measure family responses to a handicapped member. *Journal of Community Psychology, 2,* 92–94.

Korsh, B.M., & Gozzeric, F.V. (1968). Gaps in doctor-patient interaction and patient satisfaction. *Pediatrics, 42,* 855–871.

Korsh, B.M., & Negrete, V.F. (1972). "Doctor-patient communication. *Scientific American, 22,* 66–74.

MacKinnon, J.R. (1984). Health professionals' patterns of communication: Cross-purpose or problem-solving? *Journal of Allied Health,* 3–12.

McCubbin, H.J., Joy, C.B., Caluble, A.E. Comeau, J.K., Patterson, J.M., and Needle, R.H. (1980). Family stress

and coping: A decade review. *Journal of Marriage and the Family, 42,* 855–871.

Moore, J.A., Hammerlynck, L.A., Barsh, E.T., Spieker, S. and Jones, R. (1982). *Extending family resources: A project of national significance.* Childrens Clinic and Preschool Spastic Aid Council, Seattle, WA.

Nirje, B. (1969). The normalization principle and its human management implications. In R.B. Kugel & W. Wolfsenberger (Eds.), *Changing patterns in services for the mentally retarded* (pp. 231–240). Washington, DC: President's Committee on Mental Retardation.

Rueveni, U. (1979). The family therapist as a system interventionist. *International Journal of Family Therapy, 1,* 63–75.

Slater, M.A. (1984, May). *Survey of statewide family support programs.* Paper presented at the 108th annual conference of the American Association on Mental Deficiency, Minneapolis, MN.

Slater, M.A. (1986). Respite care: A national perspective. In C.L. Salisbury & J. Intalieta (Eds.), *Respite care: Support for persons with developmental disabilities and their families* (pp. 69–96). Baltimore: Paul H. Brookes Publishing Co.

Slater, M., Andrew, L., Naqvi, M., & Haynes, K. (1987). Neurodevelopment of monitored vs. nonmonitored very low birth weight infants: The importance of family influences. *Journal of Developmental and Behavioral Pediatrics, 8,* 278–285.

Slater, M., & Wikler, L. (1984). Normalized family resources for families with a developmentally disabled child. *Social Work, 31,* 385–390.

Wehmen, P., Everson, J., Walker, R., Wood, W., & Marchant, J. Transition services for adolescent age individuals with severe mental retardation. *Adolescent individuals with severe mental retardation.* (pp. 50–76).

Wikler, L. (1981). Chronic stress in families of mentally retarded children. *Family Relations, 30,* 281–288.

Winton, P.J., & Turnbull, A.P. (1984). Parent involvement as viewed by parents of preschool handicapped children. *Topics in Early Childhood Special Education, 33,* 11–19.

CHAPTER 11

Training Respite Care Providers

A Model for Curriculum Design, Evaluation, and Dissemination

Nancy A. Neef and J. Macon Parrish

R elief from caretaking demands and the opportunity to engage in social, personal, and vocational activities are needs that have been identified by parents of both nonhandicapped and handicapped children (Blacher, 1984a; Upshur, 1982a). The need for respite for families with a handicapped child, however, is particularly pronounced. As noted by Cohen and Warren (1985):

> The day-to-day care of a severely disabled child is difficult and stressful because it is unrelenting. Not only does it lack the natural breaks commonly found in child rearing but it also lacks a pattern of changing and decreasing responsibilities for day-to-day care over time. (p. 7).

As a result of the extended duration, increased amount, and more intense nature of the care required of handicapped children, many of these families experience inordinate stress and disruption (Beckman-Bell, 1981; Blacher, 1984a; Joyce, Singer, & Israelowitz, 1983; Tausig, 1985; Wikler, 1981).

In some cases, siblings as well as parents of handicapped children are reported to experience higher levels of stress than those of nonhandicapped children (Powell & Ogle, 1985). The frequent reliance upon siblings to assume caretaking responsibilities, and the disproportionate attention afforded the handicapped child may contribute to other negative behavioral, social, and emotional effects (Fromberg, 1984; Hayden, 1974; Klein, 1972; Seligman, 1983; Travis, 1976; Zatlow, 1982). There is some evidence to suggest that these problems, including family dysfunction, stress, social isolation, negative attitudes toward the handicapped family member, and ultimately, placement of the handicapped family member outside the home, can be attenuated by the provision of respite care (Apolloni & Trieste, 1983; German & Maisto, 1982; Joyce et al., 1983; Lawson, Connolly, Leaver, & Englisch, 1979; Pagel & Whitling, 1978; Webb, Shaw, & Hawes, 1984; Wikler, 1981).

NEEDS AND IMPORTANCE

Despite the extraordinary needs of families with handicapped children in addition to those shared with families of nonhandicapped children, there are often fewer resources available to the families to meet those needs (Salisbury, 1986a). Paradoxically, despite the fact that respite care is the need most often identified as a priority by such families (see Levy & Levy, 1986; Salisbury, 1986a), the problem most often identified by programs has been reported to be the reluctance of families to use the respite care services available (Apolloni & Triest, 1983; Slater, 1986; Wikler, 1981).

The variables that account for this gap between the identification and operationalization of needed services are complex. Results of statewide respite care surveys indicate that availability is limited by inadequate funding (Cohen & Warren, 1985; Cutler, 1986; Salisbury, 1986b; Slater, 1986; Upshur, 1982a; Webb et al., 1984), difficulties in recruiting and maintaining care providers, bureaucratic obstacles (e.g., zoning and licensing regulations), and transportation (Slater, 1986). Problems affecting utilization include the nature and quality of the services, limited awareness of their availability, financial concerns, and reluctance to leave family members with a stranger (Apolloni & Triest, 1983; Cutler, 1986; Slater, 1986; Upshur, 1982a).

Primary Importance of Training Care Providers

Perhaps the most serious and commonly reported problem related to both availability and utilization of respite care services is the lack of *adequately trained* care providers (Cohen & Warren, 1985; Cutler, 1986; Egel, Parrish, Sloan, & Neef, 1984; Salisbury & Griggs, 1983; Upshur, 1982a; Webb et al., 1984). Appropriate training of care providers can affect parents' utilization of respite care in at least two important ways: 1) parents may be more willing to seek services if they are confident that the caregiver is well-qualified to meet their child's needs, and 2) they may be more likely to continue to use respite care services if the experience is positive, and the care provider's preparation enables him or her to interact with the child constructively (Cutler, 1986; Intagliata, 1986). The nature and quality of training can similarly affect the care providers' continued availability in two ways: 1) they may be more willing to initially provide services if they are confident that the training they receive will enable them to care appropriately for the clients, and 2) they may be more likely to continue to provide respite care services if their experiences are positive.

Without the necessary initial investment in training, the problem becomes self-perpetuating; inadequate training results in insufficient opportunities to provide care, and unrewarding care-giving experiences can exacerbate problems with high turnover (Apolloni & Triest, 1983; Slater, 1986). The costs of training new recruits are thus increased and the benefits decreased (i.e., recovery of investment in previous or under-utilized staff). This, in turn, contributes to fewer or less well-qualified care providers whom parents can and are willing to utilize. The families most in need of respite remain un- or under-served.

Despite the well-established need for and importance of adequate training of respite care providers (Salisbury, 1984; Upshur, 1982a), the demand for services has preceded the development of guidelines for ensuring that those who deliver the service acquire the necessary skills. Most reports of respite-care training programs are solely descriptive and do not present detailed information regarding the content, length, method, or evaluation of training. Nevertheless, the initial efforts in this area (Neef, Parrish, Egel, & Sloan, 1985), together with the research findings on effective instructional technology and the evaluation of the available respite care services, suggest several important factors in the design and implementation of respite care training programs.

Factors in Design and Implementation First, it is essential that the content of any training curriculum be *responsive to consumer needs*. This requires the participation of consumers (i.e., families) in judgments of the appropriateness of the *focus* of training (Kazdin, 1977; Wolf, 1978). Families may be more likely to use the services of a program into which they have had input. Unfortunately, the curricular content of most respite care training programs is derived by professionals' individual judgments of what providers should know about caring for developmentally disabled persons, and few attempts have been made to verify the relevance of those skills (Salisbury, 1984). If respite care programs are to have the desired effect on families, the ecological and social validity of the training curricula must be established.

Relatedly, training programs should be *competency-based*. In such a paradigm, the emphasis is placed upon the acquisition and maintenance of skills rather than on the provision of general information designed to increase the trainees' knowledge base. (The parents of a child with epilepsy, for example, would undoubtedly prefer a care provider who had demonstrated his or her performance in appropriately handling seizures to one who could only recite the types of seizure disorders, their prevalence, and associated brain wave patterns.)

By using a competency-based approach that focuses only upon those skills that are frequently required and important in serving the target population (i.e., responsive to consumer needs), it is more likely that the training program will be cost-effective. As noted by Salisbury (1984), the remediation of assessed trainee needs, rather than the presentation of a stock curricular package, will yield the most cost-effective use of the training time. However, in the absence of data regarding the effects of training, it has been impossible to investigate the relative cost-effectiveness of alternative training methodologies. (In order to be cost-effective, not only must the goals of the training be tailored to the needs of the consumers, but the instructional procedures must be tailored to the needs of the trainee.) By conducting cost-effective analyses, the results of training activities in producing desired outcomes can be integrated with their costs in such a way that one can select those training activities that provide the best educational result for the least cost. Given that one of the greatest obstacles to the availability of respite care services is inadequate funding (Ross, 1980), it is essential that the training program be designed to produce skilled providers for the least amount of money in the shortest period of time.

The training program must also be *practical*, that is, one that can be conducted feasibly in service-oriented settings that may be lacking in time, space, money, and expertise. Unfortunately, there is a tendency to rely upon experts for assistance, which not only limits accessibility to training, but also increases the costs. Thus, a well-designed training program is one that can be maintained without extensive resources and ongoing external, expert assistance.

Finally, inherent in each of these components of a quality training program is the need for *evaluation and social validation*. Evaluation and social validation is required to: 1) determine the extent to which the program is meeting the needs for which it was intended (e.g., responsive to consumer needs), 2) generate support for the effectiveness of the program (e.g., in facilitating acquisition of needed competencies), 3) compare alternative methods or approaches (e.g., on dimensions of cost-effectiveness), 4) justify previous or planned expenditures, 5) obtain support for program expansion, and 6) "identify those factors both internal and external to the program or service that facilitate or inhibit it in making its intended impacts (Intagliata, 1976, pp. 264)."

The remainder of this chapter is devoted to specific issues and illustrations pertaining to service design and development, and implementation of respite care training programs that are responsive to consumer needs, competency-based, effective and economical, practical, and that provide for evaluation and social validation. At the conclusion of the chapter, future directions are suggested.

SERVICE DESIGN AND SUMMARY OF KEY FINDINGS

There are several types of respite care programs, which are usually classified according to the location of service provision (either in or out of the family home). Other distinctions include the nature and time period of the service (e.g., day or overnight), the type of worker providing the service, and fiscal responsibility. Models of in-home respite include homemaker/home health aide and sitter/companion services. Models of out-of-home respite include private family homes (e.g., through foster care, respite providers, volunteers, parent cooperative/family respite exchange members, or daycare); respite daycare centers, respite group homes, and residential facilities (e.g., group homes, nursing homes, pediatric hospitals, and state institutions) that maintain spaces for providing respite care. Cohen and Warren (1985) and Levy and Levy (1986) present descriptions, examples, and advantages and disadvantages for each of these models, as well as guidelines for establishing and operating respite care programs.

Regardless of the model used, the qualifications of the care provider remain an important consideration. Thus, the recommendations that follow, although based on the in-home model most widely preferred by parents (Levy & Levy, 1986; Upshur, 1982a,b), are applicable to other types of programs.

Responsiveness to Consumer Needs

Establishing the ecological and social validity of the target skills is an important step toward the development of a respite care skills training curriculum that is responsive to the needs of the families to be served. In order for a program to be responsive to consumer needs, the consumers (i.e., the target service population) must first be defined and identified. An analysis of the demographic characteristics (e.g., age and handicapping conditions) of the children of the families in need of service should provide information that will be useful in guiding the content of the training program. For example, such an analysis may reveal that the few medically fragile children in the target geographic area are being served adequately by home health aides, while there are a large number of older children with behavior disorders whose families require respite; this would indicate that the skills pertaining to behavior management and protective maneuvers with aggressive clients should receive emphasis in the curriculum, while tube feeding and suctioning procedures should not. The information yielded by the analysis may also help to guide the structure of the training program. For example, it may suggest the need to establish a generic set of competencies that are applicable across a range of handicapping conditions that would serve as the core requirements of the training program, with additional competencies delineated for the care of consumer subgroups (e.g., handicapped infants) in which a subgroup of care providers could specialize. Thus, a demographic assessment of the target population may help in tailoring a training program that maximizes resource allocation in relation to consumer needs.

Once the service consumers are identified, representatives of these groups, as well as others who provide services to these children (e.g., professionals and experienced care providers) can be polled to determine the qualifications that they consider to be important for care providers. Direct observation of the providers of respite care whom parents judge to be particularly competent may suggest additional important behaviors. The identified skills can then be operationally defined, and the input of consumers can be solicited in order to reach a consensus regarding priorities. These skills, upon being task-analyzed with the aid of relevant experts, should form the content of a curriculum that is maximally relevant. Ongoing assessment of parents' satisfaction with the services of care providers and the corresponding refinement and updating of the curriculum should help to ensure that it remains so.

A study by Neef et al. (1986) illustrates one of the few reported attempts to involve consumers in the systematic development and validation of a respite care skills training curriculum. In order to derive key skill areas, researchers surveyed the parents of handicapped children (Egel et al., 1984). The parents of the more severely impaired children who posed special feeding and physical management problems were, in particular, concerned about the need for more adequate training of respite care providers. Some of the qualifications cited most frequently as being essential for respite care providers included patience and understanding; dependability; skills pertaining to lifting, transferring, and positioning physically handicapped children; firm and consistent discipline; and management of emergencies. Members of an advisory board composed of parents of handicapped children as well as professionals also provided input regarding the content of the curriculum under development (Neef et al., 1986). Based upon survey responses, suggestions from the advisory board, and observations of actual childcare situations, a provisional task analysis of respite care skills was operationalized. This task analysis was resubmitted to advisory board members, who rated the skills pertaining to their areas of expertise according to whether each was: 1) crucial, 2) important but not crucial, or 3) neither crucial nor important for respite care providers. Skills judged to be neither crucial nor important were omitted.

The content validation process resulted in the identification of the following four major skill domains: 1) preparation and parent interaction, 2) child behaviors, 3) physical/medical management, and 4) emergencies.

Preparation and Parent Interaction   The area of training involving preparation and parent interaction included behaviors such as arriving on time (reflecting "dependability"), and soliciting from and reporting to parents key information pertaining to the care of the child. Interviewing skills were emphasized to teach the care provider to collect any information necessary (e.g., on requisite routines and procedures) to meet the idiosyncratic needs of the child. If, for example, the use of a particular piece of equipment was required, the care provider was instructed to ask the parent to demonstrate its use and then to practice the procedure in the presence of the parent. The potential advantages of this generic skill are that it allows the curriculum to be of reasonable scope while the care provider still acquires first-hand experience from the "experts" (parents), it expands the repertoire of the care provider who thereby acquires specialized competencies that may be relevant to the care of other children with similar handicaps, and it may enhance the trust and confidence of the parent that his or her child will be well cared for.

Child Behaviors The skill domain of child behavior included skills relevant to the management of behavior problems, capitalizing on educational opportunities afforded by routine care activities (thus enhancing the likelihood that the clients would directly benefit from respite care time), and managing mealtime, bedtime, and toilet routines. (Subsequent refinement of this skill area in response to consumer feedback resulted in the addition of competencies in basic manual signs for communicating with nonvocal and/or hearing impaired individuals, and in protective maneuvers with clients who are physically aggressive.)

Physical/Medical Management The area of physical/medical management included skills pertaining to positioning and handling, transferring, and feeding of individuals whose physical handicaps pose special difficulties. In addition, it included medication administration.

Emergencies The training area for emergencies included skills pertaining to the management of seizures and choking (events that are most likely to pose a risk among handicapped populations), the administration of first aid and other medical emergency procedures, and the handling of property-related emergencies.

The respite care behaviors yielded through this analysis constituted the training curriculum. The updated listed of competency areas is presented in Table 1.

Competency-Based Training

The key features of a competency-based training model include the identification and operationalization of target skills, a baseline assessment of trainee performance, the provision of systematic training in those areas in which proficiency is lacking, repeated assessments of trainee performance to determine mastery of the skills trained, and, when necessary, provision of remedial

Table 1. Target skill areas

I.   Preparation/Information/Parent Interaction
    A.   Phone call
    B.   Arrival
    C.   After parents leave
    D.   Parent return

II.   Child Behaviors
    A.   Mealtime
    B.   Toileting (for child who is being toilet trained)
    C.   Behavior problems
    D.   Handling aggressive acts
    E.   Educational opportunities
    F.   Bedtime
    G.   Communication

III.   Physical/Medical Management
    A.   Positioning and handling
    B.   Feeding a child with oral-motor problems
    C.   Medication

IV.   Emergencies
    A.   General medical/property
    B.   Seizures
    C.   Choking
    D.   Bleeding
    E.   Poisoning
    F.   Breathing difficulties
    G.   Shock

training. Unfortunately, most respite care training programs have not been competency-based. The most prevalent method of instruction has been in-service training that centered upon workshops (Salisbury, 1984). In a review of research related to the efficacy of in-service training, Ziarnik and Bernstein (1982) concluded that such training often does not produce changes in trainee performance. They found that the effects of in-service training are frequently small and transient, thereby bringing the cost-effectiveness of this form of training into question. Several strategies can be utilized to enhance the effectiveness of in-service training (Powers, 1983). These include such strategies as systematic instruction within the trainees' work setting, tailoring the curriculum to suit the idiosyncratic needs of individual trainees, the identification of content that corresponds to actual job requirements, involving the trainee in the planning, development, and evaluation of training strategies, and the use of strategies that take into consideration the milieu of the trainees (Salisbury, 1984). Thus far there appears to be relatively little incorporation of these strategies into respite care provider training via workshops.

An alternative to in-service training through

workshops is a competency-based training paradigm (e.g., Lukenbill et al., 1976; Neef et al., 1986). For instance, Neef et al. (1986) evaluated an instructional package, based on a self-directed training manual (Sloan, Neef, Parrish, & Egel, 1986), in the context of a competency-based program for training respite care providers. The manual consisted of the four major content areas delineated in Table 1. The format for each content area consisted of behavioral objectives, an introduction, specific management strategies, examples of and rationale for these strategies, a reading comprehension quiz, an answer key with referral page numbers on which the respective material was addressed, and a remedial quiz with an answer key. Each section of the manual was presented sequentially to the trainees. If, after preparation, the trainee did not demonstrate mastery of the target skills during simulated (through role-play) respite care situations, remedial training was provided. Relevant sections of the manual were reviewed with the trainee, after which the trainer modeled competent performance and then provided feedback as the trainee practiced it. Following completion of the fourth and final section of the manual, if trainees demonstrated mastery of all target behaviors during post-training simulations, a generalization probe was conducted. During the generalization probe, the trainee provided care to a handicapped child at the training site for 45 minutes to an hour, during which time data were collected covertly on the trainee's responses to several situations. These situations included arrival and preparation, parent exit, mealtime (the worker was to prepare a dinner or snack for the child), behavior problems, administration of medication and reponses to any medical problems, toileting, use of reinforcement and naturalistic teaching opportunities, and parent return.

Figure 1 shows the results of simulations of all skill areas conducted before training and after presentation of each section of the manual for six trainees (T1–T6). These data suggest that the instructional package was effective in facilitating acquisition of skills by all trainees. Typically, the percentage of correct responses steadily increased following the successive presentation of each of the manual sections, although some remedial training was necessary in order to achieve skill mastery. Results of generalization probes indicate that all trainees also demonstrated target skills in a respite care situation with a handicapped child.

Cost-Effectiveness

Analyses of cost-effectiveness are especially important at a time when funding for respite care skills training is difficult to acquire (Ross, 1980). Effectively competing for limited funds for training may hinge upon the availability of data documenting that the program is economical as well as effective. Data derived from cost-effective analyses can also be useful in planning and examining budget proposals. Levin (1983) presents several methods for analyzing the cost-effectiveness of educational programs. When using a cost-absorption formula, for example, the expenses for personnel time, materials, and trainee remuneration are totaled and divided by the number of trainees successfully completing the training program; this yields a quotient of the cost of training per trainee. The costs associated with specific training methods can then be compared in order to select the most economical training strategy.

For example, the second experiment by Neef et al. (1986) compared the cost-effectiveness of a competency-based curriculum that was centered upon an instruction manual with one that was centered upon a workshop training format. In the one that was centered upon a workshop training format, the content was derived exclusively from the information presented in the manual. During the workshops, information that was relevant to the successful completion of each item of the task analysis was presented orally and supplemented with videotaped vignettes depicting positive and negative examples of competent performance and/or in vivo demonstrations by staff. Figure 2 presents the results of a multiple-baseline analysis for trainees enrolled in manual-centered (Trainees 1–9) or workshop training (Trainees 10–18), respectively.

The data suggest that the instruction manual approach compared very favorably with the workshop approach. Both training paradigms facilitated acquisition of respite care skills in simulated (role-played) situations, and generalization to situations involving the care of a handicapped

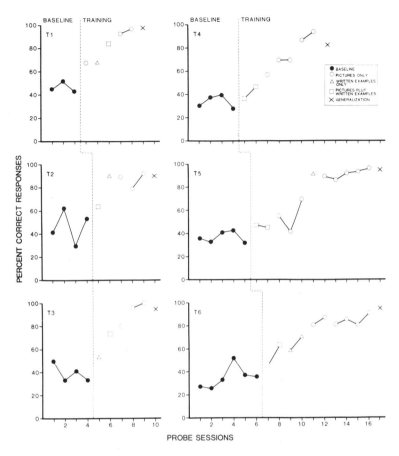

Figure 1. Percentage of correct responses on probes across baseline (closed data points), and generalization (Xs) conditions, for Trainees 1–6. During training, the four sections of the manual were presented sequentially, as indicated by separated data points; connected data points indicate skill areas in which remedial training occurred. Open circles (pictures only), triangles (written examples only), and squares (pictures plus written examples) represent the format of the manual section presented. (From Neef, N.A., Parrish, J.M., Egel, A.L., & Sloan, M.E. [1986]. Training respite care providers for families with handicapped children: Experimental analysis and validation of an instructional package. *Journal of Applied Behavior Analysis, 19* [2], p. 114. Copyright © 1986 by the Society for the Experimental Analysis of Behavior, Inc.; reprinted by permission.)

child, with remedial training required in all cases. However, the manual training package was far more cost-effective than workshop training. The average cost of assisting each trainee to attain mastery using the manual training package was $12.91 versus $43.41 to assist each trainee in workshop training.

Practicality

A training program, no matter how potentially effective, will be of little value unless it is practical to implement. For example, during the second experiment Neef et al. (1986) observed that the development and conduct of workshops was more time-intensive and difficult than the construction and distribution of the manual. Subse-

quent to the disbursement of the manual, the trainees were provided with only the needed remedial instruction. In contrast, the presentation of material via workshops required that the trainers schedule sessions at times convenient for trainees, posing conflicting schedules, repeatedly delivering instructional materials, and arranging make-up sessions. In addition, most trainees stated a preference for reading the manual over participation in the workshops. With ongoing access to the manual, trainees could advance through the curriculum at a self-determined pace, refer often to numerous examples, and test their own comprehension of the content. Furthermore, the manual served as a useful tool for remedial as well as initial training; it could easily

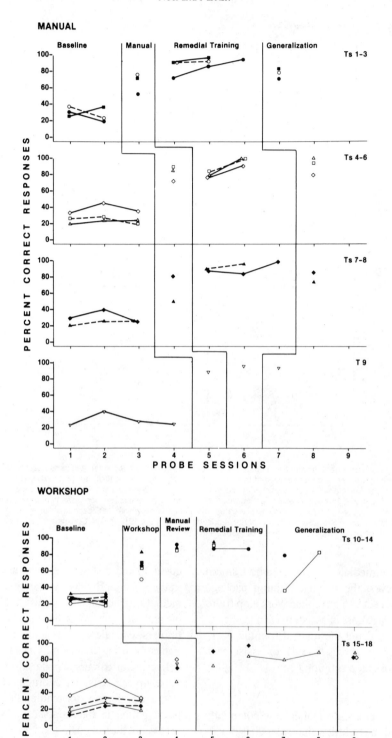

Figure 2. Percentage of correct responses on probes across experimental conditions for trainees in the manual and workshop groups. (From Neef, N.A., Parrish, J.M., Egel, A.L., & Sloan, M.E. [1986]. Training respite care providers for families with handicapped children. Experimental analysis and validation of an instructional package. *Journal of Applied Behavioral Analysis, 19* [2], p. 115. Coypright © 1986 by the Society for the Experimental Analysis of Behavior, Inc.; reprinted by permission.)

be divided into sections that gave the individual trainee more information in areas of identified deficiency.

Although the advantages of competency-based training for respite care services are clear, the resources required to conduct such training (e.g., three or more staff to role-play and observe, and a room equipped to simulate a home environment) are unlikely to be readily accessible to most respite care agencies. In two subsequent experiments, therefore, a simplified training and evaluation package was evaluated that could easily be conducted by one or two trainers, using materials that were inexpensive and commonly available. This streamlined version of the original competency-based paradigm could be effectively employed either by experienced trainers or by indigenous staff within a pyramidal training model (Jones, Fremouw, & Carples, 1977; Page, Iwata, & Reid, 1982) in community-based respite care agencies.

The streamlined training procedure consisted of several steps. First, the trainees were administered a written pretest composed of multiple-choice and short-answer questions related to the target respite care skills. Questions were derived from all of the content areas contained in the manual. The pretests were scored, but the trainees were not provided with performance-based feedback. The scores served as baseline measures prior to presenting the manual. Second, immediately following the pretest, each trainee received a copy of the manual and was informed that he or she would be allowed 6 weeks to read and study the material, and that, in order to be eligible to take the posttest, he or she would be required to show evidence that each of the quizzes in the manual had been completed. Then, approximately 6 weeks later, the trainees were administered a posttest identical to the pretest in terms of the number and types, but not content, of questions. Posttest responses were scored immediately upon completion. For each incorrect answer, the trainer recorded (on a specially prepared sheet) the corresponding section(s) and page number(s) that the trainee was to re-read. Following self-directed remedial training, failed posttest items were re-administered. This procedure continued until each trainee obtained a score of 85% or greater cor-rect on the post test. After meeting this requirement on the written test, each trainee was sent individually to a simulation area, where he or she was asked to demonstrate selected skills in response to scripted scenarios. Specifically, the skills targeted for assessment included lifting, transferring, and positioning a physically handicapped child, feeding a child with oral-motor defects, managing seizures, and handling choking episodes. Behaviors were demonstrated either with a doll (e.g., wheelchair transfers) or with the trainer (e.g., feeding a "child" with an oral-motor problem). For each scenario, the trainer described the task and/or situation, and ongoing events or conditions. No feedback was provided to the trainees until the scenario had been completed and the behaviors had been scored. At the completion of each demonstration, the trainer provided descriptive praise for correct performance and labeled errors; the trainer then modeled the correct behaviors and asked the trainee to practice them while the trainer provided feedback. This process was repeated until the trainee correctly demonstrated all target behaviors in a selected skill area, at which time the next skill area in the manual was assessed. Demonstrations with remedial training continued until mastery was attained in each of the assessed skill areas.

Evaluation and Social Validation

Continued evaluation and social validation of the program is, of course, needed to document its benefits, and thereby justify its continued operation and expansion. Perhaps most importantly, it also provides a means for systematically identifying and introducing needed refinements so that the program can more effectively meet its objectives (Intagliata, 1986).

Testing the trainees' skills before and after training is an important feature of competency-based programs. First, pre-training assessment allows the determination of those skill areas in which the trainee is or is not competent, and tailoring the program accordingly permits more efficient use of time. Second, through repeated measurement of individual trainee performance, a competency-based approach yields a rigorous assessment of whether the training results in the acquisition and maintenance of target skills; attendance at, or participation in, a training program alone does not ensure that the necessary skills have been learned. Unskilled care providers can damage the reputation of the respite care agency, as well as jeopardize the safety of the clients for whom they are responsible. Third, by evaluating trainee performance, the areas in which remedial training is required can be identified. Finally, evaluation data can serve as the basis for making subsequent adjustments in the program to enhance its effectiveness.

Unfortunately, few respite care training programs have provided for systematic evaluation of trainee performance (Salisbury, 1984). The most frequently used method for assessing mastery has been to use written quizzes (Upshur, 1982a; Warren & Dickman, 1981), with no provision for evaluating trainees' actual performance of the requisite skills. Parrish, Egel, and Neef (1986) discuss several alternative methods of evaluating trainee performance. One alternative is direct observation and recording (via a checklist) of trainee performance of target skills by an experienced care provider who accompanies the trainee in the actual respite care situations. Another method involves role-playing, in which target behaviors are demonstrated (and evaluated) under conditions that simulate the natural environment. Neef et al. (1986) found that respite care trainees who performed well in role-played situations also performed well in a respite situation with a handicapped child, although this may be affected by the extent to which actual conditions are approximated.

Social validation measures can also yield useful information in evaluating training programs. *Social validation* typically refers to whether the focus and impact of an intervention are deemed important by the various constituency groups to be served by the intervention (Kazdin, 1977; Wolf, 1978). In their series of experiments, Neef et al. (1986) sought validation from the following three groups: trainers, professionals, and consumers of respite care (parents). Measures of trainee satisfaction with the training program were obtained through a questionnaire adapted from one developed by Larsen, Attkisson, Hargreaves, & Nguyen (1979). In the questionnaire, the trainees were asked to anonymously rate

their satisfaction with training on four-point Likert scales along eight dimensions. Questionnaires were returned by all the participants. Trainees indicated a high degree of satisfaction with the training program, (i.e., all mean ratings were between positive and very positive). Parents of handicapped children who were not recipients of respite care provided by trainees and the coordinator of a county respite care agency participated in an evaluation of the overall quality of trainee performance. Each observer viewed a randomly selected pre- and posttraining videotaped simulation session for at least one trainee. The two tapes per trainee were presented in a random order, and observers were not informed of this order. After viewing each tape, observers were asked to rate the sessions on four-point Likert scales along 10 dimensions. The results indicate that parents and professionals rated trainees' performance substantially higher on posttraining than on pretraining probes in all skill areas.

Families who received respite care by trained providers were asked to evaluate the trainer's performance. The parents were asked to indicate on a stamped, addressed postcard their names, the name of the sitter, the date service was extended, and their degree of satisfaction with the care provided on a 1 (very dissatisfied) to 5 (very satisfied) Likert-type scale. Parents were asked to complete and mail a postcard each time respite care occurred. All parents indicated that they were very satisfied with the performance of trainees. The convergence in ratings across trainees, professionals, and parents, whether they are direct recipients of respite care or not, suggests that the skill acquisition and maintenance achieved through the competency-based training curriculum was considered to be beneficial.

Other Considerations The training of respite care providers, albeit of considerable importance, is not a panacea for the problems relating to the availability and utilization of services. Certainly recruitment is a consideration that interacts with training; although the availability of quality training programs might enhance recruitment efforts, sufficient numbers of persons must be available to be trained. The quantity as well as the quality of care providers is a concern;

the benefits of respite care for families of handi-capped children cannot be realized if only a few care providers are available, no matter how well they have been trained. The low wages typically associated with such roles are an obstacle to re-cruitment efforts (Slater, 1986) that might be at least partially offset by conducting more cost-effective training programs, thereby allowing more fiscal resources to be allocated directly to care providers. Recruitment might be further en-hanced by appealing to population groups who would be attracted by opportunities for part-time employment with flexible hours and to gain job-related experience, and/or who have a particular interest in persons with developmental disabili-ties and their families. High school students in work-study programs or college students en-rolled in social service or special education pro-grams at local universities might be particularly promising candidates, for example (Levy & Levy, 1986). Other potential sources for recruit-ment include civic organizations, senior citizen associations, and churches and synagogues. Re-cruitment strategies include distributing fliers or brochures, making presentations, submitting press releases and public service announcements to the media, placing advertisements in the vol-unteer or classified sections of newspapers, and contacting key individuals (e.g., high school counselors) in programs and organizations (Cohen & Warren, 1985; Levy & Levy, 1986).

A related consideration is the screening and selecting of potential respite care providers. In addition to competencies, personal qualities of the care provider can affect parents' utilization of respite care. Unlike the competencies that are the targets of training, personal qualities are treated as prerequisites. Unfortunately, guide-lines for identifying and assessing the required existing repertoires are lacking. Cohen (1980) (reported in Cohen & Warren, 1985) report 11 qualities of good respite care workers based on a survey of the literature and of the directors of re-spite care programs. Among these are "depend-ability" (e.g., punctuality, low absenteeism), "positive outlook" ("pleasant mood" and "sense of humor"), "good judgment" ("common sense"), "thoughtful consideration and warmth toward client" (e.g., "affection," "empathy," and "con-

cern"), "emotional stability," "flexibility," and "cooperation" (p. 115). It cannot be assumed, however, that these are the characteristics that parents also value most, or even that there would be agreement as to their definition of the pres-ence or absence in the individual.

Finally, the effective matching of respite care providers with families is a variable that would be expected to affect utilization. The factors that must be considered in obtaining an appropriate match are complex, and include time availability of the caregiver, geographic proximity, respite care worker and family preferences, and the worker's skills in relation to the needs of the cli-ent (Levy & Levy, 1986). This would seem to suggest the need for a respite care coordinator who is both familiar with the care providers and families and intuitive enough to use this informa-tion effectively.

FUTURE DIRECTIONS

The preceding discussion highlights the critical need for respite care for families with handi-capped children, and the aspects of service de-livery requiring attention in order to more ef-fectively meet that need. Effecting these changes and services requires educating govern-mental policymakers, administrators, and pro-fessionals staffing human service programs about these needs; it also requires educating con-sumers about *their* needs. Coleman (1972), for example, advocates conducting policy research involving:

> 1) [the identification] of parties interested in policy outcomes and with some power or potential power to affect policy; 2) [determination of the] interests of those parties; 3) . . . the kinds of information [that] are relevant to their interests; 4) . . . the best way to obtain the information; [and] 5) . . . how to report the results. (p. 16)

It is possible to appeal to the interests of pro-gram administrators by reducing financial costs, as proposed in the previous discussion of cost-effectiveness. In addition, individuals can ap-peal to the interests of potential program de-velopers or agency coordinators by reducing re-sponse costs (King, 1981). One marketing axiom explains that the more effort required of the potential consumer, the less likely it is that the product will be purchased. Validated respite care training programs, therefore, need to be packaged so that respite care agency coordinators, with relatively little effort or special training, can implement them.

The training program developed by Neef et al. (1986), although designed to be both economical and easily exportable, may present several associated limitations. Because reading is a relatively time-consuming and effortful means of acquiring information, a curriculum that centers upon this activity (i.e., via a self-instruction manual) may not appeal to a large number of potential trainees, thereby rendering it more difficult to attract and retain recruits. Therefore, it is desirable to develop alternative respite care skills training materials that will minimize consumer effort and that will appeal to potential program adopters.

The popularity of television and video media relative to books suggests that many, if not most, people prefer watching and listening to reading. Therefore, one promising means of training respite care providers is through the use of videotapes. Videotaped curricula, when carefully constructed, can be an effective means of achieving behavior change (Dowrick & Raeburn, 1977; Flanagan, Adams, & Forehand, 1979; Nay, 1975; O'Dell, Mahoney, Horton, & Turner, 1979; Webster-Stratton, 1981a, 1981b, 1982; Winett et al., 1982). Such curricula offer several potential advantages as training vehicles. They may be more economical than previously developed training programs, and can be easily duplicated and exported. The ever-increasing ubiquity of video cassette recorders also enhances dissemination. If properly equipped, agency personnel could implement videotaped training programs without much, if any, direct training by program developers. A video-centered curriculum may be easily disseminated to and maintained by service agencies lacking in time, space, money, and technical expertise. The authors are currently developing and evaluating such a curriculum.

To summarize, it is important to appeal to the legislator's need for model programs that meet special interests, the administrator's need to control costs, the educator's need for improved pedagogic tools, the agency coordinator's need for resources, and the care provider's need for a training program that appeals to their learning profiles and interests, all in order to meet the parents' need for respite.

SUMMARY

Although obtaining adequate child care has been identified as a concern by many parents, this need is particularly pronounced for families with handicapped children. Without respite from the increased demands associated with the care of handicapped children, there is a heightened risk of family dysfunction, stress, social isolation, negative attitudes toward the handicapped family member, and placement of the handicapped family member outside of the home. There is a need for quality training programs that are responsive to consumer needs, competency-based, cost-effective, practical, and that provide for appropriate evaluation and social validation, in order to increase both the availability and the utilization of respite care services. In this chapter, one training model has been presented that may serve to illustrate these important defining characteristics.

REFERENCES

Apolloni, A., & Trieste, G. (1983). Respite services in California: Status and recommendations for improvement. *Mental Retardation, 21,* 240–243.

Beckman-Bell, P. (1981). Child related stress in families of handicapped children. *Topics in Early Childhood Special Education, 1,* 45–54.

Blacher, J. (1984a). Sequential stages of parental adjustment to the birth of a child with handicaps: Fact or artifact? *Mental Retardation, 22,* 55–68.

Blacher, J. (1984b). *Severely handicapped young children and their families.* New York: Academic Press.

Cohen, S., & Warren, R.D. (1985). *Respite care: Principles, programs, and policies.* Austin, TX: PRO-ED.

Coleman, J.S. (1972). *Policy research in the social sciences.* Morristown, NJ: General Learning Press.

Cutler, B.C. (1986). The community-based respite residence: Finding a place in the system. In C.L. Salisbury & J. Intagliata (Eds.), *Respite care: Support for persons with developmental disabilities and their families*, (pp. 167–193). Baltimore: Paul H. Brookes Publishing Co.

Dowrick, P.W., & Raeburn, J.M. (1977). Video-editing and medication to produce a therapeutic self model. *Journal of Consulting and Clinical Psychology, 45*, 1156–1158.

Egel, A.L., Parrish, J.M., Sloan, M.E., & Neef, N.A. (1984, May). *A survey of respite care needs and problems in the community*. Paper presented at the Association for Behavior Analysis Convention, Nashville.

Flanagan, S., Adams, H.E., & Forehand, R. (1979). A comparison of four instructional techniques for teaching parents to use time-out. *Behavior Therapy, 10*, 94–102.

Fromberg, R. (1984). The siblings' changing roles. In E. Schopler & G. Mesibov (Eds.), *The effects of autism on the family*. New York: Plenum.

Gath, A. (1973). The school age siblings of mongol children. *British Journal of Psychiatry, 123*, 161–167.

German, M., & Maisto, A. (1982). The relationship of a perceived family support system to the instructional placement of mentally retarded children. *Education and Treatment of the Mentally Retarded, 17*, 17–23.

Hayden, V. (1974). The other children. *The Exceptional Parent, 4*, 26–29.

Intagliata, J. (1986). Assessing the impact of respite care services: A review of outcome evaluation studies. In C.L. Salisbury & J. Intagliata (Eds.), *Respite Care: Support for persons with developmental disabilities and their families*, (pp. 263–287). Baltimore: Paul H. Brookes Publishing Co.

Jones, F.H., Fremouw, W., & Carples, S. (1977). Pyramid training of elementary school teachers to use a classroom management "skill package." *Journal of Applied Behavior Analysis, 10*, 239–254.

Joyce, K., Singer, M., & Israelowitz, R. (1983). Impact of respite care on parents' perception of quality of life. *Mental Retardation, 21*, 153–156.

Kazdin, A.E. (1977). Assessing the clinical or applied significance of behavior change through social validation. *Behavior Modification, 1*, 427–452.

King, L. (1981). Comment on "Adoption of innovations from applied behavioral research: Does anybody care?" *Journal of Applied Behavior Analysis, 14*, 501–511.

Klein, S.D. (1972). Brother to sister/Sister to brother. *The Exceptional Parent, 2*, 10–28.

Larsen, D., Attkisson, C., Hargreaves, W., & Nguyen, T. (1979). Assessment of client-patient satisfaction: Development of a general scale. *Evaluation and Program Planning, 2*, 197–207.

Lawson, J.S., Connolly, M., Leaver, C., & Englisch, H. (1979). Short-term residential care of the intellectually handicapped. *Australian Journal of Mental Retardation, 5*, 307–310.

Levin, H.M. (1983). *Cost-effectiveness: A primer.* Beverly Hills: Sage Publications.

Levy, J.M., & Levy, P.H. (1986). Issues and models in the delivery of respite services. In C.L. Salisbury & J. Intagliata (Eds.), *Respite care support for persons with developmental disabilities and their families* (pp. 99–116). Baltimore: Paul H. Brookes Publishing Co.

Lukenbill, R., Lillie, B., Sanddal, N., Hulme, J., Calkins, C., & McKibben, M. (1976). *Respite care training manual*. Helena, MT: Developmental Disabilities Training Institute.

McAndrew, I. (1976). Children with a handicap and their families. *Child Care, Health and Development, 2*, 213–237.

Nay, W.R. (1975). A systematic comparison of instructional techniques for parents. *Behavior Therapy, 6*, 14–21.

Neef, N.A., Parrish, J.M., Egel, A.L., & Sloan, M.E., (1986). Training respite care providers for families with handicapped children: Experimental analysis and validation of an instructional package. *Journal of Applied Behavior Analysis, 19*(2), 105–124.

O'Dell, S.L., Mahoney, N.D., Horton, W.G., & Turner, P.E. (1979). Media-assisted parent training: Alternative models. *Behavior Therapy, 10*, 103–110.

Page, T.J., Iwata, B.A., & Reid, D.H. (1982). Pyramidal training: A large-scale application with instructional staff. *Journal of Applied Behavior Analysis, 15*, 335–352.

Pagel, S.R., & Whitling, B. (1978). Readmissions to a state hospital for mentally retarded persons: Reasons for community placement and failure. *Mental Retardation, 16*, 164–166.

Parrish, J.M., Egel, A.M., & Neef, N.A. (1986). Respite care provider training: A competency-based approach. In C.L. Salisbury & J. Intagliata (Eds.), *Respite care: Support for persons with developmental disabilities and their families*. Baltimore: Paul H. Brookes Publishing Co.

Powell, T.H., & Ogle, P.A. (1985). *Brothers & sisters—A special part of exceptional families*. Baltimore: Paul H. Brookes Publishing Co.

Powers, D.A. (1983). Mainstreaming and the in-service education of teachers. *Exceptional Children, 49*, 432–439.

Ross, E. (1980). Financing respite care services: An initial exploration. *Word from Washington, 9*, 1–23.

Salisbury, C. (1984). Respite care provider training: Current practice and directions for research. *Education and Training of the Mentally Retarded, 19*, 210–215.

Salisbury, C.L. (1986a). Parenthood and the need for respite. In C.L. Salisbury & J. Intagliata (Eds.), *Respite care: Support for persons with developmental disabilities and their families* (pp. 3–28). Baltimore: Paul H. Brookes Publishing Co.

Salisbury, C.L. (1986b). Generic community services as sources of respite. In C.L. Salisbury & J. Intagliata (Eds.), *Respite care support for persons with developmental disabilities and their families* (pp. 195–216). Baltimore: Paul H. Brookes Publishing Co.

Salisbury, C., & Griggs, P. (1983). Developing respite care services for families of handicapped persons. *Journal of The Association for Persons with Severe Handicaps, 8*, 50–57.

Seligman, M. (1983). Siblings of handicapped persons. In M. Seligman (Ed.), *The family with a handicapped child: Understanding and treatment* (pp. 147–174). New York: Grune & Stratton.

Slater, M.A. (1986). Respite care: A National Perspective. In C.L. Salisbury & J. Intagliata (Eds.), *Respite care support for persons with developmental disabilities and their families* (pp. 69–88). Baltimore: Paul H. Brookes Publishing Co.

Sloan, M.E., Neef, N.A., Parrish, J.M., & Egel, A.L. (1986). *Functional skills training for day-to-day care of developmentally disabled individuals: A guide for respite care providers and parents*. Portland, OR: Applied Systems Instruction Evaluation Publishing.

Tausig, M. (1985). Factors in family decision making about placement for developmentally disabled individuals. *American Journal of Mental Deficiency, 89*, 352–361.

Travis, G. (1976). *Chronic illness: Its impact on child and family.* Stanford: Stanford University Press.

Upshur, C. (1982a). Respite care for mentally retarded and other disabled populations: Program models and family needs. *Mental Retardation, 20,* 2–6.

Upshur, C. (1982b). An evaluation of home-based respite care. *Mental Retardation, 20,* 58–62.

Warren, R., & Dickman, I. (1981). *For this respite, thanks.* New York: United Cerebral Palsy Association, Inc.

Webb, A.Y., Shaw, H.W., & Hawes, B.A. (1984). *Respite services for developmentally disabled individuals in New York State.* Albany: State of New York Office of Mental Retardation and Developmental Disabilities.

Webster-Stratton, C. (1981a). Modification of mother's behaviors and attitudes through a videotape modeling group discussion program. *Behavior Therapy, 12,* 634–642.

Webster-Stratton, C. (1981b). Videotape modeling: A method of parent education. *Journal of Clinical Child Psychology, 10,* 93–98.

Webster-Stratton, C. (1982). The long-term effects of a videotape modeling parent-training program: Comparison of immediate and 1-year follow-up results. *Behavior Therapy, 13,* 703–714.

Wikler, L. (1981). Stress in families of mentally retarded children. *Family Relations, 30,* 281–288.

Wikler, L.D., Hanusa, D., & Stoycheff, J. (1986). Home-based respite care, the child with developmental disabilities, and family stress: Some theoretical and pragmatic aspects of process evaluation. In C.L. Salisbury & J. Intagliata (Eds.), *Respite care: Support for persons with developmental disabilities and their families* (pp. 243–261). Baltimore: Paul H. Brookes Publishing Co.

Winett, R.A., Hatcher, J.W., Fort, J.R., Leckliter, I.N., Love, S. Q., Riley, A.W., & Fishback, J.F. (1982). The effects of videotape modeling and daily feedback on residential electricity conservation, home temperature and humidity, perceived comfort, and clothing worn: Winter and summer. *Journal of Applied Behavior Analysis, 15,* 381–402.

Wolf, M.M. (1978). Social validity: The case for subjective measurement or how applied behavior analysis is finding its heart. *Journal of Applied Behavior Analysis, 11,* 203–214.

Zatlow, G. (1982). A sister's lament. *The Exceptional Parent, 12,* 50–51.

Ziarnik, J.P., & Bernstein, G. (1982). A critical examination of the effect of in-service training on staff performance. *Mental Retardation, 20,* 109–114.

CHAPTER 12

Using Cash Assistance
to Support Family Efforts

John Agosta

Families who provide care at home to persons with developmental disabilities can face a variety of extraordinary challenges. In response, a growing number of states are implementing programs to support family efforts, with approximately 20 offering cash assistance to families to offset the costs they incur (Agosta, Langer-Ellison, & Moore, 1988).

ISSUES AND UNCERTAINTIES

Plans to implement cash assistance programs often spur lively discussion that revolves around three topics.

Conflicting Beliefs
Regarding Cash Assistance

Should families be given cash to help offset the costs of providing care? This question often prompts debate among professionals and family members alike. Some argue that families are ill-equipped to spend their cash wisely, that the cash will be used to purchase items that are not care-related, or that by receiving cash the families are made needlessly dependent on public support for the long term. Others maintain that the provision of cash assures a flexible response to family needs and reflects a belief that families are responsible caregivers, capable of making informed decisions about the supports they require.

Administrative Uncertainties

Traditionally, a state agency provides for persons with disabilities by either offering services di-

rectly or by contracting with a third party service provider. Providing cash directly to families represents a significant departure from this pattern, and may not be easily incorporated into existing administrative structures. Depending on the state, certain administrative issues may first need to be resolved in order to implement a cash assistance program.

Programmatic Uncertainties

Ideally, families can receive needed supports from the public sector (e.g., public-financed programs), the private sector (e.g., employers, health insurers), and informal support networks (e.g., extended families, friends, neighbors, church groups). The challenge facing policymakers is to define a useful role for cash assistance within the context of these sources of support. Given multiple potential sources of support, how can cash assistance be used most efficiently and with the greatest results?

In this chapter, a variety of issues surrounding these topics are explored. The chapter, divided into six parts, begins with a description of the range of needs that families may have. Second, desired responses to family needs are described, within the context of an empowered family role and complementing sources of support. Third, current state level initiatives are described, along with the role cash assistance could play to help accommodate family needs. Fourth, key administrative issues and several potential limitations associated with a cash assistance approach are examined. Fifth, current information is presented regarding the evaluation of cash as-

Preparation of this chapter was sponsored in part by the Massachusetts Developmental Disabilities Planning Council (Grant #87-IV-1).

Table 1.   Potential challenges that families may face

Potential Challenges Concerning the Family Member with Disabilities:

Health status: Several types of disabling conditions require frequent monitoring of biological functions, requiring that caretakers be knowledgeable about means for coping with chronic medical needs.

Adaptive skills: Persons with mental retardation have problems with learning, while those with disabilities and normal intelligence may acquire skills at a reduced rate due to their physical condition. Regardless of the problem, such persons generally require increased opportunities for learning and can benefit from specialized instructional assistance.

Sociobehavioral skills: The inability to grasp concepts quickly, diminished capacity to communicate, or the frustrations of having a disability can result in challenging behavior. Eliminating such behavior can require extraordinary effort from parents and may necessitate consultation with a specialist.

Other developmental skills: Persons with disabilities may require specialized treatment such as communication training or physical therapy, or they may require a variety of prosthetics.

Potential Challenges Concerning Caregiving Family Members:

Natural reactions: The discovery that a family member has a disability can result in a sense of shock or numbness, denial, grief, shame, guilt, or depression.

Chronic stress: The added responsibilities can affect family interactions and functioning.

Dramatic changes in lifestyle: The arrival of a family member with a disability often affects past established social relationships within the family, or with others.

Financial costs: Lost opportunities for employment or education can challenge family members of persons with disabilities.

Extraordinary time demands: Family members are often faced with providing personal care to the family member with disabilities, finding needed specialized professionals, or negotiating bureaucratic systems.

Difficulty with physical management: Lifting, carrying, and/or handling challenging behavior of a person with a disability often confront a family member.

Difficulty in undertaking family routines: Shopping and house cleaning, or finding ample time for recreation, may require additional planning.

Lack of skills needed to cope: Parents may not be prepared for potential medical emergencies and/or to teach necessary adaptive skills.

---

sistance programs. Finally, discussion is offered concerning the future directions of cash assistance practices.

THE RANGE OF FAMILY NEEDS

Families who provide care at home must implement specialized care routines while attending to normal family functions. Because of the added responsibility, these families can face a variety of challenges over and above the normal ones associated with bringing up a child (e.g., Agosta & Bradley, 1985; Batshaw & Perret, 1986; Hobbs & Perrin, 1985; Lapham & Sherlin, 1986; Longo & Bond, 1984; Turnbull, Summers, & Brotherson, 1985; Wikler, 1986). As can be understood from numerous sources, these potential challenges pertain to the entire family unit as well as its member with disabilities (see Table 1).

Available research suggests that the difficulties actually experienced by individual families are related to many factors, including the degree of the family member's disability, the presence of challenging behavior, family characteristics, specific parenting patterns, the family's capacity for coping with adversity, and the availability of community support services (Agosta, Bass, & Spence, 1986; Crnic, Friedrich, & Greenberg, 1983; Tausig, 1985). As a result, although not all families who provide care at home have extraordinary problems, all are more at risk for having difficulties than are families without members with disabilities.

Table 2 shows a range of supports that may be needed to overcome care-related difficulties; in addition to the direct services that persons with disabilities may receive, family members may also need support to ease the day-to-day demands of providing care at home, and to enhance their capacity to function as a family. Of course, not all families require all services. Every family is different and requires a unique cluster of services, some of which may not be displayed in Table 2. Moreover, the needs of any

Table 2. List of services that might be required

Home-based services centered around the person with
   disabilities
Diagnosis and assessment
Educational/therapeutic services
Medical or dental services
Home health care
Recreational opportunity
Special clothing
Special diets
Transportation
Adaptive equipment
Housing adaptations
Adequate health insurance

Home-based services centered around family
   members
Information and referral
Temporary relief/respite
Family counseling
Parent/sibling education
Day care
Housekeepers
Cash assistance
Future financial planning
Mutual support groups
Adequate housing

given family are not fixed, but often shift in face of changing family circumstances or as the family moves through its life cycle (Konanc & Warren, 1984; Suelzle & Keenan, 1981; Turnbull et al., 1986).

An Effective Response to Family Needs

Although providing care at home to a child with disabilities can be a challenging task, most families reject out-of-home alternatives in favor of continued care at home, especially during the early stages of the child's life (Ashbaugh, Spence, Lubin, Houlihan, & Langer, 1985; Lakin, Hill, & Bruininks, 1985; Perlman, 1985). The recognition that many persons with disabilities live at home with their families prompts concern for ensuring that these persons receive the services that they need, and that the efforts of their families are supported and enhanced. For policymakers, once a commitment is made to family-based care, this often leads to concerns about the types and amounts of family-related services that should be offered, and how they should be administered.

An effective response to family needs requires that a comprehensive and flexible array of supports be made available. Furthermore, there is a growing consensus that those supports that are offered should be administered so that they are family-centered, culturally sensitive, community-based, and well coordinated (e.g., Agosta & Bradley, 1985; Turnbull et al., 1986; United States Congress, Office of Technology Assessment, 1987). Within this context, providing cash assistance directly to caregiving families is a programmatic option that must be considered carefully.

Family-Centered Approaches Many of the family-oriented models of service that have emerged in the past decade have embraced a family-centered philosophy. In reality, however, most state and local systems are just beginning to comprehend the implications of this concept. As used here, the notion of a family-centered philosophy contains three conceptual underpinnings.

First, services should *enable and empower family members to make informed decisions.* Service models must be founded on the presumption that families are potentially capable and willing to make responsible decisions, and that families want the best for their children. This stance is based in a social systems perspective (e.g., Rappaport, 1981) and suggests two subsequent conditions. The first condition is that family members who fail to display needed skills do so not because of irreconcilable personal deficits, but instead do so primarily due to an absence of sufficient opportunities to acquire needed competencies. Consequently, Dunst (1986) suggests that family members should have "enabling experiences," whereby competence can be displayed or learned. The second condition is that if family members are to claim control over their lives (i.e., become empowered), then they must attribute the changes in their lives to their own actions. Given these conditions, the challenge for service practitioners is to establish partnerships between families and professionals that enable and empower service consumers to the maximum feasible extent (Slater & Mitchell, 1984).

Of course, there are limits to the emotional, physical, and financial resources of parents. When first confronted with the reality of a disability, many family members have little understanding of the overall needs that they or their children will have. Moreover, even as time passes, some families are unable or unwilling to accept an empowered role. Yet the absence of needed skills among some or the reluctance of others does not justify the substitution of professional judgement in all cases.

A second concept of a family-centered philosophy is that services should *be responsible to the needs of the entire family unit.* Johnson (1979) notes that within a family-systems framework, the family is viewed as an interacting and reacting system that is delicately balanced and struggles to maintain that balance. A change or problem in one aspect of the system affects the entire system. Thus, family support and case management practices cannot be directed solely at the needs of the child. Rather, supports should be available to other family members as well, with the intent of enhancing the family's overall capacity to provide care.

A third concept is that services should *be flexible enough to accommodate unique needs.* No two families, with or without children with disabilities, are alike. Considerable variation exists between families regarding disability types and severity, family characteristics and resources, and family perceptions regarding the caregiving situation (Agosta et al., 1985; Sherman, 1988; Tausig, 1985; Wikler, 1986). Moreover, these factors are not static, but evolve over time (Turnbull et al., 1986). These considerations suggest that responsive programs must permit a wide array of supports (i.e., multiple support options) and must encourage each family to select those options that are most appropriate to its needs.

Culturally Sensitive No single approach to supporting families is likely to work with all families. Differences in family type, culture, income, and geographic location call for diversity in the approaches undertaken (Agosta, O'Neal, & Toubbeh, 1987; Dunst, 1986; Turnbull et al., 1986). To be the most effective, support services must be consistent with the culturally based preferences of individual families. This holds true regardless of the number of families sharing a particular belief system or the degree of difference between the dominant and minority cultures. Further, the same principle can be applied to areas other than cultural differences, including race, geographic diversity (e.g., urban

vs. rural) or socioeconomic status (McGoldrick, Pearce, & Giordano, 1982; Turnbull et al., 1986; Wells, Agosta, Berliner, Cox, & Bedford, 1988).

Community-Based Historically, the primary response to disability has been to provide services through the public sector. Present practice, however, relies increasingly on alternatives that are available in the private sector or within informal helping networks to complement public sector initiatives. To some extent, this shift is based on the belief that supports are most effective and least costly when their source is closest to the family, in terms of both geographic and personal proximity (Dunst, 1986; Hobbs, Dokecki, Hoover-Dempsey, Moroney, Shayne, & Weeks, 1984).

Many supports can and should be available through informal or private sector means (e.g., extended families, employer benefits, private health insurers) (Akabas, 1984; Dunst, 1986; Griss, 1988; Piccione, 1982). In fact, by focusing on public sector solutions exclusively, the existing support networks of a family may inadvertently be displaced or other potential sources of support may never be utilized (Hobbs et al., 1984).

The fact that informal social support can have a positive influence on family well-being is extensively documented (e.g., Cohen & Syme, 1985; Dunst, 1986; Wells et al., 1988). Such support, typically found through friendship or ongoing interaction with the extended family, can play a key role in easing the day-to-day challenges by alleviating their negative impact on the family, promoting the family's integration into the community mainstream, or promoting smooth family functioning (e.g., Dunst & Trivette, 1986, 1987; Moore, Hamerlynck, Barsh, Spieker, & Jones, 1982; Wikler, 1986).

Likewise, the potential usefulness of supports offered through more formal private-sector structures should not be ignored. Every community contains businesses or organizations that may prove helpful to families. For instance, local building contractors may find ways to make a home barrier-free. Day care operators, with some specialized training, may be persuaded to serve children with severe disabilities. And employers can tailor their benefits packages to satisfy individual family needs. Although the role that could be played by formal indigenous networks is only now being explored systematically, policy and practice in support of families can begin by encouraging a sense of community and mutual aid (Akabas & Krauskoff, 1984; Hobbs et al., 1984; Schwartz, 1987).

Existing private or informal community support structures are not likely to meet the range of complex needs of children with disabilities and their families; public funds and resources will continue to serve as a necessary complement. For example, children with severe physical limitations or chronic illnesses may require the services of specialized professionals (e.g., Batshaw & Perret, 1986; Goldfarb, Brotherson, Summers, & Turnbull, 1986; Hobbs & Perrin, 1985). Likewise, family members might benefit from formalized supports that are not typically available within natural community helping networks, such as future financial planning relevant to their member with disabilities, or disability-related information and referral (e.g., Agosta & Bradley, 1985; Parrott & Herman, 1987).

Comprehensive and Well Coordinated Approaches

Numerous programs exist for providing services to children with disabilities and their families. Examples include those offered through: 1) state disabilities agencies or Developmental Disabilities Councils, 2) the public schools as mandated by PL 94-142 (*The Education for All Handicapped Children Act of 1975*) and subsequent amendments, 3) university programs supported by federally financed demonstration projects and/or through a university affiliated facility (UAF) or project (UAP), and 4) private sector initiatives sponsored by employers, private businesses, charitable foundations, or specialty-care settings such as hospitals that offer a range of family supports.

Although these programs vary as to target population and services provided, they are part of the potential network of supports that could be used to benefit children with disabilities and their families. Taken together with informal helping networks, the challenge facing service practioners is twofold: 1) to match child and family needs with appropriate supports, and 2) to build a comprehensive circle of supports around

the family unit that takes efficient and effective advantage of all available community resources.

Match Needs to Resources Dunst (1986) explains that to maximize the positive impact of supports, a satisfactory match must be made between the nature of the support sought and the type of assistance provided, based on the unique needs and preferences of individual families. For instance, when a parent indicates a pressing need for housing adaptations to accommodate a child with severe physical limitations, and the needed modifications are made, the assistance is likely to have beneficial outcomes for the child and for other family members as well. In contrast, where there is a mismatch between the type of help desired and the supports available, family circumstances will probably not be improved. For example, when a parent's needs for periodic respite are unpredictable, respite services predicated on a two-week notice will do the parent little good. Carried further, this mismatch of resources to family need could have a serious negative impact on the family's capacity to provide care at home.

Build a Circle of Supports around Families Figure 1 shows the family unit surrounded by three potential sources of support. Families and their children can benefit from the efforts of the public sector, the private sector (e.g., health insurers, accommodating employers, day care operators, officials at local banks), and the informal efforts of a variety of caring persons. The challenge facing service practioners is to weave together these three sources of support so that the child with disabilities receives needed habilitative or health related services, the family members receive the supports they need to enhance their capacity to care and to function as a family, and potential community-centered helping networks, outside the public domain, are utilized to the extent feasible (See Hobbs et al., 1984).

STATE-LEVEL EFFORTS AND THE ROLES THAT CASH ASSISTANCE COULD PLAY

Current State Level Efforts

Using variations of the concepts described above as foundations, many states have recently imple-

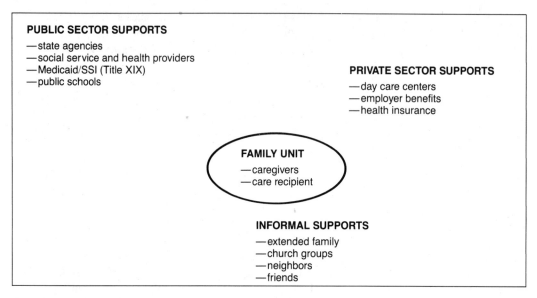

Figure 1.   The family unit and three sources of support services.

mented programs to support family efforts (Agosta, Jennings et al., 1985; Bates, 1985; Bird, 1984). In general, these programs use either a support services approach exclusively or provide cash assistance in combination with support services. A *support services approach* primarily provides families with free in-kind habilitative materials or services. In these programs, states fund various agencies, which in turn provide specified services. It is the most frequently used means of administering a family support system.

By contrast, *cash assistance programs* provide money directly to families to offset care-related expenses. In such programs, families either receive a periodic subsidy or stipend to pay for future expenses or receive reimbursement for the costs that they actually incur. Restrictions may be placed on the types of expenses to which the cash may be applied, and family members may need to show receipts to document how the cash was spent. These programs typically provide cash assistance in combination with support services, with the actual mix between the two primary approaches varying by program.

In addition, most programs are rather limited in scope and vulnerable to shifting political priorities. Although there are exceptions (e.g., Wisconsin, Michigan), such programs generally offer few services to relatively few families,

place restrictions on the types of supports that may be acquired, do little to utilize existing community helping networks, and are slow to offer family members an empowered role (Agosta, Bradley, Rugg, Spence, & Covert, 1985). Further, because these programs are usually funded primarily with state dollars, they are relatively expensive to operate from the state's perspective, especially when compared to initiatives that can utilize federal matching funds, such as the Title XIX Medicaid program (Castellani, 1987; Lakin et al., 1985). Thus the magnitude of the fiscal and programmatic resources allotted to these programs still pales compared to what is spent on out-of-home alternatives (See Agosta & Bradley, 1985; Braddock, Howes, & Hemp, 1984).

Offering families cash to offset the challenges of providing care at home could play a useful role in enhancing family efforts and in strengthening the composite effects of all available supports. The potential value of cash assistance approaches can be considered from both a family and a system perspective.

Cash Assistance from the Family's Perspective

Receiving cash assistance can provide family members with *control* over the source of the supports acquired and the *flexibility* to accommodate unique child- or family-related needs. In this regard, the administrative merits of a support service, strict cash assistance, or a combination approach can be contrasted. Although the underlying goal of each approach may be to provide families with the supports they need, the processes by which this goal is pursued differ significantly. Figure 2 displays the three administrative strategies in terms of how services are funded and ultimately secured.

Figure 2 shows that, in a support service program, the funder (e.g., state department of human services) contracts with a third party agency, which in turn provides services to families. This approach may be the least responsive to the needs of families because service agencies may not offer all those supports a family may need, such systems are not often sufficiently flexible to accommodate unique family needs, and families are not empowered so that they can choose from whom they will receive needed supports.

By contrast, in a strict cash assistance approach, the funder provides dollar resources directly to families, who in turn select and pay the support agent(s) of their choice. On its face, this approach empowers families and encourages service providers to be directly accountable to family members. However, potential problems may be that: 1) where few services exist, families may not be able to purchase needed supports, 2) family members may not have sufficient information for making informed choices, and 3) some families may not wish to play such an empowered role.

A combination of the first two approaches can

be used to offset the disadvantages of either strategy, while building on the strengths of each. With this combined approach, the funds may be provided directly to either families or service agencies, depending on the type of support needed, family preferences, or other factors. This approach may represent the most promising means of crafting an effective partnership between families and professionals, because it encourages both to be active and cooperative participants in the service delivery process. Further, while embracing aspects of a support service approach, this approach ensures that family members have some amount of cash on hand to accommodate unique needs, or to otherwise enhance family functioning.

For instance, given the availability of cash assistance, families in need of major housing adaptations, often a costly endeavor, can reach agreement with a local building contractor and finance the renovations through a bank, using the cash to make monthly payments on the loan. Other families, who have health costs that are not covered by the terms of an insurance policy, can use the cash to offset those expenses. In fact, the cash supplement may make it possible for some families to make payments on insurance premiums. Likewise, in securing temporary relief (i.e., respite care), some families may prefer to choose their own respite care providers and to pay them a fee of their own choosing.

Cash assistance may also be used to meet other unique needs. Regarding the costs associated with family care, mothers who give up their jobs to provide care at home may rejoin the work

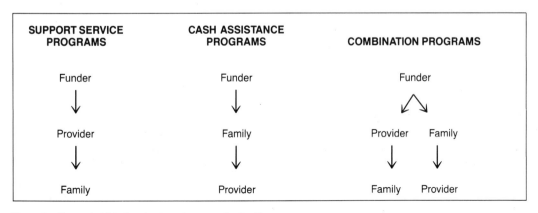

Figure 2. Three administrative structures for supporting families.

force by using the cash to pay for daycare, or they may use it to achieve previously abandoned educational goals in order to acquire higher paying employment. Others, after years of lifting and carrying a child with physical disabilities, may develop physical limitations and could use the cash to pay for adaptations or professional advice needed for themselves. Likewise, the family may use the cash to help support a family outing or simply to help with general finances.

Cash Assistance from a System Perspective

From a system perspective, providing families with cash assistance can help to extend the circle of supports around families and to fill the existing gaps in services without expanding the role of public sector interests. For instance, where respite care is needed, the state may elect not to fund formalized respite care agencies exclusively, but may opt to place some funds directly into the hands of families and encourage them to use the money to secure their own relief. Likewise, where the family requests professional counseling, providing cash may allow the family to see a counselor of their own choice, without the state or some proxy agency having to make the service available. In essence, a cash approach can simplify and enhance the service delivery process by eliminating the need in all cases for involving a vendor agency holding a contract with some office of the public sector.

KEY ADMINISTRATIVE ISSUES

Administrative Concerns

Designers of cash assistance programs must resolve numerous administrative issues, many of which are interrelated. Six such issues include: 1) deciding on the purpose of the program and the role of the family, 2) setting eligibility criteria, 3) determining how much cash will be provided, 4) deciding what the cash can be used to purchase, 5) determining how the cash will be disbursed, and 6) identifying and overcoming potential inter-agency conflicts or regulatory barriers.

Program Purposes and the Role of the Family   Toward what end should cash be offered to families? Little disagreement exists that

some primary program goals should be to prevent unnecessary out-of-home placement, to ensure that the person with disabilities receives needed services while at home, and to enhance family functioning (Agosta & Bradley, 1985). The role that cash assistance should play within this context is not universally agreed upon. For instance, the potential flexibility associated with cash assistance approaches may trouble those who believe that the cash should be used exclusively to purchase supports that are directly related to the care of the person with disabilities, and not spent on other items that are indirectly associated with such care (e.g., foodstuffs for the entire household). However, this position fails to consider that although meeting the needs of the person with disabilities is essential, enhancing overall family functioning is an important outcome as well, having been associated with continued care at home and improved family coping (e.g., Moore et al., 1982; Parrott & Herman, 1987; Turnbull et al., 1986).

A related issue concerns the role families should play in directing how their cash can be spent. Much of the policy and practice in the human services field typically discounts the family's role in providing care, presuming familial incompetence or dysfunction while relying on professional judgment (Dunst, 1986). The degree of control held by families within existing family support programs is not clear, although the addition of a cash assistance approach may carry greater potential for empowering families than can support services alone, by providing each family with greater control over the acquisition of needed supports. Yet some may question the intentions of family members or doubt their competence to make informed decisions; these concerns are not easily ignored, given that some parents may misuse the cash, either intentionally or not. Where cash programs have been initiated, however, misuse is the exception rather than the rule (Parrott & Herman, 1987; Rosenau, 1983). Moreover, if coupled with systematic feedback, actions interpreted as misuse by professionals may be translated into a concrete enabling experience for family members. In other cases, the roles may reverse themselves as family members broaden the professionals' appreciation of the wide range of activities that can be used to enhance family functioning.

Program Eligibility The question of who should receive services is a perplexing one that severely tests a society's capacity for distributing scarce resources equitably to those in need. For admittance to any family support program, prospective consumers must first satisfy the criteria established by the administering agency (e.g., Department of Human Services) concerning the person with disabilities. In addition, other eligibility criteria may also be imposed, such as those pertaining to the family's fiscal resources (e.g., a means income test), the placement status of the family member with disabilities, or an assessment of the family's need for cash.

Amount of Cash Provided Decisionmakers may elect to "cash out" the entire family support system, providing families with relatively large amounts of money to acquire whatever supports are deemed necessary. However, in an alternative approach, families may be provided a small monthly cash allotment to complement the support services that they regularly receive.

Permissible Purchases A key to the design of a cash program is to construct a set of guidelines regarding permissible purchases. Such determinations will be based on the program's underlying values and overall purposes, and the array of support services already available. Where the program's values and purposes are narrow or centered exclusively on the person with disabilities, the array of supports for which cash may be used could be restricted. Likewise, depending upon the array of supports already available, decisionmakers may choose not to undercut existing providers, opting instead to confine cash purchases to supports not already available through the public sector.

Means of Cash Disbursement and Accountability Should parents be provided cash prior to purchasing the needed services, or should they be reimbursed after they have already incurred certain service-related expenses? Receiving cash prior to purchasing services could relieve the strain on family resources. In contrast, decision makers might prefer a reimbursement strategy because it would be easier to direct and track what is purchased.

A related concern involves the level of accountability that will be expected of family members. After the cash is disbursed and the desired supports are purchased, will receipts need to be submitted? Some may argue that because public dollars are involved, family members must document exactly how their cash was spent. Others, noting that those who receive Supplemental Security Income (SSI) through the Social Security Administration need not show exactly how those dollars are spent, may claim that keeping track of how the cash is spent adds a needless demand on the family, and reflects a lack of trust in families that is unwarranted.

Overcoming Potential Interagency Conflict or Impeding Regulations Each program in a public helping network is typically assigned a specialized mission pertaining to human needs, resulting in divisions of responsibility. As needs are identified, the consumer is passed along to the appropriate agency. However, providing cash to families may undermine this tradition, because it could expand the bounds of the family support program to encompass needs that are typically met through other public sector auspices. For instance, where families have little income, should the cash acquired through a family support program be used to purchase food or shelter? Or should the family be advised to petition other components of the public system to obtain food and adequate housing, saving their family support cash for care-related expenses?

Another area of concern involves the impact of existing bureaucratic regulations or precedence. For example, in some states (e.g., Massachusetts) the public dollars that are allotted to certain social endeavors must often be spent according to the determined rates or costs associated with specific services, leaving little room for families to choose supports that are not considered previously by the state or to adjust costs. Similarly, though a state may not take issue with families who use public dollars to complete needed housing adaptations, a significant concern may surface if the adaptations enhance the value of the property. Although neither condition presents an insurmountable barrier to the implementation of a cash assistance program, these examples indicate that, in some instances, policymakers may need to tailor a program to satisfy prevailing state standards or alter impeding regulations.

Finally, how will the cash that is received by families be viewed by other public entities? For example, should the cash that is received by parents be considered taxable income? If that money is viewed as income, the state could be placed in the undesirable position of subsidizing federal tax revenues. Further, such income could jeopardize a family's eligibility for other public assistance benefits (e.g., food stamps, Medicaid). In contrast, in Michigan, where cash assistance is viewed as a public benefit, the cash received by parents is not taxable and does not affect a family's eligibility for public assistance.

Nonadministrative Concerns

The utility of a cash assistance approach may be tempered by at least four additional concerns: 1) ensuring that family members are "wise consumers," 2) meeting the needs of families facing multiple challenges, 3) the potential for fostering dependence on the cash assistance, and 4) ensuring that the needed supports are actually available for purchase.

Ensuring that Family Members Are "Wise Consumers"   A necessary foundation for cash assistance programs is the presumption that family caregivers have sufficient knowledge regarding the needs of their member with disabilities and the quality of available services. To the extent that they do, the chances of their spending their cash efficiently are improved. But some parents may be unprepared to choose and purchase services wisely, or may feel unsure of their decisions (Wells et al., 1988). Thus, complementing cash assistance programs with case consultant services and family education may be advisable, in order to provide family members with the knowledge or enabling experiences that are needed to choose appropriate services (Wikler & Keenan, 1983; Wray & Wieck, 1985).

Meeting the Needs of Families Facing Multiple Challenges   Some families are challenged by circumstances beyond those related to their member with disabilities (Wells et al., 1988). Some might include chronic unemployment of a primary wage earner, drug or alcohol dependency in a family member, criminal offenses committed by a family member, or physical abuse inflicted by a family member on other members (Parrott & Herman, 1987). As a result, a variety of public sector agencies may be involved with the family, or should be. In such cases, the role of cash assistance, and a family support program in general, must be carefully considered in relation to other family circumstances and the efforts of other human service workers.

Fostering Dependence on Cash Assistance   Providing families with a cash supplement effectively extends the family's income, especially if few restrictions are placed on how the cash is spent. Some families may choose to spend their allotment to upgrade their standard of living (e.g., move to more costly housing), or to extend their resources further (e.g., take a loan to have needed housing adaptations completed). By doing so, families may become dependent on the cash assistance for the long term, which is an undesired outcome given an overall program goal of reducing unnecessary family dependence on the public sector.

Assuring that Needed Supports Are Available for Purchase   When families are provided with cash assistance, it is presumed that the supports that are needed will be available for purchase and that they will be easily accessible. Where this is untrue, the benefits of providing cash to families may be diminished. In response, states may first need to establish certain frequently demanded services (e.g., respite care), perhaps through the existing disabilities provider network or by creating incentives for private businesses (e.g., daycare centers) to develop needed supports.

For the less frequently demanded supports (e.g., housing adaptations, special equipment), computerized information networks can be used to form a directory of available sources of support (e.g., suppliers of special equipment, building contractors) to link families with needed services, both locally and regionally. Family satisfaction with these services can also be tracked, to help families choose between competing services and to prompt businesses to provide services of the highest caliber.

EVALUATION OF EXISTING CASH ASSISTANCE PROGRAMS

Table 3 presents the dates of program inception in 20 states that presently offer families cash assistance through family support initiatives

Table 3. Twenty states offering cash assistance programs

1. Colorado (1986)
2. Connecticut (1981)
3. Florida (1978)
4. Idaho (1981)
5. Illinois (1988)
6. Indiana (1982)
7. Louisiana (1983)
8. Maryland (1984)
9. Michigan (1984)
10. Minnesota (1975)
11. Montana (1975)
12. Nebraska (1982)
13. Nevada (1981)
14. North Dakota (1981)
15. Oregon (1988)
16. Pennsylvania (1988)
17. Rhode Island (1981)
18. South Carolina (1974)
19. Wisconsin (1984)
20. Texas (1988)

Source: Agosta, Langer-Ellison, and Moore (1988).

(Agosta et al., 1988). Obtaining exact counts of such programs is a difficult task, given that the initiatives that are undertaken through the state mental retardation or disabilities service system can be complemented by supports made available through other sources (e.g., the public schools, hospitals), and that the circumstances within states are continually evolving.

As of the late 1980s, few evaluations of any family support programs have been undertaken to identify potential means for improving administrative practices or for assessing their effects. Fewer still have focused on cash assistance initiatives (Agosta & Bradley, 1985). What follows is a presentation of findings that were generated by evaluations of cash programs that have been completed thus far, from the perspective of both system-level decisionmakers and individual families.

System-Level Findings

Regarding *service processes,* the family support program in Florida has been examined to improve administrative practices. Problems were identified in the areas of staffing for family support services and the amount of time taken to reimburse parents for the costs of certain services (Bates, 1985), and steps were taken to improve such procedures. In addition, the state decided to eliminate its system for assessing parental in-

come and resources to determine the amount of cash assistance a family could receive (i.e., sliding scale eligibility). Examination of this practice revealed that it cost the state more to collect the information and allocate the services according to a sliding scale than the state was saving through the use of the information (Agosta, Bradley, et al., 1985).

The Minnesota Developmental Disabilities Council sponsored an evaluation of that state's cash subsidy program (Minnesota Developmental Disabilities Program, 1983). A stratified sample of the 38 families who were participating in the program were asked a series of questions regarding how administrative practices could be improved. Respondents suggested a range of useful improvements, including expanding the program to include adults, requiring that applications be completed once a year rather than a twice a year, providing specialized training about the program to local social and health service staff, using parents to publicize the program, increasing benefits for families with extraordinary needs, and increasing benefits for emergency respite care and care-related long-distance phone calls.

In Michigan, families of children who are aged 18 years or under who qualify for the state's cash program receive a monthly subsidy, paid through the mail by check. Based on an evaluation of that program, Parrott and Herman (1987) offered numerous recommendations for program improvement, many of which were incorporated into the program. For instance, the amount of the subsidy was initially set at $225.54 a month (based on the Supplemental Security Income (SSI) payment for an adult person in a household of one), but it was recommended and later approved that the amount be increased to $243.33 a month to match an increase in the SSI allowance for adults. Additionally, action was taken to expand the program to include previously excluded persons with severe multiple impairments, increase the appropriations set aside for complementing support services (e.g., respite), and ensure that families are informed of the full range of supports available.

For *program outcomes,* there is insufficient information regarding the effects of family support services, including cash assistance, on the overall system of services. One popular claim has been that family support services are cost-effective because they diminish the need for funding expensive out-of-home residential arrangements by making it possible for families to either keep their member with a disability at home or have him or her return home from out-of-home placement. In this regard, Michigan officials, noting institutional costs of $136.90 a day per resident compared to $7.41 a day per family receiving a subsidy, anticipated significant savings in the long term because of an emphasis on family support (Stabenow, 1983).

While such reasoning is appealing, conclusive substantiating evidence is not yet available. Several researchers have reported that receiving cash assistance can have a positive impact on family placement decisions (e.g., Herman, 1983; Parrott & Herman, 1987; Rosenau, 1983; Zimmerman, 1984). Although such findings are encouraging, they must be weighed against at least four other factors. First, the overwhelming majority of families do not place their sons or daughters with disabilities out of the home, especially during the child's early years (Ashbaugh et al., 1985; Perlman, 1985). Therefore, unless family services are successfully targeted only to families likely to seek an out-of-home placement (which is an enormously difficult task), the cost savings realized by states would not be substantial. In fact, in the short term at least, the costs of funding an extensive family support program may even add to the aggregate costs of services for persons with developmental disabilities.

Second, a review of existing services reveals that once a person with disabilities is placed out of the family home, few families bring the person back home. For instance, of the 74 children (of 3,300) participating in the Michigan cash program from 1984–1987 who were placed out of the home, only six have a goal of returning home (Parrott & Herman, 1987). Thus the cost savings to states in this regard may not be immediately recognized.

Third, available information suggests that, among people who seek out-of-home placements, there is no single overriding reason that fits all families. Instead, factors have been cited that vary from family to family, and change as

the family member with a disability ages and as the family's composition, characteristics, resources, and perceptions of the problem are altered (Agosta et al., 1986; Sherman, 1988; Tausig, 1985).

Sherman and Cocozza (1984) present an extensive review of the available literature on this issue, and show that when families do decide to place their son or daughter with disabilities out-of-home, their decision is frequently related to one or more of four factors: 1) *characteristics of the child* with disabilities, such as the level of disability, IQ, and functioning level; 2) *characteristics of the family,* such as family size, age of the parents, socioeconomic level, marital and family relations, and the presence of other family problems; 3) *perception of the problem,* as related to the level of stress that family members experience as well as its source (e.g., financial burdens, difficulty with physical management of the child, lack of parenting skills, and strained family relationships); and 4) *the availability of community services and social supports,* which can diminish the severity of the problems that are experienced by families who provide long-term care to members with disabilities. These considerations suggest that measuring the impact of family support services, or cash assistance services in particular, on placement decisions is complicated by the multiple factors that may influence the decision.

Finally, an evaluation of the effects of support programs on placement must be weighed against the recognition that all family-based care eventually ends through death or illness of primary family caregivers, or independence of the person with disabilities. Thus a more relevant issue may be whether the duration of family care is extended to the point where separation from the family is desirable and appropriate.

Therefore, the claim that family support services will save states substantial amounts of money has not been clearly documented. For some states, funding extensive family support services (including those with a cash component) may appear politically unattractive until such savings are shown. However, decisions regarding funding for these services will not be based simply on demonstrations of their cost savings to the state. Numerous other benefits to such programs have been demonstrated for families, and must also be taken into consideration.

Family Level Findings

Three primary issues concerning the efficacy of family support programs involve their impact on the family member with disabilities, the family, and family placement decisions. The family member with a disability may benefit as a function of family support services and cash assistance. Zimmerman (1984) reports that the majority of families who received cash subsidies in Minnesota think that their child improved socially, physically, intellectually, and emotionally. Similarly, a comparison between children with disabilities living with families receiving support or cash services and children living with nonparticipating families reveals that the children living with participating families showed significant increases in adaptive skills and decreases in challenging behavior, whereas children living with nonparticipating families did not show similar changes (Rosenau, 1983).

Likewise, the family unit may benefit as well. For instance, in perhaps the most extensive study of a cash program to date, Parrott & Herman (1987) reported that, during its first three years of operation, the Michigan cash program served 3,300 families, with only 74 children leaving the program for an out-of-home placement. A survey of about 1,000 of the participating families indicated that the majority of families felt that the subsidy was of sufficient size (65%), improved their ability to care for their member with disabilities (61%), eased financial worries (61%), and helped the family to do more things together (55%). Near majorities reported that the subsidy reduced the stress in family life (48%), improved overall family life (47%), and helped the family to be more like other families (42%).

Moreover, as shown in Table 4, families applied their subsidies to a great variety of materials or activities, some of which may have been impossible to secure within a program lacking a cash component. A substantial percentage of families used their subsidies on items that are not clearly tied to care-related expenses (e.g.,

Table 4. Supports purchased by 1,150 Michigan families

Expense category	Percent of families indicating use of cash
Clothing	86.0% of families
Educational aides/toys	63.0
Sitters for the child with disabilities	59.9
General household expense	59.0
Medical expenses/health related needs	55.5
Diapers	55.0
Special foods	40.8
Transportation expenses	40.0
Adaptive equipment	26.5
Respite care	20.2
Home renovation projects	14.0
Care for children without disabilities	9.0
Camp	7.7
Therapy (physical or speech)	5.7
Counseling services	3.8
Home nursing care	2.7

Source: Parrott and Herman (1987).

clothing, general household expenses). Taken together, these findings led Parrott and Herman (1987) to conclude that the Michigan cash program has had a positive effect on family functioning and placement decisions.

The newness of most family support programs makes evaluation of their long-term impact on parental placement decisions difficult. The weight of the evidence that does exist, however, suggests that support/cash services do influence decisions in favor of continued family-based care.

Rosenau (1983) describes a pilot family-support project in Michigan that served 13 families for 2 years. The project offered families a cash subsidy of $480 per month, a home trainer who entered the home for 20 hours per week to provide parent training, and cash management services. Study results showed that continued home placement for 10 of the children was achieved and three children with disabilities were returned from other environments to their natural families. In addition, through a follow-up questionnaire, eight families indicated that they "definitely" would have sought an out-of-home placement, and two other families reported that they "probably" would have sought such placement, if project services had not been available.

Herman (1983) described a meta-analysis of family support services that served 252 families for two years in three counties of Michigan, with 13 of these families having participated in the study completed by Rosenau (1983). The services varied somewhat by county and four models of family support emerged from the meta-analysis, including intensified services through cash management, intense in-home intervention, out-of-home respite and cash subsidy, and cash management with respite care and cash assistance. Study results indicated that, for the most part, families retained their member with disabilities at home throughout the course of the projects; the placement decisions of these families did not differ markedly from those of parents not participating in the projects. Further analysis, however, revealed that family perceptions and actions related to out-of-home service options were altered. Significant numbers of participating families indicated that they would have sought out-of-home placements if not for the projects' services. Furthermore, and that families with past histories of repeated use of out-of-home options used these options less. Thus, family support services, including those utilizing a cash component, appeared to have some positive effect on family placement decisions.

Zimmerman (1984) presented findings of a telephone survey of a stratified random sample of 38 families of children with disabilities receiving financial subsidies ranging between $76 and $250 per month in Minnesota. Half the families had received the subsidy for less than 2 years, and only four families participated in the subsidy program since its inception (four to six years). Results indicated that, in part due to the program, 36 of the families had no present plan for seeking an out-of-home placement. Moreover, the program had helped make it possible for one family to bring home a member with a disability.

In sum, it is apparent that much of the qualitative evidence that has been collected documents the efficacy of cash assistance approaches. Families indicate that they appreciate such services, and are satisfied with their effects (Herman, 1983; Parrott & Herman, 1987; Rosenau, 1983;

Zimmerman, 1984). Furthermore, families report that they benefit most when they are provided with multiple service options (e.g., respite care, financial assistance, and parent education) and least when they are offered fewer services (e.g., respite care only) (Moore et al., 1982). This suggests that no single service component is sufficient for achieving the goals of family support; several may be necessary.

The quantitative evidence is less conclusive. Much additional work must be done to gain a greater consensus regarding specific program objectives and to acquire sufficiently sophisticated evaluative measures and models. With these developments, the effects of support services and cash assistance on children and on the capacity of families to provide care can be determined more definitely. Moreover, existing programs can be modified so that they more effectively match the needs of individual families.

The present difficulty with this type of evaluation, however, pertains to the need for time to pass before sizeable results can be expected. Snapshot studies, or longitudinal studies of short duration, are insufficient. Due to the nature of developmental disabilities, service benefits are not always easily or promptly observed, leading Halpern (1984) to suggest that current measures may underestimate program effects. Moreover, Weiss (1983) notes that evaluations of interventions with the entire family requires measures that can assess the changes within family dynamics. Such measures have yet to be perfected (see Dunst & Trivette, 1985).

SUMMARY AND CONCLUSIONS

Since 1980, several states have initiated programs on behalf of families who have a member with disabilities, with about 20 states incorporating a cash component within their services as of the late 1980s. Establishing an effective statewide system is a complicated task requiring the consideration of several philosophical and programmatic concerns. Although there is a growing consensus that families should be offered a comprehensive circle of supports that is family-centered, culturally sensitive, community-based, and well coordinated, the substantial variance that is apparent among existing state initiatives serves as notice that little agreement has emerged regarding the most efficient and effective means of operating such programs. Some of the many administrative issues that must be resolved include the role of the family in service planning and delivery, program eligibility criteria, means of service administration, permissible supports, and the contrasting roles of the public, private and informal sectors in providing support. Within this context lies discussion over the utility and feasibility of implementing a cash assistance program.

The biggest problem facing decisionmakers is the lack of clarity regarding the goals of family support efforts. Should services be justified solely on their ability to save tax dollars for the cost of out-of-home placement, or is the goal of improved quality of life for the family as a whole

and the person with disabilities in particular a sufficient public good? Contemporary writings (e.g., Agosta & Bradley, 1985; Dunst, 1986; Parrott & Herman, 1987; Turnbull et al., 1986) on the topic suggest that the enhancement of the quality of life of the family—though not directly related to cost savings—does result in substantial benefits to the larger society, including increased family self reliance, maximization of family cohesiveness, and improvements in the productivity of individual family members and the person with disabilities. Although these goals are somewhat more ineffable, they should likewise be a part of any systematic exploration of family support practices. In this regard, the roles that cash assistance could play in helping to achieve these ends should be carefully assessed.

REFERENCES

Agosta, J.M., Bass, A., & Spence, R. (1986). *The needs of families: Results of a statewide survey in Massachusetts.* Cambridge, MA: Human Services Research Institute.

Agosta, J.M., & Bradley, V.J. (Eds.). (1985). *Family care for persons with developmental disabilities: A growing commitment.* Cambridge, MA: Human Services Research Institute.

Agosta, J.M., Bradley, V.J., Rugg, A., Spence, R., & Covert, S. (1985). *Designing programs to support family care for persons with developmental disabilities: Concepts to practice.* Cambridge, MA: Human Services Research Institute.

Agosta, J.M., Jennings, D., & Bradley, V.J. (1985). Statewide family support programs: Results of a national survey. In J.M. Agosta & V.J. Bradley (Eds.), *Family care for persons with developmental disabilities: A growing commitment* (pp. 94–112). Cambridge, MA: Human Services Research Institute.

Agosta, J.M., Langer-Ellison, M., & Moore, K. (1988). *The feasibility of implementing a MDDPC sponsored cash assistance family support program.* Boston: Massachusetts Developmental Disabilities Planning Council.

Agosta, J.M., O'Neal, M.A., & Toubbeh, J. (1987). *A path to peace of mind: Providing exemplary services to Navajo children with developmental disabilities.* Window Rock, AZ: Save the Children Federation and the Navajo Tribal Council.

Akabas, S.H. (1984). *Workers are parents too.* Child Welfare, *63*(5), 387–399.

Akabas, S.H., & Krauskoff, M.S. (1984). *Families and work: Creative workplace responses to employees with disabled children.* New York: Columbia University School of Social Work, Industrial Social Welfare Center.

Ashbaugh, J., Spence, R., Lubin, R., Houlihan, J., & Langer, M. (1985). *Summary of data on handicapped children and youth.* Cambridge, MA: Human Services Research Institute.

Bandura, A. (1977). Self-efficacy: Toward a unifying theory of behavioral change. *Psychological Review, 84,* 191–215.

Bates, M.V. (1985). *State family support/cash subsidy programs.* Madison: Wisconsin Council on Developmental Disabilities.

Batshaw, M.L., & Perret, Y.M. (Eds.). (1986). *Children with handicaps: A medical primer* (2nd Ed.). Baltimore: Paul H. Brookes Publishing Co.

Bird, W.A. (1984). *A survey of family support programs in seventeen states.* Albany: New York State Office of Mental Retardation and Developmental Disabilities.

Braddock, D., Howes, R., & Hemp, R. (1984). *Public expenditures: Mental retardation and developmental disabilities services.* Chicago: Institute for the Study of Developmental Disabilities, University of Illinois at Chicago.

Castellani, P. (1987). *The political economy of developmental disabilities.* Baltimore: Paul H. Brookes Publishing Co.

Cohen, S., & Syme, S.L. (1985). *Social support and health.* New York: Academic Press.

Crnic, K.A., Friedrich, W.N., & Greenberg, M.T. (1983). Adaptation of families with mentally retarded children: A model of stress, coping and family ecology. *American Journal of Mental Deficiency, 88*(2), 125–138.

Dunst, C. (1986). *Helping relationships and enabling and empowering families.* Morganton, NC: Family, Infant and Preschool Program, Western Carolina Center.

Dunst, C., & Trivette, C.M. (1985). *A guide to measures of social support and family behaviors.* Chapel Hill: University of North Carolina, Frank Porter Graham Child Development Center, Technical Assistance Development Systems.

Dunst, C., & Trivette, C.M. (1986). *Helping, helplessness and harm.* Morganton, NC: Family, Infant and Preschool Program, Western Carolina Center.

Dunst, C., & Trivette, C.M. (1987). *Enabling and empowering families: Conceptual and intervention issues.* Morganton, NC: Family, Infant and Preschool Program, Western Carolina Center.

Goldfarb, L.A., Brotherson, M.J., Summers, J.A., & Turnbull, A.P. (1986). *Meeting the challenge of disability or chronic illness: A family guide.* Baltimore: Paul H. Brookes Publishing Co.

Griss, R. (1988). Access to health care: Measuring the health insurance needs of persons with disabilities and persons with chronic illness (Vol. 1). Berkeley: World Institute on Disability.

Halpern, R. (1984). Lack of effects for home based early intervention?: Some possible explanations. *American Journal of Orthopsychiatry, 54*(1), 33–42.

Herman, S.E. (1983). *Family support services: Reports on meta-evaluation studies.* Lansing: Michigan Department of Mental Health.

Hobbs, N., & Perrin, J.M. (1985). *Issues in the care of children with chronic illness.* San Francisco: Jossey-Bass.

Hobbs, N., Dokecki, P.R., Hoover-Dempsey, K.V., Moroney, R.M., Shayne, M.W., & Weeks, K.H. (1984). *Strengthening families.* San Francisco: Jossey-Bass.

Johnson, S.H. (1979). *High risk parenting: Nursing assessment and strategies for the family at risk.* Philadelphia: J.B. Lippincott.

Konanc, J.T., & Warren, N.J. (1984). Graduation: Transitional crisis for mildly developmentally disabled adolescents and their families. *Family Relations, 33,* 135–142.

Lakin, K.C., Hill, B.K., & Bruininks, R.H. (1985). *An analysis of Medicaid's intermediate care facility for the mentally retarded (ICF-MR) program.* Minneapolis: University of Minnesota, Department of Educational Psychology.

Lapham, V.E., & Sherlin, K.M. (1986). *The impact of chronic illness on psychosocial stages of human development.* Washington, DC: Georgetown University Hospital and Medical Center, Department of Social Work.

Linder, T.W. (1983). *Early childhood special education: Program development and administration.* Baltimore: Paul H. Brookes Publishing Co.

Longo, D.C., & Bond, L. (1984). Families of the handicapped child: Research and practice. *Family Relations, 33,* 57–66.

McGoldrick, M., Pearce, J.K., & Giordano, J. (Eds.) (1982). *Ethnicity and family therapy.* New York: Guilford Press.

Minnesota Developmental Disabilities Program (1983). *The Minnesota family subsidy programs: Its effects on families with a developmentally disabled child* (Policy Analysis No. 18). St. Paul: Minnesota Developmental Disabilities Planning Council.

Moore, J.A., Hamerlynck, L.A., Barsh, E.T., Spieker, S., & Jones, R. (1982). *Extending family resources* (2nd Ed.). Seattle: Children Clinic and Preschool, University of Washington.

Moroney, R.M. (1983). Families, care of the handicapped, and public policy. In R. Perlman (Ed.), *Family home care: Critical issues for services and policies.* New York: Haworth Press.

Parrott, M.E., & Herman, S.E. (1987). *Report on the Michigan family support subsidy program.* Lansing: Michigan Department of Mental Health.

Perlman, R.H. (1985). *Family home care: Critical issues for services and policies.* New York: Haworth Press.

Piccione, J. (1982). *The human services option: New funding for the charitable sector.* Washington, DC: Free Congress Research and Education Foundation.

Rappaport, J. (1981). In praise of paradox: A social policy of empowerment over prevention. *American Journal of Community Psychology, 9,* 1–25.

Rosenau, N. (1983). *Final evaluation of a family support program.* Macomb-Oakland, MI: Macomb County Community Mental Health and Macomb-Oakland Regional Center.

Schwartz, D. (1987). *Re-visioning developmental disabilities councils: One council's search for the middle kingdom.* Harrisburg: Pennsylvania Developmental Disabilities Planning Council.

Sherman, B.R. (1988). Predictors of the decision to place a developmentally disabled family member in residential care. *American Journal on Mental Retardation, 92*(4), 344–351.

Sherman, B.R., & Cocozza, J.J. (1984). Stress in families of the developmentally disabled: A literature review of factors affecting the decision to seek out-of-home placements. *Family Relations, 33*(1), 95–104.

Slater, M.A., & Mitchell, P. (1984). *Family support services: A parent/professional partnership.* Stillwater, OK: National Clearinghouse of Rehabilitation Training Materials.

Stabenow, D. (1983). *The family support subsidy act: Questions and answers on P.A. 249 of 1983* (H.B. 4448). Lansing: Michigan State Legislature.

Suelzle, M., & Keenan, V. (1981). Changes in family support networks over the life cycle of mentally retarded persons. *American Journal on Mental Deficiency, 86,* 267–274.

Tausig, M. (1985). Factors in family decision-making about placement for developmentally disabled individuals. *American Journal on Mental Deficiency, 89,* 352–361.

Turnbull, A., Summers, J., & Brotherson, M. (1986). Family life cycle: Theoretical and empirical implications, and future directions for families with mentally retarded members. In J. Gallagher & P. Vietze (Eds.), *Research on families with retarded children* (pp. 45–66). Baltimore: University Park Press.

U.S. Congress, Office of Technology Assessment (May, 1987). *Technology dependent children: Hospitals v. home care—A technical memorandum,* OTA-TM-H-38. Washington, DC: US Government Printing Office.

Weiss, H. (1983). Issues in the evaluation of family support and education programs. *Family Resource Coalition Report, 2*(4), 10–11.

Wells, A.I., Agosta, J.M., Berliner, S., Cox, H., & Bedford, S. (1988). *Supporting Pennsylvania families: Strengthening the Pennsylvania family support system.* Cambridge, MA: Human Services Research Institute.

Wikler, L. (1983). Chronic stress of families of mentally retarded children. In D.H. Olson & B.C. Miller (Eds.), *Family studies review yearbook* (Vol. 1). Beverly Hills: Sage Publications.

Wikler, L. (1986). Family stress theory and research on families with children with mental retardation. In J. Gallagher & P. Vietze (Eds.), *Research on families with retarded children.* Baltimore: University Park Press.

Wikler, L., & Keenan (Eds.). (1983). *Developmental disabilities: No longer a private tragedy.* Silver Spring, MD: National Association of Social Workers.

Wray, L., & Wieck, C. (1985). Moving persons with developmental disabilities toward less restrictive environments through case management. In K.C. Lakin & R.H. Bruininks (Eds.), *Strategies for achieving community integration for developmentally disabled citizens* (pp. 219–230). Baltimore: Paul H. Brookes Publishing Co.

Zimmerman, S. (1984). The mental retardation family subsidy program: Its effects on families with a mentally handicapped child. *Family Relations, 33,* 105–118.

FORMAL SUPPORT THROUGH THE FAMILY LIFE CYCLE

CHAPTER 13

Support for Families during Infancy

Marci J. Hanson, Lynne Ellis, and Janet Deppe

The birth of a baby brings a multitude of new feelings and challenges to families, including joy, excitement, expectations, exhaustion, sibling reactions, additional financial needs, and changes in family dynamics. Most families negotiate the adaptations created by the new baby within the first several months of its arrival given adequate support systems and resources. However, for parents who deliver a baby with developmental difficulties, these feelings and challenges may be heightened and the adjustment period may be prolonged—perhaps for years. The supports and services that these families receive during the birth and early years of their children's lives can help foster positive family relationships and fruitful adaptations from the beginning. This chapter describes family needs and service options during this period and presents a model for early intervention in the first 3 years. The discussion throughout the chapter focuses primarily on families of children who are born with an established risk factor, such as a medical condition associated with significant developmental delay (e.g. Down syndrome, vision and/or hearing impairment, brain damage resulting in cerebral palsy, spina bifida).

POTENTIAL STRESS FACTORS

Families, like individuals, have different responses and needs resulting from the birth of a child with disabilities. These responses and needs are not necessarily fixed, but rather may change from day to day. Although the following discussion outlines potential stress factors that families may experience, the highly individualized nature of a family's response to the birth of a child with a disability overrides other considerations in making decisions about the provision of intervention services.

Families of infants with disabilities may experience a range of stressful factors. A number of clinical studies have outlined these factors. Briefly, these factors include fears or problems with attachment, an unresponsive or unreactive baby, early prolonged separation from the baby, fears regarding parental competence engendered from having to rely on sophisticated technology and highly skilled professionals for the baby's survival and care, and failure to produce the expected and hoped for baby (Taylor & Hall, 1979). The limitations or differences in behavioral patterns that are created by the disabling conditions may produce difficulties in interaction for parents and their infants as well (Hanson, 1984; Ramey, Beckman-Bell, & Gowen, 1980). Furthermore, many of these babies need comprehensive, specialized, and very costly services through the neonatal intensive care units. The financial costs that are associated with neonatal care are among the highest of various types of hospital costs (Schroeder, Showstack, & Roberts, 1979). Thus, families may undergo considerable stress due to economic, social, interactional, and/or typical caregiving and parenting factors. Several of these stressors are considered in greater detail.

One of the first feelings that parents may experience is a feeling of loss. Solnit and Stark (1961) likened these reactions to the mourning process, in that the parent(s) may mourn the loss of the expected child. However, unlike the process of adjusting to a death in the family, the presence of a disabling condition may necessitate a series of continuing adjustments throughout the life cycle. A great deal of clinical literature has been devoted to this lifelong adjustment, and a number of clinicians across various fields (e.g., medicine, social sciences) have hypothesized that parents pass through a series of stages in adjusting to the birth of a child with a disability. One such hypothetical model is that presented by Drotar, Baskiewicz, Irvin, Kennell, and Klaus (1975). Briefly, this model outlines five stages of parental reactions: 1) shock, 2) denial or disbelief, 3) sadness and anger, 4) adaptation, and 5) reorganization. Such models may provide useful information regarding possible parental reactions to clinicians working with families. However, family members may or may not exhibit these stages of adjustment. Furthermore, they may pass through "stages" rapidly or remain at a particular point for a long period of time. Models help to outline general considerations, but fail to predict or consider differences in the progression, magnitude, and type of response that characterize different families and individual members within the family.

Several empirical investigations also have examined the effects of specific characteristics of children with handicaps on parental (especially maternal) stress. Specifically, the rate of child progress, responsiveness, temperament, repetitive behavior patterns, and the presence of additional or unusual caregiving demands were studied with regard to their relationship to maternal stress. All of the characteristics were significantly related to the reported stress, with the exception of the rate of child progress (Beckman, 1983).

Researchers have long acknowledged the bidirectional importance of both parent and child characteristics on the interaction of the dyad. For years only the parent variables were examined. With the publication of Bell's landmark article in 1968, the effects of the infant on the caregiver also were documented. A number of studies have described parent-child interaction in dyads where the child was disabled or significantly at risk for developing disabilities due to a sensory impairment, physical impairment, Down syndrome, language delay, extreme prematurity,

and/or low birth weight. This body of research has demonstrated some interactional differences when these dyads are compared to dyads with a typically developing infant. Further, studies have documented the relationship between maternal behavior (e.g., responsivity) and child competence (Brooks-Gunn & Lewis, 1984; Crawley & Spiker, 1983). Thus, the presence of atypical behavioral repertoires in infants may affect parent-child interaction.

These factors represent several of the major issues that may pose stresses for parents of young children with disabilities. Once again, the responses of specific parents of families to these events is shaped by many other variables, such as internal and external sources of emotional support, financial support, and health considerations. However, an examination of these potential stress factors is useful in determining the type and range of services delivered through early intervention models.

ASSUMPTIONS UNDERLYING EARLY INTERVENTION

Before specific early intervention models are considered, the assumptions that underlie the provision of these services will be reviewed. Specifically, four principles are discussed: the transactional model of development, a family systems approach to treatment, the empowerment of parents in decisionmaking, and an interdisciplinary service delivery model.

Most clinicians and theorists accept the premise that developmental outcomes are attributable both to an individual's organismic or constitutional factors and to environmental factors. A more recent perspective, the transactional model of development (Sameroff & Chandler, 1975) emphasizes the active role of the child in interacting with the world. This model highlights the continual and progressive interplay between the child and the environment.

A transactional model of development is particularly appropriate for examining developmental outcomes for children with disabilities. A child that is either born with disabilities or at serious risk for developmental delays has a limited or different behavioral repertoire with which to interact with the environment, by virtue of the disabling/risk condition. For example, the child with visual impairments cannot visually explore or signal the environment and the child with physical impairments may go rigid when moved or held. These behaviors may trigger responses in parents (the major and most important persons in the environment) that are negative. The parents may feel, for instance, that the child does not love them or wish to be near them. Without interventions, maladaptive or displeasing interaction patterns may develop.

As the transactional model highlights, the child's environment is crucial to the child's ultimate developmental outcome. For the young infant, the child's family is almost entirely that environment. Furthermore, not only does the family affect the child, but the new child also affects the family dynamics. For these reasons, attention has been given to child support through a family systems approach.

The family systems approach considers the interactions of family members and the various family subsystems (e.g., parent-child, parent-parent, child-child, family-extrafamily) (Minuchin, 1974). Turnbull and Turnbull (1986) stress the importance of utilizing this approach and outline four major components to be considered in establishing parent-professional partnerships in interventions. These components include: family resources (e.g., characteristics of the disabilities, family size, cultural background, socioeconomic status); family interactions or the relationships among members and subsystems; family functions (e.g., economic, affection, socialization, domestic and health care); and the family's life cycle or the sequence of changes that affect families. Furthermore, Turnbull, Summers, and Brotherson (1984) propose that there are several implications of a family systems approach to the design of intervention efforts. These implications include the notion that each family is unique and has different characteristics and styles, the idea that the family system has boundaries that are constantly changing, the assumption that many different functions for individual members are filled by the family, and the acknowledgment that families undergo changes that affect all members.

A third principle underlying early intervention efforts aimed at family support is the notion of parent empowerment. For years, parent involvement in early intervention or educational programs solely meant parent training. Typically, in this paradigm the parent was helped to identify training goals (usually goals for remediating a child behavior) and a structured teaching regimen was developed and taught to parents. The parents then implemented the procedures and evaluated the results of the child training efforts with the help of the participating professional. Today, in early intervention efforts the focus emphasizes the parent as a true and active partner in the intervention process. This empowerment implies that parents should be given a menu of service options from which to choose and that parents should be involved in all phases of the decisionmaking process (e.g., selection and design of intervention goals and objectives for the child and the family, decisions about implementation, decisions about continuation or modification of goals). While this focus is much more difficult for professionals because of the range of services and the flexibility required, it ensures that the rights and needs of the consumers (families) are being met.

Finally, early intervention services typically focus on an interdisciplinary service delivery approach. Particularly for families of infants, the need for coordination among a wide range of professionals is great. The first concerns and contacts that families have with professionals are generally with health care professionals. Subsequently, educational and social service personnel are typically involved. Taken as a whole, these professionals and the various agencies they represent form the earliest range of intervention services. Due to the complexity of this service delivery system, families are often required to circumnavigate a cumbersome and uncoordinated myriad of services. Exemplary intervention efforts, therefore, are directed toward the provision of local, coordinated service efforts.

In summary, child development must be viewed within the context of the child's environment. For the very young infant in particular, the most important part of the environment is the child's family. It is with the child's family that early intervention efforts are made. The target, in fact, is not the child but rather the child within the context of the family. This focus on the family has created a new and broader network and range of service options than traditional services allowed. These options are considered in the following discussion.

THE SERVICE DELIVERY SYSTEM

The needs of young children with disabilities and their families are considerable and numerous. Assistance and support to families can be adequately accomplished only through a coordinated service delivery approach that involves a range of professional disciplines and agencies. Three phases of the service delivery system are outlined. They include: 1) identification/diagnosis of difficulties, 2) transition from the hospital to other services, and 3) a comprehensive early intervention program. The service delivery model described in this chapter focuses primarily upon the latter, the early intervention program. However, it is discussed in terms of its relationship to other services within the community.

Identification/Diagnosis

For parents of children at established risk, the condition(s) are often apparent at birth. A well trained health care practioner will be able to identify the difficulties and convey accurate information to families in a sensitive manner. Some risk conditions will necessitate immediate and extensive technical interventions for the babies, such as resuscitation, intubation, or monitoring of vital functions in an intensive care nursery. These critical and lifesaving medical interventions can be highly intrusive and frightening to families. Thus exemplary interventions during this initial contact period focus on two major components: the provision of crucial medical and health care services and the provision of support and information to families regarding the child's condition and the medical procedures being utilized. Supportive interventions must be immediate, adapted to the family's need and desire to obtain information, presented in a language and manner understandable to parents, and presented by a sensitive and knowledgeable health care and/or social service provider who is experienced in working with families.

Professionals employed through hospitals and community agencies may play an important role in providing early support to families. Most major hospitals employ social workers whose responsibilities include working with families of babies born with difficulties. These professionals often meet with families on a one-to-one basis as needed. They may also refer families to appropriate community resources, such as early intervention programs, social service agencies, insurance agencies, childcare and nursing services following discharge, and counseling services.

Another key role that professionals in hospitals can play is one of providing instructional services to parents. Parents may ask for accurate, factual information on their child's condition and prognosis. Further, parents may need to learn how to care for and handle their child following discharge. The new responsibilities that parents face in caring for a baby with medical and/or behavioral difficulties may be frightening and overwhelming. This early professional support can be instrumental in alleviating parental anxiety.

Transition from Hospital to Other Services

Traditionally, families have received few services after they leave the hospital. Most often they have been alone in locating other needed services in the community and obtaining information relating to their children's conditions. Today, some hospitals and early intervention programs are attempting to facilitate this transition period. This can be accomplished through an overlap of services. Typically, an appointed staff member from the early intervention program coordinates with the appropriate hospital contact person (e.g., social worker). It is important to note that family contact is made with one intervention specialist, not a range of staff members, at this point. This is done to avoid overwhelming families who at this early stage are faced with many professional contacts and a hoard of information and service needs to digest. Families may be invited at this time to visit the early intervention program, depending upon an individual family's desire to participate and the medical stability of the infant. The key issue is that families and early intervention programs make contact while families are still receiving hospital services, so that the transition to other services can be made as comfortably as possible.

Transitions can be supported also through the use of parent-to-parent networks. These services involve families of newly diagnosed children being linked to and visited by other parents of children with the same conditions. Effective parent-to-parent networks are highly organized services that are managed by parents who are well trained and skilled in working with families. Such networks are discussed in more detail in Hanson and Lynch (in press).

Early Intervention Services

Early intervention is used in this context to refer to a comprehensive set of services that are provided to children from birth to three years and their families. Services are provided by a number of different professionals representing different pediatric disciplines that include educational, health care, and social services. A variety of models for providing early intervention are available, including home-based, center-based and a combination of home- and center-based services. Some require active parental involvement and others focus primarily on the child. This chapter presents one early intervention model—the San Francisco Special Infant Services Program.

Overview of the Program This early intervention program was originally funded in 1979 as the San Francisco Infant Program (SFIP), a federal national model demonstration program under the Handicapped Children's Early Education Program (HCEEP) network. After 3 years of national funding, the program received funding through the local Regional Center services (California State Department of Developmental Services). In 1983 a second model demonstration was funded, the Integrated Special Infant Services (ISIS). This federal model program expanded the work of SFIP to include families of children born prematurely, at low birth weight, and/or with significant birth complications. Also a major focus of that model was facilitating early parent-child interactions. At the end of the federal funding period in 1986, both the SFIP and ISIS programs were combined into the present program, San Francisco Special Infant Services (SIS). Today, the Special Infant Services

program operates with state and local funding through the Regional Center system and the local school district (San Francisco Unified School District) with monies from the California State Department of Education.

Philosophy and Goals of the Program The purpose of the San Francisco Special Infant Services Program is to facilitate the development of infants and toddlers who are disabled or at significant risk for developmental delay, through training and assistance to the young children and their families. The program offers combination home- and center-based services with a transdisciplinary staffing model. The services focus on providing family support and facilitating family involvement. The components that follow characterize the philosophical approach.

1. Transactional Model of Child Development Intervention efforts are based on a transactional model of child development. The services are aimed at assisting the child to become a more competent interactor with the environment, and at designing an environment that is supportive to these early interactions. Support and assistance to family members is a crucial part of intervention.

2. View of Infant Development The young child is viewed as an active learner, regardless of the degree or type of disability. Infants are helped to actively explore, engage, and gain control over their environment.

3. Family Involvement Family involvement is viewed as paramount. Parents are actively involved in goal setting, implementation, and evaluation of the intervention efforts. Parents are given a range of service options and can select and decide what is most appropriate for their child and family. The goal is to empower parents in these early decisionmaking processes.

4. Systematic Assessment, Training, and Evaluation Goals for children are determined from a transdisciplinary assessment of the child's developmental status. These goals are formulated and implemented, and then systematically measured to determine when and how the training should be modified. Parents are actively involved as partners in all phases of intervention.

5. Developmental and Functional Curricular Goals Training goals for children must be both developmentally appropriate and functional for the child's development. The children are assisted to more competently engage their environment and obtain feedback from that environment. A major focus is on facilitating infants' social interactions and communicative abilities and on teaching them functional skills (e.g., locomotion, communication, feeding).

6. *Transdisciplinary Staffing* Services are provided by personnel from different disciplines working together as a transdisciplinary team. Team members coordinate assessment, goal setting and implementation, and provide training to one another.

7. *Interagency Coordination* The program endeavors to coordinate services with other agencies with whom the families may be in contact. This is done to ensure that the services are efficient, coordinated, not duplicated, and supportive to families.

Population Served The Special Infant Services program enrolls approximately 35 infants and toddlers. Children range in age from birth to three years and have identifiable or suspected disabilities, such as cerebral palsy, Down syndrome, spina bifida, language delays, motor impairments, or sensory impairments. In addition, children who are not diagnosed but at significant risk for developmental delay due to prematurity, chronic illness, parental substance abuse, and other pre- or perinatal complications are served. Referrals are received from hospitals, primary care physicians, the school district, other parents, social service agencies, and the Regional Center.

Staffing Services are provided by a transdisciplinary team of professionals that includes special education teachers, occupational and physical therapists, speech therapists, a psychologist, a pediatrician, and a program director. Many team members are employed on a part-time basis, and consultation with outside community resources is undertaken as needed.

The transdisciplinary team model is characterized by team effort, role release, and extensive staff development. Staff members work together with the child's family to jointly assess the child and establish intervention goals. Further, members practice *role release* in that they train one another in various aspects of their individual areas of expertise, so that each team member can

support the training goals of the other and implement the training goals that are interrelated across areas of development.

Organizational Structure and Evaluation of Services Children and their families receive services both in the home and at the center (a classroom in a local elementary school). The youngest group of children, infants ranging in age from birth to 18 months, are visited weekly in their homes. They also attend a small group meeting at the center once a week where individualized instruction is emphasized. Toddlers, ages 18 to 36 months, receive biweekly home visits and attend small group sessions at the center two to three mornings per week.

Each child is individually assessed by the team periodically, and an individual plan for services is developed (individualized education program or IEP). An individualized plan or contract (Parent Involvement Plan) is also developed with each family, whereby the staff members and the family members identify family needs together and reach an agreement on how these needs can be met.

Every effort is made to provide intervention services that are coordinated with the many other services that families are receiving. To that end, each child is assigned to one of the staff members, who functions as that child's case manager. As the liaison between the family and the other program staff and community service agencies, the case manager is able to inform the team of family issues, disseminate information as appropriate to other professionals, and ensure that all aspects of the child's and family's program goals are being addressed. Although the case manager may initially serve as the family's advocate, the ultimate goal is to assist parents to become their own advocates, thus empowering them as planners and decisionmakers.

An overall program evaluation is accomplished through measures of child change, parent satisfaction, client services and funding, and community satisfaction with and usage of services. Child progress is measured using discrete behavioral observations. Furthermore, child change is assessed annually using two standardized measures, the norm referenced Bayley Scales of Infant Development (Bayley, 1969), and the criterion referenced Uniform Performance Assessment System (UPAS) (White, Edgar, & Haring, 1978). Biannually, parents also complete a Parent Satisfaction Questionnaire on which they rate each aspect of the program on a 5-point Likert scale and provide responses to open ended questions. Additionally, primary referral sources and community agencies are asked to respond periodically to a questionnaire that analyzes their satisfaction with, knowledge of, and usage of the SIS program services. Finally, review by the funding agencies as to number and type of children served and use of funding allocations is conducted annually.

Service Provision Methods Services to infants include assessments, instruction/intervention based upon assessment information, and evaluation of the instructional program. Formal assessments are conducted annually with the Bayley Scales and the UPAS. The child is also informally assessed by the team, utilizing criterion-referenced checklists. From these assessments and observations, the IEP is developed.

Training goals are set in all areas of development—fine and gross motor, cognitive, communication, self-help, social-emotional—as needed. Instructional strategies are designed to coordinate training goals, recognizing that all areas of development are integrally related. Intervention is aimed at looking at the child as a whole and within areas of development that are interrelated, rather than looking at the child's disability or area of weakness. Further, emphasis is placed on helping the child to communicate effectively, relate socially, and initiate to and control aspects of the environment. Goals are typically organized according to a normal developmental sequence, with more complex skills built upon less complex ones. However, skills targeted for instruction must not only be developmentally appropriate, but also be functional for that child's daily living.

Services for families are provided in four major areas: information, support, training, and assistance in parent-child interaction. The parent's needs are assessed upon enrollment using both a questionnaire and informal interviews. Information and support are provided through both one-to-one discussion with staff members and a parent support group that meets twice monthly. Staff members endeavor to assist parents in ob-

taining the information they may request, such as information on their child's disability and prognosis or services in the community. Parents are referred to other agencies or services (e.g., counseling services) as the need arises. Further, they are encouraged and supported to maintain their own informal networks of support (e.g., relatives, neighbors, churches, clubs).

Parents also may receive direct instruction or training on specific aspects of their child's development and care. For example, most parents want to learn how to therapeutically position and handle their children during play, feeding, bathing, and dressing. Further, many parents wish to learn how to teach their children specific goals and how to communicate with their children through speech and/or manual communication means.

Many parents express frustration at certain aspects of their child's behavior. Thus, intervention services also focus on facilitating mutually satisfying parent-child interactions. This intervention process involves examining the components of the interaction (e.g., affect, pace, turn-taking, contingent responsiveness) and the competencies that both infants and parents bring to the interaction. For example, both infant abilities (e.g., responsiveness, signaling) and parent abilities (e.g., awareness and attitudes about the child's development and disability) are observed. Parents then are helped to read and understand their children's unique cueing systems and behavioral needs and communicate with their infants. This intervention framework is more fully described in Hanson and Krentz (1986).

Challenges Encountered The San Francisco Special Infant Services program has encountered some particular challenges in delivering services to families. Most of these difficulties or challenges are typical to other early intervention services as well. These challenges fall into four areas: eligibility requirements for available funding, coordination with and transition from birthing hospitals, coordination with other service providers, and transdisciplinary teaming.

The SIS program operates with funding from two major public sources. One provides payment on an hourly basis only for the direct hours in which children are served, and the other bases payment on an overall program operation basis. The former system, through its funding structure, fails to allow for the provision of family services. Thus, the program provides these services without receiving specific payment for them.

A second challenge is coordination, referral, and service transitions from the birthing hospitals to early intervention programs when appropriate. The staff has endeavored to facilitate this process by initiating services in the hospital in coordination with the appropriate hospital contact in the nursery. Members of the staff visit families in the hospital as needed and continue to coordinate with hospital personnel as the families make the transitions to home care and to the intervention program. In-service training of hospital staff through presentations and personal contacts is conducted by the program staff to ensure continuous collaboration and mutual awareness of resources.

Third, most children are involved with a variety of other service providers, such as primary care physicians, social service workers, and other public agencies. Often no one agency has responsibility for coordinating these services and the parent is left to organize as best as possible. This can create a tremendous burden for families and can also result in an inconsistent program for the child and families. Thus, the case manager for each child in the program makes contact with all the other service providers for that child and family, and develops a plan to coordinate services.

Finally, a major challenge faced by the program involves the organization and maintenance of the transdisciplinary team. This type of staffing model requires much more intensive staff development on an ongoing basis than does a model that requires less coordination. Further, the transdisciplinary model can only succeed if individual members are willing to work collaboratively with one another and with parents, and if they are willing to relinquish various aspects of their traditional professional roles and identity. The SIS program endeavors to provide intensive training activities both within and outside the program on a continuous basis, and also to schedule weekly staff time for communicating with one another and coordinating services for children and their families.

EVALUATION OF FAMILY SERVICES IN EARLY INTERVENTION PROGRAMS

Evaluation Practices

Outcome measures of early education programs have focused primarily on children's cognitive gains. More recently, measures of family attitudes and behavior have been examined. Both Bronfenbrenner's (1975) and Lazar and Darlington's (1982) evaluation of early intervention program effectiveness (primarily for young children at environmental risk), reviewed changes in family behavior and attitudes, as well as outcomes that measured children's cognitive performance.

Federal initiatives, such as the passage of PL 90-538, *The Handicapped Children's Early Education Assistance Act of 1968*, required that an emphasis be placed on parent participation in model demonstration infant and preschool programs for children with disabilities. Although parent involvement has long been identified as a crucial program component, evaluation studies concerning the benefits and the importance of the caregiver-child relationship on early intervention have been meager. A few of those investigations that have attempted to evaluate both child and parent behavioral outcomes in intervention programs for handicapped and/or at risk infants and their families are reviewed below.

Several evaluation studies of programs funded through the Handicapped Children's Early Education Program (HCEEP) network have included measures of parent change. One such program is the Peoria 0–3 Replication Project (Trohanis, Cox, & Meyer, 1982) for children with disabilities from birth to three years. The program demonstrated developmental gains for children and changes in parent behavior as well. The parents showed a greater acceptance of the child's handicap, greater attendance and participation in parent meetings and workshops, a greater frequency of parent-initiated work with their children, and a greater frequency of constructing adaptive equipment.

Bromwich and Parmelee (1979) investigated the effects of an early intervention program for high risk preterm infants and their families. Infants were divided into two groups, an intervention and a nonintervention group. To assess intervention outcomes, the researchers used the

Home Observation for Measurement of the Environment (HOME) scale (Caldwell & Bradley, 1978), the Bayley Scales of Infant Development, the Gesell Developmental Schedules, and measures of receptive language and cognitive abilities. The Parent Behavior Progression (PBP) and the Play Interaction Measure (PIM) also were developed and given to the intervention group.

The investigators found significant differences on the HOME scale in favor of the intervention group. The intervention group was further divided into two subgroups, including those in which interventions were felt to be successful and those in which interventions were felt to be largely unsuccessful. To assess the differences between the successful and the unsuccessful intervention groups, the HOME, PBP, and the PIM were used; the successful intervention group scored higher on the PBP, PIM, and HOME assessments.

In another investigation of home-based intervention for infants at high risk, Ross (1984) found that children in the program scored significantly higher on the Mental Scale of the Bayley Scales of Infant Development than did children in a control group that received no home stimulation. In addition, families that received home visits scored significantly higher on the quality of the home environment as measured by the HOME, and those mothers demonstrated more involvement and a greater emotional and verbal responsiveness to their infants.

In a study to assess the effects of home- and center-based intervention on teenage mothers and their offspring, Field, Widmayer, Stringer, and Ignatoff (1980) used infant developmental measures, measures of maternal stress, and maternal assessments of their infants. They found that the growth and development of infants from both the home and center intervention programs exceeded that of the control group infants. The intervention program also had an impact on the mothers in that the mothers in the center-based program were characterized by a greater rate of return to work or school and a lesser incidence of repeat pregnancies.

The importance of family variables is also underscored by the work of Dunst (1985). At Project SUNRISE (Support Network of Rural Intervention Services), Dunst investigated the effects of specific parental characteristics, family characteristics, and child characteristics on parent, family, child, and parent-child functioning variables. Child diagnosis variables were found to be not generally related to measures of parental emotional and physical problems or well-being, but they were consistently correlated with both time demands and family integration. Further, most social support measures were significantly correlated with these parent/family dependent measures. For instance, an increased provision of support was related to decreased emotional and physical problems as well as time demands for parents. Personal characteristics, family characteristics, child diagnosis, and intrafamily support also were consistently correlated with family outcome measures. Finally, as ages of parents, educational levels, family income, child's developmental quotient, and intrafamily support increased, family opportunities increased and financial problems decreased.

These studies represent some of the investigations on the effects of early intervention on family variables. Such analyses are difficult to interpret unequivocally, given that early intervention as a concept involves a variety of services to children and families. Further, many different programmatic models have been utilized. Only recently have the programs begun to concentrate on directly assisting families to interact with their infants and on examining family supports and resources.

San Francisco Special Infant Services Evaluation

For a number of years the SIS program has been collecting information on child change as a result of early intervention procedures. The program also has endeavored to look at some parental behavior change variables and the relationship of family functioning variables (e.g., degree of stress experienced) to child measures. Hanson (1985) reported the effects of the first years of the program using several child and parent measures. Specifically, child progress was measured utilizing the Bayley Scales of Infant Development, the Uniform Performance Assessment System, and a Curriculum Objectives Checklist; parent behavior was measured on the Parent

Behavior Progression Scale (PBP). The PBP (Bromwich, 1978) was developed to examine the following parent behaviors: 1) sensitivity and responsiveness to the child's behavioral cues, 2) the quality of the interaction, 3) awareness of appropriate materials, activities, and experiences for the infant, and 4) the ability to generalize information and past experiences to provide novel activities and experiences for the child.

All of the measures were administered at the beginning and the end of each intervention year. Complete data for 24 infants and their mothers were reported. Pre- and posttest comparisons indicated statistically significant, positive behavioral changes for both the children and their parents on all measures. Furthermore, analyses were conducted on the relationships between parent behavior and child behavior, and on the relationship between the amount of child change and the amount of parent behavior change. Correlations between the parent PBP scores and the child UPAS scores were low, indicating little relationship. This is not surprising in light of the fact that the children studied had moderate to severe handicaps, and while the children showed modest developmental gains, the parents' gains were more dramatic.

The relationship between parent-child interaction variables and family stress was also studied (Hanson, Deino, & Krentz, 1986). The interaction patterns of 25 mother-infant pairs were examined using the Nursing Child Assessment Teaching Scale (NCAT) and the PBP. The NCAT (Barnard, 1978) is a behavioral rating scale consisting of 73 binary items; it is designed to measure both the mother's and the infant's contributions and responses during interactions. It is appropriate for use with infants from birth to 36 months of age, and involves a mother teaching a task to her infant. The scale is organized into six subscales that include: 1) a parent's sensitivity to the infant's cues, 2) a parent's responses to the child's distress, 3) a parent's social and emotional growth fostering, 4) a parent's cognitive growth fostering of the child, 5) a child's clarity of cues, and 6) a child's responsiveness to the parent. Maternal stress was measured utilizing the Revised Questionnaire on Resources and Stress (QRS-R) (Friedrich, Greenberg, & Crnic, 1983). This parental report questionnaire con-

sists of 52 true/false items and assesses areas of adaptation and coping, including parental difficulties (e.g., lack of social support, poor health), family difficulties (e.g., financial problems, lack of shared consensus), and child difficulties (e.g., physical incapacitation).

Relationships were analyzed between the two parent-child interaction measures and between each interaction measure and the QRS-R. The results indicated that a statistically significant correlation existed between the interaction measures, indicating that they were most likely tapping the same interactional phenomena. However, correlation coefficients for the relationship between the PBP and the QRS-R and between the NCAT Mother Score and the QRS-R, failed to reach significance. Thus, the amount of stress reported by these mothers appeared not to be related to their interactional patterns with their infants.

In the last several years the program has emphasized facilitating parent-child interaction in the early intervention curriculum. In an effort to evaluate the effects of these efforts, a pilot study was conducted on a small sample of families ($n = 10$). To measure potential changes, the PBP, the NCAT, and also the Nursing Child Feeding Scale (NCAF) (Barnard, 1978) were used. The QRS-R was again utilized to examine whether or not these intervention efforts affected the parent report of stress on this measure. Results indicated significant pre- to posttest changes on the PBP, but no statistically significant pre- to posttest changes in maternal behavior on either the NCAF or the NCAT. Nor were any pre- to posttest changes noted on the QRS-R. Either these measures were not effectively evaluating the intervention phenomenon, or the intervention was not effective in changing interaction patterns as measured on these scales. Furthermore, stress (as reported by mothers on the QRS-R) was not affected. Given the small sample, few conclusions can be drawn.

However, these studies do demonstrate how difficult it is to measure the impact of a comprehensive early intervention program on parental behavior variables. First of all, few measures are available for observing parent-child interactions or examining the family environment. Many rely on parental reporting, such as the stress and support measures. Others rely on an evaluation of the home environment (e.g., HOME scale) but may only be culturally appropriate for a middle class sample. This has been a distinct problem for the SIS in San Francisco, where the population of families includes members from many different socioeconomic, ethnic, and cultural groups. Although goals related to improving family functioning, providing support to families, and enhancing parent-child interactions are undoubtedly among the most important early intervention goals, they are also the most elusive to study.

FUTURE DIRECTIONS

Public Policy

Public policy regarding the inclusion of family services in early intervention programs was redefined with the passage of PL 99–457 (*The Education of the Handicapped Act Amendments of 1986*). This landmark piece of legislation authorized new discretionary state grant programs for early intervention services for infants and toddlers *and their families.* As such, this law establishes that family services be included as part of the child's educational program. In fact, the law calls for the development of individualized family service plans (IFSP) for children and their families participating in services funded through this legislation. Although the law is discretionary, all states have elected to participate in the beginning planning phases of implementing the program.

Direct Service Practices

Family services have long been acknowledged as important to the delivery of services for young children. In fact, for almost two decades, the Handicapped Children's Early Education Program network of projects has emphasized the provision of services to infants and preschoolers and their families. With the passage of the new federal legislation, this commitment to serving families has been underscored. It is likely that this emphasis on the importance of the family to the child's development will continue, and in fact be strengthened. Not only is this focus supported by developmental theory, but also now by

years of clinical experience in the education, health, and social service fields.

The commitment to family services within the broader field of early intervention is strong, and has been for years. Issues that have not been resolved, however, include the identification of the service provider (i.e., who should be the early interventionist?) and the development of a network of locally based, coordinated services. It appears that, just as for children, a menu of services is needed for families, so that family needs can be defined and families can be matched to the appropriate assistance agencies in the community. Such a menu must take into account the changing needs of individual families, and also the diversity of needs experienced across families and across the life cycle of families.

Research

Given the commitment to the provision of services to young children and their families, what remain to be identified are the most fruitful types of interventions for particular children and their families. The approach in early intervention has been to fund a variety of models for providing services to a heterogeneous group of children and their families. Given the funding and research design restraints, most of the attention has been placed on providing rather than evaluating the services. Thus, today the effectiveness of early intervention in general and specific components in particular is being questioned and studied more systematically (Casto & White, 1984).

Evaluation research studies are finding that more structured and intensive efforts are more effective (Casto & White, 1984; Mahoney, Finger, & Powell, 1985). Furthermore, the outcomes of early intervention are being examined on a broader scale. As was previously discussed, the sole use of child cognitive measures has been disputed, and more ecologically sound variables are now also being considered, such as parent-child interaction, parental attitudes, and family functioning. Researchers such as Dunst (1985) suggest that these variables may be among the most important in determining the effects of early intervention. Dunst's (1985) investigations, for instance, demonstrated the relationship between family informal and formal support systems and parent, child, parent-child, and family functioning variables.

Although direct service program providers increasingly recognize the need for systematic evaluation of program efforts, several barriers preclude adequate empirical investigation. First of all, few service providers have the funding or expertise on staff to implement an extensive evaluation plan. In addition, the children and families served often represent a variety of disabilities, cultures, ages, and socioeconomic groups (to name only a few variables) making research attempts difficult with these small heterogeneous samples. Further, the selection of instrumentation is difficult. Cognitive measures have probably been utilized predominantly because they are methodologically sound and available. Measures appropriate to the analysis of the ecological context of early intervention, particularly the family, are less available or well developed. Many of these measures, for example, involve a parent report on a questionnaire regarding attitudes or stressful events. Such reporting is fraught with difficulties, such as the reliability of reporting. Finally, most of the measures utilized have been developed for other purposes, such as studying family systems or personality development. Thus, their appropriateness for use as measures of program effectiveness and behavior change can be called

into question. In summary, few ecologically valid measures suited to evaluating early intervention program effects are available. This lack of appropriate methodology poses legitimate difficulties and restraints on current attempts to evaluate the effects of intervention regimens.

SUMMARY

Family services are an inseparable component from other early intervention services. This emphasis is grounded in child development theory, extensive clinical practice, and public policy. Today exemplary early intervention service delivery models provide services to children who are disabled or at risk for developmental delay through the context of the child's family. Although the importance of family services has been recognized increasingly, few research efforts have attempted to determine which services or cluster of services are appropriate for which group of families. Further, the methodology for studying the effectiveness of these family oriented services is lacking. Further directions must focus, therefore, on more systematic appraisals of service delivery efforts, and on refining and defining those interventions that are the most efficient and appropriate to family needs for children in the infancy period.

REFERENCES

Barnard, K. (1978). *The nursing child assessment satellite training.* Seattle: University of Washington School of Nursing.

Bayley, N. (1969). *Bayley scales of infant development.* New York: Psychological Corporation.

Beckman, P.J. (1983). Influence of selected child characteristics on stress in families of handicapped infants. *American Journal of Mental Deficiency, 88*(2), 150–156.

Bell, R.Q. (1968). A reinterpretation of the direct effects of studies of socialization. *Psychological Review, 75,* 81–95.

Brooks-Gunn, J., & Lewis, M. (1984). Maternal responsivity in interactions with handicapped infants. *Child Development, 55,* 782–793.

Bromwich, R. (1978). *Working with parents and infants.* Baltimore: University Park Press.

Bromwich, R., & Parmelee, A. (1979). An intervention program for pre-term infants. In T.M. Field, A.M. Sostek, S. Goldberg, & H.H. Shuman (Eds.), *Infants born at risk* (pp. 389–411). New York: Spectrum Publications.

Bronfenbrenner, U. (1975). Is early intervention effective? In B.Z. Friedlander, G.M. Sterritt, G.E. Kirk (Eds.), *Ex-*

ceptional infant (Vol. 3), (pp. 449–475). New York: Brunner/Mazel.

Bronfenbrenner, U. (1979). *The ecology of human development.* Cambridge, MA: Harvard University Press.

Caldwell, B., & Bradley, R. (1978). *Home observation for measurement of the environment.* Little Rock: University of Arkansas, Center for Child Development and Education.

Casto, G., & White, K. (1984). The efficacy of early intervention programs with environmentally at-risk infants. *Journal of Children in Contemporary Society, 17,* 37–48.

Crawley, S.B., & Spiker, D. (1983). Mother-child interactions involving two-years-olds with Down syndrome: A look at individual differences. *Child Development, 54,* 1312–1323.

Drotar, D., Baskiewicz, A., Irvin, N., Kennell, J.H., & Klaus, M.H. (1975). The adaptation of parents to the birth of an infant with a congenital malformation: A hypothetical model. *Pediatrics, 56,* 710–717.

Dunst, C.J. (1985). Rethinking early intervention. *Analysis and Intervention in Developmental Disabilities, 5,* 165–201.

Field, T., Widmayer, S., Stringer, S., & Ignatoff, E. (1980).

Teenage, lower-class black mothers and their preterm infants: An intervention and developmental follow-up. *Child Development, 51,* 426–436.

Friedrich, W.N., Greenberg, M.T., & Crnic, K.A. (1983). A short-form of the Questionnaire on Resources and Stress. *American Journal of Mental Deficiency, 85,* 551–553.

Hanson, M.J. (1984). Parent-infant interaction. In M.J. Hanson (Ed.), *Atypical infant development* (pp. 179–206). Austin, TX: PRO-ED.

Hanson, M.J. (1985). An analysis of the effects of early intervention services for infants and toddlers with moderate and severe handicaps. *Topics in Early Childhood Special Education, 5*(2) 36–51.

Hanson, M.J., Deino, D.M., & Krentz, M. (1986). Family stress: Its relationship to parent-infant interaction. In D. Gentry and J. Olson (Eds.). *The family support network series (Monograph 3): Research in family involvement practices* (pp. 23–29). Moscow, ID: University of Idaho.

Hanson, M.J., & Krentz, M. (1986). *Supporting parent-child interactions: A guide for early intervention program personnel.* San Francisco: San Francisco State University, Department of Special Education.

Hanson, M.J., & Lynch, E.W. (in press). *Early intervention: Implementing child and family services for infants and toddlers who are at-risk or disabled.* Austin, TX: PRO-ED.

Lazar, I., & Darlington, R. (1982). Lasting effects of early education: A report from the Consortium for Longitudinal Studies. *Monographs of the Society for Research in Child Development, 47*(2–3), Serial No. 195.

Mahoney, G., Finger, I., & Powell, A. (1985). Relationship of maternal behavioral style to the development of organically impaired mentally retarded infants. *American Journal of Mental Deficiency, 90,* 296–302.

Minuchin, S. (1974). *Families and family therapy.* Cambridge, MA: Harvard University Press.

Ramey, C.T., Beckman-Bell, P., & Gowan, J. (1980). Infant characteristics and infant-caregiver interactions. In J.J.

Gallagher (Ed.), *New directions for exceptional children: Parents and families of handicapped children* (No. 4, pp. 59–84). San Francisco: Jossey-Bass.

Ross, G. (1984). Home intervention for premature infants of low-income families. *American Journal of Orthopsychiatry, 54,* 263–270.

Sameroff, A.J., & Chandler, M.J. (1975). Reproductive risk and the continuum of caretaking causality. In F.D. Horowitz (Ed.), *Review of child development research* (Vol. 4, pp. 187–244). Chicago: University of Chicago Press.

Schroeder, S., Showstack, J., & Roberts, H. (1979). Frequency and clinical description of high cost patients in 17 acute care hospitals. *New England Journal of Medicine, 300,* 1706–1709.

Solnit, A., & Stark, M. (1961). Mourning the birth of a defective child. *The Psychoanalytic Study of the Child, 16,* 523–527.

Taylor, P., & Hall, B. (1979). Parent-infant bonding and opportunities in a perinatal center. *Seminars in Perinatology, 3,* 73–79.

Trohanis, P., Cox, J., & Meyer, R.A. (1982). A report on selected demonstration programs for infant intervention. In C. Ramey & P. Trohanis (Eds.), *Finding and educating high-risk and handicapped infants* (pp. 163–191). Baltimore: University Park Press.

Turnbull, A.P., Summers, J.A., & Brotherson, M.J. (1984). *Working with families with disabled members: A family systems approach.* Lawrence: Kansas University Affiliated Facility, University of Kansas.

Turnbull, A.P., & Turnbull, H.R. (1986). *Families, professionals, and exceptionality: A special partnership.* Columbus, OH: Charles E. Merrill.

White, O., Edgar, E., & Haring, N.G. (1978). *Uniform Performance Assessment System.* Seattle: College of Education, University of Washington.

CHAPTER 14

Supporting Parent Involvement in Early Intervention

A Role-Taking Model

*Kristine L. Slentz, Barbara Walker,
and Diane Bricker*

By the late 1970s, both practice and research in the area of parent involvement reflected a conceptual framework that regarded parents as a valuable and capable resource in the education of young children with special needs (Bronfenbrenner, 1974). The prevailing theoretical position supported parent involvement for three reasons: 1) the great amount of potential time available to parents for teaching their young children, 2) the tendency of parents to be highly salient and reinforcing to their own youngsters, and 3) the increased probability of generalization and maintenance of skills taught in the home environment (Bricker, Seibert, & Casuso, 1980). The concept of parents as interventionists also established a foundation for parent-professional partnerships that reduced professional dominance and control over the lives of disabled children.

EVOLVING MODELS OF PARENT INVOLVEMENT

The theoretical focus on educational aspects of the parent-child dyad evolved to a broader ecological perspective that emphasized the powerful influence of the affective relationship between young children and their caregivers (Lewis & Lee-Painter, 1974). Considerable attention was directed to conceptualizing the impact of the

quality of parent-child intereactions on children's development (Bromwich, 1981; Goldberg, 1977; Kaiser & Hayden, 1984). Theories of parent-child interaction were translated into global variables such as attitude and knowledge of developmental principles (Moxley-Haegert & Serbin, 1983), in addition to specific teaching skills.

The most recently articulated theoretical perspective in the area of parent involvement in early intervention further expands the concept of ecological context to include a variety of social systems that may have an impact on the child's development and family's adjustment. The adoption of a more comprehensive view of the young child and family as part of a dynamic environmental context suggests a shift in focus in the area of parent involvement; the entire family system becomes the most appropriate target of intervention (Foster, Berger, & McLean, 1981). Rather than focus exclusively on the needs of the disabled child, an array of personal and social services is then indicated to promote and support each family member.

Current theoretical and conceptual orientations in the area of parent involvement show evidence of an evolving appreciation for the complexity of child, parent, family, and societal interactions (Wikler, 1986). The changes in theoretical and

Support for this chapter came in part from Grant No. G008300637 awarded to the Center on Human Development, University of Oregon from the Office of Special Education and Rehabilitation.

conceptual perspectives on parent involvement over more than a decade appear to have been a process of evolution, rather than the replacement of one orientation by another. The rationale for successful involvement of parents in their children's educational programs has provided a strong foundation for more theoretically complex and programmatically sensitive approaches to parents and families of disabled children.

PARENT ROLES

Parent involvement activities cast parents in many roles, including, but not limited to, advocate, learner, interventionist, client, and decisionmaker. Individual programs combine the variety of roles into plans of service to parents and families. Rather than attempting to identify select programmatic models among the many available, the discussion here focuses on the most obvious roles that parents may assume.

Parents as Advocates

For the first half of this century, the prevailing practice was to institutionalize young children with handicaps. Medical personnel were primarily responsible for encouraging these placements. The rationale for removing the child from the home included the prevention of dysfunction within the family as a result of the stress and burden of caring for a child with handicaps (Aldrich, 1947). Parents were thus cast in the passive, nonparticipative role of needing protection from parenting their children with special needs. The expectation was that parents would comply with professional decisions and surrender control of their children's habilitation to others (Turnbull & Winton, 1984).

With the advent of advocacy groups such as the National Association for Retarded Citizens (NARC), the "quiet-saint" characterization of parents of children with handicaps changed dramatically in the 1950's and 1960's (Healy, Keese, & Smith, 1985; Turnbull & Winton, 1984). Advocacy remains an important role for parents who support educational services for preschool children, and who champion active involvement of parents in developing services. At local, state, and federal levels, parents have been an important force in developing services and shaping the

legislation that currently governs early intervention practice (Bricker, 1986).

Of the many models that exist nationwide to develop and assist parents in advocacy activities, few specifically target the parents of preschoolers. Similarly, few early intervention programs train parent advocates as a primary involvement strategy (Walker, Slentz, & Bricker, 1985). Nonetheless, advocacy constitutes an important avenue for parent involvement during the preschool years. Those parents who enjoy the political process and/or are comfortable with taking an activist role can make meaningful contributions to the field as a whole, as well as to improving the quality of available services for their own children.

Parents as Learners and Interventionists

The role of parents as learners has also been widely recognized in preschool programs for children with handicaps, which involve parents in curricula designed by professionals to enhance parenting and teaching skills. A frequent approach has been to provide specialized information to parents on topics such as developmental hierarchies and positive parenting approaches, specific disabilities, the individualized education program (IEP) process, and services available for children.

Teaching parents skills that enable them to become more effective change agents appears to be the most frequent strategy for parent involvement in early intervention programs described in the literature (Baker, 1984; Kaiser & Hayden, 1984; Walker et al., 1985). In this role the parents are cast as resources to foster growth and development in their young disabled children. Parents have entered into frequent partnerships with professionals in a variety of diverse programmatic contexts. Parents tend to serve as primary interventionists at home for infants and toddlers and to move toward classroom involvement as the child reaches preschool age. Combined home and center involvement often spans the middle range of 18 months to 3 years, easing the transition from home to classroom (Filler, 1983).

In addition to developing teaching skills and providing information, a few programs in the early 1980s developed involvement strategies wherein parents were trained to perform specific tasks other than teaching children. For example, parents may have been trained to observe and assess their own children. Some programs also describe components that assist parents in developing skills for working with other parents in the areas of intervention, advocacy, and mutual support (Walker et al., 1985). Although specialized training beyond a teaching role for parents is currently infrequent, a trend that expands and enhances the options of parents as learners is apparent.

The role of interventionist is an appropriate avenue of involvement for those parents who like to teach, value their ability to develop skill and knowledge in others, and have time in their lives to devote to helping others learn. The seemingly logical notions of carrying instructional activities into the home, increasing training opportunities, and developing parents as skilled interventionists can place unreasonable demands on the schedules of families. In addition, a focus on skill development at home may be successful at the expense of more normalized parenting interactions. The demonstrated success of parent training models makes it easy for early interventionists to assume that "inside every mother is an enthusiastic therapist with time on her hands" (Kaiser & Hayden, 1984, p. 304).

Parents as Recipients of Specialized Services

A more recent and less common phenomenon that is apparent in the literature is an approach to parent involvement that seeks to address the needs of parents directly, as a separate component of early intervention services. This perspective involves parents as legitimate clients in their own right, by providing specialized services for adults in conjunction with early intervention services for their children (Fine & Johnson, 1983). Examples of this approach to parent involvement include support groups and individual counseling or therapy sessions. Participation in these specialized services offers opportunities for sharing reactions to the child's disability, exploring the impact of the disability upon the family, and developing successful coping mechanisms.

A rather recent development in parent involvement in early intervention is the inclusion

of family members other than the mother in the program. A few programs have developed models designed to involve fathers, siblings, grandparents, and other extended family members (e.g., see Gabel & Kotsch, 1981; Moore, Hammerlynck, Barsh, Spieker, & Jones, 1982; Vadasy, Fewell, Meyer, Schell, & Greenburg, 1984). Other programs (O'Neill & Levy, 1981; Smith, Edwards, & Gibson, 1981) describe culturally responsive programs that approach early intervention using both a familial and cultural perspective. These models attempt to provide relevant services to any person who is involved with the disabled child.

The existence of family-focused services does not necessarily promote parent involvement, however. Parents whose personal and cultural values promote individualistic, family-oriented solutions are unlikely to become enthusiastic about counseling services just because they have a child with special needs. In a similar vein, poverty-level and/or dysfunctional families may not welcome the presence of even the most well intentioned professionals in their homes. Parents are most likely to assume the role of receiving services for themselves if they perceive the service as facilitative rather than evaluative, and if their particular interests, needs, and concerns are addressed directly and individually.

Parents as Decisionmakers

Parents of infants and toddlers with special needs are often cast, willingly or not, into the role of decisionmakers. Parents often become case managers by default, having a strong vested interest in the integration and coordination of available medical, educational and social services on behalf of their own children. Parents ultimately decide which professionals to believe and trust, and which treatments to undertake. In addition, parents are responsible for the hundreds of decisions that go into accommodating the needs of any child in the family unit, and maintaining the family in the community. Parents decide what the family's priorities are, and how having a child with a handicap will affect those priorities.

The national policy toward parent involvement places strong emphasis on the role of parents as decisionmakers. Public Law 99-457 (*The*

Education of the Handicapped Act Amendments of 1986) grants parents of preschoolers decision-making rights concerning evaluation, placement, and IEP development. The Handicapped Children's Early Education Program (HCEEP), a federal agency that funds demonstration programs in early intervention, has guidelines that identify parents as planners and advisors, in addition to their roles as learners and teachers (Turnbull & Winton, 1984). Decisionmaking options for involvement appeal to some parents who become skilled and energetic members of planning and advisory boards for local, state, and national programs.

Parents can be successfully involved in early intervention programs in a number of roles. They can provide a multiplicity of resources to their own children, themselves, their families, and early intervention services, if involvement roles can be matched with abilities, interests, preferences, and schedules.

CURRENT CONTEXT OF PARENT INVOLVEMENT EFFORTS

The evident, long-term impact of the home environment on a child's education and habilitation provides a compelling reason for professionals to include parents and families in early intervention efforts (Gottfried, 1984; Meyers, Nihira, & Mink, 1984). As parents and professionals have interacted and worked together on behalf of young children, the preferences, needs, resources, and concerns of a child's family have emerged as an important context for the delivery of early intervention services (Turnbull & Turnbull, 1986; Wikler, 1986).

Despite the general acceptance of family involvement in early intervention programs, there is no single consensual model for the meaningful inclusion of families in these programs. In this chapter, issues are addressed that have emerged from various parent involvement efforts, and a model implemented at the University of Oregon's Early Intervention Program is presented.

Heterogeneity of Families

Eligibility for participation in early intervention programs is generally based on child, rather than family, characteristics. While eligibility criteria

for identifiable handicaps and delays may ensure predictable composition in the population of children from year to year, this may not be true of the families involved. The heterogeneity of families is increasing with the trend toward inclusion in early intervention programs of children who are at risk due to environmental factors such as prenatal addiction, poor maternal nutrition, abuse, and neglect. Professionals working with this population of high risk, multiproblem families are often faced with divergent systems of values and beliefs, as well as unfamiliar cultural backgrounds. Providing services to parents and families in the 1980s has become a far more complex endeavor than providing information about disabilities and teaching skills designed to improve the young child's developmental outcome.

Diversity of Interventions

Passage of PL 99-457 reflects a growing acknowledgment of the role of parents and families in the education and development of young children. The requirement for an Individual Family Services Plan (IFSP) for children from birth to 2 years of age is a clear indication that, at least on a conceptual level, the field recognizes the need for family focused intervention. Strategies for the implementation of the IFSP remain to be developed, however, before its impact on parent/family involvement can be evaluated (Vincent, 1987). Often the individual educational needs of the child, as viewed by interventionists, are at odds with the healthy functioning of the family unit (Turnbull & Turnbull, 1986; Vincent, 1987). For example, specific training activities with the disabled child may interfere with more global family activities. Early intervention personnel are being required to consider the challenge of involving parents without adding to parents' levels of stress and to family disruption.

The content of parent/family involvement efforts currently ranges from teaching skills to stress-management to advocacy (Walker et al., 1985). Intervention formats vary in duration and frequency, and include many combinations of group and individual meetings, at the child's home or at school, with attendance being voluntary in some programs and mandatory in others. The nuclear and extended family, and even unrelated significant others (e.g., neighbors, baby-sitters) have been the focus of parent/family program components (Moore et al., 1982). Individual family members, interactions between people in the home, or the entire family system may be intervention targets (Bristol, 1988).

Changing Professional Roles

The diversity of parents and families in the population, as well as the range of intervention format and content, calls into question some of the traditional roles of early interventionists. The skills and expertise that are required to work successfully with adult family members are quite different from those needed to intervene with young children (Bricker & Slentz, 1988). Professionals from special education, counseling psychology, social services, and allied health specialities are still exploring interdisciplinary models that will minimize professional overlap while maximizing efficiency of services to preschool children and their families (Healy et al., 1985; Thornton & Frankenburg, 1983).

Evaluation Concerns

The evaluation of parent/family involvement in early intervention programs remains a dilemma. Practitioners are still struggling to identify what to measure (appropriate outcome measures) and how to measure it (proper instrumentation). Many professionals have lamented the dependence on child change data and encouraged the expansion of evaluation emphasis to include parent and family variables as outcome measures (Bricker, Bailey, & Bruder, 1984; Dunst & Rheingrover, 1981; Sheehan, 1982). At present, however, few resources are available to assist the conscientious practitioner in determining the impact of service components that are designed specifically to address parents and other family members.

The success of efforts to involve parents is typically measured by rates of parental attendance or participation in program activities, such as parental involvement in IEP development. The assumption that meaningful parent involvement is best reflected in attendance and active participation in program-driven activities ignores the fact that parents are often involved in other aspects of their children's overall develop-

ment and welfare. Current evaluations of parental involvement do not provide information on those parents who actively choose not to participate in program activities. Nor does the current definition of meaningful involvement address important questions about whether efforts to involve parents are sufficiently sensitive to families' individual circumstances, cultural differences, value structures, and belief systems.

The principles of an individualized approach to parent involvement within a family-focused context form the basis for a parent component at the University of Oregon's Early Intervention Program. The parent component was designed to develop numerous involvement roles and provide the training and support necessary for parents to assume preferred roles successfully. A primary focus was the evaluation of the project impact on parents, the results of which are presented in the following pages.

SERVICE DESIGN

The Parent-to-Parent Project was a federally funded, three year grant awarded to the Early Intervention Program (EIP) at the Center on Human Development, on the University of Oregon campus. The Center on Human Development is a University Affiliated Program (UAP) housing numerous evaluation, service, research, and personnel preparation programs in the area of developmental disabilities. The EIP served approximately 50 children and families in two classrooms and in weekly parent-infant groups.

Population

Children served by the EIP were between the ages of birth and six years. The population of children that was served displayed a variety of delays and identified handicaps. Because Oregon mandates services for preschoolers with severe handicaps, the Early Intervention Program provided services to children whose disabilities were less severe than the eligibility requirements for state funded services. Parent-to-Parent services were also open to parents whose children were enrolled in other early intervention programs.

The population of families varied considerably over the three years of the project. There were single parents, two-parent families, and extended families as primary caretakers. Income and education of parents varied along a wide continuum, with a large number of low-income families participating actively in the second and third years.

Philosophy and Goals

The Parent-to-Parent Project was designed to provide an opportunity for the parents of young children with developmental disabilities to interact with the program staff in a broad range of activities that focused on child and family needs. Project goals were generated from a philosophy that acknowledged the validity of legal and educational rationales for involving parents in intervention programs for children. In addition, the project was dedicated to a service model that was capable of offering a broad and flexible menu of services that would be sensitive to needs and resources that individual families presented.

The Parent-to-Parent Project provided services that the parents themselves identified as useful. Considerable attention was devoted to assessing parental needs, interests, skills, and resources. Care was taken to identify and respond to both educational and support needs, and to offer an array of services that project resources could realistically address. In cases where parental needs exceeded project resources, the project staff assisted parents in locating appropriate referral agencies or services in the community.

One major goal of the program was to encourage parents to become involved in their children's intervention programs. Activities were designed to assist parents in acquiring information and skills that were related to understanding their children's developmental needs. An equally important goal was to facilitate participation in informal discussions with other parents, with a focus on the rewards and responsibilities of parenting young children with special needs. A third goal was to encourage parents to take roles that would permit them to act as resources for child- and family-focused interventions, and for other parents.

Program Organization

Services for parents were divided into two coordinated areas identified as *education* and *support*

tracks. The *education track* was structured to offer parents instruction and skills acquisition in areas of child development, parenting, and teaching. The *support track* was similarly structured to give parents an opportunity to evaluate and improve their communication and problem-solving skills, to assess and consider alternative strategies for managing child care and coping with personal and family stress.

The division of the content into two tracks was admittedly arbitrary, as it was recognized that many issues that were presented initially in either track would surface appropriately in the other. This overlap was seen as favorable, because it gave parents an opportunity to address major concerns from two perspectives. For example, difficulties with a child's behavior were initially addressed in the education track, where parents learned strategies for effective behavior management; concurrently, or at a strategic time, the affective impact involved in carrying out behavior management programs was addressed in the support track.

Because parents presented considerable diversity in terms of knowledge and skills, a graduated-steps model was developed to allow a logical progression of educational and support-oriented content, starting with basic information and advancing to skills training and role-taking. Most parents elected to start at the entry level and proceed to a preferred role. Occasionally parents demonstrated sufficient knowledge, skills and/or motivation to move quickly into the more advanced levels of participation. The four stages of the program shown in Table 1 provided the framework for sequencing information and the training content. Parents who participated in all levels became qualified to assume a variety of roles at the EIP or in the community.

Stage I: Program Entry Orientation services were provided during this stage for parents whose children with handicaps were newly enrolled in local intervention programs. The activities of this stage included assessing parental concerns, interests, and needs, and gathering information regarding the intervention program and the parental rights and responsibilities related to the individualized education plan process. The objectives of Stage I were to conduct intake and orientation, and to identify individual needs and interests.

Table 1. Parent-to-parent training sequence

Stage	I. Program entry	II. Change agent	III. Aide/assistant	IV. Interventionist
Objectives	Complete program intake and orientation. Identify individual needs, interests, resources.	Develop parent's skills and resources as change agents within each family.	Support parent performance in preferred roles.	Develop parent skills as interventionists for other parents.
Activities	Assess parent needs, interests, resources. Provide information re: program policies and procedures. Review rights and responsibilities.	Provide service and instruction in areas of parent education and parent support. Conduct small group and individual sessions.	Instruct parents in requirements for performance of roles, education or support. Supervise parents on-site. Coordinate with on-site staff.	Instruct parents in group management, organization, and supervision. Consult with parent interventionists to address issues and evaluate progress.
Outcomes	Signed consents, releases, Individual Family Plan	Successful completion of family plan objectives	Successful performance by parents in a variety of education and support roles	Parents as interventionists for peers

Typically, the parents attended an initial meeting with a small group of other parents whose children were enrolling in the same early intervention program. These intake sessions occurred while the children were undergoing developmental assessments. In addition to securing informed parental consent for both child and parent participation in the intervention program activities, the Parent-to-Parent staff described options for involvement. Parents completed a *Family Interest Checklist* from which data were aggregated to guide subsequent plans for services offered to parents. Materials that described the Early Intervention Program (EIP) were distributed at the initial meeting, and time was devoted to addressing parents' concerns about children's adjustment to the classroom experience.

Soon after the children's enrollment in the intervention program, parents were invited to attend several parents' meetings. At one of these meetings, classroom teachers welcomed parents, introduced classroom staff, and described classroom routines as well as the program's philosophy and policies. Other parent meetings provided information on parental rights and responsibilities that were contained in current legislation, and on the purpose of the IEP process. Emphasis was placed on the variety of opportunities for parental participation in the

planning, implementation, and review of their children's educational programs. In addition, parents were invited to consider participation in the activities available through the Parent-to-Parent Project.

At a time that was scheduled to coincide with the IEP meetings, parents were asked to participate in an *Individualized Family Plan Interview* conducted by the project staff. This interview was structured to collect information in several areas: parental understanding and concern about their child's development; family resources, needs, and functioning; parental feelings and experiences pertaining to meeting their child's needs; the history of experiences related to special services; the history of parental involvement in intervention services for their child; and participants' interest in working with other parents or in activities to support their child's intervention program.

The result of the family interview was a set of goals that featured family and/or parent involvement. An *Individualized Family Plan* was created, with the responsibilities for implementation divided among parents and project staff. This plan was then shared with classroom interventionists, and where appropriate, project staff facilitated collaboration between classroom staff and parents in working parents' priority goals into the overall program for the child. Progress toward parent/family goals was then monitored and reviewed with parents at quarterly intervals.

Stage II: Change Agent During Stage II, the initial education and support services and instruction were provided weekly to small groups of parents. Training focused on assisting parents in the implementation of ongoing parenting or teaching tasks that were related to meeting their children's specific developmental needs. The objective of this stage was to develop parents' resources and skills as change agents, within the context of each family's strengths and needs.

In both the parent education and the parent support tracks, the lesson plans were designed to ensure sequential treatment of basic concepts and skills that were identified as core content. The time allotted to each lesson varied, as different groups of parents progressed at different rates through the planned agendas. The 8-week plan for the parent education track was designed to cover topics that included an introduction/ orientation, information on early development, information on parents as teachers, teaching strategies and content, and monitoring progress.

Stage III: Aide or Assistant During Stage III, parents received training that was designed to prepare them for roles as aides or assistants in either EIP classrooms or in Parent-to-Parent Project activities. After initial instruction was provided for specific roles, parents were supervised by project personnel and on-site staff to ensure comfortable transitions and satisfactory maintenance of skills from the training setting to the on-site work location. The objective of Stage III was to support parents in their performance of a variety of roles in EIPs.

Training during Stage III was conducted in the form of a practicum experience. The project staff conferred with classroom personnel, for example, to ascertain the skills that parents would need to function as aides in each specific classroom. These skills were then described, demonstrated, and practiced until parents met performance criteria set by the classroom and project staff; parents were then assigned roles in the classroom. Continuous supervision was provided by project personnel, as was feedback about performance from classroom staff. For parents who demonstrated interest and ability, additional training and supervision was provided

to allow them to assume more responsibility in activities such as leading instruction for small groups of children and collecting data on child performance.

Some parents elected to become involved in training for support roles within the Parent-to-Parent Project. They received training and supervision in skills that prepared them for roles as intake and orientation assistants, parent group co-leaders, social event organizers, and library managers.

Stage IV: Interventionist Parents who completed Stage III training and demonstrated continued interest and sufficient success in their roles were invited to participate in Stage IV training. The objective of this final training stage was to assist parents in acquiring skills that were necessary to become interventionists with other parents. Depending on interest, prior training, and work experience, parents could elect to become instructor/trainers for other parents. Parent instructors provided information and on-site training for peers who were pursuing roles in classroom settings or in support component services.

The training that was provided during Stage IV consisted of individual meetings between project staff and parents who qualified and elected to assume leadership roles as trainer/interventionists in Stage II activities. The training content and supervision for Stage IV participants were organized as follows: Orientation; Teaching Skills and Group Management; Organizational Skills; and Consulting with Supervisor.

Summary of Training Stages Considerable variation in parental interest, ability, and circumstances affected the participation and the rates of progress through the stages. After completing initial needs, demographic, and attitude assessments, parents could elect to begin or not begin participating, or to defer participation to a more convenient time. Parents progressed through the training stages at rates that were determined by their mastery of requisite content and skills.

Personnel and Staff Skills

The director of the Early Intervention Program (EIP) assumed administrative responsibilities for the project, and two program coordinators were responsible for service delivery and supervision of project staff. One program coordinator was an early childhood development specialist, and the other was a counselor who had experience working with families with disabled children; they were responsible for service delivery in the education and support tracks, respectively. In addition, part time staff were recruited from masters level students in early childhood special education, and eventually from parents who had completed Stage II and III training. The program coordinators were responsible for supervision of part time staff and parents.

The primary activities that were conducted by program coordinators required expertise in adult and family assessment, in development and implementation of educational and support services, in supervision of parents and staff, and in program evaluation. Staff working in the education track of the Parent-to-Parent Project had experience related to child development, behavior management, the IEP process, activity-based instruction for young children with special needs, and methods for integrating educational objectives comfortably into home and community environments. Staff working in the support track were qualified in areas pertaining to support, communication skills, and coping skills such as problem-solving and stress-management. In addition to presentation and instruction, skills in small group leadership and individual consultation were critical to effective program implementation in both tracks.

Project staff were required to adapt the available programmatic materials and training methods to the specific population of parents. Instructional materials that were designed for college courses or for service providers were frequently unappealing and inappropriate for use with parents. The ability to locate, adapt, or develop materials and training formats that would meet the changing needs and interests of the group was important to the project's success.

In order to procure jobs for parents as aides in early intervention settings and parent group meetings, Parent-to-Parent staff were required to negotiate with other service program personnel to ensure an appropriate match of parent capabilities to program needs. Negotiation and supervision skills were therefore critical to the successful integration of parents into work settings. For example, classroom teachers at the Early In-

tervention Program requested frequent assistance from the project staff in managing the parents' transitions into the classroom. Staff time was needed for briefing parents, for assisting the transition from training into classroom aide roles, and to ensure appropriate ongoing supervision of parent aides.

Initially, many parents did not consider themselves likely candidates for roles in service programs. In this project, therefore, effective training and supervision of parent participants required considerable sensitivity to parents' needs for encouragement, and a willingness to adapt customary performance evaluation procedures. Strategies that were developed and revised frequently included building confidence, frequent recognition of progress, and constructive feedback when improvement was needed.

In addition to providing training for parents at sites with center-based services, project staff assisted in community outreach efforts to provide training to parents who were involved in parent services in the community. The ability to adapt program elements and to develop strategies for successful interface with community agencies was important to effective collaboration.

Methods and Techniques

Within the training stages described above, strategies for assessment and training were tailored to achieve a dynamic interplay between parental request for services and use of project resources.

The 8-week agenda for the support track included the following topics: introducing/orienting parents, addressing issues in obtaining and maintaining support, enhancing communication skills, improving problem-solving ability, and managing stress.

Various materials were developed to supplement the content for each instructional session. Techniques that were designed to encourage participation also varied, with frequent use of discussion and problem solving formats, role-playing, and worksheet exercises.

PROGRAM EVALUATION

During the second and third years of the Parent-to-Parent Project, the evaluation procedures measured: 1) parent participation, 2) parental attitudes, 3) parent satisfaction, and 4) training impact. Data were collected from several sources, including program documents, parent self-report measures, and supervisors' reports. Demographic data and measures of attitudes and satisfaction were collected only on parents whose children were enrolled in the Early Intervention Program (EIP) classes. Evaluation of the training impact included ratings from EIP parents and from parents in the local community who participated in program activities.

The sample sizes vary across evaluation analyses, reflecting changes in the absolute number of parents participating from year to year, and differences in the relative return of evaluation measures. For example, demographic measures were completed by all parents during the EIP intake process, yielding a total of 31 families for Year 2 and 39 families for Year 3. The rate of return on self-report measures was always less than 100%, resulting in a smaller sample for the evaluations of attitude and satisfaction. The number of participants in the evaluation of the training impact reflects a subset of EIP parents and those from other programs who were trained to assume various education and support roles.

Evaluation data were collected using multiple measures, for the purposes of improving services to families. In order to evaluate possible trends, data were analyzed separately for the 2 different years. Since many of the same families participated for consecutive years, the data sets were not independent samples.

Population Description

Demographic data were collected in categories that included the child's handicapping condition, the family structure, and socioeconomic variables. Table 2 shows selected characteristics of the families served in the second and third years of the Parent-to-Parent Project.

Classification of Parents for Analysis

The project staff were interested in determining if parents who differed on the variables of participation, income, and interaction style also differed on measures of attitude and program satisfaction. Criteria were established and parents were assigned to appropriate categories in the three selected variables. Parents were divided

into two groups based on participation status: 1) participants (parents who participated regularly in elective as well as required program activities) and 2) nonparticipants (parents who did not participate beyond required activities such as IEP meetings). Program attendance records and activity checklists provided data on parent participation in both required and elective program activities. Parents were grouped according to two income levels, including higher income parents (annual incomes > $10,000) and lower income parents (annual incomes < $10,000). Parents were also categorized according to a rating of interaction style, which included difficult interactions, moderately difficult or variable interactions, and easy interactions. These interaction ratings were based on reports by classroom staff, Parent-to-Parent project staff, and other parents.

Table 3 shows the distributions of parents on the variables of participation, income, and interaction style for Years 2 and 3. In Year 2, more parents were nonparticipants, while in Year 3 more parents were classified as participants. In both Years 2 and 3, more parents had incomes that exceeded $10,000. The distribution of interaction style is relatively even, except that in Year 3 more parents were judged to have an interaction style that was categorized as easy.

Analyses were conducted to determine if the parents who were classified as participants differed from those classified as nonparticipants on any of the following variables, including income level, interaction style, family type, or child's disability. Chi square analyses indicated that, for both years, participation rates were unrelated to differences in those characteristics. Parent-to-Parent activities were successful in eliciting participation across a broad range of family types and socioeconomic situations. In addition, the rate of parental participation in EIP activities rose from below 50% in Year 2 to 66% in Year 3.

Evaluation of Parental Attitudes

Parental attitudes were assessed at the beginning and the end of the school year. Evaluation focused on shifts in parental attitudes about their knowledge and competence as parents of children in a special education setting, and satisfaction with the Early Intervention Program.

Two instruments were used to measure paren-

Table 2. Characteristics of EIP families for years 2 and 3

Family characteristic	Year 2 N^a	Year 2 % of Group	Year 3 N^a	Year 3 % of Group
Degree of impairment of child				
Nonhandicapped	9	31.0	7	17.9
At risk	4	13.8	10	25.6
Mild	7	24.1	11	28.3
Moderate	8	27.6	9	23.1
Severe	1	3.5	2	5.1
	29		39	
Type of family				
Single parent	8	25.8	11	28.2
Partnership	23	74.2	27	69.2
Extended family	0	0.0	1	2.6
	31		39	
Annual income				
Less than $5,000	10	33.3	10	31.3
$5,000–$10,000	3	10.0	2	6.2
$10,001–$15,000	5	16.7	2	6.2
$15,001–$20,000	4	13.3	8	25.0
$20,001–$25,000	4	13.3	3	9.4
Greater than $25,000	4	13.3	7	21.9
	30		32	
Level of education (father)				
Under 7 years	0	0.0	1	3.7
Junior high school	1	3.6	2	7.4
Partial high school	1	3.6	1	3.7
High school	7	25.0	3	11.1
Partial college	9	32.1	8	29.6
College	7	25.0	8	29.6
Graduate school	3	10.7	4	14.8
	28		27	
Level of education (mother)				
Under 7 years	0	0.0	0	0.0
Junior high school	0	0.0	1	2.6
Partial high school	2	6.5	2	5.1
High school	10	32.2	6	15.4
Partial college	12	38.7	21	53.8
College	2	6.5	5	12.8
Graduate school	5	16.1	4	10.3
	31		39	

^{a}Total N varies due to missing data for selected questions.

Table 3. Number and percent of parents classified on the variables of participation, income and interaction style

	Participation Participants	Participation Nonparticipants	Income <$10,000	Income >$10,000	Interaction style Easy	Interaction style Moderate	Interaction style Difficult
Year 2 ($N = 31$)	14 (45%)	17 (55%)	13 (42%)	18 (58%)	12 (39%)	10 (32%)	9 (29%)
Year 3 ($N = 39$)	25 (64%)	14 (36%)	16 (41%)	23 (59%)	17 (44%)	11 (28%)	11 (28%)

tal attitude, including a modified version of the *Parental Self-Appraisal Inventory (PSAI)* (Carter & Macy, 1978) and the *Parent Survey* (Roberts, n.d.). For analysis, program staff generated five scales for the PSAI: *child, home, planning, adjustment,* and *other* (general competence), while three scales were created for the *Parent Survey: comfort* (with child's development and behavior), *attitude* (toward services and the child's prospects for improvement), and *needs* (degree to which needs were perceived as satisfied). Correlated *t* tests were conducted on attitude scores from the PSAI and Parent Survey in both Years 2 and 3 to discover if there were any pre- to posttest within-group changes for the total group of parents with children enrolled in the EIP. In addition, the subgroups defined by participation and income characteristics were examined for pre- to posttest differences in attitude. *T* tests were also conducted to examine between-group differences at both pre- and postparticipation assessment.

PSAI total scores for each year's total group of parents indicated no significant differences between pre- and posttest. However, as Table 4 shows, at pretest in Year 2 on the other (general competence) scale, the nonparticipants group rated themselves more positively, indicating a

higher global rating of self-appraisal. This difference may have played a role in these parents' decisions to participate in parent-oriented activities. At posttest, this difference on the other (general competence) scale was no longer significant between nonparticipants and participants, suggesting that participation may have had some impact in elevating global self-appraisal.

In Year 3, nonparticipants reported a significant, positive change in self-appraisal on the child scale over the school year, a measure that reflects an increase in perceived ability to manage child-related problems. While the change on this scale was also positive for participants, it was not significant. On all other PSAI scales, there were no significant differences either between or within groups for Year 2 or 3.

Table 5 shows that, for subgroups defined by income level, significant differences were found at the posttest in Year 2, with higher income parents consistently reporting more positive self-appraisal on the child, future plans, and adjustment scales of the PSAI scales ($p < .05$). These findings confirm general expectations that parents with more adequate financial resources feel more positive about their ability to manage family life and to adjust to parenting responsibilities.

Table 4. Within and between comparisons of participant and non-participant groups on the other (general competence) and child PSAI Scales

		PSAI Scales			
		Child		Other	
Year 2					
Participant group	(N = 11)	Pre	Post	Pre	Post
Mean		14.27	14.36	3.91[a]	4.18
SD		2.09	3.72	2.07	1.80
Nonparticipant group	(N = 11)				
Mean		15.36	15.09	5.64[a]	5.27
SD		1.92	2.50	.64	1.21
Year 3					
Participant group	(N = 13)				
Mean		13.46	14.15	4.15	4.54
SD		2.85	2.82	1.61	1.50
Nonparticipant group	(N = 9)				
Mean		12.56[b]	15.00[b]	4.56	3.78
SD		2.06	2.45	.83	2.15

[a]Between-groups difference significant at $p < .05$, two-tailed t test.
[b]Within-groups difference significant at $p < .05$, two-tailed t test.

Table 5. Within and between comparisons of higher and lower income groups on child, plans, and adjustment PSAI Scales

	Child		Plans		Adjustment	
	Pre	Post	Pre	Post	Pre	Post
Year 2						
Low income						
(<$10,000)						
N = 9						
Mean	14.22	13.00[a]	11.44	10.44[b]	8.11	7.78[a]
SD	2.15	3.83	2.22	1.77	.74	1.40
High income						
(>$10,000)						
N = 13						
Mean	15.23	15.92[a]	13.08	13.38[b]	8.54	8.77[a]
SD	1.93	1.90	2.56	1.82	.75	.42
Year 3						
Low income						
(<$10,000)						
N = 7						
Mean	12.29	13.00	11.71	11.43	7.57	7.29
SD	1.03	2.20	2.25	2.66	1.29	1.58
High income						
(>$10,000)						
N = 18						
Mean	13.47	15.20	11.33	12.00	7.13	7.40
SD	2.99	2.64	2.65	2.78	1.82	1.70

[a]Between-group difference significant at $p < .05$, two-tailed t test.
[b]Between-group difference significant at $p < .01$, two-tailed t test.

These differences were not replicated, however, in Year 3.

Parent Survey scores, summarized in Table 6, indicate that, for Year 2 only, a significant decrease in the comfort scale ($p < .05$) occurred for the total group of parents with children in the EIP. For the subgroups defined by participation, participants reported significantly more discomfort on the comfort scale than nonparticipants at posttest ($p < .05$) in Year 2. These results sug-

Table 6. Within and between comparisons of participants and nonparticipants on the comfort, attitude, and need scales of the *Parent Survey*

	Comfort		Attitude		Need	
	Pre	Post	Pre	Post	Pre	Post
Year 2						
Participants (N = 12)						
Mean	60.00[a]	55.08[a,b]	33.67	33.92	23.58	24.08
SD	5.77	3.23	2.56	2.84	4.94	3.75
Nonparticipants (N = 11)						
Mean	59.91	59.27[b]	34.64	34.45	25.18	25.73
SD	4.10	5.29	.88	2.71	4.24	4.16
Year 3						
Participants (N = 16)						
Mean	57.44	56.81	34.13	34.63	24.63	24.00
SD	3.76	5.54	3.08	2.39	4.03	4.37
Nonparticipants (N = 9)						
Mean	58.89	60.22	34.44	35.11	24.78	25.56
SD	4.51	4.39	1.83	2.81	3.94	3.62

[a]Within group difference significant at $p < .05$, two-tailed t test.
[b]Between groups difference significant at $p < .05$, two-tailed t test.

gest that child attendance at the Early Intervention Program increased the amount of discomfort that parents felt concerning the development of their young children with handicaps and delays. Parents who participated in program activities reported feeling less comfortable about their children than those parents who were nonparticipants.

As shown in Table 7, for the groups defined by income, low income parents reported a significant decrease on the comfort scale during Year 2. While high income parents also reported a decrease on the comfort scale that year, it was not significant. Also, in Year 2 high income parents showed a significant increase ($p < .05$) on the need scale. That is, high income families reported significantly more needs met after a year of involvement. Low income parents did not change on this dimension. These data suggest that in Year 2 the Parent-to-Parent program was more successful at meeting the needs of high income parents. In Year 3, no differences between income groups were found on the Parent Survey.

It appears that during Year 2, parents whose preschoolers were enrolled in the EIP experienced an increase in their discomfort, an effect that may be a result of parents learning new and unsettling information about their young children. The fact that higher income parents reported lower levels of discomfort and higher need satisfaction than low income parents may reflect differences in comfort and need in the broader context of their lives. The more stable scores in Year 3 are difficult to interpret in terms of program impact. An optimistic interpretation is that the program may have been more successful in Year 3 in addressing problems presented by low income families.

Evaluation of Parent Satisfaction

Parents with children in the Early Intervention Program completed a *Parent Satisfaction Questionnaire* that asked them to rate their satisfaction with participation in program activities, and how participation in the program had improved their knowledge of child development, changed their attitudes, improved their child's behavior, and benefited their children.

Table 7. Within and between comparisons of low and higher income groups on the comfort, attitude and need scales of the *Parent Survey*

	Comfort		Attitude		Need	
	Pre	Post	Pre	Post	Pre	Post
Year 2						
Low income (<$10,000) (N = 10)						
Mean	59.20[a]	55.20[a]	33.50	33.80	23.00	23.00[b]
SD	4.71	4.14	2.38	2.56	1.20	3.74
High income (>$10,000) (N = 13)						
Mean	60.54	58.54	34.62	34.46	25.38[a]	26.31[a,b]
SD	5.21	4.80	1.50	2.93	4.78	3.65
Year 3						
Low income (<$10,000) (N = 7)						
Mean	58.57	55.29	33.86	36.14	22.57	23.29
SD	4.34	3.24	3.18	2.80	4.03	4.16
High income (>$10,000) (N = 15)						
Mean	57.72	59.11	34.39	34.28	25.50	25.06
SD	3.98	5.69	2.48	2.26	3.67	4.09

[a]Within-group difference significant at $p < .05$, two-tailed t test.
[b]Between-group difference significant at $p < .05$, two-tailed t test.

General ratings of program effectiveness fell in the *very good* to *excellent* range for more than 90% of parents completing evaluations. No parent rated the program below average, and *t* tests indicated no significant differences in effect as a function of participation status, income level, or quality of interaction.

In one section of the Parent Satisfaction Questionnaire, parents rated items about program impact on specific areas of child development, attitudes, child behavior, and benefits to families. In Year 2, high income parents' ratings of program benefits to families were significantly higher (p < .05) than those of low income parents. There were no differences between income groups in Year 3.

These results suggest that in Year 2, income level had an impact on parent satisfaction with services offered by the program, as well as on attitudes. In Year 3 this effect was not evident, suggesting that efforts to modify service delivery to meet the needs of individual families were successful.

Evaluation of Training

Four parents from the EIP took part in Stage III aide training. Nine parents whose children were not enrolled in the EIP participated in community-based workshops and completed evaluations of their training experience.

EIP parents completed a *Trainer/Trainee Satisfaction Questionnaire*, a measure developed by the staff to obtain parent ratings of the usefulness and effectiveness of the training provided by the project. Other parents completed a two-page evaluation form asking them to rate (using a 5-point scale) the effectiveness of various training components and presenters.

In general, EIP parents found that staff and parent interventionists presented the materials at an appropriate level of difficulty and were adequately prepared for the roles they assumed. Most parents indicated that they liked the lecture presentations and group discussions, although two parents responded with a neutral rating of the reading materials. Scores from the evaluations of the parents trained in networking skills showed the group's mean score (with 1 representing the lowest rating and 5, the highest pos-

sible) to be 4.27. Means of individual scores ranged from 3.60 to 5.00.

Summary

Data were collected to evaluate program impact on parent participation, satisfaction, and attitudes, and to evaluate program activities that were modified and revised based on evaluation results. Changes in participation data from Year 2 to Year 3 show that the program grew increasingly effective in eliciting parent participation, although the impact of participation on attitudes was less clear. While subtle differences in attitudes were detected among parents and between parent groups defined by participation status and income, they were not systematic across groups or years. Nonetheless, the disappearance in Year 3 of several negative effects for participants (Parent Survey: comfort scale) and for low income parents (PSAI: child, future plans, and adjustment scales) suggests that efforts to enhance individualization of service delivery to better address the concerns of individual families were successful. Unfortunately, the measurement period of 2 years was not sufficient to validate this trend. Parents' ratings of program effectiveness improved somewhat in Year 3 as well.

Caution must be exercised in interpreting these results, since the psychometric qualities of the instruments used to measure parent attitudes and satisfaction have not been clearly established. Furthermore, parent satisfaction ratings (program effectiveness) are known to be typically positive and may not provide a sensitive measure of parent attitudes.

OBSERVATIONS AND RECOMMENDATIONS

As with any model, the actual implementation of the role-taking approach to parent involvement required some refinement in order to produce a workable system of service delivery. The primary problems that were encountered in the first year related to the assumptions that groups of parents involved in early intervention programs would progress as cohorts through the four tracks of role-taking. Following the program intake and training to become change agents, it was anticipated that a subset of parents would choose to become interventionists themselves with other parents. The expectation was that these parents would continue in orderly progression to the next stage of training, and develop skills to work with other parents, thus beginning another cycle.

The model was originally organized to accommodate a range of interests and needs through the options for participation in education and/or support components. Similarly, variability in entry skills and rates of progress through the stages of training was expected to be handled through more intense schedules for the most needy participants. The first group of parents soon made it all too clear that the orderly progression of the group through predetermined stages of training was not possible.

Individual differences in demographics, resources, outside demands, and values seemed to interact strongly with the skills and interests of participating parents. The constantly changing needs and priorities of the group and the individuals who were involved were often determined by needs, problems, and concerns extraneous to the Parent-to-Parent Program. The interplay of a number of variables created the demand for a more flexible and dynamic model, if the participation of a diverse sample of parents was to be maintained.

The second major problem related to the process of assessment and evaluation. An array of instruments had been proposed, from family interviews to pre- and postmeasures of topic area content, to consumer satisfaction surveys. This product-oriented evaluation plan failed to take into consideration important factors in the process of collecting information from families. Timing, reactivity to instruments and methods, and the types of evaluation questions that were asked emerged as issues to be resolved. For example, family interviews yielded guarded information when parents were new to the program, and pre- and postmeasures were threatening, invalid, and unreliable with parents in the sample who were illiterate or poorly educated.

Because the goals of the Parent-to-Parent Project included participation of many types of parents, rather than a select, homogeneous few,

progression through the key components of the model became a more individualized process. The stages of training that were available were presented as a continuum of involvement options, rather than a lock-step progression from stage to stage. As a flexible menu of activities, the model was tailored to meet the needs of individual families. The family interview was used to develop an individualized plan of services based on the parents' interests and preferences.

The originally proposed group instruction format was expanded to include individual sessions, provision of written information, and strategic noninvolvement options. The latter allowed staff to coordinate participation in IEP planning and ongoing communication without excluding working parents or those whose primary need was respite from a difficult child. The provision of a variety of options successfully captured the participation of an increasing number of families. Parents developed and negotiated numerous avenues of meaningful, comfortable, and useful involvement.

The positive aspects of the original model that were sustained and reinforced throughout three years of operation were those that provided parents with options and acknowledged their efforts directly. The core concept of role-taking created for many parents an avenue of involvement that minimized professional dominance and control, while allowing an opportunity for meaningful contribution. Parents seemed to find or create roles that reflected their individual needs and abilities. While a number of parents chose to work as classroom aides or facilitate support groups, many others developed creative roles for themselves (e.g., making a songbook/tape, writing monthly newsletters, organizing and managing a toy library).

Parent-to-Parent funding allowed hourly pay for parents whose involvement roles replaced or augmented those of project staff. Experience demonstrated that parents perceived themselves as more capable partners when the value of their time and effort was acknowledged with a paycheck. Although program resources do not usually allow the luxury of an hourly wage, there are other ways to legitimize and acknowledge parent contributions to program operations, such as inclusion in staff meetings, public acknowledgment at social events, or vouchers donated by local merchants. Based upon previous experience, incentive and/or remuneration is an important alternative to expecting parents to become involved solely because of the characteristics of their children.

The provision of both educational and support tracks gave staff continued flexibility in presenting a range of requested content. The support track was able to directly acknowledge and address issues relating to child education content. For example, while training in behavior-management in the education component, parents were able to discuss in the support component some interpersonal issues regarding other family members' consistency. Coordination between education and support staff was a key fac-tor in maximizing the benefits of both group and individual efforts across the two components.

In conclusion, providing a continuum of options for parent involvement in early intervention programs is strongly recommended. It is no longer feasible in service delivery settings to offer or require a singular, delimited role for parents.

The development of dynamic models of service that are designed to meet the needs of a range of families is well within the reach of most early intervention programs. The Parent-to-Parent Project illustrates how relatively minor changes in an existing model can have an impact on the ability of a program to maintain the involvement of parents.

REFERENCES

Aldrich, A. (1947). Preventative medicine and mongolism. *American Journal of Mental Deficiency, 52,* 127–129.

Baker, B. (1984). Intervention with families with young, severely handicapped children. In J. Blacher (Ed.), *Severely handicapped young children and their families: Research in review* (pp. 319–375). Austin, TX: PRO-ED.

Bricker, D. (1986). *Early education of at-risk and handicapped infants, toddlers, and preschool children.* Glenview, IL: Scott, Foresman.

Bricker, D., Bailey, E., & Bruder, M. (1984). The efficacy of early intervention and the handicapped infant: A wise or wasted resource? In M. Wolraich & D. Routh (Eds.), *Advances in developmental and behavioral pediatrics* (Vol. 5, pp. 373–423). Greenwich, CT: JAI Press.

Bricker, D., Seibert, J.M., & Casuso, V. (1980). Early intervention. In T. Hogg & P. Mittler (Eds.), *Advances in mental handicap research.* London: Wiley.

Bricker, D., & Slentz, D. (1988). Personnel preparation: Handicapped infants. In M. Wang, H. Walberg, & M. Reynolds (Eds.), *The handbook of special education: Research and practice* (Vol. 3, pp. 317–345). Oxford, England: Pergamon.

Bristol, M. (1988, February). *Bringing a family focus to early intervention, the impact of PL 99–457.* Workshop, Developmental Disabilities Preschool Committee, Portland, Oregon.

Bromwich, R. (1981). *Working with parents and infants: An interactional approach.* Baltimore: University Park Press.

Bronfenbrenner, U. (1974). *Is early intervention effective? A report on longitudinal evaluations of preschool programs* (DHEW Publication No. OHD 75–25, Vol. II). Washington, DC: U.S. Department of Health, Education and Welfare.

Carter, J. & Macy, D. (1978). *Project Kids study of parenting competency.* (Report No. SP 78-105-52-08). Dallas, TX: Dallas Independent School District.

Dunst, C., & Rheingrover, R. (1981). Discontinuity and instability in early development: Implications for assessment. *Topics in Early Childhood Special Education, 1*(2), 49–60.

Filler, J. (1983). Service models for handicapped infants. In G. Garwood & R. Fewell (Eds.), *Educating handicapped infants* (pp. 369–381). Rockville, MD: Aspen Systems.

Fine, M., & Johnson, F. (1983). Groups for parents of children with Down syndrome and multiple handicaps: A pilot project. *Canadian Journal of Occupational Therapy, 50*(1), 9–14.

Foster, M., Berger, M., & McLean, M. (1981). Rethinking a good idea: A reassessment of parent involvement. *Topics in Early Childhood Special Education, 1*(3), 55–65.

Gabel, H., & Kotsch, L. (1981). Extended families and young handicapped children. *Topics in Early Childhood Special Education, 1*(3), 29–36.

Goldberg, S. (1977). Social competence in infancy: A model of parent-infant interaction. *Merrill-Palmer Quarterly, 23,* 163–177.

Gottfried, A.W., (1984). *Home environment and early cognitive development: Longitudinal research.* Orlando, FL: Academic Press.

Healy, A., Keese, P., & Smith, B., (1985). Early intervention: Themes for services. *Early services for children with special needs.* Iowa City: The University of Iowa.

Kaiser, C., & Hayden, A. (1984). Clinical research and policy issues in parenting severely handicapped infants. In J. Blacher (Ed.), *Severely handicapped young children and their families: Research in review* (pp. 275–318). Orlando, FL: Academic Press.

Lewis, M., & Lee-Painter, S. (1974). An interactional approach to the mother-infant dyad. In M. Lewis & L.A. Rosenblum (Eds.), *The effect of the infant on its caregiver* (pp. 21–48). New York: John Wiley & Sons.

Meyers, C., Nihira, K., & Mink, I. (1984). Predicting retarded students' short-term growth from home environment. *Applied Research in Mental Retardation, 5,* 137–146.

Moore, J.A., Hamerlynck, L.A., Barsh, E.T., Spieker, S., & Jones, R.R., (1982). *Extending family resources: A project of national significance.* Seattle: Children's Clinic and Preschool.

Moxley-Haegert, L., & Serbin, L., (1983). Developmental

education for parents of delayed infants: Effects on parental motivations and children's development. *Child Development, 54,* 1324–1331.

O'Neill, S., & Levy, L. (1981). *Simple justice: A case for mainstreaming the severely emotionally handicapped bilingual preschool child.* Paper presented at the Council for Exceptional Children conference on the exceptional bilingual child, New Orleans, LA.

Roberts, T. (n.d.). *Parent attitude assessment.* Tempe, AZ: Arizona State University.

Sheehan, R. (1982). Infant assessment: A review and identification of emergent trends. In D. Bricker (Ed.), *Intervention with at-risk and handicapped infants* (pp. 47–62). Baltimore: University Park Press.

Smith, O.S., Edwards, L., & Gibson, F.C., (1981). *Working with parents of Hispanic severely handicapped preschool children.* Paper presented at the Council for Exceptional Children conference on the exceptional bilingual child, New Orleans, LA.

Thornton, S., Frankenburg, W. (1983). *Child health care communications: Enhancing interactions among professionals, parents and children,* pp. 61–68. Skillman, NJ: Johnson & Johnson.

Turnbull, A., & Turnbull, III, H. (1986). *Families, professionals, and exceptionality: A special partnership.* Columbus, OH: Charles E. Merrill.

Turnbull, A., & Winton, P., (1984). Parent involvement policy and practice: current research and implications for families of young severely handicapped children. In J. Blacher (Ed.), *Severely handicapped young children and their families: Research in review* (pp. 377–400). Orlando, FL: Academic Press.

Vadasy, P., Fewell, R., Meyer, D., Schell, G., & Greenburg, M., (1984). Involved parents: Characteristics and resources of fathers and mothers of young handicapped children. *Journal of The Division for Early Childhood, 8,* 13–25.

Vincent, L. (1987, November). *Extending services to handicapped and at-risk infants and preschoolers.* Keynote address, National Early Childhood Conference on Children with Special Needs, Denver.

Walker, B., Slentz, K., & Bricker, D. (1985). *Parent involvement in early intervention.* Washington, DC: Rehabilitation Research Review, National Rehabilitation Information Center, The Catholic University of America.

Wikler, L.M. (1986). Family stress theory and research on families of children with mental retardation. In Gallagher, J.J., & Vietze, P.M. (Eds.), *Families of handicapped persons: Research, programs, and policy issues* (pp. 167–195). Baltimore: Paul H. Brookes Publishing Co.

CHAPTER 15

Facilitation of Family Support through Public School Programs

Lori Goetz, Jacki Anderson, and Sherry Laten

The neighborhood school, as a social system, provides the context for both informal and formal support services to families. Some of the services are intended goals of the schools, while others are unintended outcomes that occur naturally when groups of people who share basic human needs for self-esteem, affiliation and friendship, belonging, contributing, and achievement come together (Maslow, 1968). Members of all families, including those with a child with severe disabilities, share these basic human needs. All families of school-aged nondisabled and disabled children also share many other specific needs related to child, adult, and family development (Laten, 1981; Vincent, Laten, Salisbury, Brown, & Baumgart, 1980). Historically (and in many communities today), families with children who have severe disabilities have been considered to be disabled families (Vincent et al., 1980) and received specialized services to meet needs that are common to all families with school-age members, needs that are typically met for nondisabled families via the regular education public schools system.

THE SCHOOL AS A NATURAL SUPPORT SYSTEM

A variety of family support services are provided to nondisabled students as a part of the educational process. The educational system takes responsibility for providing a formal education that prepares students for productive adult lives in the community. They may receive additional assistance in this educational process from school counselors, social workers, psychologists and resource teachers. The hidden curriculum also prepares them for life by teaching social, behavioral, problem-solving, decisionmaking, and leadership skills. As a microcosm of society, the school imparts to the students certain attitudes regarding the differences and similarities of people, and gives the students an awareness of who is considered to be a part of the human community and their role in relationship to others (Kirp, 1982; Rist, 1979).

As part of their school experience, nondisabled children develop close friendships within their classrooms and through extracurricular activities such as scouting, sports, and music. They also have the opportunity to observe a variety of peer models and to develop relationships with a variety of adults. During grade school and junior high school, students develop the sense of belonging to their school through participation in extracurricular activities. The whole family is brought together in pride when the school wins the basketball game or the math olympics, or during holiday pageants and parades. By offering opportunities for volunteer work, the school also provides an opportunity for parents to fulfill needs for achievement, affiliation, and contribution, all of which contribute to the continued development of their

This chapter was supported in part by USOE Contract #300-82-0365; however, no official endorsement should be inferred.

self-esteem (Cochran & Henderson, 1986; Maslow, 1968). By observing students who are older than their own children, parents gain vital information regarding reasonable expectations for their own children as they get older. Casual and close social relationships are often formed as a result of children's friendships from school, extracurricular, and community activities. Expansion of the social network also provides parents with added opportunities for gathering and sharing information about child and family development and activities. Parents are afforded opportunities for emotional support, personal affirmation, socialization, and for expansion of contacts that will be useful in other aspects of their lives. The school, therefore, becomes a central forum from which support services and opportunities for families of regular education students are negotiated and secured (Cochran & Henderson, 1986).

Because of the change in the configuration of the family within the last few decades (i.e., an increase in families that are headed by a single parent, or contain two parents with careers), and because of the attention now given to families with cultural/linguistic differences, the regular education community is becoming aware of the need to provide a variety of different support systems for families. In a massive study in Syracuse, New York, Cochran and Henderson (1986) worked with a group of parents as facilitators for a wide range of other regular education parents. The parent facilitators aided other parents in organizing their activities with their children, provided positive feedback to parents regarding their parenting knowledge and abilities, and established opportunities for parents to increase their social networks. These interventions were successful, for many groups within the study, at increasing parental self-esteem and social contacts. The intervention was also successful at increasing child school performance, perhaps through increasing parental self-confidence so that they would respond early to their children's school difficulties.

As a segment of the greater school-age population, parents of children with severe disabilities could benefit from many of the same interventions and other supports that are available to families of nondisabled children. Fortunately,

with the mandate of PL 94-142 (*The Education for All Handicapped Children Act of 1975*), for which parents of disabled children with disabilities diligently lobbied, and section 504 of PL 93-112 (*The Rehabilitation Act of 1973*), the resources described above are increasingly available to students with severe disabilities and their families. The remainder of this chapter will provide a description of current educational practices that facilitate, for families with disabled children, the access to the support mechanisms available through regular education. The focus throughout will be on school-age children (3–16 years) with severe and profound disabilities as well as their families.

THE SCHOOL AS A SUPPORT FOR FAMILIES OF STUDENTS WITH SEVERE DISABILITIES

Through the enactment of PL 94-142, the public school is the institution that manages the educational program of children with disabilities. As part of a child's total educational program, the school is responsible for the provision of needed *related services*, several of which might fall into the category of family support services, including parent training and family counseling. Public schools thus provide a variety of support services, some of which are required by law and some of which are not legally mandated, to families of children with disabilities. The school's role in supporting families in coping with both stresses specific to their child's educational needs, and stresses that fall outside of a child's specific educational program, has been discussed from a variety of perspectives (Espinoza & Shearer, 1986; Turnbull & Turnbull, 1986; Vincent et al., 1980).

Some evidence supports the idea that schools do in fact function as long-term coping institutions for families. The validity of the school's role as a source of support for families of children with severe disabilities, for example, is reflected in a large-scale investigation reported by Meyers and Blacher (1987). Based upon interview data from 99 families having young (three–eight years old) children with severe disabilities, a majority of parents were found to have high satisfaction with the overall school program (which reflected answers to questions concerning the teacher, school staff and administrators, therapy, and home-school communication). A high level of involvement, as reflected in answers to questions concerning participation in IEP, assessment, parent activity, and school observations was also reported. While noting that their sample may reflect a bias (families were self-selected), Meyers and Blacher (1987) nevertheless conclude, ". . . the great majority of parents of children with severe handicaps were pleased with the school and would certainly regret it if the school program . . . ceased to exist" (p. 448).

While the public school's role as a coping institution is generally acknowledged, the nature and quantity of support that is provided by local education agencies varies widely. Espinoza and Shearer (1986) note that the amount of support services that a family receives from a public school agency will vary greatly according to the interrelationship of at least five factors, including size and location of the school, local and state funding structures, family demographics, characteristics of school personnel, and characteristics of the disabled child.

The types of support that are provided by schools can also vary widely. One category of support is through the direct provision of services that are adjunct to the child's educational program, including parent training groups, parent support groups, and linkage to other resources including respite programs, voluntary groups such as the YMCA, or social service agencies (cf. Halvorsen, 1983). Provision of information and technical knowledge regarding a child's disability is another example (Espinoza & Shearer, 1986). A second broad category of support might be considered to be the less tangible but highly salient emotional and moral support offered by school personnel (i.e., Garguilo, 1985). Espinoza and Shearer (1986) discuss this as "a shared concern for the child's welfare" (p. 261); Turnbull and Turnbull (1986) describe it as ". . . no more (or less) than well-placed empathic comments and moral supports" (p. 304).

A third type of support that is offered by public schools specifically relates to the child's educational program. Parent participation in identification and evaluation activities has been

discussed in detail by several authors (Bronicki & Turnbull, 1986; Vincent et al., 1980). The development and actual delivery of appropriate instructional programs for an individual child, however, is an aspect of school services that has received comparatively less attention in the family support literature (see Turnbull & Turnbull, 1986, for review). The participation of families as partners in the development of a child's IEP (individualized education program) is mandated by law, but implementation of the IEP has generally not been discussed as a potential source of family support.

The following section of this chapter focuses specifically on the educational practices that the school program can engage in to foster family support, such as curriculum development and direct instruction in functional skills within an integrated school context. The community intensive curriculum model of instruction (Sailor, Anderson, Halvorsen, Doering, Filler, & Goetz, in press; Sailor, Goetz, Anderson, Hunt, & Gee, 1987) is the basis of these practices. Finally, the school's role in providing support services adjunctive to the educational process is considered.

The Community
Intensive Curriculum Model

Community intensive instruction represents a synthesis of what are currently held to be the best practices in the education of students with severe disabilities. Sailor et al. (1987) describe the model as follows:

> The community intensive instructional model is based on the assumption that all individuals, including the most severely disabled, should be taught the skills to enable them to live, work, and recreate successfully in integrated environmental settings. By this definition, the purpose of education is to ensure normalized community participation by providing systematic instruction in skills essential to success within the social and environmental contexts in which those skills ultimately will be used by the student. Thus, instruction within our model takes place across three broad types of environmental settings: classroom, integrated school settings outside the classroom, and in the community at large. (pp. 69–70)

A number of features thus typify this model, including instruction in chronological age-appropriate functional life skills (Brown et al.,

1979), use of multiple natural environments for instruction (cf. Brown et al., 1983; Snell & Browder, 1986), integration with nondisabled peers through sustained structured and incidental interactions (Halvorsen & Sailor, in press), and adherence to the principle of partial participation and adaptations (Baumgart et al., 1982). Commitment to the values of parental participation and the likelihood of a non-sheltered future life are also characteristics of this model (Sailor et al., 1986).

While not all aspects of this model necessarily facilitate parent support, a number of components do appear to function as support strategies for families of children with severe disabilities. A discussion of each of these, along with available supporting evidence, follows.

Assessment and Curriculum Development Process   In a community intensive model, decisions about what to teach are based upon several information sources, including ecological inventories (Brown et al., 1979) of activities that typically occur in the places where a particular student is expected to live, work, and play, and assessment information from various disciplines such as physical therapy, audiology, occupational therapy, and so on. A crucial source of information, however, is a structured parent interview process (Holowach, 1985), in which the teacher and parent (or other significant other) systematically review a student's entire day, from the time of awakening until the student goes to bed.

The focus of the interview is to review the usual activities that the student engages in throughout a typical day. Because the goal of instruction is to increase the student's participation in domestic, community, recreational, and vocational settings outside of school, the teacher's role in this interview process is to solicit rather than to provide information to the parents. The caregivers, rather than the educational personnel, have the most relevant information and experience concerning a student's participation in the world beyond the classroom.

An excerpt from a sample interview protocol is presented in Figure 1. Beginning from the time the student awakens, the environment (home, school, community) and subenvironments (i.e., bedroom within the home, or grocery store in

the community) are noted, along with a description of the student's participation in each major activity of the day. The teacher also notes whether the activity is chronologically age-appropriate, and asks if the parents' preference is high, medium, or low that the student increases independence in each specific activity. In the example provided, the care provider (a foster parent in a group home) felt it was a low priority for Dan, the student, to wake up independently to an alarm clock; however, high priority was cited for increased independence in specific aspects of self-care skills. Discrepancies in skill performance may also emerge as the result of a systematic review of the student's typical day, as was noted, for example, in Dan's dressing skills.

Similar protocols are completed for weekend days and for routine events that may not occur on a daily basis, such as shopping for groceries once a week, or attending a biweekly community recreation group such as Boy Scouts. The result of this documentation is a rich and yet detailed and specific record of the student's current levels of participation across the actual environments in which he or she lives. This record forms the basis for determining IEP objectives.

By seeking information from parents about their preferences for skill learning, the IEP team (including parents) can develop instructional objectives that meet both the student's needs (for enhancing independent skill acquisition) and parental preferences. This strategy encourages the team to avoid common discrepancies between teacher and parent, such as those described by Roos (1985), in which the teacher's priority was successful color matching, while the parents' priority was reducing self-destructive behavior.

Parental preferences may reflect not only what parents believe is important for their disabled child to learn, but also the needs and priorities of the family as a system (Hoffman, 1980). Numerous authors have proposed that the family of a disabled child be viewed from the perspective of family systems theory (Benson & Turnbull, 1986; Vincent et al., 1980). This perspective is based on the assumption that families are interrelated units, of which the child with a disability is only one part; intervention with any one member of the family unit, including the handicapped

Worksheet 3 (Weekday Schedule)

Student: Dan

List information from the time the student gets up and goes to school to the time he arrives home from school and goes to bed.

Environment	Subenvironment	Activity	Approximate Time	C–A App?	Description of student's performance in activity	Prefer-ence H,M,L	Comments
Home	Bedroom	Wakes up	6:30	Yes	Care provider wakes Dan up. Dan gets up willingly.	L	
	Bathroom	Uses bath-room			Care provider tells Dan to go. Watches to make sure Dan does not play in toilet.	H	
	Bathroom	Showers			Showers with care provider help. Water is turned on, ad-justed, physical prompt through shower. Care provider assists drying.		
	Bedroom	Dresses			Care provider physically as-sists in all steps of dressing ex-cept shoes.		At school Dan dresses when given clothes.

Figure 1. Sample interview protocol.

child, will inevitably have an effect upon the unit as a whole. Thus, a parental preference for their child to learn skills that are related to morning grooming rather than meal preparation may reflect the needs of a new sibling who requires parental attention during the morning hours.

While participation of parents as partners in the general IEP process has been widely discussed in the literature, investigators have reported that parents are frequently not perceived as partners by professionals (Lynch & Stein, 1982), or, alternatively, that some parents may prefer that teachers assume primary responsibility for their child's education (Turnbull, 1983). From a family systems perspective, the significant other interview process, which focuses upon the student's participation in real events and activities in the family's daily life, and upon parental

perceptions of which activities are high priority for mastery within that family system, appears to be a specific educational practice that functions logically to support families, although direct evaluation data are not available. (For discussion of the actual interview process and interview techniques, see Garguilo, 1985; Holowach, 1985.) As an example, despite the fact that her child had several specific skill needs in the curriculum domains of domestic, recreational, vocational, and community functioning, one parent considered the mastery of specific domestic and community activities as a medium priority, commenting instead, "For me and [my husband] *social* integration is the key thing. . . . [We want] our kids to go to recess, lunch in the cafeteria, attend assemblies. . . ." (Porter Beckstead & Goetz, 1987). The shared values of the family, rather than those of the educational personnel, thus determined the nature of specific IEP objectives.

Age-Appropriate Objectives Taught within Multiple Natural Environments

Greater demands for caretaking have been identified as one factor that differentiates families that have a developmentally disabled member from families that do not (Dunlap, 1979). Respite care services that provide short-term relief from increased caretaking responsibilities have been shown to reduce family stress (Cohen, 1982). The very existence of a public school program (regardless of type or content) functions as a potential respite opportunity for parents because it provides daily relief from caretaking functions, enabling family members to pursue sustained vocational or educational pursuits or intermittent personal, social, or recreational activities (cf. Salisbury & Griggs, 1983). If relief from caretaking functions is extended to include the time that a child with disabilities spends at home, the family will be further supported; teaching generalized, age-appropriate, functional life skills that contribute to that child's independence across nonschool contexts is one way in which school programs can extend and elaborate their respite function.

Research supporting the community intensive model as an instructional model that builds generalized functional skills has been extensively discussed by Sailor et al. (1987) and is reviewed only briefly in this chapter. However, evidence does indicate that students with severe disabilities acquire functional skills when these skills are systematically instructed in natural environments, including domestic, recreational, social, community, and vocational environments (see Snell & Browder, 1986 for review). The critical role of teaching in the natural environment as a strategy for generalized functional skill acquisition (in which learned skills are actually used in nontraining environments) has been further analyzed by Horner and his colleagues (see Horner, McDonnell, & Bellamy, 1986, for discussion). While efficacy research that compares a community intensive model with other instructional models remains to be done, the role of direct instruction in real community environments in contributing to generalized skill performance has been demonstrated (McDonnell, Horner, & Williams, 1984).

From the perspective of family support, an equally important question involves family perceptions of skill acquisition and increased student independence as a function of community-based training in functional skills. Freagon et al. (1983) sent a questionnaire to all 55 parents whose children participated in a 3-year model demonstration project that established integrated, community-based instructional programs for elementary, middle school, and high school classes of students with severe disabilities. Sixty-four percent of the sample responded to the questionnaire; of these, over 80% reported that their children were more independent in the community and demonstrated more age-appropriate behaviors. Over 65% of the families reported that they also felt more comfortable in taking their child into the community. Thus, according to parents, students participating in a community intensive model are perceived as acquiring increased independence and age-appropriate behaviors in the community; the reported increase in comfort when taking their child out into the community suggests that decreased caretaking responsibilities may in fact reduce familial stress. Hanline and Halvorsen (1987) similarly reported that skill enhancement, particularly of social skills, was identified by all of the families that they interviewed as a primary benefit of an integrated, community-based school program.

Integration

An integrated school program is one in which school-age students with severe disabilities attend a self-contained class that is centrally located on an age-appropriate regular campus, in accordance with the rules of natural proportion. Structured and incidental interactions between students with severe disabilities and their nondisabled peers occur on a sustained basis in all classrooms and in the school and community at large (Sailor, 1984).

Integration as a component of community intensive instruction has been widely investigated as an independent variable that affects disabled students' learning outcomes, parental family expectations and perceptions, nondisabled students' attitudes, and social interactions between students (see Halvorsen & Sailor, in press). An integrated (vs. segregated) school program appears to facilitate parental and familial strategies in coping with the stress associated with having a family member with a disability through at least three different mechanisms.

Improved Familial Perceptions Numerous investigators report that familial perceptions of the family member with a disability improve as a result of integrated school placement. Anderson, Halvorsen, and Farron-Davis (1987) conducted a longitudinal study, utilizing a structured interview format, to obtain information about: 1) what types of environments across the categories of home, respite, eating, personal fitness/health, religious, vacation, cultural, sports, recreation, occupation, education, and transportation that the family participated in, and with what frequency the disabled child participated with the family, 2) what level of assistance was required by the student in these environments, and 3) the parents' expectations for the student's future level of independence in the settings.

Subject attrition from an original sample of 20 matched pairs over a 4-year period resulted in data from two groups, five parents each of integrated and segregated students that were matched by age and disability. Even with this small sample, some trends were suggested. The results indicated that parents of students in the segregated group perceived their children to need higher levels of assistance across the range of activities. This perceived level of needed assistance increased over time (but was not statistically significant). In contrast, the perceived level of assistance needed by integrated students decreased over the 4-year period. However, the small sample precludes generalization from these findings.

Data from interviews with 13 parents that were conducted by Hanline and Halvorsen (1987) also indicated that transferring a child with disabilities to an integrated setting increased the family expectations for that child's future functioning. The sample included both families who actively sought integrated placement for their child and families who were uncertain during the placement process, although sampling bias is still a possibility in this descriptive study. Anecdotally, however, many parents have attributed the increased health and independence of their children to an integrated environment (Turnbull &

Turnbull, 1986; Vesey, 1986). As one parent in the Hanline and Halvorsen (1987) study noted, the biggest benefit of integration for her family was their daughter's increased ability to be independent.

The Disability Rights Education and Defense Fund (DREDF, 1985) examined the educational equity of disabled high-school-age students in order to ascertain factors that influence the future plans of disabled students, their families, and their teachers. An analysis of interviews with 130 parents revealed strong correlations between parental expectations for postschool living/working opportunities and the extent to which their children were integrated, both at school and in social situations outside of school. Approximately 27% of the total sample were parents of students with severe disabilities. Analyses indicate that for all skill levels, school segregation had a strong, negative relationship to parent expectations for independent living and full employment.

Increased parental expectations may reflect actual student behavioral changes, although direct evidence is not available. The positive effects of higher expectations have long been speculated to contribute to improved learning outcomes (i.e., Rosenthal & Jacobsen, 1968) and the topic is an important one for future research. Improved perceptions of competence and raised expectations, regardless of actual student outcomes, reflect in part a significant coping strategy of reframing, or redefining a situation to make it less stressful. As Turnbull and Turnbull (1986) note, reframing skills are a vital part of coping strategies for any family responding to stress.

Increased Social Support Increased social support is a second way in which an integrated school program facilitates family support. While individual families will of course differ in their range of social support networks, families of children with severe disabilities are especially at risk for social isolation (Dunlap, 1979). If their child is served in a segregated, "handicapped only" school setting, then family members are also restricted to "handicapped only" options; PTA meetings, school social and sports functions, fund raising drives, and the myriad of choices available to families at the regular ed school are denied. As one parent notes, "If you have a disabled child, you enter a whole disabled world. Special schools, clinics, recreation centers, camps, special swim classes. . . . Other people have baby sitters; we have respite workers" (Lipton, 1983, p. 28).

The psychological effects of such isolation for the family may be considerable. While parents may express fear and concern about the physical and emotional security of their child in making the transition from segregated to integrated settings (Hanline & Halvorsen, 1987; McDonnell, 1987), parents may also feel the stigma of being persistently identified as different. Placement of children with severe disabilities onto regular school campuses provides families with increased tangible social support networks (as described earlier); it also affirms the intangible emotional message that they, and their child, are accepted. At a Bay Area conference on integration, a mother of an elementary school-age daughter with severe disabilities ended her keynote address with the following comment:

> . . . what I think integration really means to parents, is the idea that it is *OK to have a disabled child*. That is really, as a parent, what I feel when I see my child going to school with all the other kids in our neighborhood. It's OK that my child can't walk, it's OK that my child has whatever difficulties that she has. She is still part of the community and part of our world. . . . [I]t is very important to keep in mind what you are really saying and that is, "all right, it's OK, there is nothing to apologize for and it is not necessary for any of us or for you to hide your child." (Lipton, 1983, p. 29)

Established Peer Friendships   A third factor that offers the potential for a coping strategy for families is the development of friendships between a child with severe disabilities and his or her non-disabled peers. Hanline and Halvorsen (1987) report that several parents in their sample commented that contacts between students after school hours were a benefit of integration; teachers in San Mateo and San Francisco Counties reported the development of friendships outside of school hours at the elementary school level as reflected in invitations to birthday parties, overnights, and so on (Porter Beckstead & Goetz, 1987).

Friendships that extend to shared activities between disabled and nondisabled students outside of the school context may contribute to family support in several ways. Participation in birthday parties, overnights, school dances, and other community functions by a disabled child offers a very real respite function to families, just as those same kinds of activities offer parents of a child without a disability the opportunity to pursue individual or recreational interests apart from their child. A child's participation in activities away from home thus may enable parents to utilize a generally recognized coping strategy, relaxation (Turnbull & Turnbull, 1986). When the logistics of child care have been accomplished through highly normalized means, parents are more likely to take time for themselves.

The development of friendships also offers social support (tangible and intangible) to parents; the validation and acceptance implied by their child's attendance at a regular education school is further supported by social interactions between their child and other children. An example from a recent videotape made to address the inclusion of severely handicapped students with profound motor and sensory disabilities in integrated school programs highlights this point. A mother of two sons with severe multiple disabilities, both elementary-school-age, who have been integrated for several years comments,

> There is no question what it means to Tim to have friends that care about him and want him to be part of their lives. . . . (F)rom our family perspective, we never dreamed of this for our kids. . . . With integration, they have real normal lives. . . . (Porter Beckstead & Goetz, 1987).

Integration thus facilitates family support in several ways, and provides an excellent example of how educational practices, which have the student with severe disabilities as their focus, can in fact function to support families and facilitate the coping strategies available to them. In the next section, the services that schools provide directly to families are considered.

Services that Are Adjunct to the Student's IEP

Within a community intensive model, integration is more than the mere placement of a class of students with severe disabilities in a regular education campus. Successful integration of a particular child requires the active intervention of both teachers and administrators to facilitate acceptance of all severely disabled students and their families, as part of the school, so that families with a severely disabled member have access to the same supports available to other families within the school (Halvorsen & Sailor, in press).

Administrative practices such as locating classrooms centrally in the building (vs. in a "special ed" wing or portable classrooms), adhering to one school-wide schedule for all students, and including students and their families (as appropriate) in noncurricular activities such as dances, football games, school fairs, and formal organizations have all been identified as contributing factors to successful integration programs (Hamre-Nietupski, Nietupski, Stainback, & Stainback, 1984; Taylor, 1982). On-site supervision by a single administrator for both regular and special education teachers has been identified as another best practice integration marker (Halvorsen & Anderson, 1987). Teacher practices that are identified as facilitative of successful integration include the participation of the special education teacher in the regular education curriculum committee, the participation in regular duties such as hall monitoring or yard duty, and the development of interaction strategies including peer tutoring, buddy systems, and special friends programs (cf. Murray & Beckstead, 1983).

In addition to administrative practices that assist in the integration of families, schools also offer adjunct services directly to families. One aspect of adjunct services that has received considerable attention is the provision of parent training and parent support groups to allow the successful inclusion of families in an integrated school model (Halvorsen, 1983; Laten & Nye, 1986; Mendoza & Cegelka, 1988). These programs typically include parents as co-trainers, instead of relying solely on professionals as trainers for other parents. This programming strategy is extremely beneficial; it allows participants, who may experience normal feelings of isolation, fear, confusion, sadness, and intimidation (cf. McCollum, 1984), to have the opportunity to observe, learn from, identify with, and be given encouragement by competent, sensitive parent leaders who have had similar experiences and feelings. Parent-led programs also commu-

nicate to other parents that they are capable, creative, and resourceful people who can meet the challenges of parenting a child with severe disabilities. In addition, the *trainer of trainers* model, in which parents train other parents to be trainers, has been utilized in many of the selected programs to capitalize on the multiplier effect for program dissemination.

Parent and Community Together (PACT) (Halvorsen, 1983), was developed as part of a three-year project as a family support and systems-change oriented parent involvement program. It was cosponsored by San Francisco State University and San Francisco Unified School District during their three-year collaboration for the integration of students with severe disabilities, a federally funded school and community integration project entitled Regular Education for All Children with Handicaps (REACH). The goal of PACT was to provide mechanisms for parent education, linkage to specialized and generic services, implementation of a *trainer of trainers* model, and advocacy within a group context for parents of students with severe disabilities.

A unique feature of PACT was the participation by parents and family members in district-wide disability awareness education activities to assist with site preparation for integration. Halvorsen and a parent cofacilitator, who was also the chairperson of the district's advisory council on special education, recruited and provided training to two core groups of parents in strategies for disability education, such as learning stations or simulations, for all age groups within regular education (cf. Murray & Beckstead, 1983). One group of parents was available during the day for school-based activities, and the second was available in the evening for workshops with community and/or parent organizations, such as the PTA, Rotary, and so forth. Interested parents were given a stipend for their participation, with a commitment to train at least two groups in the following year, after the REACH project funding ended. The ripple effect from this strategy far exceeded expectations; 2 years after the project's end, these parent volunteers, along with a second generation of trainers that they had recruited, had provided disability awareness activities in a dozen schools, to more than 1500 students, staff, and parents. In addition, they provided training to regular education student trainers in selected schools, which led to a further spread of education.

The success of these efforts was attributed to several factors: 1) collaboration with existing organizations such as the advisory council for special education and the school volunteers group, 2) cofacilitation of the original group by a parent who gradually assumed coordination of all activities, and 3) the diverse nature of the parents involved in terms of ethnicity, interests, their child's age, and other factors, which assisted in attracting new parents to activities. By providing an avenue for self-sustaining responsible parent training and advocacy that is integrated into the fabric of the schools, these activities demonstrated that parents could creatively meet the challenges of parenting a child with severe disabilities. Employing parent leaders also exemplified the trust and respect that the administration held for parents and the administration's commitment to parent involvement and participation.

Additional outcomes of this project included facilitating parent roles as teachers of their children, consumers and advocates for educational and other services, and systems-change agents within the educational system and within specialized and generic community organizations. All models of participation were based on individualized needs assessments in recognition of the heterogeneity of families (Benson & Turnbull, 1986). The PACT can be useful to parent organizations who are advocating for a long-term community commitment to integrated public school and community programs for students with severe disabilities. An evaluation of this program demonstrates its cost-effectiveness. The training manual, available through ERIC (Educational Resources Information Center), includes descriptions on establishing, implementing, and evaluating the PACT program.

Parents as Effective Partners (PEP), developed by Laten and Nye (1986), is an 8-week course that provides parents the skills they need to effectively participate in the development and implementation of their children's special education program. PEP was developed as part of the parent training and support program, Building Home to School Partnerships, funded by the federal government and awarded to the La

Grange Area Department of Special Education, in metropolitan Chicago, Illinois.

Content of the course includes teaching parents how to communicate effectively at important school meetings so that their children's needs are met, how to write goals and objectives for their children's IEPs that will foster educational development, what classroom programs and services exist that can help their children, and what laws, policies, procedures, and informal mechanisms "make things happen" in special education in their community.

The course is led by a parent and professional, and meets weekly for 2½ hours. The class size is kept small, approximately 6–10 parents, to encourage participation and support within each session. The class format includes lecture/discussion, role-playing of communication skills in groups of three, discussion of vignettes related to parental coping skills, presentation and discussion of projects that parents design to improve their child's special education program or their relationship with program staff.

The program has been implemented with a varied group of parents from different economic and cultural backgrounds. It utilizes a *trainer of trainers* model whereby parent graduates are recruited to be leaders in future groups.

The goal of PEP is to improve parents' abilities and confidence as advocates for their children's educational needs. Parent's knowledge of the law, policies and procedures, and their perceptions of their ability to be a partner with the schools were assessed prior to taking the course, immediately at its completion, and at a later follow-up for a group of 19 parents, using a five-point Likert-type scale. At the follow-up (which for some parents, occurred 2½ years after course completion) as compared to pretest results, parents felt more confident in their knowledge of their rights, and of the policies and procedures within special education. They also felt that they had an impact on IEP decisions that they did not have before, and in fact, contributed an average of 2.3 goals to their child's most recent IEP. Their relationship with their child's special education teacher continued to be perceived as very good, yet at the follow-up they also felt very successful as a partner with the schools in their child's education. Parents indicated that they nearly always prepared for school related meetings and felt assertive in expressing their concerns and opinions.

The PEP project manual, with the evaluation scale, has been disseminated to over 30 sites within Illinois and nationally so that effectiveness data can continue to be collected. PEP and PACT are therefore two examples of effective adjunct services to families that provide support by increasing parental participation in diverse aspects of their child's school program. The PEP program empowers parents in the IEP process; and the PACT program involves parents in the actual process of creating a successfully integrated school program.

SUPPORT FOR ALL FAMILIES

The data, practices, and procedures that were reviewed in this chapter suggest that integrated public school programs can in fact function to support families both through the utilization of promising practices that are specific to the stu-

dent's educational program, and through adjunctive services such as parent training activities. One assumption throughout has been that schools are delivering quality services (cf. Meyer & Eichinger, 1987) to students with severe disabilities, including placement in the least restrictive environment and incorporation of families into the educational program on an individualized basis (Turnbull, 1983). When this assumption is lacking (i.e., Lynch & Stein, 1982), a school system may in fact function as a significant cause of stress for all family members (Hanline & Halvorsen, in press).

Alternatively, when schools incorporate students with severe disabilities and their families into a comprehensive local school program through some of the practices reviewed in this chapter, the support that is available to regular education students and families—be it through provision of social networks, individualized counseling, or referral and linkage to community resources—can in fact be successfully extended to *all* students and families.

REFERENCES

Anderson, J., Halvorsen, A., & Farron-Davis, F. (1987). *A longitudinal comparison of parental expectations for their severely disabled sons and daughters attending integrated and segregated programs.* Unpublished manuscript, San Francisco State University, Department of Special Education, California Research Institute, San Francisco.

Baumgart, D., Brown, L., Pumpian, I., Nisbet, J., Ford, A., Sweet, M., Messina, R., & Schroeder, J. (1982). Principle of partial participation and individualized adaptations in educational programs for severely handicapped students. *Journal of The Association for Persons with Severe Handicaps, 7*(2), 17–28.

Benson, H. A., & Turnbull, A. P. (1986). Approaching families from an individualized perspective. In R. H. Horner, L. H. Meyer, & H. D. B. Fredericks (Eds.), *Education of learners with severe handicaps: Exemplary service strategies* (pp. 127–157). Baltimore: Paul H. Brookes Publishing Co.

Bronicki, G. J., & Turnbull, A. (1987). Family professional interactions. In M. Snell, *Systematic instruction of persons with severe handicaps* (3rd ed.) (pp. 8–38). Columbus, OH: Charles E. Merrill.

Brown, L., Branston, M. B., Hamre-Nietupski, S., Johnson, F., Wilcox, B., & Gruenewald, L. (1979). A rationale for comprehensive longitudinal interactions between severely handicapped students and nonhandicapped students and other citizens. *AAESPH Review 4*(1), 3–14.

Brown, L., Nisbet, J., Ford, A., Sweet, M., Shiraga, B., York, J., & Loomis, R. (1983). The critical need for nonschool instruction in education programs for severely handicapped students. *Journal of The Association for Persons with Severe Handicaps, 8,* 71–77.

Cochran, M., & Henderson, C., Jr. (1986). *Family matters: Evaluation of the parental empowerment program. A summary of the final report to the National Institute of Education* (Report No. PS 016401). Ithaca, NY: Cornell University. (ERIC Document Reproduction Service No. ED 280 577).

Cohen, S. (1982). Supporting families through respite care. *Rehabilitation Literature, 43*(12), 7–11.

Disability Rights Education & Defense Fund. (1985). *Educational equity and high school aged disabled students.* Unpublished manuscript, Disability Rights Education and Defense Fund, Berkeley, CA.

Dunlap, W. R. (1979). How do parents of handicapped children view their needs? *Journal of the Division of Early Childhood, 1,* 1–10.

Espinoza, L., & Shearer, M. (1986). Family support in public school programs. In R. Fewell & Vadasy (Eds.), *Families of handicapped children: Needs and supports across the life span.* Austin, TX: PRO-ED.

Freagon, S., Wheeler, J., Brankin, G., McDaniel, K., Costello, D., & Peters, W. (1983). *Curricular processes for the school and community: Integration of severely handicapped students aged 6–21.* Project replication guide, Northern Illinois University, DeKalb, IL.

Garguilo, R. M. (1985). *Working with parents of exceptional children.* Boston: Houghton Mifflin.

Halvorsen, A. (1983). *Parents and community together (PACT).* San Francisco: San Francisco State University; San Francisco Unified School District. (Eric Document Reproduction Service No. ED 242 183).

Halvorsen, A. T., & Sailor, W. (in press). Integration of students with severe and profound disabilities: A review of research. In R. Gaylord-Ross (Ed.), *Issues and research in special education* (Vol. 1). New York: Teachers College Press.

Hamre-Nietupski, S., Nietupski, J., Stainback, W., & Stainback, S. (1984). Preparing school systems for longitudinal integration efforts. In N. Certo, N. Haring, & R. York (Eds.), *Public school integration of severely handicapped students: Rational issues and progressive alternatives* (pp. 107–141). Baltimore: Paul H. Brookes Publishing Co.

Hanline, M., & Halvorsen, A. (in press). Parental perceptions of the integration transition process. *Exceptional Children*.

Hoffman, L. (1980). The family life cycle and discontinuous changes. In E. Carter & M. McGoldrick (Eds.), *The family life cycle: A framework for family therapy* (pp. 53–68). New York: Gardner Press.

Holowach, L. (1985). *Individualized critical skills model significant other interview*. California State Department of Education, Special Education Resource Network, Sacramento, CA.

Horner, R., McDonnell, J., & Bellamy, G. T. (1986). Teaching generalized skills: General case instruction in simulation and community settings. In R. Horner, L. Meyer, & H. D. Fredericks (Eds.), *Education of learners with severe handicaps: Exemplary service strategies* (pp. 289–314). Baltimore: Paul H. Brookes Publishing Co.

Kirp. D. L. (1982). *Just schools: The idea of racial equality in American education*. Berkeley: University of California Press.

Laten, S. (1981). *Mothers of young handicapped children: Their emotional responses and their perceptions of their needs and resources*. Unpublished doctoral dissertation, University of Wisconsin, Madison, WI.

Laten, S., & Nye, J. (1986). *Parents as effective partners: A parent training program designed to strengthen the parent school relationship in special education*. La Grange, IL: La Grange Area Department of Special Education (1301 West Cossitt Avenue, La Grange, IL 60525).

Lipton, D. (1983). A parent's perspective on integration. In A. Halvorsen (Ed.), *Proceedings of the Bay Area Conference on the Integration of Students with Severe Disabilities* (LRE Module I). San Francisco: San Francisco State University, California Research Institute.

Lynch, E., & Stein, R. (1982). Perspectives on parent participation in special education. *Exceptional Education Quarterly*, *3*, 56–63.

Maslow, A. H. (1968). *Toward a psychology of being* (2nd ed.). Princeton, N.J.: VanNostrand Reinhold.

McCollum, A. (1984). Grieving for the lost dream. *Exceptional Parent*, *14*, 16–19.

McDonnell, J. (1987). The integration of students with severe handicaps into regular public schools: An analysis of parents' perception of potential outcomes. *Education and Training of the Mentally Retarded*, June, 98–111.

McDonnell, J., & Horner, R. (1985). Effects of in vivo versus simulation-plus-in vivo training on the acquisition and generalization of grocery item selection by high school students with severe handicaps. *Analysis and Intervention in Developmental Disabilities*, *5*, 323–343.

McDonnell, J., Horner, R., & Williams, J. (1984). A comparison of three strategies for teaching generalized grocery purchasing to high school students with severe handicaps. *Journal of The Association for Persons with Severe Handicaps*, *9*, 123–133.

Mendoza, J., & Cegelka, T. (1988). *Project PPACT*. San Di-

ego: San Diego State University, Department of Special Education.

Meyer, L.H. & Eichinger, J. (1987). Program evaluation in support of program development: Needs, strategies, and future directions. In L. Goetz, D. Guess, & K. Stremel-Campbell, (Eds.), *Innovative program design for individual with dual sensory impairments* (pp. 313–346). Baltimore: Paul H. Brookes Publishing Co.

Meyers, C., & Blacher, J. (1987). Parents' perceptions of schooling for severely handicapped children: Home and family variables. *Exceptional Children*, *53*, 441–449.

Murray, C., & Beckstead, S.P. (1983). *Awareness and inservice manual (AIM)*. San Francisco: San Francisco State University, San Francisco Unified School District. (Eric Document Reproduction Service No. ED 242 182).

Porter Beckstead, S., & Goetz, L. (Directors). (1987). *The way to go* [videotape]. San Francisco: San Francisco State University, Community Intensive Programs for Students with Sensory Impairments.

Rist, R. (Ed.). (1979). *Desegregated schools: Appraisal of an American experiment*. New York: Academic Press.

Roos, P. (1985). Parents of mentally retarded children—Misunderstood and mistreated. In H. R. Turnbull & A. Turnbull (Eds.), *Parents speak out—Then and now*. Columbus, OH: Charles E. Merrill.

Rosenthal, R., & Jacobsen, L. (1968). *Pygmalion in the classroom: Teacher expectation and pupils' intellectual development*. New York: Holt, Rinehart & Winston.

Sailor, W. (1984). *Integration: State of the art*. Proceedings of the Bay Area Conference on the Integration of Students with Severe Disabilities (LRE Module 1), California Research Institute, San Francisco State University.

Sailor, W., Anderson, J., Halvorsen, A., Doering, K. Filler, J. & Goetz, L. (in press). *The comprehensive local school: Regular education for all students with disabilities*.

Sailor, W., Goetz, L., Anderson, J., Hunt, P., & Gee, K. (1987). Research on community intensive instruction as a model for building functional, generalized skills. In R. Horner, G. Dunlap, & R. Koegel (Eds.), *Generalization and maintenance: Life-style changes in applied settings* (pp. 67–98). Baltimore: Paul H. Brookes Publishing Co.

Sailor, W., Halvorsen, A., Anderson, J., Goetz, L., Gee, K., Doering, K., & Hunt, P. (1986). Community intensive instruction. In R.H. Horner, L.H. Meyer, & H.D.B. Fredericks (Eds.) Education of learners with severe handicaps: Exemplary service strategies (pp. 251–288). Baltimore: Paul H. Brookes Publishing Co.

Salisbury, C., & Griggs, P. (1983). Developing respite care services for families of handicapped children. *Journal of The Association for Persons with Severe Handicaps*, *8*, 50–57.

Snell, M., & Browder, D. (1986). Community-referenced instruction: Research and issues. *Journal of The Association for Persons with Severe Handicaps*, *11*(1), 1–11.

Taylor, S. (1982). From segregation to integration: Strategies for integrating severely handicapped students in normal school and community settings. *Journal of The Association for Persons with Severe Handicaps*, *7*(3), 42–49.

Turnbull, A. P. (1983). Parental participation in the IEP process. In J. A. Mulick & S. M. Pueschel (Eds.), *Parent-professional partnerships in developmental disability services* (pp. 107–122). Cambridge, MA: Ware Press.

Turnbull, A. P., & Turnbull, H. R. (1986). *Families, professionals and exceptionality: A special partnership*. Columbus, OH: Charles E. Merrill.

Vesey, D. (1986, October). *The perspective of a parent and special education commissioner on the benefits of integration and plans for statewide implementation.* Paper presented at 13th annual TASH Conference, San Francisco, CA.

Vincent, L., Laten, S., Salisbury, C., Brown, P., & Baumgart, D. (1980). Family involvement in the educational processes of severely handicapped students. In B. Wilcox & R. York (Eds.), *Quality education for the severely handicapped: The federal investment* (pp. 164–179). Washington, DC: U.S. Department of Education, Office of Special Education.

CHAPTER 16

The Role of Parents and Family Members in Planning Severely Disabled Students' Transitions from School

Ann T. Halvorsen, Katherine Doering,
Felicia Farron-Davis, Ruth Usilton,
and Wayne Sailor

T he perspective of one parent sums up the concerns that many encounter in planning the transition from school for their child with a disability:

Jay will pass too soon from public school to adult services. He will move from a school system that must serve everyone to a nonsystem of multiple programs with usually inconsistent goals, functions, eligibility criteria, funding and governing authorities, and accountability—programs that need not serve him but must merely practice non-discrimination. He will go from a relatively protective system to one that may impose responsibilities on him that he cannot meet. And he will graduate from a system in which I can legally and functionally command services and accountability to a system that is far less amenable to my importunings. Will there be a group home for him, a job, entitlement benefits, recreation, and other opportunities for growth and protection? Frankly, the answer is unclear, and the pending transition from some certainty to great uncertainty is profoundly disquieting to me. (Turnbull, 1985, p. 119)

IMPORTANCE OF TRANSITIONAL SERVICES

For all families, the transition of a child from school to adulthood, beginning with the child's adolescent years in middle school, is a period comprising major adjustments and stress, particularly for parents (Olson et al., 1983). The impact of this life cycle transition is magnified for families with a disabled child, where the traditional markers of change (e.g., graduation) may be lacking or delayed, and the adult role of the individual unclear (Turnbull & Turnbull, 1986). When considering that this uncertainty is coupled with the historic lack of mandated appropriate services for the disabled adult, particularly for the adult with severe and profound disabilities, the need for family support and a systematic transition process becomes clear.

Federal initiatives and policies (Will, 1984) have underscored the need for a systematic process of transition that will have a significant im-

This chapter was supported in part by U.S. Department of Education Grant No. G008530143 and Contract #300–82–0365. No official endorsement should be inferred.

This chapter is dedicated to the memory of Bill Rosenberg, our colleague and friend, whose major contributions to meaningful transitions of severely disabled individuals and their families have had a lasting effect on our lives and work.

pact on the opportunities available to and accessible by all students who experience disabilities. Given estimates of 250,000 to 300,000 special education graduates annually (Will, 1984), and figures that indicate that 60% of all special education students are between 15 and 21 years old (Elder, 1985), the urgency behind these priorities is apparent, and the failure of educational efforts to ensure postschool success is painfully obvious. Mithaug, Horiuchi, and Faning (1985) cited figures on special education graduates' living arrangements that reinforce the picture of limited options available to individuals with disabilities; approximately two-thirds of these students continued living with their parents as adults. Estimates of unemployment for graduates of special education range from 50%–67% (Hasazi, Gordon, & Roe, 1985) and are as high as 80% for individuals with severe disabilities. Special education can no longer afford to place the blame for dismal postschool outcomes solely on the adult service system or vice versa.

A collaborative transition process, guided by families and consumers, is the topic of this chapter. This chapter will address the rationale for transitional services to severely disabled students and their families in terms of support needs; the philosophy, purpose, and design of the proposed service model; outcomes for graduates in the San Francisco Bay Area as well as empirical data from similar transition programs; and future directions for both practitioners and researchers.

Wehman, Kregel, and Barcus (1985) note that the results of transition planning are dependent on the quality of both the foundation provided by the school program and the adult services that the student will be able to use. This fact supports the belief that a critical feature of transition is the instructional focus beginning at about age 12, and the need for early, coordinated planning in which relevant agencies participate with parents and the schools beginning when the student is age 14.

Family Support Issues

While transitions are a fact of life for everyone, even the most positive change, such as a new job, marriage, or the birth of a child may be accompanied by feelings of loss (cf. Bridges,

1980). Professionals working with families who have a disabled child indicate that important transition periods may be particularly stressful for these families, because they may highlight the child's differences and thus revive parental feelings of "chronic sorrow" (Fewell, 1986).

Turnbull and Turnbull (1986) present a detailed analysis of potential issues encountered by parents and siblings of disabled youth during the life cycle stages of adolescence and young adulthood, which is reproduced in Table 1.

As Table I indicates, families with a disabled teenager experience concerns and issues that are shared by families with nondisabled children (e.g., emerging sexuality, planning a career), and they experience issues and concerns that are unique to families of a disabled child. Families may be struggling with any or all of these issues as the transition approaches, and may increasingly need information about future options for their child as an adult, and support for the change process. With these issues in mind, educators have often focused their efforts with families on providing information and parent training that is expected to lead the parent to assume the primary advocacy role in the transition process. This chapter proposes instead an emphasis on individual families, based on parental and sibling stated needs, preferences, and resources. In their definition of roles and responsibilities for the transition process, Everson and Moon (1987) support this position, noting the need for flexibility in assigning parent roles and the continuum of potential responsibilities that may be assumed by families participating on the transition team.

An individualized transition process can acknowledge the heterogeneity of families in a variety of ways, including connecting with other parents or arranging visits to model programs (Hanline & Halvorsen, in press), involving interested parents and siblings in staff development activities focused on transition, implementing parent in-services on adult options, or facilitating school-based support groups for families of graduating students. Each of these options may be appropriate for, or desired by, individual families at different points throughout the transition process. The integral characteristic of family support for transition is individualization.

Table 1. Possible issues encountered at life cycle stages

Life cycle stage	Parents	Siblings
Adolescence, ages 13–21	Adjusting emotionally to possible chronicity of exceptionality	Overidentification with sibling
	Identifying issues of emerging sexuality	Greater understanding of differences in people
	Addressing possible peer isolation and rejection	Influence of exceptionality on career choice
	Planning for career/vocational development	Dealing with possible stigma and embarrassment
	Arranging for leisure time activities	Participation in sibling training programs
	Dealing with physical and emotional change of puberty	Opportunity for sibling support groups
	Planning for postsecondary education	
Adulthood ages 21 and up	Planning for possible need for guardianship	Possible issues of responsibility for financial support
	Addressing the need for appropriate adult residence	Addressing concerns regarding genetic implications
	Adjusting emotionally to any adult implications of dependency	Introducing new in-laws to exceptionality
	Addressing the need for socialization opportunities outside the family for individual with exceptionality	Need for information on career/ living options
	Initiating career choice of vocational program	Clarify role of sibling advocacy
		Possible issues of guardianship

From Turnbull, A. P., & Turnbull, H. R. (1986). Family Life Cycle. In Turnbull & Turnbull, *Families, professionals and exceptionality: A special partnership.* Columbus, OH: Merrill Publishing Co., p. 107.

The Purpose of Transition

Following the federal mandate that all children must be educated by the public schools, there has been a dramatic increase in the development of new curriculum models to increase the competencies of students with the most severe disabilities in integrated, adult environments (Sailor, Goetz, Anderson, Hunt, & Gee, 1988). More and more individuals with disabilities and their families are demanding that programs be available to support postschool working and living in integrated environments of the individuals' choice. Many families are unprepared for the change in coordination of and access to information when moving from the school system to adult services. Not only is the lack of services at issue, but also the lack of effective services to produce satisfying life-styles for adults with severe disabilities (McDonnell, Wilcox, & Boles, 1986).

In response to this dilemma, federal initiatives and legislation have established programs to in-

crease access to training and other support services for employment for individuals with disabilities (cf. Elder, 1985). The establishment of transitional services has also been the focus of some federal legislation. The 1984 Amendment to the Rehabilitation Act and the Carl D. Perkins Vocational Education Act of 1984 set aside funds for transitional services. More recently the Transition of Youth with Disabilities Priority of the Office of Special Education and Rehabilitation Services (OSERS) has incorporated the transition from school to working life as a national priority (Rusch & Phelps, 1987).

The word *transition* is often used almost interchangeably with the term *employment* or *supported employment*. Much of the current literature implies, either by title or content, that successful employment is the goal of the transition process (cf. Wehman, Moon, Everson, Wood, & Barcus, 1988). Gaining and keeping employment are integral to feeling successful and worthwhile as an adult, thus, vocational placement must be a major part of transitional planning (Wehman et al., 1988). However, it is the authors' position that a successful transition process includes meeting the needs of the whole person across all life areas.

Transition is a process that includes longitudinal, comprehensive planning that results in effective and satisfying outcomes when certain quality standards are met. Critical aspects of this process include at least: 1) parent collaboration in all decisions regarding school and postschool preparation and placement; 2) a quality, integrated, community intensive educational program; 3) systematic planning that begins early in the school years and becomes more comprehensive as graduation nears; 4) involvement and collaboration with all appropriate school and adult service agencies; and 5) placement into meaningful, integrated employment and living options with participation in natural community and leisure activities.

Definition of the Transition Period

Although many tend to think of a transition period as the time immediately preceding a change, most special educators would agree that beginning the planning process at age 19 or 20 for exiting school is far too late (e.g., Sailor, 1988; Wehman, Moon, & McCarthy, 1986). In the model developed by San Francisco State University and the San Francisco Unified School District, three periods of emphasis for planning are described that will be discussed later in detail:

Age 12–14—Initial focus for secondary instruction and postschool planning

Age 14–18—Primary instructional emphasis for transition

Age 18–22—Major focus of individualized interagency planning process and transition

THE TRANSITION PLANNING PROCESS

In order to attain desirable transition services for individuals with the most severe disabilities, careful planning and attention to the three-phase process (developed by San Francisco State University) are essential.

Instruction during the School Years

Longitudinal Program Planning   The educational years for a student with severe disabilities should provide the same outcome as the expected educational outcome for students who are not identified as disabled. Specifically, the student should have choices and opportunities in adulthood that he or she would not have had without the educational experience (Brown et al., 1987). For more than a decade, curricula have emphasized skill acquisition to enhance the participation of students and adults with severe disabilities in all aspects of community life. This type of curriculum is identified in the literature by a variety of terms that reflect the expectation that outcomes will enhance integrated lifestyles. Sailor et al. (1986) have described the community intensive curricular model and its application across age levels. For an overview of this model and school-based family support components, see Chapter 15 (Goetz, Anderson, & Laten).

Within the San Francisco schools, students who have reached age 18 and are no longer age-appropriate for a high school setting yet continue to require instructional services of an intensity that can only be provided by an educational program, have access to transition programs. These programs are based at the high schools; however, the curriculum strongly emphasizes extended vocational training experiences and instructional sequences across domains and natural environments utilized by the students and their families. One example of this approach is the rotational job sampling strategy.

Rotational Job Sampling   This process ensures that students are provided with instruction and evaluated across a wide variety of integrated, meaningful, age-appropriate types of work during their secondary school years. Beginning at age 15, with movement to new training sites each year, the job sampling results in up to nine different work experiences prior to the selection of postschool job placements by transitioning students and their families. As students get older, their endurance, skill repertoire, and motivation are increased in conjunction with the increase in the number of training hours and/or days spent at work (cf. Pumpian et al., 1980).

For each work experience, individualized instructional programs are implemented for both general vocational skills (i.e., work attitude, social behavior) and the specific skills required for task completion.

Through the IEP and transition planning process, parents can assist in compiling the students' resumes or work histories, which document each year of work and ensure that variety is built into the sampling process. This documentation assists families in determining students' preferences and acquired competencies over time, and provides potential future employers with data on graduates' employability. At the same time, the sampling process demonstrates both to families and to the business community the increasing competence of students through their high school and transition years.

Job Development and Implementation To implement the rotational job sampling model, teachers secure several integrated job-training sites that represent different employment categories and career options. A chronological sequence for developing community-referenced sites within local businesses is listed below. More detailed information on this process can be found in the *CTS Project Manual* (Doering, Usilton, & Farron-Davis, 1989). The site development sequence includes:

1. Site selection
2. Job development-negotiation
3. Job analysis
4. Safety and emergency procedures
5. Program implementation
6. Site maintenance

Parents may wish to collaborate with school personnel in identifying potential vocational training sites through their own business contacts or network of friends and relatives in various work settings. Their experience and insight into business or industry can be invaluable to educators, who may have had minimal background in presenting to commercial interests.

Individualized Transition Plans

Overview of the Transition Plan Students with severe disabilities will not have successful transition experiences without services and support to maintain them in integrated living and work situations as adults. The desired supports are not necessarily available on demand. Thus parents may wish to initiate planning well in advance of the time that students leave the educational system to determine what options they want for their son or daughter, to identify the resources that will be needed, and to ensure that quality services will be available to support community-based residential, leisure, and work choices. The *individual transition plan* (ITP) is a process in written form that provides the structure for these activities.

Within the ITP, which is developed and updated as a part of each annual individualized education program (IEP) beginning at age 14, all of those issues that will directly affect the individual's quality of life as an adult can be addressed. School personnel, in conjunction with adult service providers and the case manager, can assist parents to investigate residential and vocational programs. The student's transition team also develops strategies and assumes responsibility for the types of support and programing that will be needed for successful functioning within the work and living options that the student and parents select. The available services can then be compared to the needed services, in planning the student's transition.

Figure 1 provides an example of an ITP form listing many of the critical issues that must be considered for each student prior to graduation; a brief discussion of each issue follows.

The transition plan addresses the individual needs and abilities of each student across all life areas, and provides information regarding all previous skill training and current performance in each area. Any discussion of future options should include the preferences of the student and his/her parents before decisions are made regarding programing in adulthood.

Financial Issues School personnel can take responsibility for ensuring that parents have accurate, current information about eligibility for Social Security and Supplemental Security benefits, as well as Medicaid and other possible health and medical benefits. Parents must closely examine medical insurance converage so that they are aware of whether students who graduate may lose any existing coverage; the issue of receiving

Student: _____ Date: _____

Issues to be addressed: Each of the following areas should be discussed at each transition meeting. Goals, objectives and activities should be developed where appropriate.

Area:	date	concerns discussed	goal written
1. Employment Options • previous work experience • current job(s)/support needs • future options for employment • expressed preferences			
2. Residential Options • previous/current living situation • future options/expressed preferences			
3. Financial Issues • benefits/unearned income • earned income • insurance • other			
4. Recreation Options • previous experiences • current support needs • future options/expressed preferences			
5. Community Access • current skills and support needs • future options/expressed preferences			
6. Transportation • current skills/support needs • future options/expressed preferences			
7. Family/Friends/Advocates			
8. Other			

Figure 1. Individualized transition plan.

benefits such as insurance from an employer can be a major factor in job site selection if the individual has no other coverage. Information on any wages or earned income that the student receives and on the skills that this student may need to handle and budget money may also be included in this plan, and discussion of issues such as guardianship or estate planning may be raised by family members as well, thus illustrating the scope of the transition planning process.

Transportation Issues Transportation is frequently a major factor in determining the potential success of a job placement. Transportation may also be an issue in creating a social network and/or reaching other community environments for recreation, personal shopping,

and so forth. Possible transportation options to be considered may include public transportation, walking, taxi, family- or job-coach-provided, coworker-provided, and "special" transportation.

Family/Friends/Advocates Any issue or concern relating to support needs for the student who is disabled and his or her family should be addressed within the transition process. The continuity of friendships and of family relationships is an integral factor affecting the successful transition of a student into the adult world. The identification of an advocate to assist the individual and the family through the transition program process might well provide a needed support.

The members of the transition team, as described later in this chapter, must be willing to participate actively in reaching the objectives for each student. Attendance at an annual staffing is not sufficient to guarantee the success of a plan. Activities, with timelines for completion, should be written into the plan for each participating agency and individual as necessary. These timelines will provide a structure in moving toward a successful transition to adult services for each student.

Interagency Collaboration   Interagency coordination is an issue, particularly for those persons for whom employment at or above minimum wage is unlikely and who, because of their disabilities, may need ongoing lifelong support. Although collaboration between school and adult service agencies is necessary for identifying and obtaining these necessary services prior to the student's exit from the educational system, recent research indicates that coordinated planning is virtually nonexistent (Hasazi et al., 1985; McDonnell & Hardman, 1985; Wehman, Kregel, & Seyfarth, 1985).

Composition of Individual Transition Team   Identifying and selecting meaningful, integrated employment for individuals with significant disabilities requires coordinated efforts and careful delineation of roles and responsibilities for all parties involved in ensuring appropriate transitional service delivery. In order to be most effective in meeting this goal of transition, it is essential to identify an individual transition team. This core team ideally includes at least the following key representatives: parent(s), student, a special education teacher, a vocational/transition specialist, an adult service provider, a developmental disabilities case manager, and a vocational rehabilitation counselor. Certain factors, such as the severity of the disability and the extent to which an individual can work independently of adult supervision for 20 hours or more, may determine whether the Vocational Rehabilitation (VR) counselor is involved in transition planning. Where VR is not involved (usually in the case of students with severe disabilities), the developmental disabilities provider of postschool placement services participates. In every case, the postschool vocational placement should be integrated and supported, with re-

sources provided to sustain the client in the community and on the job.

Individualizing the transition process for a given student involves the following step-by-step approach (cf. LaMar & Rosenberg, 1987; Wehman et al., 1988):

1. Schedule the initial transition team meeting.
2. Hold an initial meeting, preferably on the occasion of the first IEP, to be scheduled following the students' fourteenth birthday.
3. Develop the Individualized Transition Plan (ITP) and assign responsibilities and timelines to each team participant.
4. Implement the transition goals.
5. Evaluate the ITP on an annual basis.
6. Update and improve upon the ITP at the annual IEP meeting.
7. Plan for the gradual transfer of responsibility from the school system to the targeted adult agency.
8. Collaborate in arranging meaningful employment in an integrated setting and normalized community living options.

The rate at which the team progresses through this process will vary, and may be determined by who is coordinating the transition planning, the severity of the disabilities of the individual for whom the plan is written, the degree of parent participation, the availability of appropriate adult services for integrated work and living options, and the extent to which the interagency task force is committed to and follows through with the written transition agreement.

Parent Involvement   In this model, parents are encouraged to participate actively as partners in the process of preparing their child for adulthood, and are the primary source regarding prioritization of goals and objectives (Turnbull & Turnbull, 1986). Parent input is invaluable regarding the students' present levels of performance and the students' and/or parents' preferences for community skills instruction, employment, and residential options. Individualization should be based on family needs for support and information and their willingness and comfort in making decisions regarding adult options for their son or daughter. Close contact and ongoing communication with families that begins during the preschool years and continues throughout primary and secondary programs facilitates later collaboration. Although families provide as much information to school personnel as they receive from them, a number of strategies can work to enhance parent education and transition planning:

The Parent Interview can be used to inform families of program philosophy, of integration of persons with severe disabilities into the community at large, and of the rationale for implementation of IEP objectives in natural environments (cf. Turnbull & Turnbull, 1986).

The IEP/ITP can familiarize families with the process of developing individualized educational programs and involve them in the design of a written, formal plan.

Parent Meetings (In-services) can be initiated on an annual basis by parent groups, the public schools, and/or adult agencies, and can be related to topics of concern that are identified by a parent questionnaire or a needs assessment.

Informal Meetings with families can address their specific concerns and provide them with information and resources to alleviate their anxieties and fears.

Site Visitations to Local Adult Agencies' Work and Living Settings provide parents an opportunity to learn the role of the different agencies and the services rendered, obtain information regarding alternatives for their son or daughter, and observe model programs.

Written Information/Literature helps to establish connections for families before the student leaves school.

Regarding the strategy of written information, it might be advantageous for the school system to illustrate the step-by-step process of transition via diagrams, flow charts or written guides. McDonnel and Hardman (1985) discuss the benefits of designing a "Transition Planning Guide" to assist parents in acquiring the needed services and doing so according to clearly delineated timelines. Wehman et al. (1988) have provided guidelines for parents of elementary-, middle-, and high-school-age students in transition planning steps at each age level.

If parents are to collaborate effectively with school and adult agency personnel, they will also need to be informed about the criteria that they can use to evaluate both school and adult service programs. Information regarding the components of quality programs will enable them to advocate for services that prepare the individual for work and community living.

Parent Concerns   Regardless of how well-informed they may be, parents experience a number of concerns related to transition. Educators and adult service personnel need to be aware of these issues and work with families to alleviate their anxieties and to bring about change in service delivery systems and educational policy for persons with severe disabilities. Five family concerns that are specific to the transition process follow:

1) Discontinuation of Services   Most parents do not want their child to remain idle at home once he or she reaches adulthood. Financial burdens and emotional stress for the family can be expected to result when there is an absence of appropriate adult services (McDonnell & Hardman, 1985). An interruption of necessary services may also contribute to graduates' skill regression or the demonstration of undesirable behavior due to a lack of structured, meaningful program options. At this point, parents can become overwhelmed and frustrated at sudden changes in their child's disposition.

2) Lack of Appropriate Adult Services   Although a number of adult programs are in the process of converting to supported employment models in competitive, integrated work settings, a considerable number of agencies still utilize strict entrance criteria that exclude many individuals because they do not possess certain prerequisite skills. Some parents have been informed, for example, that their son or daughter is ineligible or not skilled enough to be placed in integrated program options. This inequity imposes a hardship on families and prevents the individual with severe disabilities from having access to a meaningful and satisfying life-style.

3) Difficulty in Acquiring Information on Available Resources   Inequity in service provision results when some parents are unfamiliar with how to obtain the specific services to which they are entitled or how to utilize the system (Brewer & Kakalik, 1979). Service providers can be of tremendous assistance in presenting information in a clear, accurate, and nonthreatening manner, as well as in assisting families to locate appropriate resources. The distribution of written directories of available services can be helpful in addressing this concern. Provisions need to be made for translating materials into parents' primary languages, with additional interpretive support available.

4) Effects of Wages on Society Security Income (SSI)   It is also important that parents be given written information on how employment will affect their son or daughter's SSI and other health benefits. In addition, efforts to maintain the individual's SSI and health care benefits need to be explored within transition planning.

5) Planning for Care After Parents' Deaths Many families are planning ahead to the days when they may no longer be available to assist in advocacy for, or in the care of, their son or daughter. Often, these responsibilities are passed along to siblings or other family members. While a job for the individual with disabilities may not solve all of the problems, families feel more reassured in knowing that a consistent, supportive work environment has been arranged. At the same time residential alternatives may become significant, and placement options may need to be considered.

Since parents are the most important component in most young adults' transition from school to adult life, their involvement in all aspects of transition planning needs to be encouraged. Service providers work closely with families to determine the individual needs of the family and the extent to which they would like to be involved in transition planning. However, regardless of the parents' level of participation, formalized transition planning is most effective if it occurs several years prior to school graduation.

Placement Considerations   Transition into integrated community placements is the only logical postschool outcome for individuals who have received a functional curriculum within integrated schools emphasizing community-based instructional experiences. As these young adults near graduation, the appropriate services that are currently available tend to lead to placement in employment positions that require either *time-limited support* with a follow-up component, or *ongoing, permanent support*. School personnel

need to involve parents in the determination of projected support needs.

Parental support for the *time-limited option* is integral for those graduates who will ultimately be able to work with little or no adult supervision in *individual site placements*. The school system's transition specialist will probably assume the primary responsibility for all aspects of job development, and intensive job-site training. Once the student is stable on the job, the transition specialist will coordinate with the adult service provider, who gradually works in postschool support and provides the necessary follow-up services for graduates and their families, to ensure consistency and continuity of programming.

The job development, placement, and on-site training process that is utilized for persons who may need *ongoing, lifelong support* is more complicated. Historically, for most of these graduates, few if any integrated options have been available (Brown et al., 1987). In this model, the interagency transition task force makes a commitment to develop a detailed action plan and assign responsibilities to ensure that quality options for gainful employment are realized for these students. In this sense, the team members serve as advocates along with the family. This process is incorporated within the individualized transition plan (ITP) and usually requires a willingness on the part of school and adult service personnel to share staff and resources in order to produce the desired work and adult living outcomes. After a thorough review of the student's work experiences and individual needs, the receiving agency is usually in the best position to place the new graduate into an existing job vacancy or to develp an entirely new job site. The final placement decision is made by a consensus of the entire team and members determine who will be responsible for job development, factors (such as transportation, SSI, etc.) affecting job placement, intensive on-site training and follow-along services.

Since this chapter focuses on the parental role in the transition process, a detailed analysis of the steps that were identified for developing meaningful employment options must be saved for another discussion. (Refer to Doering et al., [1989] for specific information on determining and developing work options, job analysis and modification, placement, training and ongoing support services, as well as support and staff development components for educational and adult agency personnel.)

EVALUATION OF THE TRANSITION PROCESS

Client employment data are extremely helpful as a basis for making comparisons among programs, and thus can be of assistance to families selecting postschool options. Additionally, follow-up studies that examine the long-range effects of transition models on subsequent employment (Brown et al., 1987) or on the benefit costs of these programs (cf. Piuma, 1988), can provide information to families about the effectiveness of various programs in ensuring successful, ongoing employment for their child.

The evaluative literature on transition models, as they exist around the country and in Europe to date, is described in an excellent new book by Wehman and his associates (Wehman et al., 1988). Brown et al. also discusses this information, (1987), and the California Transition Research Fair proceedings (California State Department of Education, 1987) provides a review of evaluative data from programs in that state. Finally, Gaylord-Ross (1987) discusses a cross-cultural perspective on transition, as does OECD/CERI (1986).

Key Findings within the San Francisco Unified School District

The Community Intensive Transitional Services Project (CTS) for students with severe disabilities in San Francisco is a federally funded grant to San Francisco State University in conjunction with the San Francisco Unified School District. CTS has emphasized the development of vocational training opportunities and the transition process for students with the most severe and challenging disabilities. The integrated classrooms in which these students are placed are designed for individuals who have been labeled by San Francisco Unified School District (SFUSD) as severely handicapped. The SFUSD integrates students on the basis of a "zero-rejection" principle; no student would be too disabled to be con-

sidered a member of this group. The students that are served have multiple disabilities, including severe or profound mental retardation as well as other physical, sensory, behavioral, or health problems. More specifically, the model particularly addresses those students who have traditionally been denied services by adult programs or offered placement in segregated nonwork programs as their only postschool vocational option. All but seven of the classrooms for approximately 700 students with severe disabilities are fully integrated into regular, age-appropriate schools. For the current school year, the high school classrooms have been redistributed, with more attention to heterogeneous groupings of students with various types and ranges of disability and to placing students closer to their homes.

The chapter findings include outcome data for the graduates of the San Francisco Unified School District (SFUSD) over a 2-year period from 1986 through 1987, and descriptive data based on a transition interview protocol of parental perceptions of the transition process for families who were assisted by CTS.

CTS's involvement with the SFUSD graduates was twofold. It included working with students from specific, integrated community-based high schools, and assisting in their vocational training experiences in community environments. The second aspect of CTS's involvement included the facilitation of the transition process by developing an ITP format and participating in the process, coordinating agencies on behalf of individual students, visiting adult agencies by families, and technically assiting adult agencies that were receiving project graduates.

Postschool Placement Status of SFUSD Graduates over a Two-Year Period

Subjects and Data Collection CTS gathered data on postschool placement of graduating students with the most severe disabilities over the 1986, 1987, and 1988 school years within the SFUSD. Data on the placement of students into sheltered, nonsheltered, or home settings were derived from the teacher reports of postschool placements.

Analysis The data for 21 students were analyzed for the end of the 1986 school year by tallying the number of graduates participating in each of three types of settings. At the end of the 1987 and 1988 school year, identical analyses were made for 23 and 20 graduates, respectively.

Results The results showed that for the 1986 school year, 5 students (24%) were placed into nonsheltered, integrated work settings, 14 (67%) attended sheltered settings, and 2 (9%) remained at home. 1987 figures showed that 10 students (43.5%) were placed in nonsheltered, integrated work settings, 10 students (43.5%) were placed in sheltered settings, and 2 (13%) stayed home. Figures for 1988 indicate that 16 students (80%) attended nonsheltered integrated work settings, 4 students (20%) attended sheltered settings, and no students stayed at home.

The results (as shown in Figure 2) indicate an initial increase of 20% in the placement of students into integrated work settings, and a doubling of the number of these students placed into nonsheltered settings from the 1986 to the 1987 school year. A further examination of results from the 1987 school year showed that 9 of 11 students who attended fully integrated high school settings were placed into integrated work settings. By comparison, 10 of the 12 students who attended a partially integrated high school program were placed in sheltered workshop placements. The other 3 students remained at home. The movement of students into integrated work settings, from the 1986 to 1988 school years, reveal a major increase in students' attendance in integrated placements (see Figure 3).

Discussion

CTS has had a dual role in transition, to both assist students in acquiring real work experiences that are community-based and facilitate the process of transition into integrated work situations.

Further systematic evaluation and research that focuses on controlling for such factors as integrated or segregated school placement, and the definition of meaningful integrated vocational placements are needed.

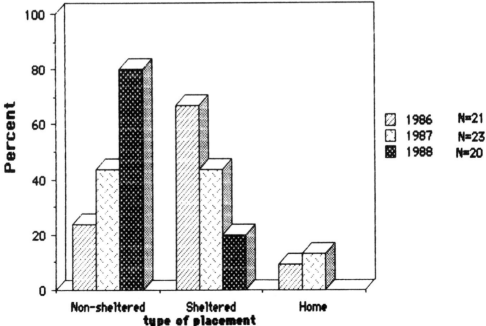

SFUSD
SUMMARY OF GRADUATE PLACEMENT OF STUDENTS FROM
THE 1986, 1987, AND 1988 SCHOOL YEARS

Figure 2. Summary of graduate placements.

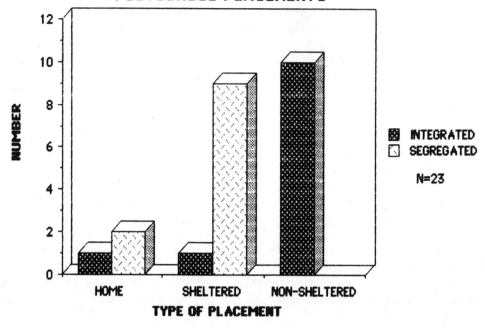

Figure 3. Status of integrated and segregated postschool placements.

The CTS data were collected from students who are considered to be "the most severely disabled." A number of these students who were in the sample have achieved successful, integrated work placements within the community. These data are of particular interest in light of the fact that students categorized as "profoundly handicapped" were once deemed ineligible for postschool vocational placement, even in most sheltered programs (Sailor, Gee, Goetz, & Graham, 1988).

Brown et al. (1987) concluded that when the population of adults with developmental disabilities in the United States is considered, too many individuals are confined to segregated environments. In fact, the number of segregated workshops, activity centers, and other day programs increased from a mere six prior to 1954 to over 4,600 in 1984 (Brown et al., 1987). The available data on successful integrated work placements indicate that conscious efforts toward creating more positions for these disabled individuals within our nation's regular work force can have the desired outcome, and these efforts

are particularly crucial given research that shows major improvements in a wide range of quality-of-life indicators when individuals with severe disabilities move from segregated to integrated environments (cf. Halvorsen & Sailor, in press).

A Descriptive Study of Parents Involved in the CTS Transition Process

Subjects and Data Collection Transition interviews were conducted with the families of two of three graduating, integrated high school students. CTS facilitated the transition process from integrated school to work settings for these students, both of whom were considered to be the students with the most significant disabilities. The parent of one student was identified as the single head of the household and the parent of the other student was a brother acting as guardian.

The transition interview protocol (adapted from Hanline & Halvorsen, in press) consisted of questions about secondary school placements, family involvement/participation in the transition process, the effects of transition on family perception of their child with severe disabilities, and information regarding the status of current job placement.

Analysis The analysis of the questions from the transition parent interview at the pregraduate level included the percentage of time spent within and across domains, as described in the community intensive model, and the degree of satisfaction with individual school placements, with a range from one (extremely dissatisfied) to seven (extremely satisfied). At the transition point, the analysis involved the degree of parental satisfaction with the process and the degree of their involvement on a scale of one to seven, as well as descriptions of influences, support, and concerns during this time. At the postgraduate level, analysis included the type of setting for client placement, the type of work for the client, the weekly time spent in social/leisure activities, the transportation used, and living arrangements.

Results An analysis of the interviews showed that students from both families had come from integrated school placements, in which parents stated that at least 55% of the school week consisted of vocational job training within the community.

In one case, a parent raised the initial issue of the potential postgraduate placement of her child, in the other case, the guardian was contacted by the CTS coordinator in order to facilitate a smooth transition to an integrated work setting. The transition started for both parents in February of their family member's graduating year. Both families agreed that the process started late, and that they were extremely involved in the process. While both families wanted their family member placed into an integrated work setting, they did have concerns. Lastly, the parents felt that the transition should be a process that is coordinated and gradual, and not an abrupt movement from one type of service to another.

Discussion Interviewing parents about their perceptions of the transition process provides invaluable input that will assist teachers, job training, and placement specialists to evaluate both the transition process and the programing. Individual family needs should be considered, and participation to the desired degree should be allowed. Families need to be acknowl-

edged as a heterogeneous group, rather than a homogeneous one (Turnbull & Turnbull, 1986).

Finally, the parent perspective is essential in determining the best possible placement for individual students. If parents do not feel that their family or child needs are being met, then a lack of communication may result in the ineffective placement of the graduating student. This can also ultimately result in dissatisfaction with work for the individual, or placement in a sheltered work option (Wehman et al., 1988).

The limitation of the present pilot interview study was the sample size ($n = 2$), which was too small to lead to any definitive statements about how parents perceive the effects of the transition process. Future research could examine the impact of family involvement and perspective on postschool placement, on the roles assumed/preferred by families in the transition process, and on the social validity of transition approaches for families of students with severe disabilities.

Relating Family Support and Transition Services

The family is the primary entity that maintains constant supervision of a young adult's needs for continued and ongoing services (Johnston, Bruininks, & Thurlow 1987). Parents need to be an integral part of the decisionmaking for placement of their child during the school years, and particularly at the postgraduate level. Parents are and need to be acknowledged as *equal* members in the transition process; they should have access to choices from a range of quality, integrated vocational placements, as well as areas of community access, recreation, and independent living. In order to make informed choices, parents need evaluative and comparative data on all of the available alternatives. Parents may wish to evaluate not only future adult services for their son or daughter, but also current school services and their potential to facilitate and promote meaningful working and living within the community.

Several specific areas need to be addressed more fully to facilitate a successful transition process for the family as a whole, and to provide information that will better equip families to make informed choices on the matter of transitions from school to work and community living.

Future research needs include an examination of how parent and child preferences and choices affect performance on a pre- to postgraduate level (cf. Guess, Benson, & Siegel-Causey, 1985). The need to individualize program planning for families during the transition process and its outcomes are also important considerations. Evaluative data on wages earned, individual motivation or affect, and opportunities for interactions with nondisabled persons are likely to prove to be significant outcome indices of transition planning efforts. Research is also needed on the extent and type of family involvement in the transition process, and those relationships to placement outcomes.

Family involvement in the transition process demands intensive time commitments, coordi-

nation with teachers and adult agencies, and emotional effort. Educators need to determine the preferred strategies for providing information to families during this period, to promote the benefits of quality integrated services and the benefits to society, as observable through indicators such as increased social skills by participants, more individualized program options, positive influences on staff and the consumer, and natural interaction opportunities (Stark & Karan, 1987). Finally, educators and adult service providers need to have a better awareness of individual family needs and concerns to ensure student participation within quality, integrated vocational work and community living environments.

REFERENCES

Brewer, G.D., & Kakalik, J.S. (1979). *Handicapped children: Strategies for improving services*. New York: McGraw-Hill.

Bridges, W. (1980). *Transitions: Making sense of life's changes*. Reading, MA: Addison-Wesley.

Brotherson, M.J. (1985). *Parents self report of future planning and its relationship to family functioning and family stress with sons and daughters who are disabled*. Unpublished doctoral dissertation, University of Kansas, Lawrence.

Brown, L., Rogan, P., Shiraga, B., Albright, K.Z., Kessler, K., Bryson, F., VanDeventer, P., & Loomis, R. (1987). *A vocational follow-up evaluation of the 1984–86 Madison Metropolitan school district graduates with severe intellectual disabilities*. Unpublished manuscript, University of Wisconsin and Madison Metropolitan School District, Madison.

Campbell, P. (1987). The integrated programming team: An approach for coordinating professionals of various disciplines in programs for students with severe and multiple handicaps. *Journal of The Association for Persons with Severe Handicaps, 12*(2), 107–116.

Conley, R.W., Noble, J.H., Jr., & Elder, J.K. (1986). Problems with the service system. In W.E. Kiernan & J.A. Stark (Eds.), *Pathways to employment for adults with developmental disabilities* (pp. 67–83). Baltimore: Paul H. Brookes Publishing Co.

Doering, K., Usilton, R., & Farron-Davis, F. (1989). *CTS project manual*. Unpublished manuscript, Community Transitional Services, San Franciso State University, San Francisco.

Elder, J. (1985). Transition from school to employment: A new frontier in work force. *Rehabilitation World*, Spring.

Everson, J.M., & Moon, M.S. (1987). Transition services for young adults with severe disabilities: Defining professional and parental roles and responsibilities. *Journal of The Association for Persons with Severe Handicaps, 12*(2), 87–95.

Fewell, R.R. (1986). A handicapped child in the family. In R.R. Fewell & R.F. Vadasy (Eds.), *Families of handi-*

capped children: Needs and supports across the life span (pp. 3–34). Bellevue, WA: Edmark Corporation.

Gaylord-Ross, R. (1987). Vocational integration for persons with mental handicaps: A cross-cultural perspective. *Research in Developmental Disabilities, 8,* 531–548.

Guess, D., Benson, H., & Siegel-Causey, E. (1985). Concepts and issues related to choice-making and autonomy among persons with severe disabilities. *Journal of The Association for Persons with Severe Disabilities, 10,* 79–86.

Halvorsen, A., & Sailor, W. (in press). Integration of students with severe and profound disabilities: A review of research. In R. Gaylord-Ross (Ed.), *Issues & research in special education* (Vol. I). New York: Teachers College Press.

Hanline, M.F., & Halvorsen, A.T. (in press). *Parent perceptions of the integration transition process, Exceptional Children*.

Hardman, M., & McDonnell, J. (1987). Implementing federal transition initiatives for youths with severe handicaps: The Utah community-based transition project. *Exceptional Children, 53*(6), 493–498.

Hasazi, S.B., Gordon, L.R., & Roe, C.A. (1985). Factors associated with the employment status of handicapped youth exiting high school from 1979–1983. *Exceptional Children, 51,* 455–469.

Hill, J., Seyfarth, J., Banks, D.P., Wehman, P., & Orelove, F. (1987). Parent attitudes about working conditions of their mentally retarded sons and daughters. *Exceptional Children, 54*(1), 9–23.

Johnson, D.R., Bruininks, R.H., & Thurlow, M.L. (1987). Meeting the challenge of transition service planning through improved interagency cooperation. *Exceptional Children, 53*(6), 522–530.

LaMar, K., & Rosenberg, W. (1987). *Synthesis of ITP format and process*. Unpublished manuscript, Sonoma County Office of Education, Sonoma, CA.

McDonnell, J., & Hardman, M. (1985). Planning the transition of severely handicapped youth from school to adult services: A framework for high school programs. *Education and Training of the Mentally Retarded,* 275–286.

McDonnell, J., Wilcox, B., & Boles, S.M. (1986). Do we know enough to plan for transition? A national survey of state agencies responsible for services to persons with severe handicaps. *Journal of The Association for Persons with Severe Handicaps, 11*(1), 53–60.

Mithaug, D.C., Horiuchi, L.N., & Faning, P.N. (1985). A report on the Colorado statewide follow-up survey of special education students. *Exceptional Children, 51*, 397–404.

Olson, D.H., McCubbin, H.I., Barrnes, H., Larsen, A., Muxen, M., & Wilson, M. (1983). *Families: What makes them work.* Beverly Hills: Sage Publications.

Organization for Economic Cooperation and Development (OECD). (1986). *Young people with handicaps: The road to adulthood.* Washington, DC: Centre for Educational Research & Innovation.

Piuma, C. (1988). *A benefit cost analysis: The economic impact of integrated and segregated educational service delivery models on the employment of individuals with severe disabilities.* Unpublished manuscript, Institute for Disability and Rehabilitation Research, San Francisco, CA.

Pumpian, I., Daumgart, D., Shiraga, B., Ford, A., Nesbit, J., Loomis, R., & Brown, L. (1980). Vocational training programs for severely handicapped students in Madison Metropolitan School District. In L. Brown, M. Falvey, I. Pumpian, D. Baumgart, J. Nesbit, A. Ford, J. Schroeder, & R. Loomis (Eds.), *Curricular strategies for teaching severely handicapped students functional skills in school and nonschool environments* (Vol. 10, pp. 273–310). Madison, WI: Madison Metropolitan School District.

Rainforth, B., & York, J. (1987). Integrating related services in community instruction. *Journal of The Association for Persons with Severe Handicaps, 12*(3), 190–198.

Rosenberg, W. (1983). *Individualized critical skills model: Career vocational training.* California State Department of Education, Office of Special Education, Sacramento.

Rusch, F., & Phelps, L.A. (1987). Secondary special education and transition for school to work: A national priority. *Exceptional Children, 53*(6), 487–492.

Sailor, W. (in press). Phase IV: Transition from school to work and community service. In W. Sailor, J. Anderson, A. Halvorsen, K. Doering, J. Filler, & L. Goetz, *The comprehensive local school: Regular education for all students with disabilities.* Baltimore: Paul H. Brookes Publishing Co.

Sailor, W., Gee, K., Goetz, L., & Graham, N. (1988). Progress in educating students with the most severe disabilities: Is there any? *Journal of The Association for Persons with Severe Handicaps, 13*(2), 87–99.

Sailor, W., Goetz, L., Anderson, J., Hunt, P., & Gee, K. (1988). Research on community intensive instruction as a model for building functional, generalized skills. In

R. Horner, G. Dunlap, & R. Koegel (Eds.), *Generalization and maintenance: Life-style changes in applied settings* (pp. 41–98). Baltimore: Paul H. Brookes Publishing Co.

Sailor, W., Halvorsen, A., Anderson, J., Goetz, L., Gee, K., Doering, K., & Hunt, P. (1986). Community intensive instruction. In R. H. Horner, L. H. Meyer, & H. D. Fredericks (Eds.), *Education of learners with severe handicaps: Exemplary service strategies* (pp. 251–288). Baltimore: Paul H. Brookes Publishing Co.

Snell, M., & Browder, D. (1986). Community-referenced instruction: Research and issues. *Journal of The Association for Persons with Severe Handicaps, 11*(1), 1–11.

Stark, J., & Karan, O. (1987). Transition services for early adult age individuals with severe mental retardation. In *Transition issues and directions* (pp. 91–110). Reston, VA: Council for Exceptional Children.

State Department of Education. (1987, May). Specialized Programs Branch, Education Transition Center, California Transition Research Fair: Proceedings. Oakland Convention Center, Oakland.

Sylvester, J., Thomas, K., Curtin, C., & Driscoll, K. (1985). Horizons: A transition to the future. In *Vermont Vocational Training Network Project Training Manual.* Unpublished manuscript, Winooski, VT.

Turnbull, A. P. & Turnbull, H. R. III (1986). *Families, professionals and exceptionality: A special partnership.* Columbus, OH: Charles E. Merrill.

Turnbull, H. R. (1985). Jay's story. In H. R. Turnbull & A. P. Turnbull (Eds.), *Parents speak out: Then and now* (pp. 109–118). Columbus, OH: Charles E. Merrill.

Wehman, P., Kregel, J., & Barcus, J. N. (1985). From school to work: A vocational transition model for handicapped students. *Exceptional Children, 52*(1), 25–37.

Wehman, P., Kregel, J., & Seyfarth, J. (1985). Transition from school to work for individuals with severe handicaps: A follow-up study. *Journal of The Association for Persons with Severe Handicaps, 10*(3), 132–136.

Wehman, P., Moon, M. S., Everson, J. M., Wood, W., & Barcus, J. M. (1988). *Transition from school to work: New challenges for youth with severe disabilities.* Baltimore, MD: Paul H. Brookes Publishing Co.

Wehman, P., Moon, S., & McCarthy, P. (1986). Transition from school to adulthood for youth with severe handicaps. *Focus on Exceptional Children, 18*(5), 1–12.

Wilcox, B., & Bellamy, G. T. (1982). *Design of high school programs for severely handicapped students.* Baltimore: Paul H. Brookes Publishing Co.

Will, M. C. (1984). *OSERS programming for the transition of youth with disabilities: Bridges from school to working life.* Washington, DC: Office of Special Education and Rehabilitation Services, U. S. Department of Education.

CHAPTER 17

Critical Parent Roles in Supported Employment

Jo-Ann Sowers

In our society, most parents hope that their children, as adults, will have opportunities to select from a wide array of fulfilling career options, and to make a meaningful and well remunerated contribution to society. Unfortunately, until the mid 1980s, parents of individuals who experienced significant disabilities were not able to share in this dream. In the past, individuals with severe disabilities have been limited to employment in a sheltered workshop or work activity center. Through the new supported employment movement, greater work opportunities are becoming available for these individuals.

EMPLOYMENT SERVICES:
PAST, PRESENT, AND FUTURE

Sheltered employment programs have two major goals. The first goal is to prepare people for movement out of the sheltered program and into community-based employment. The second goal is to provide individuals with the opportunity to work and earn a living while they remain in the program. Unfortunately, these programs have not been successful in achieving either of these goals (United States Department of Labor, 1979). The annual rates of placement for persons with mental retardation from sheltered workshops and work activity centers into competitive employment are 11.3% and 7.4%, respectively. The vast majority of individuals with more severe disabilities are served in work activity centers.

In fact, the actual placement rates of persons with severe disabilities may be even lower than 7.4%. Moss (1979), in a further analysis of the United States Department of Labor (1979) report, found that 75% of the placements occur for those individuals who were in a program for 3 months or less; only 3% of individuals who were in a program longer than 2 years were placed into competitive employment annually. The fact that 23% of people with mental retardation remained in sheltered programs for more than 5 years suggests that the rate of placement for these individuals is closer to the 3% level. The 1979 United States Department of Labor report also revealed that the average annual salary of persons with disabilities in sheltered work programs was $417, or $.43 per hour.

In response to these rather dismal outcomes that resulted from the existing service delivery system, a number of experimental research and demonstration projects were initiated in the late 1970s to determine if a more effective approach could be developed (Rusch & Mithaug, 1980; Sowers, Thompson, & Connis, 1979; Wehman, 1981). Fortunately, these efforts have been successful in documenting that individuals who traditionally have been maintained in segregated settings can work in regular settings alongside nondisabled coworkers and earn more than a trivial wage. The approach that has been used to achieve these outcomes is commonly called *supported employment*.

The movement away from sheltered employment to community-based, supported employment service models is only now being at-

The preparation of this chapter was supported in part by the U.S. Department of Education Grant No. G008730431. The opinions expressed herein do not necessarily reflect the position or policy of these agencies.

tempted on a widespread basis, as of the late 1980s. The goal of these efforts is that every individual, regardless of the severity of disability, will have the opportunity to participate fully in the American work force. A number of factors will determine the extent to which this ambitious goal is achieved. The parents of individuals with disabilities will certainly play a particularly important role. As Siegal & Loman (1987) stated:

> Situated at the center of the new programmatic developments, with a greater stake in their outcome than the policy makers who initiate them and the service professionals who implement them, are the parents of the children for whom these programs have been designed. Their assistance, support, and collaboration are conditions for the possibility that these new programmatic undertakings have the effect and impact that is expected. (p. 16)

The purposes of this chapter are to discuss the impact that parents will have in the success of supported employment, and to delineate the strategies that professionals can utilize to enhance the positive nature of this impact.

Supported Employment: Critical Factors

Traditional employment programs for persons with disabilities are based on the following beliefs: 1) that a person is "ready" for movement out of sheltered employment only after a vast array of skills that are considered essential for community employment have been mastered, 2) that "readiness" training of these skills is most effectively provided in segregated and simulated work settings, and 3) that, to remain in a community job, a person must be able to function with little or no assistance.

Sheltered programs provide classroom-based training in academics, telling time, making change, match-to-sample sorting, and numerous other prerequisite skills. Specific task training is provided in the context of the skills that individuals learn while performing work that is subcontracted to the program. This work typically involves assembly or packaging tasks, although few opportunities may exist for obtaining similar work in the local business sector. Given such beliefs and strategies, it is not surprising that few persons have been deemed "ready" to be given the opportunity to work in regular work settings.

In contrast, the supported employment approach is based on the singular philosophy that an individual should be provided with the opportunity to work in a community setting as quickly as possible. Three major strategies are essential to achieve this outcome.

Job Development The proponents of the supported employment approach recognize that the requirements for successful employment vary greatly from one worksite to another and from one job to another. Consequently, an attempt is made to identify or create a job that matches the current skills and abilities of an individual.

On-the-Job Training Supported employment programs recognize that the most important training will occur at the actual worksite where a person will be employed. Individuals are provided with intensive and systematic training, in order to ensure that they perform the assigned tasks and exhibit the social and work-related behavior critical to job success at that site.

Follow-Up and Ongoing Support Perhaps the most critical strategy of the supported employment approach is the provision of long-term follow-up and support to ensure job maintenance. In many cases, the amount of assistance may be slowly decreased over time and eventually reach a minimal level. However, a high degree of support and assistance may be required and provided for some individuals on an indefinite basis.

Supported Employment Outcomes

Several research and demonstration projects have been instrumental in the development of supported employment placement programs. A brief review of the most critical outcomes (i.e., number of placements and wages earned by consumers) of these projects follows. Wehman, Kregal, and Seyfarth (1986) in Virginia have placed and maintained a total of 71 individuals with severe to moderate mental retardation in a 5-year period. All of these individuals earned at least minimum wage (Wehman, 1986). The University of Washington Employment Training Project began training and placing individuals with severe to mild mental retardation in 1975. At the present time, 55 individuals are employed competitively, at minimum wage or better (Moss,

Dineen, & Ford, 1986). Rusch and his colleagues in Illinois have successfully placed 72 individuals in approximately 6 years (Lagomarcino, 1986). The wages earned ranged from minimum wage to over $7.00 per hour. In Vermont, the supported employment placement approach has been implemented successfully in rural areas; through Project Transition, 40 individuals with severe to mild mental retardation have been placed in a 5-year period (Vogelsberg, 1986).

The majority of supported employment program demonstration efforts focus on individuals whose only significant disability is mental retardation. Rarely have individuals who experience severe physical and multiple developmental disabilities been served by these projects. Recently, model projects are beginning to develop that address the unique employment needs of individuals who experience such multiple disabilities. Specifically, the participants in these programs experience cerebral palsy (a few have spina bifida) and mental retardation. Most also experience other disabilities such as a loss of vision and/or hearing. Through the Oregon Transition to Employment Project (OTEP), over three school districts have implemented programs to prepare students with severe physical and multiple disabilities for the transition from school to community-based employment (Sowers, Jenkins, & Powers, 1988). The three students who left high school (at age 21) and participated in OTEP are working in community-based, supported employment positions.

Alternative Work Concepts (AWC) (Sowers, 1988) is a supported employment program for adults with severe physical and multiple disabilities. AWC has been in operation for less than one year, and has successfully placed and maintained four individuals in community jobs. Three of these individuals use a wheelchair for mobility. Each also experiences severe to moderate mental retardation. All of the AWC participants work approximately 20 hours per week; two have been placed in individual job sites, while two others work in a job-share arrangement at one company. Three are paid based on their productivity through a subminimum wage contract; their hourly wage equivalent ranges from $.94 to $2.16 per hour. Although the productivity of the fourth individual is less than 50%, her employer has agreed to pay her the minimum wage.

Summary It is clear that individuals with severe disabilities can be employed successfully in community settings. In addition, a fairly well defined set of strategies prove effective in achieving this outcome. This technology includes job procurement, analysis, and matching techniques, strategies for training tasks and skills that are both effective and acceptable in public job settings, and procedures to enhance long-term job maintenance. The challenge is to move beyond university-based demonstration and model projects to implement supported employment on a widespread basis.

The Role of Parents in Supported Employment

The importance of the roles that parents play in the employment of their adult children in community settings has been widely acknowledged (Bellamy, Wilcox, McDonald, & Sowers, 1982; Goodall & Bruder, 1985; Schutz, 1986; Wehman, 1981). Two major roles are critical. First, parents typically make the final selection between sheltered employment and community employment for their young adult child. Many parents are hesitant to permit their disabled son or daughter to work in a nonsheltered situation (Hill, Seyfarth, Banks, Wehman, & Orelove, 1985; Katz & Yaketiel, 1975). A survey of parents of individuals attending day activity centers regarding their attitudes and opinions about their child's future employment (Hill, Wehman, Hill, & Goodall, 1986) showed that only 63% wanted their son or daughter to have more access to work and the opportunity to earn money. Of these parents, only 10% preferred a community work setting.

Parental concern related to nonsheltered employment is understandable for a number of reasons. First, for years professionals have told these parents that community employment was not a feasible goal for their young adult child. Parents and families accepted this judgment as fact and believed that sheltered employment best served the needs of their son or daughter. Now these same professionals indicate that community employment is not merely an option, but the preferred option. Parents, like most people who receive information that contradicts certain long-held belief systems, are skeptical of this new information.

Many parents are also afraid of the impact that the employment of their young adult child will have on the family. Like any family, those with a handicapped member tend to establish a lifestyle pattern, typically one that promotes stability and constancy (Mittler, Cheseldine, & McConachie, 1980; Schutz, 1986). Parents of a disabled individual are aware that a change in the employment status of that disabled individual has the potential to change the entire family system that they may have worked so long to achieve. In addition to the general sense of anxiety that the prospect of a lifestyle disruption may elicit, parents have identified a number of specific concerns that arise when considering community-based employment for their disabled family member. These concerns include transportation to and from work, loss of SSI financial and medical benefits, lack of opportunities for recreational activities typically provided by sheltered programs, and what will happen in the event that the job ceases to exist (Schutz, 1986; Siegal & Loman, 1987).

The resistance of parents to community-based employment is changing. Siegal and Loman (1987), in a survey of 184 parents of individuals currently in sheltered programs, found that 79% would like to see their child have an opportunity to work in a community setting. In fact, 90% of the parents who were 40 years of age and younger wanted their son or daughter to have this opportunity. In the same survey, 29% of 43 sheltered work providers indicated that parents' objections would be a factor that would hinder the employment of the individuals served at their facility in a community setting; perhaps parents' fears of community employment are decreasing more rapidly than are professionals' fears.

The influence that parents can have on the success or failure of their young adult children who are given the opportunity to work in community settings has also been addressed (Kochany & Keller, 1981; Schutz, 1986; Wehman, 1981). Kiernan and Koegal (1980) found that individuals who had families who were not supportive were less likely to be employed successfully than those with supportive families, regardless of the amount of support provided by a service provider. Kochany and Keller (1981) found that 4 of 18 job losses (22%) by individuals with mental retardation resulted from lack of parental support.

One specific and critical role that parents and families can play is to assist service providers to find employment for their sons or daughters. Hasazi, Gordon, and Roe (1985) found that 80% of the jobs found by former special education students were obtained through a family connection. Wehman, Kregal, and Seyfarth (1985) have estimated that in two out of three cases, the family or close friends contribute to the acquisition of a job for the family member with a disability. Other critical roles that parents frequently must play in supporting the employment of their young adult children include assistance in getting to and from work, ensuring proper grooming and dress, and perhaps most importantly, reinforcing the importance of work and job performance (Schutz, 1986; Wehman, 1981).

In the following section, specific strategies are delineated for achieving parental support of community-based employment. These strategies have been derived from the experience of the chapter author in developing supported employment programs. They serve as critical components of the Alternative Work Concepts Program.

SERVICE DESIGN

As of the late 1980s, community-based employment programs have been conducted on a very small scale by university-based demonstration projects. These programs have the luxury of working only with those individuals whose parents are committed to, and have few concerns about, community-based employment. In addition, grant-supported projects typically have the financial resources that permitted the provision of most of the supports that an individual might need on the job; consequently, the importance of parent and family supports may be diminished. Most non–grant-supported programs will not have the financial resources that are available to demonstration projects. These programs will need to take advantage of every possible resource, to supplement the support that their staff can provide to assist individuals in maintaining their jobs. Therefore, it will be imperative for a program to use systematic strategies to gain parent support. In this section, specific suggestions and strategies will be described that service providers can utilize to assist parents to overcome their concerns related to community-based employment, as well as to enhance parental involvement and support of their child's employment.

Parents' Concerns and Strategies in Selecting Community-Based Employment

The availability of programs that offer severely disabled individuals the opportunity to work in community-based settings will increase in the future. Sheltered workshops and work activity centers will continue operations as well. As a result, when students leave school their parents will have to choose between these two types of employment options. Similarly, the parents of individuals who have been receiving services in sheltered programs will also have to decide if their young adult child should remain in that service or move to community-based employment.

The supported employment movement will succeed only if a significant number of parents believe that it offers more benefits than does sheltered employment. In order to make their decisions, parents will need assistance in identifying the relative value of the programs. Descriptions of the concerns that parents frequently voice, and the strategies that supported employment providers can implement to diminish each, follow.

Concern 1: Is Community-Based Employment a Feasible Goal?
Many parents may accept the potential value of community-based employment, but still have difficulty believing that their son or daughter could work successfully in a regular business. They may fear that their child will lose his or her job and feel like a failure. Or they may fear that the person with disabilities will experience stress when placed in a regular business, due to high performance demands.

To help alleviate these fears, service providers must keep an open dialogue with parents. Parents should be provided with a clear description of the supported employment approach, and be assured that every effort will be made to place their young adults into jobs where they will have the greatest likelihood of succeeding. It should also be explained that program staff will provide continuing intensive and systematic training after placement, to ensure success and decrease the stress that may accompany first attempts to learn a job. Finally, parents should understand that the program will provide ongoing support and assistance to their sons or daughters, in order to ensure that these young adults maintain their jobs.

Even with a clear description of the supported employment approach used by a program, some parents may still find it difficult to believe that their young adult can work successfully in a community setting. One of the most powerful strategies for assisting parents to overcome these doubts is to provide them with examples of other individuals who have similar disabilities and are successfully working in community settings. Parents will relate best to examples of people in their own community. If this is not possible, successful placements in other communities can be described or shown to parents during visits to programs in these communities, by attending conferences, or by reading case examples in books or articles related to supported employment. There are also a number of videotapes available that describe supported employment programs and provide illustrations of their success.

Concern 2: Will My Son or Daughter be able to Keep His or Her Job?
Perhaps the major advantage of sheltered programs from a parental perspective is the security and stability that they offer. Rarely will a person be fired for poor performance or inappropriate social skills. Also, people are not likely to be laid off due to lack of work. A sheltered workshop or work activity center always provides somewhere for a person with disabilities to go on Monday through Friday.

Although the supported work approach to community-based employment is designed specifically to decrease the likelihood that a person will lose a job, a few individuals will still do so even when all the components of this approach are implemented as effectively as possible. Parents are legitimately concerned about what will happen to their son or daughter in this event. They will find it particularly troublesome if the only option is for their child to remain at home until another job is found. When a parent works during the day and does not feel comfortable leaving a son or daughter alone all day without supervision, this issue alone can produce a reluctance to opt for community-based employment. Even for a parent who is home during the day, the impact of having an adult son or daughter constantly at home may be stressful. Parents will also be concerned about the effects that remaining at home for a substantial period of time will have on their adult children in terms of skills lost, boredom, possible increase of behavior problems, and a loss of motivation.

Therefore, it is imperative that programs provide a back-up option so that individuals who lose their jobs can receive services while waiting to be placed again. Placement services operated by sheltered programs can often have individuals return to the facility between jobs. Some supported employment programs have preplacement training sites that typically operate in regular business environments. For example, the Employment Training Program (Moss, Dineen, & Ford, 1986; Sowers, Thompson, & Connis, 1979), provides short-term or preplacement training at a restaurant located on the University of Washington campus. In the event that an individual who has been placed loses a job, he or she can return to the training site.

Many programs, however, do not have a preplacement component. These programs present the greatest risk regarding job loss. Such services can attempt to establish options that accommodate individuals while they are waiting for a new placement. One possible solution would be to develop an agreement for a sheltered program to provide temporary services to a person from the placement program who has lost a job and is waiting for a new one. A more appropriate strategy might be to locate a number of community businesses where individuals who are between jobs can be work in a volunteer capacity.

Termination of the client from a supported employment program presents similar problems. Programs need specific policies related to the circumstances under which a person will no longer be served. The policies can state clearly what will be done to assist a person who leaves

the program. This issue will be of particular concern to parents who are considering taking their adult child out of a sheltered program and to those who are passing up an opening in a sheltered program that has a lengthy waiting list. People who lose their place on such a list often must wait for months or years to regain it in the event that a community-based job does not work out.

Concern 3: Will My Son or Daughter Lose SSI and Medical Benefits? At the age of 18, individuals with disabilities are eligible to receive financial (SSI) and medical (SSDI) benefits. Although the actual amount of money may not be great, it can make a significant contribution to the income of many families, particularly those with elderly parents or others who must live on a fixed income. Of even greater importance are the medical benefits that are made available to people with disabilities, because the high cost of private medical insurance is prohibitive for many families. Given the importance of these benefits, parents are understandably concerned about the potential impact that community-based employment for their young adult may have on their family's financial stability.

One of the major advantages of community-based employment is the potential it offers for higher wages than in sheltered employment. Paradoxically, this prospect of higher wages may worry a parent due to the potential impact of this income on financial and medical benefits. In fact, until very recently, the regulations related to benefit eligibility served as a major disincentive to community-based employment. Prior to 1981, a person who earned more than approximately $300.00 per month (considered "substantial gainful employment") would lose all SSI income and medical benefits after a short, trial work period. Fortunately, the regulations have changed. As of 1988, under Section 1619(a) and 1619(b) of the Social Security Act, people continue to be eligible for benefits unless they earn a fairly significant income (approximately $735.00 per month).

Information about the new regulations has not been widely disseminated to persons with disabilities, their families, or even service providers. Clearly, it is imperative that parents be provided with information about these new regulations so that their concerns relating to the loss of benefits will be decreased.

Despite the provisions in Sections 1619 a and b, however, a person in supported employment can remain in jeopardy of losing benefit eligibility. The specific regulations regarding eligibility vary from state to state. In addition, the interpretation and application of the regulations often varies between Social Security offices. Due to these discrepancies, it is imperative that service providers become thoroughly acquainted with state regulations as well as with the manner in which their local Social Security Office interprets and applies them.

Attempts to place individuals in positions that include medical benefits are one way to address these issues. Such benefits often are not provided for the entry-level positions into which persons with developmental disabilities are frequently placed. Nevertheless, programs can target benefits as a high priority when attempting to find jobs for their consumers. Although it may take longer to find a job that offers benefits, the interests of the individual are better served when this time is taken.

Concern 4: What Transportation is Available? Many sheltered programs provide transportation to and from work. In most cases, this service will not be available once the person is placed into a community-based job. Understandably, parents will be concerned about how their son or daughter will get to work once a placement is made.

In a community where a public bus system is an available alternative, parents will be concerned about safety issues related to public transportation; there are a number of genuine risks involved in bus riding. To alleviate this concern, programs can develop systematic and intensive training regimens to ensure that consumers are able to use the public bus safely to get to and from work. Descriptions of how to accomplish transportation training are available (Rusch & Mithaug, 1980). That the supported employment service make a commitment to remain with the person until he or she has demonstrated consistently the ability to get to and from work safely is of greatest importance.

Public transportation will not be an option for everybody. In some communities, no bus system

is available for persons using wheelchairs, and buses often are not accessible. Some parents may be willing and able to transport their adult children to and from work; however, this will not be possible for many families. Even when it is possible, programs should realize the burden that daily transport represents to many families. Some parents simply will not be willing to devote the time to arrange transportation. Consequently, programs must be prepared to assist parents in arranging alternative transportation. Options to consider include: 1) the use of a cab, 2) the use of a private, wheelchair-accessible van, 3) arranging for a ride with a coworker or neighbor who works in the general vicinity, and 4) finding a job for the person that is close to home.

Concern 5: Will Recreational Activities Still Be Available? Many sheltered programs provide people with recreational activities during the time that they attend the program. These activities include bowling, swimming, field trips, and so forth. Students in school are also provided with daily recreational activities as a routine part of their school programs. Parents may be concerned about whether recreational activities will be available for their son or daughter who is placed in a community-based job. This is a legitimate concern, and one that many supported employment programs have failed to address when placing individuals into jobs.

Community-based employment is intended to positively affect a person's quality of life. If choosing a community job over a sheltered program results in decreased access to recreational opportunities, this outcome will not be achieved. In some cases, parents may be willing to assist in identifying, setting up, and transporting their son or daughter to recreational activities; others, however, will not. Some supported work programs may take the position that their role is to provide only vocational training and support, and that other agencies must take the responsibility for recreational activities. Although in theory this is how an ideal system would operate, few communities have a well-developed program that assists individuals with disabilities to participate in leisure activities. The work program, therefore, can take an active role in advocating for improved recreational services for persons with disabilities. Programs can assist parents in gaining access to these activities for their son or daughter. Such efforts are really in the best interest of the program, because they can influence the willingness of parents to select community-based work options, and they will enhance the disabled person's satisfaction with work and life.

If the recreational activities available at the sheltered program are extremely important to parents and their adult children, it may be possible and appropriate to find a job with hours that would permit a regular return to the facility to participate. For example, if bowling is scheduled in the afternoon, a morning job might be found so that the person with disabilities could participate in the recreational activities at the sheltered program. It is certainly true that many professionals (including this author) would prefer that individuals with disabilities participate in integrated leisure activities, rather than in those arranged for and attended only by persons with disabilities. It may be too much, however, to ask a parent to take the major step required in permitting a son or daughter to move into a community-based job, and to give up those sheltered program recreational activities.

In some communities the City Parks and Recreational Program, the Association for Retarded Citizens, or other organizations offer leisure programs and activities for persons with disabilities. Parents can be made aware of these activities and provided with assistance in arranging for their son or daughter to participate.

Frequently, the most difficult aspect of recreational activities will be transportation. The program could assist in this regard by training the person with a disability to ride the bus to the activity. Another transportation strategy might be to identify two or three parents, living in the same vicinity, who attend these activities and arrange a carpool whereby driving duties can be shared.

A recreational program may not be available for persons with disabilities in a given community. Or, the one that is available may be limited in the type, number, or regularity of activities offered. One strategy that can be used to change this situation is to recruit volunteers who are in-

terested in participating in leisure activities with an individual in the program.

Enhancing Parental Support of Community-Based Employment

The importance of family support in the employment of persons with disabilities has been established (Kochany & Keller, 1981; Schutz, 1986; Wehman, 1981). For the most part, however, community placement programs generally approach the issue of family involvement in an unsystematic fashion. Program staff may tell parents how important their support is and then hope that parents will provide it. Given the critical importance of parental support, it is imperative that providers give as much attention and effort to developing a systematic intervention approach for gaining the support of families as is given to other program components. The following discussion provides a description of seven activities that can be utilized to increase family involvement in support of job placement and maintenance.

Activity 1: Obtain Information about Parents' Needs and Desires Relating to Placement A widely practiced technique for determining placement involves assessing the skills and behavior of a person who will be placed in a job, and then finding the job that best matches those skills. However, the needs and desires of parents and family members often are not taken into account. For example, families may have specific desires related to the hours when their son or daughter will work, the amount of time that he or she works, the type of job, the location of the job site, and so forth. Parents and families are also an excellent source of information about their son's or daughter's behavior and the types of situations in which he or she will be successful. Information from parents will be particularly useful for program staff who have little or no previous experience working with the individual. For example, parents might indicate that their son or daughter likes to work outside more than inside, and performs better for male than for female supervisors.

One of the best strategies for obtaining input from parents regarding their desires related to their adult child's placement is to use a structured interview approach (Schutz, 1986). The purpose of this approach is to provide a systematic yet flexible means to ask parents about their desires. The questions shown in Table 1 provide examples of those that might be included in the interview. It is important that they understand the issues facing them. For example, if a parent indicated that they had no preferences regarding the hours when their son or daughter works, the interviewer could confirm this by asking, "You wouldn't mind if he or she works at night?"

Also, a parent's initial response may be modified after discussion and clarification. For instance, parents may indicate that they do not want their son or daughter to work in a downtown area due to safety concerns. Program staff can explain that eliminating placement possibilities in businesses downtown will dramatically decrease the opportunities and increase the amount of time to locate an appropriate job. Staff members may also provide examples of individuals whom they have placed downtown with no problems.

Through the structured interview, program

Table 1. Sample questions to ask parents regarding job placement performance

1. Do you have a strong preference regarding the type of work that your child will perform? Are there any jobs that you would be strongly opposed to your child performing?

2. Are there any jobs that you know that your child likes to perform? Are there any jobs that you know your child strongly dislikes performing?

3. Are there any areas of town where you would prefer your child to work, or where you would be strongly opposed to your child working?

4. Do you think your child would prefer to work inside or outside?

5. Does your child work better at tasks that require moving around a lot, or tasks that allow him or her to sit or stand in one place?

6. Do you think your child will work better for a male or a female supervisor, or does it matter?

7. Does your child like to work around a lot of other people, or does he or she work better alone?

8. What hours would you prefer that your child work? Are there any hours that you would definitely not want your child to work?

9. How many hours per week would you prefer that your child work? Would you be willing to consider a job for your child that had a different number of hours than your preference?

staff can gain a clear idea of the parents' desires related to placement. This process communicates to the parents the importance of their involvement if employment is to be successful. It also enhances their confidence that the program is interested in, and responsive to, their views.

Activity 2: Obtain Possible Job Leads from Parents and Family The likelihood of obtaining a job is enhanced if the job seeker has a personal contact in the company. Parents and other family members typically have friends, relatives, and business contacts in numerous companies throughout a community. These individuals can be of great assistance in finding an appropriate job. Parents can be asked to identify any individuals who may be able to assist in gaining entry into a particular company and who may be willing to advocate for the hiring of their son or daughter, or other individuals with disabilities.

Activity 3: Keep Parents Informed of Placement Activities In some cases it may take weeks or months to find a job for a person. In order to maintain parents' interest and motivation in placement during this period, it is useful to provide them with regular updates on job search efforts. This can be achieved by calling the parents weekly or once every two weeks and describing the companies that have been contacted and analyzed, the reasons why they did not work out as a placement, and those that are targeted for contact during the next few weeks.

Activity 4: Review the Details of a Potential Job before Proceeding with Placement Activities The review occurs when a job has been located that may be a potential placement for a person. The program staff should meet with the individual's parents and describe all aspects of the job, including the tasks, hours, pay, social environment, vacation policy, sick leave policy, and grooming requirements. If there is more than one potential placement, each can be described and the parents can be given the opportunity to select the one that they prefer.

Parents have certain responsibilities if they agree to the placement; their commitment to fulfill them should be obtained. For example, if a job starts at 7:00 A.M., they may have to make a commitment to assisting their son or daughter to get up, get dressed, and to the bus by 6:15. The parents may also need to make a commitment to assist the individual to wear a clean uniform each day. Also, if a company's policy directs that employees not be given time off for doctor's or dentist's appointments, the parents will have to commit to making these appointments on their son's or daughter's day off. Delineating these responsibilities, and gaining a commitment from parents before a job is accepted, will ensure that dif-

ficulties related to parent cooperation do not arise later, jeopardizing job success.

Activity 5: Provide Critical Information in Writing about the Job and Parents' Related Responsibilities   If parents do agree to a particular job, the program can proceed in making the final arrangements with the employer regarding the placement. Before the individual begins the job, it is useful to provide parents with a Job Information Form (see Figure 1). This form pro-

---

Page 1

Name of company	Acme Insurance
Address	197 Division
Supervisor name	John Smith
Telephone	963–2121
Job coach name	Sally Jones
Telephone (8 A.M.–5 P.M.)	932–7890
(after 5 P.M.)	516–1823

Page 2

Days/hours	M-F, 8:30–12:30
Salary	$4.35 per hour
Pay schedule	Paid every 2 weeks on Friday
Pay procedure	Supervisor will give Donna her check and make sure she puts it in her purse. If the check is not in her purse when she arrives at home, call Sally, her job coach, immediately.

Page 3

Vacation policy	She will be given 1 day paid vacation for each month she is employed. Vacation days cannot be taken until after 6 months on the job. Vacation day must be arranged at least 2 weeks in advance.
Sick leave policy	After being employed for 3 months she will be given 1 day paid sick leave for each month employed.
	Call supervisor and job coach as soon as possible to inform them that Sally is ill and will not be at work.
Dentist/doctor appointment policy	Employees should always attempt to make dentist/doctor appointments during nonworking hours.
	If taken during working hours it will be counted as sick leave time.
Dress policy	Clothes should be freshly washed and ironed. Type of clothes should be appropriate for office job.
	No jeans, tennis shoes, sweat shirts, T-shirts. A nice pair of pants or a skirt along with a pullover sweater or shirt will be acceptable. Sally will visit with you and help you identify the clothes in Donna's wardrobe that are appropriate.

Figure 1.   Completed job information form.

vides a clear description of the critical information about the job. The purpose of this activity is to avoid difficulties that may arise due to a lack of understanding of the job. Program staff should review the information on the form with the parents, in order to make sure that they understand it completely and to clarify any points of confusion.

Activity 6: Provide Specific Suggestions for Supporting and Reinforcing Job Performance The family is probably the most powerful influence on a person's attitude, motivation, and behavior related to work. Program staff can provide parents with specific suggestions on how to reinforce and support their son or daughter for working and performing well at a job. Providing the suggestions in writing for parents is especially helpful. Table 2 provides an example of such a document. It offers suggestions that can serve as a guide to parents for reinforcing their sons or daughters.

Table 2. Suggestions for reinforcing and supporting employment

1. Give your child a few words of encouragement before he or she leaves for work each day.
2. Talk with your child about how things went at work when he or she comes home each day.
3. Tell your child on a regular basis how proud you are that he or she has a real job.
4. In front of your son or daughter, tell your neighbors, relatives, and friends about his or her job and how proud you are.
5. Be particularly enthusiastic each time your child brings home a paycheck.
6. Make depositing his or her check a particularly big event. Make a special trip to the bank. Make sure he or she understands that the money he or she earned at work is going into the bank. Have your child get at least a small amount of cash when depositing the check and to spend it on something he or she would like such as a special treat, a record, tape, or article of clothing.
7. If a portion of your child's earnings are used to contribute to basic family expenses such as rent, food, and utilities, make sure that you and other family members reinforce him or her on a regular basis for the important contribution that he or she is making to the family.
8. Set aside a portion of your child's earning to be spent on activities and items that he or she wants, and provide him or her with the opportunity to purchase these items and participate in these activities. The program staff will provide specific suggestions and assistance in doing this.

Staff can go over the suggestions with parents and emphasize the importance of following them as much as possible. It might be recommended that the document be posted in a location in the home where family members will see it and thus be reminded to do these things. During routine phone contacts with parents, staff can ask if they are following these suggestions and reinforce them for doing so. During the first few months of their son's or daughter's job, the phone calls can be made on a weekly basis, after which they may occur monthly. It is useful to send a duplicate document to parents every month or two in case they have misplaced or discarded the original, and as a reminder of the importance of their support.

Activity 7: Provide Ongoing Information about Job Performance and Status It is important to provide parents with ongoing information about how their son or daughter is doing at work. Some of the types of information that should be shared with parents about their son's or daughter's performance include progress in learning the assigned task, social and survival skill performance, progress learning to ride the bus to and from work, coworker relations, any feedback from supervisors, any changes that occur in the job (i.e., new coworkers, supervisors' tasks assignment change, and enjoyment of the job).

This information can be shared with parents during the same phone calls that are used to prompt them about their role in reinforcing their son's or daughter's work performance. Progress reports can thus be used as the basis for feedback that the parents provide to their son or daughter.

Summary Parents frequently express a number of concerns when considering community-based employment for their young adult sons and daughters. Supported employment programs should address these concerns in a proactive manner, in order to increase the opportunity for as many individuals with disabilities as possible to work in nonsheltered settings. In addition, because many parents' concerns reflect real service delivery weaknesses, responding to these concerns will help ensure the success of the supported employment movement for people with disabilities.

Parents can positively or negatively influence

the employment of their son or daughter in community settings. Programs must develop and implement systematic approaches in order to increase parent involvement and support. These strategies should be initiated before a job is sought for an individual, and continue throughout the job placement, training, and maintenance phases of the employment process.

IMPLICATIONS

Research Implications

Given the important roles that parents have in the success of supported employment, increased attention to this topic is needed. In particular, there are two areas of research that should be addressed. First, as more individuals are placed into community jobs, it will be critical to evaluate parental satisfaction with and perceptions of community-based employment for their adult children, in a manner similar to the parent surveys conducted by Wehman (1981) as well as Wilson and Brodsky (1988). If parents' satisfaction with their adult children's experiences in community jobs continues to be positive, this information will provide powerful evidence for the viability of supported employment. As a result, other parents who are hesitant to permit their son or daughter to work in a community setting might be more willing to do so. This information can also serve to encourage the continued support of these programs by funding and policy-making agencies.

From a different perspective, the information obtained from these surveys could reveal the types of problems that parents encounter when their son or daughter is placed on a job. Supported employment programs can flourish only if they are actively responsive to parents' views and concerns.

In this chapter, a number of strategies have been delineated that may be helpful to programs for enhancing parental support of a son's or daughter's job performance. These are strategies that the author has used and that appear to be effective. However, no attempt has been made to determine experimentally the extent to which these or any other strategies actually affect parent involvement and support. Research is needed to identify the strategies that programs can most

effectively and efficiently use to gain parent support.

Public Policy Implications

Programs should attempt to alleviate the concerns that parents may have regarding the impact of community-based employment on all members of the family. However, in many cases, existing policies limit what programs can actually do. An example of this situation involves the regulations that determine eligibility for SSI and medical benefits. Programs can only assist people to maintain eligibility by ensuring that they do not earn over the current allowable amount. Fortunately, the recent changes in the regulations reduce the risk of benefit loss significantly. Public policy related to benefit eligibility is always open to change, and is influenced by public opinion and the philosophies of legislators and other politicians. Parents will be willing to permit their son or daughter to gain community-based employment and to earn a significant wage only if policymakers continue to establish regulations that do not jeopardize the financial security of families.

Programs also may be limited in solving transportation concerns. If there is no public transportation system available that an individual can use to get to work, then programs can attempt to identify and arrange for an alternative mode such as a cab or special van. However, both of these options are expensive, and the amount of money typically offered to cover transportation costs to and from supported employment programs is minimal. Funding agencies must provide greater amounts of money to cover transportation costs in order to remove this barrier to employment.

The availability of programs to assist individuals with disabilities to participate in recreational activities is limited or nonexistent in most communities. In part, this is due to the fact that, in the past, sheltered programs have been willing to incorporate recreation into their programs. However, this option will not be feasible or appropriate for supported employment programs. Parents understand the important contribution that leisure and recreational activities make to the quality of life, and may hesitate to allow their son or daughter to be placed into a community job if those recreational activities will no longer be available. Consequently, policymakers must recognize the need to fund programs that assist individuals who are working in community-based jobs to participate in leisure activities.

Concluding Remarks

In recent years, the importance of parent-professional partnerships in the education of school-age children with developmental disabilities has been recognized. However, parents have typically had little involvement in the employment programs of their adult children. Given the highly structured and protected nature of sheltered employment programs, as well as the lack

of expectation for movement out of them, there was little need or motivation for parent involvement in the past. In the late 1980s the adult vocational service system is experiencing a dramatic change in focus and expected outcomes. Through the supported employment approach, individuals with even the most severe disabilities are working in community settings. Due to the nature of community jobs and the supported employment approach, parents' roles take on a great deal of importance. Professionals must be prepared to identify and utilize the strategies that will increase parent involvement in supporting the employment of their sons and daughters.

REFERENCES

Bellamy, G.T., Rhodes, L.E., Bourbeau, P.E., & Mank, D.M. (1986). Mental retardation services in sheltered workshops and day activity programs: Consumer outcomes and policy alternatives. In F.R. Rusch (Ed.), *Competitive employment issues and strategies* (pp. 257–271). Paul H. Brookes Publishing Co.

Bellamy, G.T., Wilcox, B., McDonald, J., & Sowers, J. (1982). *Improving vocational services for severely handicapped individuals: Strategies for parent involvement.* National Parent Conference Proceedings: Education of children requiring extensive special education programming.

Bourbeau, P. (1985). Mobile work crews: An approach to achieve long-term supported employment. In P. McCarthy, J. Everson, S. Moon, & M. Barcus (Eds.), *School-to-work transition for youth with severe disabilities* (pp. 151–166). Richmond: Virginia Commonwealth University School of Education.

Goodall, P.A., & Bruder, M.B. (1985). Parent involvement in the transition process. In P. McCarthy, J. Everson, S. Moor, & M. Barcus (Eds.), *School-to-work transition for youth with severe disabilities* (pp. 43–63). Richmond: Virginia Commonwealth University.

Greenleigh Associates, Inc. (1975). *The role of the sheltered workshops in the rehabilitation of the severely handicapped.* Report to the Department of Health, Education, and Welfare, Rehabilitation, Services Administration. New York: Author.

Hasazi, S., Gordon, L., & Roe, C. (1985). Factors associated with the employment status of handicapped youth exiting high school from 1979 to 1983. *Exception Children, 51*(6), 455–469.

Hill, J., Seyfarth, J., Banks, P., Wehman, P., & Orelove, F., (1985). Parent/guardian attitudes toward the working conditions of their mentally retarded children. *Exceptional Children, 54*(1), 9–24.

Hill, J., Wehman, P., Hill, M., & Goodall, P. (1986). Differential reasons for job separation of previously employed persons with mental retardation. *Mental Retardation, 24*(6), 347–351.

Katz, S., & Yaketiel, E. (1975). The vocational adjustment of graduates of two sheltered workshops for the mentally

retarded. *British Journal of Mental Subnormality, 21*(4), 71–78.

Kiernan, K., & Koegal, R. (1980). *Employment experiences of community-based mild retarded adults.* Working paper No. 14, Socio-Behavioral Group. Mental Retardation Research Center, School of Medicine, University of California, Los Angeles.

Kochany, L., & Keller, J. (1981). An analysis and evaluation of the failures of severely disabled individuals in competitive employment. In P. Wehman, *Competitive employment: New horizons for severely disabled individuals* (pp. 181–198). Baltimore: Paul H. Brookes Publishing Co.

Lagomarcino, T.R. (1986). Community Services: Using the supported work model within an adult service agency. In F.R. Rusch (Ed.), *Competitive employment issues and strategies* (pp. 65–75). Baltimore: Paul H. Brookes Publishing Co.

Mittler, P., Cheseldine, S., & McConachie, H. (1980). *Roles and needs of parents of handicapped adolescents.* Paris: Organization of Economic Cooperation and Development, Center for Educational Research and Information.

Moss, J.W. (1979). Post secondary vocational education for mentally retarded adults. Final report to the Division of Developmental Disabilities, Rehabilitation Services Administration, Department of Health, Education, and Welfare, Grant No. 56P 50281/0.

Moss, J.W., Dineen, J.P., & Ford, L.H. (1986). University of Washington employment training program. In F.R. Rusch (Ed.), *Competitive employment issues and strategies* (pp. 77–85). Baltimore: Paul H. Brookes Publishing Co.

Rhodes, L. & Valenta, L. (1985). Industry-based supported employment: an enclave approach. *Journal of The Association for Persons with Severe Handicaps, 10*(1), 12–21.

Rusch, F., & Mithaug, D. (1980). *Vocational training for mentally retarded adults.* Champaign, IL: Research Press.

Schutz, R.P. (1986). Establishing a parent-professional partnership to facilitate competitive employment. In F.R. Rusch (Ed.), *Competitive employment issues and strategies* (289–302). Baltimore: Paul H. Brookes Publishing Co.

Siegal, G., & Loman, L. (1987). Enhancing employment opportunities for persons who are developmentally disabled. *Journal of Job Placement,* Summer/Fall, 16–20.

Sowers, J. (1988). *The Alternative Work Concepts: Supported employment for persons with physical and multiple disabilities.* Unpublished manuscript, Oregon Research Institute, Eugene, OR.

Sowers, J., Jenkins, C., & Powers, L. (1988). The training and employment of persons with physical disabilities. In R. Gaylord-Ross (Ed.), *Vocational education for persons with special needs* (pp. 387–416). Palo Alto, CA: Mayfield.

Sowers, J., Thompson, L., & Connis, R. (1979). The food service training program: A model for training and placement of the mentally retarded. In G. Bellamy, G. O'Connor, & O. Karan (Ed.), Vocational rehabilitation of severely handicapped persons (pp. 181–205). Baltimore: University Park Press.

United States Department of Labor. (1979, March). Study of handicapped clients in sheltered workshops (Vol. II). Washington, DC: Author.

Vogelsberg, R.T. (1986). Competitive employment in Vermont. In F.R. Rusch (Ed.), *Competitive employment issues and strategies* (pp. 35–49). Baltimore: Paul H. Brookes Publishing Co.

Wehman, P. (1981). *Competitive employment: New horizons for severely disabled individuals.* Baltimore: Paul H. Brookes Publishing Co.

Wehman, P. (1986). Competitive employment in Virginia. In F.R. Rusch (Ed.), *Competitive employment issues and strategies* (pp. 23–33). Baltimore: Paul H. Brookes Publishing Co.

Wehman, P., Kregal, T., & Seyfarth, F. (1985). Employment outlook for young adults with mental retardation. *Rehabilitation Counseling Bulletin, 29*(2), 90–99.

Wilson, D. & Brodsky, M. (1988). *Report on supported employment.* Salem: Oregon Development Council.

CHAPTER 18

Guardianship, Trusts, and Protective Services

Tony Apolloni

The movement to provide community-based services to persons with mental retardation essentially began after the conclusion of World War II (Murray, 1969). Aided by economic prosperity and a greater acceptance of handicapping conditions (due to the number of polio victims and disabled veterans), the parents of children with mental retardation began organizations for their benefit. These pioneer parents held the attitude that public support for their children was a privilege and that parent-to-parent assistance was the most appropriate approach for helping.

Due to their self-reliance and cooperation, parents made significant advances. School and social recreational programs were started in church and school basements. Camp programs were initiated, and parents began organizing what would eventually become a potent political base (Katz, 1961).

Gradually parents' attitudes began to change and their expectations began to rise (Roeher, 1984). Support for the charity model declined, and the belief that taxpayers have no obligation to assist those in need became widely accepted. Parents began to demand help from public agencies; a second wave of parent leaders adopted the view that public support for disabled children was an inherent responsibility of society.

The period from the early 1960s to the mid-1970s was truly a time of unprecedented growth for the field of services for persons with disabilities. Parent organizations grew from tiny, charitable groups to become huge, multifaceted service corporations. Consumer expectations increased, as did the pressure for an expanded public role; for example, pressure for permissive legislation gave way to demands for mandatory legislation. The trend toward an ever increasing reliance on government support was accelerated by recognition of the significance of the problems associated with mental retardation and by sweeping legislative and judicial mandates for government assistance to persons with disabilities.

Pioneer parents initially focused on securing school services for their children that were often run by parent cooperatives. Gradually, many public schools were persuaded to play a more active role. As their children grew older, parents began struggling to initiate activity centers and sheltered work programs for their adult children. Moreover, they began to concentrate on establishing out-of-home living arrangements. At first these living arrangements were often large, congregate settings that served fifty or more persons, sometimes hundreds of miles from parents' homes. Eventually, more typical group living arrangements for six or fewer persons were created in geographical proximity to parents' homes. By the late 1960s and early 1970s parent organizations often continued to operate adult day training and community living arrangements, but the funding base for these services increasingly shifted from private, charitable contributions to government funds. As of the late 1980s, many of these services have come under

The author gratefully acknowledges the input that has been provided on the topic of this chapter by the directors of the corporations listed in the Appendix of this chapter. Moreover, Gunnar Dybwad, Donald Sappern, William Dussault, and the late Dr. G. Allan Roeher have made significant contributions toward designing and implementing the National Continuity Program described in this chapter.

the control of public agencies and professionally managed corporations that may or may not emphasize parental representation on their governance boards.

The trend toward increasing public support for and influence over services for persons with mental retardation has become even more pronounced during the past decade. Supported by legislation such as PL 94-142 (*The Education for All Handicapped Children Act of 1975*), PL 93-112 (*The Rehabilitation Act of 1975*), PL 94-103 (*The Developmental Disabilities Assistance and Bill of Rights Act of 1975*), and subsequent extensions of these acts, the combined efforts of parents and professionals have resulted in the development of a wide range of service options. While variations in the comprehensiveness of services and utilization patterns still exist across states and counties, publicly supported services for basic living arrangements, education, and habilitation are currently available in most locations across the United States.

It may be argued, however, that despite the plethora of service agencies and services that currently exist, one prominent service need remains: namely, there is a need for ensuring that persons with severe disabilities will have someone they can depend upon to guard and personally advocate their best interest once their parents can no longer serve in this capacity.

The issue of how to provide advocacy and guardianship to vulnerable persons once their parents can no longer look after their well-being is extremely personal and sensitive. It is a question that is foremost in the minds of many parents, particularly older parents. This chapter reviews this issue and describes alternatives that are available for parents to consider when planning for the long-term security of their disabled child. Particular emphasis is placed on a relatively new service phenomenon, private guardianship corporations (Apolloni, 1984, 1987). In this chapter, the general characteristics of the programs in this category are described and the pros and cons of this emerging trend are discussed. Finally, a national corporate guardianship model is presented that is proposed as an approach for improving the stability and quality of existing and future corporate guardianship programs.

TRADITIONAL SOLUTIONS TO THE OLD AGE QUESTION

Pioneering parents had little time or energy to contemplate the long-term future of their child with mental retardation; the struggle to obtain appropriate educational and health care services for their child was enough of a challenge. They worked to help their child and joined efforts with other parents to help all other children with similar disabilities. They believed that their child's future well-being would be ensured by loving friends and relatives and felt optimistic that younger parents with retarded children would join their organizations to ensure continuity of effort in the future. Parents also felt certain that if all else failed, public institutions would always be available as an approach for protecting their severely disabled children.

It now appears likely that those pioneering parents misjudged the future. Demographic, economic, and political factors have conspired to undermine the stability of the solutions that they envisioned. Many people with mental retardation simply do not have friends or loved ones who are willing and appropriate advocates and guardians. In general, families are becoming smaller and geographically dispersed. Trusted relatives and friends have grown older along with parents and they generally are not knowledgeable enough to advocate effectively for appropriate services. In addition, the organized parent movement is not robust. As parent organizations have matured, some have become stagnant, professionalized, and overly influenced by public funding agencies. In recent years the parent movement in the United States has been severely weakened due to a division among parents over the issue of deinstitutionalization. As Roeher (1984) has observed, "It appears that many of the leading consumer organizations in the field of developmental services are weakening and that adequate voluntary replacement bodies are not on the horizon" (p. 25). Finally, public institutions for the mentally retarded in the United States have been substantially decreased since the early 1970s (Hill, Lakin, & Bruininks, 1984; Scheerenberger, 1979) with many former residents relocated to living arrangements in community settings. Fewer and fewer people are being considered for residence in public facilities, and many institutions are actually being closed (Braddock & Heller, 1985).

ASSESSING A DEPENDENT PERSON'S NEED FOR PROTECTION

What are the alternatives available to parents when planning to safeguard the quality of their child's life on a long-term basis? To answer this question parents must first examine their child's future need for protective services. If a person with a disability recognizes when decisions need to be made, knows alternatives for making decisions, is able to weigh the potential outcomes of various alternatives, and is able to make sound decisions, then he or she does not need protective services. If he or she can partially handle these responsibilities and has someone to turn to for occasional guidance when making decisions, then he or she probably does not need a guardian, particularly if there are no substantial assets to be managed. But if that individual cannot make sound decisions and this inability is likely to seriously jeopardize his or her well-being, then guardianship may be necessary. This is especially true when the person: 1) might face significant health care decisions, 2) might need publicly supported living arrangement services, 3) has a substantial inheritance, or 4) is easily influenced by others and has a history of being abused, victimized, or exploited by unscrupulous people.

ALTERNATIVES FOR PROVIDING PROTECTION

Once a parent has determined that his or her child with disabilities is likely to need assistance throughout life, and whether such assistance pertains to the child's personal needs, financial management needs, or both, the parent must weigh the alternatives that are available for providing protective services. Russell (1983) has provided an extensive discussion of various alternatives available to parents. These alternatives may be classified in terms of two categories: personal protective services, and financial protective services.

Personal Protective Services

Personal protection refers to the supervision of the life experiences of a person with a disability to ensure quality and decency. Attention might be needed in many areas, such as the appropriateness of the person's living arrangement and daytime settings; the quality of the developmental stimulation he or she receives; the nutritional value of his or her diet; the availability and quality of the mental health, medical, and dental care; the integration of his or her social and recreational experiences; and the general comfort of the psychological climate that he or she experiences. When appropriately delivered, protective services can maximize life quality and minimize external control over the personal choices of individuals with disabilities. Several major sources exist for providing those personal protective services.

Personal Advisor/Friend   Most people with mental retardation can live independently or semi-independently, with only an occasional need for outside guidance from a friend or relative. Wolfensberger (1977) has advocated the creation of a formal agency model, much like Big Brothers and Big Sisters, for pairing volunteer advocates with mentally retarded individuals, and a number of such programs have been established. The most typical approach, however, is for a relative or family friend to follow parents in the role of advisor.

Professional Advocacy Agents   Many formalized advocacy agencies have been established for providing temporary advocacy services to people with mental retardation. The services of these agencies tend to be crisis-oriented and their staffs tend to be professional advocates. The names of potential agencies may be obtained from local or state chapters of parent organizations and from state councils on developmental disabilities.

Guardians   Once a person reaches the age of majority, which is 18 in most states, courts are responsible to care for individuals who are incapable of caring for themselves. Courts fulfill this responsibility by appointing an agent, termed a guardian (or conservator in some states), to protect the dependent person. Guardians may be individuals who are relatives or friends of the disabled persons, or any paid or voluntary person or agency that is deemed appropriate by a court. The actions of a guardian in respect to the interests of the person with a disability, termed a ward, should be guided by two considerations; the guardian must make decisions that are in the best interest of the ward, and the guardian should make decisions based on what the ward would presumably decide under similar circumstances (Rogers, 1984).

In appointing a guardian, courts may award the guardian total responsibility over the ward's personal affairs, an arrangement termed plenary guardianship. Increasingly, however, courts are recognizing that people with disabilities may only need help in selected areas of their lives but not in other areas, and are limiting the authority of guardians to the particular needs of wards. This could include one or more, but not necessarily all, of the following responsibilities:

Ensuring that the ward receives the full benefits of government entitlement programs

Approving or negating plans regarding medical, dental, psychological, educational, and/or habilitation services to be provided to the ward

Determining the ward's place of residence

Having the right of access to confidential records on the ward that are needed for making decisions

Negotiating and approving contracts on behalf of the ward and canceling contracts inappropriately signed by the ward

Controlling the ward's social/sexual relationships, including bestowing or withholding consent to the ward's marriage

Initiating or defending the ward's interests in lawsuits.

The decisionmaking authority of a guardian always has some limits. Some decisions (e.g., consent to sterilization, other surgery, and certain behavior modification procedures) potentially have such a serious impact on a ward that a court may have to approve them.

Financial Protective Services

Parents often want to leave assets to their child with a disability, but are concerned about making the child ineligible for government benefits and services, and/or are concerned about their child's ability to appropriately manage a bequest. At least six major alternatives are available to parents, such as the transfer of property to another for the benefit of the person with a disability, assigning a power of attorney, using a joint bank account, assigning a representative payee, employing a guardian of the estate, and making trust arrangements.

Transfer of Property to Another Perhaps the most frequently used approach involves parents disinheriting their disabled child and willing their property to a trusted relative or friend with an informal understanding that this person will use the assets for the benefit of the child with a disability. This approach has merit because the parent's bequest will not affect the son's or daughter's entitlements. The shortcomings of the approach, however, are noteworthy. They include the fact that the person with disabilities has no legal claim on the assets of his or her parents, should the administrator choose to ignore the needs of the disabled person and use the assets for personal betterment. Similarly, the disabled person has no rights should the administrator's creditors or heirs make claim to the assets. This approach places a great deal of trust on the stability, credibility, and integrity of the administrator and his or her family.

Power of Attorney Under a power of attorney, parents may arrange for some trusted administrator to be legally appointed as the authority to act in certain matters on behalf of their child with a disability. A power of attorney may be established in relationship to almost all financial management actions that can be undertaken. The major strengths of this approach are that it is relatively simple and inexpensive to institute, the disabled person retains ownership of his or her own property (i.e., the property should not become merged with that of the administrator), and the power of the administrator is limited to certain matters that are defined in writing. The major disadvantages of this approach are that it does nothing to protect the person's eligibility for government assistance, the arrangement would be invalidated should the disabled person be determined incompetent by a court, some health care practitioners concerned about malpractice lawsuits may not be willing to honor a power of attorney, good agents may be hard to identify, and future changes in agents may create difficulties.

Joint Bank Accounts Most people have experience with bank accounts from which two or more people may remove the money. Withdrawal arrangements may be set up so that the disabled person and the co-owner of the account can independently remove money, or so that both signatures are required to remove funds. The primary advantages of this approach are that it is familiar to most people, it is a very low cost arrangement, and it allows the person with a disability freedom in relationship to all other areas of his or her financial affairs. Pertinent disadvantages are that the assets in the account are fully considered when determining the disabled person's eligibility for government entitlements and, when a single signature is needed, a co-owner may remove all of the money in a joint account without the other person's permission. Problems can also arise when two signatures are required and one of the signatories dies.

Representative Payee The only asset owned by many people with disabilities is the monthly SSI check that they receive from the Social Security Administration. A representative payee is someone who is formally designated by the government to receive a person's financial benefits and to account for the expenditure of the benefits. The advantages of this approach are that representative payee status is relatively easy to establish and review of the payee's behavior is ensured by the Social Security Administration on at least an annual basis. The weaknesses of the model are that it is only useful for a single type of income (government paid benefits), good payees are sometimes difficult to find, and weaknesses in the government's supervision of payee performance may sometimes permit the victimization of disabled individuals.

Guardian of the Estate A guardian of the estate is appointed by a court to make all or some of an individual's financial decisions. When appointed, the guardian of the estate is usually instructed by the court to:

File a surety bond to protect the ward's estate from malfeasance.

File an initial inventory of the assets of the ward's estate with the court, and make annual reports to the court on the status of the ward's estate.

Demonstrate reasonable care and judgement in conserving, investing, and dispersing the assets in the ward's estate.

Keep the ward's assets separate from his or her own and use them solely for the ward's benefit.

Demonstrate reasonable care and judgment in conserving, investing, and dispersing the assets in the ward's estate.

The major advantage of this approach is that the guardian's behavior is closely regulated by a court. The disadvantages are numerous, including the fact that the establishment of a guardianship generally requires labeling a disabled person "incompetent," the approach does not protect a ward's assets from government creditors, the assets managed by a guardian are usually considered accessible to the disabled person and hence he or she may be judged ineligible for government entitlements, the court supervised nature of the arrangement can be expensive, and the inflexibility of the approach can result in inferior investment performance.

Trust Arrangements A trust is a legal arrangement in which property or assets are given by a person (a grantor) to another (a beneficiary) with the condition that a third party (a trustee) is responsible to administer the assets or property in keeping with the grantor's directions. A trust can be created during a parent's lifetime or in his or her will. It can be funded with any asset owned by the parent, including the proceeds of life insurance.

A trust can be a very important planning tool. Even parents with modest assets should consider explicitly disinheriting their disabled child in their will and establishing a specialized trust. Appropriately designed trusts can offer a number of important advantages:

Trusts can be designed to protect assets from government creditors and allow beneficiaries with disabilities to retain access to government benefits and services.

Trusts do not require declaring a beneficiary competent.

Trust assets and property may be managed and

spent independently of public disclosure, court supervision, and related expenses.

A trustee (trust administrator) may serve without posting a bond, thereby avoiding this expense.

Trustees may exercise considerable flexibility in managing investments, which can sometimes result in increased principal growth.

Cotrustees may be appointed, whereby one person or institution is assigned responsibility for investing, managing, and disbursing trust assets, and a different individual or agency with information on the beneficiaries' personal needs is empowered to authorize disbursements from the trust.

Trusts can be written to include the specific preferences of the grantor parent.

Trusts can provide a large measure of protection and assistance to a person with a disability, yet still allow him or her to make some personal financial decisions.

Trusts can be written to allow grantor parents to retain control over the distribution of remaining trust assets after the death of a disabled beneficiary.

Trusts may be established on an irreversible basis that allows tax reductions for the grantor parent.

Trusts are better than simply leaving assets to another for the benefit of a disabled person, because they formalize the grantor's intention and thereby provide a basis for public intervention if the trustee violates the grantor's intentions.

Not all trusts are effective for providing resources that benefit persons with disabilities, protecting their assets from government and private creditors, and safeguarding their eligibility for government benefits and services. To achieve these purposes, a trust should incorporate five components. First, an *explicit statement of purpose* is important. Trusts should state that it is the grantor's expressed intention that a disabled beneficiary be provided trust assets to improve his or her quality of life. Second, it is imperative that the trustee be granted full *discretionary power* regarding the distribution of trust funds. The beneficiary must not have any power to de-

mand that the trustee spend funds from the trust. Third, well designed trusts have a *spendthrift clause* that disallows the beneficiary from spending trust funds not already in his or her possession and prohibits the trustee from distributing substantial liquid assets to the beneficiary. Fourth, effective trusts clearly state that it is the grantor's intention that trust resources *supplement,* not supplant, goods and services that are available from government agencies. Finally, good trusts include a *fail-safe (or poison pill) provision* that serves to discourage potential attempts by creditors to seize trust assets. One such provision involves naming one or more additional individuals or organizations along with the disabled person as beneficiaries of the trust. Since the trustee has discretion as to when and how much to disburse to multiple beneficiaries, the trustee may pay all of the assets to a nondisabled beneficiary should an external raid of the trust appear imminent. Another approach that is useful for protecting trusts from creditors involves naming nonprofit charitable organizations as remainders (recipients of assets remaining in a trust at the death of the original beneficiary). The theory here is that creditors, particularly government creditors, will be less likely to seize trust assets that are earmarked for future charitable use.

Some may feel that such extraordinary efforts to protect trust assets from government creditors are unethical, because government creditors are only seeking repayment for the costs of services delivered to the disabled beneficiary. It can be argued, however, that legal estate planning approaches such as a special needs trust arrangements are no less ethical than standard efforts to minimize income and estate taxes.

When a trust is used, parents should take care to have it drafted by an attorney who is familiar with disability estate planning. Standardized trust language such as that found in model trust forms from stationary stores is not adequate. A special needs trust is an excellent vehicle for parents to use when they want to provide assets that will improve their child's future life quality, protect assets from government creditors, and maintain their son's or daughter's eligibility for government benefits. Achieving these purposes requires the advice of a competent attorney.

Public Guardianship

Recognizing that many people with disabilities need a guardian but do not have a relative or friend to fulfill this role, some states have established public guardianship programs. Under these programs, a state official, usually the state director of services for persons with mental retardation, is appointed guardian by a court. This public official, in turn, delegates actual day-to-day guardianship responsibility to a state, county, or regional caseworker. This arrangement has the strength of assigning someone to act as guardian who is professionally trained, knowledgeable about services, and backed by the authority and stability of a government organization. Moreover, a successor guardian is guaranteed throughout the dependent person's life, and conflicts of interest that sometimes occur when family members act as guardian are avoided.

Public guardianship models are not without weaknesses. Most are understaffed and encounter high turnover rates. Furthermore, some programs delegate guardianship responsibility to already overworked case managers and place guardianship duties low in terms of organizational priorities; these conditions inhibit personal attention to wards. Perhaps the most serious problem with public models is the fact that the parties responsible to guard the quality of the ward's direct services often also employ the people, albeit one desk removed, who are responsible to deliver or pay for the ward's direct services. This situation can lead to problems, for example, when an in-house guardian is responsible to advocate for his employer to purchase or provide discretionary services for a ward. A related conflict emerges when a ward has assets that a public guardian could use over time to improve the ward's life quality, but the guardian must first protect the ward's assets from seizure by his or her employer, the state.

As currently operated, most public guardianship models should be viewed as last resort alternatives. Improvements are needed to implement public guardianship models that afford competent, personalized representation in ways that minimize potential conflicts of interest.

Private Guardianship Corporations

A new service model has emerged in the United States for addressing the protection and advocacy needs of people with mental retardation. Private corporations have been formed to act as advocates and guardians. The first such program was begun over twenty years ago in Seattle, Washington—the Foundation for the Handicapped. Now at least 26 similar programs exist, and many more are being planned. (Contact information for these programs is listed in the Appendix of this chapter.)

The one characteristic shared by existing corporate advocacy and guardianship programs in the United States is that they make a lifetime commitment to safeguard the quality of their clients' lives. Aside from this common feature, the programs differ in terms of their histories, services, funding sources, and client populations. For example, 13 of the 26 programs listed in the Appendix are operated by parent-controlled corporations, while 13 others are not. Their length of existence averages 10 years, with a range of 1 to 24 years. Most rely heavily on volunteers and have a staff of three or fewer. 22 accept guardianship and 4 do not, preferring only to act as advocates. Of the 22 that accept guardianship, 12 serve only as guardian of the person, while 10 others also accept other forms of guardianship. The number of wards/clients per program varies from 10 to 500, with an average of 90. Twenty of the organizations serve only individuals with mental retardation, six also serve mentally ill individuals, and two also serve elderly individuals who are not mentally retarded or mentally ill. The programs derive their funding from a combination of sources. Nine programs rely on service fees or require trust arrangements, ten depend heavily on charitable fund raising efforts, and seven receive government assistance.

Private advocacy and guardianship programs offer many strengths. First, they are usually administered by competent professionals who do not have conflicts of interest in relation to the estates of wards/clients. Second, they tend to offer more individually tailored arrangements than public models and are more apt than public models to incorporate approaches for sharing representative status with a ward/client's friends and family members. Third, many corporate programs provide services to orphaned and abandoned persons, using charitable contributions and/or government payments to support services. Finally, some corporate programs offer excellent advocate-to-ward ratios through the use of volunteer advocates supported by professional staff.

The national movement to develop corporate and advocacy services for persons with mental retardation is being hampered by several fundamental problems. Perhaps the most serious of these problems is the paucity of professionals who understand the multidisciplinary body of knowledge necessary to effectively develop and administer such programs. Originators and administrators must be well versed in terms of service systems, advocacy services, financial and estate planning approaches, protective services, organizational development and management, and fund raising. Other significant impediments to the corporate advocacy and guardianship movement include a general absence of start-up funds for new programs, the failure of most programs to capitalize adequately to ensure lifetime services, the absence of guiding quality standards and procedures for this relatively new form of service, and the fact that support provisions do not exist for maintaining the ongoing operation of services should local provider corporations cease to exist. This last problem is particularly significant since the hallmark of corporate advocacy and guardianship services must include a lifetime of quality services.

THE NATIONAL CONTINUITY PROGRAM

The California Institute on Human Services of Sonoma State University has worked for almost a decade in collaboration with the Security Connecticut Life Insurance Company, the Connecticut Bank and Trust Company and Donald Sappern, Inc., to design a national service model, termed the *National Continuity Program (NCP)*, for addressing the major problems that are evident in the corporate advocacy and guardianship movement. The primary goals of the NCP are: 1) to provide a stable, long-term funding mechanism for local advocacy and guardianship ser-

vices, 2) to assist local programs in defining and enforcing quality service standards, and 3) to ensure service continuation in the event that a local advocacy and guardianship corporation defaults. The NCP serves developmentally disabled beneficiaries through service contracts with local advocacy and guardianship organizations.

As shown in Figure 1, the funding and service patterns for the NCP consist of six steps.

Step I   Parents pay an enrollment fee and establish a trust (discretionary, spendthrift, supplemental benefits) funded either by investing in a specially designed permanent life insurance program, or through an *inter vivos* or testamentary transfers of cash assets. (Actuarial projections indicate that a $50,000 trust in 1987 dollars is necessary to provide income adequate to insure lifetime advocacy/guardianship services given other features of the program, to be explained below.)

Step II   Upon the death of a participating parent, the proceeds of his or her life insurance policy or equivalent cash assets are paid directly to a national trustee, the Connecticut Bank and Trust Company. A disability provision also exists that allows the commencement of advocacy and guardianship services prior to the death of participating parents under special circumstances.

Step III   Funds are distributed directly by the national trustee, in accordance with instructions from the NCP, to advocacy and guardianship programs that then act as advocates to disabled beneficiaries under the terms of contractual agreements with the NCP. The NCP is responsible for ensuring that the assets in each beneficiary's trust are spent on behalf of the beneficiary, and not in a manner that affects his or her eligibility for public assistance.

Step IV   Local advocacy and guardianship programs deliver services to beneficiaries in keeping with predefined service quality standards that are established and monitored by the NCP. Beneficiaries thus receive guardianship and advocacy services from a local advocacy and guardianship program.

Step V   Upon the death of the disabled beneficiary, the assets funds remaining in his or her trust pass to a master trust for the benefit of all surviving program beneficiaries.

Step VI   Funds are paid to local programs from

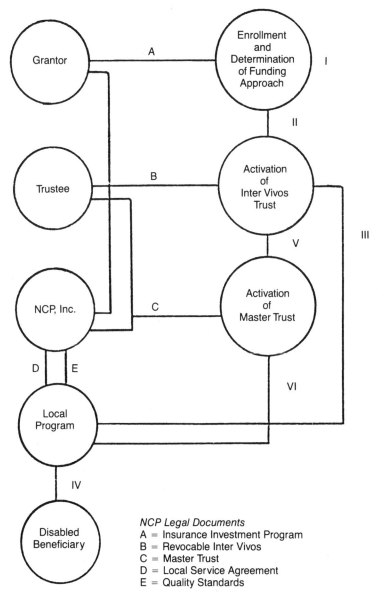

Figure 1. Funding and service patterns of the NCP.

the master trust as necessary to ensure ongoing advocacy and guardianship services to all beneficiaries throughout their lives.

Alternatives for Funding NCP Trusts

A life insurance policy that was designed specifically for the NCP has been underwritten by the Security Connecticut Life Insurance Company (Best A-Rated). This company has agreed to issue policies with liberal underwriting requirements. However, it is not necessary that parents purchase life insurance to enter the NCP's program; parents may also enter the program using existing life insurance or by making an *inter vivos* or testamentary transfers of cash assets (e.g., the proceeds of the sale of a parent's home after his or her death).

The trustee of the NCP model is a corporate fiduciary with trust powers, the Connecticut Bank and Trust Company. Although each beneficiary's trust is maintained separately throughout his or her life, all trust funds are pooled for investment diversification and management economy.

Combating Inflation

Under the NCP's program it is anticipated that
many beneficiaries will die with significant sums
remaining in their trusts. This is true because the
advocacy and guardianship services envisioned
for the NCP primarily will be supplied on the
basis of the annual income from a 1987 participating trust of $50,000 and because the
amount that eventually will be paid to a participating trust will be increased by 4% each
year. The NCP's insurance program under Security Connecticut Life includes a 4% cost of
living adjustment, without any increase in premium payments over time. Even with this consideration, however, participants living long
lives could see their trusts eroded by inflation.
Since no one can predict individual life expectancy, or changes in the cost of living across future years, a parent and the NCP cannot determine with certainty the amount of funding
necessary for each individual participant. The
NCP's design addresses this problem by considering the predictability of a large group.

Pooling is initiated upon the death of a beneficiary. The funds remaining in each beneficiary's account are transferred upon his or her
death to a master trust, also managed by the
Connecticut Bank and Trust Company. The
funds in the NCP's master trust will be used to
ensure ongoing services for a lifetime to all surviving beneficiaries under the NCP's program.
In this manner beneficiaries will be afforded financial protection for a longer lifespan without
imposing an extra burden on individual grantor
parents. Most importantly, a significant capital
increase should occur in the master trust over
time, and this increase may eventually allow for
those surplus funds (i.e., funds in excess of
those needed to assume lifetime services to surviving beneficiaries) needed to provide scholar-
ships for persons with developmental disabilities
whose families cannot otherwise afford to enroll
in the NCP's program.

The Services of the Program

The seven services provided by the NCP (via
contracts with local programs) to participants
and their families are as follows:

Immediately upon enrollment, a current file is
    established on each beneficiary with periodic

updates to ensure proper services upon the
    death or disability of the beneficiary's parent.
Once the parent dies, or becomes permanently
    disabled, the local program monitors the ben-
    eficiary's receipt of government benefits and
    intervenes if needed benefits are not being
    received.
The beneficiary is provided with competent rep-
    resentation at individual planning sessions
    with service agencies.
Each beneficiary is visited on a twice-monthly
    basis to monitor his or her quality of life, and
    an advocate acts to correct any deficiencies.
The delivery of all services that are specified in
    the beneficiary's individualized service plan is
    monitored, and an advocate acts to correct
    problems.
The provision of a guardian is ensured when the
    appointment of a guardian is deemed neces-
    sary by a court and no appropriate alternative
    to the local program is available.
Legal, dental, and medical services that supple-
    ment entitlement services are made available
    to beneficiaries up to a maximum amount es-
    tablished each year by the NCP Board.

Strengths of the Model

The NCP offers important advantages to persons
with developmental disabilities and their families. These advantages include ensuring that:

A local agency that is credible to the parent will
    supply an informed personal representative to
    assist their child in maintaining the quality of
    his or her life once the parent is no longer able
    to advocate.
Creation, finance, and management of advocacy
    and guardianship services is maintained, and
    that the services of local agencies are deliv-
    ered in accordance with agreed quality
    standards.
Local agencies will be funded adequately to pro-
    vide advocacy and guardianship services
    throughout the lives of disabled participants.
Provision of an arrangement for funding trusts is
    affordable for middle income families.
The trust parents have established for their dis-
    abled child will not impair his or her receipt of
    government benefits.
Direct training is provided for severely disabled
    persons on how to identify their service needs,

advocate on their own behalf, and live with as much independence as is appropriate.

The likelihood exists that surplus funds in the NCP's master trust will someday be available for use in assisting persons with developmental disabilities who lack family resources.

Target Population

The target population for the NCP is that portion of the United States population that includes persons with disabilities and severe handicaps (approximately one percent of the overall population [United States Bureau of Census, 1975]) whose families can afford to establish a $50,000 trust and pay an enrollment fee. While this may appear to create a situation that favors middle income and wealthy persons, a national, private-fee-based advocacy and guardianship model such as the NCP should also benefit all developmentally disabled persons, including those whose parents earn lower incomes or are indigent. First, it is possible that private donors can be convinced to support scholarships for poor families, particularly scholarships that permit temporary guardianships in emergency situations. The founders of the NCP have created a sister corporation termed the National Continuity Foundation, Inc. for the explicit purpose of promoting and managing a scholarship program for indigent persons. Second, it should be possible in the future, depending on the extent of inflation and the costs of services to NCP participants, to use surplus funds from the NCP's master trust to assist disabled persons whose families cannot afford to join the program. Third, the public sector, including probate courts, may be convinced to fund services for individuals who are severely disabled, particularly when a temporary guardian is needed by an individual who loses a parent or guardian. Fourth, the im-

proved quality of life and the increase in personal contacts experienced by NCP program beneficiaries would seem likely to offer indirect benefits to nonbeneficiaries who share living quarters with NCP participants. Many NCP beneficiaries will receive advocacy and guardianship services in the context of publicly supported living arrangements and other government financed services. It is likely that the problems that are addressed by NCP supported advocates in beneficiaries' schools, homes, and work sites will also improve the life quality of all other persons in the same setting.

CONCLUSION

This chapter has reviewed various alternatives that are available to the parents of children with disabilities who are planning for their child's long-term care and well-being. However, one final point warrants emphasis. It is extremely important that the parent of a disabled child prepares a valid will drafted by a competent attorney. State laws direct the disposition of a decedent's estate when an individual dies without a will, which could create problems for a disabled person. The person's government benefits could be terminated (including his or her health care benefits), an unintended bequest could be seized by the state to pay for the person's services, and a person who needs assistance could be forced to manage assets that make him or her vulnerable to victimization. Parents should take care to develop a will that does not leave substantial cash or other assets to their disabled child if he or she is not capable of managing such assets, and parents should talk to their relatives to be sure that no other family member makes a similar mistake.

REFERENCES

Apolloni, T. (1984). Design elements of corporate guardianship models. In T. Apolloni & T.P. Cooke (Eds.), *A new look at guardianship: Protective services that support personalized living* (pp. 141–164). Baltimore: Paul H. Brookes Publishing Co.

Apolloni, T. (1987). Assuring a legacy of care: Corporate advocacy and guardianship programs offer parents a new planning alternative. *Ways*, Spring Issue, 11–13.

Braddock, D., & Heller, T. (1985). The closure of mental retardation institutions I: Trends in the U.S. *Mental Retardation, 23* (4) 168–176.

Frolik, L.A. (1979). Estate planning for parents of mentally disabled children. *University of Pittsburg Law Review, 40,* 305–357.

Hill, B.K., Lakin, K.C., & Bruininks, R.H. (1984). *Trends in residential services for mentally retarded people: 1977–*

1982. Minneapolis: Center for Residential and Community Services, Department of Educational Psychology, University of Minnesota.

Katz, A. (1961). *Parents of the handicapped.* Springfield, IL: Charles C Thomas.

Massey, J. (1981). Protecting the mentally incompetent child's trust interest from state reimbursement claims. *Denver Law Journal, 58,* 557–566.

Murray, D. (1969). *The rising tide. History of the National Association for Retarded Children.* Unpublished manuscript.

Roeher, G.A. (1984). The changing context of the human services movement: Implications for the disability field and the need for more adequate backup systems. In T. Apolloni & T.P. Cooke (Eds.), *A new look at guardianship: Protective services that support personalized living* (pp. 13–33). Baltimore: Paul H. Brookes Publishing Co.

Rogers, P. (1984). Understanding the legal concept of guardianship. In T. Apolloni & T.P. Cooke (Eds.), *A new look at guardianship: Protective services that support person-alized living* (pp. 35–45). Baltimore: Paul H. Brookes Publishing Co.

Russell, L.M. (1983). Alternatives: *A guide to legal and financial planning for the disabled.* Evanston, IL: First Publications, Inc.

Scheerenberger, R.C. (1979). *Public residential services for the mentally retarded.* Madison, WI: National Association of Superintendents of Public Residential Facilities for the Mentally Retarded.

Townsend, M.G. (1980). Avoiding an unwanted invasion of trust. *Albany Law Review, 237,* 237–259.

U.S. Bureau of Census. (1975). *Current Population Reports,* Series P–25, No. 601. "Projections of the Population of the United States 1975 to 2050." Washington, DC: U.S. Government Printing Office.

Wolfensberger, W. (1977). *A balanced multi-component advocacy/protection schema* (Law and Mental Retardation Monograph Series). Toronto, Canada: Canadian Association of Mental Retardation.

Appendix

Corporate Guardianship Programs

Association for Retarded Citizens
Dade County Florida Guardianship Program
8405 N.W. 66th Street, Suite 100
Miami, FL 33166
(305) 539-0807

Corporate Guardianship Project
Greater Boston Association for Retarded Citizens
1249 Boyston Street
Boston, MA 02215
(617) 266-4520

Corporation of Guardianship, Inc.
P.O. Box 13742
Greensboro, NC 27405
(919) 275-9567

Family Advocacy Center
P.O. Box 1067
Marshfield, MA 02050
(617) 837-6572

Foundation for the Developmentally Disabled
2114 Anson Road
Dallas, TX 75235
(214) 634-9810

Foundation for the Handicapped
1550 W. Armory Way, Suite 205
Seattle, WA 98119
(206) 283-4520

Guardian Advocate Program
Association for Retarded Citizens of New Mexico
8210 La Mirada, NE, Suite 500
Albuquerque, NM 87109
(505) 298-6796

Guardianship, Advocacy, and Protective Services
Program
Association for Retarded Citizens, Oregon
1745 State Street
Salem, OR 97301
(503) 581-2726

Kent County ARC Volunteer Guardian Program
1331 Lake Drive SE
Grand Rapids, MI 49506
(616) 459-3339

Kindcare, Inc.
611 East Wells Street
Milwaukee, WI 53202
(414) 271-8110

Macomb-Oakland Guardianship, Inc.
16200 Nineteen Mile Road
Mt. Clemens, MI 48044
(313) 286-8400, ext. 484

Maryland Trust for Retarded Citizens
5602 Baltimore National Pike
Baltimore, MD 21228
(301) 744-0257

Massachusetts Association for Retarded Citizens
Retardate Trust
217 South Street
Waltham, MA 02154
(617) 891-6270 or (617) 471-0845

Monitoring Council
310 South Eastern Road, Suite A217
Glenside, PA 19038
(215) 886-4069

National Continuity Program (NCP)
The Anchorage
253 Riverside Ave.
Westport, CT 06080
(203) 226-9911

New York State Association for Retarded Children   Guardianship Program
393 Delaware Avenue
Delmar, NY 12054
(518) 439-8311

Oakdale Guardianship, Inc.
P.O. Box 541
Lapeer, MI 48446
(313) 664-2951

Office of Public Guardian
6 White Street
Concord, NH 03301
(603) 224-8041

Pact, Inc.
166 W. Washington Avenue, Suite 300
Chicago, IL 60602
(312) 641-6363

Permanent Planning
2530 University Avenue
Waterloo, IA 50701
(319) 232-6671

Planned Lifetime Assistance Network (PLAN)
509 Park Street
Charlottesville, VA 22901
(804) 295-0653

**Protective Services Council for the Retarded of
    St. Joseph's County**
Logan Center
P.O. Box 1049
South Bend, IN 46624
(219) 289-4831

South Dakota Guardianship Program
P.O. Box 794
Pierre, SD 57501
(605) 224-9647

Star Systems Consultation and Training
1011 70th Avenue
Philadelphia, PA 19126
(215) 549-5440

**Virginia Beach Community Trust for
    Developmentally Disabled Individuals**
Pembroke Six, Suite 218
Virginia Beach, VA 23462
(804) 499-7619

We Four, Inc.
1046 N. 12th Street
Milwaukee, WI 53223
(414) 277-7775

Treatment for Maladaptation

CHAPTER 19

A Contextual Approach to the Clinical Treatment of Parental Distress

Anthony Biglan

Many parents of handicapped children, like many other people who have difficult or distressing circumstances to deal with, often find themselves deflected from pursuing significant directions by thoughts and feelings that they do not want to have. This chapter is about an approach to assisting parents of handicapped children in dealing with this kind of dilemma. The approach is an emerging synthesis of two lines of thinking in behavior analysis: a problem-specific approach to treatment of depression and related problems (Biglan & Campbell, 1981; Biglan & Dow, 1981; McLean & Hakstian, 1979) and comprehensive distancing (Hayes, 1987). The problem-specific approach involves careful delineation of behavioral goals in collaboration with clients, precise specification and monitoring of client's between-session assignments, and treatment strategies for specific problems that are chosen on the basis of the evidence about their efficacy. Comprehensive distancing is an approach that may be especially valuable in working with people who have become locked in a struggle to get rid of their distress and see this outcome as an essential precursor to any other changes in their life. Through metaphors and experiential exercises, comprehensive distancing prompts people to experience thoughts and feelings that they have been working to avoid, and to perceive those experiences differently. The approach provides a unique therapeutic context that contrasts with the traditional societal and clinical context for understanding problems of distress. As such, it may provide a framework for people to pursue specific changes in their lives in ways that do not increase their distress and efforts to control that distress. It appears to reduce the risk that therapeutically prompted activities will become part of "the problem."

PROBLEMS OF PARENTS OF HANDICAPPED CHILDREN

Parents of severely handicapped children have higher levels of self-reported distress than do parents of nonhandicapped children, but do not have a higher prevalence of diagnosable psychological conditions (Breslau, Staruch, & Mortimer, 1982). It might be argued, then, that there is no need to provide these parents with the kind of services described here. However, the relevance of these techniques to the problems of parents of severely or multiply handicapped children should not be determined on such a narrow basis. Stress that does not rise to the level of diagnosable pathology may nevertheless put a person at risk to be diagnosable at some time in the future, and it may reduce parents' ability to be effective parents (Hops, Sherman, & Biglan, in press). At a minimum, further investigation is needed to determine whether the amelioration of these kinds of psychological distresses could contribute to better outcomes in other areas of family functioning.

Requiring that psychological services be provided only when difficulties meet diagnostic cri-

The author would like to thank Chris French for help in preparing this chapter and Jim Monroe for feedback on it.

teria may provide a basis for limiting the escalating cost of such services. But reliance on the traditional diagnostic system tends to divorce problems from their context. It is only by understanding the relationship of parents' distress to the other aspects of the family situation that service providers can help in effective ways. And, when these problems are examined in their social/familial context, service providers are forced to deal with the material and social problems that contribute to psychological distress and deleterious outcomes for children.

A CONTEXTUAL APPROACH TO TREATMENT

In the approach to treatment that is described here, people's behavior is seen as occurring in a (primarily) social context. During treatment, the clinician becomes a small part of that context and can directly affect the person. The clinician also can have indirect effects on the client by prompting him or her to engage in behavior that alters other aspects of his or her context. The approach described here is based on behavior analysis of the kinds of problems that have been traditionally labeled as psychological distress. From a contextual viewpoint, psychological distress is understood (and treated) only within the context of other aspects of a person's behavior; distress and other behaviors are viewed as functions of the context in which they occur.

Clinical interventions are only one part of what might be done to reduce the incidence and prevalence of distress among parents of handicapped children. For example, research indicates that parents of handicapped children may face any or all of the following problems: 1) poverty, 2) difficulties with social service agencies, 3) lack of respite care, 4) health and health insurance problems, and 5) social conflict and isolation (Singer & Irvin, Chapter 1, this volume). Clinical intervention may have a direct or indirect—but limited—impact on these problems. Other strategies, such as the provision of adequate respite care, changes in how social services are provided, and improvement of financial support, will likely be needed. Moreover, even if clinical intervention could ameliorate all of these problems, it is unlikely that the re-

sources are available to provide such services to every family that might need them.

Problem-Specific Treatment

The essential feature of the behavior therapy revolution that swept clinical psychology in the 1960s and 1970s was an emphasis on delineating specific problems and empirically evaluating the effects of well-defined treatments on those problems (Biglan & Kass, 1977). This was the starting point for development of the treatment program that is described here. It was developed by the chapter author and four other psychologists who worked extensively with adults with problems involving depression and anxiety (Biglan & Campbell, 1981; Hawkins & Biglan, 1981). The approach has been influenced equally by research on anxiety and depression problems (e.g., Biglan, Hops, & Sherman, 1988; Glaser, Biglan, & Dow, 1983); the strategy in much of this research has been to identify the specific problems that are characteristic of people with anxiety or depression problems, and to develop interventions to ameliorate those problems (Biglan & Dow, 1981). The problems for which interventions were developed include chronic anxiety (Lewis, Biglan, & Steinbock, 1978), social anxiety and skill deficits (Dow, Glaser, & Biglan, 1981; Glaser et al., 1983), low rates of pleasant activities (Biglan & Craker, 1982), and insomnia (Alperson & Biglan, 1979).

The appropriateness of a problem-specific strategy is suggested by the fact that the problems among people who fit diagnostic criteria for affective disorders are much more diverse than the existence of a single diagnostic category would suggest (Biglan & Dow, 1981). The effectiveness of specific interventions that have been advocated for the treatment of depression depends, in part, on the specific problems the person is having (McKnight, Nelson, Hayes, & Jarrett, 1984). A random control trial comparing such a problem-specific approach to psychotherapy, pharmacotherapy, and relaxation training in the treatment of depression found that this treatment was more effective than these comparison conditions (McLean & Hakstian, 1979).

Limitations of the Problem-Specific Approach Treatment failures are seldom discussed, even in research involving true experimental designs. However, Weissman's (1979) review of the outcome literature on the treatment of depression underscores the fact that many people do not respond to treatment or relapse soon after treatment. Their conclusions are consistent with the author's experience in doing problem-specific treatment. A subset of the people who were treated seemed not to respond to any interventions that were provided. Hayes's (1987) description of comprehensive distancing provided a possible explanation of why these clients did not respond to intervention, and it presented some new approaches to treatment that seemed particularly germane to this subgroup of clients. For the past two years, the chapter author and colleagues have been grappling with the implications of this view of people and their problems.

Of the people for whom a problem-specific approach has not seemed to work, the cardinal characteristic is that they have made repeated and sometimes life-long efforts to solve their problems, all of which have failed in their view. Typically they were people who had *views of themselves and their problems* that not only mitigated the effect of potentially helpful interventions, but even turned problem-specific interventions into contributors to the problem. For example, one man had been in treatment intermittently for over 10 years for a severe public speaking phobia and a strong and consistently negative view of himself. He was very sensitive to whether he was becoming distressed, and he organized virtually all of his activities in ways that would help him avoid distress. He avoided attending meetings where he would have to introduce himself. He monitored his tension constantly in such situations because he believed that it was essential to avoid the extreme levels of distress that he sometimes felt. If he could not avoid a situation where he would have to introduce himself, he would spend large amounts of time worrying about it and trying to prepare himself for it. What no one realized at the time was that it was the very effort to avoid distress that was the problem.

Relational Frames Analysis of Cases that are Difficult to Treat

Recently, Hayes (in press) has articulated an analysis of the verbal control of behavior that provides a general theory within which the problems of clients who are difficult to treat can be understood. The key concept in that analysis is the *relational frame*. In essence, a relational frame is an arbitrary or socially defined relationship between two stimuli. A key frame is synonymy. There is evidence that responses of language-able humans to an object or event can be modified when the object or event is placed in a synonym relationship with other stimuli (Hayes, in press). For example, when a person is told the name of an object, he or she is able to name the object when asked what it is, and to point to it when asked where it is by name. It is perhaps a fundamental accomplishment of human language learning to respond under the control of relational frames such as synonymy. Once an individual is able to do so, he or she can respond to the features of the world without going through direct training.

But the ability to respond under the control of relational frames can also create problems. Experience with clients who are struggling to control their thoughts and feelings suggests that they are responding as though feelings such as guilt, anger, anxiety, and depression are equivalent to words like "bad," "awful," "terrible," and "terrifying." They fail to separate the verbal reactions from the situations that they have been connected with in their past experience, such as others responding with anger.

Procedures in Comprehensive Distancing

Consistent with this analysis, Hayes (1987) has developed a number of techniques that are designed to help a person out of the trap of trying to be "normal" by not feeling negative emotions. All of the procedures relate to making the synonymy conditional between people as they experience themselves and their negative thoughts, feelings, and evaluations. That is, intervention is a matter of changing the relationship between the concept of self and other concepts; it is also a matter of decreasing the avoidance of feelings. Someone who is struggling might reason that his or her mental health depends upon whether his or her feelings are positive or negative. In such a situation, much work goes into controlling or eliminating those feelings. However, using comprehensive distancing, someone might reason that he or she can have the feeling of sadness but understand that it is a feeling rather than a characteristic of his or her identity. In this way, a certain distance or conditionality is established between the individual and the events that make them a little less troublesome; then when an individual labels a particular feeling as "bad," it is no longer a definition of self. Thus, if an individual can accept these feelings rather than struggling not to have them, the experiences change and the individual can get on with life, rather than trying first to control these thoughts and feelings before taking significant action in his or her life.

A word should be said about the concept of emotion, based on the analysis of verbal behavior that underpins this approach; a stimulus is verbal if it is in a relational frame. Emotional events are themselves stimuli; even when visceral arousal occurs, it is experienced in light of its relationship to prior verbal labeling (Skinner, 1945). For example, a person who expresses his or her anxiety has a history of reinforcement for such expression in the presence of specific bodily events. The events may be experienced by the person as anxiety, but the entire experience is dependent on a conditioning history in which those bodily sensations have been related to words like "anxiety" (and probably "terrible," "bad," "I don't want this," "I have to stop feeling this way," etc.).

The treatment procedures that Hayes has developed based on this analysis are designed to assist people to change from avoidance to acceptance of their own thoughts and feelings. Thus, therapy that is intended to change a person's response to his or her emotion necessarily involves prompting the experience of bodily sensations and the verbal behavior that goes with them, and placing both the verbal and visceral experiences in new frames that alter the entire experience and its influence over other aspects of behavior. Extensive use is made of metaphors that suggest new ways of thinking about or relating to thoughts and feelings. Exercises are used in the sessions to prompt new ways of experiencing emotions and thoughts. The metaphors and exercises are described briefly.

Hopelessness When a person is in therapy to strive to control or avoid thoughts and feelings, almost anything that is said by the therapist will be taken as instructions regarding how to achieve this goal. Unfortunately, this goal is probably not attainable. One may be able to avoid situations that prompt certain thoughts and feelings, but this occurs at the cost of not being able to experience those situations.

It is important that the therapist not imply that this goal of mastering feelings can be achieved. It is even more essential for the therapist to interfere with the person's traditional ways of viewing the problem. Indeed, people who are particularly obsessed with controlling thoughts and feelings will also be obsessed with how to solve this problem. Thus almost anything that a therapist says to a person that makes sense will be understood in the context of solving the problem and may contribute to the person's continued obsession.

To the extent that this analysis is correct, it is both therapeutic and a matter of providing informed consent to tell the client that he or she cannot achieve a goal of controlling certain thoughts or feelings. Following a number of sessions in which the therapist has made efforts to understand the chief concerns of the client and the particular ways in which the client views problematic thoughts and feelings, the intervention begins with a discussion of the futility of the client's current and past efforts to get out of the situation. Most of a lengthy session (2 or more hours) is devoted to discussing and explaining this possibility. Each of the possible reactions that people might have to the therapist's assertion is likely to repeat their previous efforts to solve their problem. The reactions may include crying, complaints of great anxiety or depression, anger, threats, or confusion.

The attempt in this session is to meet each effort on the part of the client to determine a solution with a firm but gentle review of the facts that indicate that the individual's attempts to control his or her feelings have been unsuccessful. This is admittedly a frightening endeavor for the therapist. Therapists are, after all, members of the same social-verbal community as the client (one that places a great premium on the control of thoughts and feelings); and much of the tradition of therapy has been to help people control thoughts and feelings. In a sense, taking this stance with a client involves an abandoning of a therapist's own efforts to control thoughts and feelings.

At the same time, the therapist communicates that there is a way to change, but that to discuss it at this juncture would not work because it would be heard (by the client) in the context of the client's frame of "avoid and control." Hayes (1987) uses a metaphor of a person who falls into a hole and has a shovel as the only available tool. That person is so motivated to get out that he or she begins digging with the shovel; although much effort is made to get out, a shovel is the wrong tool for the job. Unfortunately, in his or her current state that person would try to dig with any tool. The person in the hole is so caught up in digging that if someone gave him or her a ladder, he or she would dig with it. Likewise, a client who has spent so much time and effort trying to solve problems by controlling thoughts and feelings will use whatever is available to continue to try to achieve that control.

A case example may illustrate the struggles in which some people engage. One mother of a child with multiple handicaps fit the criteria for a major depressive disorder. She indicated at the outset of therapy that virtually all of her waking hours were spent thinking about whether or not she should continue her marriage, why she felt so frustrated with her husband, why she didn't feel more loving toward him, whether or not there was something wrong with her for feeling like leaving him, and whether or not her friends and coworkers approved of her. There was a labyrinthine quality to her discussions of these issues. Each topic overlapped with the other, always with a sense that she needed to and could figure it all out and reach a conclusion that would clearly indicate whether or not she should leave her husband and how she could satisfy everyone. She clearly expected that therapy would give her the answers that she needed and still her anxieties.

A discussion of the hopelessness of controlling feelings prompted a good deal of distress and confusion for her. Yet by the end of the session and over the subsequent weeks she found that she struggled less. In a sense, she was resigned to her fate of having these problems, but as she stopped struggling, the feel of those problems changed.

While the effect of talking to people about the hopelessness of their current efforts to rid themselves of problems often has dramatic effects, people do not stop struggling permanently. From a behavioral perspective, the struggling includes a repertoire of verbal behavior that is prompted by a broad range of stimuli, including thoughts and feelings; intervention is a matter of modifying responses to these situations. A single session can have a dramatic effect because it can prompt people to abandon their mobilization to avoid thoughts and feelings. A person who has been working very hard to control thoughts and feelings may stop struggling and become willing to experience those thoughts and feelings, but this will probably create other thoughts and feelings that have also been avoided, which is likely to start the struggling again. Thus, therapy is a matter of assisting a person to learn how to approach situations with a "hands-off" attitude toward thoughts and feelings.

Control is the Problem Much of the intervention is focused on helping people notice the ways in which they attempt to control their thoughts and feelings. The word "notice" is used to convey the "hands-off" attitude. Hayes (1987) uses the metaphor of a freight train going 80 miles an hour; people can notice how it works, but they cannot try to stop it.

An initial discussion of hopelessness may increase the person's willingness to have unpleasant thoughts and feelings, which in turn will allow his or her dissatisfaction to decrease. But as the person notices that change and likes it, he or she becomes motivated to keep this state; unfortunately, that is tantamount to becoming less willing to have unpleasant thoughts and feelings. The result is that as soon as unpleasant thoughts or feelings occur again, the person gets locked into the struggle by virtue of his or her reluctance to have these experiences.

One client was the mother of a child with a life-threatening handicap who had been raised in a family that stressed the importance of not showing emotion. Her family had given her the impression that there was something wrong with her and, as a teenager, she had been sent to a number of psychiatrists. For many years she read books and went to therapists to solve her problems. After her child was born, she spent a good deal of time reading books about families with handicapped children. Reading and seeking therapy were her efforts to arrive at ways that she could rectify the psychological shortcomings she felt she had to overcome in order to proceed with her life. Had she not had such real difficulties as a critically ill child and substantial debt, she might have been able to manage her distress. However, when she responded to these very real sources of distress with intense efforts to understand and control, she was locked into a nearly constant state of distress. Because she was unwilling to experience the thought that she was sick, crazy, or a bad mother, she found herself almost constantly faced with those very thoughts; her life was focused on not being sick.

As might be expected, this woman asked frequent questions about whether her experiences were "normal," and she frequently asked if the therapeutic approaches that she read about might help her. These questions were typically met by suggestions to examine whether these questions reflected efforts on her part to get rid of thoughts that she was "sick," "bad," or "crazy." As therapy progressed, she devoted less effort to controlling her thoughts and feelings.

Building New Responses   Most therapy involves exercises to assist a person in developing new ways of responding to thoughts and feelings. The first exercise in comprehensive distancing is designed to increase the extent to which people can experience thoughts and feelings neutrally, rather than as reflections of the world in which they live; people need to develop a sense of self that is distinct from their experiences.

The first exercise is adapted from Zen meditation, and it prompts people to notice the way in which they are observers of thoughts, feelings, sensations, behaviors, or roles. People are asked to close their eyes and listen as the therapist asks them to think about the sensations, roles, thoughts, and feelings that they have had over the years, and to notice the sense they have of being the same person now that they were then—the same person across all of those very different experiences. The purpose of the exercise is to give people the sense of a "safe" place from which to experience the thoughts and feelings that they have been experiencing as overwhelming. It is also helpful to have clients actively label their thoughts and feelings. For example, rather than saying, "I can't stand this,"

the person would be prompted to say, "I have the feeling that I can't stand this."

The metaphor of the person as a chess board illustrates the "hands-off" approach to thoughts and feelings that is described here. In this metaphor the individual is asked to imagine that life is a chess board stretched out in all directions and that thoughts and feelings are the pieces that have been placed on the board by experiences in life. Clients are asked to consider the possibility that they are not any of these pieces, but rather that the chess board is doing its job when it simply holds things.

At this point in treatment, much of the discussion concerns the feelings that the person experiences in daily life. Specific assignments typically focus on doing something that is likely to produce negative thoughts and feelings, so that the person can experience them in the "hands-off" way that is being taught. For example, one mother was given the assignment to notice and make a note of the times when she felt angry, but to try not to do anything in particular about her feeling of anger.

At this stage, a typical session focuses on what has happened in the past week that seemed significant to the person. More often than not these situations involve emotions that the person has not experienced in some time, which often prompt the person to struggle to control his or her thoughts and feelings again. The discussion and exercises are intended to help the person recognize the struggling and adopt the same "hands-off" stance toward these reactions.

A metaphor that illustrates this new stance toward emotions and thoughts is "the bum at the door" (Hayes, 1987); it compares an individual's thoughts and feelings with a bum that might try to crash a party. Since the door is unlocked so that the guests can come in, if a person wants to keep the bum out he or she will have to stand at the door. This will keep the bum out, but the individual can no longer enjoy the party. However, the person can truly welcome him, even if he or she does not like the fact that he is there, and then be free to enjoy the party. The same is true of negative thoughts and emotions. There is a sense in which people can welcome their feelings; and, if they really hate the fact that they are experiencing them, those are just more feelings to be accepted—the bum's chums.

In essence, therapy is organized to provide a social context in which negative thoughts and feelings can be experienced without the avoidance behaviors that have been typical in the person's past. As the individual becomes willing to experience feelings, new and even more negative emotions come up. From a behavioral standpoint, emotions that have been frequently occurring may have been helping the individual to avoid other emotions that were even more aversive. For example, the mother who began therapy struggling to not feel that she was a bad person, began to feel anger toward her husband and her father as she began to let go of the other struggle. At the same time, this new acceptance of feelings typically increases the experience of positive emotions. People become more responsive to their immediate environment as they become less focused on monitoring their thoughts and feelings in order to control them. Rather than being locked into one emotion much of the time, people often become much more labile.

A Gentle Approach?   In working with this approach the author and associates have been exploring the possibility that this reframing of the way in which people experience their emotions might be done gently. In some discussions of it, Hayes (personal communication, January, 1986) seems to suggest that therapy will inevitably create quite intense emotions. However, from a behavioral standpoint, what is loosely labeled an "emotion" in nontechnical terms consists of physiological, verbal, and overt behavioral components (Lang, 1968). Because other people do not have direct access to many of the events that can influence a person's verbal labeling, there is a good deal of inter- and intrasubject variability in the verbal labels that occur in response to emotions (Skinner, 1945). For example, a person may say, "I am anxious" in response to diverse bodily sensations. From this view, a person might complain of having emotions that are "too strong" because of any or all of the following: 1) a high amplitude physiological response, 2) various physiological events (e.g., heart pounding, hands shaking, reverse peristalsis), 3) persistence of the "emotional" reaction, or 4) persistent thoughts that are part of what the

person labels as "this emotion" (e.g., "I am very upset"). In addition, much of what is happening when people say that an emotion is "too strong" involves the behavior in which they are engaging in order to stop that emotion. This becomes apparent when people calm down in a session on the hopelessness of struggling with these emotions. Thus, it is conceivable that therapy could prompt a person to experience new emotional reactions in small steps. This could happen both by introducing themes and experiences that evoke emotions in small and controlled doses (as is done in systematic desensitization for phobic behaviors) and by strengthening the person's repertoire of responding in the newer "hands-off" way. This "gentle" approach may be particularly relevant to using these techniques in group therapy.

A danger with this line of thinking is that it seems to imply that it is a bad thing to experience strong emotion. To the extent that this notion is conveyed in therapy, it may interfere with a person's acceptance of the experience of emotion; however, this aspect of the approach does not need to be communicated to the client at all. The emotional experiences that are prompted by therapy can be approached within the context of this new "hands-off" frame. What is ultimately important is that therapy progresses toward the goal of helping people accept their emotions related to life experiences. Further research is needed to explore the efficacy of different approaches to this goal.

Going Forward   As a person becomes better able to accept emotional reactions to situations, he or she can begin to examine some desires and goals for his or her life. For a person who has been struggling with thoughts and feelings, life previously centered around the control of those experiences. At this stage, behavioral procedures for specifying overt behaviors and increasing the occurrence of those behaviors become relevant. Thus, the next step involves establishing explicit goals.

Goal Setting

Since what happens in behavioral treatment flows from the determination of goals, it is important to have a clear understanding of goals and their functions. Research on rule-governed behavior suggests the value of thinking of goals as specific verbal stimuli (Riegler, Kohler, & Baer, 1985). The statement of a goal is a verbal event. Its relationship to subsequent behavior is apparently a matter of a person's prior experience in responding to such stimuli. For example, there is evidence that reinforcement for responding in a manner consistent with a verbal statement increases compliance with those statements (Baer, Rowbury, & Baer, 1973; Israel & Brown, 1977; Risley & Hart, 1968). Evidence that verbal stimuli affect behavior only when the person knows that others are aware of the verbal stimulus (Hayes & Wolf, 1984) also implies that social consequences for adhering to stated goals are a factor determining the control of those goals over behavior.

No research is available on why a person states or chooses a particular goal. From a behavioral perspective, what people state as goals are the result of their past experiences with stating their plans and encountering consequences for those statements (Biglan, 1987). Clients often state their goals in terms of experiences that they don't like (e.g., "I don't want him to get so angry," or, "I don't want to be so anxious"). Such statements may be part of a more general class of behaviors—commands, requests, and complaints—that are reinforced, at least intermittently, by events such as changes in the source of the complaint. However, as discussed above, people often fail to distinguish statements that have some hope of being reinforced ("I am going to fix this window") from those that do not ("I am not going to think about that").

In any case, it seems that people come to therapy with a repertoire of verbal statements about what they would like to change in their lives. This repertoire is the starting point for establishing goals. The therapist has the responsibility to assist the individual in arriving at a set of goals that have some possibility of being achieved.

The author and associates have developed the following guidelines for this goal-setting process:

1. Therapists assist clients in clarifying possible outcomes of therapy that might be desirable.

2. Possible goals that are indicated by a person's description of a situation, but that the person might not mention, should be suggested by the therapist.
3. The possible consequences of achieving goals should be reviewed.
4. The therapist should indicate what treatment procedures are available to help achieve each of the possible goals and how effective they have been for others, based on empirical evidence.
5. The risks associated with those treatments should be clearly stated.
6. Having been informed about the possible consequences of pursuing the stated goals, the client should make the ultimate decision about what the goals of therapy should be.

This approach to setting goals defines the role of the therapist as one who is expert in the analysis and modification of behavior, but one who does not make judgments about what clients should do. Individuals can come to therapists for assistance in changing characteristics that they want to change, but they will not be told what changes they should make. This is not to say that clients' decisions are undetermined. From a behavior-analytic perspective, minimizing the degree to which the therapist determines the goals for therapy simply leaves the determination of those goals to other variables in the history and current environment of the client.

This may seem like a strange position to take within the context of the deterministic position of behavior analysis. Moreover, to those who are working to ensure the welfare of handicapped children through the provision of services to parents, this stance may seem to abandon any concern with the child's welfare. Although it has not been general experience that parents use therapeutic services to pursue goals that are contrary to the best interests of the child, these rules ensure that the possibility exists. For example, it is conceivable that parents would adopt a goal of getting their handicapped child placed in foster care or an institution.

The value of this approach to setting goals has to be examined within the context of the cultural system in which it is embedded. Viewed narrowly, it may make sense to only provide therapy

for goals that seem likely to benefit the handicapped child. But to do so would diminish the
degree to which people can feel uncoerced in
seeking therapeutic assistance. Given the evidence that many parts of the social service system are aversive to parents (Wahler, Leske, &
Rogers, 1979), the interests of the system and the
people served by that system seem best addressed by having at least one service provider
whose role is to be entirely at the service of the
goals and aspirations of the parent. For example,
in most states there are other features of the system that make it difficult or unlikely that parents
can institutionalize their child simply because
the child is a burden. And, to the extent that the
system provides respite care, the motivation to
pursue such an option will probably be diminished. Therapy that is clearly at the service of the
parents may actually reduce parents' tendency to
see themselves as hopelessly burdened.

There may be strategic value in this approach
as well. It is likely that framing the goal-setting
in terms of doing what the parents want to do
rather than what the therapist thinks they should
do will reduce their reactance (Brehm, 1966).
People may be more likely to regard the goals as
their decisions, not as someone else's demands.
There is reason to believe that this increases
compliance, as is discussed below.

Enhancing Compliance

Analyses of rule-governed behavior (e.g.,
Riegler et al., 1985) can increase the likelihood
that clients will work between treatment sessions
to accomplish their goals. An assignment to do
something such as monitor one's social encounters is a verbal stimulus. Behavior occurs in conformance with it to the extent that the contingencies for conformance favor such consistency.
There are a number of things that the therapist
can do to sharpen the contingencies for following
through on such plans.

First, it is useful to have an explicit agreement
with the client regarding the rules for developing
and complying with between-session activities.
In a sense, this is simply a description of the contingencies. Compliance may also be enhanced
by eliciting explicit agreement to the procedures
that are followed, which may also reduce reactance to those procedures (Brehm, 1966).

Second, giving the client the ultimate choice
of which between-session activities to engage in
makes it more likely that the activities are ones
that the person believes will be useful and makes
the situation less one-sided. It is typically proposed that the therapist will only "suggest" activities. The client is encouraged to indicate
ways in which the suggested activity might be
altered to make it more useful or appropriate,
and to reject proposed activities outright when
necessary. This stance may be particularly valuable in working with people who are inclined to
argue or denigrate proposed activities; the therapist's clear statement that he or she is willing to
be wrong about the usefulness of proposed
between-session activities probably makes it less
important for the client to prove the therapist
wrong.

Third, precise and written specification of the
tasks to be accomplished between sessions
makes it much more likely that they will be completed. During the session, a list is made of each
of the items that the person agrees to complete
during the coming week. A copy of the list is
kept by the therapist. The activities are defined
in such a way that there can be little ambiguity
about whether or not there has been completion. For example, an assignment that suggests,
"Try to have two pleasant interactions with your
son each day—ones where you are not trying to
get any particular thing accomplished. Note each
interaction," would be preferable to one that simply says, "Try to have positive interactions with
your son this week."

Precise lists of the activities will not function
as controlling stimuli for between-session behavior unless there are consequences for compliance. For this reason, a key activity in each
session is the review of the activities that were
planned in the previous session. This is not done
in an accusing tone, but the person is asked how
each of the plans worked out. The implication is
that the activity occurred; the only question concerns its success. It is assumed that it is reinforcing for clients to describe their activities. Reports of failures to comply are never overlooked,
but they are not met with disapproval; for most
people, the very fact of having to report noncompliance is mildly punishing. Typically, it is
useful simply to suggest that the plan be revised

in light of any problems the person confronted in following through.

Therapists are sometimes asked if they really trust what clients tell them about their compliance. In most cases, clients have little reason to lie, since the activities to which they agreed are seen by them as relevant to achieving important goals. Therapists are very accepting of whatever clients report. Most activities result in some kind of record of what was done. It is certainly possible to fake such records, but inspection of them over the years has seldom suggested that people are dishonest. There is empirical evidence that examinations of self-monitored records can reveal noncompliance (McConnell, Biglan, & Severson, 1984).

Repeated failure to comply needs to be examined in terms of the "reasons" that the person offers. The fundamental question is whether keeping a commitment can occur only if a person's thoughts and feelings are compatible with action. Thus, when people say they have not accomplished something that they committed to accomplish, there is an occasion to discuss exercises about keeping commitments.

Money penalties may be appropriate on some occasions. For example, one client was not following through on plans to exercise three times a week and to limit the number of desserts. She agreed that failure to adhere in the subsequent week would result in her having to pay $20.00 to a political candidate she detested. She completed her goals in subsequent weeks.

Interventions for Specific Targets

This section presents a very brief description of three specific treatment procedures that have been useful in working with parents of handicapped children: 1) defining and pursuing life goals, 2) changing social behavior, and 3) increasing activity. The procedures were developed on the basis of clinical research and general experience. However, it should be stressed that an empirical evaluation of the efficacy of these interventions with parents of children with handicaps has not been accomplished. Thus, while most of the interventions have been shown to have some effects with other populations, determination of their efficacy with the parents of

children with disabilities requires further study. There are two useful treatment procedures that are not described here because they are described in Chapter 5 by Hawkins and Singer: self-monitoring and relaxation training.

Defining and Pursuing Life Goals People often find it useful to enumerate and set priorities among their long-term goals for life. This is a little different from establishing goals for therapy, because accomplishments may cover a longer range of time and are often not goals that a therapist could help them achieve. The behavior analysis of therapy goals that was presented above is applicable, though, because goals are verbal statements that will control behavior only if contingencies are established that provide for such control.

The author and associates have found it helpful to follow steps outlined by Lakein (1973) about time management that suggest listing all the goals that an individual wants to achieve under three time frames: 1) with 6 months to live, 2) in the next 5 years, and 3) in a lifetime. Priorities can then be established among the items on each of these lists, and ultimately all lists are combined.

Once a person has clarified his or her priorities, it is useful to introduce some simple principles of time management. These include defining activities that help to achieve the goals, breaking the activities into small steps that can be accomplished in an hour or so, making "to do" lists for the day or week, consulting the list of goals whenever "to do" lists are made, and putting some effort into at least one goal each day. Usually the client is assisted in putting these principles into practice through between-session assignments. Therapist attention to the completion of these activities by the client is gradually decreased once the activities are established. Presumably, the reinforcer that maintains these time management activities is the progress toward stated goals.

Changing Social Behavior Often people find it difficult to specify what their problems with others are. In this case, they are asked to monitor the social interactions in which they feel some dissatisfaction and to report on: 1) who was involved, 2) what they said, 3) what the other person said, and 4) anything they think they might have done differently. Specific behavioral targets are established based on reviews of these records, interviews about the situations, and evidence from empirical studies regarding the effects of different social behaviors. Typical targets include: initiating conversations, self-disclosing, making demands on others, and giving compliments. Then role-play (Hollin & Trower, 1988) and covert rehearsal procedures (Glaser et al., 1983) are used to assist the person in developing targeted ways of responding in problem situations. It is stressed, however, that one cannot be sure what behavior will be effective in advance. Clients are encouraged to prepare themselves for upcoming social situations by covertly rehearsing whatever behaviors they feel are likely to help.

Increasing Activity   Increasing pleasant activities is useful for many depressed people, although the efficacy of this approach may depend on the way the person labels reasons for engaging in activities (Biglan & Craker, 1982). Just because an activity might be considered pleasant does not mean that it will make the person feel better. It is important to identify life goals and establish time management routines to help people find time to enjoy pleasant activities.

A CASE DESCRIPTION

The author and associates have incorporated comprehensive distancing into their treatment program because it seems so relevant to the problems of people who do not typically responded to the problem-specific approach. In order to give some indication of the effect of comprehensive distancing, the outcomes of the treatment of one mother follow.

K. T.'s Treatment

K. T. was married and the mother of two daughters with handicaps. One of her daughters had spina bifida, a congenital deformity in which the spinal column is not fully formed. That daughter was paralyzed from her chest down, and her intellectual development was delayed. She was not expected to live past puberty, and death was a possibility at any time. The other daughter had Type I diabetes and required daily insulin injections and careful monitoring of her blood glu-

cose level. Both K. T. and her husband were out of work and had accumulated medical bills for their daughters that totaled over $60,000.

K. T. was distressed in the ways that were previously described. At the time that treatment was initiated, she met the diagnostic criteria for major affective disorder. For the previous 3 years she had been taking imipramine to relieve depression and panic attacks. During most of her waking hours, she was worrying about her mental health and whether or not she was going crazy. She read books about these issues in an effort to relieve her distress. She avoided other people, and particularly feared hearing something sympathetic about her difficult situation, such as, "I don't know how you cope so well." She was quite inactive, and one of the things that she did in response to her situation was to eat; she had gained 55 pounds over a 4-month period prior to the beginning of treatment, and was 70 pounds overweight.

Treatment following the techniques described previously was associated with a distinct reduction in K. T.'s struggling with concerns about herself. As she abandoned those struggles she began to take action. She sued her first husband, who was the father of her children, for child support and eventually got a $60,000 settlement. She found a job and began to initiate contacts with other people. At a session that was held 6 months after treatment began to review her progress, she was not depressed as assessed by a standardized measure of depression or her own report. At that time, the one remaining goal that appeared to be appropriate was to decrease the number of interactions she had with members of her family in which she got angry. A plan was developed for her to make notes about these occasions so that an intervention could be developed in the next session.

Unfortunately, both of her daughters became ill. During a 3-month period, K. T. cancelled a series of scheduled sessions. She said that it was impossible for her to come because of her children's illnesses, but she later indicated that she avoided coming because she was quite distressed and was avoiding sessions because she thought they would make her feel worse.

When treatment did resume, it was apparent that K. T. had begun struggling again. She had decided to quit her job as a result of the medical crisis and the distress that was associated with it. Her standardized depression test score was again elevated, and she was worrying about her sanity; it was clear that further treatment was appropriate.

As therapy progressed, she continued to report a good deal of distress, but reported also that it was no longer immobilizing. She began to have many positive experiences with others. A series of experiential exercises involving K. T.'s reactions to people being warm or loving toward her appeared to be particularly important to her. Her experiences were framed in terms of the possibility that what she had been taught by her family about not showing distress, and their not being supportive to her, did not have to stand in the way of her having these experiences. After this session she began to have many more warm and frequent contacts with others. Her parents were dead, but she had two sisters and two brothers with whom relations had been strained; following this session, she began making more contact with them and she initiated warmth in these contacts. Her oldest brother had been made the trustee of a trust fund that her father had established. Although she knew of its existence, she was unaware of how much money was in it or the fact that she could have access to it. As a result of contacts with that brother, she received over $160,000 in cash and securities.

Therapy is continuing with focus on the way in which thoughts and feelings tend to get the struggle started. She has continued to have many distressing thoughts and feelings, but she has also had many very positive experiences—ones that she feels were not occurring previously. These include the development of new friendships and the renewal of old ones.

Based on her descriptions, it appears that she is developing a generalized skill of responding to her emotions in a "hands-off" way. She recently described an incident that she said was typical of her new stance with respect to her thoughts and feelings. She had become quite angry as the result of a conflict with a coworker, which would traditionally have prompted her to express great anger, sometimes in fairly counterproductive ways. Rather than doing this, she decided to exercise and let herself feel what was there to be felt. She said that she noticed that the anger soon turned to sadness, and as she let herself feel sad, that too, soon went away.

K. T. has also developed long-term goals for herself, including finishing her bachelor's degree, working in a law office, and going to law school. Therapy is being tapered and she continues to make progress on her life goals; she has also lost 55 pounds, although weight loss was never specifically discussed in therapy.

During therapy she decreased her use of imipramine on her own initiative. At this writing, she has not taken any in 2 months. She indicated that she feels anxiety occasionally, but does not experience panic attacks. She related this to a greater willingness to experience these feelings of anxiety.

OUTCOME

Empirical evidence for the efficacy of the approach described in this chapter is quite limited as of the late 1980s. Zettle (1984) conducted a controlled comparison of comprehensive distancing and two variants of Beck's cognitive therapy (Beck, Rush, Shaw, & Emery, 1979) in the treatment of depressed persons. Zettle found that, on some depression measures, subjects receiving comprehensive distancing improved significantly more than those receiving the cognitive treatment. In light of the substantial evidence for the efficacy of cognitive treatment, this is encouraging evidence. However, that is the only controlled study completed thus far.

REFERENCES

Alperson, J., & Biglan, A. (1979). Self-administered treatment of sleep onset insomnia and the importance of age. *Behavior Therapy, 10*, 347–356.

Baer, A.M., Rowbury, T.G., & Baer, D.M. (1973). The de-

velopment of instructional control over classroom activities of deviant preschool children. *Journal of Applied Behavior Analysis, 6*, 289–298.

Beck, A.T., Rush, A.J., Shaw, B.F., & Emery, G. (1979).

Cognitive therapy of depression. New York: Guilford Press.

Biglan, A. (1987). A behavior-analytic critique off Bandura's self-efficacy theory. *The Behavior Analyst, 10,* 1–15.

Biglan, A., & Campbell, D.R. (1981). Depression. In J. Shelton & R. Levy, (Eds.), *Behavioral assignments and treatment compliance* (pp. 111–146). Champaign, IL: Research Press.

Biglan, A., & Craker, D. (1982). Effects of pleasant-activities manipulation on depression. *Journal of Consulting and Clinical Psychology, 50,* 436–438.

Biglan, A., & Dow, M.G. (1981). Toward a second-generational model: A problem-specific approach. In L.P. Rehm (Ed.), *Behavior therapy for depression* (pp. 97–112). New York: Academic Press.

Biglan, A., Hops, H., & Sherman, L. (1988). Coercive family processes and maternal depression. In R.D. Peters & R.J. McMahon (Eds.), *Marriages and families: Behavioral-systems approaches* (pp. 72–103). New York: Brunner/Mazel.

Biglan, A., & Kass, D.J. (1977). The empirical nature of behavior therapies. *Behaviorism, 5,* 1–15.

Brehm, J.W. (1966). *A theory of psychological reactance.* New York: Academic Press.

Breslau, N., Staruch, K.S., & Mortimer, E.A. (1982). Psychological distress in mothers of disabled children. *American Journal of the Disabled Child, 136,* 682–686.

Dow, M.B., Glaser, S.R., & Biglan, A. (1981). The relevance of specific conversational behaviors to ratings of social skill: An experimental analysis. *Journal of Behavioral Assessment, 3,* 233–242.

Glaser, S.R., Biglan, A., & Dow, M.G. (1983). Conversational skills instruction for communication apprehension and avoidance: Evaluation of a treatment program. *Communication Research, 10,* 582–613.

Hawkins, N.E., & Biglan, A. (1981). Parenting skills. In J. Shelton & R. Levy (Eds.), *Behavioral assignments and treatment compliance* (pp. 331–346). Champaign IL: Research Press.

Hayes, S.C. (in press). An analysis of relational frames. In P. Chase & L. Hayes (Eds.), *The analysis of verbal behavior.* Springfield, IL: Charles C Thomas.

Hayes, S.C. (1987). A contextual approach to therapeutic change. In N. Jacobson (Ed.), *Psychotherapists in clinical practice: cognitive and behavioral perspectives* (pp. 327–387). New York: Guilford.

Hayes, S.C., & Wolf, M. (1984). Cues, consequences, and therapeutic talk: Effects of social context and coping statements on pain. *Behavior Research and Therapy, 22,* 385–392.

Hollin, C.R., & Trower, P. (1988). Development and applications of social skills training: A review and critique. In M. Hersen, R.M. Eisler, & P.M. Miller (Eds.), *Progress*

in behavior modification (pp. 166–214). Newbury Park, CA: Sage.

Hops, H., Sherman, L., & Biglan, A. (in press). Maternal depression, marital discord, and children's behavior: A developmental perspective. In G. Patterson (Ed.), *Depression and aggression: Two facets of family interactions.* New York: Lawrence Erlbaum Associates, Inc.

Israel, A.C., & Brown, M.S. (1977). Correspondence training, prior verbal training and control of nonverbal behavior via control of verbal behavior. *Journal of Applied Behavior Analysis, 10,* 333–338.

Lakein, A. (1973). *How to get control of your time and your life.* New York: New American Library.

Lang, P.J. (1968). Fear reduction and fear behavior: Problems in treating a construct. *Research in Psychotherapy, 3,* 90–102.

Lewis, C., Biglan, A., & Steinbock, E. (1978). Self-administered relaxation training and money deposits in the treatment of recurrent anxiety. *Journal of Consulting and Clinical Psychology, 46,* 1274–1283.

McConnell, S., Biglan, A., & Severson, H.H. (1984). Adolescents' compliance with self-monitoring and physiological assessment of smoking in natural environments. *Journal of Behavioral Medicine, 7,* 115–122.

McKnight, D.L., Nelson, R.O., Hayes, S.C., & Jarrett, R.B. (1984). Importance of treating individually assessed response classes in the amelioration of depression. *Behavior Therapy, 15,* 315–335.

McLean, P.O., & Hakstian, A.R. (1979). Clinical depression: Comparative efficacy of outpatient treatments. *Journal of Consulting and Clinical Psychology, 47,* 818–836.

Riegler, H.C., Kohler, F.W., & Baer, D.M. (1985, May). *Rule-governed behavior: A discussion of its origins, functions and maintenance.* Paper presented at the 11th annual convention of the Association for Behavior Analysis, Columbus, OH.

Risley, R.T., & Hart, B.T. (1968). Developing correspondence between nonverbal and verbal behavior in preschool children. *Journal of Applied Behavior Analysis, 1,* 267–281.

Skinner, B.F. (1945). The operational analysis of psychological terms. *Psychological Review, 52,* 270–276.

Wahler, R.G., Leske, G., & Rogers, E.S. (1979). The insular family: A deviance support system for oppositional children. In L.S. Hamerlynck (Ed.), *Behavioral systems for the developmentally disabled: I. School and family environments* (pp. 102–127). New York: Brunner/Mazel.

Weissman, M.M. (1979). The psychological treatment of depression. *Archives of General Psychiatry, 36,* 1261–1269.

Zettle, R.D. (1984). *Cognitive therapy of depression: A conceptual and empirical analysis of component and process issues.* Unpublished doctoral dissertation, University of North Carolina, Greensboro.

CHAPTER 20

Ecobehavioral Interventions for Abusive, Neglectful, and High-Risk Families

John R. Lutzker, Randy V. Campbell,
Maxine R. Newman, and Mark Harrold

Annually, an estimated 1.7 million children in the United States have been reported to child protective service agencies as abused or neglected. This is equivalent to approximately 27.3 children per every 1,000. These serious family/societal problems were functionally ignored or hidden until 1962, when Kempe, Silverman, Steele, Droegemuller, and Silver (1962) published their paper, "The Battered Child Syndrome". Public attention was heightened when Kempe and Helfer (1972) published a book on the subject. Probably the most important outcome of this attention was that all 50 states developed hotline services so that professionals and concerned individuals could report suspected abuse or neglect, and so that those reports would receive follow-up child protective service or law enforcement investigations. Most states ensure anonymity in such reporting.

A NEED FOR COMPREHENSIVE SERVICES

Despite the recognition of these child abuse problems and the legal actions taken, *treatment* programs with good evaluation methods and data to document effectiveness have not met the need (Helfer, 1982; Lutzker & Newman, 1986). To truly meet a community's needs, a treatment program should be community-based and should view the problems of child abuse and neglect as multifaceted ones in need of multifaceted ser-

vices (Lutzker & Newman, 1986; Rosenberg & Reppucci, 1985). Such has been the basic tenet of Project 12-Ways, an ecobehavioral approach to the treatment and prevention of child abuse and neglect (Lutzker, 1984; Lutzker, Frame, & Rice, 1982). By ecobehavioral, it is meant that many factors contribute to these family system problems; thus, several in-home, *in situ* treatment services are necessary. An in-depth review of two ecobehavioral approaches is presented in this chapter. However, an expanded rationale for the need for this kind of approach precedes that review.

Theoretical Premises

After Kempe et al. (1962) exposed the professional community to the prevalence and severity of child abuse and neglect, theories tried to account for the occurrence of such aberrant behavior. Early explanations of child abuse focused primarily on the personality characteristics of parents. These explanations tended to be psychodynamic in orientation and attributed child abuse and neglect to pathological characteristics of the parents, such as distorted perceptions of the nature of childhood, difficulty in handling aggressive impulses, impulsivity, rigidity, low self-esteem, and a history of having been abused or neglected (Kempe & Helfer, 1972). While certain parental characteristics may contribute to child abuse and neglect, these theories did not consider environmental predictor variables, nor did they offer much of a solution beyond long-term psychotherapy, a process that holds little immediate advantage for a child victim of abuse or neglect. From the parental characteristics account, however, it is clear that many parents that become involved in child abuse and neglect have difficulty coping with stress. Thus, training in stress reduction would seem to be a logical therapeutic technique, in conjunction with a comprehensive treatment approach.

More recent theories on abuse or neglect consider two other very important variables: sociological factors (the environment), and the social learning or social interactional factors (the child and family). The sociological model focuses on the prevention and alteration of societal factors that encourage abuse (Gil, 1970). These factors include the socially sanctioned use of force in child-rearing, and stressors such as unemployment and poverty that may decrease parental ability to control anger and frustration. Additional sources of stress that might also influence abuse include poor health, poor housing, too many children, and isolation from helpful social systems (Garbarino & Sherman, 1980).

The social learning or social interactional model focuses on family interaction (Burgess, 1979; Dubanski, Evans, & Higuchi, 1978; Parke, 1977; Patterson, 1982). This model emphasizes systematic observation rather than self-report alone for evaluation. The social interaction perspective acknowledges the growing body of research indicating that not only do parents influence children, but children influence parents as well (Bell & Harper, 1977; Rutter, 1979). Characteristics of the child that increase the risk of abuse include developmental disabilities or physical handicaps, colic, high pitched whining and crying, and noncompliance; a multifaceted treatment approach needs to provide services to the child and the family that lower risk by changing some of these behaviors or characteristics. For example, children who have been the victims of abuse or neglect often lag behind their age mates in developmental skills. Therefore, providing training in basic skills such as toilet training, personal hygiene, and communication may help lower the risks of additional abuse to the child. Similarly, helping parents to procure medical care and other habilitative services for the child

would also seem to lower risks. Also, teaching parents how to manage their children's behavior without using severe punishment techniques is another necessary component of a multifaceted approach.

Child abuse and neglect is precipitated by many interrelated factors, some of which parents may be unable to change, such as their own history of abuse as a child (Gil, 1975). However, other precipitating problems may be more easily addressed, such as a lack of knowledge about child development or parenting skills (Blumberg, 1974; Green, Gaines, & Sandgrund, 1974; Wasserman, 1967), unemployment (Gelles, 1973), marital discord (Bennie & Sclar 1969; Green et al; 1974; Ory & Earp, 1980), community insularity (Wahler, 1980; Wahler, Leske, & Rogers, 1979), and parental attitudes toward children and violence (Crozier & Katz, 1979; Doctor & Singer, 1978; Nurse, 1964). Treatment programs that do not take these systems factors into account by offering services to try to remediate some of these problems seem necessarily deficient.

PROJECT 12-WAYS

With social learning underpinnings and an eco-behavioral philosophy and approach (Lutzker & Newman, 1986), Project 12-Ways started in 1979 as a service and research project aimed at the treatment and prevention of child abuse and neglect in rural southern Illinois, an economically depressed area where high-sulphur coal mining has been the major industry; in that year, Project 12-Ways served 27 counties. In each of the subsequent years, 10 counties have been served. The goal was to provide a multifaceted service to tackle the multifaceted predictors and contributors of child abuse and neglect. The empirical goal was to reduce the future likelihood of abuse or neglect in families who entered the Project having been *indicated* for child abuse or neglect (families who have been brought to the attention of a protective service agency and either adjudicated or considered high risk), or to prevent child abuse or neglect in poor single mothers who were at particular risk. Further goals were to reunite families, to avoid out-of-home placements, and to achieve favorable clinical outcomes from objectives set by the Project 12-Ways direct service providers (staff) and the families served. In addition, the Project was created in order to provide training and financial support to graduate students in the Behavior Analysis and Therapy Program in the Rehabilitation Institute at Southern Illinois University at Carbondale (SIU-C).

Population

Most of the clients served by Project 12-Ways present a picture of the descriptions found in the literature. For example, most are poor, insular, single mothers with less than a high-school education. They are usually agency-dependent, living in unkempt environments, and often have a history of intergenerational abuse (Burgess & Youngblade, in press). The modal client is a 30-year-old, single white mother with two children who was referred for abuse. Also, frequently intimate partners of the mother were the perpetrators of abuse, rather than the mother.

The typical Project 12-Ways family lives on public aid, receives around $200 in cash per month and about $250 in food stamps. Monthly rent is between $150 and $175, leaving $25 to $50 in cash. Typically, this cash is used for cigarettes, and the food stamps are used to feed family members. Most families eat very well during the first two weeks of the month, after which they either borrow money from friends or eat what food the family can bring home through fishing, hunting, or procuring from the local food mission or church. Project 12-Ways staff find themselves trying to help families manage their money and/or food stamps. If the family is able to provide food through fishing or hunting, it becomes difficult to address the problem of money management.

Parental attitudes toward children can be best described as nonnurturing. Parents spend little or no time in developmental in-home activities or family excursions.

Funding

Federal Title Purchase of Service Funds, allocated by the State of Illinois under a program known as the Governor's Donated Funds Initiative (whereby the recipient of funding contributes 25%), provide the fiscal support for Project 12-Ways. From 1979 to 1988 this amount totaled over $5 million.

All referrals came from the Department of Children and Family Services (DCFS) and represent cases of indicated child abuse or neglect, or families considered at high-risk for abuse or neglect. The regional team leader of each DCFS field office discusses potential referrals with caseworkers. After deciding what cases are at high-risk, the team leader makes a referral to Project 12-Ways. Project 12-Ways receives occasional self-referrals that must still go through the screening process.

Staff

A hierarchical system of supervision and training is utilized in Project 12-Ways. In 1987, the structure of the organization changed. The Project Coordinator directs the project, and the Program Manager is responsible for writing additional grants and managing the day-to-day operation of the Project. Now, there is a Program Evaluator and Clinical Administrator, and instead of six counselors, there are two senior counselors (who are responsible for clinical supervision on a daily basis) and four counselors.

The Project Director provides leadership and supervision to all personnel on the project. Faculty in the Behavior Analysis and Therapy Program (BAT) at SIU-C have provided paid (summer) and *gratis* supervision to Project 12-Ways staff members. Additionally, the BAT coursework provides a critical academic foundation for Project 12-Ways services. New staff members on the Project are provided with an intensive 2-week in-service course/workshop on child abuse and neglect. This course is followed by a careful monitoring of skill acquisition for four months, as well as a personal development contract.

The daily operation of the project is provided by a program manager with a Masters Degree specializing in behavior analysis. The program manager provides administrative supervision and supervises one counselor team. Two Chief Rehabilitation Counselors, also holding Masters Degrees specializing in behavior analysis, provide supervision to counselor teams.

Direct client services are provided by counselors; most of the counselors on Project 12-

Ways are advanced students in the graduate program who have been promoted to this position. Counselors generally work from 60% to 100% of full-time, averaging 75 percent. Each counselor is a graduate assistant who has little seniority and experience in the program and the project. Graduate assistants collect data, keep children occupied in the homes while counselors work with parents, and assist in a variety of in-home services provided by the counselors. Additionally, the lengthy drives to client homes and the stressful nature of working with these families makes pairing counselors and graduate assistants a necessity in order to help prevent staff burnout.

Staff training can be conceived of as a mentorship that is academic and systematic. The BAT coursework comprises the academic component of training. The mentorships exist in the counselor-graduate assistant pairings. Systematic training involves staff training packages in counseling and problem-solving skills, parent training, stress reduction, child abuse and neglect reporting law, home safety, and home cleanliness.

The counseling and problem-solving training program consists of three groups of skills: general counseling skills (active listening, etc), opening and closing a session (greeting, scheduling next appointment), and problem-solving skills (generally alternatives). Each staff member is presented each skill group individually; the instructor then models and role-plays each group of target behaviors, and the staff members are asked to practice within their groups until mastery is achieved. Next, staff members role-play with the instructor until 100 percent acquisition is achieved. Follow-up observations are conducted in Project 12-Ways families' homes. Staff training in the areas of parent training, stress reduction, home safety, and home cleanliness are all conducted in a similar way. Upon demonstration of skills, staff are asked to perform and monitor with a Project 12-Ways family.

Overview of FIRST Program Family Interaction-Relationship Systems Training (FIRST) was developed for Project 12-Ways staff to use as a standardized parent training intervention. FIRST combines several important behavioral parenting strategies into one easy-to-implement training program and emphasizes an ecobehavioral approach to parent-child training. Family relationships are interactive in nature, and many variables contribute to and influence the members' behaviors. These variables include parent behavior, child behavior, parent-child interaction, family structure, and daily routine, to name a few. Given that family relationships and interactions are controlled by many factors, it is important to intervene with any or all variables that contribute to the dysfunction of the family system. As of the late 1980s, behavioral research and related program development in the area of child abuse and neglect has focused on modifying singular aspects of the family system, rather than providing multifaceted treatment programs.

In order to address the many variables that contribute to child abuse, FIRST utilizes five training components. Discussions of those five components follow:

1. Interaction-Compliance Training (ICT) The foundation of FIRST is the ICT, which is designed to improve parents' interaction skills with and their verbal control over children. The target behaviors involved in the Interaction-Compliance Training includes three different elements, based on available research. Compliance training (Forehand & McMahon, 1981), activity training (Twardosz, Schwartz, Fox, & Cunningham, 1979), and teaching adults interaction skills such as leveling, voice intonation, and active and passive touch (Lutzker, Megson, Webb, & Dachman, 1985) are all part of ICT.

2. Omission Training and Rule Setting (OT) The OT program enables staff members to increase positive child behaviors that will functionally support the parent training. The OT program, which utilizes an in-session sticker chart, can later be expanded into a token economy designed to increase the overall density of reinforcement in the family environment.

3. Activity Training Activity training is also provided and is programmed into FIRST during the pretreatment phase by conducting interaction-compliance observations and practice trials within the context of planned activity sessions. Parents are required to plan daily activities with their children to promote the maintenance of newly learned skills between Project 12-Ways home visits.

4. Review of Discipline In reviewing discipline, the area of problem-solving is addressed. Staff members try to have the parent pinpoint a specific problem area or behavior, then encourage the parent to generate alternative solutions for that specific problem. Further, parents are taught to select an appropriate alternative by evaluating the benefits and disadvantages. Role-playing is then used in selecting the alternative with the therapist, and in implementing the solution.

5. Providing Support Services The mulifaceted aspects of these interventions are reviewed with parents in a counseling format.

Progress through FIRST depends upon the acquisition and demonstration of specific skills by both the parents and their children. During each phase, the client is evaluated and the client's progress is assessed by analyzing information from both a Parental Daily Report (PDR) and direct in-home observations.

Assessment Procedures within FIRST

FIRST conducts an initial assessment of a family's needs, skills, stressors, and skill deficits. FIRST has a suggested standard battery of assessment devices that include:

1. Daily routine
2. Parent-child inventories
   a) Parent-child behavior inventory
   b) Parental knowledge of behavioral principles
   c) Child expectations questionnaire
   d) Parent daily report
   e) Parent opinions questionnaire
   f) Reinforcing events schedule
3. Behavioral measures
   a) Interaction-compliance training data
   b) Activities selection and scheduling
   c) Time out observations.

Treatment Services

Parent Training Most families that are referred to Project 12-Ways receive parent training, which has taken several forms. With some families, staff used structured training programs that were adapted from the model provided by Forehand and McMahon (1981). This involves teaching parents to use clear, concise commands

and to reduce their use of vague commands. Furthermore, they learn to attend more consistently to appropriate child behavior and use time out for inappropriate behavior. Structured parent training benefits families with children in the 3- to 9-year-old range; older children tend to find it boring, and younger children lack the prerequisite attention skills. This model focuses on antecedents as well as on consequences in child behavior management. Also, a priori criteria are established for moving parents through each level of training. An example of the success of the adaptation of this model was described by Dachman, Halasz, Bickett, and Lutzker (1984). They provided parent training to a low-income, single mother who was referred for neglect of her 7-year-old son. Multiple assessment measures were used and several corollary behaviors were continuously monitored throughout treatment. For example, data were collected on the frequency of the mother's criticism of her son's behavior, although that was never directly treated. A multiple baseline across three settings showed that the training was effective in increasing the mother's frequency of descriptive praise, and in producing demonstrable change in the untreated criticisms. Maintenance probes that were conducted 2 and 6 months after the end of training showed durability in the treatment effects.

Stress Reduction The literature is replete with suggestions that parents who are involved in abuse and neglect have particular difficulty coping with stress (Green et al., 1974). The parents served by Project 12-Ways are introduced to one of three kinds of in-home stress reduction approaches. *Progressive muscle relaxation* (PMR) (Jacobsen, 1983) involves teaching the client to distinguish between tension and relaxation in each of the major muscle groups. Through guided verbal imagery from the counselor, the client learns to produce deep levels of relaxation. *Behavioral relaxation training* (BRT) (Schilling & Poppen, 1983) teaches relaxed posturing. The counselor reviews a checklist of relaxed postures with the client and provides the client feedback about his or her relaxation. In-home *biofeedback* is used with clients who have difficulty with verbal techniques (PMR and BRT). Auditory feedback is provided to the client who has an electrode placed on the frontalis muscle; as muscle tension is progressively reduced, the tone indicates each reduction to the client.

A good example of the use of stress reduction within this ecobehavioral perspective is illustrated by Campbell, O'Brien, Bickett, and Lutzker (1983). A mother had been referred to Project 12-Ways after expressing a sincere concern that she might kill her 4-year-old daughter because of the child's hyperactive behavior at home. Although parent training was an obvious necessity in this home, it was learned that the mother suffered from debilitating migraine headaches. Neurological examinations proved negative; thus, prior to putting this mother through the added stress of structured parent training, the first treatment service provided for her was progressive muscle relaxation. After reducing her frequency of headaches from a weekly average of 13 to nearly zero, structured parent training was introduced. After parent training, a variation of reciprocity marital counseling (Azrin, Naster, & Jones, 1973) was used with the mother and father. No reports of abuse have ever occurred in this family. The mother's relief from headaches was monitored and maintained for over 1 year; she found a job, and ratings of marital satisfaction moved from the dysfunctional to the functional range.

Assertiveness Training Because a lack of assertiveness has been shown to create or exacerbate anxiety (Wolpe & Lazarus, 1966), assertiveness training has been provided to 7%–23% of the families served by Project 12-Ways. It is used most frequently with single mothers, to teach them to request clarification of health concerns from medical personnel and professionals, interact more assertively with friends and family members who may create added anxiety, and apply problem-solving to stressful situations.

Self-Control Training Anger control (Novaco, 1986), weight control, and smoking cessation represent some of the self-control treatment strategies that have been offered to some Project 12-Ways parents and adolescents. For example, a 15-year-old was taught to reduce verbal and physical outbursts in his special education high school class (Lutzker, 1984) by using strategies similar to those described by Novaco (1986). This involved teaching him to identify anger-provoking situations, to avoid some of those situations and to use on-the-spot stress reducing exercises for others. Seldom have self-control strategies been offered first in the sequence of services; however, when employed after other family problems have been successfully treated, self-control programs provide an important adjunct to those services. For example, if a mother's self-esteem has suffered because of a weight problem, a successful weight-reduction program is likely to improve her self-esteem and could, in turn, help her improve both her attitude and behavior toward her children.

Basic Skill Training Abused and neglected children often lag behind their age mates in developmental skills. These delays may also frustrate parents and further contribute to the possibility of abuse or neglect. Therefore, a variety of basic skill training programs have been adapted or developed, such as rapid toilet training (Azrin & Foxx, 1974), nighttime enuresis training (Azrin, Sneed, & Foxx, 1974), and teaching basic grooming and bathing skills (Lutzker, Campbell, & Watson-Perczel, 1984; Rosenfield-Schlichter, Sarber, Bueno, Greene, & Lutzker, 1983). For example, Rosenfield-Schlichter et al. (1983) taught two severely neglected children to bathe, wash and comb their hair, and dress in clean clothes on a daily basis. Teachers at school rated the children's cleanliness and an older sibling was taught to monitor, prompt, and reinforce his siblings' grooming and hygiene behaviors. In another example, mildly retarded parents and their children were also taught a variety of hygiene skills (Lutzker, Campbell, et al. 1984). Special contingencies were utilized with the parents in that situation, such as showing educational filmstrips to the mother (which she enjoyed) as reinforcers for following through with the hygiene programs that had been developed for the children.

Activity Training Sanders and Dadds (1982) have shown the value of structured family activities in facilitating outcome in parent training. Therefore, parents are taught to engage in activities with their children as part of their training. A sample list of activities that can be shared with parents appears in Table 1. Lutzker (1984) describes a method in which index cards describing simple activities are placed in pocket

Table 1. Examples of structured activities

The following list of activities can be performed by all members of your family. Many of the activities require little in materials or equipment in order to participate. Many activities can be adapted to fit children of different ages. The activities have been arranged, in general, in order of difficulty from simple to complex. The list presented here is by no means exhaustive and you can add as many activities as you wish.

Category	Activity/description
A. Books	Use is age appropriate
B. People games	Mother May I
	Simon Says
	Follow the Leader
	Musical Chairs
	Duck-Duck-Goose
	Exercises: Stretching, Jazzercise
	Ring Around the Roses
	Chase
	Telephone
	Charades
	Tell A Story
C. Paper and pencil games	Cutting
	Pasting, making collages
	Drawing
	Painting
	Tic-Tac-Toe
	Connect the dots
	Hangman
	Paper bag puppets
	Alphabet
	Make your own book
D. Household games	Tea parties
	Picnics
	Camping
	Cleaning
	Washing dishes

envelopes on the refrigerator in order to prompt daily interactions. In addition, activity training allows other service components to be incorporated; for example, a set of activities for parents and children to prepare different "fun" nutritious snacks each day could be developed. These kinds of activities may be at least as important as behavior management parent training (Lutzker, McGimsey, McRae, & Campbell, 1983).

Marital Counseling and Problem-Solving

Marital conflict or difficulty in dyadic relationships is a frequent problem cited in child abuse and neglect families (Isaacs, 1981). In the first few years of the Project, reciprocity counseling (Azrin et al., 1973) was used with a few families who were good candidates for this approach.

Briefly, this approach involves teaching couples to identify and increase the mutually reinforcing behaviors within their relationships. Each partner monitors these behaviors, and his or her happiness on an assessment scale before *each* session. Also, a variety of *quid pro quo* strategies involving household chores and child care responsibilities have been used (Tearnan & Lutzker, 1980). This involves having couples identify responsibilities, and having each partner complete them as reinforcers for the other partner performing his or her agreed-upon responsibilities. However, more recently the problem-solving strategies outlined by Borck and Fawcett (1982) have been adapted.

In problem-solving, the most important first step is to define the problem in a way that produces behaviors (i.e., How can I get . . .).Stating the problem in a "how-to" form sets the occasion to generate alternatives. Generating alternatives (brainstorming) is the second step; most parents have problems with this step, because they typically focus on one solution. The parents are asked to generate as many solutions as possible. The subsequent steps include reviewing the benefits and disadvantages of each alternative, rating each alternative on a 3-point Likert scale (1 is poor, 2 is fair, 3 is excellent), selecting the best alternative, evaluating whether the selected alternative addresses the problem, and determining a treatment plan to implement the selected alternatives.

There are seven steps to teaching a parent to problem-solve. The counselors first define the target steps (discussed previously), then models it. After modeling the step, the counselor explains what was done and how it was done. The parent is then asked to perform the target step. The counselor provides feedback during and after the parent completes the target step. The task of teaching a parent problem-solving is very repetitive, because the parent is asked to chain previously targeted steps together. At the end of a session, the parents are asked to do homework assignments by picking a current problem and implementing the problem-solving procedure. The counselors review the homework assignment with the parents on the next scheduled appointment, and monitor the implementation of the selected alternative.

Alcohol Treatment Referral Although alcohol abuse is a frequent problem among parents who abuse and neglect their children, it is in need of its own intensive treatment. When alcohol abuse is seen as a serious problem for a Project 12-Ways client, the client is referred to a community treatment program. However, as noted by Lutzker (1984), alcohol use and abuse seems to be a way of life in the group served by Project 12-Ways. Thus, in many cases counselors are forced to work around the problem.

Job Search Unemployment occurs frequently among parents indicated for child abuse and neglect; furthermore, unemployment in southern Illinois has been higher than the national averages. Many Project 12-Ways clients live in remote rural areas, possess few job skills, and lack high school educations. And for many, finding a job is often not even economically in their best interests, if it pays means minimum wage and creates a new need to pay for child care. Nonetheless, some clients benefit from participating in an individualized adaptation of the Job Club (Azrin & Besalel, 1980). This involves helping the client prepare a resume, telephoning prospective employers for interviews, and role-playing interview techniques.

Money Management Training Individualized money management training teaches clients how to live within their limited (usually public aid) means, how to handle creditors, and how to shop economically. This service tends to interface with nutrition training; for example, clients are taught that packaged foods such as potato chips lack nutrients and are more costly than nutritious homemade snacks.

> As with most of Project 12-Ways' services, the success of this component is dependent upon the clients' motivation . . . among . . . eager clients, the interactions between the counselors and themselves have produced clear successes. Through such efforts, families have been taken out of debt and have even managed to produce some small savings. (Lutzker, 1984, p. 279)

Health Maintenance and Nutrition Training Hygiene and nutritional deficiencies are cited as factors frequently associated with child abuse and neglect (Tizard, 1975). In addition to hygiene training as previously described, nutrition training is also provided. Sarber, Halasz,

Messmer, Bickett, and Lutzker (1983) describe a single-case experiment involving an illiterate retarded mother and her 4-year-old daughter. The woman was referred because of neglect based upon her inability to provide nutritious meals to her daughter. The first phase of treatment involved match-to-sample procedures to help the mother plan three daily meals with the four basic food groups. The second phase involved using match-to-sample procedures to teach the mother how to use a pictorial shopping list. Finally, through role-playing and social reinforcement, the mother was taught to shop for the items on her specially designed shopping list. Similar strategies have been used with other families.

Home Safety Training The hazardous conditions of homes often lead child protective caseworkers to charge families with child neglect (Lutzker, 1984). Furthermore, accidents are the leading cause of death in children. Tertinger, Greene, and Lutzker (1984) developed and validated the Home Accident Prevention Inventory (HAPI) to measure safety hazards in homes. The HAPI assesses 26 items that are accessible to young children among five safety hazard categories, including: 1) fire and electrical, 2) suffocation by mechanical means, 3) suffocation by ingested objects, 4) guns, and 5) poisoning by solids and liquids. The initial use of the HAPI and an in-home safety education program, which was implemented by a counselor, was evaluated using multiple baseline designs across hazard categories with six families that were served by the project. The safety education program was effective in dramatically reducing safety hazards in the families' homes; however, the program was also time consuming and relied on well trained counselors. Barone, Greene, and Lutzker (1986) developed and assessed a slide/cassette program and manual that required considerably less time and training. Using a multiple baseline design across three Project 12-Ways families, the streamlined safety program produced even more dramatic reductions in safety hazards than had the counselor-implemented program. Social validation data collected from the parents involved in these studies indicated their satisfaction with the programs.

Multiple-Setting Behavior Management Training An ecobehavioral program serves clients in whatever *in situ* setting is required and in which the project is allowed to serve. Besides natural homes, this may include schools, daycare facilities, residential facilities, and foster care placements. In doing so, as much as possible, Project 12-Ways has relied on direct observation of behavior and programs that are implemented by parents, teachers, foster parents, and other caregivers.

Single Parent Program Young single parents are at highest risk for child abuse and neglect (Taylor, 1973); therefore, Project 12-Ways has provided a number of prenatal and postnatal services to young single parents. These included maternal and infant nutrition training, preparation for childbirth (counselors have served as Lamaze coaches), family planning, infant stimulation (Lutzker, Lutzker, Braunling-McMorrow, Eddleman, 1987), and health care education and training (Delgado & Lutzker, 1988). These single parents have also been provided with other Project 12-Ways services when necessary, such as stress reduction.

It is believed that providing the array of services described previously facilitates FIRST and reduces stress in the family ecosystem.

PROJECT ECOSYSTEMS

Project 12-Ways represents an attempt to examine whether or not treating child abuse as an ecobehavioral problem in need of ecobehavioral services reduces the likelihoood of further abuse or neglect by families who are referred from the state's child protective service. Although out-of-home placement of children with developmental disabilities is a different social problem than child abuse and neglect, the reasons for such placement can also be considered ecobehavioral and in need of ecobehavioral services. Parents of children whose behavioral excesses or deficits put them at risk for out-of-home placement are faced with added stress, needs for problem-solving and basic skill training for their children, health maintenance issues, the need for parent training, and in some cases the need for money management and job search skills. Thus, the ecobehavioral tenets of Project 12-Ways are also applicable to families whose children are at risk for out-of-home placement; children with de-

velopmental disabilities and/or multiple handicaps are at high risk for placement into more restrictive settings.

Parents of children with disabilities are known to feel considerable stress and are frequently depressed (Friedrich & Friedrich, 1981; Wikler, 1986). The child's slow development, constant demand for attention, greater susceptibility to illnesses, dependence upon medical regimes, greater likelihood of noncompliance to rules and discipline, and lack of responsiveness to parental affection are problems not usually experienced as severely by parents of nonhandicapped children. These stresses, combined with the environmental issues of social isolation and financial strain, are pressures that can lead to an abusive and/or neglectful situation, or a desire to have the child placed out of the home.

Families served by Project 12-Ways are referred from DCFS for child abuse and neglect or the prevention of it. Many of these families have children with mental retardation, and often the parents themselves experience some degree of mental retardation; however, Project 12-Ways was designed to serve any family that is indicated for child abuse or neglect, regardless of whether a family member has mental retardation. Project Ecosystems was designed to systematically replicate the Project 12-Ways ecobehavioral model in Orange County, California, by serving families who have children with disabilities who are at high risk for abuse or neglect, or at high risk for placement into a more restrictive setting because of their severe behavior problems and/or multiple handicaps. Other systematic aspects of the replication are: urban (Orange County) versus rural (Southern Illinois areas; and staff from Project Ecosystems are primarily clinical psychology doctoral students from the California School of Professional Psychology, Los Angeles (CSPP-LA), and other local universities versus the staff of Project 12-Ways from the Behavior Analysis and Therapy Program at SIU-C.

Funding for Project Ecosystems

In its first year, 1987–1988, Project Ecosystems was funded by an Experimental Cycle 10 Professional Development Fund Grant from the California Department of Developmental Services to the Developmental Disabilities Center of Orange County. Continuation funding is provided through vendorization, whereby the state approves a service from a vendor and regional centers purchase service from the vendor. These services have been expanded to the San Fernando Valley, the Antelope Valley, and the San Gabriel Valley in the greater Los Angeles area.

Staff for Project Ecosystems

Clinical Psychology Graduate Assistants from CSPP-LA were the first direct service providers trained and utilized by Project Ecosystems under the supervision of a program manager. Subsequently, a hierarchical system of supervision and training similar to that for Project 12-Ways was developed. Furthermore, with geographic expansion, graduate students from other local universities have been sought. Training is similar to Project 12-Ways, although even more intensive hands-on training is employed, because Project Ecosystems staff do not have the breadth in behavior analysis and therapy that the Project 12-Ways staff have. Intensive training in behavior management and communication skills is provided to Project Ecosystems staff through work with profoundly retarded residents of Fairview Development Center. This experience has prepared staff especially well to subsequently provide treatment in the homes of less severe clients.

Referrals

All families are referred by the Developmental Disabilities Center of Orange County for Project Ecosystems. The program coordinator (caseworker) makes a recommendation to the unit psychologist; if both agree that services are necessary and Project Ecosystems is able to meet those needs, a referral is then made to the unit program director. The program manager of Project Ecosystems and the unit program director meet monthly to review cases and referrals. Typically, in order to be selected for Project Ecosystems, the family must be amenable to in-home services, and must be at risk of out-of-home placement or of child abuse or neglect. The typical target child is of school age, preferably 3 to 11 years old, with some acting-out behaviors (i.e., temper tantrums, aggressive acts, fire setting, stealing, or noncompliance). Older adolescents are also served. The parents and the children should be free of drug dependency, and should not have a history of schizophrenic behavior. Upon receiving the referral, Project Ecosystems graduate assistants and counselors initiate home visits.

Treatment Services

Most of the treatment services provided by Project Ecosystems are adaptations of those used by Project 12-Ways. They have been adapted for developmentally disabled children and their parents, and descriptions follow.

Basic skill training becomes even more salient than it is in Project 12-Ways, because of the more obvious and more frequent deficits of the children served by Project Ecosystems. Included are toilet training, nighttime enuresis, control of encopresis, self-dressing, self-hygiene, communication skills, and self-feeding.

The same stress reduction strategies described in Project 12-Ways families are used. Parents of developmentally disabled children are known to show higher levels of stress and depression than parents of nonhandicapped children. Beck Depression Inventories (Beck, Ward, Mendelsohn, & Erbaugh, 1961) are administered and monitored with all parents served.

Parents who have difficulty solving problems such as how to arrange child care and find transportation are provided with the structured *problem-solving* program used in Project 12-Ways.

Job search, *money management*, *nutrition training*, and *parent-child relationships training* are identical to the Project 12-Ways' services. However, *behavioral pediatrics* is a new category of service; if children fear medical procedures, symbolic modeling techniques are used to allay their fears, and parents are taught to monitor and comply with required medical regimens of their children.

Finally, *home safety and cleanliness* services are provided. The home safety program utilized by Project 12-Ways is also used on Project Ecosystems. A specially tailored home cleanliness program (Watson-Perczel, Lutzker, Greene, &

McGimpsey, 1988) provides education and training in reducing health hazards in homes.

RESULTS

Four levels of evaluating projects such as these (Lutzker, 1984; Lutzker, Wesch, & Rice, 1984) have been described. Clinical assessment and evaluation is defined as meaning that, whenever possible, data are collected directly on target and corollary behaviors. Although the majority of the data have little scientific merit, they provide tangible information for service providers to share with clients on their progress. Graduate assistants and counselors use data for supervision, and data can also be used therapeutically. For example, a mother may criticize her child less frequently after being asked to monitor the frequency of her criticisms. The second level of assessment is through single case experiments, or case studies (Lutzker, Campbell, & Watson-Perczel, 1984). These efforts produce sufficient and reliable data on individual families to be published in research periodicals. Publishing single case experiments, even with their limited external generality, provides the professional community with techniques and programs that might be replicable elsewhere.

Research using single subject designs with more than one family and research using group designs each represent a third level of assessment. Research of this kind suggests generality across families served, and provides suggestions for systematic replications in other settings.

Program evaluation represents a fourth level of evaluation. To date, the program evaluation data of interest on Project 12-Ways has been an examination of recidivism data. Clients served by Project 12-Ways in fiscal years in which they were terminated from services have been compared with clients served by DCFS in the same region, but who did not receive Project 12-Ways services. Each family is followed by the state for a maximum of four years, if there have been no subsequent incidents of abuse or neglect reported. Data have been gathered by sending code numbers of both groups to the Springfield State Central Register, where they are entered into the computers that record all indications of abuse and neglect.

Although this kind of program evaluation is replete with possible confounds, it offers some perspective of the overall impact of this multi-faceted project. Of additional interest would be data on the severity of abuse and other measures of outcome such as success in reaching clinical goals. Program evaluation for Project Ecosystems is taking the form of examining placements, reports of abuse or neglect, and cost-comparison data.

Three analyses of program evaluation of Project 12-Ways have shown significant differences in the number of indicated abuse and neglect incidences between Project 12-Ways clients and comparison groups (Lutzker & Rice, 1984, 1987; Lutzker, Wesch, & Rice, 1984). Lutzker and Rice (1984) compared 51 families served by Project 12-Ways to 46 DCFS comparison families. They found a 2% rate of abuse or neglect for Project 12-Ways families during treatment and an 11% rate for the comparison group. One year after services had been terminated, the Project 12-Ways families showed a 10% rate, while the comparison group was 21%. A chi-square analysis determined this difference to be significant at the .05 level. Lutzker, Wesch, and Rice (1984) reported on families over three different fiscal years. The first group of families was followed for 3 years posttreatment, the second group for 2 years, and the third group for 1 year.

For the 1980 groups, recidivism and repeat data were described cumulatively across years 1980–1983. The 1980 data report incidence results whereas the 1981, 1982, and 1983 data reflected recidivism data, that is, incidences reported after the termination of services. For 1980, the Project 12-Ways group rate of abuse and neglect was 3.9%; the comparison group was 26%. For 1981, the 12-Ways recidivism rate was 11.7%; the comparison group was 28.2%. For 1982, the Project 12-Ways group rate was 21.6%; the comparison group rate was 31.4%. For 1983, the Project 12-Ways group recidivism rate was 25.5%; the comparison group rate was 34.5%.

For the 1981 groups, the 1982 rate of recidivism for the Project 12-Ways group was 8%; the comparison group rate was 5%. The 1983 rate was 19% for the Project 12-Ways group and 17% for the comparison group. The one year follow-up on recidivism for the 1982 groups showed a 21% rate for the Project 12-Ways group, and a 31% rate for the comparison group.

Finally, Lutzker and Rice (1987) looked at 352 families over 5 different fiscal years. Once again significant differences were seen in that the overall rate of recidivism for Project 12-Ways was 21.3% and the comparison group rate was 28.5%.

To determine whether this difference was statistically significant, 2 x 2 chi-square analysis of independent samples was performed (Siegel, 1956). Project 12-Ways families were compared to comparison families, and families who were and were not recidivistic were compared. The obtained chi-square statistic was 4.894, df = 1, $p \leqslant .05$, which confirms the hypothesis that these groups are, indeed, statistically different. Because these data were cumulative, an analysis across years following termination could not be performed.

Overall, more than 1,000 families have been assisted by Project 12-Ways in 10 years. Although the differences between Project 12-Ways and the comparison group are less pronounced over the years, they still appear. Funding arrangements prevent "booster" treatment sessions for families who may become recidivistic. Also, it is important to bear in mind that the Project 12-Ways families examined in these comparisons include families who were terminated from services for a variety of reasons. Some were terminated because treatment was deemed to be successful, some because of failure to cooperate with treatment, and some because they refused treatment. Thus, it would be particularly interesting to know if families who were terminated because they reached their treatment goals were more successful (less recidivistic) than families who terminated services for other reasons.

As of Spring 1989 in Project Ecosystems, 75 high-risk families have been served. That is, in all cases the children were sufficiently handicapped that they were at risk for placement into a more restrictive setting or for abuse or neglect;

none have been placed out of the home and only one case of abuse/neglect has been reported.

FUTURE DIRECTIONS

Ecobehavioral approaches seem only logical; they are difficult to manage, yet offer the hope of success. Child abuse and neglect is a community problem in need of community solutions (Lutzker & Newman, 1986). Projects 12-Ways and Ecosystems each represent strong community involvement. Close cooperation with DCFS and other local health and mental health agencies facilitates Project 12-Ways' efforts. Similarly, the close cooperation with the Developmental Disabilities Center of Orange County enables Project Ecosystems to find and treat families in their homes. Working in close concert with the schools has also been necessary on both projects. Cooperation has generally been very good; many teachers having willingly collected data and helped to implement treatment programs.

Clinic-based university research without a service component certainly has its merits. Much can be learned from such endeavors; however, it is the authors' thesis that ecobehavioral approaches, utilizing the four levels of assessment that are presented in this chapter, can provide services that may actually lead to a reduction in risks for children. Future efforts should continue in this direction and need to focus more on prevention.

The authors' future research efforts will involve both systematic replication of previous work, and new directions.

Two new areas need exploration: 1) strategies to promote generalization of skills taught to *staff and parents*, and 2) the nature of functional families, such as how they spend their time and what activities they engage in with their children. At one level, staff are creative at developing new programs; however, they do not teach specific skills well, nor do they generalize teaching skills well unless specifically taught to do so (McGimsey, McRae, Helfer, Greene, & Lutzker, 1983). Thus, additional research must focus on this dimension of staff training. Also, much is to be learned from functional families. Collecting data about them and then finding ways to produce behavior change in dysfunctional families based upon that data represents a great challenge (Lutzker, Touchette, & Campbell, in press). Furthermore, through developing more careful and comprehensive assessment strategies it may be possible to better predict the particular services that might benefit a given family.

Finally, the age of electronics will continue to affect human services. Computer assisted instruction and video technology using self-modeling strategies (Dowrick & Dove, 1980) will become more dominant in these kinds of services.

REFERENCES

Azrin, H.H., & Besalel, V.B. (1980). *Job Club counselor's manual: A behavioral approach to vocational counseling.* Baltimore: University Park Press.

Azrin, N.H., & Foxx, R.M. (1974). *Toilet training in less than a day.* New York: Simon & Schuster.

Azrin, N.H., Naster, B.J., & Jones, R. (1973). Reciprocity counseling: A rapid learning-based procedure for marital counseling. *Behavior Research and Therapy, 11,* 365–382.

Azrin, N.H., Sneed, T.J., & Foxx, R.M. (1974). Dry bed training: A rapid method of eliminating bedwetting (enuresis) of the retarded. *Behavior Research and Therapy, 11,* 427–434.

Barone, V.J., Greene, B.F., & Lutzker, J.R. (1986). Home safety with families being treated for child abuse and neglect. *Behavior Modification, 10,* 93–114.

Beck, A.T., & Steer, R.A. (1984). Internal consistencies of the original and revised Beck Depression Inventories. *Journal of Clinical Psychology, 40,* 561–571.

Beck, A.T., Ward, C.H., Mendelsohn, M.J., & Erbaugh, J. (1961). An inventory for measuring depression. *Archives of General Psychiatry, 4,* 561–571.

Bell, R.Q., & Harper, L.V. (1977). *Child effects on adults.* Hillsdale, NJ: Lawrence Erlbaum Associates.

Bennie, E., & Sclar, A. (1969). The battered child syndrome. *American Journal of Psychiatry, 125,* 975–979.

Blumberg, M.L. (1974). Psychopathology of the abusing parent. *American Journal of Psychotherapy, 28,* 21–29.

Borck, L.E., & Fawcett, S.B. (1982). *Learning counseling and problem-solving skills.* New York: Haworth Press.

Burgess, R.L. (1979). Child abuse: A social interactional analysis. In B.B. Lahey & A.E. Kazdin (Eds.), *Advances in clinical child psychology* (Vol. 2). New York: Plenum.

Burgess, R.L., & Youngblade, L.M. (in press). Social incompetence and the intergenerational transmission of abusive parental practices. In R. Geles, G. Hotaling, D. Finkelhor, & M. Straus (Eds). *New directions in family violence research.* Beverly Hills: Sage Publications.

Campbell, R.V., O'Brien, S., Bickett, A.D., & Lutzker, J.R. (1983). In-home parent-training, treatment of migraine headaches, and marital counseling as an eco-behavioral approach to prevent child abuse. *Journal of Behavior Therapy and Experimental Psychiatry, 14,* 147–154.

Campbell, R.V., Twardosz, S., Lutzker, J.R., & Cuvo, A.J. (1983, May). Teaching child interaction skills to child abusive parents. Paper presented as a part of a symposium, *Project 12-Ways: An ecobehavioral approach to child abuse/neglect.* Paper presented at the ninth annual conventional of the Association for Behavior Analysis, Milwaukee, WI.

Crozier, J., & Katz, R.C. (1979). Social learning treatment of child abuse. *Journal of Behavior Therapy and Experimental Psychiatry, 10,* 213–220.

Dachman, R.S., Halasz, M.M., Bickett, A.D., & Lutzker, J.R. (1984). A home based ecobehavioral parent-training and generalization package with a neglectful mother. *Education and Treatment of Children, 7,* 183–202.

Delgado, L.E., & Lutzker, J.R. (1988). Training young parents to identify and report their children's illnesses. *Journal of Applied Behavioral Analysis, 21,* 311–319.

Doctor, R.M., & Singer, E.M. (1978). Behavioral intervention strategies with child abusive parents. *Child Abuse and Neglect: The International Journal, 2,* 57–68.

Dowrick, P.W., & Dove, C. (1980). The use of self-modeling to improve the swimming performance of spina bifida children. *Journal of Applied Behavior Analysis, 66,* 394–397.

Dubanski, R.A., Evans, I.M., & Higuchi, A.A. (1978). Analysis and treatment of child abuse: A set of behavioral propositions. *Child Abuse and Neglect, 2,* 153–172.

Forehand, R.L., & McMahon, R.J. (1981). *Helping the non-compliant child: A Clinician's guide to parent training.* New York: Guilford Press.

Friedrich, W.N., & Friedrich, W.L. (1981). Psychosocial assets of handicapped and nonhandicapped children. *American Journal of Mental Deficiency, 85,* 551–553.

Garbarino, J., & Sherman, D. (1980). Identifying high-risk neighborhoods. In J. Garbarino & S.H. Stocking (Eds.). *Protecting children from abuse and neglect: Developing and maintaining effective support systems for families.* San Francisco: Jossey-Bass.

Gelles, R.J. (1973). Child abuse as psychopathology: A sociological critique and reformulation. *American Journal of orthopsychiatry, 43,* 611–621.

Gil, D.G. (1975). Unraveling child abuse. *American Journal of Orthopsychiatry, 45,* 346–356.

Green, A.H., Gaines, R.W., & Sandgrund, A. (1974). Child abuse: Pathological syndrome of family interaction. *American Journal of Psychiatry, 131,* 882–886.

Helfer, R.B. (1982). A review of the literature on the prevention of child abuse and neglect. *Child Abuse and Neglect, 6,* 251–261.

Isaacs, C. (1981). A brief review of the characteristics of abuse-prone parents. *The Behavior Therapist, 4* (5), 5–8.

Jacobson, E. (1983). *Progressive relaxation.* Chicago: University of Chicago Press.

Kempe, C.H., & Helfer, R.E. (Eds.). (1972). *Helping the battered child and his family.* Philadelphia: J.B. Lippincott.

Kempe, C.H., Silverman, F.N., Steele, B.F., Droegemueller, W., & Silver, H.K. (1962). The battered-child syndrome. *Journal of the American Medical Association, 181,* 105–112.

Lutzker, J.R. (1984). Project 12-Ways: Treating child abuse and neglect from an ecobehavioral perspective. In R.F. Dangel & R.A. Polster (Eds.), *Parent training: Formulations of research and practice* (pp. 260–291). New York: Guilford Press.

Lutzker, J.R., Campbell, R.V., & Watson-Perczel, M.

(1984). Utility of the case study method on the treatment of several problems of a neglectful family. *Education and Treatment of Children, 7,* 315–333.

Lutzker, J.R., Frame, R.E., & Rice, J.M. (1982). Project 12-Ways: An ecobehavioral approach to the treatment and prevention of child abuse and neglect. *Education and Treatment of Children, 5,* 141–155.

Lutzker, S.Z., Lutzker, J.R., Braunling-McMorrow, D., & Eddleman, J. (1987). Prompting to increase mother-baby stimulation with single mothers. *Journal of Child and Adolescent Psychotherapy, 4,* 3–12.

Lutzker, J.R., McGimsey, J.F., McRae, S., & Campbell, R.V. (1983). Behavioral parent-training: There's so much more to do. *The Behavior Therapist, 6,* 110–112.

Lutzker, J.R., Megson, D.A., Webb, M.E., & Dachman, R.S. (1985). Validating and training adult-child interaction skills to professionals and to parents indicated for child abuse and neglect. *Child and Adolescent Psychotherapy, 2,* 91–104.

Lutzker, J.R., & Newman, M.R. (1986). Child abuse and neglect: Community problem, community solutions. *Education and Treatment of Children, 9,* 344–354.

Lutzker, J.R., & Rice, J.M. (1984). Project 12-Ways: Measuring outcome of a large in-home service for treatment and prevention of child abuse and neglect. *Child Abuse and Neglect, 8,* 519–524.

Lutzker, J.R., & Rice, J.M. (1987). Using recidivism data to evaluate Project 12-Ways: An ecobehavioral approach to the treatment and prevention of child abuse and neglect. *Journal of Family Violence, 2,* 283–290.

Lutzker, J.R., Touchette, P.E., & Campbell, R.V. (in press). Parental positive reinforcement might make a difference: A rejoinder to Forehand. *Child and Family Behavior Therapy.*

Lutzker, J.R., Wesch, D., & Rice, J.M. (1984). A review of Project 12-Ways: An ecobehavioral approach to the treatment and prevention of child abuse and neglect. *Advances in Behaviour Research and Therapy, 6,* 63–73. Indexed in the *Inventory of Marriage and Therapy*, Vol. *XI*, Family Resource Center. 1985.

McGimsey, J.F., McRae, S., Helfer, S., Greene, B.F., & Lutzker, J.R. (1983, May). *The parent-trainer: Conductor and engineer aboard the behavioral express.* Presented as a poster at the ninth annual convention of the Association for Behavior Analysis, Milwaukee, WI.

Novaco, R.W. (1986). Anger as a clinical and social problem. In R.J. Blanchard & D.C. Blanchard (Eds.), *Advances in the study of aggression*, (Vol. 2). New York: Academic Press.

Nurse, S.M. (1964). Familial patterns of parents who abuse their children. *Smith College Studies on Social Work, 32,* 11–25.

Ory, M.G., & Earp, J.L. (1980). Child maltreatment: A analysis of familial and institutional predictors. *Journal of Family Issues, 1,* 339–356.

Parke, R.D. (1977). Socialization into child abuse: A social interactional perspective. In J.L. Tapp & F.L. Levin (Eds.). *Law; justice and the individual in society: Psychological and legal issues.* New York: Holt.

Patterson, G.R. (1982). *Coercive family process.* Eugene, OR: Castalia.

Rice, J.M., & Lutzker, J.R. (1983). Group and individual feedback, public posting, and prompting to increase counselor supervision. *The Clinical Supervisor, 1,* 77–90.

Rosenberg, M.S., & Reppucci, N.D. (1985). Primary prevention of child abuse. *Journal of Consulting and Clinical Psychology, 53,* 576–585.

Rosenfield-Schlichter, M.D., Sarber, R.E., Bueno, G., Green, B.F., & Lutzker, J.R. (1983). Maintaining accountability for an ecobehavioral treatment of one aspect of child neglect: Personal cleanliness. *Education and Treatment of Children, 6,* 153–164.

Rutter, M. (1979). Protective factors in children's responses to stress and disadvantage. In M.W. Kent & J.E. Rolf (Eds.), *Primary Prevention of Psychopathology* (Vol. III) Hanover, NH: University Press of New England.

Sanders, M.R., & Dadds, M.R. (1982). The effects of planned activities and child management training. An analysis of setting generalization. *Behavior Therapy, 13,* 452–461.

Sarber, R.E., Halasz, M.M., Messmer, M.C., Bickett, A.D., & Lutzker, J.R. (1983). Teaching menu planning and grocery shopping skills to a mentally retarded mother. *Mental Retardation, 21,* 101–106.

Schilling, D., & Poppen, R. (1983). Behavioral relaxation training assessment. *Journal of Behavior Therapy and Experimental Psychiatry, 14,* 99–107.

Siegel, S. (1956). *Nonparamentric statistics for the behavioral services.* New York: McGraw-Hill.

Taylor, C. (1973). The battered child. In D. Clifton & J.G. Wells (Eds.), *Deviancy and the family.* Philadelphia: F.A. Davis.

Tearnan, B., & Lutzker, J.R. (1980). A contracting "package" in the treatment of marital problems: A case study. *American Journal of Family Therapy, 8,* 24, 31.

Tertinger, D.A., Greene, B.F., & Lutzker, J.R. (1984). Home safety: Development and validation of one component of an ecobehavioral treatment program for abused and neglected children. *Journal of Applied Behavior Analysis, 17,* 159–177.

Tizard, J. (1975). Three dysfunctional environmental influences in development: Malnutrition, nonaccidental injury, and child minding. *Postgraduate Medical Journal, 51,* 19–27.

Twardosz, S., Schwartz, S., Fox, J. & Cunningham, J.L. (1979). Development and evaluation of a system to measure affectionate behavior. *Behavioral Assessment, 1,* 177–190.

Wahler, R.G. (1980). The insular mother: Her problems in parent-child treatment. *Journal of Applied Behavior Analysis, 13,* 207–219.

Wahler, R.G., Leske, G., & Rogers, E.S. (1979). The insular family: A deviance support system for oppositional children. In L.A. Hamerlynck (Eds.), *Behavioral systems for the developmentally disabled: I. School and family environments*, New York: Brunner/Mazel.

Wasserman, S. 1967. The abused parent of the abused child. *Children, 14,* 175–179.

Watson-Perczel, M., Lutzker, J.R., Greene, B.F., & McGimpsey, B.J. (1988). Assessment and modification of home cleanliness among families adjudicated for child neglect. *Behavior Modification, 12,* 57–81.

Wikler, L.M. (1986). Periodic stresses of families of older mentally retarded children: An exploratory study. *American Journal of Mental Deficiency, 90,* 703–706.

Wolpe, J., & Lazarus, A. A. (1966). *Behavior therapy techniques: A guide to the treatment of neuroses.* Oxford: Pergamon Press.

EVALUATION AND POLICY

CHAPTER 21

Evaluating Family Support Programs

Larry K. Irvin

Because this book presents descriptions of model demonstrations of family support programs, it will be helpful to describe how evaluation relates to those demonstrations of support and education services for families that include a member who has handicapping conditions. Paine, Bellamy, and Wilcox (1984) have described ways that necessary and useful social services can be developed based on social scientific research, field testing, and evaluation. The initial phase of such model development involves identifying specific techniques that alleviate a social problem. The technologies (e.g., effective teaching, motivation, and learning strategies) are most often established initially under experimental and controlled circumstances. A second phase is required if these techniques are to be useful in a practical sense; they must be tested and documented (or evaluated) as feasible and ecologically valid within an actual service delivery system.

These phases of model development are illustrated throughout the preceding chapters. For example, in the family support work of Singer and colleagues involving stress management, parent training in child behavior management/ teaching, and volunteer support, techniques were first identified that previously had been documented as effective under certain circumstances. Progressive muscle relaxation, self-monitoring, and self-control have been researched widely and demonstrated as effective techniques for stress reduction by adults (Wool-

folk & Lehrer, 1984). Similarly, other research documents that volunteers facilitate the creation of social support networks for children with severe handicaps (Voeltz, 1982). And behavioral parent training in child management and teaching has been implemented effectively with a wide variety of parents (Baker, 1984).

Model demonstration efforts then proceed through several related steps. For example, Singer and colleagues assembled a novel application of techniques is assembled to address the family support goals of increasing child participation and integration in home and community activities, and decreasing parental distress in families that include children with severe handicaps. These family support and education efforts were designed for delivery within an existing service system; the family supports fit the missions of local agencies serving families with children who have handicaps. Finally, the family support programs with those local agencies have been field tested in order to evaluate it from a variety of perspectives.

Many contributions to this volume describe such an approach to development of family support program services. This chapter presents the foundations of an evaluation strategy that many have used to develop, describe, improve, and document the effects of our model demonstrations of family support programs.

Before a full-scale description of the evaluation of family support programs is presented a definition of evaluation will be helpful.

This chapter was developed in part with funding from Grant #008730149 from the U.S. Department of Education. The views stated herein are not necessarily those of the funders.

EVALUATION

The prospect of a program evaluation seems to cause many people involved in that program to consider everything that they might be doing wrong, and to expect that someone will judge them harshly when the evaluation is done. This pattern illustrates a fundamental misunderstanding of evaluation; from such a perspective evaluation is viewed narrowly as judgment of inadequacy, inefficiency, or ineffectiveness.

Although judgment of value is one of the purposes that evaluation can serve, it is certainly not the only, nor even the main purpose for evaluating family support efforts. Judgments about value represent only one application of evaluation. Program development, description, monitoring, modification, documentation, and validation are other applications of evaluation that are equally useful. Evaluation is a multifaceted tool for obtaining information that can be useful for making a variety of decisions.

This chapter is a forum for the gospel of multiple evaluation, or the multiple uses of information to enable different types of decisionmaking. Multiple evaluation concerns are always relevant. Goals, resources, and program processes are as important to evaluate as the outcomes or effects of family support and education services. And, to be useful, evaluation of family support program efforts ultimately must be able to serve the needs of many participants and decisionmakers, including those to whom the program provides services, those who provide and deliver the program services, those who administrate the program, and those who develop and fund the program.

Information needs vary among participants and decisionmakers based upon what types of interest(s) they have in program efforts, and what types of decisions they must make. Both family members and professionals make day-to-day decisions about needs for diversity and individualization of family support efforts. Program developers and administrators make policy decisions and changes in support and education programs as needed. Others make decisions about eligibility for services, staffing, and general guidelines for service provision. All of these types of decisions involve people continually in

formative evaluation, or using information to learn about and improve program quality.

Other decisions focus on the political viability and social value as well as the funding of entire programs. These latter uses of information to make decisions about the success or failure of programs, and other judgments of value, are known as *summative* evaluation. These involve documenting and defending all aspects of family support to those who decide the fates of such programs.

In any family support effort, needs exist for information to facilitate decisionmaking in all of these areas. Meeting those information needs requires evaluation from multiple perspectives. To describe and/or judge the quality of family support services for any purpose, evaluation strategies need to be developed that help people to view those programs in terms of impact on, and perceptions of, all people who participate in and make decisions about the programs, including parents, children, families, professionals, and funders.

Multiple measures are essential for addressing each evaluation concern, because the accuracy and validity of any single type of measurement are not by any means perfect. Multiple measures of different types—ratings, surveys, in-depth interviews, and direct observations—enable convergent and divergent evaluative interpretations based on source and type of measurement. Assessments of program effects or outcomes can be isolated from measurement error due to different types of measurement, including self-report, observations, and so forth. This is the "multitrait, multimethod" approach to measurement that Dunst and colleagues use in their assessment efforts, described in Chapter 8.

Evaluation is not unitary. It takes different forms for different purposes. To know which forms of evaluation to use, and how to apply evaluation tools in the development and demonstration of family support programs, at least three general types of questions and their corollaries need to be answered. First, what types of decisions about which aspects of the program need to be made and when? Are program goals, resources, processes, and/or effects the focus? And is the program currently being developed and/or field tested, or is it in place and ongoing?

Second, who will make which decisions and in what decisionmaking roles? Are the decisionmakers in the role(s) of program administrators, program implementors, program consumers, and/or program developers and funders? And are they deciding about program development, modification, and improvement, or about program value and viability? Finally, what kinds of information are needed and in what formats for decisionmaking? Is information from self-report surveys or questionnaires sufficient, or are direct and independent observations required? The answers to these questions enable and guide the design of appropriate evaluation strategies for model demonstrations of family support programs.

DEFINING FAMILY SUPPORT

Before detailing specific strategies for evaluating model demonstrations of family support programs, the issue of defining family support should be addressed. Clarity is essential not only for the purposes of guiding program development and implementation, but also for the purposes of directing program evaluation efforts.

Just as evaluation is multifaceted rather than unitary, so is family support. The possible variations in the forms that family support can take are numerous, as the contributions to this volume demonstrate.

The clear implication of this diversity is that a conceptual framework is essential, not only for development of needed family supports, but also for subsequent evaluation to be meaningful, and for all aspects of family support programs to be understood in the most comprehensive manner possible. A conceptual framework provides a basis for decisions about development, delivery, and evaluation of family support programs. Goals that guide program efforts, strategies and resources that enable programs to provide services, processes that are used to implement actual services, and effects and outcomes that should result from services are all guided by conceptual vision, whether or not that vision is made explicit. The same conceptual framework is important in subsequent evaluation, because it directs decisions about: which evaluation questions are meaningful, which measurements

should be used to assess goals, resources, processes, and outcomes; and how to approach interpretation of the results of evaluation. The utility of evaluation of family support program efforts is optimal when it is directed by the same vision that guides the development and implementation of the program itself.

Effective evaluation cannot occur outside the substantive context of family support programs. Both program development and evaluation should be based on the same underlying conceptual framework—whether it is made explicit or remains implicit. And, the more explicit the conceptual framework for program development purposes, the better the subsequent foundations for evaluation to characterize interdependencies among program goals, resources, processes and outcomes (Dunst & Trivette, 1988).

A couple of examples are useful here. Dunst et al. (1988) have been involved in the development and evaluation of early intervention services for mitigating the potentially deleterious effects of developmental disabilities and delay on children and their families. Dunst and his colleagues have adopted an integrated social systems framework to guide both their early intervention program development efforts and related evaluation activities. They have defined their conceptual foundation operationally as comprising social network, human ecology, help-seeking, and adaptational theories. Child development, parent-child interactions, parent well-being, and family integrity have served as conceptual guides to the development of social support program goals and resources. And program processes to reach those goals, as well as desired outcomes of intervention efforts, have been derived directly from the overriding integrated social systems framework. Additionally, Dunst and colleagues' selection of measurements to evaluate any aspect of program development, implementation, and effect has been guided by the same conceptual foundations.

A second example comes from the work on development and evaluation of community-based family support and education services at the Oregon Research Institute. As is detailed in Chapters 1, 5, 6, 9, and 19, Singer, Irvin, Hawkins, Biglan, Cooley, Irvine, have used family systems (Turnbull & Turnbull, 1986) and demoralization theories (Breslau & Davis, 1986) as

Table 1. SAEF model evaluation

Model components	Multiple evaluation concerns	Specific evaluation questions	Measures
Participants	Family characteristics	Structure Income Education	Demographic questionnaire
	Child characteristics	Age Adaptive functioning Maladaptive functioning	Demographic questionnaire Behavior Development Survey
	Family stress and coping	Social networks and satisfaction Marital relationship Sources of strain and personal resources	Inventory of Parents' Experiences Dyadic Adjustment Scale Questionnaire on Resources and Stress Parent Stress Questionnaire "Hassles" Scale
Case management services	Fidelity of implemention of case management services	Nature and frequency Elapsed Time	Tracking of services by case managers
	Social validation	Family satisfaction Family valuing of case management goals and roles Family perceptions of effectiveness	Social validation questionnaire
Parent training	Fidelity of implementation	Quality of training	Implementation checklist
	Parent involvement	Parent attendance Homework assignments	Project records
	Parent change	Clear directions to child Praising child	LIFE Observational Codes
	Child change	Follow parent directions Maladaptive behavior	LIFE Observational Codes
	Social validation	Family valuing of training Family perceptions of effectiveness Family satisfaction	Social validation questionnaire
Behavioral counseling Stress management	Fidelity of implementation	Quality of counseling	Implementation checklist
	Parent involvement	Parent attendance Relaxtion practice Cognitive modification practice	Project records Homework 2-week log
	Parent change	Psychosomatic Mood/affect Stressors	Beck Depression Inventory State-Trait Anxiety Inventory "Hassles" Scale

(continued)

Table 1. (*continued*)

Model components	Multiple evaluation concerns	Specific evaluation questions	Measures
	Social validation	Family valuing of stress management goals Family perception of effectiveness Family satisfaction	Social validation questionnaire
Depression treatment	Fidelity of implementation	Quality of treatment	Implementation checklist
	Parent involvement	Parent attendance Parent practice	Project records
	Parent change	Mood/affect Stressors	Beck Depression Inventory State-Trait Anxiety Inventory
	Social validation	Family valuing of depression treatment goals Family perception of effectiveness	Social validation questionnaire
Respite/volunteer services	Fidelity of implementation of respite/volunteer services	Hours billed to respite providers Records of volunteer activities	Respite provider records Volunteer logs
	Social validation	Family valuing of respite/volunteers Family perceptions of effectiveness Family satisfaction, Volunteer satisfaction	Social validation questionnaire and testimonials
School/home coordination	Extent of requests for school/home coordination	Consultation Information/referral IEP Assistance	Tracking by case managers
	Parent/teacher interactions	General: Nature and frequency IEP participation Communication skills	Parent/teacher interviews and logs
	Social validation	Family valuing of home/school coordination Family perceptions of effectiveness Family satisfaction	Tracking by case managers and social validation questionnaire
		Teacher valuing of home/school coordination Teacher perceptions of effectiveness Teacher satisfaction	Social validation questionnaire

conceptual foundations for guiding program efforts with families of school-age children who have developmental disabilities. Table 1 shows how the conceptual framework (model components) has been used as a basis for identifying multiple evaluation concerns that lead to specific evaluation questions, which have been the basis for specific multiple measurements for all model components. The selection of a skills focus for interventions with multiple members of families came directly from previous theoretical work and empirical demonstration regarding amelioration of demoralizing effects of chronic stress and strain in families of children with disability. Thus the program goals, processes, and desired outcomes all have their foundations in preventions of the sequelae of demoralization in multiple subsystems of these families, including out-of-home placement of children with disabilities, family break-up, abuse and neglect, and so forth. And, the selection of multiple measures for evaluation of program goals, implementation, and outcomes has been directed by the same conceptual foundations that have guided program development and improvement.

Dunst et al. (1988) note that at least two major benefits derive from the use of conceptual foundations for program development and evaluation: 1) clearer specification of support interventions is facilitated, and 2) contribution is made to theory development (for ongoing refinement and clarification of information about supporting families). Thus, conceptual frameworks should and do guide program development and implementation. And the same conceptual frameworks enable educated predictions about the aspects of support interventions that are likely to influence the outcomes of concern. As a result, conceptual vision then dictates which evaluation questions to ask, and what measurement strategies as well as specific instrumentation to use for valid reflections of relationships among goals, resources, processes, and outcomes.

DECISION-ORIENTED EVALUATION OF FAMILY SUPPORT PROGRAMS

Now that some clear definitions are established with regard to evaluation, model demonstration, and conceptual frameworks surrounding family support, a discussion of evaluation of family support programs will be more meaningful. A comprehensive decision-oriented evaluation approach that is known by the acronym CIPP—for Context, Input, Process, and Product evaluation (see Stufflebeam, 1983) is well suited to application in family support programs. Use of the CIPP approach facilitates multiple perspective evaluation. After a description of the components of the overall CIPP strategy, an illustration is provided to demonstrate how CIPP evaluation has actually been applied in a demonstration of a community-based family support program.

Throughout the preceding pages of this chapter, evaluation has been characterized as equally applicable to any aspect of family support programs, such as goals/objectives, strategies and necessary resources, implementation processes, and outcomes or effects. This multiple perspective is an essential foundation, if evaluation is to lead to comprehensive understanding of family support programs and their effects on those they serve.

An indisputable reality of family support programs is that multiple and often competing interests and agendas exist among the families who are consumers, the professionals who are service providers, the politicians who are funders, and the other audiences and decisionmakers who assume a variety of different and influential roles in human service efforts. For example, families may see direct cash disbursements to be spent at family discretion as the most useful of possible family supports, but funders may be motivated primarily by budget consciousness in their deliberations, and service providers may feel that their guidance in identification and selection of supports is essential to assure optimum benefit and avoid abuse of the service system. The implication here is that before setting family support program goals and designing and delivering support services, decisionmakers need to be aware of the multiple contexts in which such a program will operate. Multiple perspective evaluation can provide that necessary information.

CIPP is especially applicable as a multiple evaluation strategy because it enables individuals to view programs from at least four different perspectives that any or all decisionmakers may find important: *context* (the goals and objectives that guide the design and delivery of programs), *inputs* (the system capabilities, alternative strategies, and resources that are necessary to enable delivery of a program's services), *processes* (what actually happens as programs are being implemented), and *products* (the outcomes or effects of programs).

In Chapter 8, Dunst and colleagues have noted briefly their use of a CIPP evaluation strategy as the guiding structure for their program evaluation efforts. That discussion is expanded here to provide a more detailed description and demonstration of actual application of CIPP evaluation within a family support program.

In the CIPP approach, *evaluation* is defined essentially as it is in this chapter, as the provision and interpretation of information to enable program development, design, and delivery decisions by those who must decide about why, whether, when, and how services will be fashioned and provided. Therefore, evaluation exists to serve any of a number of different kinds of decisionmaking.

Context Evaluation   Some decisions must be made about the *context* in which programs will operate. That is, information is sometimes needed about goals and objectives that guide programs as they exist from day-to-day and across larger time frames. Typically, the type of evaluation that occurs to assist in the setting of program goals and objectives is called *needs assessment*. This type of evaluation is guided by questions such as: What are the goals of the family support program of interest? What should they be, according to any or all individuals or groups who have an interest in the program? How can consensual goal priorities be set, especially if different stakeholders have different values for what family support should try to accomplish and how it should do so? What needs attention in the family support program of interest? What should the family support program try to accomplish? The goals and objectives that direct family support program efforts can be determined empirically through evaluation that accomplishes needs assessment. Evaluation to assist in setting goals and objectives can also focus on making explicit the conceptual foundations (the vision) that will guide program efforts.

Another approach to evaluation of the context of family support programs is called *social validation* (Wolf, 1978). In social validation, the significance, acceptability, and/or importance of goals and objectives are evaluated by the people who are affected by their use. In addition to simple documentation of the nature and extent of the values and consensus therein, the idea behind such evaluation is ultimately to enable demonstration of the degree to which program processes and effects are influenced by social valid-

ity, that is to show to what degree the consensual valuing of goals influences outcomes of interventions. Table 1 shows that the SAEF program at the Oregon Research Institute has attempted to accomplish social validation of every model component. In context evaluation of this type, family members rate the acceptability, importance, and effects. Goals and objectives of each model component, as each component has occurred to families, volunteers, and so forth have been presented, and ratings of importance have been requested. As data presented in Chapters 5 and 6 show, the participants in our SAEF model family support programs valued all component goals highly.

Input Evaluation   Other decisions need to be made about what strategies to use in the design and delivery of family support programs. In a related manner, decisions need to be made about alternatives regarding the resources that will or should be used and how to allocate them. Information is often needed about how programs can maximize the likelihood of being successful, and conversely, about how to avoid program designs that will predictably fail or, at a minimum, waste resources. This type of evaluation is often called a *systems* or *feasibility study*, and is guided by questions such as: What plans of action are required to meet identified needs of families served by the program? Are some better suited to certain families than to others? What different approaches to program design and delivery are available? What is the value of each to different participants and decisionmakers? What are actual and potential problems, barriers, constraints, and limitations related to each alternative? What is the likelihood that a potential strategy can be implemented as proposed and will achieve desired results? What training and levels of staffing or other resources will be required to ensure quality implementation of a family support program?

Examples of input evaluation can also be drawn from the SAEF program. These have taken the form of clear documentation of who is served by the family support efforts (e.g., a high proportion of lower income families) and the level of expertise required by staff for adequate provision of those services.

Process Evaluation   Other decisions need

to be made about the day-to-day activities that define a program. Information is often needed about what is actually occurring, regardless of what was planned. Using information to make decisions in this manner is called *implementation evaluation* or *program documentation*. This type of evaluation is used most often to facilitate decisions about how to change or adjust programs to make improvements, or simply to record and document what is actually happening. These evaluation efforts are guided by questions such as: How many families are being served? When, how often, and where are they being served? Are services provided on schedule, and if so, whose schedule? What services do families actually get? Is there variability in services depending on where families live? Are budgets for services being used effectively?

In the SAEF program process evaluation is accomplished in several ways. The primary effort in this regard is the use of a Fidelity of Implementation Checklist to document what actually happens as each of the model components is implemented. Another type of process evaluation that is used involves tracking of participation by families (see Chapter 5 by Hawkins and Singer), case managers, educators (see Chapter 7 by Walker), and volunteers (see Chapter 9 by Cooley) in the different program components. Also, attendance, homework, practice, and variety and cost of activities are all documented.

Product Evaluation Finally, some decisions need to be made about the continuation, expansion, or termination of the various aspects of family support programs. Information is needed to determine the effects that family support programs have and how those effects occur. Product evaluation is guided by questions such as: How effective is the program? How does it reach its goals (or other outcomes)? Is it worth what it costs (worth can be referenced to any relevant consideration—money, time, political value, effort, returns, etc.)?

The SAEF program measures the effects of: 1) stress management and parent training on demoralization (see Chapter 5 by Hawkins and Singer, for documentation of significant effects of stress management and depression interventions); 2) behavioral parent training on parenting skills, as well as on child participation, follow-

ing directions, maladaptive behavior, and integration (see Chapter 6 by Singer, Irvin, & Irvine for documentation of significant effects of such intervention); 3) communication and cooperation training on teachers' and parents' interaction skills (see Chapter 7 by Walker for documentation); and 4) participation in program activities on parent, teacher and volunteer perceptions of program impact.

Using CIPP for Program Improvement and Accountability

A principal feature of the CIPP approach to evaluation is its flexibility for application to decisionmaking needs that are related to either program development and improvement (formative evaluation) or program documentation and accountability (summative evaluation). As Table 2 shows, Context, Input, Process, and Product evaluation can all be applied for both formative and summative purposes.

Table 2 demonstrates that "formative" evaluation of Context, Input, Process and/or Product involves the provision and interpretation of information to assist in decisionmaking for purposes of planning, monitoring, controlling quality, and improving programs. Table 2 also shows that "summative" evaluation of any of these types involves the provision and interpretation of information to assist in decisionmaking related to documenting and defending programs. All aspects of family support programs are related to CIPP in some manner: needs, goals and objectives; strategies for implementation and related resources; actual methods of service delivery; and interim as well as final results. Any or all of the aspects of family support programs can be evaluated for either the general formative purposes of planning and changing, or the summative purposes of documenting and defending.

An Example of Application of CIPP

The Support And Education for Families (SAEF) model demonstration project has been developed, implemented, and evaluated using the CIPP decision-oriented approach. Chapters 1, 5, 6, 7, 9, and 19 by Singer, Irvin, Hawkins, Biglan, Cooley, Irvine, and Walker (respectively) have presented descriptions of model components and related empirical outcomes in

Table 2. Formative and summative evaluation for decisionmaking

	Context (or goal-related) Decisions	Input (or design-related) Decisions	Process (or implementation-related) Decisions	Product (or outcomes-related) Decisions
Formative evaluation for program development and improvement	Provides information to assist in identification of needs, and development of goals, objectives and values.	Provides information to assist in identification, development, and improvement of alternative plans for use of strategies and resources to achieve goals.	Provides information to assist in identification and improvement of actual implementation processes.	Provides information to assist in identification and improvement of results for quality control.
Summative evaluation for program documentation and accountability	Provides information to assist in documenting and justifying goals, objectives and values.	Provides information to assist in documenting and justifying actual strategy and resource plans used to guide program activities.	Provides information to assist in documenting and justifying the actual program processes used, including modifications.	Provides information to assist in documenting and justifying all results of program.

detail. A summary is presented that demonstrates how the CIPP approach has been applied.

The SAEF model has several major components: 1) behavioral counseling for stress management and depression (see Chapter 5 by Hawkins & Singer, and Chapter 19 by Biglan); 2) parent training in child behavior development (see Chapter 6 by Singer, Irvin, & Irvine); 3) case management, respite care, and volunteer services (see Chapter 9 by Cooley); and 4) school-home coordination (see Chapter 7 by Walker). The conceptual framework from which these components are derived has two primary foundations (see Chapter 1 by Singer and Irvin): 1) amelioration of the deleterious effects of stress in families, and 2) integration of children with severe handicaps into home and community life.

Table 1 (see p. 332) presented the SAEF model components in detail, with related multiple evaluation concerns and multiple specific evaluation questions, as well as the names and sources of the multiple measurements that are used to address each question.

Table 1 also demonstrated that this approach includes *context*, *input*, *process*, and *product*

evaluation. For example, to evaluate the stress-management part of the behavioral counseling component, social validation measures (for context evaluation), parent involvement data (for input evaluation), Fidelity of Implementation and Parent Involvement measures (for process evaluation), and parent change data (for product evaluation) have been collected.

Table 3 illustrates how needed information was identified to assist in making decisions related to the contexts, inputs, processes, and products of the SAEF program for both formative and summative purposes. The entries in Table 3 are the specific evaluation questions from the third column of Table 1.

As Table 3 shows, some information has been used for both formative and summative purposes. Context data on the value and/or importance of goals and objectives has been used just as effectively for program planning or modification purposes as for justification of program foundations after the fact. Similarly, process data have been used to improve programs and to document what happened during program implementation.

Table 3. Questions guiding CIPP evaluation of SAEF program

	Context (or goal-related) Decisions	Input (or design-related) Decisions	Process (or implementation-related) Decisions	Product (or outcomes-related) Decisions
Formative evaluation for program development and improvement	Importance or value of goals to those affected by SAEF Program (parents, teachers, volunteers, etc.)?	Who should the SAEF Program serve? Expertise needed by parent trainers, behavioral counselors, respite and volunteer services providers, and educators? Necessary backup referral and treatment services?	Fidelity of Implementation? Satisfaction with process? Parent attendance, involvement and practice? Acceptability of program processes?	Interim effects: quality of homework and practice? parent perceptions of effects?
Summative evaluation for program documentation and accountability	Importance or value of goals to those affected by SAEF Program (parents, teachers, volunteers, etc.)?	Characteristics of families served? Family satisfaction with competence of staff? Cost effectiveness of family services?	Fidelity of implementation? Satisfaction with Process? Parent Attendance, involvement and practice? Acceptability of program processes?	Parent change on communication, stress, depression and training measures? Child change on integration, following directions and maladaptive behavior measures? Parent, teacher, and volunteer perceptions of effects?

The CIPP strategy has been useful in the SAEF program development, refinement, and evaluation efforts, largely because it is decision-oriented. The CIPP approach has served to focus thinking about program design and improvement into practical and functional evaluation questions. Rather than trying to ask questions about overall SAEF model viability and value, the evaluation process has involved identifying types of decisions that need to be made (both formative and summative) and the information necessary to make them. And the CIPP approach enables selectivity regarding the evaluation questions that are asked; only the questions that facilitate decisions about the SAEF program and related concerns are presented.

ISSUES AND PROBLEMS IN THE EVALUATION OF FAMILY SUPPORT PROGRAMS

In this concluding section, a brief discussion of relevant issues and problems is presented. The discussion is not intended to be exhaustive, but rather serves to identify and emphasize the most important concerns. Two general types of evaluation issues and problems exist: conceptual and methodological.

Conceptual Issues[1]

Typically, little disagreement exists regarding the broad goals of family support programs. They are usually aimed at: 1) enabling people

---

[1]John Agosta, author of Chapter 12, contributed substantially to these analyses of conceptual and methodological issues. His insightful contributions are gratefully acknowledged.

with disabilities to live at home with their families, 2) ensuring that people with disabilities get necessary services, and 3) enhancing family functioning. Although these broad goals are probably consensual, and common belief is that achieving them is worthwhile from social and economic perspectives, there are many variations in translations of goals to actual forms and substance of services. No wide agreement exists as to what programs should accomplish in terms of specific outcomes, and how program goals should be realized (Agosta & Bradley, 1985). The variety of program goals and processes in the family support efforts described in this volume reinforce that assertion.

This variation in actual practice makes it difficult to develop a definition of family support that has even relatively general application across family support efforts nationally, or even within a state or region. As a result, no consensual reference points or anchors exist as definitions upon which to base evaluation efforts. Researchers may not share a view of what they are evaluating. This issue of clarity exists on both the system and individual family levels.

Operationalizing program objectives is problematic at the family level (especially for evaluation purposes) because of increasing individualization of services. In recognition of the uniqueness of each family and their needs for varying types and amounts of services, many programs have moved toward involving families more in making decisions about the services that they receive (Weiss, 1983). With this increase in individualization of services, evaluation becomes more difficult because no clear set of standards exists by which to gauge the nature, effectiveness, and efficiency of service goals, resources, processes, and outcomes, especially as they affect individuals and families.

On the system level, programs vary according to availability of financial resources, political climate, and service philosophy. For example, in a program where preventing out-of-home placement is an important goal, eligibility criteria would have to define "at risk for being placed out-of-home." "At risk" could be defined broadly to include more families, or narrowly to best use restricted resources. A question, however, is which of these definitions is most likely to reduce out-of-home placement.

These types of definitional issues require solutions in order to understand what is being evaluated. Otherwise, a given conceptual foundation may be used to evaluate program efforts that derive entirely or in part from a different framework.

Similarly, operationalizing service system goals that address families' caregiving capacities into specific service plans and processes is a complex task. Even to begin requires considering how much of the caregiving burden the state can reasonably expect families to assume, and how the state decides that a given amount of support is unjustifiable. Because service planners and providers differ on answers to such questions, family support takes many and varied forms around the country.

As a result of such disparity in operational definitions of family support, evaluation of family support efforts does not have a clear and unitary focus. In evaluation efforts, researchers must somehow account for and address the effects of such variations in goals and actual processes of services at the system level.

Methodological Issues

Evaluation of family support programs can also be problematic because of concerns related to design and measurement. For example, because of the lack of a comprehensive and consensual framework within which to work on model development and evaluation, causal models to guide quantitative investigations are frequently inadequate. As a result, certain statistical tools that acquire much of their explanatory power from theoretical foundations cannot be applied; any outcomes are difficult to interpret because of the lack of context within which to understand them. The best examples of notable exceptions to this state of affairs are presented in the explicitly theory-based contributions to this volume by Dunst and colleagues (Chapter 8), Turnbull and colleagues (Chapter 2), and by Singer and colleagues (Chapters 1, 5, & 6).

Another problem that frequently limits interpretation of model demonstration and other family support program efforts is the size of samples from which results are obtained. Small sample sizes, difficulty in applying random sampling and/or random assignment of families to types of services, and variability in the characteristic of families and their members with disabilities all contribute their share to problems of external validity or generalization of results beyond the samples from which data are derived.

Yet another issue is the need for adequate longitudinal evaluation. Immediately observable processes and results may not endure. Or, conversely, the lack of immediately observable outcomes may signal the need for evaluation across a larger span of time, especially if conceptual/ theoretical frameworks lead researchers to believe that observable changes take time to occur. However, any of a number of problems can complicate the interpretations of results of longitudinal evaluation, for example, attrition of participating families, maintenance of standardized services (even if services are individualized) over time, and applying and interpreting appropriate statistical tools for understanding change over time.

Uncontrollable, mitigating circumstances can also affect evaluation efforts adversely. Tausig (1985) and Herman (1983) both note that several states operate within policies that actively discourage out-of-home placement into institutional settings. However, other states do not do the same. The differential impact of varying policies on placement decisions by parents complicates the evaluation task considerably.

Finally, and perhaps most directly of interest within ongoing family support programs, the actual measures of process and effects that are used may be insensitive or only partially sensitive to the phenomena of interest, that is, family dynamics. Weiss (1983) has observed that to understand the effects of interventions designed to enhance entire family functioning, measures that are sensitive to changes within family dynamics are needed. Essentially, no such measures are widely available that meet even conventional psychometric standards for reliability and validity (Dunst and Trivette, 1985).

Some efforts are underway to broaden the nature of available design, measurement, and analysis strategies to enable meaningful investigations and measurements of family dynamics. For example, Skinner (1987) describes a family systems approach to assessment of family functioning in which separate measurements are taken from individuals in families that provide reports

on individual, dyadic, and general family functioning. Also, Dunst and Trivette (1988) have recently reported on their efforts to assess family functioning via comparisons of spouses' ratings of extent of and satisfaction with responsibilities for various roles within the family. As these and other such efforts to develop measures of family variables eventually result in available standardized instruments, measures that are more appropriately sensitive to the family dynamics that are the focus of service interventions will be available.

To guide this effort toward adequate measurement of family phenomena, Christensen and Arrington (1987) have proposed that the "natural units" of family functioning be discerned. To do so, they note that clear distinctions among and decisions about five methodological aspects of measuring and understanding families must be made: objects of study, units of study, units of observation, units of measurement, and units of analysis. Objects of study in family support programs are *families* because family dynamics and/ or functioning are the focus of many interventions. However, most studies use individuals as the units of study because most available and convenient measurement tools are designed for that application. Researchers have been limited to interviewing, surveying, and observing individuals in order to learn about families. And, the units of observation comprise only some aspects of individuals' views or behaviors related to family functioning or dynamics. In addition, units of measurement vary in a number of ways; they are structured or unstructured, categorical or dimensional, and of varying sizes—from molecular to molar (from direct observations of verbal interactions to global ratings of communication ability), and from individual or dyadic to whole family units. Finally, units of analysis are often different than the units of measurement in family studies. In order to try to reflect the family as a unit of study, composites of measurements of individuals are used, perhaps without knowing from theory or experience whether the whole is truly equal to the sum of the parts.

These unitization issues, and the other problems and concerns described previously, are all part of a larger issue: the validity of conclusions (and resulting implications for program design, development, delivery, and improvement). To develop useful measures of family functioning, researchers need to be clear in distinctions among the objects and units of study, observation, measurement, and analysis. By doing so, misinterpretation and overgeneralization of data on family functioning can be avoided. To derive meaning from evaluation results, researchers need to account for and explain the influences of conceptual and methodological concerns.

REFERENCES

Agosta, J.M., & Bradley, V.J. (Eds.). (1985). *Family care for persons with developmental disabilities: A growing commitment.* Boston: Human Services Research Institute.

Baker, B.L. (1984). Intervention with families with young, severely handicapped children. In J. Blacher (Ed.), *Severely handicapped young children and their families* (pp. 319–375). Orlando, FL: Academic Press.

Breslau, N., & Davis, G.C. (1986). Chronic stress and major depression. *Archives of General Psychiatry, 43,* 309–314.

Christensen, A., & Arrington, A. (1987). Research issues and strategies. In T. Jacob (Ed.), *Family interaction & psychopathology: Theories, methods & findings* (pp. 259–296). New York: Plenum Press.

Dunst, C. & Trivette, C. (1988, May). *Measures of ecological congruence in research on families of the mentally retarded.* Paper presented at the meeting of the American Academy of Mental Retardation, Washington, DC.

Dunst, C., & Trivette, C. (1985). A guide to measures of social support and family behavior. *Monograph of the Technical Assistance Development System* (No. 1). Chapel Hill, NC: TADS.

Dunst, C.J., Trivette, C.M., McWilliam, R.A., & Galant, K. (in press). Toward experimental education of the family, infant, and preschool programs. In H. Weiss & F. Jacobs (Eds.), *Evaluating family programs.* New York: Aldine.

Herman, S.E. (1983). *Family support services: Reports on meta-evaluation studies.* Lansing: Michigan Department of Mental Health.

Paine, S.C., Bellamy, G.T., & Wilcox, B. (1984). *Human services that work: From innovation to standard practice.* Baltimore: Paul H. Brookes Publishing Co.

Skinner, H.A. (1987). Self-report instruments for family assessment. In T. Jacob (Ed.), *Family interaction & psychopathology: Theories, methods & findings* (pp. 427–452). New York: Plenum Press.

Stufflebeam, D. (1983). The CIPP model for program evaluation. In G. Madaus, M. Scriven, & D. Stufflebeam (Eds.), *Evaluation models* (pp. 117–141). Boston: Kluwer-Nighoff Publishing.

Tausig, M. (1985). Factors in family decision-making about placement for developmentally disabled individuals. *American Journal on Mental Deficiency, 89,* 352–361.

Turnbull, A.P., & Turnbull, H.R. (1986). *Families, professionals, and exceptionality: A special partnership.* Columbus, OH: Charles E. Merrill.

Voeltz, L.M. (1982). Effects of structured interactions with severely handicapped peers on childrens' attitudes. *American Journal of Mental Deficiency, 86,* 380–390.

Weiss, H. (1983). Issues in the evaluation of family support and education programs. *Family Resource Coalition Report, 2*(4), 10–11.

Wolf, M. (1978). Social validity: The case for subjective measurement, or how applied behavior analysis is finding its heart. *Journal of Applied Behavior Analysis, 11,* 203–214.

Woolfolk, R.L., & Lehrer, P.M. (Eds.). (1984). *Principles and practice of stress management.* New York: Guilford Press.

CHAPTER 22

Implications for Policy Development

Valerie J. Bradley

There is a surprising unity of perceptions and findings that emerges from the varied chapters that appear in this book. Such a consensus would seem to suggest that the "field" of family support has approached an initial stage of maturity and coherence and thus is able to impart some guidelines for the development of public policy.

POLICY IMPLICATIONS AND NEXT STEPS

Major Themes

Some of the themes that are woven through the discussions of family theory and model programs are:

In all realms of intervention on behalf of families and children with disabilities, parents and professionals should be viewed as partners and collaborators.

Assessments of family functioning should no longer merely examine the impact that a child with a disability has on the family, but should also examine the multiplicity of relationships among family members and the relationship of the family to the surrounding community.

Interventions should be tailored to the individual circumstances of each family and should be governed by the family's expressed needs and assessments of family functioning within the natural environment.

Instead of viewing the child with a disability as a "problem," interventions on behalf of families should concentrate on the strengths of the child and the family unit, and should focus on the development of instrumental skills and positive coping.

Families should no longer be viewed as the passive recipients of services, but rather as playing a potential range of roles including case manager, advocate, interventionist, and peer teacher.

In the past, services on behalf of families and children with disabilities have tended to engender "system dependence" and have failed to build on natural supports.

The provision of services in integrated settings that maximize community involvement enhances the self-esteem of parents, reduces the isolation of the family, and increases the child's ability to participate and benefit from the same social relationships as his or her nondisabled peers.

These compelling themes suggest the need to reassess the role of public policy in the support of families of children with disabilities. The critique indicates that the policies of the past have yielded resources, but have failed to capitalize on the unique strengths of families and to impart to them a sense of efficacy and competence. This is a particularly propitious time to rethink the mission of publicly supported services and the roles that professionals should play in the facilitation of more individualized and responsive services.

In order to translate these themes and the particular discussions that have preceded this chapter into public policy recommendations, it is useful to break policy concerns into several areas: 1) income support and assistance, 2) direct service and intervention strategies, 3) evaluation and research, and 4) public-private partnerships.

Income Support and Assistance

Many of the authors in this book discuss the need for a flexible array of services that is dictated by the expressed needs and individual circumstances of families (e.g., Slentz, Walker, & Bricker, Chapter 14, this volume; Hanson, Ellis, & Deppe, Chapter 13, this volume). The availability of such infinite variety through established public and private agencies is clearly problematic. While the formal system can generate a richer menu of services than is currently evident, it is unwise to assume that formal services will ever fully meet family needs. There is a need, therefore, to put resources directly at the disposal of the family so that they in turn can purchase what they need. Agosta (Chapter 12, this volume) describes the rationale behind such support and indicates the virtues of placing money directly in the hands of the family.

There are several ways in which the level of resources available to families can be increased. First, at the federal level, eligibility for Supplemental Security Income (SSI) for children with disabilities could be expanded by eliminating the requirement that parental income be deemed to the child. The current deeming provisions essentially limit the number of eligible families to those whose incomes fall below or very near the poverty line. Since eligibility for SSI gains entry for the child into the Medicaid program, this change would also expand the availability of needed medical care to families with children with disabilities.

Furthermore, with respect to the Medicaid program, there is a need to broaden the definition of covered services to include those that are of most direct benefit to families, including respite, in-home supports, transportation, home adaptation, and other forms of assistance that will make it easier for families to support children with disabilities in their homes and in their communities. The additional availability of such supports has been a major plank in the Medicaid reform activity associated with Senator John Chafee (R.) of Rhode Island.

Another means of providing income support to families with children with disabilities is to institute a family allowance for all families. The family allowance, which is part of the welfare system in many countries in Europe, is made available regardless of need. The adoption of an income support system for all families has the virtue of being generic and decreasing the stigma and separateness of a welfare payment.

Several of the authors comment on the special problems of low income families (e.g., Lutzker, Campbell, Newman, & Harrold, Chapter 20, this volume) and Signer and Irvin (Chapter 1, this volume) note that many of the interventions described can only prove beneficial to low income families once their basic needs have been met. These observations strongly support the need to develop an adequate national level of support through the Aid to Families with Dependent Children (AFDC) program, given the vast differences among states in levels of support and the politically difficult task of raising benefits at the state level. Making such support available to two-parent families as well as single-parent families would also prove beneficial. Further, the self-esteem of parents is critical to their sense of efficacy in assisting their child with a disability (Summers, Behr, & Turnbull (Chapter 2, this volume). Such self-esteem is particularly problematic among those depending on welfare. This suggests the importance of job training and placement programs as adjuncts to the AFDC program, as well as an increase in the availability of integrated day-care for working mothers.

In the aggregate, these recommendations for more responsive federal income support policies add up to a mandate for a national family policy that does not pick and choose among those who are "truly needy" and those who are not, but rather supports the family in its multiple guises, respects and values the idiosyncrasies of families, and—while maintaining support—minimizes the dependence of families on formal assistance and systems.

Direct Service Strategies

As Slater, Martinez, and Habersang (Chapter 10, this volume) suggest, the professional working with families should play a facilitating role that strengthens the ability of the family to gain access to needed services while increasing what Summers, Behr, and Turnbull (Chapter 2, this volume) call the family's mastery. Chapter 10 (this volume) describes several new roles that professionals should play, including systems assessor, systems convenor, systems activator, systems trainer, and family therapist. Chapter 13 stresses the coordination role, the virtues of collaboration, and notes the importance of brokering and service mobilization.

These role descriptions vary substantially from the more conventional dyad of interventionist and family and require both system restructuring and retraining to achieve. The revamping of service systems must include the design of mediating structures that have the ability to draw together the diverse services needed by families. No one agency, whether it is a school system, the welfare system, or the disability system has the ability to meet all of the needs of the family at the varying developmental stages. Establishing case coordination agencies whose staff have the ability to move easily among relevant programs and to draw together disparate resources is necessary to support new staff roles such as systems convenor and system activator.

PL 99-457, *The Education of the Handicapped Act Amendments of 1986*, with its heavy emphasis on interagency collaboration and coordination, provides an excellent opportunity for the development of new coordinative and mediating structures that can provide bridges among the diverse agencies providing services to families whose children have disabilities. Such structures will also facilitate the collaboration necessary to develop the individualized family plan required in the legislation.

An independent agency structure would also give staff the autonomy necessary to advocate on behalf of families. Family agents who are part of a direct service agency may find it difficult to be critical of services or to propose alternatives to the services provided by the agency that employs them.

Training will also be required to introduce the many professionals who provide services to families to the values reflected by the authors in this book. Notions of shared responsibility and empowerment are not concepts generally included in medical school or special education curricula. Furthermore, the issues of collaboration and team participation—though beginning

to emerge in professional training—are still not sufficient to bring about the sort of interagency collaboration envisioned in this book. This is especially the case among entities who traditionally have not related to one another, such as ICU staff and early intervention programs or special education personnel and generic human services agencies. Federal and state funds allocated for the support of professional training (including funds from the Administration on Developmental Disabilities, the National Institute on Disability and Rehabilitation Research and the National Institute on Mental Health) should be provided on the condition of the development of training curricula that embody the above values and that assist the professional-in-training to understand the larger context within which he or she works.

The development of training curricula for individuals who work directly with families should, as pointed out by Neef and Parrish (Chapter 11, this volume), include the participation of families both in the design of training regimens and in the actual training. Further, training appears to be most relevant when it is tailored to the needs of the individual trainee as well as to the particular needs of the family or families with whom the individual will work. Finally, training programs need to equip staff with the ability to mobilize natural and informal as well as formal support systems.

Virtually all of the authors note the importance of family participation in decisionmaking and planning. Specifically, Halvorsen, Doering, Farron-Davis, Usilton, and Silor (Chapter 16, this volume) stress the utility and advisability of including family preferences and assessments into the implementation planning for the transition of young people from school settings into work life. To ensure that such participation takes place, federal regulations governing both special education and vocational rehabilitation can be altered to require such participation prior to and during the process of transition. The primacy of the preferences of the person with a disability, however, should be maintained in order to reinforce the self-esteem and ultimate independence of the emerging adult.

With respect to the strengthening of parent and professional relationships, Walker (Chapter

7, this volume) in particular noted the barriers posed to such relationships—specifically parents and teachers—by the sometimes adversarial character of mandatory due process proceedings. In terms of policy implications, this strongly suggests the need to stress mediation techniques as a positive precursor to full due process and the need for dissemination of information regarding successful mediation approaches. This is not to suggest that the availability of due process hearings should in any way be diminished, but that alternative dispute resolution mechanisms be aggressively pursued.

Taylor, Knoll, Lehr, and Walker (Chapter 3, this volume) describe compellingly the need for a firm mandate regarding the right of all children, regardless of disability, to be raised in families. Such an orientation has several policy ramifications. First, it suggests that states should limit admission to conventional residential programs to individuals over 21 years of age. Second, it supports the need to refocus out-of-home placement activities to a concentration on securing a permanent home through specialized adoptions. Third, it reinforces the need to redouble efforts to move children currently placed in public facilities into natural homes. Further, in those instances where permanent homes cannot be found, policies should be developed to recruit and train specialized foster home providers.

Additionally, given the benefits noted by Goetz, Anderson, and Laten (Chapter 15, this volume) of integrated school programs and the community intensive instructional model, there is certainly an argument for strengthening the requirements surrounding the implementation of PL 94-142 (*The Education for All Handicapped Children Act of 1975*) to include rewards for the development of nonsegregated educational opportunities for special education students and the creation of curricula that is functionally based and geared to individual, contextual needs.

Finally, policymakers must make decisions on a range of questions that will affect the scope and magnitude of family support and intervention strategies. In addition to the location of services, described above, these decisions primarily revolve around eligibility for services. For instance, what families will be targeted? Will all

families, regardless of the nature of the disability of their child, be included? Should families with children with chronic or terminal illnesses and emotional disabilities be included? Should the program be means tested or should it be available to all families regardless of income? The answers to these complex questions implicate resources, the types of agencies that should be involved, and the nature of the interventions that should be pursued.

Research and Evaluation

Several suggestions for public support in the area of research and evaluation emerge from the discussions in this book. They can roughly be catalogued as follows: 1) further investigations of positive family coping strategies, 2) additional evaluations of model approaches to family support and family intervention, and 3) dissemination of information about efficacious approaches.

Summers, Behr, and Turnbull (Chapter 2, this volume) describe the positive ways in which families with children with disabilities have adapted and coped. Rather than focusing on the "chronic sorrow" of families, recent theorists tend to concentrate on the strengths of families and the ways in which their adaptation can be maximized. Furthermore, Lutzker, Campbell, Newman, and Harrold (Chapter 20, this volume) note the importance of understanding the ways in which some families have achieved *bonadaptation* in order to teach high-risk families efficacious coping strategies. Public support is required at the federal level to assess positive family functioning and to identify variables that are likely to predict such positive adaptation.

As noted by many of the authors and as stressed in Chapter 13, there is a continuing need for information about what works for different kinds of families and children. Therefore, a strong recommendation might be to develop a federal research agenda that supports a range of studies and methodologies aimed at assessing the outcomes of family support and intervention. One of the key issues in such studies concerns the criteria required to determine success. As Slentz, Walker, and Bricker (Chapter 14, this volume) point out, using more conventional indices such as improvement on child development scales may not illuminate the full impact that services have on both the child and other family members. Additional measures should include the family's report of increased competencies, altered expectations regarding the child's capabilities, reduction in perceived stress, increased self-esteem, or expanded community connections. Certainly, the views of the child with a disability should also be solicited whenever feasible, to determine the impact of family interventions.

The final area noted has to do with dissemination. One important area of "technology transfer" appears to be in the area of informal supports. How do professionals facilitate connections with generic community agencies such as YMCAs, Boy Scouts, 4H clubs, and so forth? One way is to focus energy at the agency level directly through national networks and conferences. Films depicting successful integration into community settings could be used both in professional training as well as with generic voluntary agencies. Dissemination is also clearly needed in the area of training, where many of the materials have been prepared on an ad hoc basis and have had only limited circulation. Finally, public support is needed to inform a wide audience of the results of the outcome-oriented assessments noted above.

Public-Private Collaborations

There are several ways that public policy can encourage and support private sector services for families with children with disabilities. Through tax incentives, legal mandates, and other forms of public subsidies, the federal and state governments can support the initiation of a range of corporate benefit programs that would assist families in general, and families with children with disabilities in particular. Some of these programs include:

The development of individually tailored "flex-time" arrangements that make it possible for parents to schedule work hours around the needs of their child.
The availability of maternity and paternity leave that makes it possible to stay at home with a

newborn during the first several months after birth.
The creation of subsidized work site day-care that makes it possible for parents to be near their children during the work day.

Several collaborations involving the use of technology—especially computer technology—to assist children and families are currently in operation. For example, Apple Computer has developed a line of software for families who are part of a training network. The software helps parents to understand the ways in which computers can be used to assist their child with a disability. Apple has contributed funding to the network and also has contributed computers to key individuals within states. Further, the National Institute of Disability and Rehabilitation Research has recently funded a collaboration between United Cerebral Palsy Association and IBM to develop a computer and technology assistance network in the Southeast.

Unanswered Questions

Some of the issues raised in this book remain problematic. One is the special challenge posed by minority, low income, and high-risk families. Many of the authors note that such families do not derive as much benefit from the models described (e.g., Slentz, Walker, and Bricker (Chapter 14) and may be overwhelmed by the pressures of meeting basic needs. The interventions described in the book require a certain level of commitment, energy, and, in some instances, basic academic skills to participate fully. While these are qualities possessed by most middle class and upper middle class families, the circumstances of poverty mean that many parents will not bring such qualities to bear.

As economic and social factors drive a widening wedge between the poor in this country and everyone else, it is especially important to examine policies proposed for families with children with disabilities to make sure that they do not unwittingly exclude families that are poor or culturally different. Specifically, this may mean that approaches aimed at the withdrawal of formal supports in favor of informal supports may place families without resources or natural support networks at a disadvantage. Further, given the needs of these families for a broad range of income supports, health services, job training, and so forth, models aimed merely at reducing the caretaking load may not be sufficient.

Another major issue, which is touched on by Neef and Parrish (Chapter 11, this volume), is the long-range availability of staff to serve the multiple roles reflected in the models described. While it is true that the maximization of natural supports will in part solve the problem of recruiting paid staff, these networks will not always be adequate to meet the needs of families with children with multiple support needs. The recent experience in many states—especially those with low unemployment rates such as Massachusetts, indicates the increasing difficulty of recruiting staff to a range of human services jobs, including day-care and other family and children's services.

One way of ameliorating the problem of staff shortages is to rely on volunteers. As Cooley's discussion (Chapter 9, this volume) suggests, however, the use of volunteers, while enriching and positive, also has problems. For instance, volunteers cannot necessarily provide a long-term relationship with families. Furthermore, the resulting termination of volunteers as supports to families can be traumatic. Finally, the recruitment, supervision, and training of volunteers is time-consuming. These facts suggest that while "no cost" and more informal service substitutes—like bartering and volunteering mechanisms—are valuable assets to family support, they cannot be relied on as the stable core of family assistance.

Finally, the Slentz, Walker, and Bricker (Chapter 14) discussion raises some initial warning signals about intervention "overload." In their report of the evaluation of the Oregon Parent-to-Parent project, the authors note that some families reported increased discomfort following the training regimen. This may indicate the importance, as other authors note, of balancing the level and intensity of intervention against other pressures and expectations placed on the parents. It may also suggest that some families may not be able to become equal partners or parent interventionists and that publicly supported back-up systems will be required, such as expanded respite, in-home supports, and intensified school programs. Family support should not become an exclusive alternative to other forms of direct service.

Conclusion

The authors in this book have, as a group, described a new set of theoretical and practical conceptions regarding supports to children with disabilities and their families. In so doing, they have assisted in recasting the role of public policy and those who carry it out. Simply put, future policy should emphasize family strengths, support not supplant families, recognize the individuality and complexity of need, and have as its goal empowerment, integration, and autonomy of the family.

Index

preliminary findings of, 136–138
   comparative analysis, 136–137
   independent exchanges, 137–138
   needs met, 137
problems/challenges in, 135–136
staff roles/responsibilities in, 133–135
Protective services, 283–293
   assessing need for, 285
   financial, 286–288
      bank accounts, 287
      estate guardian, 287
      power of attorney, 286–287
      representative payee, 287
      transfer of property, 286
      trusts, 287–288
   National Continuity Program, 290–293
   personal, 285–286
   see also Guardianship programs
Public policy issues, 19–21, 343–348
   direct service strategies, 344–346
   early intervention programs, 217
   enhancing professional-parent cooperation, 117
   family themes affecting, 343
   income support/assistance, 344
   parental stress management, 80
   public-private collaborations, 347
   research and evaluation, 346–347
   supported employment, 280–281
   unanswered questions, 347–348
   volunteerism, 155–157

Quality assurance
   changes in, 56
   parents' roles in, 64

Relaxation training, 76–77
Research
   on behavioral parent training, 99–100
   on early intervention programs, 217–218
   on ecobehavioral family interventions, 324–325
   on improving professional-family interactions, 116–117
   on normalized family resources, 172
   on parental roles in supported employment, 271
   Project SHaRE and, 139
   on stress management, 81–82
   Support and Education for Families Program and, 153–154
Respite care provider training, 175–186
   applicant selection for, 185
   competency-based approach to, 176–177, 179–180
   cost effectiveness of, 177, 180–181
   design and implementation of, 176–185
   evaluation/social validation of, 177, 183–184
   future directions in, 185–186
   importance of, 176
   need for, 175–176
   practicality of, 177, 181–183
   recruitment for, 184–185
   responsiveness to consumer needs, 176–179
   skill areas in
      child behaviors, 180
      emergencies, 180

physical/medical management, 180
      preparation and parent interaction, 179–180
   use of services, 175–176
   vidotaped curricula for, 186

SAEF, *see* Support and Education for Families Program
San Francisco Special Infant Services Program, 211–216
   challenges encountered by, 213–214
   evaluation of, 212–213, 215–216
   methods of, 213
   organizational structure of, 212
   overview of, 211
   philosophy and goals of, 211–212
   population served by, 212
   staffing of, 212
School
   adjunct services of, 246–249
   community intensive curriculum model, 241–246
      assessment and curriculum development process of, 242–244
      features of, 241–242
      integration of, 244–246
      teaching within natural environments, 244
   family training/support by, 247–249
      Parent and Community Together, 247–248
      Parents as Effective Partners, 248–249
   integrative administrative practices of, 246–247
   as natural support system, 239–240
   role as coping institution, 240–241
   support for all families by, 249
   support for families of disabled students by, 240–249
   transition from, 253–266
      see also Transitional planning
   types of support by, 241
Social isolation, 12, 46
   behavioral parent training and, 90
State Trait Anxiety Inventory, 79
Statement in Support of Families and Their Children, 41–43
   adoption, 50–51
   community integration, 49–50
   existing social networks and natural supports, 46–47
   family control, 47–48
   family reunification, 50
   foster care, 51–52
   permanency planning, 42–44
   whatever it takes, 44–46
      cash subsidy, 45
      service vouchers, 46
   whole-family support, 48–49
Stress, 3–14
   adaptation to, 12–14
   family theory of, 10–14
      child abuse and, 12
      divorce and, 12
      indicators of distress, 11–12
      out-of-home placement and, 11–12
      social isolation and, 12
   individual theory of, 6–10
   models of, 5–6
   stressors, 7–10
      after birth of disabled child, 207–208
      appraisal of, 9–10
      identification of, 7–9